Running the Show

By the same author

Hongkong Bank
Docklands
Olga's Story

Running the Show

Governors of the British Empire 1857–1912

STEPHANIE WILLIAMS

VIKING
an imprint of
PENGUIN BOOKS

For William

VIKING

Published by the Penguin Group

Penguin Books Ltd, 80 Strand, London WC2R ORL, England

Penguin Group (USA) Inc., 375 Hudson Street, New York, New York 10014, USA

Penguin Group (Canada), 90 Eglinton Avenue East, Suite 700, Toronto, Ontario, Canada M4P 2Y3
(a division of Pearson Penguin Canada Inc.)

Penguin Ireland, 25 St Stephen's Green, Dublin 2, Ireland (a division of Penguin Books Ltd)

Penguin Group (Australia), 250 Camberwell Road,
Camberwell, Victoria 3124, Australia (a division of Pearson Australia Group Pty Ltd)

Penguin Books India Pvt Ltd, 11 Community Centre,
Panchsheel Park, New Delhi – 110 017, India

Penguin Group (NZ), 67 Apollo Drive, Rosedale, Auckland 0632, New Zealand
(a division of Pearson New Zealand Ltd)

Penguin Books (South Africa) (Pty) Ltd, 24 Sturdee Avenue,
Rosebank, Johannesburg 2196, South Africa

Penguin Books Ltd, Registered Offices: 80 Strand, London WC2R ORL, England

www.penguin.com

First published 2011

1

Copyright © Stephanie Williams, 2011
Maps copyright Stephanie Williams and Zoë Shinnick, 2011

The moral right of the author has been asserted

Set in 11/14.25pt Bembo Book MT

Typeset by Palimpsest Book Production Limited,
Falkirk, Stirlingshire
Printed in Great Britain by Clays Ltd, St Ives plc

A CIP catalogue record for this book is available from the British Library

Hardback ISBN: 978–0–670–91804–1
Trade Paperback ISBN: 978–0–670–91805–8

www.greenpenguin.co.uk

MIX
Paper from
responsible sources
FSC™ C018179

Penguin Books is committed to a sustainable
future for our business, our readers and our
planet. This book is made from paper certified
by the Forest Stewardship Council.

Contents

List of Illustrations   vii

List of Maps   xi

Map of the British Empire   xii–xiii

Introduction   1

1. Dispatch   13

2. Commander Glover on the Slave Coast: Lagos 1863–72   26

3. The loneliness of the righteous governor: St Lucia 1869–77   49

4. Captain Douglas settles Palmerston: South Australia 1870–73   70

5. Fever and delusion: The Gold Coast 1874–6   91

6. White stalkers on the beach: Fiji 1875–82   108

7. The washing of the spears: South Africa 1877–80   139

8. 'The mind of heaven and earth': Hong Kong 1877–82   167

9. The death of Thomas Callaghan: Falkland Islands 1879–80   191

10. The Marquess of Lorne and the Indians: Canada 1881   202

11. Sweet talk and secrets – the rise and rise of Frank Athelstane Swettenham: Malaya 1874–1903   224

12. Lady Tennyson at home: South Australia 1899–1903   256

13. A marriage of imperialists: Northern Nigeria 1901–6   275

14. Where the land was bewitched: Uganda 1906–10   308

15. A socialist in the West Indies: Jamaica 1907–12   333

16. Letters from Nairobi: British East Africa 1909–12   356

17. Running the show: Ceylon 1907–12   386

18. Going home   411

Acknowledgements   421

Notes   423

Bibliography   463

Index   475

List of Illustrations

Text illustrations

p. 5 The island of Heligoland, from C. H. Spurgeon (ed.), *The Sword and the Trowel: A Record of Combat with Sin & Labour for the Lord,* London, 1867

p. 19 Governor's dress uniform, from M. V. O. Trendell, *Dress Worn at His Majesty's Court,* London, 1912

p. 31 The Reverend Samuel Crowther, from Jesse Page, *Samuel Crowther: The slave boy who became bishop of the Niger*, London, 1889

p. 49 The Pitons of St Lucia, from C. Kingsley: *At Last*, London, 1889

p. 55 Map of the sugar plantations of British Guiana, from E. Jenkins, *The Coolie, His Rights and Wrongs*

p. 66 Chinese indentured labourers sketch their abuses in British Guiana, from E. Jenkins, *The Coolie*

p. 98 Bearing the wounded across a river from Kumasi, *Illustrated London News,* 28 February 1874

p. 99 Arriving over the surf below Cape Coast Castle, *Illustrated London News,* 10 January 1874

p. 101 Street scene, Cape Coast, *Illustrated London News,* 10 January 1874

p. 121 The island of Ovalu, Fiji, with Government House and the jetty, by Constance Gordon Cumming, from C. F. Gordon Cumming, *At Home in Fiji*

p. 123 King Cakobau in 1885, painted by P. Spence, in Philip Snow and Stephanie Waine, *The People from the Horizon,* London, 1979

p. 155 Cetewayo, *Illustrated London News,* 22 February 1879

p. 159 Delivering the ultimatum on the banks of the Tugela River, *Illustrated London News*, 8 February 1879

p. 181 View of Hong Kong towards the harbour, *Illustrated London News,* 5 May 1866

p. 210 Lorne and Princess Louise arriving in state by sleigh in Ottawa, *Illustrated London News,* 11 January 1879

p. 211 Lorne's sketch of his snowshoe club descending through the woods in Indian file, from *Canadian Pictures* by the Marquess of Lorne

p. 214 Governor-General's party crossing the Lake of the Woods. Sketch by Sydney Prior Hall, 1881, Canadian National Archives

p. 235 Smoking the mosquitoes. Isabella Bird, *The Golden Chersonese*

p. 244 Swettenham at breakfast, from Chong Keat Lim, *Frank Swettenham & George Giles: Watercolours and sketches of Malaya 1880-1894,* Malaysian-British Society, 1988

p. 246 Meta Rome and Sydney Swettenham, from Lim, *Swettenham & Giles*

p. 257 Plan of Adelaide, 1838, from Henry Capper, *South Australia,* London, 1838, courtesy of King's College, London. Foyle Special Collections Library, Rare Books Collection, QA803.A2

p. 271 Government House, Melbourne, from *Australian Pictures* by Howard Willoughby, London, 1886

p. 290 Lugard, the celebrity, by Spy, December 1895

p. 298–9 A view towards Kano, *The Sphere,* 23 February 1903. Lugard Papers, MSS BRIT EMP S.99n/N 2288 b.34, Bodleian Library of Commonwealth and African Studies, Rhodes House Library, Oxford

p. 316 The laboratory where the causes of sleeping sickness were traced to the tsetse fly, *New York Times,* 20 March 1904

p. 342 An idealized vision of a sugar cane plantation from Revd William Moister, *The West Indies, Enslaved and Free,* London, 1883

p. 372 'Mummy and the dead buffalo', courtesy of Mark Girouard

p. 384 Norman Leys's sketch maps, from Norman Leys, *Kenya*

p. 401 Clifford the celebrity: *The Review of Reviews,* March 1911, in Clifford Papers, Bodleian Library of Commonwealth and African Studies, Rhodes House Library, Oxford

p. 404 'A soothing draught': *Amicus,* 19 February 1909. Clifford Papers

p. 412 'Tropical Life', November 1925, Clifford Papers

Plates

SECTION ONE

1. Inset: John Hawley Glover, administrator of Lagos, 1863–74 (*Life of John Hawley Glover*)

2. Government House, Lagos (Royal Geographical Society)

3. A house on the track to Abeokuta from Lagos (Royal Geographical Society)

4. 'Over the bar': the harbour at Lagos (Royal Geographical Society)

5. William des Voeux being hauled up the rapids, British Guiana, *c.*1864 (des Voeux, *My Colonial Service*)

6. Des Voeux on a visit to a local chief, Canimapo (des Voeux, *My Colonial Service*)

7. Castries, St Lucia, with Morne Fortune beyond (Getty Images/Caribbean Photo Archive)

8. Des Voeux and family at Government House, Nasova, Fiji, 1881 (des Voeux, *My Colonial Service*)

9. Larrakia camp at Palmerston, 1874 (South Australian Museum Archives, AA96/No 61)

10. William Bloomfield Douglas, two years after he left Palmerston, as Resident of Selangor, *c.*1876 (Bill Potter)

11. The beach below Government House, Palmerston (State Library of South Australia, B 4650)

12. The first telegraph pole at Port Darwin, 15 September 1870 (History SA, GNO 3363)

13. Government House, Palmerston (State Library of South Australia, B 9746)

14. Captain George Strahan, *c.*1874 (National Archives)

15. Market at Accra, Gold Coast, *c.*1874 (National Archives)

16. Sir Arthur Gordon and Captain Knollys, Fiji, 1875 (*The People from the Horizon*)

17. Rachael Gordon, shortly before she set off for Fiji, 1875 (*The Career of Arthur Hamilton Gordon*)

18. Government House at Nasova, Fiji, *c.*1876 (*The Fiji Journals of Baron Anatole von Hugel*)

19. Freshwater bathing near Government House, Fiji (*The Fiji Journals of Baron Von Hugel*)

20. Sir Bartle Frere (Sarah Frere)

21. Lady Frere (Sarah Frere)

22. A Zulu delegation listens to Frere's ultimatum, 11 December 1878

23. Isandlwana, photographed during a burial expedition, June 1879

24, 25. Thomas Callaghan and his wife, Alice, 1879 (Gravesend Historical Society)

26. Stanley Harbour, the Falkland Islands, 1875 (Cameron and Layman, *The Falklands and the Dwarf*, 1881–2)

Section Two

27. Government House, Labuan (Pope-Hennessy, *Verandah*)

28. Hugh Low, 1869 (Pope-Hennessy, *Verandah*)

29. Kitty Low, 1867 (Pope-Hennessy, *Verandah*)

30. John Pope Hennessy and his son, Johnnie, *c.*1872 (Pope-Hennessy, *Verandah*)

31. Government House, Hong Kong (Royal Geographical Society)

32. The drawing room of Government House, Hong Kong, *c.*1877 (Pope-Hennessy, *Verandah*)

33. The Marquess of Lorne, at the time he became Governor-General of Canada (National Archives of Canada)

34. Princess Louise as a young woman (National Archives of Canada)

35. Crowfoot, chief of the Blackfoot, addressing the Marquess of Lorne (National Archives of Canada)

36. Frank Swettenham and other British officials, Malaya, 1874 (Pakenham, *Out in the Noonday Sun*)

37. Frank Swettenham and John Birch (Pakenham, *Out in the Noonday Sun*)

38. Sydney Holmes on her wedding day, 21 February 1878 (Harrow School Archives)

39. The view from the Residency at Kuala Kangsar, sketched by Frank Swettenham, *c.*1884 (Lim, *Frank Swettenham and George Giles*)

40. In the garden of the Residency at Kuala Kangsar, July 1897 (Pakenham, *Out in the Noonday Sun*)

41. Sir Frank Swettenham by John Singer Sargent, 1904 (Ormond, *John Singer Sargent*)

42. The Tennyson family at Adelaide Station, 1899 (State Library of South Australia, B 7810)

43. The Tennyson family, 1903 (State Library of South Australia, PRG 280/1/15/394)

44. Audrey Tennyson (Selzer, *Governors' Wives in Colonial Australia*)

45. The Queen's Home, Adelaide

46. Lord and Lady Tennyson, their children and soldiers as they were about to depart for the Boer War

47. Flora Shaw, colonial editor of *The Times* (Perham, *Lugard*)

48. Frederick Lugard, *c.*1895 (Perham, *Lugard*)

49. Lugard working at his desk in the Emir's palace, Kano, 1903 (Perham, *Lugard*)

50. A ruler in Northern Nigeria arriving to meet Lugard (Perham, *Lugard*)

SECTION THREE

51. Henry Hesketh Bell among his animal trophies, Uganda, *c.*1909 (Royal Commonwealth Society Collection)

52. The view of Entebbe and Lake Victoria from Government House, Uganda, 1908 (Royal Commonwealth Society Collection)

53. One of the first medical missionaries in Uganda, 1892 (Royal Commonwealth Society Collection)

54. Bell's new Government House at Entebbe (Royal Commonwealth Society Collection)

55. The drawing room at Government House, Entebbe (Royal Commonwealth Society Collection)

56. Sir Henry Hesketh Bell departs from Kampala, 3 May 1909
57. Sir Sydney Olivier as Governor of Jamaica, 1907 (Pippa Harris)
58. Margaret Olivier in Jamaica, *c.*1908 (Pippa Harris)
59. The Olivier girls with their father in Kingston, Jamaica, *c.*1901 (Pippa Harris)
60. Earthquake damage, Jamaica, January 1907 (Getty Images/Caribbean Photo Archive)
61. Loading bananas, Kingston, Jamaica, *c.*1900 (Stark, *Jamaica Guide)*
62. Sir Percy Girouard and his *syce* in British East Africa, 1909 (Mark Girouard)
63. Gwen Girouard on safari, 1909 (Mark Girouard)
64. The hunt assembles before Government House, Nairobi, 1909 (Mark Girouard)
65. Staying with the Delameres at Elmenteita, December 1909 (Mark Girouard)
66. Fording a river on safari, December 1909 (Mark Girouard)
67. Hugh Clifford, aged twenty-four (Clifford Papers)
68. Clifford towered over the Malays in the province of Pahang (Clifford Papers)
69. Hugh Clifford and his new wife, Elizabeth, on honeymoon, 1910 (Clifford Papers)
70. Sir Hugh Clifford, not long before retirement (Clifford Papers)
71. The King's Pavilion, Kandy (*Souvenir of the Royal Visit to Ceylon*)

List of Maps

p. 35 Lagos, Colonial Office List, 1868
p. 52 The Leeward Islands, Colonial Office List, 1895
p. 71 South Australia, Colonial Office List, 1895
p. 92 Gold Coast, Colonial Office List, 1878
p. 110 Fiji, Colonial Office List, 1875
p. 144 South Africa, 1879
p. 168 Hong Kong, Colonial Office List, 1877
p. 193 The Falkland Islands, Colonial Office List, 1895
pp. 216–17 Canada, 1881, showing Lorne's journey to the north-west
p. 228 Malay States, 1874
p. 294 Northern Nigeria: adapted from 'Nigeria showing approximate areas of main tribal groups', in Margery Perham, *Lugard*, vol. I
p. 314 Uganda, Colonial Office List, 1910
p. 334 Jamaica, Colonial Office List, 1878
p. 357 British East Africa, 1909
p. 387 Ceylon, Colonial Office List, 1878

GREENLAND

Alaska

CANADA

GREAT BRITAIN

Newfoundland

UNITED
STATES

ATLANTIC
OCEAN

Bermuda

Gibraltar

Bahamas

AFRICA

WEST INDIES

Jamaica   St Lucia

Belize   Barbados
             Trinidad   Gambia   Nigeria
             Guiana
                            Sierra Leone
                                          Gold Coast

EQUATOR

• Ascension Island

SOUTH
AMERICA   • St Helena

Tristan da Cunha

Falkland Islands

S. Georgia

S. Orkney Islands

Graham Land

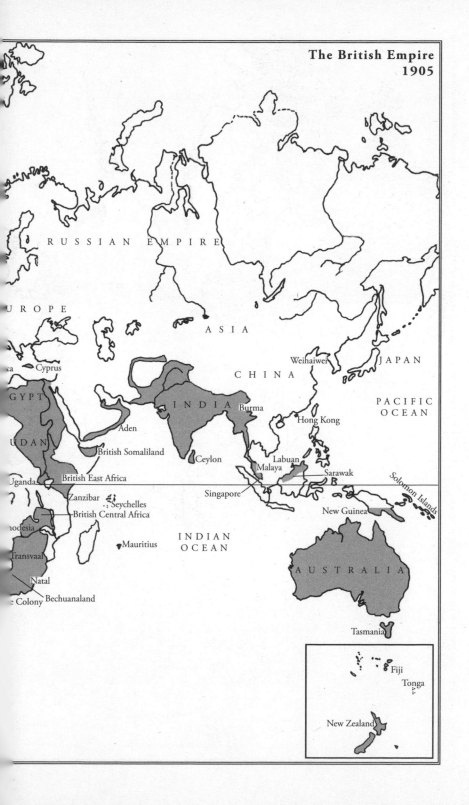

**The British Empire
1905**

RUSSIAN EMPIRE

EUROPE

Cyprus

EGYPT

SUDAN

Uganda

Aden

British Somaliland

British East Africa

Zanzibar

Seychelles

British Central Africa

Rhodesia

Mauritius

Transvaal

Natal

e Colony Bechuanaland

ASIA

CHINA

Weihaiwei

JAPAN

INDIA

Burma

Hong Kong

Ceylon

Labuan
Malaya

Sarawak

Singapore

New Guinea

Solomon Islands

PACIFIC
OCEAN

INDIAN
OCEAN

AUSTRALIA

Tasmania

Fiji

Tonga

New Zealand

'Crawley, I congratulate you.'

'What do you mean?' said the Colonel.

'It's in the Observer and the Royalist too,' said Mr. Smith.

'What?' Rawdon cried, turning very red. He took up the paper and, trembling, began to read . . .

'Governorship of Coventry Island. – H.M.S. Yellowjack, Commander Jaunders, has brought letters and papers from Coventry Island. H. E. Sir Thomas Liverseege had fallen a victim to the prevailing fever at Swampton. His loss is deeply felt in the flourishing colony. We hear that the Governorship has been offered to Colonel Rawdon Crawley, C.B., a distinguished Waterloo officer. We need not only men of acknowledged bravery, but men of administrative talents to superintend the affairs of our colonies, and we have no doubt that the gentleman selected by the Colonial Office to fill the lamented vacancy which has occurred at Coventry Island is admirably calculated for the post which he is about to occupy.'

Coventry Island! Where was it? Who had appointed him to the government? *The next moment, an official arrived from the Colonial Office.*

'You have seen this gratifying announcement in the papers this morning, Colonel? Government has secured a most valuable servant, and you, if you accept office, as I presume you will, an excellent appointment. Three thousand a year, delightful climate, excellent government-house, all your own way in the Colony, and a certain promotion. I congratulate you with all my heart. I presume you know, gentlemen, to whom my friend is indebted for this piece of patronage?'

Thus Becky Sharp's husband, Rawdon Crawley, is disposed of in Vanity Fair *by William Makepeace Thackeray, first published in monthly parts in 1847–8.*

Introduction

I am a white child of the British Empire, a descendant of a family which emigrated – seven of them, from three generations – from an old white-washed stone house in Cumbria to the wilderness of southern Ontario in Canada around 1837. They took up a piece of Crown land near the little town of Port Hope, soon after the first handbooks on how to be a pioneer began to be published in England. They cleared the land, and built a log cabin. My great-grandmother baked loaves of bread for the Indians, which she would leave on the fence at the edge of the woods. How hard their life must have been, how huge the shock of dislocation, from the soft light and gentle rains of the Cumbrian hills to the harsh rock and deep forest, big snows and long winters of Canada, has been lost in time.

But I sometimes wonder how they might have felt had they been present, more than 125 years later, when my class at school in the small Ontario town of Kingston would meet for history and geography lessons. Before us at the front of the room was a big map of the world, dominated by a large pink bit: Canada. Other pink bits – Australia, New Zealand, India and South Africa; large chunks of central and east Africa, and in the west of that vast continent, places like Ghana, Nigeria and Sierra Leone; most of the West Indies, Fiji, Tonga and dozens of other islands around the globe – were all part of the British Commonwealth, we were told, the countries with which we, as Canadians, had more in common than any other places in the world. At its head was Queen Elizabeth, and Britain – one of the smallest, most obscure pink bits, tucked in on the edge of Europe – was in charge. On other maps you could see Britain, from where thick lines of shipping routes (it was too early for flight paths) and undersea cables emanated and spread around the world.

Twenty-five years later I was living in Britain – having myself endured the dislocation of making a new life across the Atlantic – browsing through files in what was then the old Public Record Office in London's Chancery Lane for an article I was writing on the history of Government House in Hong Kong. It was then that I came across four bound volumes, intriguingly classified as 'Miscellaneous', among the vast series of nineteenth-century Colonial

Office files. They contained the answers to an early survey: a two-page printed questionnaire that had been dispatched in March 1879 by the Secretary of State for the Colonies, Michael Hicks Beach, to British governors around the globe.

The questions were simple, detailed and copious. How much are you paid? Describe your house/gardens/carriages/horses. How many servants do you have? Does your house have heating and lighting? How much land is there? Is there a country house available? How much, Hicks Beach wanted to know, does your establishment cost to maintain? Finally, the big opener: please supply 'any other details which it may be useful for a Governor to know'.

As I read the answers, an unknown world unfolded. You hardly need to go beyond the indexes of all the volumes that have been written about the history of the British Empire to discover how little has been written about the men who governed the colonies. Even in local histories they appear as little more than ciphers, remembered as founders or innovators or villains, in the names of towns or, more usually, streets.

By 1879 Britain had more than 300 years of colonial experience, which had begun with a first (failed) attempt at an overseas settlement in Newfoundland in the time of Queen Elizabeth I in 1583. This was followed by success at Jamestown, Virginia, in 1607. Meanwhile, from the beginning of the seventeenth century, the East India Company had begun establishing a network of 'factories', or warehouses, throughout the south and east of Asia. For the next 150 years, Britons settled new colonies along the eastern seaboard of today's United States and Canada, and in the islands of the West Indies, where they built plantations to grow sugar. Gibraltar was captured in 1704. The defeat of France in the Seven Years War in 1763 brought Britain Quebec; seven years later Captain Cook claimed Australia for King George III. By the time Queen Victoria came to the throne in 1837, besides having assumed a firm hold on the Indian sub-continent, Britain also held much of southern Africa, Mauritius and other assorted islands.

The reasons for this series of apparently random acquisitions were primarily commercial, spurred by private enterprise and the quest for riches – gold, sugar, cotton, spices. Safeguarding them became political. There had never been any government strategy of building towards Empire, and by the middle of the nineteenth century, after conducting a major fight to abolish slavery and its trade, the acquisition of any more overseas responsibility was viewed with a jaundiced eye. 'These wretched colonies will all be independent, too, in a few years,' Prime Minister Disraeli famously declared in 1852, 'and are a millstone round our necks.' By the 1870s he was in power again, and although Britain continued to colonize new lands – in west Africa, Malaya and the southern Pacific – it was with considerable reluctance.

The survey of 1879 which I found myself reading 100 years later was the first attempt in almost three centuries of imperial administration to gather information on the private life and day-to-day concerns of the men sent to run these strange places. Here was a brave and solitary military man living in a 'mean and sordid' farmhouse in Griqualand West (next door to the province of the Transvaal in today's South Africa); here another who had adapted thoroughly to the lazy pace of the lovely Caribbean island of St Vincent, where Lieutenant Governor George Dundas, formerly of the Rifle Brigade and one-time member of parliament, aged sixty, lived with his wife in a ramshackle bungalow 'more or less rotten throughout' called 'The Garden'. They looked out to sea from their verandah in the midst of one of the world's earliest botanical gardens – stocked by Captain Bligh of the *Bounty* from islands in the Pacific in 1793 – which Dundas maintained with the help of a convict gang. His bath, he delighted in reporting, was 13½ feet by 8 feet and 4 feet deep. 'Water, of which there is an ample supply of excellent quality, runs continually through it.'

In Newfoundland – the vast island on the eastern seaboard of Canada, past which Arctic icebergs flow in summer – you find a whole household sick with typhoid, scarlet fever, diphtheria and blood poisoning caused by the squalid conditions in Government House. The Governor, Sir John Glover, past hero of the ferocious Ashanti wars in the Gold Coast, complained: rain beat through the walls whenever there was a strong gale. Not only had the state of the house ruined the health of his wife, but it was 'far too large for the salary of the Governor unless half of the house only be in occupation'.

The frankness of the governors' remarks amazed me. Some sounded appropriately disdainful: the costs of maintaining the Governor's household in Jamaica were 'those of a large gentleman's establishment anywhere'. Others maintained ludicrous expectations – such as the need for a perfectly trained English butler in the diamond rush of South Africa's Transvaal. There, thirty-six-year-old Colonel Lanyon was living in nothing more than a small rented bungalow lit by oil lamps and candles, with an earth closet and tents for his servants outside. Or, in the warmth of the Bahamas:

'A governor should import, through a licensed importer, *all his Wines* . . . There is . . . fine sailing' – but 'unfortunately there is no good yacht'. None of these were the dry and dignified remarks that I expected of a governor. Many sounded exhausted, beleaguered and ill. Most were surprised that London took any interest in their personal situation at all.

Some reports spoke of extreme isolation. Dr John Treacher, aged sixty-four, was the colonial surgeon and acting governor of Labuan, a tiny triangular island six miles off the coast of Borneo – today a popular diving destination in eastern Malaysia. 'Neither stores nor servants can be procured and there is no hotel of any kind,' he wrote. 'There is a communication every three weeks by steamer with Singapore, on which Labuan is dependent for supplies. Servants (Chinese), horses and carriages can be obtained there. With the exception of the officials and of one or two Gentlemen in the Service of the Coal Company, there is no European society.'

What visions of lost dreams were going through Treacher's mind as he penned his reply? No British governor ever went to Labuan willingly. It had been ceded in perpetuity by the Sultan of Brunei in return for naval protection against pirates in 1846, and Treacher had been there as a doctor ever since. With its rich seam of coal and a fine natural harbour, Labuan had seemed to London to be an ideal coaling station for ships en route to Hong Kong – an island that had been taken from China for the merchants operating there. Only later was Labuan's fundamental drawback revealed: the place was so stifling, fever-ridden, and covered in pestilential swamp that even local fishermen regarded it as uninhabitable.

But Treacher had, in the phrasing of the time, long since 'gone native'. A former naval surgeon with a penchant for Sarawak girls, his fitness to be medical officer for the colony had been queried with London by an earlier governor. A morning of doctoring exhausted him for the rest of the day. Treacher was white-haired and jolly, but he suffered from frequent attacks of malaria and rheumatism, and was unable to walk or ride any distance. Now he was filling in, until a proper candidate could be found to govern remote and deadly Labuan at a salary of £800 a year – about £60,000 today.

Henry Fitzhardinge Maxse, at twenty-two, was the gilded aide-de-camp to Lord Cardigan, who carried the fatal order from Lord Lucan to launch the disastrous Charge of the Light Brigade. Now he was Sir Henry, full-faced and choleric, the governor of a pinprick of an island in the North Sea that today is known as Helgoland – 'Holy Island' – tucked into the armpit of the German Bight at the foot of Denmark. Seized from the Danes in

1807, and formally ceded to Britain under the Treaty of Vienna in 1815, Helgoland is distinguished by precipitous cliffs, a vertical stack of red rock on its northern tip, and a flat plateau on the top. It takes less than ten minutes to walk its length. Sir Henry spent his days translating Bismarck's letters to his wife and sisters into English. By 1879, 'Heligoland', as the British called it, was 'five minutes sail' from a second tiny island, with a fine sandy beach that had become a fashionable English bathing place. 'The Governor's expenses are considerable,' wrote Maxse. 'He has to buy everything in the dearest market almost anywhere, viz. Hamburg, and convey his things over 100 miles of sea and on arrival, everything has to be carried up the cliffs on men's backs, and for which no light charge is made . . . with Royal Highnesses, Generals etc etc constantly calling, it is impossible to avoid a great deal of entertainment for which there is NO ALLOWANCE.'

In 1879 Britain's smallest possession was the North Sea island of Heligoland,
off the south-west coast of Denmark

Together the governors' replies added up to a snapshot of Empire. The sheer diversity of Britain's colonies around the globe – and the characters who governed them – was to me astonishing. India did not figure here – nor does it in this book. The place was so vast and complex, it was in a class of its own. It was also governed differently. After the Rebellion of 1857, Britain took over the responsibilities of the East India Company for governing India. In 1858 a separate government department, the India Office, was created.

Elsewhere, there were governors all around the globe: in the Gold Coast – now Ghana – in Sierra Leone, Singapore and exotic provinces of today's Malaysia. There were a number in the Mediterranean: the military bastions of Malta and Gibraltar, and the blissful Ionian Islands. Far to the east were Hong Kong and Ceylon – today's Sri Lanka. Deep in the south Atlantic were St Helena, where the Emperor Napoleon was condemned to spend his last days, and the Falkland Islands. The former slave islands of the West Indies, and the great dominions, the settler colonies of Canada, Australia and New Zealand: each place was as different from the others as it was possible to be in climate, peoples and character.

The finest government houses, in places the nation regarded as the most important, were wonderfully grand. With smoking and billiard rooms, libraries and schoolrooms, and offices for the Governor and his staff, they were reminiscent of the English country houses they imitated, often self-sufficient, with extensive kitchen gardens, stabling, dairies, and laundries. In Melbourne, Australia, in 1879, Government House was newly built. When the Queen was told that the ballroom was to be as big as Buckingham Palace's, she was not pleased. In Hong Kong the heat, white ants and mildew led to the design of a plain, stone-built Greek Revival house, with vast high-ceilinged bedrooms, each with its own bathroom (and large stone-built bath tubs which drained through open holes in the walls), and special drying rooms to preserve linen, books and shoes against mould. Rideau Hall in Ottawa, Canada, had a hot air furnace, three conservatories, and two skating rinks. At the King's House in Jamaica, a pretty two-storeyed house with open verandahs and curlicue trim, there were twenty-six rooms for black under-servants, and a large swimming bath. A dispatch cart ran between the King's House and the Colonial Secretary's office daily – and 'a Telephone erected between these two places'.

A clear hierarchy of governorships emerges from the questionnaires. Ottawa and Melbourne, the capitals of fully-fledged, self-governing dominions, came top, with salaries of £10,000 a year – the equivalent of around £750,000 today. Next Ceylon and New South Wales on £7,000 (£525,000) a year, followed by Jamaica, Malta, Hong Kong, Singapore, the Cape and Gibraltar at £5,000 (£375,000). The Falkland Islands were worth £1,200 a year (£90,000), and then things descended to the West Indian islands, where a governorship fetched a few hundred a year.

These were jobs not unlike those of today's top chief executives. But wherever you were, flying the flag did not come cheap. From Tasmania, Governor Weld (salary £3,500; and the income from his considerable sheep stations in New Zealand) replied to the questionnaire on 6 June 1879. Government House was twenty years old, a handsome neo-gothic country house built of rosy sandstone, with seventy-three rooms and forty acres of ground. He had twelve children, and an aide-de-camp who misused the Governor's household account. In four years he had spent more than £10,000 over and above his pay and allowances to entertain, travel, keep up the garden and cover his ordinary living expenses. In his opinion, 'it would not be advisable for anyone to take the position who is not prepared to find £2,000 a year out of his own pocket' – around £150,000 at today's prices.

As time went on, details in the four volumes of files were updated, and information on other, more recently acquired, colonial possessions was added: Zomba, the home of Rider Haggard's *People of the Mist*, in British Central Africa, now Malawi – gloriously set on the slopes of a forested mountain, where a 'hammock crew' was kept; and on Zanzibar, Nairobi and Entebbe, Uganda, newly acquired outposts in the 1890s. In October 1894, Francis Winter wrote from Port Moresby, in today's Papua New Guinea, then notorious for its man-eating inhabitants: 'Without a little additional explanation some of the answers might be misleading to a gentleman whose life had ... been spent in civilised parts of the Globe.' Government House was built on piles and walled with galvanized iron. It did for 'a couple of single men but is hardly adequate for a family'. There was not a complete set of furniture or domestic utensils in the house. Vehicles of any description were practically useless and the only servants, while 'good-tempered and pleasant', were 'unskilled and careless'.

'Clothing: probably the same as is worn in India or Africa will do. Sun not so dangerous here as I understand it is in India. No tailors, shoemakers, barbers etc in the Possession.'

The fast-paced, crowded, multicultural London that I came to live in was so unlike the empty wildness of provincial Canada where I grew up that I was struck, reading what these governors had to say, by how tumultuous it must have been for a man to find himself suddenly catapulted into the position of governing a place of which he knew nothing, away across the seas. Who would do the job? How was he chosen? What was he like? What did he think? What was he *actually* doing, so far away from home?

I began to dig: Colonial Office dispatches, private letters and diaries, nineteenth-century memoirs and dusty biographies from the early twentieth century. The people that I began to uncover were nothing like what I expected. Men like John Glover, who left home at the age of eleven to go away to sea, and by the age of twenty-five was in the forefront of the fight against slavery, in charge of Lagos. Arthur Charles Hamilton Gordon, cosseted younger son of the fourth Earl of Aberdeen and prime minister of England, confounded expectations as the first British governor of Fiji, living in a house made of reeds and thatch alongside chieftains who twenty years before had been cannibals. Yet he declared them every ounce his social equal, and devised a system of liberal government that uniquely combined their traditions with British justice. Then there was fifty-year-old William Bloomfield Douglas, first resident of today's Darwin in northern Australia, reported as a hard-drinking bully to his subordinates. Yet he recorded a relentless battle against fever, dysentery and mental illness in his diary. There was no *typical* Victorian governor.

In fact our picture of the British colonial governor – haughty, stoic and pristine, in smart dress uniform, helmet topped with waving plumes – is an Edwardian stereotype. Most governors before the First World War grew up in modest circumstances, many in the colonies or in Ireland, and were officers in the army or the navy, members of parliament who had failed to be re-elected, or – emerging during this period – young administrators who started out as colonial clerks or magistrates and worked their way up. Only in Singapore and the Malay States, Hong Kong or Ceylon, where entry to local service was, like in India, by examination, was a young man offered training as an 'Eastern Cadet'. They were very few.

Once in post, governors had few resources – a handful of troops and not much cash. Written communications with London took weeks. Many lived surrounded by potentially hostile inhabitants. The best governors came to terms with them, accepted and understood them. In west Africa they led an ongoing fight against slavery. In the West Indies, and colonies like Mauritius and British Guiana – today's Guyana – governors had to stand up for the rule of law, defending the weak against the power of the few, often facing a costly personal battle with the vested interests of white planters and businessmen who used powerful connections to raise protests at home in the newspapers and in parliament. Other times their actions provoked riots and even wars.

In spite of its unvarnished confidence in British racial superiority, the

Colonial Office in London, to whom the governors were responsible, consistently stood up for what the officials saw as fair play and justice towards subject peoples. When Anthony Trollope dined in Jamaica in the winter of 1858–9 the Governor's table was the only one in the colony where black and white dined together. It is striking how many governors of the period should call attention to the abusive connotation of the word 'nigger'; how many deplored the offensive behaviour of ordinary white men in the presence of other races, to the extent that, in Fiji in the late 1870s, the Governor insisted in keeping them away from any ceremony of importance. 'The whole tone of the white population of the Colony . . . shows a complete indifference to [the] tradition of honour,' wrote Hugh Clifford, as he tried to grapple with the issues of racial tension as acting governor in Trinidad in 1906.

The picture of the colonial governor that began to emerge was one of a man operating with his shirt sleeves rolled up, working long hours, living by his wits, riding hard, commissioning surveys and systems of sanitation, negotiating with tribesmen, drafting laws that would form the basis of a society to come, and losing sleep at night. The danger of disease was a constant theme in memoirs and letters: these were men obsessed with their health. No one knew what caused malaria and other tropical fevers. Large doses of quinine, the remedy of the time, were almost as painful as the attacks themselves. For scores of governors recurring illness took a terrible toll, and permanently ruined their health.

But their freedom of action was remarkable. Many governors had exceptional power to make of a place what they would. They laid out towns, built railways, created assemblies, drafted laws, set up schools, hospitals, galleries and learned societies: things that we now take for granted, but which defined the character of places and the societies that came after them. Some drank too much, or were irascible or difficult. Others were weak and incompetent. But – surprisingly – scarcely any were corrupt.

Power was the attraction, but the personal costs were high. Everything the Governor said and did was noted and discussed. It was one thing for a junior officer in the colonies to conduct a liaison with a local girl; another for the Governor, the leader of society. Governors tended to marry late – when on home leave, well into their forties. Many then spent months, even years, separated from their wives and especially their children, who were sent back to relatives or to school in England. Many suffered heartbreaking loneliness. They were exasperated with the formality of their lives and the requirements of precedence. All agreed that no one in London understood their jobs, or appreciated the difficulties that they had to face.

'Why, some of them seem to think that you can govern a West Indian colony with a fiddle and a ham-bone,' Sir Courtenay Knollys remarked to a fellow governor when he arrived to take over Antigua in 1895. Finally, the job was expensive, and it often cost a good deal of private income to keep the flag flying.

Meanwhile back home in England, the Colonial Office rested in the shadow of the India Office. The loss of the American colonies in 1776 had been a huge blow to its prestige. In 1801 responsibility for the colonies – hitherto administered by a committee of the Privy Council called the Board of Trade and Plantations – had been united with the war department. However, the gravity of the Crimean War, which broke out in 1854, called for a dedicated Minister of War. A separate post of Secretary of State for the Colonies was created.

Unlike India, most of the places the Colonial Office administered were regarded as beyond the pale of civilization – if anyone had heard of them at all. Its mandate was to administer the nation's overseas dependencies with as little trouble and expense as possible. A position as governor in the colonies had nothing like the glamour of India, with its vast wealth and vice-regal status. With the exception of governor-general of Canada, the Cape, or commander-in-chief of Gibraltar or Malta, a colonial governor was usually seen as someone who had been passed over at home, relegated to a small provincial society of second-raters abroad.

Thus, when at last they returned home to Britain to retire, governors found themselves unacknowledged. From high command and travel around the Empire, their worlds had shrunk. Few in England cared in the least who they had been, what sights they had seen, or what they had achieved.

This book is about what it was like to be a governor – 'the officer appointed by the Crown to administer' a British colony between 1857 and 1912, during the years when Britain was still shopping for raw materials and looking for new markets, of ad hoc regulation and uncertain policy, fervent exploration, and free-for-all acquisition of territory – especially in Africa. The reluctance of the Disraeli government which fell in 1880 to add to Empire was swiftly overcome when an international scramble for central and eastern portions of that great continent began. It was a time when horizons were vast and much of the world was still pristine, the last time that a governor, acting alone, could still put his personal stamp on a town, a region, or a country.

By 1901, when Queen Victoria died, the idea of a unified British Empire was firmly established. In the Colonial Office an eight-year regime under the Birmingham businessman Joseph Chamberlain, as Secretary of State, increasingly rationalized and streamlined the administration of the colonies. In 1906 the office of colonial governor reached its zenith. He became 'the single and supreme authority responsible to, and representative of His Majesty'.

The first protestors against British rule began taking to the streets more than 100 years ago. Today any discussion of colonialism is fraught with controversy; talking about the men in charge, who created its legacies, is even more so. But the Empire happened. Extant material from those who were governed during this time is scarce; this is necessarily 'white man's' history. This is a book about ordinary men, set down in strange places, among strange peoples, facing circumstances and events they could never have imagined – and how, for better or worse, they made attempts to order them. Like us, they made promises they did not keep. Their views are not our views, and many of their actions cannot be condoned. But it is in the details of their lives, and with a knowledge of who they were, that we can begin to understand our own world better.

In the period between 1857 and 1912 there were over 300 governors, or lieutenant governors, administrators, high commissioners and presidents, as they were called, depending on where they served. I wanted to look at the impact of personality on situations and places and policies; to give the reader a sense of the randomness and accident that I was uncovering beneath the surface of the history of Empire as we have come to know it, by looking at brief episodes in the careers of a variety of men.

My search for characters began with the fifty-nine men who answered Michael Hicks Beach's questionnaire in 1879. From these, I selected an initial seven: Thomas Callaghan, the son of an Irish woollen draper from rural County Cork, ordinary, unremarkable, the backbone of the service; John Glover, swashbuckling hero of the Ashanti wars, who became known as 'Oba Golobar', King Glover, on the west African slave coast; and Arthur Gordon, son of a prime minister, gawky, conceited, and compulsively fascinated by the people of Fiji whom he governed. Sir Bartle Frere, enormously eminent after a lifetime of service in India, set off one of the bloodiest encounters with Zulu warriors Britain had ever seen while resident at the Cape in South

Africa. John Pope Hennessy, selfish, disastrously impetuous and devastatingly charming, carried on a career as a governor so wildly erratic it would be impossible to make up. The Marquess of Lorne, in Canada, was married to Princess Louise, the daughter of Queen Victoria. Romantic, naïve, and probably gay, he set off on a modern royal progress across the prairies complete with a press corps to hold councils with the Indians, to try to save them from extinction. Later, Henry Hesketh Bell, an amusing and compulsive diarist, built a stockbroker Tudor government house at Entebbe while serving in Uganda, where he wiped out a pandemic of sleeping sickness.

Bell's rival in East Africa was Sir Percy Girouard, a Canadian railway engineer who gave away the lands of the Maasai to the British. Frank Swettenham, Frederick Lugard (with his formidable wife Flora Shaw) and Hugh Clifford were huge figures in the colonial pantheon. Venerated as model governors even after the demise of the Empire in the 1960s, they were powerful, effective, vain, righteous, highly intelligent and deeply complicated men. Meanwhile I could not resist finding out more about Sydney Olivier, a founding member of the Fabian socialists and close friend of George Bernard Shaw, who went to be governor in Jamaica. Next to nothing is known of George Strahan, whose few letters from the Gold Coast, telling of men dying of fever, I found in the private correspondence of the Secretary of State, Lord Carnarvon. Hallam Tennyson had no qualification to be a governor other than that he had been private secretary to his father, Alfred, the poet laureate – but it was his wife Audrey, quiet, unassuming, who wrote long letters to her mother when they served in Australia, that caught my eye. I wanted these people to speak for themselves.

1 Dispatch

To the nerve centre of Empire, the Colonial Office: in 1857, a crumbling warren of offices at the end of Downing Street, where the steps now run down to St James's Park. Numbers 13 and 14 were like numbers 10 and 11 today, venerable seventeenth-century houses. Twenty years before, a survey had declared them unsafe and beyond repair. Now, passages had been knocked between the two buildings on the first and second floors to provide the offices of the Secretary of State and two under-secretaries, their private secretaries and the senior clerks. Up in the attics were the junior clerks and servants, while the basement was inhabited by copyists, bookbinders, the library and the living quarters of the housekeeper. Rain poured through the roof and the sky was visible through cracks in the walls. Ceilings bulged, fires smoked and foul smells rose from a medieval sewage ditch nearby. The following year, when twenty-six-year-old Lord Carnarvon arrived to take up his post as Under-Secretary of State for the Colonies, the department did not possess a decent map – or even enough chairs and tables to operate properly.

Fifty colonies (or so) around the world: in London there were sixty-two employees. Of these, nine were copyists, five were messengers and four were porters. Only six people were graded above the level of assistant clerk. Boys – 'drawn from a rank in society to which liberal education & cultivated address belong as a matter of course' – came into the office from school and after ten or fifteen years of poor pay (a fourth-class clerk began on £100 a year, considerably less than it took to live as a gentleman in London), copying, sorting papers, and running errands, they gradually worked their way up. The office operated with pens and ink, paper held together with pins and files bound up with red tape. Staff normally worked a five-day week, from eleven to five. From this, time off was taken for lunch, 'prepared in the kitchen and carried up to the gentlemen between two and three – and for tea'. This was still the normal pace in 1873, when the Permanent Secretary directed that clerks *must* arrive at work no later than twelve. Annual vacations – of several weeks – were liberal.

Even the most senior clerks were not too sure of all the places the nation had laid claim to over the past 250 years, much less how they were run. The first official attempt to catalogue 'Her Majesty's Colonial Possessions' was in 1839; a second was begun in 1860. Such was the difficulty experienced in collecting information from the colonies that the clerks viewed their efforts – published two years later in the first edition of the *Colonial Office List* (an annual publication that would go on until 1966) – as only 'an approximation of what they at first expected to achieve'. They tried to codify and sort: North America with the West Indies, Europe – which besides the military bastions of Gibraltar, Malta and Cyprus also included little known outposts in Africa. The Indian Ocean possession of Mauritius was slightly muddled with Australia, while Hong Kong and the Falkland Islands were tucked in at the end. As Herman Merivale, the Permanent Under-Secretary, said in a lecture on colonies and colonization in 1861: 'so strangely various are the circumstances of the colonial societies . . . so powerful is that taste for piecemeal legislation, so instinctive that dislike of systems and uniformity, which have ever characterized the political mind of England', that the scale and character of colonial government was nowhere the same.

Colonial Office ministers were junior, and they changed frequently. Office routine was geared to periodic work crises provoked by the arrivals and departures of the monthly mails, and the demands of parliament. From the point of view of the Secretary of State the most important issues of the day were based in the white settler colonies of Canada, Australia and South Africa: how to manage emigration, how best to settle them, and once settled, to organize them with forms of constitutional government. The affairs of lesser colonies – especially those populated by people who were not white – were negligible, remote, usually disease-ridden, and generally regarded as dreadful spots. At any time, though, tensions could explode. Spain encroached on Gibraltar; the French claimed the fisheries of Newfoundland; scandal, corruption and race riots would erupt in the West Indies. The fight against slavery, corruption and disease in west Africa was unending. Colonies were expected to be self-supporting; the cost of a garrison, or funds awarded for other purposes, had to be repaid out of local taxes, customs revenues and other fees.

Governors were not easy to procure. True, the position had a certain social cachet – but even for plum posts, men were difficult to find. Especially to the tropics, the prospects of isolation, the climate and the dangers of drink, combined with disease, malarias and other fevers, made the most promising posting seem like a death sentence.

The India Office had a system of recruitment inherited from the East India Company, which began with a two-year training course at Hailey-bury College. This led into a formal career structure administered in India. In the Colonial Office, making appointments came under the title of 'Patronage', granted 'at the pleasure of the Crown', which meant effectively that all posts were in the personal gift of the Secretary of State. Indeed, it was virtually impossible to become a governor unless you were known to him, or, at the least, one of the permanent secretaries.

The top three appointments in any colony – the governor, the chief justice and the colonial secretary – were all controlled from London. Once in post, the Governor's powers of hiring and firing his officials were limited: any sus-pension from office, and the appointment of anyone who was paid more than £100 a year, had to be referred to the Secretary of State, who could substitute someone else instead. There was no sense that good work in one colony nec-essarily brought promotion to another. Magistrates in the West Indies, for example, could be assigned to the same remote district for an entire career. In 1869 the Colonial Office introduced a competitive examination to recruit a very few young men to train as 'Eastern Cadets' in Ceylon, the Straits Settle-ment and Hong Kong – territories previously regarded as part of India's purview. Until well after the First World War, the functions of what we would today call 'Personnel' were decidedly vague and ramshackle.

In spite of these drawbacks, day after day petitions arrived in Downing Street from the parents or friends of hopeful young men seeking appoint-ments in the colonies – most of them unsolicited and invariably rejected. 'His Lordship regrets that the vacancies are very few and the list of candi-dates is already long.' A former acting governor from the Gold Coast – 'a well meaning gentlemanlike man with some small amount of talents fitted for a small place' – who had been unemployed for four years as a result of 'noxiousness of the climate' was given 'the usual answer' (if an opening occurred he would be advised) when he requested another appointment. Widows whose husbands' pensions had never been paid could wait in vain for help from the Colonial Office.

Sir Rawson Rawson, Governor-in-Chief of the Windward Islands, based in Barbados, was passed over, admittedly at the age of sixty-four, after a lifetime working his way up through clerkships in the Board of Trade, to civil secretary to the governor-general of Canada, colonial secretary of the Cape of Good Hope and governor of the Bahamas. He was told he had been in subordinate positions too long to make a satisfactory chief. His colleague, William des Voeux, then administrator of St Lucia, saw his principal defect as fearing responsibility, 'but this he has in common with several special favourites of the Colonial Office and he is at least a gentleman, which is for governors evidently not a *sine qua non*'.

In the case of a governorship, when mistakes could be so costly, it was immensely comforting, enormously helpful, to appoint someone the Secretary of State knew personally. Explorers, military commanders, former politicians and experienced local administrators all basically qualified. A governor's term was limited to six years. The best way to find one, when there wasn't someone suitable close to hand, was the old boy network.

Two months after he took up office as Secretary of State for the Colonies for the third time, in 1874, Lord Carnarvon wrote to Sir Bartle Frere at the India Office for his advice on whom he would recommend for the tricky assignment of governing the Gold Coast, where the noble kingdom of the Ashanti had been freshly sacked by British troops, and warring tribes continued to fuel the slave trade with captives.

'There could be no better school for frontier *war* than that of the Punjab,' Frere replied. The kind of man Carnarvon required was at his best aged thirty to forty, 'or 45 at the outside', for 'if they have not the ballast and discretion you require at 30 or 35, they will never have it'. Frere went on to produce a list of candidates that reads like a racing card from the Grand National:

- Major Brabagon Pottinger: Cadet of season 1857. Married, an excellent officer with plenty of ability and sound common sense – served for sometime in command of the Sind Frontier Artillery – a nephew of the defender of Heart, and like him in character –
- Captain C. S. Reynolds: Bombay Staff Corps. Married. Cadet of Season 1859. Serving with the Sind Horse and as assistant political on the Sind Frontier. An officer of good ability and sound good sense. He has shewn great tact and temper on several occasions in his present appointment . . . well acquainted with the Sind system of managing the wild frontier tribes.
- Captain W. Reynolds . . . Plenty of common sense – with great perseverance and steadiness of character and always ready for work.
- Captain A. L. McNair . . . Steady, with plenty of energy in him –

But by the time Carnarvon received this list from Frere, it was too late: time had been too critical. Carnarvon had no choice but to choose the man closest to the troubles, and transfer the man in charge of Lagos.

Once selected, the name of a prospective governor was submitted to the Queen. She took an interest: of some she would have heard, a few she might have met. A governor, unlike a Foreign Office minister to even the most obscure nation, was almost never summoned to an audience. Her Majesty's agreement secured, the governor's letters patent would be issued in her name: 'Victoria, by the Grace of God, of the United Kingdom of Great Britain and Ireland, Queen, Defender of the Faith, to Our Trusty and Well-beloved . . .' And so would commence the pages of the new governor's instructions, in rolling Elizabethan phrases, 'and further know you, that We reposing especial trust and confidence in the prudence, courage, and loyalty of you . . . Our Governor . . . in and over Our said Settlement of . . .' each adapted according to the place he was to govern.

This was heady stuff. To the governor was given overall responsibility for law and order, revenue and expenditure, and leading society in his colony. He had the power to prorogue legislative bodies and pardon criminals. At all times he was to make sure the Secretary of State knew what was going on. He was to tour the country, open new buildings, confer honours. Most governors were given one or two overriding tasks to perform. His job was to succeed and generally leave a place better than when he arrived.

There were different classes of governor. Governors-in-chief or governors-general were responsible for several colonies. Those answering to them might be lieutenant governors, administrators, or presidents of councils. Workloads varied enormously depending on where a man was going – 'in inverse rather than in direct proportion to the importance of what is governed', drily observed Sir William des Voeux after his experience in five governorships. 'The higher the place in the official hierarchy, the more capable as a rule are the subordinate workers; the lower the place, the greater is the amount of drudgery to be undergone by the administrator, who is obliged to do much which is ordinarily done by subordinate officers, and has also to exercise a much closer supervision over his assistants.'

In Canada and Australia, and the Cape and Natal in South Africa, parliamentary governments had been established. Here a governor walked a razor's edge. He was like a constitutional monarch, his powers 'brittle if too heavily pressed, a shadow if tactlessly advertised, substantial only when exercised discreetly in the background', wrote the author John

Buchan – who would later hold the office himself – of the governor-generalship of Lord Minto in Canada from 1898 to 1904. In places like Ottawa, the governor-general had so little power that he could scarcely order a lock for a door in Government House without the authority of the Department of Public Works, much less make appointments. It was even becoming unusual for him to have the power to pardon prisoners, or commute a sentence of death.

The most taxing jobs were in the Crown colonies, where, with few exceptions, the ruling white Briton was vastly outnumbered by people of other races. Here the governor was personally responsible for every decision and the work of all government departments, often operating virtually on his own. At the Colonial Office there was a long-standing principle that the governor, their man on the spot, should be supported in almost any situation not covered in his instructions. Everywhere, however, the day-to-day manner of government differed.

On important issues the governor of a Crown colony was instructed to consult his Executive Council, an advisory body of the most senior government officials in the colony: the chief justice, ranked next to him in precedence; the colonial secretary, the head of the bureaucracy and his real number two, who stepped up to act for him if he was taken ill or away on leave; the treasurer and the attorney-general. Their mandate, however, was purely advisory. The governor's say was final.

Des Voeux is frank. To grant suffrage to the 'non-European races' in Crown colonies would 'render the position of Europeans precarious, if not altogether untenable'. To give the vote to the Europeans, however, 'would almost certainly be prejudicial to the interests of the majority'; hence, the widespread instrument of the Legislative Council. Chaired by the governor, it was made up of the members of the Executive Council, plus a number of 'unofficial' members, representatives of key interest groups in the colony – nominated by the governor. 'Unofficials' were never permitted to outnumber 'officials' of the government: for it was the governor, and his servants, who were to speak on behalf of the great, unrepresented, non-white, majority of the population. Thus did the white man pick up his burden.

A governor's support system was slim. In his own office he would have a private secretary or two, often a relative he brought with him. His aide-de-camp (ADC) was his adjutant, perhaps his younger brother or that of his wife. The ADC took charge of the smooth running of Government House, and of protocol: placing the guests, introducing them, making sure no one monopolized the governor.

Signing the contract for a governorship involved paying substantial fees and stamp duties in connection with the appointment. A governor's passage and that of his private secretary and their servants were paid, and their travelling expenses within the colony – but not those of his wife and family. No presents were to be accepted. Beneath him, his colonial secretary was not paid until he had produced the annual 'Blue Book', the report of the colony laid before parliament every year. The same applied to the treasurer until he had rendered the accounts. Leaves of absence of up to a year, when only half salary was paid, confined as far as possible to cases 'either of serious indisposition or of urgent private affairs', were discouraged until the end of a term. Otherwise, officials were permitted six weeks holiday a year. Pensions were first introduced in 1865.

Governor's dress uniform: black silk cocked hat dressed with plumes of white swan over scarlet feathers; a 'coatee' of blue cloth with scarlet collar and cuffs trimmed with silver embroidery. In the tropics, a coat of white drill trimmed with gold braid topped with a white helmet did for ordinary ceremonial occasions

All sorts of checks and balances seem to be in place: a host of rules and regulations accompanied the governor – from how dispatches should be written, to what uniform he should wear when, to how and when he should fly the flag. Elaborate tables of precedence were supplied, which dictated in what order which people should process in to dinner, and who was to be seated next to whom. 'Persons entitled to precedence in the United Kingdom or in Foreign Countries, are not entitled as of a right, to the same precedence in the British Colonies . . .'

'I have elaborate instructions from the Colonial Office as to the custody of treasure,' wrote Arthur Gordon when he first moved into his house of reed and thatch in Fiji in 1875. 'It ought to be kept in a fireproof stone vault with three different locks, each key in the keeping of a different person. As a fact, the treasure boxes I brought down are piled close to my bed, in a room which would burn like flax . . . and which has no key. But on the top of the pile is a basket containing Snip and her puppies . . .'

The Colonial Office kept in constant touch with its governors through a stream of circulars, keeping them up to the mark on responding to dispatches within a month, giving them news on new postal routes, instructions on how to handle deserters from merchant seamen, repatriating pauper lunatics (they could not recommend any general system) and assigning new badges to colonies. Many issues had come before the Queen herself in Council, and circulars would be headed as if they had come directly from the Court at Windsor, giving governors the sense of a direct link with the monarch herself.

Governors were to be on the lookout for important escaped prisoners and Fenian outlaws from Ireland. Every assistance was to be given to the artist Miss Marianne North on her visit to Australia, New Zealand, South Africa and Mauritius to make paintings 'of remarkable trees and plants' for the Royal Gardens of Kew. They were kept up to date on the latest findings on leprosy, advances in sanitation, and instructed in detail, courtesy of the director of public gardens in Jamaica, on sowing plantations of cinchona, the tree from South America that produced quinine.

In 1881 Secretary of State Lord Kimberley wrote that several examples of 'revoltingly botched executions' had come to his attention, which 'in the interest both of humanity and decency' had to be prevented. He attached a detailed memorandum on 'the Execution of Prisoners by Hanging with a long Drop'. That year too, governors had received instructions to hold a census in April, as in Britain, and according to identical methodology. Sample enumerator forms, laying out names and addresses, professions and occupations, from the British Registrar-General were enclosed.

The results were shambolic. Only Canada managed properly to comply, while across the globe, governor after governor adapted the instructions to his own circumstances. In Western Australia the Governor forgot to include the Aborigines, which made nonsense of his crime figures. The Gold Coast's figures were based on the Governor's estimate; in a subsequent attempt, he enlisted the help of his native kings: calabashes filled with Indian corn were used to count the males; cowries for females.

However inaccurate the numbers, the single table that resulted, placed at the back of the 1881 Census of England and Wales, brought the true enormity of what the Colonial Office and its governors in the field were dealing with into focus for perhaps the first time. 'The territory occupied by the 254,187,630 inhabitants of the British Empire is estimated as consisting of slightly over eight millions of English square miles, – an area more than twice as large as Europe, larger than North America, almost half as large as Asia, and not very far short of one-sixth of the land surface of the earth.'

In 1875 the Colonial Office moved into substantial – if plain – new offices in the corner of the grand building on Whitehall which George Gilbert Scott had built for the Foreign and India Offices. The workload increased. Britain had acquired the Straits Settlements – today's Singapore and Malaysia – while the laying of telegraph cables both east and west prompted a series of reorganizations. By 1879 work was divided into three departments: 'Eastern and West Indian', 'North American and Australian' and 'African and Mediterranean'. Thus, bizarrely, Jamaica and British Honduras (today's Belize), as well as Hong Kong, Ceylon (Sri Lanka), Mauritius and the Falkland Islands – all fell under the eye of the Permanent Under-Secretary, Charles Cox, who had risen through the Colonial Office from his appointment as a clerk, fifty years before. In spite of a near doubling in scale of the amount of correspondence, by 1890 the number of staff had increased by only three. Before long, typewriters would come into use, and the powerful Joseph Chamberlain, with his business brain and sense of imperial mission, would come into office as Secretary of State in 1895.

Governors in post kept a constant watch on openings that appeared, writing repeatedly to Downing Street for news of possible chances for promotion. Most of them knew their contemporaries – if not personally, certainly by reputation. Service in the islands of the West Indies brought many governors together. When in London, they gravitated to hotels or rooms near St James's, close to clubs like the Travellers, the Athenaeum and the Carlton and within walking distance of the Colonial Office, where they would call in to discuss affairs with the under-secretary and clerks with whom they had been corresponding. In 1887 the first conference of colonial governors from around the globe was held in London. Gradually a new breed of professional governor was emerging. Whereas in the 1850s only three men had risen through the ranks of colonial administration in different colonies to become governors, by the 1890s, half had done so.

'Up to now I have been entitled, as Administrator of Dominica, to wear the Civil uniform of the third class; a rather simple affair of dark-blue cloth with gold-embroidered cuffs and collar. But now that I am, to all intents and purposes, a pukka Governor I can wear the uniform of the second class, which is a much more imposing suit,' wrote Henry Hesketh Bell as he anticipated his promotion to Governor of Uganda in 1905. 'There is a good deal of gold lace on the chest and coat-tails, and it costs, I find, a pretty penny. There is also a white undress uniform, for the tropics, which will be a great comfort in Uganda. A white helmet with a plume of scarlet and white feathers goes with it together with a Court sword . . .'

The moment a governor heard his name had been submitted to the Queen, it was time to prepare to move. Unless he happened to be in England on leave, there was no time for a briefing beforehand. Many went directly to their posts from somewhere else in the Empire. They culled their information about their destination from government Blue Books and headlines in the newspapers.

The Army & Navy stores, shirt-makers and tailors were ready for the departing colonial servant. Recommended, more or less for everywhere, was the following list:

COMPLETE

INDIA OUTFIT

FOR

£45

12 White Shirts, Linen Fronts

24 " Collars

6 Saratta Shirts, Collars on

6 Flannel Shirts

6 Sleeping Jumpers

6 Pair Sleeping Pyjamas

12 Gauze Banians [a loose fitting jacket]

6 Pair Gauze Drawers

12 Pair Merino Socks

12 " Cotton "

2 " Braces "

24 Irish Cambric Handkerchiefs

1 Anti-Cholera Belt [flannel waistband]

1 Pith Helmet

1 Felt Hat

2 Puggaries [cloth that goes round the brim of a hat]

1 rug

1 Soiled Clothes Bag,
Frame & Lock

1 Housewife [sewing kit]

1 Cabin Portmanteau

1 Overland Trunk

12 Towels

4 Bath Towels

2 Pair Canvas Shoes

1 Mosquito Curtain

Sponge and Bag

1 Coloured Flannel
Suit

1 Serge "

2 Brown Holland "

2 " Extra Trousers

Advertisers in the colonial press offered every kind of stationery and portable writing case, inkpots and stands, stamping presses and seals; seeds; tobacco, cigarettes and snuff; 'Ellis & John's new long cloak, made of patented "Solaro", the new sunproof cloth' was 'a wonderful combination of bed, hammock and stretcher, in a great coat'. There were 'Tents for All Climates', 'Watertight boxes', pianos – 'specially constructed for extreme and trying climates', safes, shipping, hotels and insurance. No one could do without Dr Collis Browne's chlorodyne, one of the period's most popular patent medicines for the treatment of cholera. A potent mixture of laudanum, tincture of cannabis and chloroform, it was also recommended for a host of other ailments, from sleeplessness and 'calming the system', to consumption, asthma, bronchitis, diarrhoea and whooping cough.

And then there were sad, sad, sad advertisements like this one, laid out across a half page in the front of the *Colonial Office List* for 1879, in soft Kate Greenaway style typeface: 'Mrs Jacob, The Close, Salisbury, offers a home to little girl or boy as companion to her own two children. Beautiful large old House and Garden . . .' for the children of the governors who could not go with them, or had to be sent home to be schooled.

With experience, the challenge of tackling Africa and other tropical locations began to be collected into handbooks that started to appear in the 1880s. 'Look upon the sun as an enemy, and never go into the direct rays without having the head covered by a pith helmet,' the newcomer was advised. Such headgear, 'light in weight, with a broad brim, and made so that they afford shade to the back of the neck', was essential, along with mosquito nets, hot water bottles (indispensable in the treatment of malaria) and water filters. While governors often revelled in feasts of local produce – Lady Glover reports eating bullfrogs, land crabs and cabbage palms, 'each dish costing the life of a tree', as well as turtle, flying fish, and 'yams and fruit of every kind' when she was wife of the Governor in Antigua – it was considered impossible to live without European staples. For Africa a European provision order for a year would include tins of meat and fish, fruit, jams and biscuits; plain biscuits such as 'water' and 'soda' often took the place of bread on the march. 'In a country like Africa every person should take a tepid bath at least once a day.' It was necessary however to guard against chills of every kind. Only flannel was to be worn next to the skin, under a white cotton suit. 'To protect the region of the abdomen from constant chills . . . the flannel belt or "Kamarbund" is usually worn . . . 10 inches wide, 6 feet long, unshrinkable flannel – wound around the waist at least twice.'

William Denison was forty-two when he went with his pregnant wife, Caroline, and their five young children to his first post as governor to Van Diemen's Land. The only way for the Denison family to travel to Tasmania in 1846 was via a regular trader by way of the Cape of Good Hope. Their experience was little different from the Gordons travelling to Fiji in 1875, the Freres to the Cape in 1879, or the Tennysons to Australia in 1899. Vast preparations had to be made for long voyages and stays away from home that could last for many years. Denison packed up his library of nearly 2,000 books. 'Every article of furniture, plate, crockery, glass, household utensils, saddlery, harness, etc., had to be purchased, for I was told that it would not be wise to trust to the local market for the supply of these.' No allowance for this expenditure – some £2,000 – was provided by the government.

At last, having seen their servants and their household goods – 'no small portion of the cargo' – on board, 'we bade adieu to those whom we were not destined to see again for very many years', Caroline Denison wrote sadly. They set sail from the Port of London, on the greasy brown waters of the Thames.

For days the Denisons were becalmed in the Channel. Ten days out from Portsmouth, they ran into a 'fearful gale' that lasted three days and nights. At its height, a heavy sea struck the ship and washed over the deck, carrying away a foresail, and a man off the jib-boom. 'I shall never forget the impression of horror produced by the awful sound of the sea striking the ship, followed almost instantly by the terrible cry, "a man overboard!" Everything was done that could be done, but it was of no use; in such a tremendous sea, one felt there could be but little hope,' wrote Caroline. A month later, the pain of leaving England and everything she knew had not left her. 'Alas!' she wrote after an evening spent star-gazing on the deck, days south of Madeira. 'Our northern stars are fast descending in the sky and soon we shall have lost sight of them . . . the last link between us and England.'

The Denisons, like generations of governors, before and after, were now on their own.

2 Commander Glover on the Slave Coast

Lagos 1863–72

Sailing south past the Cape Verde Islands on a tiny steamer called the *Day-spring* in June 1857, twenty-eight-year-old John Glover found himself slowly being seduced by the suffocating heat, the damp luminous air, the sea, 'as smooth as a lake', and the 'strange things [that] come up to look at us, the monsters of the deep: sperm whales and porpoises and the pretty dolphins'.

'This morning,' he wrote in a diary he was keeping for the woman he loved, but whose name we never learn, 'we sailed through a whole fleet of beautiful nautilus with their delicate sails of silver silk.' At night the cool air, the 'phospheric appearance of the water', the 'glorious splendour' of the Southern Cross, the intense brightness of the moon, at once soothed and enraptured him.

'A man of dash and daring, a negotiator gifted with the power of ingratiating himself with strangers', as his fond wife later described him, over the next seventeen years John Glover was to become famous along the whole of the west coast of Africa, his name (transposed to 'Golobar'), 'like Livingstone's', known among all the peoples of the interior, an action-hero, selfless leader of men, resourceful, enterprising and a fighter against slavery – in short, the ideal Victorian governor.

But in 1857 he was just a part of a ten-man expedition funded by the Foreign Office at the behest of the Royal Geographical Society to chart the Niger, one of the world's epic rivers, whose history stretches back into myth. For centuries, not even the Arab traders who sailed along its reaches knew where it began and ended. In 1795 the British explorer Mungo Park set out to reach the mouth of the Niger from its source, high in the east of Sierra Leone on the west coast of Africa. But after a year, over 1,200 miles of arduous travelling, and the loss of almost all his men, Park was able to discover only that the legendary river flowed east. Ten years later, he returned to continue his exploration. On a six-month journey of unspeakable suffering, forty of the forty-five Europeans with him died. Park went on with four of the survivors, only to meet his death in mysterious circumstances on the river near Boussa, in the north of today's Nigeria. Between 1806 and 1857 thirteen more expeditions cost the deaths of almost entire companies – twenty-nine out of thirty-four, nineteen out of twenty-three – from fever or dysentery.

The *Dayspring* expedition was led by Dr William Balfour Baikie, a protégé of Roderick Murchison, one of the founders of the Royal Geographical Society. Thirty-two-year-old Dr Baikie, a naval surgeon and keen naturalist, had headed an attempt on the Niger three years before. That expedition had made medical history because not one of the twelve men died of fever, due, Baikie was convinced, to his novel use of half a glass of quinine wine early in the morning as a prophylactic against fever. On this new expedition, Glover, a naval lieutenant and experienced surveyor, had volunteered to serve as his deputy.

As the *Dayspring* sailed south through the Atlantic, Glover prepared for his ordeal. After an early morning bath and a cup of coffee, he spent the day reading about the exploration of Africa, and learning Hausa, the language of some of the peoples he would meet along the Niger, from the ship's doctor. On 11 June, thirty-five days out from Liverpool, he had his first sight of the west African coast.

'All day we were steaming along with the endless heavy swell that is ever rolling on this to me (though I can hardly tell you why) fascinating shore . . . The richness and rank luxuriance of its dark green weeds makes a pleasant background under this scorching sun to the sandy shore and the racing surf. [The land is not high but] so varied by slopes between which numberless rivers find their way to the sea, or are lost in lagoons teeming with animal and monster life, while the thick jungle . . . and the forest of mango and palm by which the whole country is bound affords shelter to birds of gorgeous plumage which only display their gay colours in the glare of a tropical sun. In spite of its fevers and mosquitoes all this has a charm for me.'

The following day, the *Dayspring* anchored off Cape Palmos to take on a crew of fifty black 'Krumen' for the voyage up the Niger. Dawn broke on a scene of dozens of long canoes setting out from the shore, full of 'hooting, screaming, fighting and bargaining' fathers, eager to hire out their sons. Men were so eager to get on board the little *Dayspring* they jumped into the sea and swam. 'Arrived on board, the Kru-man takes a cloth and dries himself,' recorded Glover. 'He then takes his *full* dress from round his head' and wraps about two yards of cotton 'not ungracefully about his loins . . . These are *gentlemen*, who having saved enough to buy from 2 to 4 wives, are rich men, and have given up the sea.' The deals being struck (two months' wages and two pieces of cloth, fourteen yards long, in advance), the sons were stripped of every possession by their fathers, and locked in the hold until the ship sailed.

'Once *away*, they *must* remain with us, for if they were to run away the people among whom we are going would make slaves of them,' wrote Glover. Released from the hold, 'there is no hardship in their fate. In 3 or 4 voyages they too will have enough to purchase their wives and in course of time will do as their fathers are now doing by them; "It is our custom," they say.'

In those two days of wild chaotic pleading, laughter and argument with soaking wet black men, Glover's love affair with Africa and her peoples was born.

John Hawley Glover was born on 24 February 1829 in the quiet Hampshire village of Yateley, the eldest of four sons of the Reverend Frederic Glover, an eccentric and uncompromising man of considerable versatility. The Glovers were an ancient military family that traced its roots back through the Plantagenets to Charlemagne. Before taking holy orders, Frederic Glover had seen action as an infantry officer on the Gold Coast – today's Ghana – in the first Anglo-Ashanti war of 1826, and his vivid accounts of life in the African jungle became part of family lore. He wrote books on the great pyramid of Egypt, and invented a type of ambulance. Meanwhile Glover's mother, Mary, a descendant of Henry VIII's sixth wife, Katherine Parr, was the daughter of an admiral. The couple had one daughter, who died young. Their four boys were destined for the army.

But from an early age John showed that he would choose his own way. At the age of three he disappeared while lagging after his nurse on a family visit to his grandparents in Bath, enticed away, in the Victorian mother's worst nightmare, by the promise by a stranger of a ride on a pony. Later he was found happily eating sausages in a gypsy camp. As he grew, his father took charge of his education, teaching him to draw maps and plan fortifications, and planned his entry into the Royal Engineers at Chatham. But John, enraptured by his grandfather the admiral's stories of the sea, pleaded to be allowed to go into the navy. His father refused. At the age of eleven Glover decided to run away to sea.

Fortunately, his mother discovered his plan and managed to get him a position as a 'first class volunteer' on the *Queen*. His father, however, remained adamant, and virtually cut him off; his grandmother provided his uniform. On 4 December 1841, Glover left home. Before the turn of the year, his mother was dead.

In the year that followed, Glover's father married again and took up a new post, as the Anglican chaplain in Cologne in Germany. John, away at sea and acutely lonely, received news of these momentous events in an abrupt letter in which his father told him that he wished John to call his new wife 'Mother'. Heartbroken, John refused. His father stopped his allowance.

Glover's captain took pity on him. If he began to train as a surveyor, he told him, he could earn enough to pay his keep and no longer have to pay for naval instruction. From the age of twelve, John was brought up by the navy, learning the discipline, playing practical jokes. On one occasion he fell off the yardarm of the *Queen* and hit the water from seventy-four feet. By the age of seventeen he was a midshipman, surveying the eastern Mediterranean; a year later, he took his first command of a naval cutter. In his spare time he devoured books – Scott, Byron and the English poets – and explored the cities where they landed, visiting churches, and, over-wintering in Malta one year, going nightly to the opera.

Glover's career prospered. By 1851, at the age of twenty-two, he was a lieutenant. The year before, he had paid a visit of reconciliation to his father and his second wife in Cologne. There he met a lady 'older than he was, clever and refined', whom he hoped to marry. But before he could do more than declare his intentions, he was dispatched, first to St Helena and the Cape, and next, to the East Indies. There, in September 1852, he was ordered to join the *Sphinx*, sailing up the Irrawaddy River to survey enemy activity in the midst of a new war the British had declared against Burma. On 4 February 1853, Glover was caught up in a disastrous attack on the Burmese near Donabew. More than eighty Europeans were killed, and Glover was severely wounded, hit by a bullet beneath his right eye that shattered the bone and passed out by his ear. Throughout a chaotic retreat in intense heat through dense jungle, harassed by the Burmese, Glover, fainting with pain and loss of blood, repeatedly roused himself and rose from his stretcher, to walk on and cheer the men safely back to their ship.

Four years later, on Monday, 22 June 1857, Glover landed from the *Dayspring* at Clarence Cove, a seedy trading post dealing in palm oil and slaves on the island of Fernando Po, nominally held by the Spanish, off the south-east coast of today's Nigeria. He had grown into a thick-set man with brooding good looks, close-cropped dark hair, trimmed beard and moustache, and a great hole from his Burmese wound beside his right eye. He was lithe and fit, a splendid horseman, and such a superb marksman that on the expedition he was to shoot birds while sparing their plumage, to preserve and send back for scientific investigation to London. At Fernando Po there were two black clergymen who were to accompany the expedition. 'I liked Mr Crowther's appearance very much,' wrote Glover, 'as well as that of a Dr Taylor, also black, who goes with us.'

For his part, the Reverend Samuel Crowther found Glover courteous and kind. Crowther was an exceptional man. Captured as a small boy with his mother and younger brother in a Muslim Fulani slave raid on his Yoruba village in 1821, he was sold to Portuguese traders and packed on board a slaver bound across the Atlantic. By good fortune, the Royal Navy intervened and Crowther and his mother and brother were taken to Freetown in Sierra Leone. There he was delivered into the hands of the Anglican Church Missionary Society, who taught him English, baptized him, and in 1826 dispatched him to England for a year at Islington Parish School in north London.

Returning to Africa, Crowther discovered a flair for languages, studying Latin, Greek, Temne and Hausa. Fifteen years later he went to England again, to be ordained into the church. The following year, in 1843, he opened a mission with an Englishman, Henry Townsend, in the important town of Abeokuta, some fifty miles north of Lagos. Here scores of Christians who called themselves Saro, freed slaves, like himself, from Sierra Leone, had returned to Nigeria. He began translations of the Bible and the Book of Common Prayer into Yoruba, and work on codifying other Nigerian languages. So successful was Crowther and Townsend's mission, and a second founded by the Methodists, that soon the Church Missionary Society and the Wesleyans were advertising Abeokuta in England as 'Sun Rise in the Tropics'. By the time Crowther met Glover he was in his late forties, destined to become Africa's first Anglican bishop seven years later.

The *Dayspring* landed in Fernando Po on a Monday. On the following Sunday, 'I was seized at about 3 in the morning with the most dreadful vomiting, cholera and pain. Nothing that the Doctor gave me would remain on my stomach.' Medical practice of the time believed that an early dose of 'seasoning' fever would stand him in good stead. The expedition set off that

Samuel Adjai Crowther
Bishop, Niger Territory
Oct 19 1888

The Reverend Samuel Crowther, later the first Anglican bishop in Africa

evening in a heavy swell and torrential rain, every member of the eleven-man party, except for Glover who had recovered, sick, battened down in the stinking hold.

'The whole is one entire swamp covered at high water and exposed at low . . . displaying the richest and as I should think the most stinking mud the earth can produce . . . and yet withal it is very pretty, sometimes, beautiful.' Through the daily downpours between 11 a.m. and 4 p.m., Glover sat in the bow of the *Dayspring* as it manoeuvred the Niger delta, with his instruments and drawing board, captivated by the intense green of the trees, 'their fantastic stems and roots, with the branches and many creepers hanging gracefully over the stream', and everywhere the birds: gorgeous parrots, long-legged cranes and white egrets fishing on the edges of lagoons lined with palms. Despite careful soundings, the little ship ran aground time and again in the swampy, labyrinthine creeks, lined by dense mangroves, of the delta. The men took occasional pot-shots at crocodiles and hippopotami, and were devoured by mosquitoes and sand flies. It took the *Dayspring* twelve days to reach the Niger River proper.

No one was well. In spite of – possibly because of – taking daily doses of quinine in the hope of preventing fever, all the Europeans experienced recurring attacks of sickness, vomiting and diarrhoea. As a drug, quinine is fatally toxic at high doses (2–8 grams); taken daily, its side-effects included ringing in the ears, vertigo, blurred vision and nausea, vomiting and diarrhoea. Glover had had fevers before, in the Mediterranean. But now they were much worse. His answer was to work through the attacks: 'I had had fever two days previously, but I put my lips together and would not *give in*. I can do this unless it is accompanied by ague, and indeed it is best if you can.' By mid-August, the expedition was 400 miles upriver. By then, 'malaria had begun to fasten on the Europeans in real earnest', dissent was breaking out, and the 'Krumen' were on the verge of mutiny. Glover and Baikie were exhausted with the tension of dealing with the sullen, unpredictable peoples they were now encountering.

How to behave? A Nigerian king who had presented Dr Baikie with a bullock was terrified when Glover came to collect it, rifle in hand, half the town following at his heels. 'This is a land of war, distrust and rapine; you never take a cup of water without making the donor taste it before. [The King] led the way evidently with the greatest distrust of poor me. As we approached nearer the ground, I cocked my gun to examine the priming, for it had been loaded for some days, and how you would have laughed could you have seen the start poor frightened Majesty gave!'

Glover was returning to the town 'when an eagle soared over our heads, and my ball brought it to my feet . . . I had performed a feat which in their eyes stamped me at once a necromancer.'

But his attitudes were rapidly changing. In this strange, dark, and superstitious land he had become a royal emissary, with a direct, almost mystical link to the great majesty, Queen Victoria herself. By mid-September: 'I am almost mahogany in colour and certainly not a white man, while my two companions are. The greatest compliment which my guide and admirer Abdul Kader can pay me is that I am an Arab . . .' While Baikie was laid up with fever, Glover visited village chieftains with the Reverend Crowther. At night, listening to the chorus of cicadas and the beat of distant drums, he shared grass-roofed huts with Crowther, talking long into the night – 'I smoking and he on his back with his feet high above his head, resting against one of the posts of the hut'.

Alas, the voyage of the *Dayspring* was as ill-fated as every previous Niger expedition. On 6 October, the ship foundered on a rock near the town of Jebba and sank. By nightfall, among swarms of mosquitoes, the party had pitched tents on shore – but their clothes, books, instruments, most of

Glover's original survey papers and his collections of birds and plants had gone. Baikie and four other Europeans settled down with Crowther to wait rescue from their supply ship, the *Sunbeam*, due in January. Glover, his servant and guide Abdul Kader, a Fulani Arabic scholar, and the expedition's botanist, Mr Barter, continued upriver by canoe, surveying the river. They reached Boussa, the famous spot where Mungo Park had lost his life, just before Christmas.

'Christmas morning – Early came a large white cock from the king, with bowls of milk, *fufu* and yams.' The King wished 'his stranger friend' to drink some palm wine with him. Sitting with him in front of his palace, thousands of people flocked in, throwing dust on their heads before him. Slave girls bore calabashes of water, the drums began, and men started dancing before him. On the 28th, after a day of receiving callers, and a visit to the King's stud of splendid horses, Glover said farewell. The King, mounted on a horse whose head was covered in bells, and 'half the town' accompanied him to his canoe. Glover parted from the King of Boussa, telling him he had been a father to him during his stay.

Glover was immersed in a world of disturbing contradictions: against the warmth and kindness of the King of Boussa, he saw canoes on the river loaded with slaves on their way to market. The people worshipped trees and rocks in eerie ceremonies, 'and yet the name of God is ever in their mouths'. He saw weird and sinister masks of witch-doctors and was told of blood feuds, unsettling fetish superstitions, poisonous concoctions and ghastly human sacrifices. He carried a white sheepskin for visiting chiefs to sit on, and gifts of beads and bags of cowries to pay for services rendered.

On 5 January 1858, having travelled further up the Niger than any white man before, he returned to the wrecked *Dayspring* to find Baikie and the remains of the party sick with fever and fighting among themselves. There was still no word from the *Sunbeam*. In the midst of this vast and forbidding wilderness, Glover volunteered to travel overland to Lagos and then by sea to Sierra Leone to get help.

It was while he was in Freetown that he came across a group of Hausa who had been seized as slaves from eastern Nigeria. Rescued and set free in Sierra Leone, they were eager to return to their homeland. But they were terrified of crossing the territories of their enemies, of being recaptured and sold once more. Glover engaged them as porters and took them back to Lagos. There, rumours that a party of freed Hausa had landed seeped into the slave quarters, and more Hausa slipped out to join them. By the time

Glover's entourage arrived at the gates of the town of Abeokuta, en route back to the *Dayspring*, there were over 450 of them.

Abeokuta, the town where Crowther had set up his mission, was the capital of the Egba, who had fled from Ibadan in 1830 at the time of the Yoruba wars. Glover entered the city alone, on his horse. All at once he found himself surrounded by crowds of furious slave owners brandishing swords and spears. Armed men, 'thirsting for his blood, yet not one daring to touch him', hemmed him in on all sides. Just then Glover noticed a gap in the wall, guarded by a number of men with spears. He drove his spurs into the horse's flanks, 'and the horse responding to his rider broke over the formidable array of spears, and was out into the countryside beyond'.

Glover was never able to trust the Egba again. Reading the fear in the Hausa's eyes, at once he began to train them in British methods of military defence. From that day, he earned from them undying loyalty and a permanent bodyguard.

The expedition did not end upon his return to the wreck of the *Dayspring*. Glover, Barter and Baikie continued to explore the Niger delta until the end of 1859. By the time Glover returned to England in March 1861, he was thirty-two, thin and ill, and his diary of letters to his beloved in Germany – who perhaps, after an absence of almost ten years, had written to release him from his obligations – had ceased.

That summer the British government annexed the island of Lagos. Sheltered by a great sandbank, Lagos provided the only safe harbour on more than 600 miles of west African coastline. From its lagoon, scores of creeks and further lagoons extended inland to a lush network of rivers, fostering a rich trade in slaves with the interior. By the middle of the nineteenth century it was notorious as the most flourishing slave market on the west African coast.

This is how the traveller Richard Burton described it: 'Those were the merry days . . . The slavers had nothing to do but sleep and smoke . . . the tradesman made all the bargains; the doctor examined the contrabands and they were shipped off by the captain and the crew.' Many of these slaves had come from Abeokuta, fifty miles inland. From there the Anglican missionaries Crowther and Townsend began petitioning London to put an end to the slave market in Lagos as soon as they arrived in 1843. Prospects improved when in 1845 the King of Lagos, Akitoye, was ousted in a coup and began

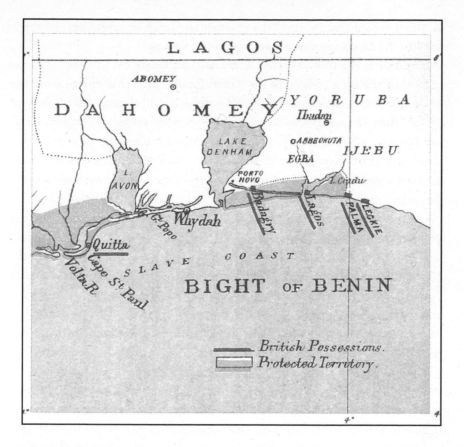

cultivating British traders and the missionaries in Abeokuta. Then as demand from Cuba and the southern United States began forcing prices of slaves to new heights, Akitoye promised he would close the slave market if the British navy would help him recover his throne in Lagos.

John Beecroft, the British Consul on the Bight of Benin, keen to increase Britain's authority on the coast, sailed to Lagos in 1857 for talks with Kosoko, the man who had usurped Akitoye. When Kosoko refused to put an end to the slave trade, the navy attacked. After two ferocious battles, Akitoye was restored to the throne, and an English consul was installed in the town to ensure he complied with the ban on slavery. Kosoko retreated across the lagoon.

In 1853 Akitoye's son Dosunmu succeeded him. Friction continued between him and Kosoko. Then, in January 1861, a French frigate sailed into the Lagos lagoon. Rumours spread that the French were negotiating a new market exporting 'labourers' to work in their own colonies.

When reports of the French activities reached London, the years of pleading from the region to take possession of Lagos finally bore fruit. In August, the acting consul, a trader, William McCoskry – 'Oba Apongbon' or 'Chief Redbeard' – brought the British cruiser HMS *Prometheus* over the sand bar and into the harbour, with its guns primed and aimed at the King's palace. McCoskry struck a bargain with King Dosunmu: in return for a pension of £1,000 a year, Dosunmu yielded the island to Britain. From London, Henry Stanhope Freeman sailed as the first governor of the new colony. In command of the gunboat *Handy,* newly commissioned to defend the Lagos lagoons, was John Glover.

Richard Burton, who sailed into Lagos just weeks before Glover arrived, described the scene: 'Arriving over the "bar" to the muffled roar of the sullen surf . . . [at] Beecroft's Point curlews and plovers rose screaming wildly . . . Pass[ing] alongside the shrimp stakes, the town came into view.' It was a disordered mass of huts and houses with mud walls and lumber walls, barred casements and holes for windows, and huge sloping roofs of dry palm leaf.

Sailing on, round Fetish Point, 'a growth of gigantic trees indicated holy ground'. This was the site of King Dosunmu's palace, 'a red tiled and partially white washed barn backed by trees of the noblest stature and fronted by water perilously deep'. Then, 'as if a hole had been hollowed out in the original mangrove forest that skirts the waters', a thin line of European buildings, topped by flags: the French *comptoir,* surrounded by gardens, then a 'large, pretentious white and light yellow building', home of a Sardinian merchant. Next, the Wesleyan Mission House, a German trading company, the Wesleyan chapel, and finally the British consulate: 'a corrugated iron coffin . . . containing a dead consul once a year'. Inland was a racecourse.

Burton hated Lagos, this 'pestilential island', its people suffering from yaws, leprosy, fever, dysentery and dracunculus, its town 'native to the last degree . . . [where] everything has the squalid, unclean look of an idle people'. At an early hour he saw a man 'shamelessly making himself drunk with "hashish"'. Just offshore lay 'three lumps of land', the 'Sacrifice Islands' from the executions common in the recent past: 'the victim . . . fastened to a rude cross, clubbed and impaled'.

Yet the lagoon glistened in bright sunshine, and the horizon was fringed with tall groves of palms. 'The redeeming feature was the mixture of country with town which all can admire . . . it is a city of palms: the cocoa grows almost in the salt water; the broad leaved breadfruit (from Polynesia) has taken root like an indigen, and in the branches of the pawpaw nestle amadavats, orioles and brilliant palm birds.' In the marketplace, women hunched over piles of sun-dried shrimp for sale, mullet and oysters. Tall Ibadans from the interior bartered ivory and palm oil for gunpowder and other necessities. The currency was cowrie shells, sackfuls of which might give you change from a sovereign. The local people, a tribe of the Yoruba, called the place 'Eyo'.

Lagos proved as deadly for Governor Freeman as it had been to three of its previous consuls. Needing frequent bouts of leave for his health, his effective time as the first governor of Lagos lasted no more than eighteen months. By April 1865 he was dead at Tunis, en route to England.

For Glover, his arrival in Lagos at the helm of the *Handy* had been a turning point. He had been promoted to the rank of commander – but this entailed a six-month period on half pay while he awaited his new ship. Lagos might be 'a humble and miserable place', but Glover was convinced it had a great future as a port of trade. With Freeman keen to bring him into his embryo administration, Glover volunteered to become harbourmaster. Within months he was colonial secretary, delegated to take charge of the colony in Freeman's absence.

But London was not happy to see him in a permanent position of command. An exchange of letters with London took at least two months, and Glover was not a man whose strong suit was patience. Too often he acted first, and sought permission afterwards. He was reckless, too eager, and had no regard for the rules. But competent officers with knowledge of west Africa were rare. After over three years of being de facto in charge of the colony, Glover was officially appointed its administrator, with all the powers, if not the title, of 'Governor', in 1863.

Glover moved into Government House, accompanied by his devoted Hausa servant, Harry Maxwell. This iron-built residence, with its delightful garden of oleander and acacia trees and a tree-fringed verandah overlooking the lagoon, was so stifling and hot at night that 'the Governor and his guests frequently met each other wandering from one part to another in quest of sleep with mattress and pillow in hand'. At last Glover would doze off, half in, half out of his room, in a passage on the ground floor, given over as an armoury for his Hausa troops.

Glover's orders were to defend the inhabitants of Lagos and to suppress the slave trade by trying to create peace on the mainland. The problem was that no one knew exactly how far the borders of Lagos extended. Customs posts had been established forty miles on either side of Lagos: at Badagry in the west and Lekkie in the east. The rest of the shoreline, low, marshy and malarious, was impossible to police; bush and jungle concealed movement on land. Beyond Badagry, the King of neighbouring Dahomey – today's Benin – made annual raids for slaves on the Egba at Abeokuta. They in turn waged wars with the Ijebu to the south-east, and the Yoruba based at Ibadan. The fruits of war – 'the noble trade' as the chief of the Egba described it – continued. Whole cargoes yielded vast sums of £100,000, or £1,200 a head: more than £6.5 million today. Now that Lagos was closed to the trade, the slavers – mainly Portuguese and Brazilian – centred the trade in Whydah (today's Ouidah) in Dahomey, and at Porto Novo – just twenty miles west of the customs post at Badagry.

The immediate community Glover governed was tiny: 30,000 – chiefly Yoruba, incestuous and volatile. Many were close followers of King Dosunmu, who was vain and suggestible, 'much given to pomp and show [and] possessed of a hundred wives or so, and innumerable suits of apparel', Mrs Foote, the wife of the last British Consul, wrote. 'Visitors were always regaled with champagne'– or European-style breakfast parties. Heavily influenced by his medicine men, Dosunmu played a diddling game, outwardly amenable to the British while secretly supporting the slaving of the Egba and stirring up trouble. Glover detested him as a rogue and a fool.

The rest of the population were Muslims, freed Hausa slaves, Amaros, 'those who had left home'– artisans returned from Brazil and Cuba – and nearly 1,500 Saro, freed slaves who had flooded back to Lagos from Sierra Leone during the 1850s, western educated and Christianized – they were an elite. Europeans numbered no more than a handful. Half a dozen formed Glover's administration; the rest were a jealous group of European and British traders. There were, perhaps, no more than five European women. Among Glover's closest confidantes were Bishop Crowther's daughter, Juliana Thompson, and her sister-in-law, Marian, with whom he would often take tea. On his staff, his closest friend was the doctor, Samuel Rowe. Rowe was twenty-eight years old when he first arrived in Lagos, handsome, well built, with a genial smile and a remarkable beard of silky light red hair. Fluent in French, with good Italian and Portuguese, he was invaluable to Glover in his dealings with foreign traders. Besides being the colony's chief medical officer, he was also a stipendiary magistrate, who enjoyed a joking rapport with the Yoruba and the Saro.

Glover ruled Lagos like he commanded a ship: with discipline and hard work, bonhomie and sheer force of personality. Now in his late thirties, his figure had filled. Powerful, bull-like, he was a man of spartan habits (notwithstanding a penchant for pink silk vests) with exceptional physical stamina. He worked through malarial fevers and rode for hours through the jungle, wearing a small dark blue forage cap on his head in the sun and sleeping on a black ram-skin rug in village huts. There were no precedents for a white man dealing with the issues he faced.

Every morning after breakfast for two or three hours 'Oba Golobar' could be seen comfortably dressed in light Turkish breeches and a short tunic, sitting on his verandah smoking a cigarette and listening to noisy cases of breaches of promise, marital disputes, arguments over land, and unpleasant cases of fetish and witchcraft. These were interpreted if need be by Henry Willoughby, Superintendent of Police and government interpreter to the new British administration, and one of the first Saro to come to Lagos, a well-to-do trader, intelligent and educated.

Every two or three weeks there was a meeting of the Legislative Council to discuss key issues and pass ordinances: Glover, the chief justice, the commanding officer and two traders – one the former acting Consul, William 'Red Beard' McCoskry. Behind the scenes, Glover prepared budgets and reported to London. There was constant housekeeping: pensions, appointments to recommend, the need to send people home because of their health; approving the servicing of tugboats and disciplining officers. The War Office was warned of Major Leveson, 'a decorated officer', who was 'in the habit of carrying in his pocket daguerreotype likenesses of women of the town', offering his services as a procurer.

Later Glover would ride out along the esplanade he was extending along the waterfront and on to the broad new streets he was building through the town. His horse, Gunner, was celebrated, an almost mythical animal presented to him by the chiefs of Ikorodu, readily visited by ferry across the lagoon, for his having defended them against a raid by the Egba. Glover kept the Europeans amused with sport and entertainments at Government House – croquet parties, receptions, dinners and dances – plying his guests with fine food and good drink. He was an attentive host, famous for mixing his own Christmas puddings, popping champagne corks with brio and caring for guests himself when they were taken ill with fever. He kept up traditions from home: Dosunmu and other chiefs were bidden to dine on the Queen's birthday, with invitation cards requesting 'the pleasure of your company'. A chief who took him at his word arrived with fifty retainers for a dinner laid for twenty. He rewarded the kings and chiefs who helped him restore peace on the mainland with flags and silver swords sent from London, presented before large crowds, troops drawn up, flags flying and bands playing.

A detachment from a West Indian regiment was assigned to Lagos for protection, but as yet there was no permanent barracks. For security and information Glover preferred to rely on his Hausa, whom he was training into a police force with the sanction of the Colonial Office. He commanded them personally and kept them occupied by moving them about the mainland, policing customs posts and the entrance to the treacherously swampy and rugged tracks that led to Abeokuta. They lived in a separate cantonment that they had constructed themselves, under their own non-commissioned officers. Discipline was maintained by a system of fines for faults and disobedience, which grew into a fund used to benefit needy Hausa. But as the Colonial Office was only too aware, the Hausa might be faithful 'to some one Person in whom they have learned to have confidence, but [it was hardly safe] to leave the destiny of the Colony dependant on any one man's presence'.

Running like a constant drip feed of anxiety for Glover was domestic slavery. 'The natives consider exchanging men for goods a perfectly fair sort of barter, and in war, the victorious party make slaves of prisoners as a legitimate part of their success. The love of enslaving his fellow beings is so innate in man, that even freed slaves, if they get on in this world, spend their first money in buying a slave,' Mrs Foote had written. All along the west African coast, human beings were no more than collateral. You would like a pledge of goodwill? Here, take my sister, or my brother. Security for a debt? Have my son or my daughter. If someone had a grievance against you, your relations were seized, violently. From the moment Lagos became British territory, however, slavery became illegal.

Immediately after the British annexation a slave court was set up. In less than two months, almost 500 domestic slaves from Lagos were registered – three-quarters of them women. Most of them, it was agreed, would remain apprenticed to their owners until they worked off a redemption – in the meantime, their working conditions would be regulated, and they were guaranteed the right to purchase their freedom. Rumours of these happenings rippled through slave quarters. It soon became clear that if all the slaves on Lagos acted on their rights, there would be revolt.

In 1865 a Select Committee of the House of Commons met to consider the 'State of British Establishments on the Western African Coast'. Testifying before it, red-bearded William McCoskry described domestic slavery at Lagos as a mild institution. Slaves were more like dependants or clansmen of their owners, 'treated more as servants' than as slaves, even though a master had the right to repossess a slave if he ran away. The position of women, particularly as concubines, was ignored altogether. The Committee concluded that 'the native practice of domestic slavery' in Lagos was 'at variance with British law'. It demanded 'the serious attention of the Government, with a view to its termination as soon as possible'.

Nothing happened. In the vacuum Glover proposed various forms of apprenticeship leading to freedom. His ideas were rejected by London. Nor would the Colonial Office outlaw child slavery, so Glover adopted those he came across and educated them at his own expense. Meanwhile, he issued quiet instructions to his Hausa, who policed the tracks from Lagos to Abeokuta, not to prevent – even to assist – any runaways trying to reach the island. Those who did so could present themselves at the slave court which met every Tuesday and obtain their freedom. His most trusted lieutenant, Samuel Rowe, was in charge of the court.

Trickier cases required Glover's personal attention: firing a collector of customs for introducing the 'system of Pawns [slaves]' for debt; dispatching an emissary to the King of Dahomey to ransom a missionary taken as a slave on behalf of Bishop Crowther. Then there was the case of the woman, Awa, who had escaped as a slave from the Christian enclaves of Abeokuta.

First captured in Ibadan, Awa was brought to Abeokuta, where she was sold to a black pastor and wealthy trader, Henry Robbin, to be one of his ten mistresses and twenty slaves. Like her sisters, she was treated as a concubine and worked as a bearer. For being late for work one day, she was imprisoned for hours; for being 'saucy' she was shackled to a post in the sun for six days and starved. She went on to be traded three or four times before finally escaping when she ran into a fellow fugitive in Lagos. He brought her to the slave court.

'From the enclosed statement of the woman "Awa",' a furious Glover wrote to the Secretary of State in London, 'it would appear that the Church Missionary Society's Agents in Abbeokuta [*sic*] cannot but be aware of the system of slave dealing and concubinage which exists among their congregation.' Until their supporters in England were made aware of this system, 'there can be no hope of any amendment in the morality of the Christian Church which they are endeavouring to establish in this country'.

Robbin, of course, denied the charges. And who would the authorities in England believe: an English-speaking minister of the church, or a black woman in his 'employ'?

Glover had no more than his personal influence to bring to bear in his negotiations with the King of Dahomey to stop his slave-raiding and make peace, or to persuade the Egba and the Yoruba to end their wars. Like the kings he was dealing with, Glover conducted his negotiations in parables and flowery language. He called himself 'Golobar, Chief of the Forces of the Great Sultana Queen of England'. He was the 'Emir of Eyo', the 'Commander of all the Great Fire Ships on the wide ocean'. His Hausa messengers carried special staffs to identify the fact that they came from him. Inland he met with great assemblies of chiefs beneath the shade of the sacred groves of trees that towered over the heart of every village. One time, when a particularly recalcitrant group of elders refused to talk peace, 'Golobar' threatened to cut down the palm trees in their market-place.

'So great was the consternation of the chiefs and principal men of the town that they came on bended knees, throwing dust on their heads, to beg of him to spare their sacred trees. "Golobar" said he would think it over; and when they came to know his decision, replied: "Yes, I will spare these trees; but, mark you, I will put a white fowl's feather in the topmost branches, and when at night you sit by your firelight and talk of the Great White Queen in the North, and say that man's blood must flow, that your warriors will go forth on their war-paths, then this fowl's feather will whisper in my ear and tell me what you will do, and I will come, I and my chiefs, with the army of the 'Great White Queen', and I will wipe you out of the land, and there will be wailing in your camp."' The town ceased its aggression on its neighbours.

With the King of Porto Novo and the Egba in Abeokuta, he had to take a tougher line. In the short space of a year, Glover informed London in June 1865, the King of Porto Novo had 'killed and sacrificed' more than 200 people, mainly women, and butchered more than 600, mostly slaves. 'British subjects, Natives of Lagos, were continually chained, plundered and sold to Whydah [in Dahomey].' Glover, so angry that he was scarcely coherent, laid his gunboat, the _Eyo_, off the port and begged London to sanction his takeover of the place. European and Brazilian traders protested to London.

Meanwhile, to try to force the Egba to make peace with the Yoruba at Ibadan, he installed an armed blockade on the three trails that ran north to Abeokuta. Now a stream of bitter grievances from Manchester-based companies whose cargoes of cotton lay rotting on the tracks reached the Colonial Office. Missionaries who could not get their newspapers and tinned food from England complained. A number claimed they had been beaten and intimidated by Glover's Hausa police. They demanded his recall.

In London officials were baffled by the conflicting accounts of strife between Abeokuta and Ibadan, the Egba and the Yoruba. They knew nothing of the peoples and places Glover talked about. Glover was often too pressed, perhaps too ill with fever, and too prone now to speaking in parables, often to make his dispatches clear. Spellings and titles – were the King of the Yoruba and Bashorun of Ibadan one and the same person? Passionate, short-tempered, peremptory and defensive, he was criticized for 'a want of patience and candid consideration'. Often the under-secretaries at the Colonial Office found his rambling explanations incomprehensible. 'How long ought a man to take before he believes himself a good judge of the relative merits of obscure African Tribes and villages?' asked Frederick Elliot, Assistant Under-Secretary of State.

Some time later, Glover pleaded again for permission to put an end to the 'drunken and bloodthirsty rule of the King' of Porto Novo. Threading through his long hand-written dispatch, the clerks in the Colonial Office concluded that the King had been angry with an African missionary for starting to build a chapel without his permission, and had put one of his people in prison. Subsequently, the missionary and his wife had been beaten by the King's slaves in a dispute over a sheep, in which the King refused to interfere. 'These literally are the only recent cases known to us, on which Commander Glover proposes to depose one King and set up another, and virtually annex Porto Novo.'

'Sheep?' minuted another official. 'A territory is to be annexed and a war is to be waged over a *sheep?*'

In Lagos itself, an uneasy entente prevailed between Glover's administration and King Dosunmu's court, where the counsel of masked witch-doctors prevailed and dark idols were worshipped. One result of the Select Committee's investigations in 1865 was that the Colonial Office decided to centralize its west African administrations for Lagos, the Gambia, the Gold Coast and Sierra Leone under a single governor-in-chief at Freetown, Sierra Leone – 1,100 miles from Lagos.

Rumours of these changes – surely now the British would leave Lagos? – set the place on edge. Secret emissaries transferred back and forth between the Egba in Abeokuta and King Dosunmu in his palace at Lagos. 'The king and his partisans cannot forget the lucrative benefits of the Slave Trade, and long for the re-establishment of Native rule,' Glover reported early in 1866. He warned of retribution. 'This morning the people in the King's Quarter are already naming those who are marked off for vengeance when the Troops shall have left Lagos.'

Slowly, however, Glover was making progress in bringing peace to the region. When he returned from six months' leave in early 1867, he learned that the Bashorun of Ibadan had driven off a raiding tribe who had stolen and killed over 200 of his people. But true to the promise he had given Glover, he had not pursued them and captured their towns. 'When I showed [the Bashorun] the Stick with the Knot [the sign that an understanding could not be undone],' Glover's lieutenant told him, 'he gave me a good shake by the hand for you, and said his heart was right with yours and that he would do anything in his power to serve you; that he was glad you had returned to Lagos and that he thanked the Queen of England for sending you back. "You see," he said, "I have kept my word with you."'

Lagos was prospering. Under Glover's administration the population doubled, revenues rose and sewage and clean water supplies were introduced. His Hausa police force had expanded and was sufficiently well trained that the garrison of West Indian troops had been able to be withdrawn. By 1872 the place, with its modern wharves and warehouses, shops, a hospital and three churches, was becoming, in 'striking contrast' to other settlements like Cape Coast and Freetown, a rare example of 'a neat and tidy African town'. If only he could stop the human butchery at Porto Novo, and persuade the Egba to settle down and stop the slave trade, Glover saw a mighty future for Lagos as a second Liverpool, *the* port of central Africa, shipping palm oil, ivory and cotton.

On 24 April 1872, as the fierce rains and intense heat of the wet season set in, a newly appointed governor-in-chief of the West African Settlements, John Pope Hennessy, sailed into Lagos. Hennessy's approach to government was the antithesis of Glover's. A man whose world revolved entirely around himself, he had landed in Africa for the first time in his life, at Freetown in

Sierra Leone, less than two months before. Hennessy's views on emancipation were exceptionally enlightened. But he was also Irish, Catholic, had a weakness for the underdog and a ready ear for grievance, and had an absolute conviction in the correctness of his own point of view.

For Glover the year had begun with more violence, killings and robberies at Porto Novo. Again, he ordered the stationing of the *Eyo* off the harbour to safeguard the lives and property of British traders, prompting Portuguese and Brazilian slave traders to protest vehemently to the Colonial Office once more. Meanwhile, the French were engaged in a war on the Upper Niger. London had ordered Glover to enforce a strict arms embargo to the interior. In February Glover had left Lagos 'in order that he might by his presence insure the safe starting' of a huge caravan of former slaves and refugees, 'joyfully returning to their long lost homes' on a newly opened overland route to Ibadan, ninety miles to the north.

All had gone well until Glover's return to Lagos. In protest at the arms embargo, and the opening of the first direct overland route from Lagos to Ibadan, the Egba had closed the trails to Abeokuta and blockaded the port. On 18 March trade on the lagoon came to a standstill. When Hennessy arrived five weeks later, a dozen large vessels were standing outside the bar waiting for cargo, and a number of wealthy English traders were cooling their heels in Lagos.

Short, energetic and very urbane, Hennessy was thirty-eight, with a beautiful twenty-two-year-old wife, Kitty. He was in a fragile and dangerous state. Soon after arriving in Freetown they had lost their only child, an adored three-year-old son, from dysentery. The couple eschewed Glover's hospitality at Government House, and slept on board the steamer *Sherbo*, beyond the bar.

At first meeting Glover and Hennessy got on well. Hennessy was impressed with Lagos, and, it seemed, with Glover. 'It is impossible not to see that Captain Glover is a zealous officer who has devoted his energies to the improvement of the place,' Hennessy reported to London. But Hennessy was always suspicious of another's apparent success. The principal traders lined up to see him: the Yoruba praised Glover and begged Hennessy 'not to listen to the white merchants'. The European merchants—French, Italian, Portuguese, as well as British — were adamant that Glover's interference with Egba affairs and the embargo on the export of arms to the mainland were to blame for the trade blockade. Furthermore, there was a lot they did not care for about his administration: a new system of standard

weights and measures, laying the *Eyo* in threatening manner off Porto
Novo, and Glover's control of the Hausa. Why, for example, were they
stationed at so many places outside of British territory?

Glover patiently explained to Hennessy the answers to all these questions and more. The Egba blockade represented a familiar tactic: another
way of putting pressure on the British to induce the government to withdraw from Lagos. At the root of the dissatisfaction in Lagos, and on the
mainland beyond, was, Glover told Hennessy, 'the question of Slavery'.

Five days after he arrived in Lagos, Hennessy was urgently recalled to the
Gold Coast, where fierce riots had broken out. Before he set sail – relieving
Glover of seventy of his Hausa for protection – Hennessy ordered the
withdrawal of the *Eyo* from Porto Novo, and wrote to the chiefs of the
Egba at Abeokuta offering his compliments and best wishes as 'Your good
friend'. 'I find there is no trade at this moment between Lagos and Abbeokuta [*sic*],' he wrote casually. 'Why is this? Speak fully and freely to me
about it.'

In Lagos, rumours about the future blazed. At a stroke, the fear of civil war
between Glover's supporters and the Yoruba at Ibadan, and those of King
Dosunmu and the Egba at Abeokuta, flared. Great trees were felled across
the 'roads' leading north from the lagoons. The market at Ikorodu across
the lagoon from Lagos was set alight, and surrounding tribes massed
towards the British customs stations on the mainland. No canoes carrying
provisions crossed the lagoon. The British were to be starved out.

Glover warned Hennessy: even those who were well disposed towards
the British were now getting angry. The people needed a public declaration
from the Governor-in-Chief that the British were in Lagos to stay. By the
middle of May, two weeks after Hennessy had sailed, Glover still had had
no word from him. With only four other European officers at Lagos, Glover
summoned assistance from the British consuls at Benin and Fernando Po.
Then slowly, patiently, he began the work of trying to restore confidence
in Lagos and the lagoon. After three weeks, a faltering trade was resumed.

Now Hennessy dispatched a blistering letter to Glover. He alone was
responsible for the stoppage of trade at Lagos. In every respect he had failed
to carry out his instructions. Hennessy was certainly not going to make 'a
public declaration that the British Government does not intend to withdraw from Lagos'. The merchants and traders of Lagos were 'far too sensible
and patriotic not to be ashamed of any Administrator in chief who would

be so weak as to contemplate the necessity for such a declaration as you have suggested to me'. On 14 June he returned to Lagos.

'Captain Glover,' Hennessy told him. 'I want neither to hear nor read anything, I know all and have heard all. Merchants, missionaries, and natives have both written and spoken, and I must tell you, you know nothing of the country, the place, or the people. It is *not* the slave question. It is *you* and *your aggressive policy!*'

In honour, Glover could no longer remain in post in Lagos. Handing Hennessy a stiff request for six months' leave, he sailed the next morning for England. To the public at large Hennessy pronounced an end to the embargo of arms to the mainland, wrote to the Egba reassuring them that the British would no longer be interfering in their affairs, and was pleased to begin the partial restoration of King Dosunmu to his throne of Lagos. Of Glover he wrote without hesitation to anyone who inquired that he appeared 'to have misunderstood the state of affairs at Lagos', and reported his position terminated. Appointing Henry Fowler, a former collector of customs and an Irish Catholic like himself, as temporary administrator, Hennessy sailed away from Lagos.

Within a month, the trade with the mainland that Glover had just managed, painfully, to restart before he left Lagos came to a standstill. To the sound of King Dosunmu's bellman wandering through the town, charms and witchcraft spread and the slave market reopened. It was rumoured along the trails to Ibadan that Glover had been sent back to England in chains, to be tried for maladministration. Meanwhile slaves who had escaped to Lagos were being recaptured and dragged away by their old owners. Women threw themselves and their children into the lagoon rather than face the same fate. Glover's closest associates, including his police chief, Willoughby, were put out of their jobs and persecuted.

King Dosunmu celebrated by commissioning two fetish priests to invoke 'Olokun', the goddess of the sea. A bullock and other creatures were killed and thrown into the waters of the lagoon. Never again, he prayed, would Commander Glover return to Lagos.

Like a great wounded bear, Glover nursed his wounds in London's Bruton Street. Day after day new reports arrived from Lagos telling him of more abuses and atrocities. Glover never forgave Hennessy. Within weeks, the Colonial Office had become seriously alarmed at what was happening in Lagos. At the end of 1872 Bishop Crowther arrived in London to plead the case for humanity. By then the Colonial Office had realized a grave mistake had been made. But it was the end of Glover's career in Lagos.

The following year, Glover was once more dispatched by the Colonial Office to west Africa, this time to recruit and lead black forces in a military campaign against the Ashanti, who, largely as a result of Hennessy's ineptitude, had attacked Elmina Castle on the Gold Coast. The famous journalist Henry Stanley, covering the war for the *New York Herald*, found him on the banks of the River Volta.

'I discerned the sturdy form of Governor Glover striding hither and thither, and recognized his cool, calm voice giving orders. He was superintending personally the loading of the "The Lady of the Lake" for an upriver trip with ammunition; he was giving orders to a blacksmith; he was showing a carpenter what his day duties were to be; he was speaking to the engineer about his boilers; he was telling the coloured captain at what hours to be ready . . . he was assisting a man to lift a box of ammunition on to his shoulders; he was listening to a Yoruba complaint about some unfairness . . . inspecting the crews of the steam launches . . . questioning . . . rebuking . . . he was here, there, and everywhere – alert, active, prompt, industrious.'

Glover would go on to become a national hero, fêted all over London, and knighted for his contribution to the Ashanti campaign. His Hausa police force would go on to form the model of police forces used all over west Africa. Three years later, at the age of forty-seven, he fell in love with Elizabeth Scott, 'a slip of a girl' aged, perhaps, eighteen, who nursed him as he recovered from a near fatal railway accident while on leave in Ireland. They married, and she went with him to govern Newfoundland and Trinidad. But the malarial fevers that he contracted in Africa recurred constantly. In 1885, after seven brief but happy years of marriage, he died in London of a weakened heart at the age of fifty-six. Lady Glover set down the stories he had so often told her, compiled his papers, and retraced many of his footsteps. The chronicle of his life she wrote is her memorial to him.

3 The loneliness of the righteous governor
St Lucia 1869–77

Early on the morning of 12 July 1869, William des Voeux, the new administrator of the tiny sugar island of St Lucia, arrived at the port of Castries, the capital, from Barbados. He had just completed a bruising five-year assignment as a magistrate in the courts of British Guiana, an obscure colony of rainforest and sugar cane – today known as Guyana – on the north-east coast of South America. It had been tough training: exactly what was needed for the future he now faced in St Lucia.

The Pitons of St Lucia

Des Voeux's voyage had taken him north-west. As his ship rounded the southern tip of St Lucia two giant pyramidal rocks rose sheer from the sea, bringing sudden gusts of wind, unexpected squalls: the Pitons – the famous peaks on which a British sailor had once planted the Union flag, 'the peep of the town of Soufrière nestling between them at their base'. The sea was a brilliant blue; beaches bordered with coconut palms were powdered white. 'The views of the west coast of the island, as we steamed along it, seemed inexpressibly beautiful,' des Voeux was to write in a memoir many years later. Steep valleys covered in dense tropical forest rose up mountainsides. The lighter colour of cane fields shone on their lower spurs. 'The harbour of Castries seemed almost equally striking as regards natural beauty.' But as he neared the wharf and watched a handful of dignitaries of the island descend awkwardly into a boat and row out to greet him on board his ship, he could not help but see signs of disrepair and rotting timbers. Approaching the shore the town presented 'a very forlorn appearance'.

Macnamara Dix, the treasurer of the island, led the small party of officials. It was he who had been administering the island since the departure of des Voeux's predecessor seven months before. Dix, a man of lugubrious humour, had served in the West Indies for over twenty years – for the past ten on St Lucia. His annual reports submitted to the Governor-General of the Windward Islands, based in Barbados, had prepared des Voeux for the situation that he was about to meet: a deeply impoverished tropical island, a mere forty miles long by fifteen miles wide, inhabited by 35,000 people of whom around 900 were white: mostly Roman Catholics of French descent.

Discovered by Columbus, St Lucia had generally been under French control from the early seventeenth century. Increasingly bloody attempts by the British to wrest the island from the French had finally succeeded in 1803. The majority of the people, whom des Voeux described as 'more or less of African blood', spoke a French patois. There were two small towns: Soufrière, with 1,800 souls, and Castries, with 3,500. With torrential rain for half the year, hurricanes and droughts, products of rum, sugar, molasses and a little coffee and cocoa grown on large plantations, St Lucia was a typical small West Indian island. From London's point of view, it was utterly insignificant.

'The planters were again doomed to disappointment,' seemed a favourite refrain of Dix's whenever he had cause to report the harvest. Other highlights of his annual reports were a militia that persistently refused to turn out, roads washed away by deluges of rain every year, and the death rates of labourers imported from India, who seemed to die at an annual rate of about 20 per cent. The aftermath of the great cholera epidemic of 1854 that claimed the lives of over 2,000 people still persisted, flaring up from time to time, while deadly venomous snakes infested the island.

Those employed by the colonial government in this damp and overheated climate numbered no more than thirty, including the postmistress.

Fuelled by brandy and racked with fevers, the administration was chronically short of staff. Treasurer Dix also served as the comptroller of customs and navigation. Now he swore in des Voeux, introduced him to Monsieur Beausoleil and J. S. Moffat, the only two 'unofficial' members of the Executive and Legislative Councils, and escorted him down to the government offices in Castries. Except for a Demerara parrot named Jocko, and his black Barbadian valet, Samuel Cox – a man with an eye for the ladies – des Voeux travelled alone. He had no private secretary; no aide-de-camp; his own job on St Lucia was to act not only as administrator, but as colonial secretary and registrar. Two callow clerks named McHugh and Peter, a fly-blown office and heaps of mildewed papers greeted him.

'After transacting some affairs requiring immediate attention, I rode up to the Government House on Morne Fortuné, by the steep bridle-path which ascends over 700 feet in less than half a mile.' Near the summit of the hill, he came upon a large open space of rough grass and low guava bushes, and the long façade of what passed for Government House: a single-storey building fifty yards long, built as a military hospital. On each side was a long stone gallery, faced by brick arches. A rusty iron railing ran parallel to each side of the house, enclosing the ruins of a long, narrow garden. Inside, a deep gloom prevailed. There were a few pieces of dilapidated furniture and a smell of mildew. The black servants of the house believed the ghosts of dead soldiers paraded the galleries at night.

The views from both sides of the house, however, were magnificent. To the north, 'a shoulder of the Morne, covered with pasture, shut out the view of the town and most of the harbour at its foot', des Voeux wrote. But the far side of Castries Bay was visible, and wide views out to sea. On fine days des Voeux could see the whole west coast of the French island of Martinique, some twenty-four miles away, while in exceptionally clear weather, 'which occurred two or three times a year before heavy rain, there could be seen what looked like a round rock in the sea . . . in fact . . . the summit of the highest peak in Dominica, over a hundred miles distant'. To the south, a valley curved round from a high mountain on the east to blue ocean in the west. Beyond lay a ridge of mountains, shading from green to blue, and in the distance, the twin peaks of the Pitons.

Above the house, on the summit of the hill, was a fort, occupied by the police. Just below were the old officers' quarters, which housed the local magistrate and the Superintendent of Police. Nearby was an old mess house, the home of Mr Dix.

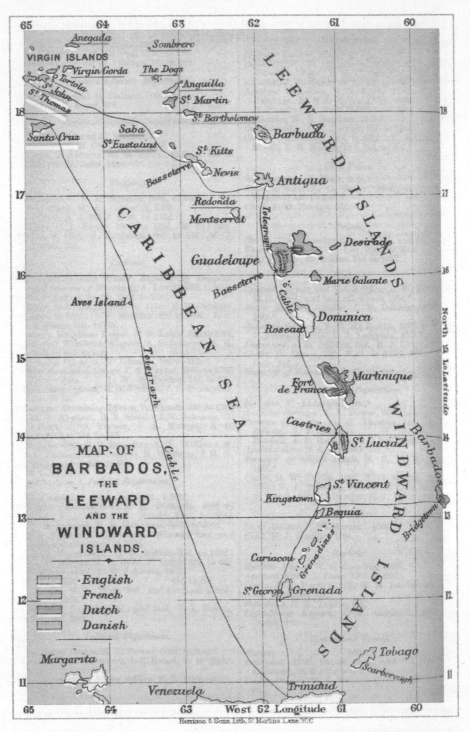

MAP. OF
BARBADOS,
THE
LEEWARD
AND THE
WINDWARD
ISLANDS.

- English
- French
- Dutch
- Danish

Harrison & Sons. Lith. St Martins Lane. W.C.

That night des Voeux dined with Dix and his family, listening to the ladies telling stories of the deadly venom of the *fer-de-lance,* the long grey-brown snakes with pointed heads that infested the island; of how the vipers slept during the day, and would go hunting at night, and how they gave birth to as many as 100 young at a time. Taking good care with a lantern to look where he trod, des Voeux made his lonely way home to bed at Government House.

William des Voeux was thirty-five years old. He was tall and lean, a lanky man of fourteen stone, with dark hair, a high forehead, a long moustache and the generous sideboards fashionable at the time. He was a sensitive and squeamish man. He was conscientious, upright, and not a little prone to anxiety. He loathed injustice, hated to see a man in pain, or cruelty inflicted on animals, and, subject to recurring bouts of malarial fever, was consumed with worries about his health. He had a horror of snakes.

The morning after he landed on St Lucia he ordered the whole of the ground on the top of the Morne, and the garden around Government House, cleared and restored. In the process forty snakes were killed, and a number of cast skins were found in the cellars of the house. In due course, he would initiate a government bounty for the snakes (12,000 heads in the first seven months), and successfully introduce the mongoose – 'the well-known enemy of the Indian cobra' – to the island. But not before a vicious test fight on the lawns of Government House, at the end of which the mongoose, bitten on the neck, jumped on the snake's back. The mongoose fed on its prey for days.

Des Voeux came from a well-to-do family of Huguenots, who had emigrated to Ireland at the beginning of the eighteenth century. One hundred years later, the des Voeux family had developed formidable English connections. William was born in Baden-Baden on 22 September 1834, the son of a retired clergyman who spent his days in foreign travel. When he was two his mother died. His father obeyed his wife's dying wish and married her closest friend, Julia Denison, whose father came of a long line of successful wool merchants from Leeds. At a stroke, young William inherited a vast and varied family. By the time he had grown up, four of his step-uncles were powers in the land: the controversial high-Anglican cleric George Denison, Archdeacon of Taunton; the speaker of the House of Commons; the Bishop of Salisbury; and Sir William Denison, who had sailed with his family to govern Tasmania more than twenty years before. By the time des

Voeux landed in St Lucia, Sir William had recently retired as Governor of Madras.

The des Voeux family moved between houses in London and Leamington Spa, vacationed by the sea, and visited William's stepmother's Denison relations. But 'being the eighth of a family of nine', des Voeux recalled, 'I was hardly, even harshly, brought up.' A freezing preparatory school at seven, followed by public school, Charterhouse, at eleven. There, a gangling, ungainly figure, he worked in fits and starts, severely bullied and frequently flogged. He emerged, having been appointed a monitor and taken a firm stand against bullying, a six-foot boy of nineteen with a place at Balliol College, Oxford.

He was two years into his studies –'the happiest of the first forty years of my life' – when his father gave him an ultimatum. If William agreed to enter the church when he finished at Oxford, he would continue to maintain him. If not, he was to leave at once and chance his hand on his own, making a living in the colonies.

Des Voeux found it impossible to assent to articles in which he did not believe. His choice of the latter was regarded as banishment. He decided to go to Canada – not that he knew anything of the country – because it was the shortest sea passage from England, and the place where he had been offered the best letters of introduction.

Every time he sailed on board a ship, des Voeux was seasick. The stormy passage to Canada lasted fifteen days: for more than a week he was unable 'to eat a single morsel'. Landing in Montreal in October 1856, the snows were beginning to fall. One look at the brutal reality of farming in the wilds of Upper Canada persuaded him that he would be better off training as a lawyer in Toronto. He had just turned twenty-two.

Five years later, he emerged at the Toronto bar having passed the best law examination of the year. But having been working as a clerk all through the time he was studying for his exams, the idea of spending half his life in 'solicitor's business' and the other in 'the close air of the Courts of Justice' did not appeal. When he was chatting to chums in the Rifle Brigade, one of the captains offered to write to his father, the Duke of Newcastle, Secretary of State for the Colonies, on des Voeux's behalf. In the autumn of 1863, des Voeux was offered a job as a stipendiary magistrate in British Guiana, and a salary of £700 a year – some £50,900 today.

'I was at the time, under the impression that the colonial service was like that of India, in which under ordinary circumstances good work brought promotion. It was well that I was thus ignorant; for had I known what I had to face in British Guiana, and that no magistrate of that colony had ever been promoted to another, I should probably have declined,' des Voeux wrote.

British Guiana was a low, swampy little colony famous for its sugar, with hazy borders to the west with Venezuela, and somewhere south with Brazil. It was hot and oppressive, infested with rattlesnakes, yellow fever and gigantic mosquitoes. Fifty miles out from its shore, the waters of the Atlantic acquired a hue of sludgy green, tinged by the silt of the mighty Essequibo and Demerara Rivers. Sailing closer, a blur of distant shoreline could be seen, barely rising out of the sea.

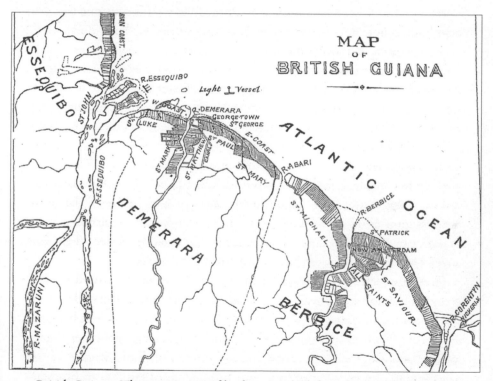

British Guiana. The narrow strips of land running back from the coast and rivers were sugar plantations

Des Voeux was twenty-nine when he first landed on the mudflats at the capital, Georgetown, and took lodgings with an old black woman. It was a few days before Christmas, 1863. Old wooden houses, two-storeyed structures on brick pillars, lazed in the sun; jalousied verandahs hung closed against the heat. Flowering oleanders, tamarinds and sweet frangipani trees grew lush in tangled gardens. Wide straight streets were intersected by canals fringed with grass. Heat shimmered over an atmosphere of decay. Fetid smells rose from open drains along the roads.

The governor, Francis Hincks, a sober, thin-faced man, appointed him to cover the region of the Upper Demerara River – one of ten magistrates' districts in the colony – and made him superintendent of rivers and creeks. As this job included the protection of the Indian tribes of the interior, des Voeux's jurisdiction extended from about ten miles south of Georgetown 'without any definite limit', deep into the rainforest on the borders with Brazil. He would spend most of the next four years on the move, living on a long narrow timber boat, powered by oarsmen, with a flat-topped wooden 'tent' with canvas sides erected over the stern to sleep in.

And so a row of twenty-five miles, or five hours, his oarsmen singing to the rhythm set by the 'cox' in the stern: the Union marching-song of 'John Brown's Body', up the wide green Demerara River. For the first eight or nine miles out of Georgetown, the chimneys of sugar plantations rose above the mangroves on both banks of the river. Vast flocks of wading birds grubbed in the shallows. Then, rowing on, scrubby trees began to line banks which were almost level with the water. Before the prevailing green of the forest marched long lines of moka-moka, a tall arum lily with large yellow-white flowers. Here and there a few coconut palms would show signs of some freed slave's holding. Except for flights of parrots at dusk or in the early morning, all signs of life gradually faded from the scene, and virgin forest rose high from the edge of the turbid water.

His first stop was at a three-room police station on the banks of the river at a place called Hyde Park. Here, where a few isolated cottages sheltered among the dense foliage, he would spend the night. Only in the policeman's room was there furniture of any kind. Silence reigned. 'No human sound, save from occasional boats passing': it seemed to des Voeux as if he now existed in some kind of 'primeval solitude'. He slept in a vast Indian-made hammock of soft cotton, in which he could stretch out any way he liked and wrap himself up against the chill, cocooned below a mosquito net. Such was the damp that overnight his boots turned white with mildew.

The next morning, he would hold court outside the police station. The parties were black and dark-coloured people, an occasional Portuguese shopkeeper, sometimes an Arawak Indian. The charges – mainly assaults and abusive language – were rarely serious. The maximum penalty he could give was six months' hard labour or a fifty-dollar fine. But this was rare. Getting the truth out of his witnesses was no mean feat. Excited plaintiffs exaggerated their cases; the defence always lied. Meanwhile, 'it was generally assumed . . . that the magistrate, who had probably never seen either party before, knew by intuition all the preceding facts and circumstances'. Question after question: des Voeux was patient. Slowly the truth would emerge from obscurity. The worst insult that could be traded in an escalating war of abuse, he wrote, was the word 'nigger' – a climax which invariably led to blows.

Wearing a solar topee on his head, a long loose-sleeved shirt and trousers, his face covered with weeks' worth of beard, des Voeux would try twenty or thirty cases in a day. Then a start would be made in the evening for the next courthouse, four or five hours up the river. This was a three-roomed cottage manned by a corporal in the gloom of a small clearing on the edge of the river. Then on to the next, another five hours, and a warm welcome in the home of George Allen, the black chief constable at Dalgin – 'a most worthy man, who quickly became a friend and strong supporter of mine'.

At Dalgin the clearing was much larger than at Hyde Park. There were several small buildings, and a schoolroom that doubled as a church. 'In return for the honour and the small pay attached to the office [Allen] gave the use of his house for a court-room.' Another round of cases, and then on upriver: another two hours to Christianburg, with a large sawmill, where des Voeux would be given a bed by the proprietor and his family, in 'the only civilized residence in the whole district', and hold court there the next day.

Now it was a long haul, twelve hours with the chanting boatmen, the forest closing in on the river, to the rapids at First Falls. Des Voeux would travel lying on the wooden roof of his 'tent' before the sun rose above the forest, then take his turn at the oars. On the way upriver, the boatmen had to haul his boat up over the rapids; on the way back down, des Voeux would hire a local Indian coxswain who knew the waters and would race them down in minutes.

From First Falls it was then four hours to the home of Charles Couchman. He and his brother, George, four miles further at Yawaribaro, were logging timber. Charles was black, George might easily have passed for white. It was George Couchman, married to an Indian woman, who taught des Voeux as much as he would learn of the Indians in these parts.

'In the many days and nights when my hammock hung in his verandah,

I had comfort rarely experienced elsewhere.' Fresh fish pepperpot, roasted deer, a clean house. Couchman was a justice of the peace, marshalling complaints for des Voeux to hear. Beyond George Couchman's there was only one other black grant holder, and then the jungle closed in above the Great Falls, 250 miles from Georgetown.

All along the river, in the places where he stayed, ants pillaged his rice supplies. At night, when he stayed at First Falls, bloodsucking vampire bats would flutter around his hammock. Everywhere, cockroaches rushed about the thatch, gecko lizards, centipedes and termites climbed the walls. Jager ants marched down ropes. Snakes fell from trees, and electric eels threatened des Voeux's early morning bathes in the river.

Inspecting the boundaries of a new logging grant he had his first experience of walking through tropical rainforest. 'I am bound to say that at first all other sensations were subordinate to an instinctive fear of snakes. The least stir in the herbage around seemed to indicate the presence of the dreaded enemy.' In fact it was lizards, 'big bloated iguanas' with their homes in trees, and others 'more slender . . . even longer than five feet' that lived in the ground, which disturbed him. Eighty, one hundred feet above his head, the trees towered over him as he and his men attempted to cut a straight line through the forest.

'Every foot of progress . . . involved severe cutlass work.' He tripped over roots, fell down gullies, and got covered, head to foot, with *bête rouge*, tiny red bugs called jiggers in the southern United States. Drenched by the rain, assaulted by ticks, and sliced by razor grass; all about him the constant hum of insects droned. One day he left an umbrella and a couple of pairs of boots on the shores of the Demerara to collect on his return. Only the seams of his boots remained.

Later des Voeux made longer journeys guided by Indians, who used arrows to shoot fish and blowpipes to hunt game. He ate *manioc*, bread made from cassava root, drank water 'the colour of porter' from streams and slept alongside his guides in hammocks under the trees. The night forest was full of weird sounds: of paddle frogs and nighthawks; the melancholy call of the whip-poor-will, and the shrieks of monkeys. The Indians told him stories of the lost city of Manoa, and the mountain plateau of Roraima, site of a legendary settlement of Amazon-like women who admitted men to their society only once a year.

It was at George Allen's at Dalgin, in September 1864, that des Voeux nearly died of yellow fever. He had already had doses of chills and fever before. Now he was caught at night in tremendous rains on the river, shivering and feeling sick. At last his boatmen managed to carry him into George Allen's house, where he overdosed on quinine and calomel. When, two days later, he regained consciousness, his hammock was soaked with blood, which they told him had come from his eyes and ears. The next morning his men rowed him without stopping the eighty miles to Georgetown to save his life. Gradually his landlady nursed him back to health. But his fevers kept recurring. The only treatment for malaria, it was then believed, was to return to a temperate climate. Late in 1865 he was given six months' leave to go to England to recover his health – where he was still troubled by unexplained attacks that would leave him prostrate for days.

Des Voeux had never had much time for the society of Georgetown, with its gossip and its iced 'swizzles' of gin or brandy, sugar and a dessertspoonful of Angostura bitters to down in one at the Club. He thought of himself as a man of the forests, a bit of an explorer. Here on the coast, everyone was in the sugar business. The plantation owners, the government committee that voted supplies: the whole revenue of the colony depended on the sugar crop. That the five government officials on the Court of Policy – the ten-member legislative body of the colony – were allowed to own interests in sugar estates stank to him of corruption.

In February 1867, Governor Hincks moved des Voeux to a new district that took in Georgetown, the east coast, and the east bank of the Demerara River: the heart of Guiana's sugar production. The coast and river shores were lined with plantations, places like 'Leonora', 'Land of Plenty', 'Aurora' and 'Bel Air', worked by thousands of indentured Indian and Chinese labourers. For four years after emancipation in 1834, former slaves in Guiana, Trinidad and Jamaica were required to serve 'apprenticeships', to prepare them for working lives as free men. After that, the supply of cheap labour in the colonies abruptly came to an end. The blacks who had cut cane for generations no longer cared to work for white masters.

Where to get the labour from? The British government stepped in with assistance. In 1838 the first ship carrying indentured Indian workers landed in Guiana from Calcutta. More workers followed, from Madras, and then from China. Recruited from pockets of destitution, men, women and children took up offers of free housing, regular work and steady wages. There was hospital treatment when they were ill, medicines free of expenses; a magistrate to hear their grievances, and an immigration department to oversee their good treatment. How could anything go wrong?

In his three years in Guiana des Voeux had seen enough abuse of indentured labourers. He wanted nothing to do with enforcing the draconian laws that applied to them. For a worker to breach his contract – and any excuse would do – was a criminal offence. The law was so wide, and its net, 'covering all possible offences, was woven so closely, that not even the smallest peccadillos could escape its meshes'. A manager could always point to some offence that would lead to a fine or a sentence of imprisonment with hard labour. Prison sentences, fines, wage cuts and prolonged indentures were handed out liberally. But Governor Hincks was insistent: des Voeux was one of only two magistrates in the colony with a legal training. He needed him there.

Now des Voeux found himself facing far greater difficulties than he had ever experienced in his remote police courts on the Upper Demerara. Murders and wounding with intent – these were frequent, but could be referred to the Supreme Court. Before him came case after case of assault by estate managers, of arrest without warrant, of theft and debt. Pregnant women expected to work as they neared their date of confinement; whole gangs of workers charged together with breaching their contracts. Stories – related through hesitant interpreters from Hindi, Urdu and a host of African and Chinese dialects – were incomprehensible. Witness after witness lied. Bribery was routine. Facing the workers across the courtroom were their bosses, the estate managers.

Des Voeux could not understand how other magistrates seemed to get through sixty to eighty cases in three or four hours. Confronting a half-starved Indian or Chinese worker in the dock, he wondered: what kinds of appalling conditions were they actually living under?

A Chinese man, caught in the act of stealing, was so badly beaten by an Indian watchman that both his legs and arms were broken. He died after the estate doctor ordered his removal in a cart back to his home. An open verdict was recorded by the doctor on the death of a boy, 'about twelve years old, a general favourite on his estate', who had been robbed for the silver and gold trinkets that he wore. When des Voeux ordered his body exhumed, he was found to have had one of his arms cut off. 'The medical man who was thus neglectful of his duty had one of the best, if not the best estates' practice in the colony,' he wrote.

Planters hectored him in court when he pronounced that arresting their workers had been illegal. He refused to permit estate managers – who expected to do so – to sit alongside him on the bench. Every time he argued with a planter or a manager they took it as a personal insult. Tension rose. Overwhelmed with work, deeply dispirited that he was not doing justice to the workers, des Voeux had only two friends in whom he could confide: James Crosby, the head of the Immigration Department, whose job it was to defend the indentured labourers, kind-hearted, educated and a hero to the workers; and the Chief Justice, a man called Beaumont, who had a profound disregard for what des Voeux called the 'settled principle' of the courts that the evidence of white men should prevail. Crosby and Beaumont were speaking out in sympathy with the workers; both were abruptly removed from office by the Court of Policy, with the active support of Governor Hincks. Des Voeux's reward was to be assigned to a new magistracy on the west bank of the Demerara, where the planters were among the most powerful in the colony, united and hostile.

West Demerara was too far from Georgetown for him to continue to live in town. Des Voeux was forced to rent a dreary half-abandoned plantation and to purchase a coach and horses, in order to drive over 100 miles a week from one court to the next.

Before long, the manager of 'Leonora', the largest estate in the area, was brought before him, charged by a worker with beating him up on a Sunday morning. The man, who had refused to work on his day of rest, had been working for almost twenty-four hours. Des Voeux fined the manager heavily, and warned him that a second offence would bring him before the Supreme Court. A second manager, who had knocked down and kicked a worker – behaviour for which he had already many times been brought to court – was given the same warning.

'Beginning with the withdrawal of ordinary courtesy', one after the other, the plantation managers began dropping casual insults in des Voeux's direction and subjecting him to 'petty annoyances'. Living alone on his decaying plantation, he was snubbed by the neighbours and attacked in the white press. One day des Voeux was holding court at a police station when an important planter, who was also a justice of the peace, appeared with a menacing crowd. Among them were several estate managers. Three of the planter's workers were charged with breaching their contracts. Des Voeux found the men had been dragged out of their quarters and arrested illegally. As he declared his verdict, the planter hurled an insult at him. Des Voeux ordered him from the court and went to see Governor Hincks. 'While listening courteously to my representations that Executive support to the magistrates was absolutely necessary for securing a decent measure of justice to the subject races', the Governor refused to stand up for des Voeux by demanding an apology from the planter, or withdrawing his commission as a justice of the peace.

By the end of eighteen months as a magistrate among the sugar plantations, des Voeux was acutely depressed, lonely and isolated. He became so ill with repeated attacks of fever that he could hardly walk. Yet he refused to resign. He was however, fortunate in his connections at home. While on his last leave he had seen much of Lady Jocelyn, the stepdaughter of the late prime minister, Lord Palmerston. She backed his application to Lord Granville, the Secretary of State, for a transfer — anything, anywhere, even at a smaller salary, if it might offer some chance of promotion. Within two months he was offered the post of administrator, running the island of St Lucia: the same pay, more expenses, but he would be his own master.

Des Voeux learned bitter lessons in British Guiana. The first, as he was to write years later, was that, however much he wanted to, a governor could not 'or ought not to — become intimate with any of the residents'. Crown colonies especially were so small; the educated population were so few and the decisions to be taken were so various — vacancies for office, issues of discipline, questions of taxes, the treatment of indentured labourers, fines and penalties — that they were bound to affect almost everyone whom the governor came to know at one time or another. 'Terms of exceptional intimacy' were sure to be put down to favouritism, 'and a loss of respect is incurred in consequence.

'But apart from all this, the friendship of the possessor of so much local power is so eagerly sought by those who hope to gain something from it, that if accorded to one it is certain to cause heartburning in others who consider themselves equally entitled to it.' Landed in St Lucia, des Voeux recognized 'the necessity for such isolation from the first'. But how complete this was to be, he was shortly to learn.

Living high up on the Morne in his dilapidated Government House, his time was spent in solitude. Every day he rose at six. Often he had not slept, but had risen much earlier to deal with papers sent up to the house the night before. Four days a week he rode down to the Colonial Secretary's office for meetings. He would see his neighbour, the treasurer, Macnamara Dix, and make sudden, surprise visits to inspect the gaol and the different asylums – one for the poor, another for lunatics and a third for patients who suffered from yaws, a contagious, syphilis-like disease, marked by nasty skin eruptions. 'The necessary day's work done, before going home I usually rode a few times round the top of the Morne, that being the only level spot within easy reach for a gallop.' Two or three evenings a week he might have guests. Otherwise he passed the evening alone, reading or working. On moonlit nights he would pace the galleries on either side of his house, thinking over the problems that faced him, wondering what to do next.

The administration was a shambles. Everywhere an atmosphere of apathy seemed to pervade the offices. He had to go over every letter written by his clerks. At the Registry heaps of musty papers – births, marriages and deaths, deeds, mortgages, properties bought and sold – had yet to be registered and filed. His deputy registrar was a popular man, but he was rarely sober. The lawyers of the island charged with making searches were delighted to add the extra time it took to find a document to their bills.

Meanwhile, the courts were in a state of bedlam. The chief justice, John Athill, had been formally charged with drunkenness ten years before. Despite the damning testimony of witnesses, he had been acquitted of all charges. Now he drowsed on the bench, milking the courts as he had done for years. Having tried a man for burglary he sentenced him for rape. Lawyers from one side hurled insults at those from the other while he looked on benignly. Whole proceeds from the sales of the property belonging to persons deceased or bankrupt were eaten up by legal costs.

Des Voeux anguished over what he should do. Six months earlier, he had been a lowly magistrate in British Guiana: now it was clear that he was going to have to sack the most powerful man on St Lucia after himself – one with a wife and daughters who were well known all over the island. Bringing Athill to book took des Voeux many months. As he launched an inquiry – which had to be sanctioned by London – Athill asked to retire and take up his pension. When des Voeux refused, Athill's doctor produced a certificate declaring he would commit suicide if he were not permitted an immediate leave of absence from the island. Des Voeux let him go. But even with the chief justice out of the way, witness after witness would say one thing in private and another on oath. It took almost a year, but eventually des Voeux's persistence won through. The chief justice was dismissed.

Athill had not been alone in his habits of drink and corruption. In less than six months des Voeux cut a deep swathe through St Lucia's officials. Sacking a number of junior officials, he then fired a magistrate (the island had three), the chief (and only) medical officer, the head of the revenue, and an unofficial member of the Executive Council (there were only two) who had been smuggling rum produced by his distillery. In December, seven months after des Voeux first arrived, his deputy registrar expired from the effects of drink.

By this time des Voeux was functioning in almost complete isolation. Protests from friends of those who had been sacked mounted. In the meantime, soon after des Voeux's arrival, a young man whom he only describes as F. Grey landed, with a commission from London as a stipendiary magistrate. By a freak of coincidence, des Voeux had known him since childhood; Grey had been his fag at Charterhouse. He appointed Grey to Soufrière, in the heart of the island's sugar production, where, as in Guiana, the magistrate was expected 'to mete a different "justice" to different classes'. Like des Voeux, Grey stood firm on his principles.

Now the leading planters of the island joined the embittered allies of the sacked chief justice against des Voeux. News that des Voeux had stopped one morning while riding down from the Morne, dismounted from his horse and helped an old woman struggling to put an enormous load of bananas and yams back on her head swept round the island like wildfire. The blacks were as stunned as the whites that a white man, let alone the governor of the island, should have behaved in such a way. Attacks against des Voeux rose in the press, and anonymous hate letters were delivered to Government House. Meanwhile he was amazed to learn that the story of his assistance had spread so far that it was reported in *The Creole,* the black newspaper in Guiana.

Christmas Day, 1869: in the peace of the day, alone at Government House on the Morne, des Voeux took his first moment of spare time to write to the Secretary of State, Lord Granville. 'My Lord,' he wrote, 'I should not more delay the performance of what I conscientiously believe an obligatory duty.' In the autumn indentured workers from India and China had started rising on the plantations in Guiana. Governor Hincks had applied to Barbados for troops. Now des Voeux was going to tell Lord Granville how the plantation workers were treated. At the same time a copy of the letter was being transcribed for des Voeux's old friend, Frederick Cavendish, the Earl's former private secretary, who he knew could lay it 'without the least delay under . . . Granville's own eye'.

It was 134 paragraphs, over 10,000 words long, and laid out all the injustices that des Voeux had seen in the courts in Guiana. He told how magistrates, often from inferior positions, had been residents of Guiana so long 'they have . . . insensibly acquired awe of the powerful planting interests'; how they could not hope to be independent. Less well educated than the plantation managers, certainly less well paid, it was easy for managers 'to soften the harsher features of the magistrate's life, and have larger means of heaping upon him trouble and annoyance'. In the same way, doctors commonly discharged sick and injured workers from hospital before they had properly recovered – leading to cases of 'idleness', brought before the court. Doctors were entirely dependent on the estate managers for their employment.

Planters, government servants, the abuses of the whole 'coolie' system: des Voeux's letter sent shockwaves through London. His accusations were appalling; 'so appalling and involving such cruelty and oppression done in the name of the law, under a tropical sun, against so many thousand British subjects, that . . . there has', *The Times* declared, 'been no such indictment preferred against officers of the Crown since Hastings was impeached of tyranny.' In March 1870, Lord Granville implemented a commission of inquiry into the treatment of immigrants in Guiana.

By then, des Voeux's health was even more fragile than usual. Not long after writing to the Secretary of State, he had taken a brief holiday on Trinidad with the Governor, Sir Arthur Gordon, and his wife, Rachael. There he had been so badly concussed in a riding accident that he lost all memory of the preceding weeks, the details of what he had written to the Secretary of State, and was sleeping only with laudanum. 'I write you one line . . . to wish you God-speed under your present difficulties,' Gordon wrote to wish him good luck. 'I am hearing you abused as I write.' With trepidation des Voeux sailed for Georgetown to give evidence to the inquiry in June 1870.

Guiana was electric with tension. An old Oxford friend of des Voeux's, the prominent businessman Walter Morrison, had put up money to enable the Aborigines Protection Society and the Anti-Slavery Society to engage a barrister from London – Edward Jenkins – to represent the workers at the inquiry. In the meantime, the planters had marshalled their forces. To impress the commissioners from England, estates that had been run down were now immaculate, awaiting their inspection: tanks for water, new barracks, bigger, better hospitals and clean yards. In white Georgetown des Voeux's name was reviled. Hotels and lodging houses were threatened by boycotts if he so much as set foot in them. A new governor, who had taken over from Francis Hincks, spurned him and took no notice of his official call. Only two white men – one a merchant, and his old friend James Crosby, the former immigration agent – had the courage to visit him during his stay.

Friends in the garrison permitted him a little house on the edge of the barracks. From dawn to dusk crowds of Indians and Chinese besieged him, eager to put their complaints. So many were exhausted with the distances they had come, so hungry and thirsty, 'my slender purse was continually being drained to supply what appeared to be very urgent want'. Des Voeux, Jenkins and his clerk took down statement after statement, while petition after petition was delivered.

'Your Commissioners we give God the Glory, who pitied the children of Israel in their house of bondage, and sent Moses for their deliverance. So the same God sent you Commissioners to deliver us from out of the house of bondage. We we[re] brought into this Colony by our planters. From the [year] 1845. By thousand From the land that is ful of Hindoos superstitions and Moh'ommedanism into a land of lights as it's called. But we were thrown into pastures like beasts in total darkness by managers on the estates.'

Chinese indentured labourers sketch their abuses in British Guiana

Time after time the small team registered the same old abuses: assault, arbitrary cutting of wages, refusal of admission to hospital or ejection from it; being forced out of their homes to work overtime; the uselessness of appeals to magistrates.

Only with difficulty was des Voeux able to get permission to see the lists of cases he had tried in the past. Access to the files, which would have given him detailed evidence to substantiate his arguments, was denied. All at once he found himself in a room packed with his enemies, his head reeling, his mind incoherent, standing before the commissioners with little concrete evidence to support him. For three days he was cross-examined.

It took a year for the inquiry to publish its findings in June 1871. Des Voeux's contribution was severely criticized for lack of concrete evidence. Nevertheless, the commissioners brought to light more abuses than des Voeux had expected. Laws were changed, executive 'vigilance' over the magistrates increased; doctors became public servants. The reforms were passed on to Mauritius and Trinidad. 'Thus ill as was performed my part in this coolie question,' des Voeux wrote later, 'I have never for a moment regretted that I undertook it.'

Returning to St Lucia, slowly, painfully, des Voeux began to make progress. It took him four hours one 'intensely hot afternoon' to at last persuade the Legislative Council that if they did not sanction a subsidy of £500 a year to a telegraph company, whose ship was even then off the port laying cable, they were unlikely ever to get the link with the island. It took much more argument to change the law to allow a black village that had grown up over generations along the 'Cinquante Pas du Roi', an ancient public right of way around the coastline of the island, to remain. He reformed the ancient French tradition of *corvée* – so many days' labour per year from every citizen – for repairing the roads. A central hospital was built at Castries, and two auxiliaries at Soufrière and Vieuxfort. He drafted new laws, argued them in the legislature, explained them to the Secretary of State, all the time in the absence of a shorthand writer, making copies and recording the minutes of meetings himself. A new chief justice was appointed from Canada, and a new medical officer arrived. As a new registrar he appointed a black, 'about the best educated man on the island', whom he pointedly invited to dinner when he heard that 'whites' had slighted him. He found one of the planters to be much more enlightened than he had thought, and made a good friend of John Goodman.

He still worked twelve hours a day, and it was only later that he learned that often he would be so absorbed in his work that when his valet, Sam Cox, mischievously told him he had already eaten breakfast, he would believe him. But beyond the piles of official work, the long hours of drudgery, only the most elusive clues in his memoirs allow you to see how much des Voeux liked good company, how attracted he was to clever, vivacious women, and how fond he was of dancing. He loved it when the fleet came into harbour and he could entertain the officers up on the Morne. He collected anecdotes and jokes. In the summer of 1872, he was sent again on leave in England. Shooting in Scotland, golf at St Andrews, house parties at Chatsworth, balls in London, dinner parties in Eaton Square and Grosvenor Place, trips to Brighton, the Pyrenees and Cannes. Meanwhile, he arranged for Sam Cox to be given cooking lessons by the chef at the Carlton Club, and was much amused one Sunday morning to realize that the black man 'with a good-looking English girl on each arm' crossing St James's Park was in fact his valet. Cox was hugely popular at servants' balls, and had to be dragged out of the arms of several maids one morning when des Voeux decided unexpectedly to leave a country house before dawn for London.

As for des Voeux himself, a day or two before he was about to sail for St Lucia in January 1873 his eye fell upon the sixteen-year-old, dark-haired daughter of Sir John Pender, a wealthy businessman whose companies had laid most of the world's telegraph cables. Her name was Marion, but he had no time to do more than briefly bow over her hand before he had to leave.

Des Voeux landed at Castries to a 'cordial' reception from the officials, and 'noisy and somewhat embarrassing demonstrations' by the blacks. 'They followed and surrounded my horse as I rode up the Morne, cheering, screaming, and waving handkerchiefs.' The planters wished to build a central sugar factory for the island, modelled on a successful effort in Martinique. This proved a fortuitous project for des Voeux, for, after exploratory investigations in Martinique, another trip to England five months later was required to persuade the Colonial Office and raise the capital for the company in London. These were all discussions which Sir John Pender could usefully expedite. Des Voeux returned to St Lucia in March 1874 engaged to Marion. It was six months before his fortieth birthday. The following year, he married her.

'The continual presence in the house of a sympathetic companion made now a vast difference in my life. First I was relieved from household worries and management, and in social duties I had tactful and valuable assistance . . . I came to take a calmer view of delinquencies and difficulties; and though my troubles were still great, I regarded them with comparative equanimity. My rides now were rarely or never solitary. We had a daily gallop round the Morne [and] in our longer excursions there was a continual pleasure in introducing to an appreciative companion the scenic beauties of the tropics.

'Save in one quarter, my wife was greeted everywhere with effusive warmth.' His old Demerara parrot, Jocko, was seized with a fit of 'extraordinary jealousy', while on their voyage out to St Lucia, his servant Sam 'deliberately assumed an attitude of unprecedented insolence'. Marion was not fooled. Afterwards des Voeux learned enough about Sam's naughty doings to fill a book. In the meantime, he 'was compelled to discharge him at his native Barbados, evidently his secret object'.

As soon as he became engaged to Marion, des Voeux began making every attempt to secure a promotion, even though he felt an obligation to see the completion of the sugar factory – in which he and Pender had heavily invested – on the island. 'Natal is vacant,' he wrote to her on 18 December 1874. '*The Times* of the 5th December announces the appointment of Arthur Gordon to Fiji,' he told her five days later. 'I envy him the chance of making a new colony "off his own bat" under entirely unprecedented conditions.' By the end of the year, he reckoned it was eleven years since he had first arrived in the West Indies, 'yet after all my work I am pecuniarily worse off'. All the same, as he looked back over his time and in spite of all the enemies he had made, 'I have made some warm friends. I have survived without, I hope, permanent damage to health, and above all, I have one prospect which compensates fully for all actual ills.'

Two years after his marriage, in early 1877, des Voeux accepted the offer of the Secretary of State to become acting governor of Trinidad. With his reputation in Guiana and St Lucia known, his reception 'proved frigid beyond anticipation'. He would go on the following year to relieve Sir Arthur Gordon as Governor of Fiji. From that point des Voeux developed a reputation as one of the most steady and reliable governors of his generation. He moved from the South Pacific to Newfoundland in 1886, and to Hong Kong from 1887 until his retirement in 1891. Returning to England, he and Marion lived quietly, mainly in London. In spite of his recurring attacks of malaria, sunstroke, seasickness and accidents, he lived until the age of seventy-five.

4 Captain Douglas settles Palmerston
South Australia 1870–73

The idea of creating a British settlement somewhere along the endless shores of the north Australian coastline had beckoned like a siren from the time the first Admiralty surveyors began to chart the lengths in 1818. Tantalizing, scarcely imaginable, all this virgin land, just off the sea routes of south-east Asia: here, surely, was a site for a second staging post to China, another Singapore? Over the next forty years, three attempts were made to establish a base. But each time, first at Melville Island, south-east across the sea from East Timor, next at places now lost to time – Raffles Bay and Port Essington – the problems were apparently intractable: shortages of water, infertile soils, a climate that was hot, steamy and atrociously wet for half the year. Then there were the sicknesses: scurvy and fever, and bloody confrontations with Aborigines. Worst of all was the isolation. Fleeting and rare were sightings of the legendary Muslim traders from Makassar, on the southern tip of the Indonesian island of Sulawesi, who were rumoured to arrive every year to fish for *trepang* – sea cucumbers – to take to China, and who might be persuaded to scoop up English goods and export them. Meanwhile, European ships bypassed the north coast, sailing from the Cape to Sydney directly via the southern trades across the oceans to Adelaide, and then around to the east, via Melbourne, up the coast to Sydney.

Under the aegis of the Colonial Office and the Royal Geographical Society, the North Australian Expedition, led by Augustus Charles Gregory, was launched in 1855. After sixteen months, and travelling over 7,000 miles by sea and land, Gregory returned to Sydney to report to the Governor-General, Sir William Denison. Denison was blunt. 'It is evident that, of this great continent, more than three-fourths is an absolute howling wilderness,' he wrote to Sir Roderick Murchison at the Royal Geographical Society in London. But Gregory also reported crossing at least 3 million acres of grazing land suitable for sheep in the region of the Victoria River, flowing north into the Timor Sea.

Then John MacDouall Stuart, a man who had spent almost twenty unremitting years exploring the burning wastes beyond the territory of southern

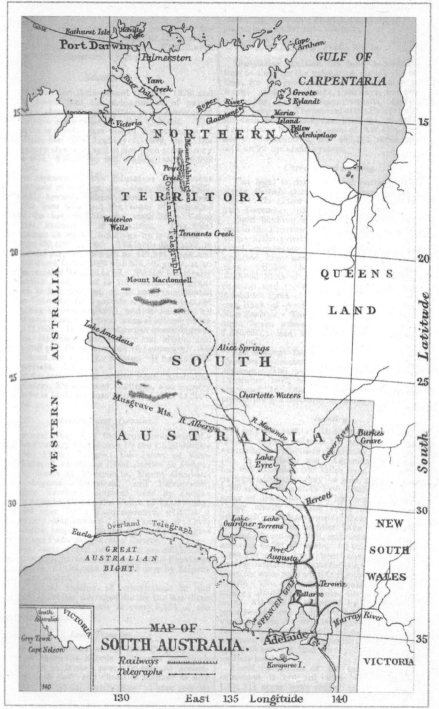

Australia, returned safely to Adelaide after his fifth attempt to cross the continent – more than 1,800 miles – from south to north. On 28 June 1862 he had reached the Roper River, 250 miles south-east of today's Darwin. 'The water of this river is most excellent; the soil is also of the first description; and the grass, although dry, most abundant . . . this is certainly the finest country I have seen in Australia,' Stuart recorded in his diary. A month later, he reached the north coast. 'Delighted and gratified to behold the waters of the Indian Ocean', he first dipped his feet, then washed his face and hands in the sea, and marvelled at the land about him.

On his return to Adelaide, sunburned, thin and exhausted, he was greeted with wild enthusiasm. The north coast was not only well adapted for European settlement, he declared, but the climate was 'in every respect suitable, and the surrounding country of excellent quality and of great extent. If this country is settled,' Stuart went on, 'it will be one of the finest colonies under the crown, suitable for the growth of any and everything – what a splendid country for growing cotton.' A gala procession and huge banquet were laid on to celebrate his triumphant return. People in Adelaide were talking. Could Stuart's country be the Promised Land?

The territory of South Australia was unique on a continent that had first been settled by British convicts. This was a British province specifically planned by an act of parliament in 1834 to be a centre of civilization, free from religious discrimination and poverty, for free emigrants from the nation's overcrowded cities. It was to be settled by 'systematic colonization' financed by the sale of land to investors. As plans were laid for the foundations of today's city of Adelaide – a clean grid of straight streets, laced by wide boulevards, large public gardens and surrounded by parkland – few realized that north of its splendid harbour on the coast lay vast wastes of arid, uninhabitable uplands.

On Stuart's return, Sir Richard MacDonnell, the bullish Governor of South Australia, who had sponsored his expeditions and urged the expansion of South Australia beyond its apparently worthless borders, had just concluded his five-year term. Now in London, he went to call on the Duke of Newcastle, Secretary of State for the Colonies. He successfully applied for an extension of the modest borders of South Australia as far as the north coast of the continent. On 1 October 1863, a bill to colonize the Northern Territories was introduced into the thirty-six-member House of Assembly in Adelaide.

Adelaide was to provide the model for settlement. The costs of establishing the new colony would be borne by selling half a million acres – packaged as half-acre town lots with 160-acre 'country' lots for farming, priced at £60 each. Half the lots were to be sold in England. In London, MacDonnell became chairman of the new North Australian Company, whose shareholders pledged to take up any orders not purchased by private buyers. The first sale was held simultaneously in London and Adelaide, on 1 March 1864. According to the deal, the purchasers, 'land-order holders', were to be able to select their holdings within five years: in the circumstances, based on no more than Stuart's twenty-four hours' observation at a single point on the coastline, this was a daunting timetable.

With cash now in hand, MacDonnell's successor as governor in Adelaide, Dominick Daly, immediately dispatched a surveying expedition to Port Essington, where in the past a settlement had been attempted. But this site and several others were found to be full of hazards – either short of water, or flooded half the year during the 'wet'. By late 1866, cash was running short. Doubts about the whole northern venture were increasing. The British land-order holders threatened to mount litigation.

One last place might possibly do. Early surveys had discounted the attractions of Port Darwin – a fine natural harbour, named for Charles Darwin when the *Beagle* called there in 1839 – because of its low mangrove shores, lack of water, and doubts about the health of its climate. But poring over charts of the northern coastline, George Goyder, South Australia's forty-three-year-old surveyor-general, could see potential in the magnificent sheltered bay. Early in 1869 Governor Daly dispatched him north by sea to investigate. In a little more than six months, Goyder, who had years of mapping the outback behind him, surveyed almost 700,000 acres. He returned to Adelaide to draw up an outline plan for a new city and suburbs. The design was every bit as artificial as Adelaide's had been thirty years before – and just as ambitious. The centre was laid out around a central square flanked by parks, surrounded by a grid of narrow streets with more than 1,000 allotments, running back from the sea in parallel lines. The new town would be called Palmerston, after the late British prime minister. Like Adelaide, it was to be the main port for a whole new region.

The next task was to settle it.

William Bloomfield Douglas was the forty-eight-year-old harbour-master of Adelaide, collector of customs, holder of various other civic posts and a prominent man in government circles. Lightly built, a smile in his eyes, flecks of grey in his hair, with long side-whiskers merging into a full moustache, Douglas had been in Adelaide for over sixteen years. Enthusiastic, intelligent and plausible, he had considerable charm. But Douglas was also known to be mercurial and bad-tempered, with a weakness for money, a fondness for drink and a handsome talent for reinventing himself.

No one was quite sure of his history. The local newspapers described him variously as Captain, Lieutenant or Major. His wife, Ellen, however, was dignified and gracious; they had two lovely teenaged daughters, the elder of whom, Harriet, was walking out with the son of Governor Daly, and five young children, one of whom was no more than a toddler. As early as 1862, Douglas had offered his services in the colonization of 'Stuart's country' in the north. He quoted long experience of exploration and European settlement in the tropical East Indies, and a particular expertise in fighting the cut-throat Malay pirates who it was believed might threaten the north coast.

Each time an expedition headed north, Douglas put himself forward as the man to head a new colony. When Goyder's surveying expedition returned to Adelaide, Douglas lobbied John Hart, the premier of South Australia, in earnest. On 22 March 1870, his dream was realized: Lieutenant Bloomfield Douglas (or so he appears on his formal instructions) was appointed first government resident of the new Northern Territory.

Douglas's appointment had nothing to do with the Colonial Office in London, although they were informed of it. The venture at Palmerston was entirely in the hands of the South Australian government. Even though the site was 1,800 miles north across a trackless desert, or four or five weeks' sailing round the continent, no thought was given to how the settlement was actually to be administered. The founding of Palmerston was seen as no more than a question of property development, a project of the Office for Crown Lands. Douglas, however, had seen a governor in operation before.

Douglas was the son of an army officer who never had enough money – an unfortunate propensity which seemed to run in the family. His grandfather, too, a gentleman clergyman and sometime chaplain to the Prince Regent, had held a sequence of unsatisfactory livings in south-east England, while spending his days reading, painting and pioneering British field archaeology. Douglas asked for half his first year's salary of £700 at Palmerston to be paid in advance, but all the same, it seems, he managed to take ship from Adelaide without clearing all his debts.

In fact, the Douglases, with their long tradition of relying on connections, could have walked out of any of Jane Austen's novels. Douglas's mother was the sister of a Dorset clergyman whose wife, Emma, was the beloved sister of James Brooke. By the time Douglas was offered the post of government resident in Palmerston, Brooke had become the stuff of Victorian legend: the first white raja of remote and exotic Sarawak, on the north-west coast of Borneo.

James Brooke was eighteen years older than Douglas. Born in India, schooled in England, a spoiled and wilful child, Brooke had returned to the east, where he became an officer with the East India Company. In 1822, at the head of irregular cavalry, he saw action first in Burma and three years later in Assam, where he was seriously wounded. Forced to take time off, Brooke resigned his commission and began exploring the islands of southeast Asia, tasting the China trade which ran between Penang, Malacca and Singapore. When his father died in 1835, leaving him a small fortune of £30,000, Brooke bought a former schooner of the Royal Yacht Squadron which he christened the *Royalist*. Flying the white ensign, armed with half a dozen six-pounders, Brooke cruised the waters of what is today's Sabah, exploring its resources, and dreaming of founding a British settlement that would link Singapore and Hong Kong with a place like Port Essington, then under development, on the north coast of Australia.

Meanwhile, at the age of eighteen Bloomfield Douglas signed on with HMS *Wolverene*, sailing for the East Indies and Hong Kong. He was the captain's steward – not even a midshipman – in and out of the galley on board, privy to all that went on in the captain's cabin. Irrepressibly enthusiastic, and a quick learner, Douglas quit the *Wolverene* in Hong Kong and made his way to Sarawak to join his uncle by marriage. Brooke took him on as second mate on the *Royalist*. In September 1842 Brooke finally achieved his long-dreamt-of ambition. In return for helping Raja Muda Hassim, the uncle of the Sultan of Brunei, suppress a rebellion, he was rewarded with the territory in the Indies which he had so long desired As Bloomfield Douglas celebrated his twentieth birthday, Brooke was installed as the Raja of Sarawak, in today's eastern province of Malaysia. Here he and his descendants – the first of whom would be Douglas's cousin Charles – were to rule their own private kingdom until 1946.

Brooke captivated Douglas – as he did almost all the Europeans who chanced upon the exotic milieu he had begun to create in Sarawak. With his sardonic good looks, his charm, charisma and considerable swagger, Brooke presided over his headquarters in a traditional Malay house raised on stilts in a clearing of thick jungle on the banks of a river. It was surrounded by a ditch and high palisades to protect poultry, sheep, goats and other live-stock. There Brooke lived alongside a gentle tribe called the Dyaks, a handful of European henchmen, and servants of several different nationalities. 'The cooking-establishment was perfect, and the utmost harmony prevailed,' wrote Brooke's friend Keppel, captain of the *Dido,* which supported Brooke's own gunboats in his battles with pirates.

'A large room in the centre, neatly ornamented with every description of fire-arms, in admirable order and ready for use, served as an audience and mess-room; and the various apartments round it as bed-rooms, [it was] comfortably furnished with matted floors, easy chairs, pictures and books . . . The great feeding time was at sun-set, when Mr Brooke took his seat at the head of the table, and all the establishment . . . seated themselves according to their respective grades . . . all Mr Brooke's party were characters – all had travelled; and never did a minute flag for want of some entertaining anecdote, good story, or song to pass away the time; and it was while smoking our cigars in the evening, that the natives, as well as the Chinese who had become settlers, used to drop in, and, after creeping up according to their custom, and touching the hand of their European raja, retire to the further end of the room and squat down upon their haunches, remaining a couple of hours without uttering a word, and then creep out again. I have seen sixty or seventy of an evening come and make this sort of salaam.'

It was a big talking group, engaged in the heady business, no more, no less, of shaping a new nation. They had gunboats, and were soon to have – Brooke was negotiating – the full weight of the British Crown behind them. Brooke's ambition was to develop the island of Borneo according to his view of the world: 'to extirpate piracy by attacking and breaking up the pirate towns . . . to correct the native character, to gain and hold an influence in Borneo Proper. To introduce gradually, a better system of government. To open the interior. To encourage the poorer natives. To remove the clogs on trade. To develop new sources of commerce. I wish to make Borneo a second Java!'

Meanwhile, the balmy tropical evenings were filled with the heavy scent of frangipani, and the silent figures of beautiful girls slipping among the shadows, enticing the white men away.

Douglas picked up Malay, and eagerly volunteered for raids against the piratical tribes who threatened Brooke's beloved Dyaks. He quickly made himself useful, taking sabre in hand to fight with the pirates who threatened the coast, plundering ships and taking slaves, and, within a year, taking command of at least one of Brooke's schooners. He captained the *Jolly Bachelor,* a large boat built by the Dyaks, fitted with a brass six-pounder and a long gun.

There is just a whisper that Brooke did not find Douglas altogether reliable: by September 1843 he had got command of the *Royalist,* 'which would be an excellent thing provided it was permanent', Brooke confided to an old friend in London. By 1848, Douglas was back in England, working for the coastguard, taming smuggling on the coast of Northumberland. There he met and married Ellen, his 'Elli', the daughter of a yeoman farmer. Two daughters were born and Douglas returned to the sea. In 1854, in command of the mail steamer *Bosphorus,* he landed in Adelaide.

Initial news of Douglas's appointment as Resident of the Northern Territories in early 1870 was greeted in his household with jubilation. 'For a time he was undecided whether he would not leave his family in Adelaide,' wrote his eldest daughter, Harriet, who was about to become engaged to Governor Daly's son. For her the news rapidly turned to dismay, for 'the idea of separation from those nearest and dearest to him was so distasteful that it was arranged that we should accompany him to Port Darwin'. With bitter tears, she and her seventeen-year-old sister Nell forswore balls and dancing for 'exile, hard work, and monotony'. But for the younger children – five of them under the age of twelve, including 'pretty, curly haired, bright-eyed' two-year-old Johnnie – 'the prospect of going to such a wild country ... seized [one and all] with an irresistible longing to read every book treating of new countries and daring adventures that came in their way'.

For Douglas, the appointment came just in time. 'He never said a word about the £100 I lent him,' the premier of South Australia, John Hart, confided to his diary on 28 April 1870, after seeing the family off on the government schooner, the *Gulnare.* 'I suppose he now looks upon it as a gift.' The family took with them only one servant, their maid, Annie, whose '*affaires de coeur*' on board the tiny *Gulnare* 'were so numerous, and followed each other with such startling rapidity, that nothing short of a conquest of the entire ship's company seemed likely to happen'. The only other passenger for whom there was room was a solitary trooper.

★

On 24 June 1870, as the *Gulnare* sailed into the harbour at Port Darwin, glassily smooth in a pearly light, Douglas and his family absorbed the sight of a world unlike anything they had ever encountered before. Shores thick with mangrove gave way to smooth white beaches, and cliffs spread with palm, ironbark and lush green milkwood trees. 'The place looked what it was, – a land of perpetual summer,' wrote Harriet. 'Beautiful it certainly was; but oh! So lonely and desolate . . . It was all . . . just as it had remained from the beginning of time – untouched and untrodden by the foot of man.'

From the rail of the ship they could see flat-topped Fort Hill, with a flagstaff flying the Union Jack. Close by was a grave, 'the last resting place of a young surveyor who had been murdered by the natives the year before' (speared in revenge for the shooting of two Aboriginal men). To the left was a second hill, covered with green shrubs. There, staring intently at the ship, were dozens of wiry black men – some perched on one leg, hands holding bundles of spears – and women, while children swarmed through the bush. These silent unclothed spectators were the Larrakia, 'the oldest inhabitants of this part of the world'. All the Douglases had met Aborigines before, but 'here the aboriginal presented himself in an entirely new aspect', recorded Harriet, with a keen eye on her audience. 'We were the smaller number, they the greater, and moreover, this crowd of savages was armed to the teeth.' Below the Larrakia on the hill lay a sandy gully and a scattered handful of log huts. Beyond loomed a mass of dense forest.

Two ships were coming in at once, for during the voyage the *Gulnare* had been damaged by a hurricane and had had to put into Brisbane for almost a month. The *Bengal* was loaded with their furniture, seven 'land-selectors' bent on inspecting the whole of Goyder's lands before finalizing their selection of allotments, and a handful of settlers. Along the shore were ranged the local population: the acting government resident, Dr Millner; Goyder's nephew, surveyor George MacLachlan; and Mr Hood, the storekeeper. The police inspector, Paul Foelsche, and four troopers in smart blue uniform stood to attention, while a ship's carpenter, a couple of masons, a blacksmith, and assorted boatmen and labourers who had been left behind from Goyder's expedition formed up as a guard of honour. There were no more than a handful of women, wives of the labourers.

Douglas landed in as much state as he could muster. Seven shots were fired, in loose and sporadic fashion, from an obsolete old cannon that Goyder had left to scare away the blacks. These were returned from the *Gulnare*. From the moment he was sworn in by Dr Millner, who had been in charge for the past six months, Douglas was known as 'The Governor'.

Walking up the sandy track that led from the shore, Douglas and the family found that on closer inspection, the 'Camp' was neat and well laid out. Beyond was a stable, in a long shed roofed with sheets of bark, and the police barracks. Two rough huts had been erected for them near the sea. The first, of thin log palings plugged with paper bark from gum trees and roofed with sheets of bark weighted down with huge stones, was for sleeping. The windows were made from calico, propped open by a stick, and the floor was mud – 'a great trial of patience, for every clean dress we put on became soiled round the edges immediately', wrote Harriet. A covered way led to a sitting room – a galvanized iron hut, about twenty feet long, lined with deal, and a wooden floor, with 'windows of sheets of iron propped open in the usual way; there was a door at each end and we habitually sat in a draught for the sake of air'.

Elli, Harriet and Nell were stunned. After the civilization of Adelaide, this was the most rudimentary of campsites. No nearby water, no kitchen range; suddenly they were confronted with cooking, cleaning, laundry and looking after young children – with only Annie to help.

Douglas ordered the immediate construction of a verandah, made of saplings and covered with canvas, and into this improvised accommodation the Douglases piled their furniture, tables, chests of drawers, sideboards and chiffoniers – and a piano. There was no time for the 'Governor' to draw breath before the land selectors were upon him, eager to set upon the job of selecting their allotments in the town. Then they headed off, out into the countryside to choose their land there.

A stout heart was needed to pioneer Australia. 'Palmerston' and its flimsy huts lay behind a shoreline infested with crocodiles and a sea full of sharks. There were pythons, snake-eating cobras and deadly tiger snakes. The land, Douglas quickly discovered, was barren of foodstuffs: there was no kind of fruit, vegetables or meat, and very little fresh water. The Camp subsisted on bread baked by two government cooks, canned meat, known as 'blanket', dried potatoes from the government stores, and the occasional gift of fresh fish caught by the Larrakia. The Aborigines haunted the settlement, dogging the white men's footsteps, appearing uncannily in the Douglases' new verandah, following any expedition out along the shore or into the jungle.

Not long after the Douglases arrived, Davis, a young police trooper – a favourite with Harriet and Nell – disregarded the ban on swimming. He was taken by a crocodile in full view of the crew of the *Gulnare*. Boats were lowered, oars thrashed the water, but the crocodile had Davis's head in its jaws. His ghastly death traumatized the little settlement. For the majority of the men at Palmerston, almost all of whom had left their wives and children in Adelaide, Douglas's act in bringing his wife and small children to such a crude settlement verged on the irresponsible. The first hints of resentment stirred.

With the exception of the surveyor, George MacLachlan, and police inspector Paul Foelsche – who was responsible for protecting the white settlers – all the men were under Douglas's complete control. On the bigger issues, his hands were tied: neither he nor MacLachlan could make any changes to the town plan of Palmerston without approval from Adelaide. In any case, the best lots had already been sold. He had no instructions to develop any kind of civic administration that would serve as the basis of a permanent colony to come. Indeed, when Lord Granville, Secretary of State for the Colonies, wrote to the new Governor of South Australia, Sir James Fergusson, to inquire what 'additional measures for promoting immigration to the Colony' were intended, the Governor was advised by his ministers 'that nothing be proposed at present'. Douglas was to hold a temporary bridgehead, supplied by Adelaide, keep meteorological information and collect botanical samples.

First thing every morning Douglas recorded the weather, and then inspected the Camp. Commandeering all the labour, he attacked the task of settling Palmerston with energy. First was to select a fine site for a Residency: the green plateau where the Larrakia had gathered to watch his ship sail into harbour. Before a month had passed, not only had Ellen laid the foundation stone of the new Residency, but a mass of planting – over 1,000 sugar canes, and samples of coffee, tea, ginger and breadfruit, melons and pineapples, coconuts – in experimental gardens around the settlement was under way.

On 5 September 1870, the land selectors returned from their inspection of the countryside. The land more than lived up to their expectations. They spread Goyder's plans out on a table in the stables, and under the eye of the Governor and surveyor MacLachlan, began selecting their lots. By the evening the best land in Palmerston had been snapped up – most of it by one man, William Henry Gray, who already owned much of suburban

Adelaide, and who, along with his descendants, would refuse to sell key sections of Palmerston, freezing development, until after 1960.

The sun set soon after six every evening. Listening to the washing of the waves on the shore, Douglas would sit, as Brooke had done in Sarawak, with Dr Millner, George MacLachlan and the land agents, in freshly laundered white shirts and splendid neckties, among clouds of mosquitoes and sand flies, smoking, drinking and planning the future of the Territory. With the land agents on the *Bengal* had arrived dispatches, and the glorious news that the government in Adelaide had signed an agreement with the British Australian Telegraph Company. A cable connected to London was to run beneath the Indian Ocean to Java, and on to Australia. Landfall was to be at Port Darwin, and the new settlement of Palmerston! Rich with the fruits of the land and the convenience of the new telegraph, there was nothing they could not do in Palmerston. Cheap coolie labour was close at hand on Java. They could work cotton plantations – and sugar cane. And what about supplying India with horses bred in the Territory? There would be shipping and freight and trade with the Indies. From beneath a tree in the middle of the Camp the sweet sounds of music rose, whistles, flutes and concertinas, and the voices of the men raised in song.

Hardly had Douglas spoken when, four days later, the steamship *Omeo* sailed into the harbour, with six officers and eighty men, seventy-eight horses and ten bullocks – landing in great confusion from boats on the beach, to build the British Australian Telegraph. With a feast of mail, books, and newspapers were new orders for Douglas. He was to forget any plans for importing indentured labour from neighbouring islands to work the new plantations of Palmerston. Now nothing mattered more to South Australia than the construction of the telegraph, Darwin to Port Augusta, 1,800 miles – to be finished in just over a year, by 31 December 1871. Unlike the sales of land in the Northern Territory in London, shares in the British Australian Telegraph were subscribed three times over. Douglas was not to leave the settlement until the line was completed.

A new camp for the telegraph men was raised on the tableland of Fort Hill, opposite the rising Residency. A week later, on 15 September 1870, Harriet rammed the earth around the first pole of the line into place. That evening the captain of the *Omeo* held a small reception. Douglas was in loud good humour. Harriet and Nell danced with the officers. Then the telegraph party packed its tools and headed south, heavy drays loaded with supplies, equipment, and tons of wire, pulled by bullocks and heavy draught horses. The men felled trees to clear a route ahead through the bush, on into the unknown. The next day the land agents set sail back to Adelaide on the *Omeo*.

Douglas and the small community of Palmerston were left alone.

Palmerston's sponsors had imagined its climate would be like the benign south of Australia. No one imagined the horrific transformation of the land as the 'wet' set in, early in November. Every day at the same time, magnificent storms built up over the opposite shore, 'rising like an inky arch' as they swept across the harbour. Thunder rolled, trees lashed in the wind, doors and windows slammed, and lightning flashed. Twenty, maybe thirty, minutes would go by. Then rain fell like stair rods. In the Camp it was difficult to keep dry. Everything was getting covered in mould: boots, books, paper. Mildew and weevils got into supplies of flour and oatmeal. Cockroaches devoured currants, jam and sugar; white ants consumed clothing, books and wood. At night Harriet lay in bed in their sleeping hut, listening to the bodies of crocodiles grating on the shingle as they moved off into the water. The rain poured.

Inland, the flooded lands turned to swamp. In the bush, work on the telegraph was turning to disaster. Once the rains began, it would take a whole day for a team to cover more than 100 yards. Exhausted horses, covered in mud, lay down on their sides in the treacherous swamps and did not get up again. Men collapsed with fever. White ants feasted on the poles. It would not be until the following June, when eight or nine men marooned for weeks by floods on the Roper River, sick with fever, managed to get back to Palmerston, that word of the tragedy would reach the outer world.

For a man like Douglas, extrovert, used to being in the centre of bustling affairs, the daily routine of Palmerston in the rains rapidly began to pall. The days fell into a tedious round of camp inspections. He regarded the handful of settlers who had landed from the *Bengal* with a jaundiced eye: they were lazy, useless and a drain on the government stores. One, Christian Schmidt, had introduced a herd of Timor swine that got into the government gardens, creating havoc and destruction. Douglas lost his temper, jumped on to his horse and mounted a furious hunt for the pigs across the tableland, joined by a crowd of Larrakia brandishing their spears. Schmidt protested to Adelaide.

Douglas became more and more concerned with minutiae: jealously guarding building supplies, inspecting his works, keeping a tight eye on the dispensation of stores, stamping on excess drinking. On Sundays, kindly Dr Millner read Divine Service, while Harriet and Nell formed the choir. Douglas noted attendances.

Building the Residency – designed by the shipwright of the *Gulnare* as a bungalow centred on a large central hall, with a roof 'decidedly Biblical in style' – was proving a difficult, makeshift job. The only building material to hand was stone – but there was no lime for mortar, until it was realized that coral from the reef would do. Ironbark trees were too tough to cut by hand; Douglas dispatched the *Gulnare* along the coast to bring back cypress. But the timber, cut before it was properly seasoned, warped and shrank. Keeping the rain out was proving impossible, and after timber and canvas had been tried, a flat concrete roof was laid.

There was little trouble with the Larrakia. Once over the shock of living in such close quarters with apparently terrifying savages, the family began to get to know them. On washing day all the women would arrive, bringing their babies and supplies of fresh water with them. Washing with soap and water, let alone the concept of clothing, was unknown to them, but they would empty tubs, rinse clothes, and hang them out. 'One of the greatest marks of friendship was changing names with the white people in camp,' wrote Harriet. She became Billymook, while Nell was known as Miranda, 'a classical but strictly Larrakiah name'.

Douglas kept track of their comings and goings, negotiating the return of pilfered axes and tools to the settlers. To him they were wild creatures, possibly a genus of aberrant child. As plants began to take in the government gardens, some were discovered thieving. The old gun on Fort Hill was fired twice, and the police and 'all other hands' marched to the Aborigine camp to find it deserted. When later, the gardener caught a boy stealing melons, Douglas ordered 'one of the old blacks' to give him a horse-whipping in front of the whole tribe. It was not until Douglas had been in Palmerston for almost a year that the first ugly incident took place. A man speared Dr Millner's favourite hack, which had to be put down. Questioned, the whole tribe stood silent. Douglas knew that to round up the elders, and hold them hostage until the offender was given up, would not work. Instead, Douglas invited all the men of the tribe for a feast on board the *Gulnare*. Scores of canoes paddled out to the schooner. After all the men were on board, the canoes were cut adrift. In an instant, the Larrakia jumped overboard, but not before two of them had been captured.

They were held on board, until at last the tribe gave up the name of the real offender.

Six months after the telegraph ship *Omeo* sailed, Douglas had still had no word from Adelaide. Day after day, he and Elli, or Harriet and Nell, rode out to Fannie Bay, searching the horizon for signs of a sail. People were heartily sick of subsisting on the pale, flavourless 'blanket', reinvented endlessly as stew, hash or curry. Stores were running short. By the end of March 1871, with still no sign of a ship, Douglas dispatched the *Gulnare,* the settlement's only link with the outside world, to East Timor for mail and supplies. 'Can it be credited that the whole Franco-Prussian war had been fought,' wrote Harriet afterwards, 'before we had even heard of there being a prospect of a war at all?'

The day after the *Gulnare*'s return on 8 May, a second ship arrived in port from Adelaide, with horses for the telegraph contractors. Huge excitement gripped the Camp. Letters, boxes, fresh food, new faces and drink: for almost a month the tiny settlement revelled. Then the *Gulnare* set sail for Adelaide. All but two of the settlers had decided to quit. Another six months would go by before there was news again from Adelaide. By that time, Ellen had been reduced to making dresses for herself and the children from the last of Palmerston's unbleached calico. Their shoes, outgrown or worn out, were replaced by canvas shoes cobbled together by one of the teamsters.

By the return of dry weather, ten crude houses, made of palings and roofed with bark, had been built. The Residency was finished. 'No one rejoiced more in the move to the hill than my mother,' wrote Harriet. Ellen had a passion for animals: dogs, cats, and especially for keeping fowl. At last she had a poultry yard that she had designed herself, for the 'Queen of Sheba', the 'Czar of Russia' and the 'Chief Secretary'. Pigeons fluttered down to rest on her shoulders at feeding time.

Meanwhile, inland, the swampy ground dried, then fissured in the harsh dry heat. The rivers shrank to trickles. The previous December, some telegraph men had uncovered a lump of gold while digging to place a pole. As soon as the worst of the 'wet' was over, surveyor George MacLachlan had set off to explore the country towards the Roper River. Waiting anxiously for his return, the heat and ennui began to afflict everyone. Douglas was irascible, often unpredictable. 'He sometimes almost sentences men to be hung and discharges them from the staff one day and takes them on again the next,' noted trooper Edward Napoleon Buonaparte Catchlove. Douglas exercised no leadership. There was not enough real work for anyone to do. The police troopers, the boatmen and the labourers watched the family 'lolling about' in easy chairs and drinking tea, playing cards and billiards in the evening in the comfort of a proper, if ramshackle house, or riding out during the day on horses that were not their own, but – Catchlove was careful frequently to note – 'belonged to the government'.

After weeks away – so long that Douglas began to fear for his life – MacLachlan returned at the end of July. He not only repeated Stuart's glowing claims for the land as a fine place for breeding cattle and horses – but had found more gold. Douglas was elated. 'A really payable gold field is ready for occupation,' he reported to Adelaide. This was the impetus the settlement of the country needed! The men in the Camp were so excited, they could hardly be contained. All were preparing to resign their appointments and take their chances on the diggings, Douglas warned Governor Fergusson. He himself set off with a party on the *Gulnare* for a day shooting buffalo and a prospecting tour on nearby Melville Island.

Then all at once it seemed that steamer after steamer began to arrive in port, discharging fresh cargoes of men, and hundreds of horses and bullocks for the telegraph party. A new push south was to be made from the Roper River. The *Gulnare* ran back and forth to the mouth of the river, carrying men and stores. As the weather grew sultry with the promise of rain, late in October, three steamships carrying the submarine cable and the staff – educated English gentlemen – to operate the telegraph in Palmerston arrived. Round bell tents, tarpaulin shelters, and a temporary office of galvanized iron were hastily erected. A round of dinners, billiard games, and drives into the country in buggies began. Soon Nellie would be engaged to Enston Squier, the superintendent of the telegraph. On 7 November, the end of the great steel cable was landed on the beach. Salutes were fired from the ships offshore. Then they steamed away to the east coast of Java, uncoiling the cable as they went. Two weeks later, the cable was landed in Batavia. Imagine! Communication to England in just ten minutes! At a stroke, the world seemed to shrink. But for the tiny, lonely community at Palmerston – what good could it do them?

Douglas was in the habit of keeping a journal, of which one leather-bound volume for 1872 survives. Morning, noon and evening he meticulously recorded the winds, temperatures and general weather conditions. Every time a ship came into harbour, he reset his instruments with the ship's chronometer. 'Clouds and close,' he wrote. 'Strong monsoon.' The 16th of January was the first fine day after over a month of rain.

In the diary there are no mentions of his schemes for settling plantations, for importing labour, or signs of settlement. Instead, there is monotony – stifling monotony – and a catalogue of complaints. Day after day, he inspected the Camp, 'settled into the accounts', rode out, reprimanded drunkards, flogged the Larrakia boy 'Pickles' and his father for stealing, sentenced a deserter from the *Young Australian* to pay £20. But he was not well. Catchlove noted that he was keeping to his room 'with prickly heat'.

Meanwhile, the headquarters for the telegraph company, handsome, well-finished buildings of stone, with a billiard room and a tennis court, were nearing completion. Douglas wanted to get to his diggings and he did not want to give up his horse transport to the telegraph men. His temper was deteriorating and so was his health. By May, his meteorological records were becoming erratic, his handwriting was thinning, and he himself was almost inarticulate. Paranoia set in. 'Mr Little's [a telegraph officer] manner is most offensive and dictatorial so much so that his requisitions like the form of an order as if I were a mere storekeeper to the OT [Overland Telegraph] and that I am not allowed to have an opinion of my own requirements.'

By the end of the month he was still ill, complaining to Dr Millner of not feeling well, of bleeding. He was weak, faint, 'very ill all day', and unable to sleep. After a day off on Saturday the 25th, he still felt very weak. He began to fear that he would have to leave his post 'on a medical certificate'.

For three or four days in early June, he rallied. But on the 12th, his horse, Charlie, died. This was Douglas's tipping point. Tired and depressed, the next night he suffered a new attack of bilious fever. While the telegraph men played cricket, he lay sick in bed. By the 18th, Douglas had been ill and confined to his bed for a week, very sick 'vomiting, [with] dreadful depression & almost entirely comatose. Suffering very much in my mind.' On Wednesday the 19th he felt better towards evening, but by the time he went to bed he was hallucinating.

Douglas woke at three in the morning, consumed by fears. He bathed, breakfasted and visited the Camp, but was convinced the police had taken a warrant out against him. Mr Foelsche, the police inspector, hastened to assure him that this was not the case, but 'nothing would persuade me to the contrary'.

Douglas barricaded himself in his office and loaded his shotguns. Convinced that he was under attack by everyone, even his own family, he was at last gently coaxed out to dinner. Afterwards, he rode out with one of the surveyors, 'who was kindness itself', but soon, convinced that police troopers were chasing him, he galloped home, 'taking the 3 rails at the bottom of the Garden. I then got home & Dr Millner took charge of me kept me in his quarters & put me under the influence of Chloral Hydrate which gave me 17 hours sleep. I awoke and dressed the next day much refreshed but weak. I was then attacked with violent bilious diarrhoea. I did not sleep well but better than I expected. This was a holiday but a very poor one for me.'

In nine days Douglas recorded a weight loss of 9lb. It is probable that today he would be diagnosed with bipolar disorder. One day he was up, manically energetic and cheerful, cooking up grand schemes; the next, in the depths of depression. His fragile mental state was not helped by illness: two weeks later, towards the middle of July, he was ill again with fever – probably malaria – and a massive abscess in his right ear, excruciatingly painful. Millner was prescribing quinine and opiates. Again he wondered if 'I shall have to give up the place'. But the abscess burst, the weather turned cool and fine, and Douglas was back on his feet and in command.

While he had been ill the *Mary King* had landed, laden with gold-diggers. The tiny camp was overwhelmed with men and horses, drays and supplies. The excitement brought him out of his malaise. He was up before breakfast, inspecting the stores, giving orders, inviting tenders for provisions, imposing customs duties for the first time, riding out to Fannie Bay with his children, and playing billiards in the evening with the telegraph men. On 4 July he had received the first telegram from across the continent from the Commissioner of Crown Lands. He had been ordered to survey and inspect the Roper River region himself. He was rounding up horses, and making preparations to set off.

Douglas's trip to the Roper River nearly killed him. No sooner had he landed than his old symptoms of acute depression and fever attacked. The temperature in his tent was 104 degrees at midday. He was drinking heavily. Somehow he retained enough lucidity to realize that the country around the Roper was nowhere as beguiling as the explorer Stuart had reported. 'Not having during my long experience in tropical countries seen any

country like that I am now visiting, I feel diffident in offering an opinion
. . . But I am convinced the Government has not been correctly informed
of the nature of the [land] they have undertaken to survey & to present to
the public.' This crucial – and accurate – assessment seems never to have
been transmitted to Adelaide. The 25th of September was his birthday. '*I
am 50*,' he noted with dismay, and went on to describe a long and confused
haul across the country in merciless heat and glare, drays stuck in mud, a
thief of a driver intoxicated, himself sour, bad-tempered and full of bile.
Then he collapsed again, so ill with fever and dysentery that a month later
he had to be carried on board the *Larrakeyah to* return to Palmerston.

Douglas was too ill to land at first. The camp was in havoc. In the time
that he had been ill since May, more than 500 gold-diggers had arrived.
Bark huts and timber shanties had sprung up all along the gully. There was
still no proper jetty in the harbour, only three wells for fresh water, and no
area for bathing safe from alligators or sharks. The diggers were a motley
assortment of young Englishmen fresh out to the colonies, pale uncertain
boys from the Melbourne shops, and rough, hard-drinking types, keen to
let off their revolvers. Nights were broken by the sounds of drunken carous-
ing. The keeper of the government store, still the settlement's only outlet,
was threatened daily as prices rose to fabulous heights. Meanwhile, land
agents, shopkeepers, hoteliers, and the keepers of drinking saloons were
landing, keen to take up leases, which Douglas had no authority to issue.
After all, the best land on the peninsula had all been taken up – by owners
who were far away. For the first time in Palmerston there came an epidemic
of malaria. Only the tracks of the telegraph's drays led off into the interior.

Douglas's days as Government Resident of the Northern Territories could
not last. Complaints about his administration and volatile behaviour multi-
plied in Adelaide. So miserable and erratic had he become that Dr Millner
was forced to contrive to keep him at sea under strict surveillance. In May
1873 Thomas Reynolds, the Commissioner of Crown Lands, himself
arrived in Palmerston to investigate. He was appalled at 'the shamefully
disorganised state of things'. Financial records were in disarray, records of
mining claims equally confused, regulations had been ignored or misinter-
preted. Douglas himself had been living from the government store on
credit.

For months Douglas had realized that he could no longer cope. Heart-
sick and exhausted, he wrote to Reynolds. At first he blamed the difficulties

of his position: 'The division of authority such as Customs, Telegraph, Police, Warden of the Gold-fields and to a certain extent the Survey department has really placed me in a position of much embarrassment,' he wrote. 'Almost every difficulty here may be traced to the anomalous position I have occupied. I have been the head where it has suited the public or others to accord me that position but as a rule my authority has been so divided and refined that I scarcely knew where it commenced or ceased, or as to what I could, or could not do.' In fact, he had had enough of responsibility. Two days later he told Reynolds he craved 'to be free for almost the first time in my life'. He quit.

Having formed his own gold-mining company, Douglas set off to his diggings, accompanied by two Malay servants. Ellen and the children returned to Adelaide, where, two years before, his daughter, Harriet, had married her sweetheart, the son of Governor Daly. Not long afterwards, he followed them. He was broke. In April 1874, the government of South Australia dispatched him to Singapore to recruit Chinese miners for the Northern Territory. He hired almost 200, who were shipped to Palmerston. But Douglas had always hankered after a job in a Malay state, so reminiscent of the years he had spent in Sarawak. He stayed on in Singapore, taken on by the British administration as an acting police magistrate. There Ellen and the family joined him. As British control extended in the Malay States, Douglas's fortunes rose once again. In April 1876 he was named resident of the state of Selangor, where we will meet him acting as a governor later in this volume. There he was remembered for the same erratic behaviour he had shown in Palmerston. After six years he was forced to resign – some scandal over land sales, it was rumoured. But his fragile mental state and his reputation for bad, unpredictable behaviour continued. Douglas died on 6 March 1906, at the age of eighty-four, in Halifax, Nova Scotia, where he had lived for almost twenty years, working for the Ministry of Marine. There a kindly obituary recalled him as 'a familiar figure . . . kindly and courteous and liked by those with whom he came in contact.'

The Northern Territory of Australia has never realized all the dreams of its early pioneers. Mining gold turned out to be as treacherous as building the telegraph line, as poor as farming proved. Leached of every nutrient, the soils that on George Goyder's first surveys had looked so rich and promising turned out to be useless for agriculture. As late as 1882, the 'Camp' of Douglas's days was still being used by bachelor officers in Palmerston. In

1911, when confederation came to Australia, Palmerston was renamed Darwin. By then there were no more than 3,000 non-Aborigines living in the whole Northern Territory – half of these were Chinese.

In February 1875, eighteen months after Douglas left the Territory, the steamer *Gothenburg,* sailing from Palmerston, ran aground on the Great Barrier Reef and was then swept up in a hurricane. Out of 117 people on board, only twenty-two were saved. Among the dead were Dr Millner and his three children, and Thomas Reynolds, the Commissioner of Crown Lands who had condemned Douglas. Three thousand ounces of gold went down with them.

5 Fever and delusion

The Gold Coast 1874–6

On 3 February 1874, for the first time, the British invaded a black African capital. Kumasi was the capital of the kingdom of the Ashanti, in what is now central Ghana. There they defeated the young King, Kofi Karikari, known as the Ashantehene, and sacked and burned the ancient city. The troops were commanded by Major-General Garnet Wolseley, small, bright-eyed and energetic, backed up by the redoubtable Commander John Glover, a little more than eighteen months after he had quit as governor of Lagos, and a cohort of his finest Hausa officers. Glover circled round the rear of Kumasi with his African forces in order to surprise the retreating enemy. But publicly the triumph in this swift and effective campaign was all Wolseley's. His meticulous organization and splendid demeanour brought him enduring fame as Gilbert and Sullivan's 'modern major-general', while Glover would be knighted for his efforts.

Accounts of the war dominated the newspapers at home for months. The *Illustrated London News* sent the special artist Melton Prior. G. A. Henty, who would write a host of adventure stories for boys, was there for the *Standard*. The famous journalist and explorer Henry Morton Stanley filed bombastic accounts for the *New York Herald,* while *The Times* ran over 400 articles on the campaign. Thousands came down to the docks in Portsmouth to cheer the Black Watch as they returned home in triumph at the end of March. In homes throughout England, the Ashanti war fuelled popular imagination, gave birth to eight books on the campaign, and established a vision of imperial adventures, and a 'Boys' Own' *gloire* of Empire.

Meanwhile Britain was in the midst of a general election campaign. Five days after news of the military triumph reached London, on 17 February, the Conservative Party under Prime Minister Disraeli swept to power with a majority in the House of Commons. At the Colonial Office Lord Carnarvon, aged forty-three, took up office as Secretary of State.

Carnarvon had done the job before. Fine-boned and sensitive, he was articulate and cultured. He had all the responsibilities of an earldom: a vast Elizabethan-style castle, Highclere in Hampshire, which had been

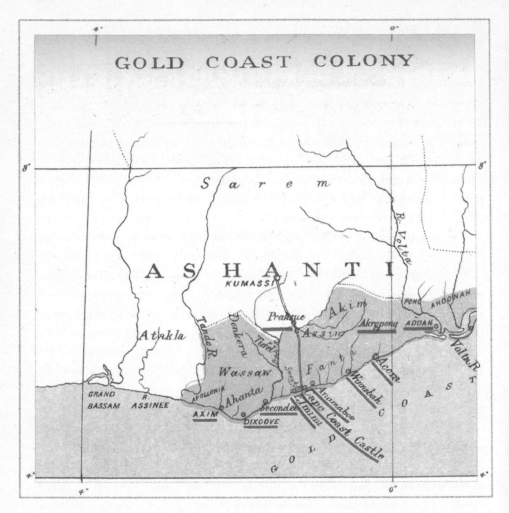

re-modelled for his father by Charles Barry, designer of the Houses of Parliament; estates in Wiltshire and Somerset; an important position in society, a wife and four children. Carnarvon had grown up travelling in Greece, Italy and the Middle East. In his youth he had ventured overland to Babylon. At the age of twenty-three he delivered his maiden speech in the Lords, from which time he took a keen interest in colonial affairs. In 1858, aged twenty-six, he had been appointed Under-Secretary for the Colonies. Eight years later he was Secretary of State, presiding over the federation of Canada.

Now that he was back in office he was extraordinarily busy. 'I hardly remember a time when my own hands have been more full,' he told his old tutor, John Kent, on the eve of the election. 'Much going on at Highclere – at Pixton – the house rebuilding in London – a yacht half-finished at

Cowes – a great deal in Nottinghamshire – the reorganisation of the County Police in Hampshire – the choice of a Headmaster for a public school –.'

Running the Colonial Office as permanent secretary was his cousin and close friend Robert Herbert. Urgently, Carnarvon set to work on the department's top priority: to redraft British policy – such as it was – on the Gold Coast. For all his experience of travelling the Mediterranean and reading colonial dispatches, Carnarvon could scarcely conceive of this part of Africa, with its torrid heat, dripping humidity, solid curtains of rain, dense jungles and tall rainforests, or of its coastal peoples – such as the Fantees, of whom the worst reports of laziness and disaffection had emerged in Wolseley's reports of the campaign.

The whole position of the Gold Coast was so anomalous that until Wolseley's sacking of Kumasi the British might just as easily have walked away from it. It was gold – which Wolseley watched old women washing from the gutters in the town of Cape Coast – that first drew European traders to this part of Africa: English, Portuguese, Dutch, French and Spanish. From as early as the late fifteenth century they had begun building toeholds along the coast: robust fortresses with sinister dungeons, warehouses for the growing slave trade. The ground was leased unwillingly from local kings and paid for every year in handsome tributes of gold. The Europeans were not welcome. They heard stories of dense forests that began about twenty miles from the sea, and the fabled wealth and gold ornaments of the inland Ashanti, feared by the peoples of the coast. But no white man dared venture on the tracks that led inland. In the year that Britain abolished the slave trade, 1807, the Ashanti swept down to the coast for the first time, nearly overwhelming the British in a little fort at Anomabu beside the sea. There were two more wars; an attempt to negotiate. A British commander-in-chief who struck up 'God Save the King' to unnerve the Ashanti was beheaded in the bloody fight that followed. After that, missionaries – including John Glover's friend, the former Yoruba slave and Africa's first Anglican bishop, Samuel Crowther – began to move inland. In 1848, the first British governor made his way to the kingdom of gold at Kumasi, where he recorded fulsomely the courtesy and lavishness of his reception to the Colonial Office. Apart from the invading General Wolseley, no other British governor would do so again until 1900.

By 1850, Europeans still held no jurisdiction outside their castle walls. Underlying their bonds with the kings was the growing expectation that they would protect their peoples in case of war. That year the British bought two Danish forts at Accra and Quittah. Then, in 1872, in spite of the strict recommendations of the 1865 Parliamentary Select Committee on West Africa that Britain should take on no more responsibilities in the region, a deal was done to take over the Dutch fortress of Elmina, nine miles west of Britain's headquarters at Cape Coast Castle. The bond for Elmina was held by the Ashanti. Now they wanted the fortress back.

The Governor-in-Chief of the West African Settlements, John Pope Hennessy, conducted the handover of Elmina by the Dutch in the unfortunate month that he fired Commander Glover at Lagos. In characteristic fashion, instead of appointing a British military officer to administer Elmina as he had been advised, he selected an educated native of the town, George Emile Eminsang – unaware that as he was of mixed race his nomination was a grave insult to the people. Three weeks later serious rioting broke out. Hennessy now installed a British officer in the castle, and without inquiring into the inclinations of the former King of Elmina, restored him to his throne. This king, Kobina Edijan, had resolutely opposed the British take-over from the Dutch, and was a firm friend of the Ashanti. In January 1873, six months after Hennessy's interventions, the Ashantehene sent forth an army of 40,000 men to reclaim Elmina: the first step in the chain of events which led to Wolseley's brutal sacking of Kumasi.

Abandon the Gold Coast, or annex it? 'A very evil choice to have to make,' minuted Carnarvon. The former was 'too charming to be capable of execution'; the latter was 'too ghastly to contemplate'. Something like the 'halting tentative half measures' of a protectorate, as his cousin Herbert suggested, would have to be attempted.

Carnarvon, who was keen on ideas like confederation, decided he would unite the Gold Coast and Lagos to create a new colony that would be properly administered. His first task: to find a governor. Wolseley had tried. 'What this place wants now is an able man who will remain here for some years, as changes of Governors are most injurious, especially at a time [of] transition from a state of war,' Wolseley had advised the War Office. Four army officers had already turned the position down. A fifth candidate was invalided home a fortnight after arrival, and died at sea on his way home. Carnarvon canvassed the opinion, as he usually did on matters of Africa, of Sir Bartle Frere, Britain's most eminent authority on India. But Frere's candidates were all too far away to be put in place in time. Carnarvon turned to the next man along the coast: Captain George Strahan of the Royal Artillery, who had taken up the post of administrator of Lagos the previous October.

Strahan had sailed out in September 1873 with General Wolseley and his staff on the *Ambriz*, its saloon full of publications about the west coast of Africa. 'He is a very nice fellow, and has the smallest and best shaped hands I have ever seen with a man,' Wolseley wrote in his diary, going on, it seems wrongly, to describe him as the son of an eminent banker who had gone bankrupt in one of Victorian England's most spectacular cases of fraud. In fact Strahan, who was thirty-six years old, was the son of a Scottish minister from Fraserburgh, a remote granite town on the northern tip of Aberdeenshire, facing full into the gales of the North Sea. Aged eighteen, he had passed a competitive examination at King's College London to enter the Royal Military Academy at Woolwich. There he fast-tracked through the course, emerging one year later as a full lieutenant in the artillery. His father must have had some powerful clerical connection with William Gladstone MP, for Strahan next achieved a brilliant coup: a post as his aide-de-camp in Gladstone's role as Lord High Commissioner of the Ionian Islands, resident in a splendid palace in Corfu, in January 1859. Shortly afterwards Gladstone went home, but Strahan stayed on to serve the next governor. Over the next ten years he moved on to Malta and the Bahamas in a steadily rising career – to colonial secretary, then acting governor of the Bahamas in 1871. Strahan was an expert on protocol; he was cautious, ambitious, presentable, and knew how to deliver the answers London wanted to hear. He had been in Lagos – the second man to succeed John Glover in less than nine months – for half a year.

Carnarvon was in the habit of writing to all his governors privately. On 15 May 1874 he wrote Strahan his letter of appointment. 'One of my principal anxieties is to secure a Governor for the United Settlements in whose judgment energy and ability confidence can be placed.' Even under the most favourable circumstances the task of setting up the new government at Cape Coast was going to be difficult. 'So important is this duty and so necessary is it to take every precaution against every possible failure of administration that I have come to the conclusion that . . . it would be impossible that any one who was not equal to the task should continue to hold the office.'

This letter, with gracious apologies that he had not made Strahan's acquaintance personally nor written it by hand, was dictated on a Friday. Carnarvon had no time for a response. The following Tuesday he announced his new policy for west Africa in the Lords. Staying on at the Gold Coast was not a question of 'selfish interests or the ambition for larger empire'. It was a case of 'obligations to be redeemed and of duties to be performed'.

★

Running in the background of Wolseley's campaign and the government of
the Gold Coast was an obsession with health. Such was west Africa's reputation as a death trap that in the late eighteenth century convicted criminals
were sentenced to garrison duties as a form of delayed death sentence.
Between 1822, when the British government first took over responsibility
for the handful of Gold Coast forts from the African Company of Merchants, and 1874, there had been forty-five governors who, with two or
three exceptions, served no more than an average of nine months each. Half
the troops sent out from England either died or had to be invalided home.
In an earlier war against the Ashanti in 1862–3, a quarter of the white troops
had been hospitalized with fever, dysentery and diarrhoea during the rains.
Many more were left 'sick and weakly'. 'Why ought we perversely to cling
to a place where Englishmen must die and Africans cannot be civilised?'
Frederick Elliott, who had recently retired as under-secretary at the
Colonial Office after forty-three years of reading dispatches from west
Africa, wrote to *The Times*.

After exhaustive analysis the Victorians were convinced that it was not
so much the climate of west Africa – although it was 'especially enervating
to the European constitution' – that was so dangerous, but the air. 'Mal
aria', from the Italian 'bad air', was the suspected cause of the fatal fevers
that had plagued Rome's summers for centuries, in particular air hanging
over marshy land and swamp. 'Pestilential morasses' bred 'malarial effluvia'
and the noxious gases that caused fevers. On the Gold Coast, when the
worst of the rains began to subside in August, 'exhalations from the wet
earth rise and hang over it like sheets of fog'. The wind was uncertain,
malaria accumulated: the chances were that before long the newly arrived
European would be down with the first dose of fever – 'the seasoning', as it
was called on the Coast.

Everyone with experience of Africa was familiar with the symptoms.
Just before the fever came on, 'the new-comer imagines himself in rude
health, has a voracious appetite, and scoffs at anyone who suggests the possibility of his having a fever'. Quite suddenly he would feel heavy and
feverish. A dizzy headache, a succession of slight chills, then diarrhoea and
vomiting. As the chills passed, 'a scorching fever follows, the tongue
becomes parched, and the thirst and longing for cooling drinks is excessive:
racking pains in the head, back, and loins preclude all attempts to sleep.'
Hours later, there would be a delicious sense of relief as the skin burst with
perspiration and the patient fell asleep. But twenty-four hours later the

fever would return, and again 'for two or three alternate days'. Under favourable circumstances an attack lasted no more than eight or nine days.

What was really happening would only begin to be discovered twenty-five years later. As we know now, malaria is caused by threadlike parasites injected into the bloodstream by the bite of the female anopheles mosquito. They head straight for the liver, where they form a cyst and quietly replicate. Two weeks later the cyst bursts. The young parasites (now known as merozoites) invade the red blood corpuscles. The fever cycle begins: first the chills, then, as the temperature rises, white blood cells swamp the parasites. The pause in the illness which follows varies according to the malaria parasite: twelve to twenty-four hours, forty-eight, even seventy-two. But recovery is only a delusion. Shivers and sweats invariably return, as more and more red blood cells are invaded with parasites.

What makes malaria potentially so dangerous is the voracious appetite of the merozoites. In hours they can consume 100 grams of haemoglobin from red blood cells. As this happens blood cells become sticky, and start to glue themselves to one another and then the linings of the capillaries of the brain.

Englishmen living on the coast went through this cycle repeatedly. They lost their fresh, pink complexions and took on a 'wretched sallow look . . . as if they . . . had been just bleached a pale lemon colour'. Their features turned pinched and sharp, and the skin was drawn like parchment over the bones of the face – the signs of chronic anaemia.

These were the observations of Albert Gore, a surgeon-major with Wolseley's offensive, who made a study of the medical history of Britain's west African campaigns. He knew that, for reasons that are still not fully understood today, only a large dose of quinine might stop the course of fever in its tracks. But too often there were complications: boils and ulcers, jaundice, acute bronchitis and pneumonia. Combined with dysentery, fever was almost invariably fatal. Besides 'the constant breathing of the malarial poison', Gore suggested that heat, exposure to the sun, too much food and drink and a sedentary lifestyle led to disease. Worst of all, getting wet virtually guaranteed a dose of fever.

Knowing this much, Wolseley had been meticulous in taking every care of his troops during the recent war, particularly on the march to Kumasi. A swift campaign, strictly limited to the dry season, from December to March: in fact the white troops were in the country five days short of two months. Men were never to march on an empty stomach; they were to drink only boiled and filtered water flavoured with tea, and not to do so during the march. Only flannel shirts – never linen or cotton – were to be worn as the best defence against fever. Every soldier wore a helmet and blue veil, a Norfolk jacket, trousers, leggings, boots and socks, as well as a cholera belt. He carried a haversack, clasp knife, pocket filter, a bayonet and short rifle.

Bearing the sick across a river on the return to the coast from Kumasi, 1874

To prevent chilling, at the halt 'the heated men' were to keep their clothes on, taking off only their valise and belts, until an hour had passed. Campfires were lit to purify the air, and 'prevent annoyance from insects, dry clothing, and . . . as security against chilliness during the night'. All the men were warned against the danger of drink, and great care was taken of the feet, bathing them at the end of a march, and washing their socks. Finally, a daily dose of six grains of quinine with coffee – which Dr Baikie and Glover on their voyage on the *Dayspring* had showed could mitigate the effects of fever – was given every morning at parade. In spite of this care and attention, out of nearly 1,600 men, 71 per cent were taken ill: almost two-thirds with fever, 40 per cent with dysentery and diarrhoea. The campaign itself only lost fifteen men (Ashanti powder was 'indifferent'), but more than 40 per cent were invalided out of the service. Not only the whites suffered. For the black troops of the West Indian regiments, 'the deadliness of the climate [still told] in a very severe degree'.

Strahan received Carnarvon's letter in the damp heat of Lagos on 10 June 1874. He was flattered to receive it, and not a little sycophantic in reply, his hand measured and clear: 'Feeling that I possess your confidence, I shall enter upon its duties with at least the determination to be successful,' he wrote.

Arriving over the surf below Cape Coast Castle, 1874

Twelve days later he sailed for the Gold Coast on board the mail steamer *Congo*, with fifty armed Hausa police. To the chanting of Fantee boatmen, he swept in on the crashing surf in a flat-bottomed boat on to the beach below the walls of Britain's headquarters at Cape Coast Castle, massed high above the ocean. Overhead a salute was fired, a guard of honour waited. The endless roar of huge breakers pounded on the shore. He walked up the streets to Government House. It was the middle of the rains: soaking days with high squalls and violent thunderstorms.

The town of Cape Coast was famous for its squalor, heaps of filth and stench of ordure. Overcrowded and littered, it was a town of narrow lanes and thick, flat-roofed, mud-walled houses. Only one European in recent years had managed to survive there for as long as two years. There were now so few that 'for one person to dine with another is now an event', wrote the *Daily Telegraph*'s correspondent Frederick Boyle during the war. Government House was in the centre of the town, whitewashed with green jalousies and a small garden. It was leased from a failing trading firm and was large, rambling and decaying. Rain streamed through leaks in the ceilings. Strahan's servants were not trained. The public offices – the courts and the customs house – were also housed in abandoned merchants' houses, and the few trading outfits that still remained at Cape Coast were in sad decline. ' Never did I leave any spot upon earth with such pleasure,' Wolseley had written when he sailed away the previous March.

Tarantulas as big as saucers thrived, but horses could not live there. The only opportunity for exercise was a stroll along the road beside the beach to a salt lagoon: the roar of the surf boomed. Men dived into the surf and people washed themselves in the sea. Transport on land, along the coast, was in a hammock, strung between two bearers. Drinking water – from waterholes in a dirty valley – had to be expensively filtered and condensed at the astonishing price of £25 to £30 a month. The beach acted as a common latrine. Except during the season of the *harmattan* in December, when dry winds blew in from the Sahara, the damp ate through iron bolts, nails, clothes and books. Shoes went mouldy and salt liquefied.

Life for the European was not improved at the nearby former Dutch castle at Elmina. While its landing stage was the best along the coast, and the nearby Sweet River provided drinking water, the only place for government housing was in the old native town, 'a spot saturated with filth . . . owing to the horrible native custom of burying the dead within the houses'. It was best avoided.

There were pleasures, of course. The women and girls of the town wore richly coloured clothes, sometimes of silk. Their hair in tall twists on their heads, they moved freely through the streets, weighed down with gold ornaments, shaking hands with friends and, if in the market for a husband, 'casting languishing glances around'. From his window Strahan had a clear view of young Jessie Cruikshank sewing on her verandah across the lane. She was 'really a very good looking girl', Wolseley had remarked. Jessie's mother washed all the Governor's linen; her slaves ironed his shirts, and they would come to call 'all got up', as Wolseley described it, 'in swell hats'. The life of the town was impossible for the Governor to escape: a man hanged for murder drew forth howls of delight, the crowds of the marketplace bartered and squabbled, people washed and cooked in the streets; sheep and fowl ran loose.

★

All life took place in the streets: scene from the town of Cape Coast, 1874

Governor Strahan's brief was to put the new colony on a secure and efficient British footing. He counted seventeen English officers in the colony, divided between the fortresses at Cape Coast, Elmina, and an old fort at Accra that had been ruined by an earthquake a dozen years before. Of these, he and six other men formed the civil administration.

He was plunged into the aftermath of the British triumph. His second-in-command, Captain Charles Lees, technically his replacement as the new administrator at Lagos, was immediately dispatched to Kumasi, from where he reported on his talks with the Ashantehene, and his efforts to collect a mass of gold tribute. There was the tedious business of rectifying inventories of stores with the War Office. The colony's accounts were so confused that no return for that year would ever be made. Strahan sat hunched, hot and sticky, over stacks of dampened papers as gusts of rain blew through the flimsy jalousies of his office.

Meanwhile, from Highclere, where Carnarvon spent a 'divine' Sunday that July, 'inhaling the perfume laden air under the limes to the murmurous music of thousands of bees overhead', came a battery of missives. How did Strahan propose to outlaw slave dealing? Domestic slavery? Organize the police? Provide defences to replace the old-fashioned fortresses? A system

of laws had to be designed, roads laid to the interior, plans made for a telegraph and a better site selected for the seat of government – Elmina or
Accra?

Carnarvon's most persistent theme, however, was health. The British
had to beat the fevers caused by bad air. He was convinced that what the
new colony needed was a fine hill station for rest and recuperation – like
India's Simla, high in the foothills of the Himalayas. What about the 'rising
ground' at the back of Elmina 'which I understand is 600–700 feet above the
sea level?' he asked Strahan, going on, 'of course you will go nowhere
except under the best medical and scientific advice that you can command,
or you might be changing a bad residence even for a worse'.

14 September 1874
Government House
Cape Coast

My Lord
I am deeply sensible of the kind anxiety shown by Your Lordship for the
health of the officers . . . Desirous as I have been to visit the several places
which have been suggested as hill residence, important matters which
have been pressing upon me daily ever since my arrival have prevented me
from leaving Cape Coast except for a few days at Elmina.

While a change of air – in most cases beneficial – was easily attained by
a visit to Elmina, I have felt it less of a necessity – more especially as I am
without the services of a competent engineer for removing even as a temporary measure the Government from Cape Coast.

As Strahan sealed this letter, a secret dispatch from Carnarvon arrived
outlining the complex challenges of abolishing slavery on the coast. What
were Strahan's views? Perhaps he might consider the course that had been
followed in India? For five days and nights Strahan worked on an exhaustive dispatch and two draft ordinances outlawing all forms of slavery.

Grey with fatigue, he rose on the morning of the 20th to pen a private note
to Carnarvon. 'I trust that I may soon have at my disposal the services of an
efficient staff of public officers, up until the present time I have been carrying
on the government almost single handedly.' Of two officers for the police
force who had just arrived, one was so ill that the colonial surgeon was
insisting he returned to England by that day's mail, the other had gone on the
sick list two days after he landed. 'I fear [he has] too much previous service on

the Gold Coast to continue well for any length of time,' Strahan wrote, suggesting that other officers appointed to the west coast of Africa should undergo a strict medical examination before leaving England. Over the next three weeks, two more officers would be sent home.

In spite of the continuous rains, fever had not got to Strahan yet. He was prudent and abstemious in his way of life. He deplored habits of intemperance, was critical of men who failed to live a disciplined life, and held himself aloof from contact with the Africans in the town. He induced the local chiefs to clean up Cape Coast, playing on their ignorance and whipping up their fears, 'a powerful element', by threatening them with an epidemic of smallpox if they did not demolish deserted mud houses, clean up pools of stagnant water, and build latrines.

The autumn in London found Carnarvon increasingly frustrated with affairs on the Gold Coast. Strahan's dispatch announcing that he was abolishing slavery throughout the new protectorate with immediate effect landed on his desk like a thunderbolt. As Strahan knew nothing about slavery in the region himself he had relied on the views of three of his officers to tell Carnarvon that the sale of slaves on the Gold Coast was far from common practice, and that the situation of domestic slaves, treated – as at Lagos – almost like family, was such that few would 'avail themselves of opportunities for self-redemption'. Along with his drafts of the new laws, he announced that he had summoned the kings and chiefs of the western and eastern districts, 'the former on the 16th October, and the latter on the 5th of November next', at which time he planned to explain to them 'the views and intentions of Her Majesty's Government'. Politically, in London, Strahan's dispatch was treated like a stunning and remarkable coup. Privately, Carnarvon feared a bloodbath. Unaware that at Cape Coast Strahan was in the process of reassuring the chiefs that no changes would be made to their existing ways of life, he summoned a naval squadron to sail for the Coast.

Meanwhile, even by pulling strings with the War Office Carnarvon was finding it 'extraordinarily difficult' to find anyone with such qualifications 'as would be likely to render real service' to join Strahan's diminishing team on the Gold Coast. After months of sounding out officers, on 22 October Carnarvon wrote to tell Strahan he was at last dispatching two men with sound experience of west Africa: Captain Lanyon, one of Wolseley's keenest volunteers, to be colonial secretary, and Dr Samuel Rowe, Glover's close friend, his stalwart medical officer and the man who had run the slave court at Lagos. Rowe was now aged forty. Carnarvon suggested him as a powerful and experienced second-in-command, either to serve as the administrator at Lagos or, better, to carry 'on negotiations with the native Kings and Chiefs . . . a service for which his experience and knowledge of the native character and customs would seem to peculiarly fit him'.

Both Lanyon and Rowe were to stay at least three months – or longer if Strahan thought fit. Early in November, Carnarvon was also able to send Strahan a Royal Engineer, Captain Sale, to identify and start designing a new and healthier site for the government. Sale's appointment was for a strict six-month period; his wages – not to mention his travel and expenses – would be £1,000. 'I need hardly say,' Carnarvon told Strahan, 'how important it is . . . that not a day should be lost in taking immediate advantage of his service.'

But by the time this news reached Strahan, he was ill, past caring. At the end of November an open steam launch carrying him, his private secretary and his black servant on a tour of the eastern districts ran aground on the Volta River. They were trapped in swamps for forty-eight hours. All three came down with serious attacks of fever. By the time Captain Sale arrived in the middle of December, Strahan was worse. Meanwhile, in a moment of doubtful lucidity, Strahan had already dispatched Rowe to Elmina, Accra and the hills beyond to carry out Sale's work for him.

Strahan spent Christmas recovering at Lagos. In London, Carnarvon was unaware of his illness. On 28 December he again wrote privately begging Strahan 'to make some arrangements – even if only provisional – for at least occasional residence on higher and healthier ground either near Elmina or near Accra . . . before the bad season begins again'. On the same day, feeling fragile, Strahan returned to his desk at Cape Coast, peevish and irritable.

Perhaps it was because Rowe's report on potential sites for a seat of government on the Gold Coast was so negative, or because the observations he made about the state of the villages, 'seldom or never been visited by any European official except to collect custom duties or Fines', implied criticism of the way he ran his government, that Strahan decided to dispense with his services when they met on his first day back at work. Rowe was wary of the whole idea of hill stations. Far better that a governor should be constantly out in his domain, visiting the different tribes and kings. 'In no country in the world is personal supervision so necessary [as the Gold Coast],' he had told Carnarvon before he left London. It was much more important 'to arrange means for visiting and communicating with the outlying parts of his Government, than to plan for retiring from the sea-board to what may be a more pleasant residence'. Nevertheless he had done his duty.

The plain around Accra offered the healthiest site Rowe had seen on the seaboard of the Gold Coast. Even so, only five miles away the spreading confluence of two rivers covered many acres 'where Mangrove bushes grow freely' and the soil [at low tide] was 'of soft, fetid smelling, black mud'. As for the town itself, the water supply was bad, and nothing had been done to improve sanitation. Aburi, 1,400 feet above sea level, nine hours' journey from Accra, might offer respite as a hill station. It was home to a group of German missionaries from Basel. But 'in their own persons and that of their Wives and Children, [they showed] the presence of enlarged Spleens with their pale Faces, decayed Teeth, and spongy Gums' – the unmistakable signs of life under unhealthy conditions.

Everything about Samuel Rowe and what he had to say made Strahan uncomfortable. Strahan was reluctant – even afraid – to travel inland. He regarded the concerns of the Africans, whom he constantly disparaged, as far beneath him. He was squeamish and fastidious. He was jealous and suspicious of Rowe's ease in the country and with the blacks around him. 'Anyone so identified with Sir John Glover' might stir up trouble, he explained later to Carnarvon. He told Rowe his services would no longer be needed on the Coast. Rowe sailed on the next ship for London on 13 January. There he delivered his report in person to the Colonial Office.

Carnarvon was livid. He had made a considerable effort to secure the 'valuable services of Dr Rowe at a time when I conceived that the administrative staff on the Gold Coast needed all possible strengthening,' he told Strahan. How dare he have sacked him?

Strahan's frail administration carried on. Two weeks after Rowe sailed, Strahan's deputy, Captain Lees, the administrator at Lagos, filed for leave on account of his health. A week later another officer died. On 20 March a police captain died and two more police officers were invalided home. By the time Strahan had been in post nine months, eight of the original seventeen British who manned the colony when he arrived were out of commission. Late in May Carnarvon wrote to press him again. 'I am very much concerned at the terrible ravages which fever and dysentery make in the health of many of the best officers whom I have sent out to you.'

Strahan was to avoid the employment of English officers as much as possible at 'the most unhealthy stations'. They must have a sanatorium and good food and water. When could he look for a change for the better? By the time Strahan received this letter three weeks later, another police officer was on his way home, ill. He wrote to Carnarvon:

> Cape Coast
> 1 July 1875

> My Lord
> Whilst I heartily concur with your Lordship as to the importance of doing all that is possible to lessen the risk to health which attends service on the Gold Coast, I have constantly brought before me the fact that there are on this Coast climatic influences radically inimical to European constitutions, and that to whatever extent those influences may admit of mitigation, there are nevertheless no grounds upon which the hope can be reasonably entertained that the death rate and especially the rate of invaliding amongst officers will not continue to be considerably in excess of the rates which prevail in healthy climates.

On 28 July the death of Mr Barkels, assistant colonial surveyor at Elmina, was reported to London. Six months later, Strahan lost his last British police officer.

How often Strahan himself suffered from fever, we will never know. Meanwhile, an increasingly petulant note began to sound in his dispatches. On 31 January 1876 he wrote privately to Carnarvon to request he come home on leave in May. By that time he would have served over two and a half years on the coast 'and altho' with the exception of occasional illnesses of no very severe type, I have hitherto enjoyed good health, the Acting Colonial Surgeon is strongly of the opinion – and I myself begin to feel – that a more prolonged residence without a change to England would be unwise.' His wish was granted.

On 7 March 1877, Strahan's new successor at Cape Coast, Sandford Freeling, wrote to Carnarvon's secretary. The letter bears a dreadful sense of déjà vu. He wanted a private secretary '*as soon as possible*. The Private Secretary here has much important work to do and he frequently has to perform the duties of other officers beside his own in the event of sickness.' Freeling went on: 'I do not know that I am expressing myself very clearly but I have my first attack of fever on me. I have been overworking myself which does not do but it is difficult to avoid.'

★

Strahan returned to England unaware of the parasites he carried within him. After six months' leave he was promoted to the West Indies as governor of Barbados and the Windward Islands. Strahan would go on, via an assignment as high commissioner to South Africa and a knighthood, to govern Tasmania. There his face was noted for its yellowish, parchment-like character. His health never recovered. Little more than ten years after he had left the Gold Coast, on 17 February 1887, he died aged forty-nine, 'attacked with a fatal cold' while waiting in London to meet the Queen, to be invested with the highest rank of the Order of St Michael and St George.

Strahan's tenure on the Gold Coast was longer than most. His legacy was the two ordinances that he composed in a tearing hurry on the abolition of slavery, which, although scholars disagree, seem to have made little impact on the reality of the lives of the people in the colony. Faint though Strahan's outlines as a man are today, his real importance is as an example of one of countless hundreds of men who lost their lives to fever and disease in the service of the Crown on the west coast of Africa.

In March 1877, the British government moved to newly built headquarters in Accra, today the capital of Ghana. Accra proved no healthier for the British than Cape Coast. The sickness and lassitude that had always characterized the administration continued into the twentieth century. Until the First World War officials were never expected to spend more than a twelve-month sojourn on the Gold Coast without a long leave in England.

In 1892 researchers working in Italy concluded that malaria was caused by parasites. In Britain, it was not until Joseph Chamberlain took over as Secretary of State for the Colonies three years later that a concentrated effort would be made to get to the heart of the fevers that took such a terrible toll on the men in west Africa. Under his instigation, the London School of Hygiene and Tropical Medicine was founded in London in 1899. A year later, a lab assistant volunteered to be bitten by a malaria-infected anopheles mosquito, and the link between the transmission of the disease from mosquito to man was proven.

6 White stalkers on the beach

Fiji 1875–82

A Fijian glossary

Bokola	a corpse to be eaten
Lotu	Christian religion
Lali	slit drum
Mataqali	landowning group, defined by descent, clan
Meke	action song
Sulu	waist cloth, kilt
Rara	village green
Tabua	whale's tooth
Yaqona	*kava*, mildly narcotic infusion from the *Piper methysticum* root

How was it that Britain ever came to lay claim to Fiji – some 300 tropical islands at the opposite end of the earth? As morning dawns on the meridian at Greenwich, the islands of Fiji, some 1,900 miles north-east of Sydney, shimmer in the fading light of the dying sun. There, every kind of coral once grew about the islands – islands fringed with palms or mangrove, ruggedly mountainous and deeply forested, or sometimes just a slip of sand, half submerged within a reef washed with crashing surf.

'Feegee, the Cannibal Isles', early navigators called them, after their powerful inhabitants with their fiercely painted war canoes, their clubs and spears, and a famous chief who was said to have consumed 999 human beings. And yet the people – handsome, statuesque, scantily clothed – lived in beautifully constructed houses of reed and grass in towns and villages surrounded by ditches and earthen mounds. They spent their time cultivating yams and *ndalo* (taro root), gathering coconuts, bananas and breadfruit – and fishing.

There were no beasts of burden and no roads in Fiji. Canoes – some no more than a hollowed-out log with simple outriggers, others enormous war craft carrying 200 men – were the only mode of getting about. Small traders from foreign lands called in search of sandalwood, coconut oil, bêche-de-mer and tortoiseshell. The couple of hundred white men who had settled by the middle of the nineteenth century were British, American, French and Germans who had run away from ships stopping at the islands for fresh food and water. They found that in spite of the heat the climate was not unhealthy, and while dysentery was present, fevers were almost unknown.

Missionaries had also come to the South Pacific – a story of gradual success in Tahiti and other islands by the 1830s. Zealous converts – especially in Tonga, with which Fiji carried on a fruitful trade, brought two Methodist missionaries to the islands in 1834. Within twenty years the entire New Testament had been translated into Fijian, over 7,000 Christians had been converted, and 228 chapels had been built – still with only seven or eight white missionaries.

Meanwhile, an American merchant had claimed soveignty of the island of Namuka. Others claimed large tracts of the land. In 1855 an American man-of-war, the *John Adams,* sailed into the harbour at Levuka on the island of Ovalau to lay a claim for the staggering sum of $45,000 – as much as $158 million today – against Cakobau, the self-proclaimed King of Fiji, in recompense for the plunder of the American consul's house after it had accidentally gone up in flames during the firing of a cannon on 4 July six years before. 'The Great Chief who has charged me with this mission presides over a country whose resources are inexhaustible,' Commander Boutwell of the *John Adams* told a terrified Cakobau. '[America's] power to punish her enemies [is] beyond the comprehension of those who have never visited her Empire.'

Cakobau had closely followed the tales of horror from the Maori wars, in which thousands had been killed in New Zealand, and knew full well the kind of treatment that could be meted out by the white men. Now he was charged with damaging US property and treating persons 'in a manner that would not be submitted to by the Government of the United States of America'. If Cakobau refused to restore the value of the damaged property with interest, he would be hanged, or taken away to America.

Cakobau turned to the only men in Fiji with the clout to assist him: the British Consul and two Methodist missionaries. An offer of 200,000 acres of Fiji was dispatched to Queen Victoria, in return for the monies to pay the Americans. The offer was reinforced in 1859, when the British Consul himself sailed for London with fine samples of cotton, and a new proposition from Cakobau: sovereignty over the islands. This time the Colonial

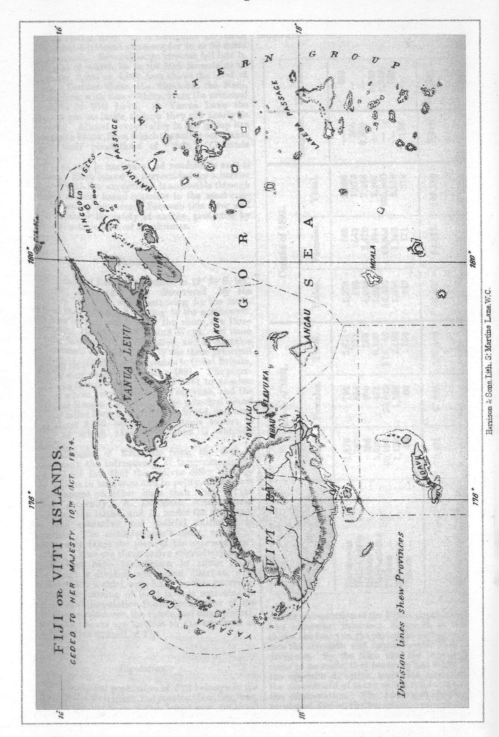

FIJI or VITI ISLANDS,
CEDED TO HER MAJESTY 10.TH OCT. 1874.

Division lines shew Provinces

Harrison & Sons. Lith. St Martins Lane. W.C.

Office decided to make inquiries. A Colonel Smythe was dispatched to investigate Fiji as a base for power and security in the Pacific, a mail station, and critically – in view of the civil war then raging in the southern United States – as a source of fine Sea Island cotton to replace supplies from Virginia.

After ten months on the islands, Smythe could not recommend Fiji. Not only were the islands far from the most direct route between Sydney and Panama, British interests in the west of the Pacific could be more than safeguarded by the presence of the navy, serviced from Australia or New Zealand. The permanent white residents were disreputable and drank to excess. As for cotton: it was true that a few moneyed planters had begun to form plantations. But there was no concept of private property in Fiji. Land was owned in common; everything was shared. 'The general habits and sentiments of the Fijians are opposed to the acquisition of property by individuals,' wrote Smythe. Planters had removed Fijians from their land; opposition was springing up. The only way to obtain labour was through the chiefs, who would send a party of people 'to perform the work agreed upon'. Such a system could not possibly meet the demand for workers on cotton plantations.

As for the task of civilizing the natives, Smythe was confident that while at the moment less than one-third were Christian, and among the remainder, 'cannibalism, strangulation of widows, infanticide, and other enormities prevail to a frightful extent', the work of the Methodist missionaries would gradually do the business of educating the Fijians. London agreed.

But the temptations of Fiji for the white man would not go away. A sudden fall in the price of wool and a succession of bad weather brought depression to Sydney and Melbourne. Advertisements luring young men from Australia and New Zealand with visions of fortunes from cotton began to appear in the press. By 1875 the number of whites on the islands had reached 2,000.

Smythe had been right. The Fijians refused to work for the white men. Plantations burned and settlers were murdered as disputes arose over the land. The planters, increasingly struggling to survive, began importing labour from other islands. Reports of kidnappings, islanders stolen for the growing labour traffic, began to haunt the South Seas. These alarmed anti-slavery interests in London. Meanwhile, vigilante parties of settlers took the law into their own hands. Appeals to the United States and to Britain to

establish some kind of protectorate fell on deaf ears. After a decade of
chaos, a handful of planters set themselves up as a ministry under King
Cakobau in 1871. Within eighteen months the islands were on the brink of
war. In January 1873 Cakobau offered Fiji to Queen Victoria once again.

In October 1874 the British Governor of New South Wales, Sir Hercules Robinson, rotund, bluff and keen on horseracing, sailed for the
islands charged with negotiating the unconditional cession of Fiji with
Cakobau and the leading chiefs. Cakobau met him with relief and resignation. 'If matters remain as they are, Fiji will become like a piece of
driftwood on the sea, and be picked up by the first passer-by,' he told
Robinson. His people had to have protection. 'Of one thing I am assured,'
he said as he signed the deed of cession on 10 October, 'if we do not cede
Fiji, the white stalkers on the beach, the cormorants, will open their maws
and swallow us.'

Covering his favourite war-club with emblems of peace, Cakobau delivered
it to Robinson to send to Her Majesty, 'the only thing he possesses that may
interest her'. Today it serves as the mace in the Fijian parliament. Then he
and his three sons sailed for Sydney with Sir Hercules to see white civilization for themselves. At Government House, Cakobau slept on his own mat
with his bible beside him and dandled Robinson's small golden-haired
grand-daughter on his knee, as she whispered to him, 'You won't eat *me*,
will you?' Across the world in London, the future of Fiji was transferred
into the hands of Lord Carnarvon at the Colonial Office. On Thursday, 26
November 1874, a small man with dark thinning hair and a wispy beard left
a gabled, red-brick house in the woods at the bottom of his father-in-law's
garden beside the racecourse at Ascot, to travel up to London in answer to
his summons.

In spite of his rather limp appearance, short-sighted and ill-at-ease, few
men moved with the assurance of Sir Arthur Gordon through London's
corridors of power. He was forty-five years old. Windsor, Downing Street,
the Commons and the Athenaeum – he was intimate with all of them. Wil-
liam Gladstone was like a second father to him; Roundell Palmer, now
Lord Selborne, the former Lord Chancellor, was a close friend; Samuel
Wilberforce, son of the famous abolitionist, Bishop of Oxford and later of
Winchester, was a constant adviser. Later that day Gordon would call on
John Delane, the editor of *The Times*, and see Lord Cardwell, the former
Secretary of State for the Colonies.

1. Inset: John Hawley Glover, administrator of Lagos, 1863–74.
2. 'A corrugated iron coffin containing a dead consul once a year':
Government House, Lagos.

3. A house on the
track to Abeokuta
from Lagos.

4. 'Over the bar': the
harbour at Lagos.

5. The twenty-nine-year-old magistrate William des Voeux being hauled up the rapids on the Essequibo River, British Guiana, *c.*1864.

6. Left, des Voeux's host, George Couchman; standing far right, des Voeux; on a visit to a local chief, Canimapo, seated, left, who was so frightened by the sight of this photograph that he tried to poison des Voeux.

7. Castries, St Lucia, with Morne Fortune beyond.

8. Des Voeux, in happier times, seated centre with his son Harry on his knee, and his wife, Marion, right, at Government House, Nasova, Fiji, 1881.

9. Soon to be displaced by European settlers, the Larrakia camp at Palmerston, 1874.

10. William Bloomfield Douglas, two years after he left Palmerston, as Resident of Selangor, c.1876.

11. The beach below Government House, with Palmerston's essential supply ship, the *Gulnare*, in harbour.

12. Harriet Douglas planted the first telegraph pole at Port Darwin, 15 September 1870. Harriet, holding a mallet, stands to the left of the pole while her mother, Ellen, and father, William Bloomfield Douglas, are second and third from the right of the pole.

13. Government House, Palmerston, stands on the hill to the right; 'The Camp' is to the left, below.

14. Captain George Strahan, Governor of the Gold Coast, left, and an unidentified officer, possibly his deputy, Captain Lees, administrator of Lagos, and Hausa officers, *c*.1874.

15. Market at Accra, Gold Coast, *c*.1874.

16. Sir Arthur Gordon, right, barefoot, bearded and wearing cut-off dungarees, with his ADC, Captain Knollys, on an expedition to the interior of Viti Levu, Fiji, 1875.

17. Rachael Gordon, aged forty-seven, shortly before she set off to live in Fiji, 1875.

18. Government House at Nasova, near Levuka, Ovalau, Fiji, c.1876.

19. Freshwater bathing near Government House, Fiji.

20. Sir Bartle Frere.

21. Lady Frere.

22. The leaders of the Zulu delegation listen to Frere's ultimatum, 11 December 1878.

23. Brooding atmosphere: the battlefield at Isandlwana, photographed during a burial expedition, June 1879.

24, 25. Thomas Callaghan and his wife, Alice, photographed in Montevideo, while he was Governor of the Falkland Islands, 1879.

26. Stanley Harbour, Falkland Islands, 1875, with ships of the South Atlantic Flying Squadron showing the flag.

Gordon's mother died when he was four. A delicate and cosseted child, he was the youngest, most cherished son of the fourth Earl of Aberdeen – at the time, Foreign Secretary in Wellington's cabinet, gentle, guileless and deeply religious. Growing up by his father's side either at Haddo, the baronial family seat in Scotland, or in their house in London, young Arthur was deemed too vulnerable to be sent away to school. Touchy, introspective and demanding, at the age of sixteen he was chided by the aunt of one of his friends for his morbidly sensitive and romantic attachment to her nephew. 'You have been a Hot House plant read beyond your years, and inheriting from your Father deep feelings, without a Mother or unmarried sister to lavish those feelings upon and therefore you exaggerate them to yourself.' She advised him to trust in religion.

Yet when he was as young as fifteen Gordon confessed to 'an excessive desire to be eminent. I believe it is wrong and . . . I have tried to subdue it, but in vain . . . I most earnestly desire greatness and power.' Proceeding to read history at Cambridge, his goal of following his older brother into the church was quashed by his father, who insisted on keeping Gordon by him. When Lord Aberdeen was elected prime minister in 1852, he made his son his private secretary. Arthur was just twenty-two. He was to spend almost ten years tethered to his father in the heady world of high politics. Standing for parliament as the Liberal member for Beverley in 1854, he kept the seat for three years. By then, his father's health was failing. But, when he rallied a year later, his father's dear friend William Gladstone invited Gordon to be his private secretary during his sojourn in Corfu as Commissioner of the Ionian Islands. There, for the first time in his life, Gordon was surrounded by people of his own age. He learned to work hard, and fell in love with Gladstone's daughter, Agnes. Not surprisingly she turned down his proposal of marriage, which he transmitted two years later in a letter to her mother. Years afterwards he confessed to Agnes's younger sister, Mary: 'I am *always* awkward and clumsy. It is the consciousness of this that makes me so still and shy, and too often disagreeable.'

Gordon returned to England to face his father's final illness and death in December 1860. Corfu had given him a taste for foreign assignment. He now determined that a colonial governorship would suit him better than anything else; the Duke of Newcastle, keen to appoint men of enterprise prepared to make governing a career, would see him. In 1861 the Duke gave him a week to make up his mind whether or not to take on the lieutenant-governorship of New Brunswick on the eastern seaboard of Canada. Gordon, now thirty-two, grasped the chance.

Gordon fell in love with New Brunswick's beauty, and its 'wild, free forest life'. He travelled hundreds of miles by sleigh in the winter, 'lightly skimming over the rock-hard snow roads, – over the frozen lakes – over the ice bound rivers, – up over the mountains – away through the dark still forests'. But he was appalled by the men in its government, whom he regarded as ill-educated, provincial and corrupt. Gordon's gawky manner did him no favours with New Brunswick's brawny citizens. A portrait shows him as slight, rather weedy, with a long pale face, his uniform liberally trimmed with gold braid. He clashed vehemently with his ministers. For their part they mocked him, as 'Thy servant Arthur', the name he had instructed should be used in prayers following those for the royal family in church every Sunday. '*Socially* I don't suppose I succeed so well. There is too much that is awkward and odd and dismal about me to be ever much liked in society,' he wrote to Bishop Wilberforce early in 1863.

He was lonely. He wanted a wife, but regarded the daughters of the colonists as 'essentially foreigners', ill-educated and unmannered. He called them 'Blue-noses'. 'I won't marry unless I fall in love and fancy that love returned,' he wrote to Wilberforce. 'Why don't you come home and try?' responded the Bishop.

It was at a London dinner party given by his friends the Roundell Palmers that, at the beginning of June 1864, he was introduced to Rachael, the eldest of the six daughters of Sir John Shaw-Lefevre, an eminent civil servant and former Under-Secretary of State for the Colonies, and his wife, Emily. Rachael herself had passed the usual age of marriage. She was thirty-five, eighteen months older than Gordon. But she was dark-haired and comely, good-humoured and patient. She had been educated with her sisters at home, a liberal London household, now one of grown-up single women – for only one of Rachael's sisters had married – full of artistic endeavour and sociable talk: of politics, the state of the poor, music, art, and the latest books.

The dinner was on Friday; on Sunday he was at lunch at the Shaw-Lefevres. On Monday they met at a garden party; on Thursday he came to dinner. And so it proceeded: teas, the Queen's Ball – by 11 June, something had been said. She answered his ideal: 'that a lady's voice should be low, soft and quiet; that she should be calm and serene, under every possible

condition of things . . .' She heard him out, and by July, as he prepared to
return to Canada, the news of an understanding between the two was
circulating within the family.

They were married by Wilberforce a year later at St Martin-in-the-
Fields. They honeymooned in Normandy and Paris, then sailed for New
Brunswick. It took almost a year for Rachael to be able to begin to settle
into New Brunswick, and her strange new role as a governor's lady. She was
pregnant, beginning a series of appalling miscarriages that would consume
her life over the next four years. Meanwhile, Gordon was obsessed with his
work. Canada was going through the process of confederation; there were
outbreaks of Fenian violence – raids by radical Irish-Americans hoping to
free Ireland from Britain. The rows with his ministers continued. Rachael
told her younger sister Madeleine he was 'utterly unfit . . . to be the Governor of a Constitutional Colony'. He could not sit by 'and submit to being
dictated to', knowing that measures that he disapproved of were being
passed, on which he was not allowed a voice.

In the autumn of 1866, Gordon was moved to Trinidad. He grumbled. It
was not a promotion, life would be more expensive, the house was meant
to be 'very small and wretched', he told Gladstone. Rachael's younger sister
Madeleine came out to New Brunswick and joined them to travel to Trinidad. Rachael was again in a 'delicate' state of health.

The tropical beauty of Trinidad, its bougainvilleas, salvias, lush ferns and
trees, its flocks of scarlet ibis and hummingbirds, the riding out, picnics and
bathing, at once captivated Gordon. He kept a macaw and a spider monkey
on the verandah at Government House. But before they had been on the
island much more than six months, Rachael had suffered two more miscarriages, one so dangerous it did her more damage than a normal birth.
Gordon took her to England to put her under the care of the best doctors.
She was pregnant again when he returned to Trinidad alone in December
1868 to wait anxiously for news of a healthy confinement.

He landed to a crowded and enthusiastic reception. 'A heap' of women,
'*splendidly* dressed, were loaded with immense bouquets meant for *you*. I
send you the ribbons . . .' Gordon had then gone to their room and there –
'oh Rachael! – I found Mrs Jones had laid on the bed your purple gown and
put out your shoes and stockings and heaven knows what articles of female
gear all ready for you! – it nearly made me cry . . . My love, it is too dreary
to be going to bed in your rooms and not to see and hear you.' On 12 July
1869, aged forty-one, Rachael safely delivered a baby girl, Nevil. 'But for

the thought of you, Mrs G, I should almost go mad,' Gordon told her. She sailed for Trinidad soon afterwards.

Trinidad was dominated by a powerful clique of white planters who ran roughshod over the local Creoles and the Catholics, and had a vast problem of squatting by former slaves. Gordon made it plain that a governor was someone who should *govern*. 'It is almost necessary to have been Governor of such a Province as New Brunswick fully to relish the pleasure or indeed fully to feel the responsibility of such a government as this,' he wrote. Trinidad was a Crown colony; he could overrule his Legislative Council. Gordon took on the planters. He refused to tolerate injustice, healed sectarian differences, improved education and transformed the lives of former slaves by implementing land reforms that turned them into landowners. In the Colonial Office in London, which was smarting over the shocking aftermath of a black rebellion at Morant Bay in Jamaica, in which British troops summoned by the Governor had killed 439 men, women and children and wounded, arrested and executed hundreds more, Gordon was making a name for himself as a talented and hard-working administrator who was good at working with 'coloured' populations.

By then Gladstone was back in office as prime minister. At his recommendation in 1870 Gordon was promoted to Mauritius, in the south of the Indian Ocean. As Gladstone saw it, the climate was like Trinidad's and the problems similar. On the eve of Gordon's departure from England, on 3 January 1871, Rachael gave birth to a son, Jack.

The voyage was so awful – a fortnight in a foul, ill-ventilated French steamer – that it would be impossible for his wife and children to reach the place alive, he moaned to Gladstone. He could not possibly serve out a term of six years without his family. Everything about Mauritius was wrong: the climate was vile, its French society – 'bourgeois – et très bourgeois' – repellent; its labourers exploited, the government unjust. Taxes fell 'almost wholly on the poor . . . whilst the rich are pretty nearly exempted . . . If for my sins I am compelled to remain any time in this detestable place, I shall feel compelled to make an attempt to remedy this evil.' Although Mauritius was a Crown colony like Trinidad, the council was so dominated by planters he was left almost as powerless as he had been in New Brunswick. Let us trade it with the French for their holdings in India, he suggested to Gladstone. 'The people . . . would hail the transfer with delight.'

Now he learned that fever was rife on the island. By the time his cable ordering Rachael to stay at home reached England, she was already on the high seas. The family came, and stayed for eighteen months. Gordon settled down. For more than twenty years things had been let slide in Mauritius, and in its dependency, the Seychelles. Under the guise of indentures, slaves were still being bought and sold. Its imported Indian labourers were wretchedly treated. Gordon set about investigating the facts, implemented surprise inspections of sugar plantations, began prosecuting the planters, and changed the law to tackle the worst abuses of the 'coolie' system. The planters loathed him, while at the Colonial Office, Lord Kimberley – who resented Gordon's intimate relationship with his Prime Minister – dragged his feet, trying, it seemed to Gordon, to stifle every initiative he suggested. In February 1874, Gladstone's government fell. Lord Carnarvon resumed the post as Secretary of State. 'You will I am sure be glad to hear that I am at last about to be released from this most unpleasant post,' Gordon wrote to Gladstone in July. The possibility of Fiji had appeared on the horizon.

'The prospect of *founding* a colony . . . the greatest chance of *individual* action I have ever yet had – probably *the* point of my career . . .' Gordon told Rachael as he savoured Fiji's potential. But the position needed negotiation. He would have preferred something grander; the possibility of the governor-generalship of the West Indies tantalized. Would accepting Fiji mean a loss of status? What he wanted, Carnarvon had told him, was an experienced governor, one with standing, someone he could trust, with considerable powers of discretion. Unlike Kimberley, Carnarvon was someone Gordon thought he could work with. Soon after he returned to England, he returned from a weekend with Carnarvon at Highclere 'much pleased with my new chief. He treats one as a gentleman, which his predecessor did not.'

Still, Gordon argued. He insisted that he, not the Colonial Office, would appoint his staff. But by late November 1874, with Hercules Robinson's confirmation of the cession of Fiji, it was time to clinch the deal. That Thursday 'I . . . went by order to Lord Carnarvon who made me the offer of Fiji . . . on Saturday morning the announcement appeared in the *Times;* complimentary.' By Monday there was an invitation waiting to dine at Windsor with the Queen the following Thursday. Gordon met Carnarvon en route: 'we talked a little of Fiji; the instructions are already prepared without my seeing them, which is contrary to promise and rather displeases me. I am also not quite easy about the personnel.'

Then it was into the castle. It was many years since he had been there as a guest, and he found it sorely changed. 'Punctuality has gone and so had decorous splendour . . . the Queen has grown old, redder, and her voice, though still full of its old clear tone, is often gruff and masculine, and she certainly has more German accent, which is odd . . . The Queen talked a little of Fiji – said I was to call the chief place Patteson' – after a bishop who had been murdered in revenge for 'recruiting' labour in the Solomon Islands three years before.

It was not until four months later, at the end of March 1875, however, that the Gordons finally set off for Fiji. 'My last day in England for long: perhaps for ever,' Gordon recorded in his journal on 22 March – Monday in Holy Week. 'At eleven there was a farewell service for us and those travelling with us – . . . about fifty people present, but the chapel was dark, and I did not recognise them all. I liked the mixture of ranks and opinions – the Duchess of Argyll and Marqués the nursemaid, Gladstone and the Dean of Westminster . . .' After the service they shook hands with their friends at the head of the stairs. It was a sombre moment. 'Gladstone . . . looked old, ill, and worn, and was muffled up to the ears in a coat with a great fur collar. Goodby at 18 Spring Gardens – a sad one; for it is unlikely we shall ever see either Sir John or Lady Lefevre again . . . then final packing and letter writing. To bed about two.'

The route was via Folkestone and Paris, then to Marseilles. Besides Sir Arthur and Lady Gordon – now forty-seven, her dark hair tinged with grey, handsome and substantial in full crinolines and black gaberdine – the party was large. There were the Gordons' two much cherished children, Nevil, now a pretty girl of six, and four-year-old Jack; and Gordon's young cousin, his namesake Arthur, to whom he had acted *in loco parentis* since he was sixteen, an awkward teenager, and who had come to live with them in Trinidad. 'A.G.', as he was called in letters home, was now twenty-eight, handsome, athletic, a talented artist, and nominally Gordon's private secretary. Miss Gordon Cumming, 'Eka', who had been introduced to them as companion for Lady Gordon, would dress in brown Holland or blue serge, with – when they got to the tropics – an enormous pith hat. Tall, rather plain, she was 'a regular globe trotter, wonderfully good tempered', but tactless and 'very pushing when she wants something done'. Cumming had already written a couple of indifferent books on her travels; she sketched ceaselessly and rather badly. In addition, there were four more young men under thirty who were to serve as members of Gordon's staff. These included a Dr Mayo, keenly interested in studying new forms of disease but who would find the Fijians terrifying, and George Le Hunte, a twenty-three-year-old lawyer. There were two nurses for the children. Finally there were Mr and Mrs Abbey and their two boys, 'a most comfortable and reliable couple' who had already served the Gordons in Trinidad and Mauritius, who would be in charge of running Government House.

The steamer was big and comfortable, French run, with first class food, but the voyage was tedious: a week to Port Said, then twenty-four to thirty-six hours on the Canal – a few hours at Suez – 'and then the dreaded Red Sea, which takes five days – a few hours at Aden, and a week to Ceylon', wrote Rachael to her mother on 3 April. At first the children were seasick, but soon took to running about the deck all day.

'Some pleasant fellow-passengers,' recorded Gordon, 'objectionable purser-commissaire. Eka rather too continually on the clack, but I think good and useful. Children well pleased and well. Captain stupid.' He, 'A.G.' and the young men spent a portion of every day learning Fijian, and the rest of the time consuming everything they could read about the islands. In Aden, they picked up Captain Knollys, who was to be Gordon's aide-de-camp, and his dog, Snip. Arthur and Rachael were captivated by Aden and its orientalism, full of 'Somaulis, and Arabs, Hindoos, Jews and Negroes, all in picturesque confusion . . . Dry, hot, confined, Aden may be, but how many with eyes in his head can call it ugly, I find it hard to conceive,' wrote Gordon, while Rachael delighted in the profusion of jars, baskets and pottery, 'which, had I been coming home, I could not have resisted getting possession of'. On 18 April, a month after leaving home, they landed in Galle in Ceylon – and finally were able to get their clothes washed.

'But it is, oh! so hot. I feel in a continued state of trickling down,' Rachael wrote to her sister Madeleine. Church was 'stifling hot. I had on my new Paris Holland and very soon found it was covered with dark lines of heat . . . I hardly know what is best to wear.' Meanwhile, Gordon was immersed in discussions with Buddhist priests, 'hearing their own account of their doctrine'. It was another week to Singapore. There the Governor was astonished to find that Rachael and the children were going to stay in Fiji too. She escaped into the Chinese town – of which her hosts would not approve – 'I longed to stop and pick up all kinds of curiousities . . . rude china pots and pans, etc . . . I don't care for fine expensive things, but these common things are most fascinating, and no one else knows of them I am sure.'

'I do not much like Sydney,' Gordon declared. They had landed in Australia. 'It resembles a third-rate English country town without the remains of antiquity such a town would possess; the streets are mean, the stores exteriorly shabby though not bad as to contents . . .' The Governor, Sir Hercules Robinson, was kind, pleasant and sensible, 'though not quite so clever a man as he thinks himself. What a thing it is to have the interest of the CO!' Gordon remarked gratefully. 'His staff is not a first-rate one. The ADC is nearly stone-deaf; slow, gentleman-like and rather good-looking. The Private Secretary is cleverish, bad form, fast, and flirts with Mrs —. My resolution never to take an Australian Colony, has been intensified by my stay here.' After a fortnight's stay at Government House they went to Pfahlert's Hotel – 'not a bad change'.

Genteel gossip about Fiji was not appealing. Many Australians had lost money on plantations, there were lamentable tales of poverty and hardship, and dangerous voyages in canoes. Rachael and the children would have to wait at least three months in Sydney while alterations were made to Government House. 'I always hear the same thing. "*You* won't like it, Lady Gordon",' Rachael told Madeleine.

But there was much worse. Towards the end of Cakobau's celebrated visit to Sydney, his two younger sons came down with a light case of measles. Carried on board ship in January, the family sailed for Fiji. Thousands gathered from all over the islands to welcome Cakobau home, sitting before him to touch his hands. By mid-March news of a catastrophic epidemic engulfing the islands had reached Sydney, but, Gordon learned to his fury, no medical aid had been dispatched. By the time he landed on the islands on Friday, 25 June, the people were drowning in grief. Measles had killed more than 40,000, a third of the population, including many of the leading chiefs who he had hoped would aid his new administration. Meanwhile, the infection continued to rage in the interior of the big islands.

> The canoe of our death has arrived among us, e!
> The foreigners have come again!

Gordon landed on the island of Ovalu at 11 a.m. on a brilliant tropical day, the sun glancing off the crystal green waters inside the reef. Beyond the white of the surf, the deep blue sea stretched towards the outlines of the islands of Wakaya and Mokongai, some ten miles off. He gave a brief speech on the jetty, then walked up the beach to Government House in the offices of Cakobau's former administration – 'large and very airy'. The walls were made of a double screen of reeds, sheltered by a thick roof of overhanging thatch which formed the roof of verandahs around the building. Behind it, great crags of rock rose into mountains covered in dense jungle.

The island of Ovalu, Fiji, with Government House and jetty, by 'Eka',
Constance Gordon Cumming

The place was alive with parrots and kingfishers, blue convolvulus, 'hoyas with their sweet waxy flowers clamber[ing] over the rocks' and gorgeous butterflies. People were constantly passing along the path in front of the house on their way to the capital of the islands, Levuka, a mile away. The town was home to about 600 whites, a ramshackle place of seedy drinking places and frail wooden houses roofed with corrugated iron strung out along a stony beach. Outrigger canoes with great brown sails sailed across the water; bands of girls in bright *pinafoas* fished before the house. Eka later recorded how envious she was of these girls 'disporting' themselves at low tide on the reef, 'bringing back baskets full of all sorts of curious, rainbow coloured fish'.

'Everything here far exceeds my expectations – scenery, climate, work, people –,' a delighted Gordon wrote to Rachael. The Fijians had surprised him: 'very different from the Hindoo and . . . as proud and indifferent as possible if not properly treated. I like [them] very much . . . Were it not for the apprehension that you will not like it as well as myself, and . . . that it may not suit the children, I should be perfectly happy . . . I am thoroughly in my element.'

Three days later Cakobau came to make what Gordon called his 'personal feudal submission'. Gordon made certain that any Europeans not directly concerned with the ceremony were kept strictly away. 'I was determined that it should not be made a show of, for the mere idle curiosity of townspeople and sailors.' Now he sat on the verandah at the head of the steps, a slight figure, white-faced and balding, his staff in uniform behind him. At his side, ready to interpret, was a pale, fine-boned Englishman with a full beard: John Bates Thurston. Thurston was 'on quite another plane' from any other white man in Fiji, Gordon would write later, utterly determined to prevent the islands becoming a 'white man's country'.

Thurston had been twenty-nine when he landed in Fiji ten years before, after being rescued from the wreck of the ship on which he had served as mate. Supplying the British Consul's need for a clerk, and in due course, a successor, he had remained in Fiji, standing up against the white settlers who argued that once they had bought land from a chief, they acquired his power and could throw the inhabitants off with impunity. Cakobau, who had been determined to show the white settlers who formed Fiji's first government that he was no puppet, had called on Thurston to join it. In negotiations with Britain, it was Thurston who insisted on measures to safeguard Fijian sovereignty. Cakobau and his chiefs awarded him with the title of *Na Kena Vai* – 'The Spearhead, the Very Bayonet'.

Now long files of Fijians approached Government House: 'strapping Tongan women full of grace and life . . . Samoan [ladies] in morning gowns of the last century's cut . . . Rotumans in scarlet and yellow, with sparkling eyes and raven hair.' On they came, Gordon wrote, 'very slowly, an apparently interminable column of natives, two and two, [the men] dressed in white kilts . . . chanting as they walked, and carrying palm-leaf baskets filled with yams.' These they piled in front of him, and as fast as their baskets were emptied, others came to carry them away, heaping them up into a huge pyramid. On they came, smoothly, easily, chanting continually, 'dragging slowly along in their midst . . . three large turtles, which also were duly deposited on their backs before me. After this there appeared Cakobau, his sons and his attendants [walking] very slowly.'

Courteous and dignified, Cakobau was now well into his seventies. For much of his life he had resisted the exhortations of the missionaries to put aside his wives and renounce heathenism. Then, twenty years ago, in 1854, a series of mass conversions had persuaded him of the expediency of taking the *lotu* and converting to Christianity.

King Cakobau in 1885: painted by P. Spence

'He is a far more striking man than the photographs would lead you to suppose – very kingly in bearing and with a most intelligent head,' Gordon told Rachael. 'He was dressed in a long wrapper of dark red (almost black) *tapa* [cloth made from the bark of the paper mulberry or breadfruit tree] with a shirt of some native manufacture. He walked with a long gold-headed walking stick . . . when he got near me he raised the salutation given by an inferior to his chief, a sort of sighing inspiration, more like the "Woh!" one says to stop a horse than anything else. This, at his lead, was taken up by all the rest in a great shout of *woh!*'

Behind Cakobau a herald carried an immense root of *kava*. 'This he now took into his own hands and laid at my feet, breaking off at the same time, rather nervously and hastily, one of the smaller portions of it and placing it on my hand. This was the decisive act of vassalage. I said, [in Fijian] "I accept this: may it be well with Fiji." Then they raised the shout of *Mâna!* and clapped hands.' The formal act was over. Gordon shook hands with

Cakobau. The old man was shaking. Not unnaturally, wrote Gordon, for, 'though he has signed treaties of cession and hauled down flags, this is probably the first time in his life that he ever performed a personal act of homage to another, and that too in the presence of his people'.

'The effect has been electric. Wherever I go now the natives shout *Woh!* and crouch down, as before their own great chiefs, and they admit and understand that I am their master.'

For the next two months, while the house was extended and before Rachael and the children arrived, Gordon bided his time, absorbing the place and its customs. Fiji was in a precarious state. Paralysed with sorrow, the Fijians were burying vast numbers of their dead. Unable to tend their crops, they were starving. Meanwhile, bad weather had ruined the crops of the white planters; cotton prices continued to fall. Gordon could go nowhere without suspicion. The Fijians would not come near his ship the *Pearl,* while the white settlers alternated between sullenness and anticipation that the advent of British rule would mean that, at last, they would be in control.

There were a lot of problems to sort out – and quickly. Young Dr William MacGregor, the son of a crofter from Aberdeenshire, who had followed Gordon at his invitation with his wife from the civil hospital in Mauritius, had been dispatched on the day he landed with a mass of medical supplies to the islands where measles prevailed. White settlers had registered 1,650 land claims – estimated at some 850,000 acres, some 20 per cent of Fiji. Almost all of them were disputed. To most white settlers, the native Fijian was a nuisance to be cleared off his holding as swiftly as possible. Gordon's instructions from Carnarvon were clear: 'the whole of the land within the limits of Fiji' had been 'absolutely and unreservedly transferred to the Crown'. They had also agreed that he would preserve existing Fijian laws, customs and structures, modifying them only where necessary.

The day after he landed Gordon ordered that anyone who wanted to obtain deeds of title had to file land claims by 31 December. He would settle all land issues. Meanwhile, the colony's revenues were in a dire state. There were many, many islands, with a scattered population, almost all of which he had to visit. Gordon had sacrificed £2,000 of his £5,000 salary to keep the costs of his administration down; he was paying his own staff as little as he could manage. He had told London he would not be needing a man-of-war or a military force, but would rely on 'cheap native police'. Even with an imperial grant, however, the colony was heading for bankruptcy.

In addition to its chiefs and hereditary office-bearers, every village had a council of elders. It would be impossible 'to deny to the natives a large measure of self-government', Gordon told Carnarvon. He was designing a structure for Fiji based on traditional gatherings of chiefs into monthly district meetings, and quarterly provincial councils. These were to be crowned by a new invention, a 'Great Council' – or *Bose Vaka Turaga* – that met once a year, what Gordon was later to call his 'native parliament'.

In every other British colony 'native affairs' were a low priority, generally delegated, as in Australia, to outlying officers in the departments of lands and surveys. For Gordon, they were his key responsibility. He threw down the gauntlet to the whites by keeping on Thurston, with his expertise in Fijian language and customs, as colonial secretary. Also by his side were Cakobau, who visited him almost daily, and Ma'afu, a powerful Tongan chief.

Early in July a young cotton planter called Walter Carew presented himself to Gordon. With an open, honest face, Carew was fluent in Fijian and, like Thurston, sympathetic to the people and their customs. Gordon took him on, dispatching him with his young cousin 'A.G.' to act as his personal representative, to travel to the neighbouring islands to try to reassure the islanders that the British had not come to steal their lands. Then: 'there is a charming fellow here – Olive, of the marines – one of *our* sort,' he told Rachael, '*good,* active and simple . . . Indeed I do not know what we should have done without him.' Gordon immediately made Olive, who was chief of police, an ADC – 'We could hardly manage the native servants without him.'

The new Attorney-General, de Ricci, appointed from India, however, turned out to be feeble and self-seeking, 'a shifty, intriguing sort of man . . . incapable of straightforwardness'. Gordon found him immediately repulsive, a sense that was soon reinforced by de Ricci's loss of temper at seeing an English sailor, clearly drunk and struggling violently, being hustled to jail '*on the shoulders* of some native policemen'. White men should only be arrested in the presence of a European constable,' de Ricci sharply instructed Olive. 'As a matter of political expediency, indeed I believe it to be most unwise that natives should be permitted to imagine for a moment that they are CAPABLE of exercising any control over the RULING RACE.' By the new year Gordon had replaced him.

Gordon was revelling in Fiji. Woken before sunrise by 'the glorious flood of golden light, which fills the eastern sky', he went to his desk to write in the tranquillity of early morning. Then: 'we generally swim about for some time, dawdle on the pier steps in that pleasantest of all garments in these latitudes, one's own skin – dive again into the clear warm salt water.' Then he dressed for the day, in thin silk and wool shirt, white trousers and white canvas shoes. Breakfast at 8.30, then the Colonial Secretary – Thurston – 'with a basket full of papers . . . which we discuss. Then come all sorts of people who want interviews; at two we have luncheon, often presaged by another short plunge in front of the house.' After: more interviews, more writing; then 'we generally tumble into the water again . . . before dressing for dinner'. In between, he had an hour's lesson in Fijian. After dinner 'we usually adjourn to Olive's or the *rara* (the open grass between us and the northern point) and go through the *yaqona* ceremony . . .'

Gordon had taken immediately to this rite. A mass of chewed *kava* root was diluted and strained through hibiscus fibre to be drunk reverently in solemn assembly. 'Nothing can exceed the grace of the strainer's movements while engaged in straining the bowl,' Gordon wrote. 'Every one of the motions of his arms, the position of his hands, etc, is regulated by strict tradition and never varies.' All the while, the assembled group, sitting in a circle, chanted old *meke*. The straining finished, there was a muffled clap of the hands, and dead silence fell.

'A youth of rank seated cross-legged before the bowl presents a cup of thin cocoa-nut shell, which is filled . . .' Silently, the youth came to kneel before Gordon, who held out his own drinking bowl with both hands for him to fill. 'As I raise it to my lips a measured clapping of hands in most exquisitely accurate time is set up by all the circle and continued so long as I am drinking. When I throw down the cup this stops . . . the drink is then taken to every one in order according to rank, and conversation and smoking are now unrestricted.'

Afterwards the soldiers sometimes danced by moonlight. 'Then the rest turn in, and so do I if I can, but I often have to steal another hour or two from the night for more writing and getting up more questions before me.'

'Have you learnt enough Fijian to know what *malua* means?' Gordon wrote to Rachael in Sydney at the end of July. '"By and by", which is its translation, is the great resource of all men, white or black in Fiji.' Little or nothing was happening with the building works on the house. It was becoming clear even to him that Fiji had its drawbacks. 'The town (which I rarely enter) is in truth thoroughly odious.' The de Riccis were dreadfully miserable. Now the weather had turned wet and 'excessively cold'; the house was terribly draughty. There were no shades for the candles, it was almost impossible to work at night with a 'flaring candle, that glimmers like a sickly hope and every second nearly goes out altogether'. Meanwhile Abbey, the butler, was in despair over the servants, 'and no wonder, for they are totally unlike anything he has ever had to do with before, have none of the submissiveness of Hindoos. But for the fact that they are all policemen . . . we should get nothing done at all.' He suggested Rachael bring two or three good sofas, as 'there is nothing in the house of that sort', and some tables for the drawing room. He was feeling unhappy and guilty that he was bringing her 'out to a place where you can have so little enjoyment'. He went on blithely, 'Still this is certainly the right sort of work for *me*.'

Rachael meanwhile was living in a Sydney hotel, required for 'oppressive' luncheons and grand dinners ('I shall take care I am not let in for another') at Government House. With only a small, awkward wagonette for getting about, and everything just like England, she could not bear to wait until 'the regular mails get going in December' to leave Sydney. On 9 September she and the children sailed with Eka for Fiji. 'We were all *horribly* sick, even *I*, – *all* from the Captain down,' Rachael told her sister, Mary. After twelve days' sailing she, Eka, the children and their nurses finally found themselves off Levuka in a tremendous storm of rain, 'so thick they can't find their way inside the reef', while Gordon waited on land, dreading her arrival in such appalling weather.

'First I went all over the house,' Rachael told Madeleine. 'It is a large one . . . but excessively rough.' Worse than the fact that it was built of reeds, so that the walls were 'nearly transparent', no partition reached the ceiling. Pigeons roosted in the roof space. Every spoken word could be heard from one end to the other. For the time being the children would live with their nurses further up the hillside – 'rather a steep pull for me to get up there'. Eka was lodged with the chief justice and his wife. All the same: 'I am most agreeably surprised at the place, and feel as if I should like it very much.'

Government House in fact had all the atmosphere of a rowdy house in an English public school. Rachael called it a large house party for which she was quite unprepared. There was not an ounce of privacy. Within a stone's throw were 100 men from the Fijian constabulary – much given to shouting and laughter in their leisure hours. Besides 'A.G.', Olive, the police constable and young George Le Hunte, the Yorkshire lawyer who would go on to serve as magistrate in one of the outer islands, living in the house were three more young men: twenty-five-year-old Alfred Maudslay, ex-Harrow and Cambridge, drily good-humoured, with a shock of wavy blond hair, whom the Gordons had rescued from the service of a decidedly camp governor in Queensland; young Captain Knollys, Gordon's ADC, and twenty-one-year-old Baron von Hügel, who had been rescued by 'A.G.' on his travels with Walter Carew in the mountains of the island of Viti Levu, sick, penniless and starving. Von Hügel was, wrote Rachael, 'collecting curiosities'.

None of them was over thirty; all of them were over six feet tall. Fit and athletic, they swam or played football and cricket in every spare moment, turned up casually in bare feet and boating flannels for meals, while Gordon himself wore a towel flung over his shoulders in case he should fancy a bathe. 'A.G.' hated his private secretary's work, 'in fact never does it', Maudslay wrote. Meanwhile Knollys was pig-headed, dogmatic, fond of arguing and thought the 32nd Light Infantry 'the finest regiment in the world'. The children, Nevil and Jack, hung on von Hügel as if he were the Pied Piper. Von Hügel possessed a discreet and languid charm. He was eagerly studying Fijian customs and collecting artefacts. In spite of being engaged to a girl whom he cherished in London, he loved to lie about on mats in Fijian houses, with pretty girls to roll cigars for him and make him *yaqona*. Maudslay would wake him in the morning with the thrust of a Fijian fishing spear through the reed partition between their rooms.

Nurse came down every morning to dress Rachael, in stays and heavy petticoats. 'Directly after breakfast the Governor and staff go off to do their work. I give the children their lessons on the verandah,' wrote Rachael. 'As for the servants, they are perfectly hopeless.' There were eight of them in the house, 'generally doing nothing. Mrs A and nurse between them make all the beds and do the housework.'

Apart from a few household things, 'I have nothing to do with dinners or actual housekeeping which Captain Knollys manages entirely.' Lunch was at one, the children at a small table at the end of the room, or she would organize picnics under the shade of coconut trees near the water's edge. Rachael was increasingly lame; walking was difficult. 'In the afternoon I generally go out boating – the new boat . . . is a *beauty* . . . We have a crew of six Fijians . . . Arthur calls it my carriage.' When she came in she and

Gordon would sit for a while on the verandah, playing with the children. But it was soon time for 'his Fiji master, who stays till dressing time'.

'We constantly have three or four extra *men* to dinner, officers of the *Barracouta*, planters, officers of the government and chiefs', but never any women, wrote Rachael. She liked Cakobau: 'such a fine dignified old man, with a most commanding manner', who, as he lived only about a mile away, frequently came to lunch or dinner. As for Ma'afu, the great Tongan chief, she thought him extremely clever 'and the handsomest of them all. If it were not for his brown colour he would be like a very high-bred, rather large Frenchman!'

By the middle of October, the house was nearly finished. The children were blooming. 'Even I!' Rachael wrote, had taken to *yaqona* drinking. 'Nurse thinks it a most "disgusting practice".' The men didn't like her to go into Captain Olive's rooms, 'but someone brings me out my bowl, which I thoroughly enjoy. It is rather like a slight mixture of Gregory's powder and soap-suds, but the moment you have swallowed it, a most delicious taste comes into your mouth, and you feel most comfortable and refreshed.'

Rachael saw little of Gordon. He was working terribly hard, writing dispatches from the moment he got up at dawn. 'Sometimes I am afraid he will get ill with working so hard. There are *four of them* now, copying as fast as he writes, and he can keep them all going . . . they will go on until midnight at least.' Her initial delight with Fiji was beginning to pale.

'I have given up the idea of having things nice, the servants are so abominably bad. Abbey has just told me that they broke twenty of his lamps – I don't mean only shades and chimneys, they are all gone, as a matter of course – but actual lamps.' Glass and china, 'cans, pails, tools etc are broken by the dozen'. Everything had to be replaced in Sydney, and 'the freight there is quite enormous; and the amount of pilfering right and left is disgusting'. The rain was drenching; there were leaks in her room. She found going to church difficult, the path was so rough and stony, and inside it was so crowded and hot. She was also worrying about money: 'our expenses are enormous, and everything we buy here is 150 per cent dearer than English prices'. Abbey was so beside himself with trouble with the servants, 'I am so afraid he will knock up altogether; and then the Governor *will* have people to dinner, and just now the kitchen is being rebuilt . . .'

Gordon, however, never cared what he ate or drank. He was working furiously. A commission under the chief justice had now been set up to investigate claims to land by the white planters. Every claim was different:

cases of joint owners of land; fraud in procuring signatures; fraud in defining boundaries; boundaries that no one could agree on. Every kind of
western legal argument was brought to bear upon the claims, none of
which recognized the fundamental problem, the sacred attachment which
the Fijians felt for their lands. Reports were forwarded to Gordon to adju-
dicate in council. Within weeks lawyers began to dispute the Crown's right
to settle land claims, arguing that they could only be settled in a court of
law. Gordon further came to realize that the chief justice seemed to regard
the duty of the Lands Commission to make good a white man's claim
whenever a plausible excuse for doing so could be found. Worse, he refused
to take up his duties if any Fijian judge were to serve. Like de Ricci, the
Attorney-General, the chief justice would have to go.

Meanwhile John Thurston was at work designing a major scheme for
taxation. In the past Cakobau's administration had raised income through
an extortionate poll tax of £1 per man and 4s per woman, feared and
loathed by the Fijians as a way of forcing them to work on white men's
plantations. Now, playing to Fiji's custom of contributing to their chief's
support by labour or in kind, Gordon and Thurston proposed to raise revenue from the sale of produce contributed by each village – according to
their ability to deliver. Prices would be set by tenders submitted by traders,
and surpluses would remain the property of the community from which
they came.

Gordon thrived on pressure. His working methods were chaotic. He jot-
ted down paragraphs on the backs of old envelopes, then procrastinated
over pulling them together. No one was allowed to touch his papers, which
were piled about his room in confusion. With Thurston, Maudslay and
'A.G.' anxious to catch the mails, he would be up on the verandah building
brick castles with the children.

Every week or so he set off on another trip around the islands, meeting
different chiefs and local *bulis*, visiting schools and seeing missions, learning
all the time, discussing his ideas for administering Fiji. Within six months,
his Fijian was fluent enough that he could understand, if not yet speak it
very well. He revelled in the exotic settings in which he found himself – 'a
new jetty decorated with arches of palm leaves'; 'a wild chief . . . a rather
handsome youth of sixteen or seventeen stark naked . . . plenty of "devils"
about with big heads of hair, blackened faces and no clothes but the *malo*'.
Evenings of drums and hollow bamboos, 300 men dancing with clubs and
spears, breastplates of whales' teeth and pearl shell, voices chanting, their

feet stamping. A typical diary entry: 'Dinner. After it reception of principal Chiefs. *Yaqona* and talk – much talk.'

For Rachael, it was a relief, though she missed him, when Gordon and his retinue set off to travel round the islands. 'Captain Knollys is away: I can give orders myself, and get things *done*.' By early December, she was cleaning up the house, 'which was in a dreadful state of dirt and confusion', and she had put the Governor's office and papers into a thorough state of order. 'Abbey has taken the opportunity of having the whole wardrobes of the six gentlemen spread out on the lawn and thoroughly scorched in the sun, to get rid of the fish moths and cockroaches which were swarming in them.'

It was the following April, ten months after Gordon landed in Fiji, that reparations for the onslaught of measles claimed their first victims. Eighteen women and children were murdered and eaten, and a dozen villages which professed Christianity were burnt to the ground. The peoples living in the remote mountain regions of western Viti Levu, one of Fiji's largest islands, had never accepted Cakobau's rule, or the cession to Britain.

Gordon did not hesitate. The only British forces in Fiji were a detachment of Royal Engineers at Levuka. Their commander, Major Pratt, objected to risking his troops in the mountains without reinforcements – and was not prepared to lead Fijian forces. Nothing was more critical to Gordon than avoiding 'a war of races'. He took command himself, sent to New Zealand for '100 Snider rifles' and sailed for the district, dispatching Knollys with eighty armed Fijian police to the north of the island, and 'A.G.' to the south, with the aim of capturing the murderers and subjugating those who sheltered them.

Gordon was once more glorying in the strange life of which he was now a part, surrounded by an army of Fijian warriors raised, in what he called 'feudal service', from every province in the islands. Gordon had called for thirty men from each *roko;* more than 2,000 volunteered. Clad in long black *likus,* faces grotesquely painted, European guns and cross belts strapped across their chests, they came to salute him in single file. 'Then they ran forward in a body, tossing up their guns into the air . . . Then they danced a formal war *meke*', and shouted, running out in twos and threes, boasting '(*bole bole*) of what they were, and what they would do'.

Dressed in a pair of unbleached drill trousers made for him by Mrs Abbey – '*reaching only to the knee*', a scandalized Rachael wrote home – Gordon took his turn on watch, and woke at daylight to the sound of his soldiers' prayers. 'We get up when it feels warm enough, for the nights and mornings are very cold. We bathe in the chill river; breakfast on beans and biscuit; do various bits of business; lunch on biscuit and beans, walk about, talk, bath again, sup on beans, biscuit and tinned beef; write letters and journal; have *yaqona* and talk to the natives until we go to bed, or rather to sleep on our mats . . .'

'I wish I could give you some idea of the intense picturesqueness of the curious events of this last month,' Gordon wrote to Rachael's brother. 'The Christian army was encamped round Bukatia, a very strong place – a vast mass of rock rising . . . above the river and the plain. This town has never been taken, and was regarded as impregnable by the cannibals. The oracles of their gods are shouted aloud by the priests speaking as in the god's name, and this night an oracle was declared. The moon shone on the white river mists, and threw the great black shadow of the rock far over the plain. Out of the stillness, from the very top of the rock, rang out the hoarse cry of the priest, audible nearly a mile off, "Fire is unknown to my house in Bukatia." With one accord the whole beleaguering host shouted out in slow and measured tones the reply, "Wait until tomorrow!" And the next day Bukatia was taken and the devil-temple burnt.'

The action lasted no more than four months. Afterwards, according to Gordon, twenty-six rebels were put to death; the rest – around 120 – had their sentences commuted to up to five years' imprisonment with hard labour. Only someone with Gordon's ego and determination to control all would have taken such a risk. He might have saved the Colonial Office money – the total cost of feeding and clothing his forces was just over £32 – but that was not the point. Carnarvon tempered his remarks to him in his letter of 14 September. 'I miss all reference to Major Pratt and his soldiers, and I fear that in this you incurred a certain risk had things gone less well . . .' In fact he was very cross indeed. Not only had Gordon apparently passed over the British officer in command, but failure would have made it essential to bring in the army – a course that would have changed Fiji's future for ever.

The uprising in Viti Levu in 1876 was Fiji's last large-scale rebellion. Gordon was a hero. The white settlers were relieved; even the normally caustic *Fiji Times* applauded him. He returned to Government House on 23 May.

Rachael had used her time well while he was away. *Lali* now beat on the *rara* beside the house, and Fijian soldiers paraded in military lines, while she had created an English capsule in which to live, her life centred around the children, who were thriving: learning to swim, running a bit wild with the Abbeys' two boys, speaking Fijian.

It had been Maudslay who had helped her arrange the house when the alterations had finally been finished. Rachael, like Gordon and all his young staff, was captivated by Fijian craft and design. Especially she found their mats, 'some of them very fine and soft', beautiful, and much cooler than sheets. She used them for everything: floors, ceilings, bedding, table covers. The high reed walls of the dining room – fifty feet long – had been white-washed. Here she hung a border of twelve huge *yaqona* bowls, and over 200 'clubs, spears, bowls, arrows, axes, paddles etc.', hung in artistic patterns.

By contrast, the drawing room had dark wood walls hung with whales' teeth and pottery. 'The effect is excellent, and so very unEnglish when well lighted', while her bedroom was decorated with baskets hung up on panels of red *tapa*. 'Even the children have their nursery walls hung with little clubs and paddles, and tiny *yaqona* bowls, fans and whales teeth,' she told Madeleine.

'The house now moves like a clock,' Eka recorded. A Hindu cook and two valets had arrived, while Rachael's Fijian footmen now glided noise-lessly through the house wearing livery she had designed: scarlet *sulus* and white short-sleeved shirts trimmed with crimson. Around their necks each wore a large white boar's tooth. 'William and Moses are so handsome and graceful that it is a pleasure to watch them, especially William, who is beau-tiful! Their waiting is quite perfect . . . they spend hours over their hair, combing, washing, liming it, tying it up in *tappa* – . . . they are exceedingly vain . . .' When they had guests to dinner, 'the Governor and staff all wear, of course, proper evening dress, Captain Knollys uniform,' but when they were on their own, dress was relaxed – white shirts, trousers and coloured sashes. There was English food for dinner, fresh fruit and vegetables from the garden – 'sucking-pig, roast turkey, rice-pudding and peaches, new potatoes, mashed turnip and salad, pineapple and bananas'.

Gordon returned to his routine of dispatches and estimates to London, liaising with his men out in the field: Knollys, Carew, Le Hunte and Baron von Hügel, whom he had now appointed to serve as magistrates on the islands. He was setting up his new 'Native Regulation Board' to make laws; drafting labour ordinances for the colony. For the Colonial Office the con-cept of Fijian law and councils had been 'rather a large pill' to swallow. They had done so 'bravely in order to give you the chance you desire of proving that you can govern the natives instead of killing them off,' Under-Secretary of State Herbert wrote to Gordon in June 1876.

The legal challenge to Gordon's right – sitting in council on behalf of the Crown – to settle land disputes had reached London. Colonial Office lawyers upheld the challenge to his authority. Any issues over land had to be settled in a court of law. Gordon knew that the Fijians could not possibly conduct their own cases, much less pay for counsel. Their cases would have to be fought by the Crown on their behalf: setting up the government against the Europeans.

'I am not given to screaming hysterics, but, I give you clear, deliberate, and emphatic warning that the course now proposed must at best entail an expenditure ... perfectly ruinous, and that it would almost certainly involve us in an unjust, calamitous, and costly war,' Gordon warned London. His fight to keep land claims out of the law courts would take another three years to win, and another six before the final report of the Lands Commission was delivered in 1882. At the end, the white planters were awarded half the acreage that they had originally claimed from the Fijians.

Meanwhile, the traders and planters hated Thurston and Gordon's new system of taxation: there was no longer any incentive for the Fijians to work on white-owned plantations, while profit on produce for export, they said, would be lost to pay for taxes. By the time their protests reached the floor of the House of Commons in London in 1878, the tax was producing such excellent revenues that the Colonial Office was unable to take the opposition seriously.

In December 1876, worried for Rachael and the children's health in the rains, the Gordons' trusted doctor, MacGregor, dispatched them to New Zealand for four months. During that time MacGregor's own young and beautiful wife died within twenty-four hours of dysentery, and young Walter Carew, Gordon's upright magistrate, took to drink. Gordon remained at Government House working on legislation and organization. 'What uphill work it all is,' he recorded in his diary on 18 February 1877, musing on how much happier he would have been 'had I contentedly sunk into being an obscure clergyman'.

Rachael found New Zealand, like Sydney, provincial and lonely. Returning to Fiji, by the following September she was increasingly out of sorts. Arthur was so absorbed in his work that there was no time to tell her what he was doing, or for him to realize 'what it is to me to be cut off from everything as I am', she wrote home. She found the situation of the house, gathered at the base of almost overhanging cliffs, increasingly oppressive. She rarely went near the unsavoury town of Levuka, and there was nowhere else to go. She could hardly write for the mosquito bites on her hands, and how she hated the heat. She possessed only one or two light sprigged cotton dresses.

'What I should *like* would be, everything clean twice a day, and nothing but white,' she told her sister Mary. Even so, what was the point? Everything got spoilt in the humidity. 'My beautiful new boots, which I have kept in an air tight tin, are quite hard.' She could never open a drawer without dozens of cockroaches running out. She had no privacy in her 'birdcage' of a house. Most of all, she longed for female companionship.

Eka didn't 'mind any amount of roughing – sleeping on mats and living on the roughest food, often only yams, and never any milk'. She was frequently away, intrepidly exploring the islands. The few colonial ladies Rachael did meet she found 'dressy, affected, [and] silly'. It was not until November 1877, after her return from New Zealand, that 'two ladies . . . the first we have had' came to dine at Government House.

Meanwhile, Rachael watched the Fijian women, tantalized. She particularly delighted in Cakobau's daughter, and the younger women that she met – one 'very tall and slim . . . has beautiful arms, hands, legs and feet, and such a fine carriage. They are my greatest interest here . . . one has a curious feeling of equality with ladies of *rank*, they are so different from the common people – such an undoubted aristocracy.' Yet she had given up learning Fijian: 'I see so little of them, for it is not considered the thing for me to go and see them in their houses,' and somehow she felt 'there is no lady here of sufficient importance for me to invite up'.

By December 1877 she was writing: 'I don't think we have ever had such a dull time as the last month or six weeks. Arthur and I and A.G. alone, nothing going on, every day the same. The Governor is so absorbed in work that he does not feel it, but Arthur and I are sometimes very tired of it, and grumble together.' By March the following year, Gordon was at last planning a visit to England on home leave. Longing for the change, Rachael found herself so excited the night before the mails were due that she could not sleep. By the time they were about to sail for England at the end of May 1878, she was beginning almost to 'dread . . . going among people again. After living so long shut up in this extreme seclusion, one feels so behindhand and out of anything that is going on.'

*

Rachael never returned to Fiji again. With Nevil almost ten and Jack seven, the children were of an age, so Gordon thought, when they should be in England to be educated. Rachael could not bear to leave them. By now almost fifty, Gordon too was desperately torn about returning to Fiji; he could envisage a happy life in Ascot with 'literary occupation, pleasant society, my books round me (dear books from which I have been nearly ten years parted . . .) and above all the sense of some permanent quiet', he told Gladstone. He began the first of many overtures to the Colonial Office to secure some kind of compromise appointment that would allow him to keep his family with him, while still governing Fiji.

As he sailed for the islands a year later, in the summer of 1879, he wrote to Gladstone with resignation: 'I quit my wife, my children, my comfortable house, my good library, my nice garden – to go and live among natives who don't know anything of one's work for them . . . and among whites who hate one for interfering with their "British Liberty" to do as they like – with the "blacks".' Nevertheless he no longer had the slightest doubt that he should return.

Thanks to Gordon, Fiji never became a European settler society. In October 1880, a key ordinance on land tenure was passed. Among other things, such as the retention of the Fijian language, it laid down in English law that the tenure of lands belonging to native Fijians, 'as derived from their ancestors, and evidenced by tradition and usage, shall be the legal tenure thereof . . . that native lands shall be inalienable to persons not being native Fijians'. Today in Fiji, over 80 per cent of land remains 'native' land, which can only be leased for twenty-one years. Gordon presided over other more controversial measures, such as the import of indentured labourers to work on white plantations, whose descendants today, some 40 per cent of the population, dominate business in the towns. But he had achieved what he set out to do. His system of taxation in kind produced far higher levels of income for the government than the Colonial Office could have conceived. It would not be until just before the First World War that cash became the accepted method of paying taxes.

At the end of Gordon's first year as governor, late in 1876, a vast gathering of chiefs from all over the islands took place over seventeen days at Vanu Levu: the first Fijian council, the *Bose*. After the formal preparation of *yaqona* Gordon made a speech, and then departed. The only Europeans allowed to be present were the Governor's Commissioner, who answered questions on government business, and his clerks, who took notes. The following year, the council stretched to twenty-five days. 'There was no longer the same passive waiting for suggestions which had been shown on previous occasions,' Gordon noted. 'Questions were freely put, and new subjects for discussion broached; for the first time the idea that the *Bose* had become a permanent institution seemed to be grasped.' For the chiefs, it was a place to meet one another, to ventilate grievances, settle disputes and make recommendations for the writing of new laws. By the time Gordon left Fiji, the role of three levels of councils – district, provincial, and the Great, or 'Chiefly Council' – the *Bose Vaka Turaga* – which still meets today, and installs the president of what is now a republic, had been fixed in law.

Cakobau was dying. Gordon still felt his work undone when, in 1880, he was promoted to be Governor of New Zealand, while also High Commissioner 'in and over' the islands of the Western Pacific. The post was a miserable and ineffectual compromise. While it meant he could be reunited with Rachael and his children in Christchurch, the role brought him no joy. He detested colonial society, and felt himself as the Governor of New Zealand 'a puppet – a leaden seal – the mere instrument of his Ministers'.

He never ceased to worry what would happen to Fiji after he had gone. A change of ministers at home, or, even more dangerous, a successor who did not have his instincts 'for understanding natives', or who could not see them as equals, would never succeed and would 'probably let the native system fall to pieces'.

Gordon was fortunate. His old friend, William des Voeux, who had fought for the rights of indentured labourers in British Guiana and served as administrator of St Lucia while Gordon governed Trinidad, had been brought in to govern Fiji while he had been on leave in 1878; now he would return as governor. In 1888 des Voeux was succeeded by Gordon's trusted Colonial Secretary, John Thurston, who would go on to govern Fiji until he died in February 1899.

Fiji had worked itself into Gordon's heart more closely than he could ever have imagined. He loved its light, its heat, 'the free unconventional dress . . . the plunge into the clear warm sea'; the trees he had planted, the house he had built, 'above all, the men who had served me so faithfully and well'. Three of them, building on what they had learned in Fiji, would go on to make outstanding contributions to the fields of anthropology and archaeology: Alfred Maudslay in Guatemala, where he uncovered and recorded the ruins of the Maya; Dr William MacGregor, who as the first

British administrator of Papua New Guinea collected more than 1,000 objects which he donated to the Anthropological Museum at the University of Aberdeen; and Anatole von Hügel, who, with the Gordons and Maudslay, gave collections of Fijian artefacts to Cambridge. There von Hügel became the first curator of the university's Museum of Archaeology and Anthropology.

Gordon left Fiji for the last time in June 1882, on a day of sheeting tropical rain, having been presented with the gift of an island by the great chief Ma'afu. He and the family returned to England, uncertain whether he would secure another appointment.

7 The washing of the spears

South Africa 1877–80

Dead was the horse, dead too, the mule, dead was the dog, dead was the monkey, dead were the wagons, dead were the tents, dead were the boxes, dead was everything, even to the very metals . . .

Birkhall, near Ballater, Aberdeenshire, 18 October 1876: in the mists and damp of the Scottish Highlands sixty-one-year-old Sir Bartle Frere was writing a letter. Straight-backed, grey-haired, he had the bright eye and bristled moustache of an ageing fox terrier.

Frere had spent a lifetime in India in service to the Crown. By now he had risen to an eminence almost beyond compare: the British oracle on all questions Eastern, his views on every aspect of the Empire were in constant demand. As commissioner of the remote province of Sind – in the south-east of today's Pakistan – during the famous Rebellion of 1857, Frere had won accolades as the virtual saviour of the British in western India. He went on to become their chief peacemaker, soothing the Europeans, placating Sikh communities, and with his wife, Catherine, by his side, taking the radical step of openly entertaining Indians in his own home. At the age of forty-seven he reached the pinnacle of the Indian civil service as governor of Bombay – only the viceroyalty eluded him. Since retiring to England nine years before, he had become a prominent member of the Indian Council in London. He and Lady Frere moved easily among the highest society; they were on the guest list for almost every banquet to meet visiting heads of state. Frere was a member of the Royal Society, and had been president of the Royal Asiatic and Geographical Societies. In 1872 he had undertaken a successful mission to negotiate the end of the slave trade with the Sultan of Zanzibar, and masterminded a magnificent trip for the Prince of Wales to India, from which he had only just returned that spring. For this the House of Commons had passed a vote of £60,000 for the personal expenses of the Prince and his suite. When Frere heard about it, he went back to argue for, and get, an increase to £100,000 – a staggering £6,600,000 today – in order to pay for gifts.

Now Lord Carnarvon, Secretary of State for the Colonies, was writing to him on 'a very important and critical matter' to ask for his services again. A strong hand, or more, a statesman, was required for an extremely delicate task in South Africa: nothing less than the creation of a confederation of the Cape Colony with Natal, and the new diamond-rich territory based on the burgeoning town of Kimberley, in a remote region called Griqualand West. At the same time, the government wanted to draw the Boers of the Orange Free State and the Transvaal into some kind of working agreement with the British Crown.

The proposal made perfect sense to Frere. He was someone who saw the big picture: the interlocking strategic interests of Empire, the lines that stretched from Afghanistan to the north of India, through to the Cape of Good Hope. He wanted it ordered, structured. Forming a tidy confederation of states to govern themselves, out of a set of rather messy colonies in South Africa, made perfect sense to him. Steeped in years of praise and flattery and every possible comfort, Frere's response to Lord Carnarvon was unctuous.

'Your letter found me here enjoying change & rest, in a charming house which the Prince of Wales has most kindly lent us, for the autumn; but quite away from all sources of information regarding the Cape of Good Hope,' he told him. 'I should not have cared for the ordinary current duties of Governor of the Cape – but a *special* duty I should look upon in a different light.' The scheme was masterly, of imperial importance.

But he would not complete his ten years at the India Office until the following spring, when he could begin to draw a pension of £500, 'which I could not feel justified in forfeiting'. There were mentions of his forty-two years of service, the 'very heavy' expenses of governing the Cape and not wanting to 'jeopardise the dignity of these'; he didn't want to go without his family, 'nor would it do for me – entrusted with such a charge – to be weighing . . . the cost of a horse or a guest more or less. . .' Two months later, Carnarvon prevailed on the House of Commons to vote Frere an extra £2,000 a year – bringing his salary to the unprecedented level for such a minor colony of £10,000.

Beyond being governor of the Cape, Frere was to be high commissioner and commander-in-chief 'more actively than customary' for all South Africa. If he succeeded in his mission to achieve confederation, he was led to understand, he would receive a peerage and stay on for a year or two in his new dominion as governor-general. It was a grand bargain, the nearest equivalent to becoming Viceroy of India Frere was likely to get.

On 6 March 1877, a fine day in early spring, two days before he was due to sail, the Queen summoned him to dine at Windsor. She was fond of him. They were of an age – she was about to be fifty-eight; the triumphs of his career had often crossed her desk and he flattered her with the importance of her forthcoming installation as Empress of India. It was he who had managed to keep the Prince of Wales in check during his triumphant tour round India. Bertie had so taken to him that he had been eager to honour him even before they sailed; Victoria had elevated his knighthood to a baronetcy less than a year before; last October there had been considerable to and fro between Balmoral and Birkhall: the Queen had come to tea with the Freres, and they had dined at the castle.

Now, the Queen recorded in her diary, Frere 'is to try & set matters right at the Cape & his conciliatory disposition, great experience & knowledge of native character & wild races, as well as his prudence, are calculated to do great good. He said L[ad]y Frere felt very much leaving England again after above 20 years in India & 12 journies [sic] there & back.'

Sir Henry Ponsonby, the Queen's private secretary, was less beguiled. Frere was old, and rather tedious. On his return from his mission to Zanzibar, he had found him interesting, but 'very long & rather twaddling', while whenever the press corps on the Prince's India tour complained of the places given to them, Frere, 'a dear old patapouf ... only made matters worse'. As for Lady Frere, 'said to be a superior person', Ponsonby told his wife, while the Freres were staying near Balmoral the previous autumn, 'she asked me more questions than I could answer all dinner'.

Bartle – originally a diminutive of Bartholomew – and Catherine Frere had been married for nearly thirty-three years. They had met in the heat and glamour of Bombay in 1842. Bartle came from steady Suffolk stock, a family whose forebears had come over with William the Conqueror. The Freres were a family of steadfast Englishness, the backbone of the nation, a long line of farmers, barristers, solicitors, vicars and the occasional army or navy officer. Bartle's father had owned an ironworks near Bath. In 1832, at the age of seventeen, he had been sent to Haileybury – where a rather Byronic portrait of him in his youth still hangs in a boarding house named after him today – to train for entry into the East India Company. He passed out, top of his year, and entered the Bombay civil service two years later.

Within a year, Bartle was attracting the attention of his superiors. Rapidly fluent in the languages and customs of almost every province in the

Bombay presidency, he was described by the Governor in 1835 as 'an orna-ment to the service'. He was practical; his views were 'at once correct and enlightened'. When, seven years later, the new Governor, Sir George Arthur, lost his private secretary to sunstroke on the voyage to Bombay, there was no person in the whole service, he was advised, 'who could be consulted . . . with more advantage or confidence', than Bartle Frere. 'He is so strictly conscientious and honourable.'

By then Frere was twenty-seven, six feet tall, brown-eyed and hand-some, a champion marksman and a talented sportsman who had once shot a tiger between the eyes when it leapt on to the head of the elephant he was riding. He was discreet, gentle and quiet, with a talent for disarming hostil-ity and a keen sense of the ridiculous. Sir George and his wife Elizabeth swept him up into their household, with its rounds of public breakfasts, dinners and balls.

Catherine was twenty-two, the Arthurs' second daughter. Her parents had met when Sir George was serving as an army officer in Jamaica. There were eight years in British Honduras – today's Belize; twelve years as gov-ernor of the penal colony of Van Diemen's Land; four years of Upper Canada. Catherine had grown up with her four sisters and six brothers trav-elling the world, in a household dominated by the ideas of her father, a strongly Calvinist-evangelical Anglican possessed of a strong sense of jus-tice, and where issues were openly debated.

She was no beauty. Her face was large and long, her eyes too small, her nose too big, her forehead narrow, her dark hair agonizingly straight. But Catherine was a determined girl: energetic, intelligent, and charming. Her mother had trained her to be a practised and easy hostess; she often helped her father with his private correspondence. Frere probably did not stand a chance. They were married two years later, on 10 October 1844, on the eve of Bartle's first home leave since coming to India, ten years before. Three weeks later they sailed for Europe – taking one of Kate's younger sisters with them, stopping in Malta to stay with Frere's elderly uncle, John Hookham Frere, a former under-secretary for foreign affairs, literary and erudite, then slowly making their way through Italy, while Frere sketched and painted, and through France by carriage, by which time Kate was preg-nant with their first daughter, May.

'My Katie', Frere called her. After two years' leave – Frere had suffered from possible hepatitis – they returned to India where he was appointed resident at Sattara at Bijapur in the central Indian Deccan. Every kind of dispute crossed his desk: charges of murder and robbery, petitions of wrongdoing, proposals for the distribution of New Orleans cotton seed, the introduction of a new breed of sheep; plans for irrigation, sanitation, the prevention of cholera – and the preservation of ancient buildings and the library at Bijapur. Kate never left her husband to spend the monsoon season in the hills, as other English women did. She knew every aspect of his affairs. They were young, charming, glamorous and inseparable.

'I noticed also his lover-like devotion to his young wife,' wrote a friend at Sattara. She was 'truly . . . [his] coadjutor in his public and social duties'. The Freres' days were spent riding early in the morning, followed by tea and breakfast over two-day-old Bombay papers, giving picnics, frequent dinner parties and the occasional ball. They introduced evening receptions at the Residency for the Raja and his court, where Indian gentry mixed with the small European community. In 1851, at the remarkably young age of thirty-five, Frere was promoted to become Commissioner of Sind, the hottest province of India, consisting of little more than the delta of the Indus River and deserts either side: damp, flat and backward, with not a mile of metalled road. It was an unenviable appointment, with a decaying government house in Karachi. There, their second and third daughters, Catherine ('Katey') and Georgina, were born. All through the 'cold weather' – when at times the temperature in his tent might read 102 degrees – he travelled constantly, Kate and the three small children often with him, travelling in carriages, tonjons or palkees; camping at night on the ground. The Freres loved everything about India: its light, the air, the plants, its peoples.

Pregnant again in the summer of 1854, and with her father in ill-health, Kate returned to England with the children. There, their son Bartle was born in the autumn. Like countless British mothers of young children, she would not return to India for another eight years. Frere wrote to each child in turn once a week, long letters about what he was doing, full of sketches and Indian myths and fairy tales. In 1856 he managed one short leave with his family, taking a lease on Wressil Lodge, a capacious and stylish gabled villa in Wimbledon, and bringing Kate's two unmarried sisters to live with her and the children, before returning to Sind on 18 May 1857, six days after the first sepoys revolted at Meerut, on the eve of the fall of Delhi and the outbreak of the Indian Rebellion.

Five years later, knighted for his role in saving the British government in western India, Sir Bartle was sworn in as Governor of Bombay, and Kate and the family returned to India. His activities were the heartbeat of their lives: the family ate, breathed and slept politics and issues of welfare. Their eldest daughter, May, now eighteen, visited women in the *zenana*, and accompanied Sir Bartle on a three-month official tour, her Indian *ayah* her only female company. May listened to the myths and fairy stories she told of her childhood, and began painstakingly to reproduce them in English. Back in Bombay, her younger sister Catherine illustrated them. *Old Deccan Days* was published in 1868, to immediate acclaim and enduring impact. Meanwhile, Frere cleared land for public buildings designed by Sir Gilbert Scott, and founded many of the city's institutions, including the university, while his wife championed education for women. He built railways, improved Bombay harbour, promoted local councils, and did all he could to enlist the goodwill of the Indian population for the crown of Queen Victoria.

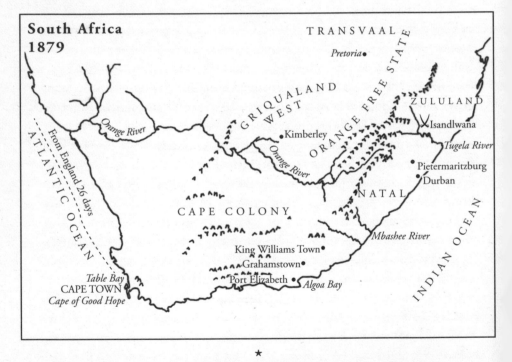

*

Arriving in Cape Town was an adjustment. From the sea the landfall looked glorious: the coastline beautifully cultivated, waterfalls tumbling into the sea, while the flat top of Table Mountain rose stupendously above the town – a picturesque, if motley collection of flat-roofed, pastel-coloured houses. In the distance, the outline of the Hottentot Mountains ranged, so jagged they hardly looked real. The waterfront was dominated by a castle built by the Dutch, but the harbour was unfinished and unkempt, and the docks far too small for large vessels. The Freres and their four daughters – sadly, their twenty-three-year-old son Bartle was serving with his regiment in Gibraltar – together with their suite, landed on 31 March 1877 in all the state that could be mustered. They were greeted by the Prime Minister, Mr Molteno, and his ministers with carriages and flags, well apart from the chaotic foreshore with its mêlée of hansom cabs and Malay drivers. In perfect summer weather they drove in slow cavalcade along a dusty road thronged with the curious to Government House, where the outgoing Governor, Sir Henry Barkly, greeted them at the door. People crowded into the stateroom, where Frere was duly sworn in.

It was two days after his sixty-second birthday. His hair was thinned and white but he was still tall and lean, his eye keen, his features sharp, his moustache brisk. His capacity for the scathing rebuke, developed during his sojourn in Sind during the terrors of the Indian Rebellion, was by now refined.

Lady Frere was fifty-seven. Over the years she had seemed to shrink. Her hair was grey, her shoulders stooped, but her energies, political acumen and charm remained formidable. Her daughters, nourished for years in a Wimbledon household dominated by their mother and her sisters, presented a redoubtable phalanx. Sophisticated, clever, travelled and serious, they had all been presented to the Queen at court, and the two eldest, May and Catherine, had been trained to serve – like Lady Frere herself – as private secretaries to Sir Bartle. By now May, dark-haired and handsome, was thirty-two. Her book of Indian folk tales had been translated into many languages; she corresponded with Florence Nightingale, and was in the habit of writing long letters to the Queen's private secretary, Henry Ponsonby. Catherine, twenty-nine, and Georgina, twenty-seven, were both accomplished artists. Only Eliza, known as Lily, who was twenty-one, still retained real hopes of a suitor; but she was very plain.

The splendid oaks around Government House, opposite the museum and the public gardens, were one of the sights of Cape Town. But the house could hardly have been in greater contrast to the glittering splendour of the family's past residence in Bombay, with its crystal chandeliers, long shaded verandahs and gliding liveried servants. Built by the Dutch in days when 'His Honour, the Governor in Chief, liked to sit with his Councillors in the "stoop" . . . only separated from the road by a row of oak trees', Frere told the Queen, it was large, rambling, old-fashioned and sorely weatherbeaten, 'hardly adapted to modern times or wants – & so bare inside, that the sole picture on the walls is an engraving of the Duke of Edinburgh, as a boy in sailor costume . . .'

'It is still Summer here, & about as warm as summer in Italy; but we are promised a bracing autumn in a few weeks,' Frere wrote. His hand was large and open: relaxed. Table Mountain was magnificent, the vegetation, even after a very dry summer, was beautiful, while the skies, 'by day or night, are finer than Sicily'.

With a population of no more than 30,000, Cape Town was small. The streets were wide, dusty and unpaved, and the footpaths on either side so taken up as Dutch *stoeps* to the houses that white-skinned pedestrians were often forced to walk in the roadway. 'Then there is the Hottentot admixture, a sprinkling of Guinea-coast negro, and a small but no doubt increasing Kafir element. The gentry no doubt are white and speak English,' wrote Anthony Trollope, who was one of the Freres' first guests at Government House a few weeks later. 'But they are not the population. Everything . . . is done by coloured persons of various races.' The workers were Malays, descendants of slaves introduced by the Dutch from Java.

Frere thought Cape Town thoroughly unhealthy. Everything about it was 'sleepy and slipshod', while the people, 'of all ranks . . . [were] singularly simple & quiet – very slow to change old habits & . . . very mistrustful of English officials,' he told Carnarvon.

The Cape was not an easy assignment. A British force had first landed in the early seventeenth century. But it was the Dutch East India Company that had settled Table Bay in 1652. During the wars with Napoleon, when Holland became a province of the French, it had been occupied by the British. They briefly conceded its return to the Dutch between 1803 and 1806 – but this toehold on the southern tip of Africa where the South Atlantic flows into the Indian Ocean was too important to the shipping routes to India and Australia to be relinquished. Besides, it was a fabulous land. In the days when Victoria first came to the throne, lions still roamed. Vast herds of game covered the veldt to the north. The climate was superb, the scenery stupendous, the distances immense, and the land so rich and fertile that it was as if Eden had at last been found on earth. From London's point of view the Cape was a white man's colony, one of the big four, along with Canada, Australia and New Zealand, to be settled by regular inputs of British settlers, funded by state emigration. In 1820, when parliament first voted a sum for the settlement of colonists, more than 90,000 people applied.

But the Dutch, who had been there for almost 200 years, were prickly and intransigent. They resented the extinction of their language from official matters in 1827; they disliked the ordinances that gave equality with the whites before the law to the blacks. 'What can be worse than this? If I give a *klopje* (cuff) to a native, he immediately runs off to a magistrate and complains, and I am sent for from the middle of my harvest work, perhaps, and am obliged to ride 20 or 30 hours to answer the complaint. And I come away leaving £5 as a fine.' The first of the Boers gathered their families and flocks, loaded their wagons, spanned their oxen and trekked away towards the virgin veldt of the eastern Cape.

When the British outlawed slavery in the colony in 1834, more Dutch decided to leave the Cape. As many as 15,000 Boer *voortrekkers* – pioneers – embarked on what became known as the Great Trek: hundreds of families and their servants, wagons, oxen and herds moved hundreds of miles to the north, over the Orange River and on, into the high veldt of the Transvaal. Meanwhile, a series of 'Kaffir wars' – eight by the time Frere arrived – expanded British control east into the province they called Natal. Then in 1867, ten years before Frere arrived, diamonds were discovered in Griqualand West, near today's Kimberley. A treaty was rapidly concluded with the Griqua to secure such valuable territory for Britain.

Governors posted to the Cape Colony had a way of falling foul of London. No fewer than three had been censured and dismissed in the past forty years over attempts to restrain violence between the Boers and the black Africans, while the threat of a 'great native war' had coloured dispatches for years. Frere's job of building a confederation was to prove an impossible task.

'Every available minute has been given to talking to Sir Henry Barkly & to the inevitable labours of settling down a large party,' Frere told Carnarvon four days after landing. John Molteno, the Cape's first prime minister, elected five years before, was sixty-three years old, a big-bearded Anglo-Italian who had lived at the Cape since the age of seventeen. His reputation for sagacity, Frere told Carnarvon, was totally deserved. Their early talks suggested that there was nothing more the government of the Cape desired than confederation – the only questions were on the process and its form.

Frere was therefore taken aback a fortnight after he arrived when the editor of the *Cape Times* bounded up the steps of Government House with a cable announcing that Sir Theophilus Shepstone, a special commissioner whom Carnarvon had dispatched months earlier to hold talks with the

Boer leaders in the Transvaal, had unilaterally issued a proclamation annexing the province. The place was so riven by faction and unrest, Shepstone declared in a dispatch to the Colonial Office, 'nothing but annexation will or can save the state . . . nothing else can save South Africa.'

'Good heavens!' Frere declared. 'What will they say in England?'

In fact, from the instant Frere landed at Cape Town, he ceased to control events. The terms of his commission gave him no clear authority outside Cape Colony beyond vague duties of supervision. His ministers at the Cape, duly elected, were happily running their own colony. The notion of confederation was something they imagined they would agree to, once it had been organized by London. Molteno told him the affairs of the Transvaal had nothing to do with them.

Frere, so cool, so confident of his authority and his ability to persuade, was slightly baffled. Catherine stood by his right hand, an irresistible force of reason, deftly influential. Apart from her and his two eldest daughters, Frere had a nice young private secretary, William Littleton, the son of an unremarkable MP, Lord Hatherton, and an energetic, good-humoured ADC, thirty-year-old Henry Hallam Parr, who far preferred being outdoors on horseback to being anywhere near a desk. He had none of his old colleagues, no support structure like the Indian civil service, or well-drilled regiments of the army on which to call.

Beyond Cape Town a great gulf of country opened out, most of it virgin land, its only tracks rough-hewn by the great ox-wagons of the Boers, over which weekly mail carts trundled for hundreds of miles. Communication, 'as of everything else' in this country, Frere told Ponsonby, was painfully slow. It took six to nine weeks for an exchange of letters with London; the telegram with Shepstone's news from the Transvaal had taken four days to arrive; his official documents another eighteen. Sir Henry Bulwer, the Governor of Natal, was unsure of Frere's role and unwilling to communicate; Frere found he was having to pick up information about the place from the newspapers, while it was soon clear to him that Shepstone's new administration in the Transvaal was in financial disarray, and frozen by bitter argument with the Boers. It was all exactly the opposite of what he had been used to in India, where the lines of command were clear, and 'half a sheet of paper' was enough to get things moving.

Some of the atmosphere in Government House that season is revealed in the memoirs of a Captain Charles Warren, who emerged from the bush after almost a year defining the boundary between Griqualand West and the Orange Free State. Fresh-faced, dark-haired and handsome, he was thirty-seven years old, a Royal Engineer who had previously spent three years surveying in Palestine, excavating Jerusalem, and publishing his findings in three celebrated books. His passage home was booked for the next day when, longing to see his wife and four children in England, he stopped briefly to call on the new Governor of the Cape. Frere knew a good man when he saw one. He wasted no time in asking Warren to stay on in South Africa, to arbitrate between the farmers settling around Kimberley, as a special commissioner on the land question. Warren politely but firmly declined. Frere told him it was his duty, and asked him to think it over.

'I was fully intending to go to England,' a desolate Warren wrote to his wife the next day. But he made the mistake of also stopping to see Lady Frere. He was Sir Bartle's first selection; she told him there was no one else so suitable for the work. 'I found that all my plans must be given up and I must sacrifice myself for the good of the State. She pointed out so clearly what I ought to do and settled it all so firmly that I felt I must give in.' By the time he called next day, Sir Bartle 'had already by that mail written to Lord Carnarvon asking for my services, [he] complimented me highly . . . and said that what they wanted for this work on the land question was "a man with backbone"'.

For the next two months Warren found himself virtually living at Government House. 'Lady Frere finds me plenty to do.' He had to stop her copying out his journal for Sir Bartle, and do it himself. Days went by: lunching with the Bishop and his sister, standing on a chair mending a gas lamp as guests arrived for dinner, giving a lecture on Palestine for the Scientific Society Sir Bartle was reviving, looking into the history of South Africa for the South African Exhibition the Frere daughters were mounting, driving out with Lady Frere and a party to Simonstown, 'the habitat of the navy'.

'We all went for a walk to see a fort which is being built here to protect the dockyard; it is being put up in a hurry. We seem always to be doing things in a hurry. It has suddenly been discovered that both Simons Bay and Table Bay are defenceless . . . they could, in the absence of our fleet, walk off with our Governor-General and the Admiral from Capetown and Simons Bay, and burn all our coal. It is so odd that it should be left to Sir Bartle Frere to find this all out.'

Meanwhile, he wrote: 'there are so many rumours of native risings in various directions that it gives a spice of excitement to our doings even if it be all untrue'. There was nothing explicit, 'only hints from old stagers, who know the natives'. It was Lady Frere who told Warren to be sure to send them word 'as to what I see as I go', when he finally departed for his new assignment six weeks later.

Early in December, as he eagerly neared the end of his agreed stay, he wrote to his wife, 'I have had an ominous letter from Lady Frere. She says that she is very anxious to know what I shall decide on, and is fully sure what it is, for that knowing the difficult work Sir Bartle Frere has had . . . she knows that his great desire will be to keep all the good and able men he can!' Warren would stay on in South Africa for another year.

In August Frere left Cape Town to visit Shepstone in Pretoria and test the views of the Boers – 'by no means bad fellows, but incredibly obstinate' – on the annexation of the Transvaal himself. On the way he would take in the eastern province of the Cape and either Natal or the diamond fields of Kimberley on the way back. It was a dauntingly arduous journey of over 1,000 miles, weeks of rough travelling by ox and cart.

On the first leg of his journey he sailed east for Port Elizabeth, settled by the first English colonists in 1820. He landed in an atmosphere thick with alarm and rumour. A drunken brawl in the Natal town of Butterworth, between rival Xhosa tribesmen, the Gcalekas, and a group of Fingoes, today the Mfengu – former 'helots' of the Xhosa, as Frere described them, loyal to the British – had escalated into raids on cattle. 'Sir Bartle says in his Telegram that he hopes it will prove only a fight between two tribes but as it is necessary to be prepared . . . he has placed three companies of the 88th Rgt . . . in readiness to leave for the Frontier,' Lady Frere reported to Lord Carnarvon. As Frere's private secretaries, Littleton and Parr, were travelling with him, Catherine was now taking care of all official administration at Government House in Cape Town, sending all cables and dispatches from her husband on to London.

Meanwhile Frere rode east, captivated by the landscape, forests 'in which Elephants still roam & where we did not see a trace of a white man', and on into countryside 'so favoured by nature . . . it is a paradise for poor sober working men'. On 30 August he reached Grahamstown. Its streets were too wide and 'the houses too far apart for it to be an English cathedral town . . . the place did not look as if it could ever be the capital of South Africa'.

From there he emerged into the heat and dust of the open road beyond, the historic scene of many bloody skirmishes.

Fighting was spreading. Frere decided to travel east to meet Kreli, the great chief of the Xhosa Gcalekas, in the town of Butterworth for talks. But Kreli eluded him. On the day Frere retreated to the border town of King Williams Town, 'swarms of many thousand' Gcalekas, led by a 'witch-doctoress' dressed in an old artilleryman's greatcoat who promised them invincibility, and armed with muzzle loaders and assegais, attacked a police post. Only superior weapons – Snider carbines, a couple of seven-pounders and some rockets – prevented Kreli's army from fatally closing in on the police.

Frere and his suite took refuge in the barracks in King Williams Town, a snug, pretty, tree-lined place, now full of families fleeing attacks on their homesteads. Every able-bodied man in the region had been drafted in to drill on the parade ground. On 3 October Frere apologized to Carnarvon for being unable to do more than send a 'very rambling' dispatch, 'written amid greater interruptions than I recollect since the Mutiny days in India . . . pressing calls to meet immediate wants, telegrams, interviews with deputations indignant, loyal, panic-stricken, fire-eating . . .'

The Cape authorities were hopeless: 'Unless I had seen it myself I could not have believed in such a state of things,' Frere told Ponsonby. Here he was on British territory, murders and cattle raids an almost daily occurrence, pitched battles being fought, scores of lives being lost, all 'in the presence of large bodies of well-armed and mounted European police, who, according to custom, quietly looked on, and reported to Government asking for orders from Capetown while the Commandant of Police, the Civil Commissioner, and Colonel Glyn, commanding Her Majesty's troops [were] all absolutely prohibited by Colonial official jealousy from exchanging opinions or even news, and all obliged to apply for orders to Capetown, four or five days distant, by a post only three times a week'.

Frere took command. He implemented a daily council with two of his colonial ministers – Mr Merriman, the Commissioner for Crown Lands and Public Works, and Mr Brownlee, the Cape's Minister for Native Affairs – and the commanders of the police, the Civil Commissioner, and the army. He was at once jokingly disparaging of the blacks and unnerved by their savagery and unpredictability. The sheer numbers of hostile tribesmen wielding assegais was chilling. The country was paying for 'the smouldering discontents of many years past', and the tradition on both sides — black and what he called 'the Dutch Command system . . . by white men, on horseback, with rifles, instead of black men, on foot, with assegais' — of 'eating up' a weaker tribe, burning down its kraal, seizing cattle and slaughtering all but the younger women and children, who grew up as 'helots'. Frere told the Queen: it was the Indian Rebellion all over again. 'Either race dreading what the other would do.'

By the end of October, Frere reported that 700 Gcalekas, including twenty chiefs, had been killed, and more than 13,000 head of cattle captured. They had been driven eastward over the border, on today's Mbashe River. In late November Frere was making plans to continue his journey to the Transvaal when their bands were reported creeping back across unguarded river fords into British territory.

There was no means of reliable intelligence. Panic and confusion rose. The countryside was deserted as women and children fled their farms. In Cape Town, all the family were caught up. 'Even as far down as Algoa Bay,' Lady Frere informed Carnarvon, 'the ladies . . . had got into such terror that . . . they had determined should the Kaffirs get so far *they* would all rush in a body into the Sea!'

For all his experience in India, Frere had never been on a military front line before. From the windows of his office, stifling in the heat, layered in dust, he watched volunteer burghers, in slouch hats and corduroys, near-naked Fingoe auxiliaries, and the 90th Regiment in their red coats marching and parading. Beyond he had a clear view of the Amatolas — the mountain stronghold of the enemy, where he could see the smoke of shells and rockets rising from the hillside. By mid-December, the situation was serious. The Gcalekas had united forces with black Africans thought loyal to the British against the whites. On Christmas Day, a hotel on the main road to the coast up which 'every ounce of flour and every cartridge had to pass' was seized and burnt.

'We do not seem to have had much decisive news this week,' Frere's youngest daughter, Lily, told her aunt in London early in the new year of 1878. 'They are enrolling all the men they can for Service on the Frontier and if only the Farmers — great strong men accustomed to the Country, will come forward and be as stout in mind as they are in body! Papa, I am most thankful, keeps well tho' he is much overtaxed and worried by the obstinacy, self-conceit, rashness and want of balance, finesse, knowledge or training of the innumerable people and authorities of various kinds whom he has to endeavour to guide and make pull together along the dangerous and much beset path upon which the Colony is now entered. The want of organization and right men in the right places is dreadful.'

Frere's outward calm was glacial. For all his legendary accessibility, kindness, courtesy and tact, he had a will of iron. He was now in serious disagreement with his colonial ministers on the handling of the war. Molteno's ministers Merriman and Brownlee favoured a merciless assault on the Gcalekas. They resented the high-handed interference of Sir Bartle, his general, and his smart British regulars. Early in January, Prime Minister Molteno arrived in King Williams Town to back up his ministers and call the Governor home. He and Frere argued for three weeks.

'It suited the . . . Ministry . . . to get up a cry against "Imperial domination" & "Military despotism",' Frere told the Duke of Cambridge afterwards. 'The attempt however signally failed. Mr Molteno, the Prime Minister, tried to set up his colleague Mr Merriman, the Commissioner of Public Works, as a kind of Military Dictator – a clever but flighty young man, with scant common sense, & no knowledge whatever of military affairs.' Merriman had no staff, no departments, no officers – only an army of volunteers who were marching all over the country, cattle-lifting, shooting 'Kaffirs', and burning kraals. Frere could barely stifle his rage.

Furious, fulminating about cabals and conspiracies, Frere took Molteno at his word when he threatened to resign and sacked him. 'You may confidently contradict any statement that I have acted or wish to act unconstitutionally,' Frere immediately cabled Catherine in Cape Town on 3 February. 'This Ministerial crisis has been forced on me quite against my will.' He told the Duke of Cambridge: 'the Prime Minister told me, in so many words, that the General & his Regulars were not needed for Colonial defence & requested me to withdraw the General at once & to send on the reinforcements of H.M. Troops to some other part of the Empire! With rebellion spreading on all sides, & an internecine war between Kaffir & Colonist already begun, this conduct was so outrageous & almost insane, that I took the only alternative & dismissed the Ministry – a very extreme step, as I need not tell Your Royal Highness, in a Colony under Responsible Govt.'

A new commander-in-chief, General Thesiger, arrived from England to take command of the war in the eastern Cape. Thesiger was now aged fifty-one, a product of Eton and the Grenadier Guards, industrious, conscientious but unimaginative. He had seen service in the Indian Rebellion and served in Bombay at the time of Frere's presidency, a better administrator than commander in the field. In spite of this, by the end of June 1878 the great Xhosa chief Kreli had been killed, an amnesty had been proclaimed, and South Africa's 9th Cape Frontier war, as the history books now call it, had come to an end.

Meanwhile Frere packed his bags to return to Cape Town. As he did so he was handed a telegram from Lord Carnarvon. Carnarvon, sickened by the bloodshed and horrors of the Russo-Turkish war, had quit the Cabinet.

This news 'has, without any figure of speech, utterly taken the heart out of me', an exhausted Frere responded. 'I try to frame all kinds of theories by which you are again at the helm in the Colonial Office till South African confederation is carried, or at soonest till my share in the work is finished, for I feel my interests in the work, and my hopes of carrying it through sadly diminished'.

White-faced and weary, Frere returned to a rapturous homecoming in Cape Town. Catherine too was worn out. 'I do not think with the load of anxiety and care on her mind that in a less good climate than this Mother could have stood it,' Lily told her aunt. For the past seven months Catherine had stood in as his deputy, fielding all dispatches, cabling London on Frere's behalf, managing Government House, entertaining important visitors including the admiral of the French fleet and Anthony Trollope while they had been ludicrously short of men to invite to their parties. Now their beloved son Bartle, on whose behalf Frere had persistently lobbied the Duke of Cambridge, head of the army, for leave from his regiment in Gibraltar, had just landed in Cape Town. But there was little time for rejoicing.

Through all the months Frere was at King Williams Town, a stream of increasingly alarming dispatches had arrived from Theophilus Shepstone in the Transvaal. There were few other white men in authority in South Africa with Shepstone's knowledge of the customs and affairs of the Africans. Like Frere, he was now in his early sixties: white-haired, broad-browed, with a candid eye. The son of an early English missionary to the Xhosa, Shepstone had lived in Cape Colony since the age of three, brought up in a village, playing with the children in their kraals, picking up their slang. On his eighteenth birthday, he began work in Cape Town as a government interpreter, getting involved in various wars going on, and then settling in the eastern Cape, living with the Fingoe and the Xhosa as British resident. When the British took control of Natal in 1845, he was dispatched, first rather as a diplomat, then to be in charge of 'native' affairs. He was there for thirty years.

The black Africans called him Somtseu, 'father'. Shepstone secured them large territories on which white settlers could not encroach. He worked through the chiefs according to their customs, and created a black police force, whose loyal commanders were rewarded with cattle and women captured in battle. In spite of Shepstone's authority over the people, he had seen too many white killings for the fear of a black uprising to leave him. The slightest opposition was ruthlessly crushed.

It was Shepstone – on behalf of the Natal government – who had 'crowned' Cetewayo as King of the Zulus in 1873. Cetewayo had fought and killed his brother for the right to succeed their father. In return for his father, Somtseu's endorsement, he had promised to end the Zulu traditions of indiscriminate bloodshed: not to kill a man without a trial and not to molest the European missionaries in his land.

Cetewayo. His portrait filled the whole of the front page of the
Illustrated London News *on 22 February 1879*

Since that day Cetewayo had entered the stuff of South African legend: as a handsome, skilful and ruthless ruler. According to Zulu custom, a warrior could not marry until he had killed an enemy. In the summer of 1876 a great marriage feast was planned to mark the wedding of hundreds of women and girls to the warriors of two of Cetewayo's senior *impis* [regiments or armies] who had been kept celibate until they were forty. Women who refused to accept the elderly husbands allocated to them were killed on Cetewayo's orders and their corpses strewn on the highways as a warning to others. When their relations stole the bodies away to bury them, Cetewayo let his warriors loose. Their kraals were 'eaten up' – every man, woman and child was put to death. Sir Henry Bulwer, governor of Natal, delivered a protest to Cetewayo over the atrocities. His response was chilling.

'Did I ever tell Mr Shepstone I would not kill? . . . I do kill; but do not consider that I have done anything yet in the way of killing . . . I have not yet begun . . . it is the custom of our nation and I shall not depart from it. Why does the Governor of Natal speak to me about my laws? Do I go to Natal and dictate to him about his laws? . . . Go back and tell the English that I shall now act on my own account, and if they wish me to agree to their laws, I shall leave and become a wanderer; but . . . I shall not go without having acted. Go back and tell the white men this, and let them hear it well. The Governor of Natal and I are equal; he is the Governor of Natal, and I am Governor here.'

Now, in 1878, Cetewayo was a great and dreadful king, whose powers were said to be even greater than those of the great white Queen. Since his coronation, 60,000 Zulus had yet to take part in battle, to 'wash their spears' in blood and be promoted from the ranks. At every feast and gala Cetewayo's warriors danced in all their pomp of war: skins, feathers, shields; rifles, spears, and leather cartridge belts – now they had the guns to meet the white man on nearly equal terms. When, in early January, a bright star had appeared on a brilliant day near the moon at noon, it was said that the day was coming soon when all the white men would be driven into the sea.

Shepstone's takeover of the Transvaal had unsettled the Zulus. What was their friend and father Somtseu doing now as head of the Boers, the Zulu's hereditary enemies, who had stolen their land? When Shepstone went to meet Cetewayo's *indunas* to open negotiations on the border where seventy-five Boer families had set up farms the previous October, he was dismayed and puzzled to find them surly and aggressive.

To Frere the threat was obvious. Missionaries had been to see him, reporting that Cetewayo was murdering their converts and had taken to torture – ordering one man's lips and another's legs and arms to be cut off. In May, a Reverend Filter begged for protection for his tiny 'colony' of 160 souls at Luneberg in the Transvaal from the Zulus who promised to 'come with the next full moon and build their kraals'. For months magistrates in places hundreds of miles apart had been reporting unease among the Africans, and behind every incident – a number of which occurred on the same day – was the same intelligence: 'Zulus had been found concealed in the neighbourhood – they were trading; they had come to buy skins, or hunting dogs, etc etc; they did not know the white men did not like natives travelling about their country without leave; they were sorry if they had done wrong, and would go back to Zulu Land if they might . . .' And then some trouble would break out. Putting all these reports together with the fighting Frere had seen with Kreli, the signs were obvious. It was just like the beginning of the Indian Rebellion – nothing less, Frere warned the Colonial Office than 'a general and simultaneous rising of Kaffirdom against white civilization'.

In the chill of the July winter, two sons of an important Zulu chief led 100 men across the Tugela River into Natal. Two of their women had taken refuge in a police station for protection. Spears in hand, they forced them out and back across the river. There they murdered them. The Governor of Natal, Sir Henry Bulwer, demanded that the perpetrators be surrendered for trial in Natal. Cetewayo excused the crime as a boyish prank, and offered £50 in compensation. Then, six weeks later, the threatened raids took place near the Reverend Filter's settlement at Luneberg. Frere dispatched an immediate request for troops from London.

'Urgent summonses come from Natal, the Transvaal, & the Diamond Fields,' Frere told the Queen on 17 September. Everywhere the Africans seemed restive: insolent, cattle-stealing and violent, while the white men in charge were prepared to let matters drift. No one was prepared to take responsibility, let alone recommend a course of action. His presence was essential to the prospects of peace. The Colonial Office directed him to Pietermaritzburg, the capital of Natal – 1,000 miles from Cape Town and seventy miles from Cetewayo's borders. He left the next day.

Two weeks later he was housed with the Governor, Sir Henry Bulwer, in the pretty English villa which passed for Government House in the small, hot, country town of Pietermaritzburg. Frere settled into 'a very dreary life . . . grumbling at deficiencies I cannot supply & delays I am powerless to shorten,' he told the Prince of Wales. 'Some time must elapse before we get the country settled in peace, & I cannot tell you what hard work it is, in the meantime.' He found the same nightmarish difficulties he had had the year

before with the officials he met. The people of Natal didn't like the Boers or
care for the Cape Colony. Frere found 'every form of selfish and narrow-
minded difficulty'. No one in Natal wanted anything to do with the
Transvaal or imperial interests in South Africa: most serious of all, no one
could see the big picture, the looming threat of a racial war.

Nobody, Frere told Carnarvon's successor at the Colonial Office, Sir
Michael Hicks Beach, could be more hospitable than Sir Henry Bulwer. He
was frank, cordial, 'almost fanatically just and loyal'. But Bulwer had never
had anything to do with military affairs, 'and many things . . . burnt in to
one after years' dealing with natives in India have to be explained to him',
he said. Nor – like Frere – was Bulwer 'facile in altering opinions once
formed'. While the British of Natal had lived comfortably alongside the
Zulus for years – Zulu 'boys' acted as nursemaids to their children, government officials arranged supplies of rifles for them – they were outnumbered
more than twenty to one.

Now that the British had taken over the Transvaal, home of the Zulus'
long-standing enemy, the Boers, Bulwer and his officials were failing to see
how the situation had changed. How their weakness of petting the Zulus,
'as one might a tame wolf who only devoured one's neighbour's sheep', as
Frere put it, might have to come to an end. While Frere easily conceded
that if 'properly treated, the Natal Kaffir is the most light-hearted, thoughtless, easily managed of animal men', and 'the Zulus are in some respect
magnificent animals – & properly governed would be a very fine race', the
people he talked to seemed to have no idea that at the present moment 'the
Zulus are now quite out of hand'. It was as if they were all slumbering on
top of a volcano.

The heat at Pietermaritzburg intensified. Frere worked on Bulwer
relentlessly to persuade him of the danger. Meanwhile Cetewayo closed the
roads into Zululand. Armed gatherings of Zulus were reported at his 'Great
Place'. As Bulwer formulated his reply to Cetewayo on his derisory offer of
compensation for the abduction and murder of the two women, the final
terms of the land settlement with the Zulus on the boundaries of Transvaal
were drawn up. The commander of the British troops, General Thesiger –
who had now succeeded to his father's baronetcy to become Lord
Chelmsford – completed an inspection of the 200-mile frontier between
Natal and Zululand. At the end of October, Frere could scarcely contain
himself as he begged London to realize the threat from the man he was now
privately calling 'the demon king', Cetewayo: '. . . the continued preserva-

tion of peace, depends ... simply on the caprice of an ignorant and blood-thirsty despot, with a most overweening idea of his own importance and prowess, and an organised force of at least 40,000 armed men at his absolute command, ready and eager at any moment to execute, in their ancient fashion of extermination, whatever the caprice or anger of the despot may dictate.'

In London the Cabinet was facing wars on two fronts: in Afghanistan and with Russia outside Constantinople. On 10 November, Frere received the news that his request for reinforcements for war against Cetewayo had been turned down. He redoubled his arguments with the Secretary of State. At last, by the end of November, he had managed to bring Bulwer into agreement. Unaware that another cable from London was en route, reiterating the Cabinet's firm opposition to any war with the Zulus, Frere insisted to Hicks Beach on 8 December that the Zulus had to be settled 'into a position clearly subordinate to Her Majesty's Government'. The time had come to deal with them.

Delivering the ultimatum on the banks of the Tugela River, 11 December 1878

Early on the morning of 11 December a group of English envoys, including Theophilus Shepstone's son, John, waited beneath an awning stretched between two spreading trees on the Natal bank of the shallow stream that was the Tugela River as Cetewayo's delegates – thirteen of them, with forty or fifty followers – crossed from the Zulu side. Away to the south, the masts of tall ships broke the skyline; to the east, the scorched plains of

Zululand rolled away into the distance. The grasses crackled under foot. It was so hot that the military escort the British had brought with them had to be dismissed.

It took more than four hours to read out Frere's ultimatum to Cetewayo. The first part dealt with the disputed lands with the Transvaal – Frere awarded them to the Zulus in return for compensation to the farmers. For a moment the Zulu delegation seemed to demur, but they had gained more than they expected. After an hour's break, a second document was read. The young men who had stolen and murdered the two girls should be given up for trial in Natal, a fine of 100 head of cattle should be paid for intimidation of two British subjects, and another Zulu wanted for crimes in Natal should be delivered for trial. To these three demands were added two more: the Zulu army was to be disbanded and the laws restricting marriage abrogated. In addition, a British resident should be admitted to reside in Zululand and missionaries who had been expelled should be allowed to return.

Cetewayo was given twenty days to comply with the first three demands in the ultimatum, and thirty for the rest. No one knew how he would respond. On 1 January 1879 the first twenty days expired. There was no word from Cetewayo.

On 6 January 1879, Frere cabled Hicks Beach. 'Still no news on C's compliance with demands . . . all well as far as we have heard on the front. Active preparations for crossing at all points.' If there was no response from Cetewayo the plan was for three columns of British troops, nearly 18,000 men, to pass into Zululand at separate points along the Tugela River, and rendezvous near Cetewayo's *kraal*. The deadline to respond to Frere's ultimatum passed.

At daybreak on 11 January, the crossing of the Tugela into Zululand commenced. The mounted men picked their way through the shallows first, their hooves clattering on the stones. Frere's private secretary, Parr, was with the central column that crossed at a place called Rorke's Drift, on the Buffalo River, a tributary of the Tugela. There were over 1,700 troops – 922 Europeans and 840 black auxiliaries. 'As soon as the cavalry . . . were well across, and had crowned the ridge on the Zulu side, the remainder of the force followed and then the wagons.' It was weary work. The river was in spate. Many men waded through, the water rising over their shoulders. Each wagon, slow, ponderous and heavy, had to be brought down to the water's edge, the oxen out-spanned and driven across, then the wagon heaved by hand on to a pontoon. Leaving behind a small camp at Rorke's Drift, the column came to rest ten miles beyond the river in the shadow of a great rock rising from the plain, the place the Zulus called Isandlwana.

It was not long after six on the morning of the 24 January that Frere's secretary William Littleton brought a message to his bedside in Pietermaritzburg. Two men, quite incoherent, had arrived from the front, garbling news of a disaster. One was quite off his head. Someone – Frere himself? – demanded they be arrested for spreading false rumours. Washed and given breakfast, the two men revived. The Zulus had swept in like cavalry, they said, swarming over the hills like bees, thousands of them. The entire central column was surrounded, overwhelmed by two sweeping horns of an advancing *impi* rounding on the British from behind the rock of Isandlwana. Hardly a man was left alive.

It was a day or two later before the full scale of the losses became clear: twenty-seven officers of the regular army, twenty-two from the colonial forces; 775 non-commissioned officers and men. Two guns, 700 stands of arms and 90 to 100 wagons. More than a whole British regiment. According to Frere's notes at the time, only six men – one of them his young secretary Henry Parr – survived.

The losses took his breath away. These were the men with whom he had lived for six months in King Williams Town. All about him in Pietermaritzburg were families who had lost a husband or a son. Frere rode about the town on horseback, his face a mask of frozen calm, comforting those who had lost a loved one. On the evening of the massacre at Isandlwana, 104 men and thirty-five hospitalized comrades had fought off over 3,000 pursuing Zulus at the camp at Rorke's Drift. This battle, immortalized in the 1964 film *Zulu,* was cleverly exploited by Lord Chelmsford – and later, Prime Minister Disraeli in the House of Commons – to downplay the huge scale of the disaster at Isandlwana. But the valiant bravery of these few, mostly English, men gave the people of Natal no comfort. Demands for immediate reinforcements were hastily dispatched to Mauritius and London. Every redcoat in South Africa was ordered to the front. The air was full of the rumble of wagons laden with stores and ammunition and the crash of hammers as barricades went up. Workmen were sinking wells, while a group of central buildings was prepared as *laagers* for defence.

'South Africa has reached its crisis, and its old temporizing policy has gone for ever,' mourned Thomas Jenkinson, the canon of Pietermaritzburg.

Like countless other citizens he had been profoundly shocked by the brutality of Frere's ultimatum. Indeed, what had happened to Frere's legendary tact and art of calm persuasion, or to his principle – reiterated two months later in a letter to his daughter May – of always considering your neighbour as your brother, as someone 'whom you are bound to know, to consider & to help in every way'?

'Ketchawayo is said to have built a new kraal, and named it "Mayezekanye", ie, "Let him come, then",' Canon Jenkinson reported. By the beginning of April the roads of Natal were thick with wagons making for the front.

News of the disaster reached London on 11 February – two weeks after details of Frere's ultimatum were received at the Colonial Office. The loss of an entire British regiment in a remote corner of South Africa confounded the nation. On 30 November a cable from the Secretary of State reiterating the Cabinet's opposition to any war with the Zulus had been dispatched to Frere. The cable was telegraphed to Madeira, where it was put on board a steamer which took two weeks to reach Cape Town. There Lady Frere transcribed it into cipher and cabled it to Pietermaritzburg. By the time Frere received it, the ultimatum had been delivered – even if he had received it in time, would he have obeyed its contents?

There is an air of unreality in the pages of self-justification that Frere now penned to London: he alone seemed to realize 'the very serious damage . . . a Zulu *impi* might do, the virtual inevitability of a Zulu attack'. Now, instead of returning to Cape Town, in mid-March he set off at last to Pretoria in the Transvaal – to begin negotiations with the Boers to try to persuade them to accept the annexation of the Transvaal and join the fold of a British confederation of South Africa.

He travelled on horseback or in a 'spider' – a light covered wagon drawn by mules with a desk rigged up for him to write on, covering twenty or thirty miles a day. It was a month-long journey of exhausting proportions. 'You must not be anxious about Sir Bartle,' the acting administrator of the Transvaal, Colonel Lanyon, wrote to Lady Frere, 'for I feel certain that all will go right. All that is required is firmness & thank goodness we have a Sir Bartle Frere who has an iron hand with a velvet glove. He has certainly had a most anxious time of it, but he stands out like a great grand glacier above the plains of mediocrity, clear, cool, & immoveable.'

Frere met the Boers on a grassy plain in the midst of magnificent rolling country. The meeting was tense. 'I was glad of an opportunity of letting them know bullying would not do – & we got on very well afterwards,' he told his wife. He arrived in Pretoria in the middle of April to the news, broadcast throughout South Africa by a Reuters telegram, that he had been censured in the House of Commons for his actions over Cetewayo.

In Britain, a storm of abuse broke over Frere's head. He had allied himself with the vilest motives of South Africa's colonists – 'their fear and hate of a savage race . . . their desire for conquest and spoil'. Sir Michael Hicks Beach's prose as he wrote to Frere was masterly in its restraint. He had waited until he was in possession of all the facts and arguments that Frere had wished to place before Her Majesty's government; 'very careful consideration' had been given to all the circumstances, to all the opinions he had garnered from other 'able and experienced persons'. He had already previously observed that the terms which Frere had dictated to Cetewayo were such that he 'might not improbably refuse, even at the risk of war'. Frere had never consulted the government on them. Nor were they able to find 'that evidence of urgent necessity for immediate action which alone could justify you in taking . . . a course almost certain to result in a war, which, as I had previously impressed upon you, every effort should have been used to accept'.

Going to war without the sanction of the Cabinet was one of the worst crimes a governor could commit. But Frere's powers in South Africa had been exceptional; he was of great experience, ability and energy, and his job had been important and difficult. 'They have no desire to withdraw, in the present crisis of affairs, the confidence hitherto reposed in you,' Hicks Beach concluded. This was a bollocking, but worse was to come.

Frere returned to a hero's welcome at Cape Town. The station was covered in flags and bunting; the streets were lined with cheering crowds. Five days later, on Wednesday afternoon 11 June, a magnificent reception was held in an exhibition building in the Goede Hoop Gardens to welcome His Excellency home. The pillars were covered with red, white and blue and 'from pillar to pillar, from wall to wall, were ropes of evergreens, intermingled with bannerets of every variety of colour'. Facing the Governor and Lady Frere, above a balcony with the band, was the motto of the Frere family, 'Traditum ab antiques servare', and Sir Bartle's monogram. Behind His Excellency's seat was a curtain of flags and the slogan, 'Progress for South Africa!'

Just before half-past one, Sir Bartle, Lady Frere and their daughters arrived. The entire company rose to their feet, and the band struck up 'God Save the Queen'. Frere's speech made clear all that he had done. 'Throughout the whole of South Africa, a movement originating with the Zulu rulers had stirred to their hearts the whole of the native population, and they only looked and hoped for some revolution which should bring about the supremacy of the black races and the expulsion of the Europeans.' When native tribes came in contact with European populations, he went on, there had to be 'a distinct understanding' of whose ideas were to rule, whose principles people were to live under. Was the Crown or the assegai 'to be the future symbol of government in South Africa'? His audience was in no doubt. The cheers were long and loud.

This was Frere's final moment of glory in a career of mounting success that had lasted forty-five years. His fall from grace was swift, tinged, for him and his family, by an increasing air of unreality. He was completely unrepentant. The Zulu war had been forced upon them, would never have occurred had there been a little more foresight in the past. The disaster at Isandlwana had been caused by disobedience to orders. Days later he was informed that General Sir Garnet Wolseley, the legendary military fixer of his time, was being dispatched to take command of the army, and replace Frere as High Commissioner of the Transvaal and Natal.

At home, the Queen was upset. 'In both Houses of Parlt most impertinent remarks were made about my message of condolence & encouragement to Ld Chelmsford & Sir Bartle Frere,' she had recorded in the midst of the furore in parliament. She was furious about Wolseley's appointment. 'Why is [he] considered the most fit person? He is not likely to be conciliatory.' Of his appointment, she told the Prime Minister, Disraeli, that she would 'not withhold my *sanction* though I cannot *approve* it'.

Frere no longer knew what was going on. Wolseley refused to communicate with him. 'I am waiting to know whether Ministers have really any plan for the future? &, if they have, what it is? & whether it is one I ought to, or can, assist in carrying out?' he wrote to the Prince of Wales on 5 August. The vision of confederation in South Africa was collapsing. Two months later: 'Irresponsible radicals, & republican newspapers urge my resignation or recall,' he told the Prince of Wales. But the government said they wished him to remain. With honour, he could not yet resign.

Not long afterwards, Cetewayo was captured after the battle of Ulundi, on 4 July 1879. That day Lord Chelmsford led 17,000 British and African troops against some 24,000 Zulus. Cetewayo was sent to prison in a large room in the old Dutch castle at the Cape and it was there that Frere came face to face for the first time with the man he once described as like 'an animal long indulged in habits of blood'.

He wrote to the Queen: 'He told me he had every thing he required, & only seemed surprized [sic] that he was not to be executed, or at any rate, tried for his life. It is impossible to give any idea of the curious mixture of sagacity & ignorance – of dignity & childishness, of fortitude & timidity which he shows in every thing.' Frere could not help but feel 'that had we begun earlier to show these people the real power which is at Your Majesty's command we might have had less need of ships & armies'.

The Queen was not pleased with the photographs he sent to her: to see a king dressed in European clothes of blue serge 'undoubtedly presented a ridiculous appearance', Ponsonby told Frere on 15 November. 'We have [no right] to make him a laughing stock.'

The final blow came with the general election in December 1879. With the defeat of the Tories, Frere's days were numbered. The following August, he was recalled to London.

The day of Frere's departure was set for 15 September 1880. Lady Frere was so ill that he thought he might have to leave South Africa without her, but she was carried on board ship early to escape the crowds. Business was suspended, and people came from long distances to bid him farewell, lining the roads of Cape Town, gay with flags, on the way to the *Pretoria*. At the dock, the horses were uncoupled and men drew the carriage with Frere and his daughters to the quay. The evening was still and clear. The guns of the castle fired a last salute, answered by ships of the fleet.

Three days after Frere reached Plymouth on 5 October, the Prince of Wales invited him to stay in Scotland. By the 10th he was with the Queen ('poor Sir Bartle Frere') at Balmoral. There was some embarrassment at the Colonial Office when he appeared there – he thought his knowledge of South Africa might be of some use. He did not meet a single politician from either side 'who does not abuse the opposite party for the way they have treated me'. All the time he hoped that there might be some trial and verdict on what had happened in the Cape, but it did not happen. The public disgrace seemed more than he could bear. Frere spent his remaining days in ignominy and sorrow – attacked by the press, writing letters ceaselessly in an attempt to correct the fallacies that he felt had been spread about him, writing articles on India and Afghanistan. Meanwhile, in January 1883, Cetewayo was restored to two-thirds of Zululand. A year later he died, widely believed from poisoning. Four months later, on 29 May 1884, Frere himself met his death from a chill, with the sad dying words, 'They would surely understand.' He was buried beneath a vast red and cream marble monument engraved with his honours in the crypt at St Paul's. Lady Frere and his two older daughters, May and Katey, spent the next ten years of their lives attempting to retrieve his reputation, assembling his papers for publication, and raising subscriptions for the statue of him that still stands today on London's Embankment.

8 'The mind of heaven and earth'
Hong Kong 1877–82

Three weeks after Sir Bartle Frere and his family first landed at Cape Town, another new governor was preparing to be sworn in, half a world away. The sun was setting over the South China Sea in a haze of mist as the P&O mailboat *Zambesi* gradually rounded the north-western side of the island of Hong Kong. It was a Sunday evening in late April 1877. As if reluctant to enter the splendour of the harbour, it selected a mooring off West Point, not far from the historical landing point of the first British officer to claim the place for Britain, thirty-six years before. The ship was decked with flags and bunting. On board was the new governor of the colony, forty-three-year-old John Pope Hennessy, small and dapper, vain and impetuous, the man who had fired John Glover from Lagos and whose ineptitude sowed the seeds of war with the Ashanti in the Gold Coast. With him were his twenty-six-year-old wife, Kitty, and their eighteen-month-old son, Bertie.

A mile or so to the east, a crowd of British officials and the principal European merchants and their ladies were gathered on the verandah of Messrs Melders and Company, merchants, opposite the colony's principal landing at Peddar Wharf to greet the new governor. The air was hot and moist. At a quarter to five that afternoon a gun had boomed out across the harbour to signal that the *Zambesi* had been sighted. Now, not only was the acting administrator of the colony, old Gardner Austin, whose job it was to go aboard and bring the viceregal party ashore, nowhere to be seen, but the Governor appeared to be landing at quite the wrong end of town.

Hastily they mounted their sedan chairs and palanquins and trotted west along Queen's Road: past the bank, the post office and company offices, then into the region of Chinese shops. On past the taverns and drinking shops, with their bands of common sailors from every nation of the earth, and on, into the strange, dense region of crowded Chinese shop houses and the stinking squalor of Tai Ping Shan. Meanwhile, Austin was borne down a steep and tortuous path from Mountain Lodge, the Governor's summer

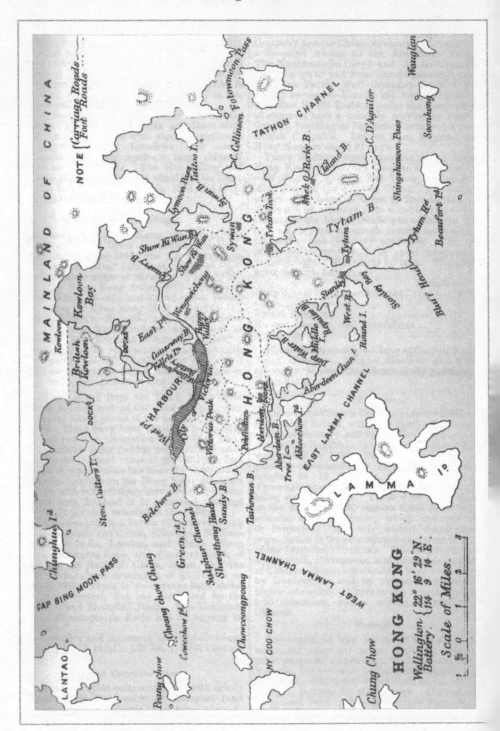

HONG KONG

Wellington ⎰ 22° 16' 29" N.
Battery ⎱ 114 9 14 E.

Scale of Miles

eyrie on the Peak, in a curtained chair lined with mirrors, by eight bearers – token of the governor's rank – in scarlet livery, dark felt hats, long pigtails and pristine white gaiters.

It was dusk before Hennessy and his wife had come ashore 'amidst cheers of those whose patience held out to the bitter end'. Only vague outlines of their figures could be made out. The new governor made a short speech, 'modest but manly, neither egotistical nor pompous'. The *China Mail* confessed, however, that looking at the matter 'impartially', 'landing Governors is not our "forte"'. Chinese geomancers would have read this uncomfortable accident of fate differently – as an ominous sign that boded ill.

The Hennessys were ushered into a waiting carriage and borne away into the hot darkness. Catching yellow gleams of shadowed lanterns in doorways, the glow of charcoal braziers and shrouded figures in the roadway, they would have been assaulted by smells: the musty mildew of their carriage, and, through the window, whiffs of cooking food, the stink of refuse and the warm stench of night-soil. The air cooled – but only slightly – as slowly their carriage wound its way up the mountainside to the east. They were conveyed past scarlet-turbanned Sikh policemen who saluted smartly, and through the gate to the white bulk of Government House, plain and four-square. Beneath the portico, the Chinese comprador, plump, inscrutable and clad in a long black gown, and his long-pigtailed staff in blue, awaited them.

Government House was set in watered lawns fringed with trees on a small plateau that had been hacked out of the granite mountainside. It turned its back on the Chinese town to the west to look out over a fine botanical garden and the brick offices of the government secretariat and the law courts below. Beyond rose the tower of St John's cathedral, a fine granite-built city hall, the cricket ground and the barracks. The view was dominated by the glittering blue of one of the world's most magnificent harbours – alive with sampans and cutters, the masts of sailing ships, high-sterned trading junks, steamers, clippers, and the wide red sails of the junks of the Hakka, who fished the south China waters. A mile across the water to the north a genteel British suburb was slowly growing on the tip of the Kowloon Peninsula. This was bounded by 'an impassable fence of bamboo eight feet high between British and Chinese territory' – for the prevention of smuggling. In the distance spread a thin margin of paddy-fields and walled villages; then a sharp range of scorched and arid mountains, barren, closed, concealing.

Different flags flew in the Hong Kong hierarchy. There was the Union flag that fluttered above Government House, and a second one at Headquarters House, home of the commander-in-chief. But others bearing strange devices flew above the residences of the *taipans*, bosses of the Hongs, the powerful trading companies that led the trade with China. Each displayed its own livery and insignia. Half a mile east along the shore was the 'Number 1 House' of Jardine Matheson, the largest trading company on the China coast, home to William Keswick, the forty-three-year-old *taipan*. Jardine Matheson had its own fleets of clippers, a private pier, a village for their workmen, and a guard of well-armed and drilled Indian troops.

'You will like to know who have got the nicest houses here,' Keswick's cousin had written home in 1849. 'As you are aware the Governor and the General have generally the finest. Here it is not so. "Who then?" Jardine's . . .'

Hong Kong was acquired to serve Britain's trade with China. European trade had first begun in the region from the quaint Portuguese town of nearby Macao, settled in 1557. Tea and silk, precious porcelains: as hunger for these luxuries grew in Europe, and the taste for tea spread across the British Isles, the British East India Company came to dominate the trade. Up the Pearl River from Macao was Canton – today's Guangzhou. In 1757 the Imperial Chinese government granted it a monopoly of trade with the west. The rules were strict: foreigners might only trade through thirteen 'Co-Hongs', groups of local merchants who were monitored and taxed by the authorities. Foreigners were confined to 'factories' on the riverfront in the south-west corner of the city, between the months of October and May. No European women or firearms were permitted, while the men were forbidden to hold any communications with local mandarins except through the Co-Hong. They were not to learn Chinese – only government-recognized Chinese linguists might translate for them – or ride in sedan chairs. Three times a month they were permitted to cross the river to visit the Fati gardens – but only in small parties. 'Obey and remain, disobey and depart; there are not two ways,' the Governor Lu K'u – today, Lu Kun – told the foreigners in 1835. He regarded them as no more than barbarians.

Still, all might have been well had it not been for opium. The drug had been known medicinally in China since the ancient Tang dynasty, but it was not until 1,000 years later, in the seventeenth century, that the practice of smoking began. By 1800 addiction was destroying the people; the drug was declared illegal. 'A harmless luxury and a precious medicine except to those who abuse it', was the general view of the foreign merchants in Canton, who could easily drop off a few cases of Indian opium on Lintin Island in the Pearl River delta, as they sailed upstream to Canton. By 1832, the British government in Calcutta was making £1 million a year from its sales, while for China losses on trade were growing. The inevitable happened.

A new imperial commissioner for the suppression of the trade arrived in Canton. He ordered up all the opium in possession of the foreign merchants. Sixteen offenders were handed over as hostages. The Europeans were forced to sign bonds, swearing that no future opium would be imported, under penalty of death. Meanwhile, they were detained in their factories until 20,000 chests of opium were finally handed over. The British superintendent of trade, Captain Charles Elliot, based at Macao, had been repeatedly rebuffed whenever he had attempted to negotiate with the Chinese. Now he demanded military intervention. 'There can be neither safety nor honour for either government until Her Majesty's flag flies on these coasts in a secure position,' he declared. Six months later, he landed and claimed the island of Hong Kong for Britain.

Just as in Canton, Hong Kong was a place where British merchants came to make money, but not to settle, and certainly, given the past history of the China trade, not to be interfered with. The place was quiet: hot and humid with typhoons in summer, damp and fog-bound in spring, and glorious with clear skies and sparkling seas in autumn and winter. Beneath the royal crest on the great seal of the colony was a waterfront piled high with boxes. Tea – or opium? Everyone continued piously to deplore the addiction of the Chinese 'to this fascinating vice', but no one did anything to stop it. By the time Hennessy arrived, the Hongs – besides Jardine Matheson, there were the Iraqi-Jewish Sassoon, Sons and Co.; Gibb, Livingstone; and the rising power of the Hong Kong and Shanghai Bank – were going from strength to strength. Companies were diversifying into shipping, insurance, banking, sugar and manufacturing.

John Pope Hennessy's reputation as a controversial and volatile governor had preceded him. Not only his adventures in west Africa, but, more recently, trouble in Barbados – in fact, full-scale race riots, which he was said to have inspired – had spawned alarming headlines around the world the year before. Like Frere in South Africa, Hennessy had been charged with implementing a confederation of the Windward Islands in the West Indies. The planters in Barbados were vehemently opposed to any step that was likely to violate their own control of the island, while the former slaves, their hopes raised by Hennessy, were convinced that an alliance with other islands would bring great things to them.

According to the *New York Times,* a deputation of gentlemen, 'who, it was stated, owned half the property of the island among them', had been so alarmed by the way Hennessy was promoting confederation to the black Barbadians that they travelled to London to meet Lord Carnarvon, to complain about the governor's conduct. Hennessy was accused of stirring up such 'agitation among the negroes, [they] had literally set the country ablaze'. For days and nights whole fields of sugar cane had been going up in flames, while 'negroes muttered insolence as the planters passed by'. The governor 'had some of the lowest and commonest people at his table'. Carnarvon professed ignorance of the whole affair. But men who had encountered Hennessy before knew better.

The man had a genius for petty feuds, stirring up trouble and causing offence. A splendid orator, he also had moments of brilliance and charismatic enthusiasm. Such was the combination of audacity, vain-glory, charm and good fortune of his early career in politics that he inspired Anthony Trollope's character of *Phineas Finn.* Like Finn, Hennessy was Irish, a Catholic and an outsider, who through his cleverness and wit captured the attention of important men.

Born in Cork in 1834, John Pope Hennessy was brought up with seven brothers and sisters in a narrow terraced house in genteel penury. His father dealt in hides, his mother was the daughter of a butter merchant. Small, delicate and suffering from bronchitis, young Hennessy was educated at home by a tutor. He was twelve when the great famine descended on Ireland in 1846, and the corpses of those who had died of starvation were collected from the streets of Cork by municipal cart in the mornings. Bred on folk-memories of ancient landed estates and past wealth, the Hennessys nursed tales of centuries of oppression, and a deep sense of grievance against the English and all things Protestant.

Hennessy grew up passionately partisan. He took up debating and developed a fascination with politics. At the age of twenty-one he won a first class degree in surgery and medicine at Queen's College in Cork – and then a place at Charing Cross Hospital in London to train for the Indian Army Medical Service.

Training as a doctor was his parents' idea. Within weeks of arriving in London Hennessy had decided to give up medicine, and was writing directly, with no introduction, to the Lord President of the Privy Council,

Lord Granville himself. Such was his eloquence that he secured himself the post of a clerk in his office. To his dismayed father he wrote, full of confidence: 'the state of the Civil Service & of political parties here at present is such, that any man who has got his foot into Downing Street, & who is determined to work hard & avoid every sort of dissipation, is certain of gaining a high position. What I have got is but the first step on the ladder. The most junior clerks in the Downing Street offices belong to the first circles of London's society. Whatever the salary may be at first, these appointments confer, as far as social standing is concerned, a very high position.'

Money, position: Hennessy lived frugally and began studying for the bar at night. He never drank. He was twenty-five when, in the spring of 1859, the Tory Prime Minister, Lord Derby, announced a general election. Hennessy seized the opportunity. 'I am going to Ireland to stand as an Irish Nationalist Conservative,' he told his Irish friend at the bar, Alfred Austin, who would later become poet laureate.

'My dear fellow,' Austin told him, 'you will die in a ditch.'

Hennessy stood for King's County and won. He became Westminster's first Roman Catholic Conservative MP. He returned to London and an invitation to dinner with Disraeli. 'Everybody here says I am the most successful new member in this Parliament,' he told his parents. 'I have got the ear of the House, and no Irish member is heard with such marked attention.'

Hennessy was small and fine-boned. His hair was thick and luxurious, dark and curly. His features were fine; he was agile, quick-moving, vivacious and graceful. Careful in the details of his dress and his manners, he cultivated an air of breeding and distinction. It was said he found it impossible to tell a dull story. It was not long before Hennessy was dining with the Duchess of Richmond, shooting at Longleat, weekending with Lord Carnarvon at Highclere. He was taken up by the wealthiest heiress in England, Angela Burdett-Coutts, and the mother-in-law of the Duke of Rutland, who engaged the family's interests in his welfare. Jane, Marchioness of Ely, lady-in-waiting to the Queen, was to come to his aid all her life. Hennessy set up accounts with the best tailors and bootmakers, acquired a brougham, and spent the winter of 1860 touring Italy as the guest of an unnamed friend, who paid all his bills. He visited Poland, and had audiences with Emperor Napoleon III in Paris and Franz Joseph in Vienna. There were other conquests: an English singer in Paris ('I often think of you, Hennessy, of your varied genius, and talents. I know of no one [who] possesses so much "savoir faire" as you do') and a certain 'A. M. Conyngham' in Barnes, who presented him with two daughters, Stella Beatrice and Mary Teodora, with whom he kept in touch all his life.

In July 1865 the high life for Hennessy came to an end. Parliament was dissolved. Hennessy stood for re-election and lost by seven votes. Ordinarily he might have waited for a safe seat in a by-election, but with only the most modest of incomes from his practice as a barrister, he had been living on credit for years. As long as he was an MP, he was immune from arrest for debt. No sooner had the election ended than he was being pursued for £700 for the cost of hiring 'jaunting cars' to take his rural constituents to polling stations during his campaign. Hennessy contested the election result, and spun out appeals for almost a year. Meanwhile he courted a wealthy heiress, a Miss Canning, and borrowed £2,000 from a Jewish moneylender on a security 'fortified by a judgment of consent', to tide him over until the happy day when he and Miss Canning were wed. Alas for poor Hennessy. Miss Canning's mother, invited to bail him out on the morning of the wedding, vanished from her hotel room in London with her daughter the same day.

Jane, Lady Ely gave him shelter in a cottage on her grouse moors to think things over. He was thirty-three years old. To escape arrest he could either exile himself in France and dispose all hope of a parliamentary future, or, with Disraeli's help, throw himself on the mercy of Lord Buckingham, Secretary of State for the Colonies, in the hope, as Disraeli put it, of 'some lucrative but quiet Governorship without any special difficulty attached to it'.

He was offered Labuan, that steamy triangular island off the north coast of Borneo. A mere coaling station? Why couldn't he have Queensland? 'You must not think I am inclined to grumble, but the more I find out about Labuan the less I like it,' he told Disraeli. He implored him to find him something else. Meanwhile, the Colonial Office was growing concerned over his requests for advances on his salary, his reluctance to pay the £70 stamp duty due for his Letters Patent, and his absurd request for an aide-de-camp in a position which Hennessy was privately calling his 'penal servitude in Borneo'.

Bidding farewell to his family in Ireland, he travelled across France, over the Mediterranean to Alexandria, thence overland to Suez to board the P&O steamer *Delhi*. He was accompanied by his eldest sister, Mary, red-haired and upright, to act as governor's lady, and his forty-year-old cousin, Bryan Cody, bald, with a croaking laugh and an ear for languages, with whom his father had been involved in business speculation, as private secretary. Hennessy landed in Singapore in early November 1867.

Onward transport to Labuan was not immediately forthcoming. Only two sailing vessels – taking between one and three weeks depending on the monsoon – plied monthly between Singapore and Labuan. Playing on his position as governor, Hennessy persuaded the navy to give them passage. Late in November they landed at Port Victoria beneath black, lowering skies in steaming heat – the middle of the monsoon. It rained, torrentially, all night, every night, and most of every day.

The more you read about Labuan, the more you realize that the presence of the British in such a place was an incredible and absurd case of colonial madness. 'I fear nothing can be worse than the financial state of Labuan,' the Secretary of State had confided to Hennessy in his final interview before leaving London. Such coal as was produced was soft and burnt too quickly; the company, the Eastern Archipelago Co., was failing. The climate was impossible, the prevalence of fever lethal, the isolation unhinging. Dispatches took six or seven weeks to reach London. No attempt had been made to repair the half-mile-long road along the harbour front for twenty years.

'Torpor and despondency', as Hennessy put it, characterized most of the handful of – there were forty – European residents. Hennessy's reaction was to adopt a Napoleonic attitude. He declared the island to be 'about the same size as St Helena, but somewhat smaller' and 'extremely beautiful'. He determined to succeed where everyone else had failed, to turn Labuan into a second Singapore.

The acting governor of Labuan when he arrived was Hugh Low. Low was forty-five, dark-haired and mustachioed, a gentle and funny man, genial and conscientious, who had for years been passed over for promotion by the Colonial Office. He had arrived on the island twenty years before as colonial secretary to the inaugural British administration. Trained as a botanist, Low had been dispatched at the age of nineteen by his father, a horticulturalist, to collect wild orchids in Borneo. There he had come to know James Brooke, the Raja of Sarawak. Five years later, in his new role with the British administration of Labuan, he sailed from England with William Napier, the new deputy governor, and his nineteen-year-old daughter, Kate. Kate, whose mother had been Malay, was a beauty. As Low and Kate danced together in the moonlight on board the *Meander* it was obvious to all how much they were in love. Landing at Singapore they were married in 'a cheery wedding'. Then they sailed on to Labuan.

Within two months of landing the whole party was sick with fever. Kate died three years later at the age of twenty-two. By then she had borne a son and a daughter. Low buried her secretly beneath a grove of orange trees in the garden of their house, to save her body from the fate of those buried in the Christian cemetery – raided at nightfall by headhunters from the mainland, who hacked off the heads of those newly buried. He sent his children to be brought up by his brother in England.

Low spent his time creating one of the finest gardens in the east, and laying out plantations of tropical fruit trees and a miniature English park around Government House. He kept pet monkeys in the house, collected tropical fish, birds and butterflies. Not far from his house was the compound of his mistress, Nona Dyang Loya, from Sarawak, and their nine-year-old girl. Six months before Hennessy arrived, Low's seventeen-year-old daughter, Kitty, her education in Switzerland complete, had returned to live with her father. Graceful and slender, with a delicate head of silky black hair, eyes that were grey and almond-shaped, she was exquisite.

One of Hennessy's first acts as the new governor of Labuan was to order a celebration to mark the twenty-first anniversary of the acquisition of the colony – on Christmas Eve. On that day he declared an amnesty for a dozen prisoners in the jail, laid the foundation for a Chinese school, and drove two stakes into the beach to mark the site for the construction of a wharf named in honour of Prince Albert. He invited all the principal inhabitants – British, Malay and Chinese. It was the first time such a mixed gathering had ever been held at Government House.

That night, there was food and drink in abundance. The band on the verandah played, 'and dancing was kept up till a late hour'. Who else would the handsome governor dance with but the most beautiful girl in the room? Five weeks later, on 4 February 1868, Hennessy married Kitty Low. 'I am glad,' Lady Burdett-Coutts wrote to James Brooke's nephew Charles, who had become his heir in Sarawak, 'he makes a marriage likely to provide *Brio* to the East.'

More than Hennessy might have liked. His sister Mary and their cousin Bryan Cody did not take kindly to the new mistress of Government House.

Meanwhile, everyone in the household kept falling ill: fever, persistent diarrhoea. 'Extremely offensive' air permeated the north-west of the house. Behind it, on slightly higher ground, were the barracks, where the Indian troops possessed the highest rate of sickness on the island.

Hennessy, the doctor, stepped in to inquire. The sepoy latrines had not been cleaned for two years. Sewage was leaking into the water supply. Summoning the officer in charge – a popular man on the island – Hennessy demanded his instant dismissal and reported him to the War Office. Then he launched a vendetta against the young surveyor-general, and rounded on his father-in-law with a twelve-page letter accusing him of withholding an old report on the sanitation of the barracks. Labuan, he informed London, was run by 'a set of incapables'.

Opposition, led by Hugh Low, rose. He placed an article in a Singapore newspaper criticizing Hennessy's policies; then told him he knew nothing of colonial administration. Poor Kitty. After seven tortuous months of marriage, she went back to her father. But she returned to Hennessy in time to give birth to a son, John Patrick, 'my Johnnie', in Government House in March 1869. Five months later, however, when Hennessy refused to recommend a rise in salary for Low, or to allow her to meet her brother from England in Sarawak, Kitty ordered her luggage and the baby and his nurse to be packed into the governor's carriage. Meanwhile she walked 'by the road and by a private path' to her father's house. When Low told his daughter she must return to her husband, she replied 'in the strongest manner' that she could never live with her husband again. Early in November, Hennessy issued a writ of habeas corpus against his father-in-law on the grounds of his illegal detention of his child. Low protested to London. Kitty returned. Both men were reprimanded. Hennessy took to referring to his father-in-law as 'the Plague'.

Hennessy was so confident of making improvements to the island in his early dispatches that London was at first delighted with his performance. As months went by, their view degenerated. Hennessy's four-year tenure in Labuan was marked with idiosyncrasies that he would repeat time and again. Energy, brilliance and obsession: as in his attempt, full of bullish confidence, to introduce a silkworm industry to the island. Seventeen mulberry trees that he planted grew so fast they produced fruit within a year; as a result of his personal devotion, silkworms were producing cocoons. Hennessy's great scheme foundered when the samples he sent back to England were so carelessly packed that they arrived mildewed and fermenting, mixed with the shattered remains of glass vials.

Hennessy darted from one project to the next. He had a talent for dramatization and magnifying the faults of others; he cleared the decks of staff he did not like, and cultivated his favourites. One dispatch would be a model of logic; another passionate and confused. Oblivious to his own imperfections, he was an autocrat one moment, the next a committed humanitarian. Officials in the Colonial Office were bewildered.

By the end of his administration in 1871, Hennessy's cousin Cody had replaced Kitty's father, Hugh Low, as colonial secretary, and his feckless younger brother, Willie, had been imported from Cork to serve as his private secretary. Relations with the Chinese – whose leading merchants he cultivated – were excellent, and revenues generated from their trade and taxes were on the rise. He imported street lamps from Singapore, and four Irish constables to create a police force, so that expensive troops could be sent home, saving the colony £12,000 a year. He was rewarded with promotion to the Bahamas.

Mr and Mrs Hennessy landed in England as Lord Carnarvon and the Colonial Office were wrestling with how to manage the settlements along the west African coast: the Gambia, the Gold Coast, Sierra Leone and Lagos. The Foreign Office was in the midst of negotiations over the acquisition of the Dutch fortress of Elmina on the Gold Coast. While in Labuan Hennessy's relations with the Dutch in neighbouring Borneo had been smooth; his attitude to those of other races was known to be enlightened. He was invited to take on a short assignment before going to the Bahamas as Governor-in-Chief of the West African Settlements, and take charge of the transfer of Elmina.

Three weeks after the Hennessys landed in Freetown, the capital of Sierra Leone, their beloved son, Johnnie, by then three years old, was dead of dysentery. He was buried beneath a black marble plaque engraved with the single word, *Baby,* in the chapel of a small convent. There at five-thirty every morning, the Governor and Kitty would hear Mass. Kitty immersed herself in the charitable work of the Catholic missions of Freetown.

It was on this assignment, a month after Johnnie died, that Hennessy took over the castle of Elmina on the Gold Coast and sacked Captain John Glover in Lagos. Meanwhile, in the short time that he was there, the reform of Freetown, founded in 1791 as a settlement for escaped or liberated slaves and taken over by Britain as a colony upon the abolition of the slave trade in 1807, provided considerable scope for Hennessy. Here he encountered hundreds of educated, English-speaking Christians, many of them former slaves returned from America. Hennessy endorsed the idea of Edward Wilmot Blyden, 'the father of pan-Africanism', of founding a west African university for Freetown, and surrounded himself with a black staff. Ignoring past cases of corruption, he promoted a number to senior positions in the administration. He suspended the colonial secretary for striking a black messenger, cleaned up the markets, put the cemeteries in order and introduced sanitary reforms. When in the midst of the rains in August 1872 he abolished a house and land tax, spontaneous celebrations broke out all over the city. Crowds of people gave thanks in the churches and gathered before Government House to cheer him.

> All dem Governor do bereh well
> All dem Governor do bereh well
> Pope Hennessy do pass dem,
> Pope Hennessy – Pope Hennessy do pass dem.

For over thirty years after Hennessy's stay of just one year, the date of 22 August was celebrated in Freetown as Pope Hennessy Day, a festival of anti-colonial protest.

'We must watch all his proceedings very narrowly,' Mr Herbert, the Permanent Under-Secretary of State, warned Lord Carnarvon on the eve of Hennessy's departure for Hong Kong. 'And when we see any tendency to bolt to the right or left from the path of established procedure in Hong Kong (which is an intricate one surrounded with special dangers arising from the Chinese character which he does not understand) he should be firmly and as gently as possible led back into it. He may cause not only terrible trouble but real danger by crude and thoughtless "improvements" in procedure.'

Hennessy's predecessor in Hong Kong was Sir Arthur Kennedy, who had served many years on the west African coast, as governor in the Gambia and Sierra Leone, as well as in Western Australia and British Columbia. Irish like himself, Kennedy had arrived in Hong Kong at the age of sixty-two. Calm, urbane, and suffering from repeated attacks of malaria, he was a tough, realistic man. The administration was smoothly run, and there was little work for the governor to do. What Kennedy wanted in Hong Kong was a place where an Englishman could dwell in peace and security. He had been content to leave vexed issues to wend their way gently through the committees appointed by the Legislative Council, and had a knack of making himself pleasant to Downing Street officials. He was especially hard on law and order as it applied to the Chinese. Taking inspiration from the mandarins themselves, whose brutal methods of punishment included the public branding and beheading of criminals, he increased flogging before the crowds on Queen's Road. He introduced the branding of criminals behind the ear and expelled miscreants from the colony. One of his last acts as governor was to implement harsher jail sentences and to reduce the quantity and quality of prison food to lower crime. The aim was, he told Carnarvon, 'to make the life of prisoners in Gaol, and of Chinese prisoners especially, as distasteful as it can possibly be made'. He was to become the only Hong Kong governor immortalized in a statue erected by public subscription.

By the spring of 1877, Hennessy was as handsome and charming as ever. Meanwhile, with almost ten years' experience as a governor's lady, Kitty had proved a match for him. Landing in Singapore after they left Labuan, she had insisted on attending a Government House garden party that afternoon, in spite of Hennessy's admonishment that, after four years on Labuan, she had nothing suitable to wear. In reply, she ordered up an ADC and the Government House carriage and went shopping. She appeared later in such a simple frock that the governor of Singapore at first mistook her for Johnnie's *amah*.

'Hers is not a common character & her beauty is quite out of the ordinary,' Lady Ely described her after Hennessy introduced them in London. 'I could not help admiring her peculiar grace & a charm which few people have.' Kitty loved music and dancing; she was graceful and assured. Three years after the tragic death of Johnnie in Freetown, she gave birth to a second son, Bertie. Meanwhile her father, Hugh Low, had, at last, been promoted – to the post of resident of the exotic jungle state of Perak in western Malaya. Her few letters that survive show a certain affection for Hennessy. They had at least reached an equilibrium.

Nine thousand Europeans; 130,000 Chinese. Europeans in spacious houses on tree-lined streets, rising up the mountainside, east of Victoria on Hong Kong island; Chinese segregated to a limited area on the lower slopes to the west, living in impossibly overcrowded shop houses, with no sanitation except a system of night-soil collection, subject to a curfew. Only in

View of Hong Kong looking towards the harbour:
behind the barracks in the foreground lie the cricket ground and City Hall

possession of a night-pass and lantern from their employer could a Chinese step out into the street after 9 p.m. There was no love between the races: the word 'barbarian' to describe the British had to be delicately negotiated out of the Convention of Peking, which ceded the peninsula of Kowloon to Hong Kong in 1860; the term 'foreign devil', and the habit of cheerfully swindling Europeans, persist to this day. Meanwhile, Europeans in Hong Kong treated the Chinese like inferior animals. They insulted and abused them, hit their servants, and struck coolies, laden with sedan chairs, with their canes and umbrellas in the street.

'A monstrous piece of class legislation', Hennessy called the night-pass system. Already, a month after his arrival, the colony was full of talk: a thirty-five-year-old Chinese, the first in history, had been appointed to the Hong Kong bar. Ng Choy – Wu Tingfang today – was the son of a Chinese merchant in Singapore, educated in Canton and at the Anglican St Paul's College in Hong Kong. From there, his father dispatched him to University College London, where he studied law. Ng was called to the bar in Lincoln's Inn in 1876. As he stood before the bench he presented a slight, modest figure, in curled white wig, stiff collar and black gown. On his feet were soft white Chinese cotton shoes.

Hennessy wasted no time in getting to know Ng. He had already begun flooding the Colonial Office with dispatches about the defects of his staff, the poor quality of interpreters, the disgraceful state of the educational system, and his plans for the creation of a new post, of Chinese Secretary to the governor. Hennessy appointed Ng to a three-man board of examiners to test candidates for a vacant position of government interpreter.

Meanwhile, Hennessy could not resist the ceaseless loading and unloading of ships in the harbour, and the energy and vitality he saw on the steep streets of the Chinese quarter. Here were shops full of porcelains, silks, shawls and lacquerware; artisans carving seals on the pavement, letter-writers, travelling barbers and fortune-tellers. It was clear from the figures that crossed his desk that revenues from trade were rising. The Chinese population was growing. Wealthy Chinese merchants were taking over British, German and American premises, whose owners were selling up and retiring from business. Before long Hennessy was telling Lord Carnarvon – in words strangely prescient of today – how Chinese merchants could put Chinese goods on the English market 'in larger quantity and at lower prices than their English competitors'. What was more, 'they also allege that they can afford to sell British goods cheaper to the natives in Hong Kong and in China than the other traders'.

'Chinomania': at first European businessmen just laughed at the new governor. Eight weeks after arriving, there was a certain frisson when he rejected the unanimous advice of his Executive Council – the colonial secretary, the commanding officer in charge of the troops, the chief justice, attorney-general and treasurer – to stop a deportation order on a young offender. But when, at the first meeting of his Legislative Council in September, he announced that he was putting an immediate end to public flogging and proposed to outlaw branding and the cat-o'-nine tails, the merchants – headed by William Keswick, *taipan* of Jardine Matheson, one of the four unofficial members of the Legislative Council – threatened to appeal to the home government. Flogging – safeguarded by the proviso that any sentence of more than 100 lashes had to be ratified by the governor – was the basis of the colony's punitive system, so habitual it was simply the norm.

'A considerable social disturbance has occurred at Hong Kong between the new Governor, Pope Hennessy, and the community,' recorded the *New York Times*. As the news reached the streets, coolies began calling him 'merciful' and 'Number One Good Friend'.

Meetings of the Legislative Council, usually ignored by the man on the street, were now packed with the public. As William Keswick predicted, the crime rate rose – terrifyingly. Within six months, a large gang of Chinese thieves raided a village on the south coast of the island. This was followed by an armed attack on the superintendent of police and several constables in May, and a series of murders of women. When Hennessy commuted the death sentence imposed on one of the culprits, protests flooded into the newspapers, and one juror swore he would never serve on a panel again. Then, on 25 September, as many as eighty armed burglars attacked a shop in Wing Lok Street. They sealed off the street, fought off police and escaped with their loot in a steam launch. The Europeans had had enough of Hennessy's 'soft on crime' policy. Led by William Keswick, they called a public meeting at City Hall to 'consider the present state of life and property in the colony'. Four days before the meeting, armed burglars broke into a European house on one of the wealthiest streets.

Hennessy, meanwhile, had continued to cultivate the Chinese. Soon after the celebrations of Chinese New Year, Ng had introduced him to the board of the Tung Wah hospital. The Tung Wah was Hong Kong's most important charity. It went far beyond treating the sick and dispensing medicine to provide welfare to the whole Chinese community. The members of its committee were the Chinese equivalent of the British *taipans*, wealthy, urbane, many with their family homes outside the colony, in Canton and Shanghai. Since the hospital had opened six years before, Hong Kong's administration had kept the institution at arm's length, fearful of its potential power, dealing with it only through the registrar-general, in his role as 'Protector of the Chinese'.

Early in the afternoon of the day of the public meeting, on 7 October, Chinese residents were seen 'streaming down in chairs' as if they were going to the races. By the time William Keswick and his protestors arrived at City Hall, the largest meeting room was filled to capacity. 'Damned Chinamen,' someone shouted. 'Throw them out!'

'A general struggle ensued', and the Europeans 'stampeded' to the cricket ground. Led by Ng, the Chinese took up position on the verandahs of City Hall overlooking the ground. Hennessy's leniency towards the criminal classes had made life and property in Victoria 'more unsafe than any town of the British dominions', Keswick declared. Ng asked him to repeat his statement so that the Chinese could understand what was going on. Keswick refused. 'We cannot speak Chinese,' he said.

By their own account, the Chinese 'swallowed the insult and left the meeting'. As the British press later told it, Ng had led 'a mob of over a thousand cut-throats and desperadoes', tacitly approved by Governor Hennessy, to disrupt the meeting.

Over 2,000 Chinese – from medical practitioners to shopkeepers – organized a petition to the Queen, praising Hennessy's benevolence. 'He embodies the mind of heaven and earth, he lives to promote life, and harsh punishment therefore is not placed in the first rank,' they said. A second petition followed from the board of the Tung Wah hospital.

After the disgrace of the meeting, Hennessy placed responsibility for all Chinese matters in the hands of forty-year-old Dr Ernst Johann Eitel. Eitel came from Württemberg in Germany, had a degree in philosophy from Tübingen university, and had been serving as a missionary with his English wife in Hong Kong when Hennessy's predecessor, Kennedy, had given him the honorary appointment of examining English students of Chinese. Recently he had published a *Chinese Dictionary in the Cantonese Dialect*. Impressed with his knowledge and sympathy for the Chinese, his stolid loyalty, Hennessy had first made him inspector of schools. Now he became acting Chinese Secretary.

The Queen responded graciously to the petition of the Chinese community as speedily as the postal system would allow. But it took almost two years, until November 1880, for Lord Kimberley, the Secretary of State, to sanction the final abolition of all branding of criminals and to repeal all ordinances permitting the flogging of Chinese except in cases where it would be administered in the United Kingdom.

One of the only Europeans to take the Governor's part at the cricket ground meeting was Thomas Child Hayllar, QC, the prosperous head of the Hong Kong bar. Hayllar had returned from leave a fortnight after the Hennessys landed in Hong Kong. Reported to have been a 'learned and conscientious' man with a 'modest and soft demeanour', he had travelled widely, and took a special interest in trees and plants; he was the president of the Hong Kong Horticultural Society. He and his wife, as prominent members of the British community, soon became frequent guests of the Hennessys at Government House. Hennessy sought Hayllar's advice on all kinds of Hong Kong issues, and began inviting him regularly to come on pleasant cruises on the government launch among the islands of the Hong Kong waters. Following the cricket ground meeting, in November 1878, he appointed him to be one of the four unofficial members of the Legislative Council.

There was another side to Mr Hayllar, with his 'frosted silken beard', who posed his 'lily white hand so gracefully' in court. People muttered how he had had to leave a post in Bombay under a cloud, and how in Hong Kong a certain Mr Alexander would not let his wife sit next to him at dinner at Government House. A day or two after the cricket ground meeting, Hayllar was invited to attend the Governor and Mrs Hennessy on a nine-day trip to Canton.

The Pearl River in November: the loveliest time of year – the humidity low, the days warm and clear, the lush green of the new rice against the golden harvest of the paddy, piled upon threshing floors, and Kitty, the lovely wife of the Governor, leaning against the rails. One month after the party returned from Canton, the celebrated lady traveller Isabella Bird – who, after the success of her books on Hawaii and the Rocky Mountains, Governor Hennessy was embarrassingly eager to know – came to dinner at Government House. There, 'Mrs H. sat in a dream, spoke to no one, and only roused herself to fire up fiercely at her husband who retorted with a cold sarcasm.'

Isabella Bird was not taken with the Hennessys. She thought him a jumped-up troublemaker, 'much overdressed ... with a mouth which smiles perpetually and sinister eyes that never smile'. After he escorted her personally through the 'simply splendid' prison at Hong Kong, it struck her 'that he is *posing* as a humanitarian'. But not long after Miss Bird dined at Government House rumours about the Hennessy marriage began to circulate in the tight, jealous colony of Hong Kong.

The following summer, Hayllar took to sending polite excuses not to join the Governor's launch excursions just as the boat was about to leave the dock. One day in September, when Hennessy was handed another note as he stepped aboard the launch, he hastily excused himself. His sedan chair hurried swiftly up to his summer residence, Mountain Lodge, on the Peak. Hayllar and Kitty were in her boudoir, looking at a book. In vain Hayllar tried to stuff it under a cushion. A volume of 'indecent prints' from the Museo Borbonico in Naples! Hennessy threw him out the house, and gave orders he was never to be admitted again. Then he wrote to the Secretary of State telling him that Hayllar was 'unfit for any post in Government Service'. When Hayllar and his wife next arrived for a Government House reception, Hennessy ordered his ADC to turn them out.

It is tempting to think that it was Hayllar's place to which, in January 1880, Hennessy appointed Ng as the first Chinese member of the Legislative

Council. Once again, the British behaved as if stunned. 'It cannot be expected that natives of the British Isles would be content to be legislated by Chinese,' declared the *Daily Press*. Officials in London were only marginally more keen on this appointment. Where would Ng's loyalty lie in the event of difficulties between England and China?

'I don't doubt his personal loyalty or worth,' Hicks Beach told Hennessy privately. 'But it seemed to me that, at any rate for the present, it would not be well to recognize Chinese representation on the Council as a regular thing.'

To the Legislative Council, and its chairman, His Excellency the Governor, Ng brought the issue of segregation in the City Hall Museum, where Chinese were only admitted during certain hours. The museum was funded by an annual grant from the Hong Kong government. Upon Ng's intervention, a new notice appeared. While Chinese would normally be permitted every morning until 1 p.m., and Europeans from two until five, 'any respectably dressed and well behaved person' could apply for admission at any time.

Never had he seen such notices in European museums, Ng declared. The Chinese press took up the campaign.

On behalf of the museum's trustees, Keswick argued. He was delighted that the Chinese of the lower classes flocked in such large numbers to the museum. But their personal habits – eating garlic with their rice, and the state of their clothing, which 'in winter is not in the cleanest state and in summer is of the very scantiest description' – would so discourage Europeans from visiting that desegregation would 'practically' close the museum.

Ng: 'If the principle of class distinction was to prevail, where was it to end?' Was there to be segregation in all public places in the colony? Would Chinese be forced to walk on one side of the street and Europeans on the other? How would Mr Keswick and other members of the museum committee like to be treated this way?

In his recommendation to the Secretary of State, Hennessy put his weight behind Ng. Unless the museum opened its doors to all comers, its grant would be terminated.

Picnics, balls, regattas, pleasure cruises, dinner parties, the races, tennis parties, amateur theatricals and afternoon teas: Victoria – then, as now – was a city of inexhaustible hospitality, extravagant living, full of gossipy cliques. 'Such was the mutual incompatibility of temperament, views and ways, between Sir John and the European community,' Dr Eitel sadly recorded in the history of Hong Kong he was to write later, 'that he deliberately assumed a position of entire isolation, whilst the European community felt, year by year, less and less disposed to disturb his insularity.'

Hennessy was not finding life easy. His mood was mercurial. In photographs his mouth was tense and defiant; his eyes glittered. He almost certainly had regular attacks of malaria. His charm was becoming perhaps a little too effusive. He prided himself on the way he entertained official guests: Mr Chung, the minister of the Chinese Imperial government, en route to Russia, and the first Chinese official to stay at Government House. General Ulysses S. Grant, the former US President and Civil War hero, thoroughly enjoyed his Government House dinners, receptions and garden parties, while Kitty drove Mrs Grant out in her phaeton with her ponies, Puck and Ariel, 'over the smooth wide roads'. General 'Chinese' Gordon, Prince Henry of Prussia, and the two young sons of the Prince of Wales: all came to stay.

In the wake of the Tory defeat in the general election of April 1880, Hennessy was knighted for reasons which, given the dismay with which he was increasingly regarded in the Colonial Office, must have seemed inexplicable even at the time. With his title, his tendency to autocratic behaviour increased. He refused to delegate. His squabbles with his personnel plumbed new depths of pettiness. He was already on his fifth colonial secretary in three years. Now he appointed steady Dr Eitel, in whom he confided information better kept private, to be his private secretary. Ever since Hennessy had permitted the sale of land to Chinese near the barracks, the commander-in-chief – who had protested about the danger of lack of sanitation to his troops – refused any longer to sit on the Executive Council or to have anything to do with him. When Hennessy requested a military band to play for the Queen's birthday dinner at Government House, the general turned him down. They would be playing at his own celebrations instead. Hennessy cabled the Secretary of State, who instructed the War Office to order the general to deliver the band.

Over the advice of his Executive Council, he continued to refuse to deport criminals whenever he felt their convictions were in doubt. Somehow, there was never time in the Legislative Council to examine the estimates. The appointment of an official shorthand reporter to record debates failed to materialize. One after the other important public works were discussed, declared urgent and rejected or postponed. At one point, thirty-nine dispatches from the Colonial Office remained unanswered. By the autumn of 1881, one official in London advised the Secretary of State that it was 'absolutely useless at present to communicate with Sir J. Hennessy, because he locks up the dispatch, shows it to no one, and never answers it'. Meanwhile, on leave in Japan, Hennessy had an audience with the Emperor, spent much 'valuable' time with his ministers, and toured Yokohama harbour on a Japanese boat, accepting ambassadorial honours and seventeen-gun salutes from the American, French and Russian flagships – while doing all he could to avoid the British minister.

It was soon after the visit to Hong Kong of the King of Hawaii in April 1881 that the final denouement occurred. William Keswick was the Hawaiian Consul in Hong Kong. He had arranged to meet the King on board his ship and conduct him to his house to be his guest. When news of what was happening reached Hennessy, he dispatched Dr Eitel to the boat, to bring the King back to Government House. As luck would have it, a few days later, Lady Hennessy was photographed at a garden party given for the King by another Hong Kong *taipan*, in the company of Mr Hayllar. Whether or not Hennessy was aware of the pictures – which Lady Hennessy made every effort to have suppressed – when he next met Hayllar, while out walking with Kitty and his son, Bertie, on a path on the Peak near Mountain Lodge, he set about him with his umbrella.

The resulting fracas fills thick volumes in the National Archives. Hayllar swore that Hennessy tried to blind him; Hennessy claimed that his wife had been insulted. He had only done 'what your Lordship or any other gentleman would have done under the circumstances'. Then the whole sorry mess began to escalate.

The contents of Hayllar's letter – 'the insane and violent demeanour of the [Governor], his disgusting Billingsgate [*sic*] and the filthiness of his insinuations lent a horror and a degradation to the transaction quite beyond my powers of description'– swirled about Hong Kong. Kitty summoned her father, Hugh Low, from Malaya. He arrived in the colony, put up at the Hong Kong Hotel, and was soon noted 'riding in chairs side by side [with Hayllar] jocularly talking together'. Low persuaded Hayllar that to bring a case of assault against the Governor would only damage Kitty.

Hayllar cabled London to rescind his accusations. Protocol required he did so through the Governor. The next day Hennessy and Kitty departed for an official six-week trip to China. Hennessy had left instructions with his private secretary, Eitel, to show his own correspondence with the Secretary of State, which went into details of the affair of the Museo

Borbonico catalogue, to any member of the Legislative Council who wished to see it. Within days, Hayllar had issued a writ for slander against Eitel. Lawyers collected in preparation for a feast.

In the end, Hennessy abandoned Eitel, handed him the blame for publishing details of the scandal and retracted his case against Hayllar. The correspondence, however, somehow ended up 'shown in a quasi public manner to leading residents in the Colony and at the Hong Kong Club'. In London, Robert Herbert, the Under-Secretary of State, concluded that both Hennessy and Hayllar had lied. There was only one solution: to advise the Governor 'to leave and quit Hong Kong as soon as possible'.

Things were changing in Hong Kong. One of Hennessy's earliest acts was to order the planting of the mountainsides, a wilderness of rock and bare orange earth. Nine government nurseries were established, and 20,000 seedlings planted. Out of his arguments with the commander-in-chief over the construction of Chinese buildings by the barracks rose an inquiry into Chinese living conditions that would introduce a sanitary board to the colony, and drains to the Chinese quarters of the town. Rickshaws were introduced in the spring of 1880, and telephones in 1881. New steamer lines connected Hong Kong with Japan, Peru and Trieste. An Anglo-Chinese debating society and a polo club were established. There were collections for the relief of famine in north China, and for floods in Canton. Six tropical storms hit the colony, but no major damage was done.

Meanwhile, over 20,000 more Chinese had moved to the colony. Whatever the attitudes of the British, the reality was that during Hennessy's tenure, Chinese companies had replaced all but three European Hongs in the list of the top twenty ratepayers in the colony.

In one of his last speeches delivered to the Legislative Council, Hennessy's intellect and optimism leaps off the page. Like the consummate orator he was, he spelt out fact after fact, long lists of talent and enterprise that the Chinese were bringing to the colony. Hong Kong having been established for no other reason than trade, he was 'bound to say ... at this moment we are in a Colony whose commercial prosperity is perhaps unrivalled'. Who would now venture to say that he was not right to encourage the Chinese to buy land and settle in Hong Kong?

Following a farewell banquet with the Tung Wah Hospital Committee, and a final, stormy debate in the Legislative Council, Sir John and Lady

Hennessy sailed for England in the spring of 1882 – ostensibly on six months' leave. When it was rumoured that Hennessy might return as governor, the British merchants sent 'the strongest remonstrances' to the Secretary of State. In December 1882 he was posted as governor to Mauritius. Said Eitel: 'Sir John carried with him the same old perverse antipathies, and roused there also, among the British community, the whirlwind and the storm.' After four years he was recalled once more to London, accused of financial maladministration, the 'persecution' of English officials and a pro-criminal bias. A long inquiry found that while he was guilty of 'want of temper and judgment', 'vexatious and unjustifiable interference' with the magistracy, he might serve out his time. In December 1889 he retired, aged fifty-five.

Hennessy bought a large house, Rostellan Castle, near Cork, which he had coveted since boyhood, and in December 1890 stood again for parliament as an Irish Home Ruler. His victory was overwhelming. He dreamed of being awarded a peerage, but fate intervened. He died suddenly ten months later of heart failure. He was buried in his father's grave, with no separate headstone, in Cork's city cemetery.

Hennessy's Chinese friend Ng did not stay in Hong Kong long after the governor left. His position on the Legislative Council had only ever been 'provisional'. With his benefactor's departure, a parcel of land which Hennessy had agreed should be leased to him was rescinded by his successor. A number of Chinese speculators who had invested with him went bust; Ng himself ended deeply in debt. Persona non grata with both the colonial government and the wealthy Chinese, Ng accepted a position as adviser to a rising Qing official in Tianjin. In 1896 he was posted to Washington DC as China's minister to the United States and went on to enjoy a successful diplomatic career.

Kitty remains elusive. Three years after Hennessy's death she married a much younger man. Always superstitious, later in life she took up spiritualism. Following instructions from a ouija board, she destroyed Hennessy's library and all their private papers.

9 The death of Thomas Callaghan

Falkland Islands 1879–80

Fourteen thousand miles from London, far away in the wastes of the South Atlantic, a keen wind whipped the icy seas. The Falkland Islands, some 400 miles off the eastern coast of Patagonia, represented one of the Colonial Office's most remote and thankless postings. Lashed by howling gales, famous for storms of tremendous fury, even ships in dire trouble had learnt to give the capital, Port Stanley, a miss. Its costs of supplies and labour were atrocious. There was no dock, and it often took days before the wind died down enough for a ship even to enter the harbour.

There were two main islands – East and West Falkland – in a group of, perhaps, 200? No one knew how many there were for sure; the islands had yet to be surveyed. With their barren windswept landscapes, vast skies and spectacular light, the Falklands held few attractions. Trees would not grow there. Instead of finding vast deposits of coal in the dark seams of the islands' graphite, surveyors had merely uncovered the skeleton of a ziphoid whale. Foxes and wolves had been exterminated but there were five species of penguin, whose eggs were voraciously consumed by the colonists. There were perhaps thirty-two glorious fine days, at long intervals, in every year.

Attempts at settlement were sporadic and miserable: first the French, who established a foothold on East Falkland in 1764. This was taken over by Spain two years later. In 1765, a British sea captain, John Byron, claimed Saunders Island and others on the western edge of the group for King George III. But all efforts to colonize the islands soon foundered. It was not until 1833 that a group of twelve stalwarts settled down to develop Port Stanley as a port of call for whalers and sealers, to provision vessels rounding the Horn with fresh water and food. Some twenty-five years later, sheep farming had been introduced, and since then, a small but steady trade had grown with England. It was a one-way thing, though. Everything but meat – from ale, beer and porter, to apparel of all sorts, woollen clothes, boots, shoes, cottons, linens, timber and nails for building, flour, butter, cheese, preserved milk, even coal – had to be imported.

Tucked into the bays and inlets of north-east East Falkland was the main harbour, Port Stanley. There was one good road along the front, and three rows of low cottages, whitewashed and grey-slated. It could have been a town in the western Highlands. At one end, like a long low manse, stood Government House, overlooking the tossing white-capped seas of the harbour.

On 13 May 1879 the Governor, Thomas Callaghan, sat huddled in shawls before the peat fire in his study. He dreaded the onset of winter. After two assignments in the tropics, his system was wracked with ague. In the Falklands flurries of snow fell all year. But in 1878, during the hardest winter in more than thirty years, deep snow had covered the ground from May until September. When the spring finally came late in October, hundreds of cattle and horses had been found dead on the Camp – the outlying pastures beyond Port Stanley. Callaghan's beloved wife, Alice, at thirty twenty-two years younger than he, had a weak chest and a horror of the cold. Having already endured three Falkland Island winters, he did not think she could survive another. The Colonial Office had given him permission to take her to Uruguay this winter, but he was worried that there was no one to whom he could leave the government. And he could not think of sending her alone in the mail schooner, 'to Monte Video, to remain amongst strangers'.

That day, the Blue Book for 1878 had been finished, written up in the neat hand of William Collins, 'acting colonial treasurer, postmaster, harbourmaster, collector of customs, clerk to the supreme court' – like Callaghan himself, a jack of all trades. For Callaghan was not only governor and commander-in-chief of the Falkland Islands but, in the absence of any other public servants, also chief justice of the supreme court, notary public, vice-admiral of the vice-admiralty court and judge of the islands.

Callaghan took up his pen and began to write his covering dispatch to the Secretary of State, the Right Honourable Sir Michael Hicks Beach. 'Sir,' he began, 'I have the honour to report upon the Blue Book of the Falkland Islands for the year 1878, which has just been submitted to me by the Acting Colonial Secretary.'

Callaghan paused, and turned over the familiar blue pages of the volume. Colonial Office Blue Books were annual reports, first introduced in 1821, almost sixty years before. Blank volumes, embossed with the name of the colony and the year, were sent out from London for completion by the end of each November. The books contained the same headings, the same forms to be completed: taxes, duties and 'other sources of Revenue'; expenditure,

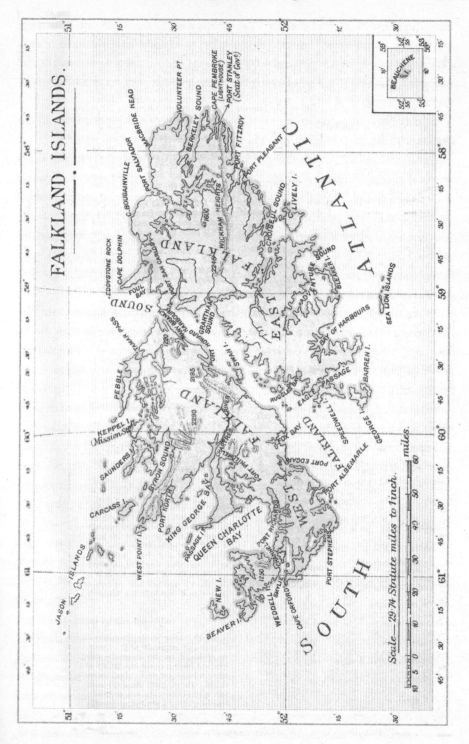

comparisons with previous years; 'the public debt'. Details of public works, legislation, the list of the civil establishment: who they were, what they did, how much they were paid. Lists of pensions, population figures, data on schools, newspapers; gaols and prisoners, criminal statistics, hospitals, imports and exports, shipping.

In sum, here at a glance was the life of a colony, a clear source for measurement and comparison reaching back for years. The deadline for completing the annual Blue Book report, like preparing the estimates for the year to come, was one of the most important dates in the colonial governor's administrative calendar. The task of collecting the information was formidable – and many administrations were content to leave much unchanged from year to year. Callaghan knew his covering letter would be laid before parliament. Governors of larger colonies often delegated the task of writing the covering commentary to the colonial secretary. Not – even if he'd had one – Governor Callaghan.

So many pages now, as Callaghan turned the pages of the slim volume, were at best half full. Even more were blank. The doings of the tiny Falklands were so limited when compared to the wider, grander schemes of more important colonies – and yet there was still so much to say. The problems facing his sheep farmers, overrun by ageing stock; the losses – up to 50 per cent – of sheep imported from Argentina not adapted to the climate. The trackless lands they could not afford to fence; the menace of scab and the merits of lime and sulphur over cheaper tobacco dips, which simply washed off in the rain. And what of the marked progress the chaplain had made to bring the membership of the Stanley Total Abstinence Society to fifty-three men and women? Nor could he fail to record the great peat avalanche at the end of last November which had engulfed the middle of Stanley. Only by the efforts of every man in the settlement ('the gentlemen finding substitutes to take their places') had disaster been averted. The work had taken eight days in bitter cold and rain.

Callaghan was fifty-two, and had been governor of the Falkland Islands for the past three years. In spite of the constant fevers he suffered, his frame had filled out since the days of his youth. His substantial jacket barely met across his chest. His face was round and genial, his beard was full and curling, his dark hair receding high from his forehead. Callaghan was a sensitive and clever man – keen above all to do the right thing.

His father had been a woollen draper in the small town of Midleton in

County Cork. As governor of the Falkland Islands, Callaghan had come a long way. But his career had not turned out quite as his youthful brilliance had promised. From Midleton he had won a place as a classical scholar at Trinity College, Dublin. Then: Barrington Lecturer on Political Economy to the Dublin Statistical Society, and counsel to the attorney-general for Ireland. Callaghan had been a rising star at the Irish bar when, at the age of twenty-eight, he decided to seek appointment with the Colonial Office – and was granted the post of chief magistrate in Hong Kong, with a seat on the Executive Council, which ran the colony.

Callaghan stepped off his ship in 1860. Hong Kong had been founded only fifteen years before; its legal hierarchy suffered from a serious lack of probity. The attorney-general had recently been dismissed for accusing the registrar-general of associating with pirates, while the registrar-general had named the superintendent of police as the man behind a number of brothels. The acting colonial secretary was accused of taking bribes in connection with the opium monopoly. Only one previous magistrate had any legal training. Some wondered if British law was even appropriate in such a setting. The chief requisite was described as 'experience in the subtleties of Chinese character'. Severed queues cut from the heads of criminals hung on display outside the Magistracy, chain gangs of felons were at work building roads. Public floggings took place in Queen's Road, or in the yard of the Land Office, where labourers gathered in search of work. Such was the power of the chief magistrate that the Chinese thought him the head of the government.

Apart from brawling sailors and soldiers, the accused brought before Callaghan were all Chinese. Translation was poor, evidence conflicting, discrimination rife. According to his predecessor, Callaghan arrived at his post only 'to break down under the responsibility of the peculiar and intricate duties which encountered him'. But his ability and concern to do the right thing had also caught the eye of the Governor, Sir Hercules Robinson, the bluff, horseracing man who, almost fifteen years later in Sydney, would go on to negotiate the cession of Fiji from Cakobau in 1874.

In July 1861 Callaghan sailed for Singapore, en route to a promotion: the governorship of Labuan. There he served, in workmanlike manner, as John Pope Hennessy's predecessor. While in Labuan his father died; he wanted to come home to tie up his affairs. There were allusions to a courtship, a desire to get married. 'It is hardly worth his while coming home, he has only just arrived,' was the essence of the Colonial Office's reply. Five years later, Callaghan was so ill with a succession of fevers that he was forced to resign.

Callaghan returned to England. There, on 27 October 1869, he married twenty-year-old Alice Arnold, the daughter of a wealthy solicitor and the mayor of Gravesend, a girl with thin dark hair and a determined eye. They set up home in lodgings in Jermyn Street with somewhat rackety neighbours: wine merchants, a retired barrister, tailors and a comedian. In 1871 Callaghan was appointed administrator of the Gambia, based at Bathurst, a hot and steamy outpost trading in groundnuts at the mouth of the Gambia River on the west coast of Africa. Here he lasted no more than eighteen months. Doctors advised him never to return to a tropical climate. After a long period of convalescence, in 1876 Callaghan and Alice sailed to command the Falkland Islands. With its robust, healthy climate it was a favoured assignment for diseased governors. Callaghan was taking over from the man who had been his predecessor in the Gambia, Colonel D'Arcy.

Unlike Colonel D'Arcy, who embraced the tempestuous climate after thirty years in the tropics, Callaghan found the rigours of the Falklands weather only added to his troubles. He had been far away from centres of civilization before, but never had he been called on to live surrounded by such furious weather, such biting cold, such angry seas, and with such a sense of bleak isolation. 'Bring warm clothing', was the first thing he said to anyone contemplating a visit.

There were fewer than 100 houses in the town of Stanley, and no more than 600 inhabitants. The government establishment numbered less than twenty, including the lighthouse keeper, a gardener and the chaplain, a Roman Catholic priest and a Presbyterian minister. Arthur Bailey, the registrar-general, receiver of wrecks and police magistrate, was Callaghan's effective number two. He had been aurveyor-general since 1848, the earliest days of the colony, and was now close to retirement.

Callaghan thought Government House 'tolerably comfortable'. It had never been finished: only the central hall and one wing had been built, some ten years before. There were carpets, curtains, 'floorcloths, etc'. But the plate was inferior, and there was not enough of it. The public rooms consisted of a drawing room in mahogany and crimson with a large portrait of Her Majesty the Queen in a gilt frame, and a dining room with seating for about a dozen, furnished at government expense. There was a breakfast room, a small anteroom, and two bedrooms upstairs. A wooden extension housed the kitchen, scullery and servants' bedrooms. There was a conservatory and a vegetable garden, and a large paddock. Domestic servants, 'even of an inferior description', were difficult to get, while it was quite 'impossible to obtain a good cook in the Colony'. Callaghan and Alice made do with William Coulson, his office keeper and messenger, as housekeeper. Their diet was simple: fish, rabbit and mutton and plenty of wild 'anti-scorbutics' – celery, scurvy grass, sorrel and cranberries.

Beyond Stanley there were no roads, and riding out, over the tussocky grasslands of the Camp towards the hills, the bogs and streams and fields of stones made journeys into the hills virtually impossible. The only other settlement on the islands that could be called a town was Darwin, headquarters of the Falkland Islands sheep operations, with a works where between 12,000 and 15,000 sheep were 'boiled down' every autumn to make tallow. Half the rest of the 1,200 population lived on the outer islands in isolated houses on sheep runs rented from the government, supplied annually by steamer. The mails from England – eight times a year via the Falkland Island Company's *Black Hawk* from Montevideo on the coast of Uruguay – took at least six weeks, often as many as ten. Letters and supplies from Stanley to West Falklands could take as long as four months. Everyone lived for the few ships that came and went. When the Callaghans arrived, everyone was talking animatedly of the legendary voyage of HMS *Challenger* the year before – the first steam vessel to cross the Antarctic Circle.

Callaghan's first year in post was dominated by three shocking shipping disasters: the first, the rescue, too late, of the captain, his wife and seven of the crew of the *Rafael* of Liverpool, which caught fire off an island at Tierra del Fuego. After heroic efforts to reach them, they were found dead among the rocks from cold and starvation. Then the arrival of the *St Elmo*, reluctantly forced into harbour, with nine of her crew with paralysed hands and feet caused by acute lead poisoning – from repairs to the pipe of the water tank with red and white lead. Not long after, the *Crown Prince* put in, her crew sick from putrid salt pork, six of them delirious and dying. Callaghan was shocked by the callous and careless treatment of the seamen. He reported to London: it would be months before any of those who survived would work again.

Two companies controlled every aspect of life on the islands: the shipping, its two largest stores, and the biggest land and sheep holdings. For transport, for work, for food, for tobacco and drink, the people were entirely dependent on the Falkland Islands Company and its rival, Messrs Dean. Instead of receiving wages, workers were paid mostly in goods, and when they did get any cash, they hoarded it away. Meanwhile the sealing industry and a once-flourishing trade in penguin oil had collapsed. It was only a few days after Callaghan arrived that he learned that Colonel D'Arcy owed the company stores more than £3,000. The colony was broke.

'Poor D'Arcy ought not to be regarded as a responsible being in matters of business,' Callaghan consoled the Colonial Office in February 1878. Not only was the colony in debt, but the accounts were in a mess, and the leases of the Crown lands, issued on the basis of three different navigational charts in *nautical* miles, were in fearful confusion.

But he saw no reason why 'the artisans and labouring classes' should have to pay D'Arcy's debts and 'put large sums of money into the pockets of the two chief Storekeepers'. He knew that the workers were pregnant with grievance. Carpenters in Stanley had recently gone on strike for higher wages. 'As might be expected the men failed to carry their point, the employers being too powerful,' Callaghan went on. Meanwhile, all government works were carried on by the Marines, rather than local craftsmen, 'a fact which has always excited a good deal of local jealousy'.

How to raise money? There was no machinery for valuing property; a tax on houses – so many islanders built their own – would be opposed. Taxing horses 'would yield very little, and create more irritation than serious import . . . there are only about two miles of road in the Colony'. The few ships that did put into harbour were 'more than sufficiently taxed by Stanley prices', to consider a levy of harbour dues. As for the sheep farmers, they were struggling. 'Any Tax would hit the people least able to bear it, while the monopolists who are making large fortunes would go comparatively scot-free,' Callaghan wrote. It was clear to London that no taxation would ever be enough 'to reduce by one farthing the debt of the colony'.

Meanwhile, Callaghan was longing for progress. He was frustrated that the Falklands should produce so much wool, but have no means to manufacture it; that as no trees grew, all wood had to be imported, that as no wheat was planted, bread had to be baked from imported flour, that vegetables were almost unknown and that 'in this paradise of cattle', as the CO put it, all butter and condensed milk were imported. Without steam communication how could the Falklands sheep farmers hope to compete, to keep up with the latest market trends, which for example said that now demand was all for fine merino rather than the coarse wool of the island sheep?

Above all Callaghan wanted to break the monopoly of the Deans and the Falkland Islands Company, which, he warned, could soon present a serious challenge to the government. But he had no powers to do more than suggest that the island should have a meat-processing plant, or that farmers might charter their own vessels to bring out supplies and export their wool to England.

He did not give up. 'The leading people here' may not entertain the ideas of taxes 'at all favourably', Callaghan told London. But at last, by threatening the Deans and the Falklands Island Company with port taxes and the list of charges he had privately rejected in his letter to London, he had succeeded in getting them 'almost to propose' a duty on tobacco – and an increase on the charges on spirits. 'I hope before long that some measure of fixing a rate upon real property may be feasible . . . this would affect the Company and Messrs Dean for whose benefit the Colony may be said in great measure to be kept up. However,' he concluded, 'it would not be wise to attempt to draw all the Dragon's teeth at once.'

Meanwhile he imposed a strict regime: no public works, cutting back the government establishment by not replacing his retiring colonial treasurer and sending home the Marines. By hiring half a dozen policemen he was saving almost £2,000 a year. He set about selling Crown land, and borrowed at moderate interest to pay the creditors back. He begged to be considered for promotion to another government, and suggested to the Colonial Office that then they might consider cutting the governor's salary of £1,200 a year – as soon as he had left.

From the Falklands Islands Blue Book 1878
Exports

VALUE of ARTICLES exported to the United Kingdom during 1878

Article	Value £
Bones, horns, etc.	8
Hides: Ox, cow, calf, and horse	5,170
Junk, metal, and old iron	106
Manufactured goods, re-exported	600
Oil: Seal and penguin	1,312
Sealskins	1,213
Sheepskins	2,040
Tallow	4,874
Wool	35,732
Total	51,055

Now the fruits of all his efforts were revealed in the Blue Book. Not only had the revenue of the islands increased, but under the heading '*Public Debt*', he wrote, 'I am happy to be able to say that at the present moment the Colony may be regarded as out of debt . . .

'Although some depression exists in the trade of Stanley,' he went on, 'prosperity is becoming more diffused throughout the Islands, and the Colony is decidedly, though, slowly progressing.'

Two months after the Blue Book was dispatched, early in July 1879, Callaghan sent his estimates for the following year. 'For the first time in the annals of the Colony the estimated Revenue I am happy to say is in excess of Expenditure required for the year,' he wrote. Winter had by then set in in earnest, and it was clear that his dream of taking Alice to Montevideo for the winter would never be realized. Bailey, the colonial surveyor and his number two, who would have acted as governor, was now so much in the pocket of the Deans and the Falkland Islands Company that he was no longer able 'to withstand the strong pressure put upon him', Callaghan told London. As governor, he could not leave the colony 'without prejudice to the public service'.

Callaghan's own health was suffering. Giving up his leave had had the 'most serious consequence' on him. What had it cost Alice? He looked forward 'with great apprehension to our having to pass another winter here', and once more applied for a promotion.

Confidentially, in the Colonial Office, minutes passed back and forth. 'I think he deserves promotion . . . but few tropical climates would suit him, and his wife cannot stand cold.' Lagos would not do, but 'if the Bahamas should be vacant . . .' Callaghan's claim to the Bahamas was seen to be strong. 'The maladministration of the late Governor left the Colony deeply in debt to local merchants . . . the accounts in a mess, and the leases of Crown Lands in fearful confusion.' Moreover, Callaghan had had to face considerable local opposition in carrying out his austerity measures. 'I believe him to be a very competent man,' minuted the Permanent Secretary, Robert Herbert. And so at last Callaghan won his promotion to the pleasant island that should be his reward for the wreck of his health and twenty years' labour in the service of the Crown.

As a result of Callaghan's entreaties, before he left the Falklands the government completed negotiations for a new mail contract with a steam company from Bremen, which would call at Stanley every second month, en route to Punta Arenas, on the coast of Terra del Fuego in Chile. On 17 June 1880, Callaghan and Alice left the Falklands for six months' leave in England. On 1 February 1881 they landed in the Bahamas.

'I can assure your Lordship that it is with the utmost pain that I ask for leave so soon after my arrival on the Colony,' he cabled to Lord Kimberley four months later. But he had been ill ever since he arrived. 'The change from such a temperate and bracing climate as the Falklands to the Bahamas has tried my constitution – which has been much impaired by Labuan and West Africa in fevers too severely.'

Early in July, Callaghan was carried on board a steamer with Alice for New York. Five days later they landed. Four hours after he was carried into a room at the Metropolitan Hotel he died – 'paralysis of the heart, caused by continued intermittent fever'. He was just fifty-four. Three days later, his coffin, enveloped in a Union Jack, was taken on board the *Elysia* bound for England. In the Bahamas, the flags were lowered to half-mast, and minute guns were fired. Public officers would wear mourning for the next three weeks.

It took a year of lobbying by Alice's uncle, Arthur Arnold MP, to obtain her a pension of £50 a year at the personal recommendation of the Queen. That Callaghan 'virtually sacrificed his life in the interests of his country through successive fevers . . . incurred in the exercise of his official duties' there could be no question. 'He was not an eminent man,' Arnold said of Callaghan, 'but he had done his best.'

10 The Marquess of Lorne and the Indians
Canada 1881

Only days after Thomas Callaghan died in New York, at 11.30 a.m. on 19 July 1881, a train massed with flowers and greenery drew out of the station at Toronto. In the heat of the day, flags waved, crowds cheered. At the centre of attention was a thirty-six-year-old British celebrity of almost god-like good looks: strong chiselled features, a thick mane of golden hair, and compelling blue eyes. He was John George Edward Henry Douglas Sutherland Campbell, Marquess of Lorne, heir to the great dukedom of Argyll, head of the powerful clan Campbell: His Excellency, the Governor-General of Canada. More than this: the Marquess was married to a princess of the realm – Princess Louise, daughter of Queen Victoria.

It was a unique moment, full of glamour. The train was heading west on the first leg of a two-month journey, by rail, ship and canoe, on foot and by horse and cart, more than 2,000 miles into a region scarcely touched by man. Six months earlier, on 15 February, Lorne had given royal assent to a bill to build the Canadian Pacific railway – a link which promised to be one of the greatest feats of engineering the world has ever known.

From the Atlantic provinces of Nova Scotia, New Brunswick and Prince Edward Island, through Quebec and Ontario, on across the breadth of the continent to the Pacific Ocean – the idea was down on paper, some $35 million of credit had been obtained and 25 million acres of land from the government had been promised for the line. But who would travel on it? The press had not been good. Yawning like a gigantic cavity across almost two-thirds of the route were two vast uninhabited territories: Rupert's Land – once the domain of the privately owned Hudson's Bay Company – and, sprawling north and west above the 49th parallel, the border with the United States, the North-West Territory. It was virtually uncharted.

These were lands – endless open plains of grass – that few white men had seen. The first Europeans had stumbled on them from the north. Stranded by Arctic ice in their search for the North-West Passage, the fabled sea route they dreamed would lead to the riches of the Orient, they found themselves in a barren wilderness. Astonishingly, the natives of these parts,

Indians and Inuit, brought forth a rich trade in furs. In 1670, King Charles II granted exclusive rights to the 'Governor and Company of Adventurers of England tradeing [sic] into Hudson's Bay'. For almost 200 years Rupert's Land, frozen for eight months of the year, remained unimaginably remote and desolate. In the words of the Welsh explorer David Thompson, only 'the Red Men', to whom 'these great Plains appear to be given by Providence . . . for ever' roamed the wide grasslands of these territories.

In December 1869, the Hudson's Bay Company sold Rupert's Land for £300,000 cash to the infant dominion of Canada. The transaction led to a fierce rebellion among the Métis, some 2,500 mixed-race people of French and Indian heritage, who had settled along the Red River, south of today's Winnipeg. It was soundly stamped out by General Wolseley. But in the end, the Métis' titles to their lands were recognized, and by the time Lorne set out on his journey in 1881, the tiny province of Manitoba, shaped like a postage stamp, had been added to the Canadian confederation. Beyond it, the rest of the country lay wide open. Lorne was to bring the Canadian West to the attention of the world, attract investors and excite emigration from Britain.

Beside his private desire to go where few white men had gone before, there was another strand to Lorne's agenda, volatile and urgent: a series of councils with Indians. The past three winters had been the hardest in living memory. In this short period, the vast herds of murmuring buffalo that had blackened the prairies since time out of mind had seemed to vanish. Buffalo supplied the Indians of the plains with their every need: food and clothing, hides, sinew and dung for fuel. Now, many Indians believed, it was as if the earth had simply opened up and swallowed them. Without government relief from Ottawa, thousands would have died of starvation.

Meanwhile, in the fledgling Canada of his day, Lorne, as governor-general, was responsible for the conduct of foreign relations – in practice, primarily with the United States, the country's big, blustering neighbour to the south. For almost three years he had been trying to persuade the Americans to allow the Indians to follow the remaining buffalo where they would, back and forth across the border line, and to treat them with humanity. His pleas had fallen on deaf ears.

For months now, the Indians had known that their 'Great Brother' was to visit them. Recently there had been reports of strange movements among them, of tribes moving to regions they never usually visited in the early summer, rumours of gatherings for a great Sun Dance, when, vilely mutilated, dancing until they dropped, the chieftains of the tribe prayed for guidance from the Great Spirit. Lorne's mission was to plead with them to change their way of life, to settle down and turn to farming, if they were to have a future.

All that long hot, dusty day on the train, hundreds of people, who had travelled miles to see him, gathered at every stopping place, eager to see and touch the Governor-General and hear him speak. For Lorne it was a succession of carpeted platforms, pavilions decorated with flowers, flags, triumphal arches, skirling bagpipes, and speeches, speeches, speeches.

He delivered seven speeches that day, each tailored for the people he met, each of his own composition. Crowds cheered the Queen; people brought him into their homes. An old man who had been in Canada for forty-seven years told him how he remembered his grandfather. Lorne had a gift for the phrase that somehow cheered the men about him, lifting them with visions of a prosperous future. He moved easily from English into French, from German into Gaelic, greeting the settlers with outstretched hands and a wide grin.

As governor-general, charged with meeting his own costs of travel, Lorne was personally bankrolling the whole operation. Beside him were his military secretary, Colonel de Winton, who for months had been overseeing every detail of the arrangements, three aides-de-camp, a doctor and his French chef. Then there was his press corps. Lorne was determined to get the maximum press coverage. Charles Austin of *The Times,* fellow of St John's College, Oxford, veteran of the Siege of Paris in 1870 and the war in Constantinople, had previously travelled across Australia and the Pacific. Sydney Hall, a swift, talented artist, represented the *Graphic.* The *Scotsman* was represented by the venerable, but irrepressibly enthusiastic forty-nine-year-old Scottish preacher Dr Hamish MacGregor, of St Cuthbert's, Edinburgh, one of the leading churchmen of his day, and a personal friend of the Queen. He doubled as chaplain to the party. Lorne himself would take care of sketches for the *Illustrated London News.* Following in their slipstream, at their paper's expense, were reporters from the *Telegraph* in London and the *Globe* in Toronto, Reuters and the *New York Times* and *Le Gaulois* from Paris.

Early in the evening Lorne's party boarded a steamer on the shores of Georgian Bay, arriving at a sleepy hamlet for a final speech at 11 p.m. 'Dust, sun and speechifying took much out of one,' Lorne confessed to his father. But the party was in high spirits. For everyone, it was a chance to go where few had ever gone before – all expenses paid. There was no doubt they were in the vanguard of a great movement.

'People have Manitoba and the North-West on the brain,' wrote Austin. All over, people were selling up to 'push on West'.

Five years before, in the snows of the winter that followed the deaths of General Custer and 260 of his men at the celebrated Battle of Little Big Horn on 25 June 1876, the American cavalry had driven Chief Sitting Bull across the border into Canada. Thousands of Sioux, men, women and children, came with him. They settled at Wood Mountain, forty miles north of the border, in what is today southern Saskatchewan: lands that belonged by tradition to the Cree and the Blackfoot. The Sioux were desperate, food so scarce they were eating their horses, so short of ammunition they had to turn their knives into spears.

'We can go nowhere without seeing the head of an American,' Sitting Bull explained to the North-West Mounted Police. 'Our land is small, it is like an island. We have two ways to go – to the land of the Great Mother [Canada] or to the land of the Spaniards [Mexico].' He swore to them he had come in peace, and that his people had no intention of returning to attack American troops or settlers. Colonel MacLeod, the commissioner of the North-West Mounted Police, accepted his word. He told Sitting Bull that the Queen recognized the Sioux as American Indians who had come to Canada for protection. But he warned him: under no circumstances must the Sioux cross the line of the border or make war.

All the same, Canadians were nervous. No other chief on the Great Plains could rival Sitting Bull. 'As ambitious as Napoleon, and brave to a fault,' one mounted policeman told Ottawa. 'He is respected, as well as feared, by every Indian on the plains; in war he has no equals; in council he is superior to all; every word laid by him carries weight, is quoted and passed from camp to camp.' From the beginning of the 1870s Ottawa had painstakingly negotiated seven treaties with the tribes of the west, by which they ceded their hunting grounds to the Crown in return for safe reservations and annual annuities. Under the terms of the treaties, the Indians were permitted to hunt upon their ancestral lands as long as the game remained. Now the Sioux had moved into the territory of their traditional enemies, the Cree, the Blackfoot, Assiniboine, the Blood, the Piegans and Sarcees, while the buffalo dwindled away.

In the winter of 1878, hundreds of Canadian Indians and Sioux, desperate for food, rode south of the border hunting for the ever more elusive buffalo. From Washington, the American government reported tales of Indian brutality and running horses over the border. Ottawa thought the stories exaggerated. Washington warned Canada she would hold her responsible for Sioux behaviour. Tensions rose. In April 1879, Lorne cabled Sitting Bull to tell him that 'the "Great Mother" would not stand attacks being made on her allies from our frontier'. That summer it was rumoured that Sitting Bull was building a grand alliance with the Blackfoot and the Cree to invade the United States. On 11 September 1879 Lorne met the US Secretary of State, William Evarts, in Toronto.

Evarts was the grandson of one of the signatories to the American Declaration of Independence, a Harvard-educated lawyer, grim-faced, self-righteous and puritanical. He was known to be fond of long, complicated legal arguments – and procrastination.

'Looks like you're expecting Indian trouble,' he told the Governor-General.

'That's exactly what we are trying to avoid,' said Lorne. Canada did not need over 4,000 foreign Indians – American Indians – while her own Indians were practically starving, he told him.

'We always feed our Indians.' Evarts was patronizing. 'Maybe you should do the same.'

Lorne told him the government had voted large sums of money to do so. They had sent the Indians a number of instructors in farming. They were doing all they could – 'but when people are hungry, they can get desperate', he warned Evarts. 'I don't want the situation getting any worse because you won't allow the Sioux to cross into the States.'

'The hostile Sioux entered Canadian territory as an armed force at war with the United States,' Evarts shot back. 'You offered them protection. According to international law you are responsible for their conduct. If you had behaved correctly you would have disarmed and interned them.'

Lorne thought it absurd to apply the strict letter of international law to a frontier of 1,000 miles where there were hardly any white men, and where for generations large bodies of Indians had been following migrating herds of buffalo north and south over the prairie. Furthermore, with no more than three or four hundred mounted police along the whole north-west boundary, Canada had not the forces that could possibly keep guard upon an Indian nation, interned, as Evarts suggested.

'Even you, with all your people and your larger military force, have found it almost impossible to keep the Indians on their reservations,' Lorne said.

Lorne wanted only one thing out of Evarts: to open up the border to allow the free movement of Indians and buffalo. Meanwhile he told him that the American terms for a Sioux surrender made it almost impossible for them to comply. That they should surrender their arms in return for government food: Lorne could just about stomach it. But 'it seemed especially hard to exact from such a nomadic people the surrender of their horses', as Evarts was demanding.

Like previous meetings, the talk accomplished nothing. Within weeks Evarts was complaining of new incursions by 'British Indians and half-breeds'. Early in 1880 a Sioux buffalo hunt strayed south into American territory. Some braves got out of hand. They attacked two American hunters, raided settlements along the Yellowstone River, and ran off a pony herd. Evarts dispatched an angry communiqué to Ottawa: the Sioux were 'fully armed and prepared for the commission of warlike acts'. Lorne insisted the Indians were only after game.

By the time the snows melted in the spring of 1881, the Sioux in Canada were living off duck eggs and roots. At the end of May, Sitting Bull met the Indian commissioner for the North West Territory in the Qu'Appelle River valley, in today's Saskatchewan.

'I shake hands with the White man on this side and I feel safe. I shake hands with the Americans and I am afraid of them,' he told him. He begged him, for the second time, to grant them a reservation. But Ottawa feared that Sitting Bull might only create a magnet for disaffected Indians. The answer was 'No.'

A month before he set off on his journey from Toronto, Lorne was told that Sitting Bull's resources were exhausted. He was unlikely to meet him on the plains. Not long afterwards, Sitting Bull set out from his camp at Wood Mountain with 187 men, women and children. On 19 July, the day Lorne boarded his train in Toronto, he crossed into the United States and surrendered to the US cavalry. They put him in prison.

'Westward Ho! for the great plains and rivers, and the wild Indians!' Lorne wrote in his diary as he set out for the prairies. He was Scottish and a romantic. To him the Indians were a species of 'wild men', nervy, unpredictable, with a tendency to lash out if surprised or treated unfairly. But he had also been brought up in a tradition of duty and service, according to codes of honour stretching back to the ancient clans of the Highlands. He sensed that like himself, the word of an Indian chief was his bond; that these people had their codes too.

Apart from his role in foreign affairs, as governor-general, Lorne's powers were nominal. The prime minister with his Cabinet ran the country. Lorne could only advise. Like the Queen, whom he represented, he signed bills into law, laid foundation stones and provided ceremonial for the state. He kept the Colonial Office informed of events, described personalities, eased the way for the realization of Canadian policy, and promoted the nation.

He had no qualifications. Lorne was only thirty-three – exceptionally young – when he was appointed in 1878, and completely untried. But he had one important attribute – his wife. 'A thrill of joy burst upon the Dominion with the announcement that a member of the Royal Family was coming to take up her abode in Canada,' wrote Charles Tuttle, an up-and-coming Canadian journalist. Lorne, 'a nobleman of well known literary tastes and ability', was rather overlooked in the rejoicing over 'the great compliment which her Majesty paid to our loyalty in sending us her beautiful & accomplished daughter the Princess Louise'.

In fact, there was not much to distinguish Lorne. He had never been an early riser; no amount of tutoring at Eton and Cambridge had succeeded in making him a student. He was a dreamer. He loved the great forest trees and superb vistas of his family's homes on the west coast of Scotland: Inveraray Castle in Argyllshire and Rosneath, an Italianate villa begun in 1803 – 'on a scale no available money could finish'. He hunted, shot and fished; he sketched and painted. He had, in the words of his younger sister, Frances, an 'astonishing facility' for composing rhyming verse and a passion for romantic poetry.

After the young Princess Louise, fourth daughter of Queen Victoria, had rejected several continental princes, she declared her intention of marrying 'someone from her own country'. Lorne's was one of a handful of names that the Queen would consider. He was so beautiful to look at, so kind and thoughtful, of such excellent and ancient family, and had been in and out of Balmoral and Buckingham Palace from the days of his childhood. After an afternoon with Louise at Balmoral and an indication that his suit would be acceptable, twenty-five-year-old Lorne declared his devotion. He and Louise were married on 21 March 1871. She was twenty-two.

Seven years after the marriage there was still no sign of children. Living in Kensington Palace, holidaying in the Highlands, Lorne and Louise took an interest in education, helping plan the Girls Public Day School Trust and fund-raising for Church of England clerics. She was painting and sculpting; he was publishing soppy poetry. Louise's elder brothers, including the Prince of Wales, did not care for him. They 'looked upon him as a regular outsider'.

Indeed, there was a difference about Lorne that no one could quite put a finger on. His manner to women was 'if anything too chivalrous'. At Eton he was remembered 'for his manly beauty of a fine Celtic type'. Was he gay? His sister Frances came closest to saying so. 'In the ball rooms of that date', dancing with his lovely sister, Elizabeth, Lorne shone: 'a bright peculiar star'.

Whispers about the marriage; Lorne in danger of becoming a dilettante; someone more important than a mere official needed to inspire and hold the loyalty of the newly formed dominion of Canada, the possibility of Louise as 'Her Canadian Majesty': the call, when it came on 24 July 1878, to meet the prime minister, held no surprise for Lorne. He had dreamed it all some days before.

'"One of 'our great Viceroyalties' was vacant," Dizzy said, "he wished me to take it. Then full stop, to see if I was surprised . . .' When Lorne suggested that other men had the administrative experience that was needed, Disraeli demurred. 'He was most anxious that I should take it, and believed I had abilities. A bow on my part, and another question.' But Disraeli had already spoken to the Queen, who, at first unhappy that her daughter would be so far, 'but considering that Canada is now only ten days off, and that you might come home . . . every year . . . she was quite in favour of the proposal. So I made my bow and left . . .'

Lorne loved Canada from the moment he and Louise arrived in November 1878. The raw, untamed land, the wide Ottawa River with its roaring cascade over the Chaudière Rocks, the sense of untapped power and the wealth of endless forests seemed to answer something in him. He had been astonished at the warmth of the welcome crowds of people seemed to give them. 'The view of Ottawa crowned by the Towers of the Houses of Parliament is really fine'; Government House, Rideau Hall, was big and comfortable, 'much superior to Kensington', he wrote home. He loved the climate, the tremendous cold, the icicles that gathered on the hair round his mouth when he walked out in the frost; the dryness of the air, and the static that collected from the rugs under his feet so he could light the gas in a lamp

The Marquess of Lorne and Princess Louise arrive in state by sleigh in Ottawa

with the snap of his fingers. The exercise: tobogganing, skating, curling, hunting for moose, camping in the wilds of Quebec, canoeing up rivers, fishing for trout and salmon. He called a little cabin he had on Lake Erie after the teeming flocks of birds, 'Duckopolis'.

The life he and Louise created in Rideau Hall was translated from country house parties in Scotland. There were skating and tobogganing parties, snowshoeing, golf and tennis. He organized amateur dramatics after dinner, and wrote poems to commemorate all sorts of events. His dog stole all the newspapers and tore them to pieces, along with his guests' slippers and socks. He and Louise regularly entertained the Cabinet, the military, the MPs, and any visiting dignitaries. He travelled constantly.

He cheerfully acknowledged his shortcomings. 'Of all things, finance to me is the most puzzling,' he admitted after meeting bankers on his first visit to Toronto. He liked to talk about farming, cattle rearing, duck shooting. He was fond of collecting novel inventions and domestic tips: a new-fangled handle for opening a gate, how to pick grapes or store apples so they lasted all winter, how to pack birds in a barrel so they would keep around a stovepipe filled with ice. He wanted to know how dogs in Labrador managed to catch fish.

Lorne's sketch of his snowshoe club descending through the woods in Indian file

As for his marriage, in tiny provincial Ottawa speculation was rife. Louise was artistic; she painted frescoes on the walls of their rooms. She was not as handsome as he was; she was cold, haughty, disparaging of colonial life. And then there was his 'peculiarity'. A little more than a year after the royal couple arrived in Canada, in February 1880, Louise was seriously injured in a sleighing accident.

Dragged for 400 yards over ice and snow by runaway horses, it was 'a wonder that her skull was not fractured', Lorne told his father. The shock and its aftermath told on her. In the summer of 1880 Louise returned to England. Lorne was constantly in touch with the royal doctors, but no one seemed to be able to get to the bottom of what ailed her. A year later there was no question that she could accompany him on his journey to the Indians.

'I fear the NW journey would certainly be too fatiguing,' he told his father. 'Flies, heat, dust and long drives across the Prairie would knock her up.'

★

Day two: the trip was going well. The party was on board a steamer sailing along the north shore of Lake Huron. The day was sunny yet cool, the water delicious. Hundreds of islands dotted the water like jewels. It was a starlit night as the party landed to the salute of a Highland piper on the sacred island of the Manitou, home of the 'Great Spirit' of the Algonquins. Here was the journalists' first encounter, face to face, with 'real Indians', men going by names like Nahgahbok, Obatonaway, Gahezheonga. They lived by fishing, berrying and basketwork.

The chief, 'very Indian in face and physique', was 'disappointingly European in his dress', Charles Austin told his readers in *The Times*. A large George III medal on a red ribbon hung from his neck – given to his ancestors for services 'rendered in our old wars' against the French and 'the revolted colonies'. 'They still spoke of themselves and their English friends as "King George's men" to distinguish themselves from the Americans, the "Long Knives".'

Slowly, deliberately, his hands spread wide, the chief welcomed Lorne as his 'dear Father'. 'When I see the beauty of the stars above us I think of the god who made them, and pray that He will prosper you and bless our meeting together this evening. All the people of the lake will welcome you.'

'I believe your words come from your heart,' Lorne replied.

The next day a flotilla of thirty canoes paddled out to greet the steamer. On the bank a line of braves fired their rifles. As Lorne stepped ashore, a mass of Indians, with their wives and families, crowded round him. 'A motley crew,' recorded MacGregor, 'some of them clad in old-fashioned military cloaks, all with the streaks of various coloured paints across their face.' Domestically, however, the Ojibeway seemed disconcertingly Europeanized, living in houses 'quite as comfortable . . . and quite as clean as that of many a small English farmer, with four-posters and dressers . . . adorned with well washed crockery', and shouting 'hip-hip hurrah' in honour of the governor-general.

'This conduct is pronounced by connoisseurs painfully un-Indian,' reported Austin. Curiosity, awe, and not a little fear runs through the British journalists' dispatches. They are superior, they are entitled to be there. Yet they note, uncomfortably, the feeling that 'the white man has corrupted his red brother'. Meanwhile, they take down every detail of these riveting and strange encounters.

The chief's face was massive, with sculpted, rugged features. His headdress was of skunk fur, eagle feathers – each one the symbol of a slaughtered enemy – and claws. He wore a long scarlet waistcoat with brass buttons, huge leather leggings that bagged over a pair of moccasins. He took from his neck a basketwork mat. On one side two figures brandished tomahawks, on the other they shook hands in peace. He offered it to Lorne, 'who at once courageously transferred it to his own neck, greatly to the delight of the old chief and the rest of the band'.

Then the chief spoke, his voice, clear and fearless, his gestures full of grace and force.

'We were many. We now are few. The white man comes, his axe cuts down one tree, he takes the fish from our rivers.' He told Lorne how he had been to Ottawa three times to ask what had happened to his land – some 700 miles from Parry Sound to Lake Superior – which he had surrendered to the Queen. 'I only want what is my own,' he said.

This was no speech drafted by some British Indian agent. Lorne's party was deeply moved.

'His attitude as he stood full in front of the Governor-General dilating on his wrongs would have made even a tailor soon forget the queer cut and jumble of clothes,' recorded Austin. Lorne solemnly promised the chief his treaty rights would be respected. His claim would be investigated.

Privately, however, he and the rest of the party were nonplussed. These people seemed so comfortable. The scale of the chief's current reserves seemed enormous – twelve miles long by three miles wide, for only 360 men, women and children? Surely the Indians could make a comfortable living from farming?

'But [this is] not much to their taste,' said MacGregor.

'Out of sight of shore, Lake Superior. We have been steaming steadily for three days and nights, and yet we cannot reach Thunder Bay at the north-west corner of the lake till tomorrow,' Lorne wrote on 24 July. 'Absolute calm has been our fortunate lot.' At Thunder Bay the expedition picked up the railway again. Here the line was still under construction. Progress was uncomfortably slow. They crawled along in the train, the road not even 'ballasted', rolling and pitching over boggy ground. Once their carriages even lurched off the rails. They were hoisted back on 'by means of clamped, sloping irons, known as "dogs"'. Around them the country seemed much wilder. The forest hugged the rail track, breaking only occasionally to reveal glimpses of lake and bog. The soil was poor. Settlers, mostly living in shanties, were few.

After two days on the train, the party transferred to canoes for the long haul up the Lake of the Woods. Everyone lay back and drank in the scenery. 'Far away from the noise and dust of civilization amid islands of every variety of shape and beauty, covered to the water's brink with forests unpeopled and wild as when they were first made, with not a sound, not even a bird-note . . . to disturb the savage solitude, save the plash and ripple of the waves against the sides of the canoe, and the regular steady sweep of the paddles, doing 50, or at a spurt, 60 strokes to the minute,' wrote Austin.

Crossing the Lake of the Woods: sketch by Sydney Prior Hall

For Lorne there were no addresses to make, no grievances to hear. He took out his notebook, sketched, and wrote. 'A night camp . . . the tawny birch-bark flotilla just floats with painted prows resting on clean sands, and the fire's glow falls on the nearer pines and firs, and a clear moon shows the more distant forest slopes backed by some huge crag . . .'

For three days they paddled, off-loaded, portaged, re-loaded, paddled. It was as the Indians had travelled for hundreds of years. The final push was a nine-mile portage. Their Indian guides trotted ahead carrying their canoes, baggage hanging down their backs from broad straps running round their foreheads. The day was extremely hot, not a breath of wind stirred. Lorne led the white men over a 'villainous path' of tree roots and boulders, infested with mosquitoes and blackfly. Enveloped in head-veils and gauntlets of caribou hide, the party soldiered on, now on the smouldering skirts of a forest fire, up over huge boulders and on, until at last they emerged from the bush on the shores of yet another lake – to be greeted by boatmen in blue caps and red jackets and a piper playing the bagpipes beside a steam tug: 'carpeted, canopied, easy-chaired, and rich in iced drinks, ready to take [Lorne] to the lovely little island on which we were to pass the night.

'Now we saw a little town of tents, most conspicuous and welcome, among them the large dinner tent, all so fresh and clean and fitted up so carefully with every comfort, from bath-towels to mosquito curtains,' wrote Austin. Every item of furniture, including the four-poster beds, had been cut from the forest a day or two before.

'Winnipeg is in a fever,' Lorne told Lord Kimberley at the Colonial Office on 3 August. The party had arrived in a splendid Pullman railway car after another 100 miles of track, at a little wooden station with a banner overhead: 'We want willing hands to work the soil!' Four hundred Swedes had just arrived, eager to take up land. All day long, Red River carts rumbled west outside their door. The price of land was rising daily.

Lorne was upbeat. 'In 18 months the Railway will probably be made to the Rocky Mountains!' he told the Queen. 'Even now they are laying a mile and a half a day, and their rate is to be increased greatly . . . Here everybody is full of confidence and hope, and no wonder with these marvellous fertile plains stretching apparently to Infinity all around them.'

For as far as the eye could see there were waving fields of wheat. The soil was a deep rich loam, 'as black as coal', the correspondents reported. The climate, they cabled east – to London, Toronto, New York, Edinburgh and Paris – was excellent.

From Winnipeg there were 100 more miles of rail on which to travel. Thirty-five miles beyond the village of Portage La Prairie, the track ran out. Beyond, a flat plain seemed to stretch to infinity. In shimmering heat, Lorne laid a couple of ties and declared a great future to the railway. At four the next morning, Monday 8 August, the expedition set off on its most challenging leg: by horse and cart for 1,200 miles across open prairie towards the Rocky Mountains.

Following a trail used by the Indians and the people of the Hudson Bay Company, it was a military march. Seventy-seven men, ninety-six horses, twenty-seven vehicles and twenty-one tents. Forty-seven of them were mounted police, dressed like dragoons: spiked white helmets, red jackets,

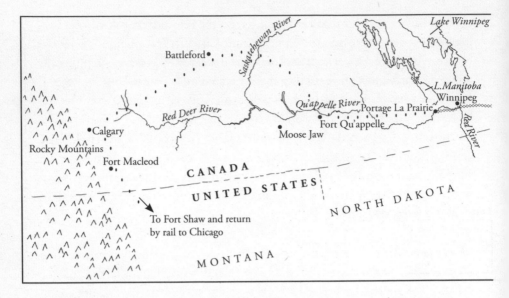

armed with carbine and revolver, and high boots; each wagon numbered,
each driver knowing exactly what to do. Reveille at four in the morning,
crawling out of sleeping bags made of buffalo hide, tucking back mosquito
nets dampened by the dew. The aim was to travel forty miles a day: from
places with wood and water, to more wood and water.

They were travelling light – a few flannel shirts, socks and a change of
suits. Lorne, dusty and travel-stained, now met dignitaries who wore white
tie and tails, in gaiters and a flannel shirt. He sat up in a specially designed
lightweight carriage beside Hamish MacGregor, whose legs were too short
to reach the floor, while he made notes for the *Scotsman*, and Sydney Hall,
sketching for the *Graphic*. Beside them rode Edgar Dewdney, a giant of a
man, wearing a fringed buckskin jacket and flaring mutton-chop whiskers.
Dewdney was the commissioner for Indian affairs: the man who had negotiated with Sitting Bull. Few other white men knew more about the Plains
Indians. They called him 'Whitebeard'.

For hours they saw no sign of human habitation. Lorne could not get
over the beauty of the prairie. The distance seemed infinite. 'You gaze and
the intense clearness of the air is such that you have never seen so distinctly
or so far over such wide horizons before.' Coming across a farmhouse, Lorne
would drop down from the carriage to question the inhabitants on every
aspect of prairie life: bushels per acre of wheat, barley and oats, on the cold
('much better than Ontario, it's dry'), the seasons, the appalling blizzards
which swept across in winter; wages, supplies of wood, machinery, the

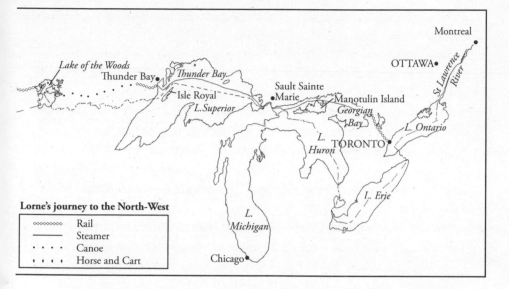

Lorne's journey to the North-West

∞∞∞∞∞	Rail
——	Steamer
· · · ·	Canoe
ı · ı · ı	Horse and Cart

labour supply, the amount of capital a farmer needed. The men were cheer-ful, the women less sanguine. The loneliness, they said – no neighbours to talk to, nowhere for the children to go to school, the nearest doctor fifty miles off. It wore them down. Then Lorne would ride on, to catch up the column as it moved across the plain.

Late in the afternoon a halt was called. The carts were unharnessed, and the horses careered away over the prairie or rolled in the long grass. Tents were pitched in a double line, camp beds were put up, and water for the nightly bath was put on to boil. Parties went out to shoot snipe or teal and widgeon, prairie hen and grouse.'You would never complain of the want of bird life in this part of the Dominion,' Lorne wrote. 'All the ponds and lakes swarmed with wild fowl.'

For three days, they saw no sign of human life. Flat, empty for as far as the eye could see, there was nothing but a waving sea of billowing grass. Some of the party were finding it hard. The solitude was oppressive, almost over-whelming. Weary and covered in dust, one afternoon, 350 miles west of Winnipeg, they arrived at the Hudson's Bay fort on the river at Qu'appelle. It was 17 August.

'Here they come, as I write, to the Great Pow-Wow in the square of the Hudson's Bay Fort,' wrote MacGregor, 1,500 Indians from 150 wigwams – Cree, Stoneys and Sioux. From as far away as 400 miles they had travelled and waited for more than three weeks to meet Lorne. 'These are the red-skins gathered in such numbers and in such circumstances as few strangers from Europe will have a chance of seeing again.'

Some had come to collect their government annuities (five dollars per head, for men, women and children; chiefs and headmen twenty-five and fifteen dollars respectively) and government presents – clothing, ammunition, flour. As their names were called out by the interpreter, each chief stepped forward to salute their 'Great Brother' as he sat beneath an awning, his officers behind him: Standing Buffalo, Loud Voice, Little Black Bear, Dark Star, Yellow Quill, and Man-who-has-got-the-stars-for-a-blanket, swarthy, black-eyed. A long silence. The smoking of pipes. And then the dance began.

'Six men almost naked, with blackened bodies, shields and long spears, decorated with feathers. Each of them has as a head-piece the bushy skin of a buffalo head with the horns. They are Sioux performing the buffalo dance, amid fierce shouting and prolonged "ughs" – the figures used by hunters to entice the buffalo into the corral.'

In the intervals, warriors came forward and narrated stories of their victories and other exploits. 'They tell Lorne their story. He replies.' He told them that the days of the buffalo were over. That they must turn their hands to the plough, must learn from the government farmers who had been employed to train them. The talks with the Sioux ended, and the ones with the Cree began. For six hours the pow-wow went on. Still the chiefs put to him the same question: 'Did I give my lands away?'

'Their incessant begging and whining', as Austin put it, grated on Lorne's nerves. But none of the white men could remain unmoved by the Indians' plight. 'It does seem hard that a man born for war and chase should be told to dig like a farm-labourer, especially by those who have practically taken from him the land he inherited from countless generations,' Austin told his readers in *The Times*. As for Lorne, these men lived by codes of honour he could understand. 'The Indian would not touch the food supply of a friend, although he himself might be almost starving,' he was to write afterwards. However apparently cruel, merciless and crafty the Indian might be against his enemies, to his friends 'he spoke the truth, and was true in his friendship'.

It was at that great pow-wow that Lorne was told of the case of Starlight, a boy who shot a mounted policeman. The story ran that as his old father lay dying he told his sons that it was the scarcity of buffalo that had killed him. And that as 'the want of the buffalo was owing to the white men, his children should revenge him. Under the impression that it was a duty he owed his father "Starlight" took his opportunity . . .' The story of the son who avenged his father stayed with Lorne for the rest of his life.

1 September: 'It is bitterly cold today, and freezing hard.' For days the rain had been cold and driving. Thick ice covered water buckets in the morning. The harsh reality of life on the plains was beginning to tell on Lorne's expedition. The vast ocean of grass 'as level and boundless as the sea' rolled on. Now the carts began to break down, horses dropped, yet still the mosquitoes swarmed. There was not a tree, a bush or a rock. There was no wood for fuel. Water, brackish and salty, was increasingly difficult to find. Overhead long skeins of geese were flying south; the game birds had vanished. The expedition was entirely dependent on two guides, a Métis called Johnnie Saskatchewan and the great chief of the Cree, known as Poundmaker, with dark olive skin and four thick plaits of black hair that dropped almost to his waist.

Everywhere now the ground was pitted by buffalo wallows, and seamed with buffalo trails, running from north to south, 'thickly sprinkled with their whitening bones', wrote MacGregor. 'But for these visible proofs, one would doubt what they so often hear of these prairies being literally covered by these multitudinous numbers.' Still not a sign of life was seen.

For a week they rode on, missing a supply of oats and fresh horses that had been sent to await them. On over the desolate ground, short of water, short of supplies, the escort now living on half rations. About ten in the morning on 7 September they reached the rough, rolling valley of the Red Deer River. Looking up over the hills and ravines, Poundmaker made a sign to Saskatchewan: a small herd of buffalo was grazing on the slope of a hill a mile away. It was Lorne's privilege to shoot one of the beasts, but he demurred: the expedition was too much in need of meat. He indicated for Johnnie Saskatchewan, the best hunter on the best pony, to lead the hunt. He and Poundmaker rode off in pursuit of the buffalo until, 'at last came the welcoming ring of a rifle shot', wrote Austin. The journalists arrived at the scene of the kill to see Poundmaker cut into the carcass, pick out a kidney and eat it raw.

Thirty-five days of continuous marching, 1,100 miles with no communications: towards evening on 9 September Lorne and his party crowned the breast of a rise. Far away in the distance the magnificent blue-grey peaks of the Rocky Mountains jumbled along the whole length of the horizon. At their feet ranged a rugged line of muddy foothills. Closer to: a belt of green trees, and glancing through it, a silver river. On the far side of the water were dotted hundreds of teepees: the Blackfoot and Sarcees.

By 9 a.m. the next morning Lorne and his police escort were scrubbed, polished, dressed in scarlet and waiting beneath an awning looking towards the mountains. Scores of Indians galloped towards them on horseback, letting off Winchester rifles into the air. They wheeled to a halt, shouting and brandishing their weapons. Leaping to the ground, they strode to where Lorne stood waiting. At their head was Crowfoot, chief of the Blackfoot, a man who Lorne was told had fought nineteen battles, been wounded six times, and rescued a child from the jaws of a grizzly bear. Crowfoot had signed a treaty with the Canadian government four years before. Behind him ranged the rest of his tribe: young warriors wearing little more than paint on their bodies, warlocks braided with brass over their temples, their hair falling from where it was gathered on the crown; and old braves, women and children. The Blackfoot settled down on the ground. There, they smoked for a long time.

After a while tom-toms sounded, and dancing began. 'Strange, weird and uncouth these dances are,' Lorne wrote. 'The braves following each other round and round a circle, strutting, stamping, bowing, howling . . . until the music ceases, when all sit upon the ground [and] eloquent and fervent harangues[begin].'

This was Lorne's seventh great 'pow-wow' with the Indians. He knew that first, long ago, the white man had given them horses; then they had given them guns. He had heard the same grievances over and over: the loss of Indian lands, the loss of the buffalo. Lorne had come to share Fenimore Cooper's view of the 'red man'. *The Last of the Mohicans* 'might exaggerate the Indian's stateliness and virtues but his main picture is a true one,' he was to write later. Now that the buffalo had gone Lorne could see no way for Crowfoot and his people to survive, unless they settled down in one place and turned to farming.

According to Lorne, Crowfoot heard his message and accepted it. He instructed his council: now the people had to plant seed and grow crops. He grasped Lorne's hand and, wrapping the cord of his horse's bridle around his arm, asked him to accept it as his gift. 'I who have been the first in fighting,' he told Lorne, 'will now be the first in working.'

Nor were Lorne's words lost on his guide, Poundmaker. In the snows of the following winter he gathered the Cree. 'Next summer, or at latest next fall, the railway will be close to us, the whites will fill the country, and they will dictate to us as they please,' he told them. 'It is useless to dream that we can frighten them. That time is past. Our only resource is our work, our industry, and our farms. Work hard, sow grain, and take care of your cattle. And send your children to school.'

'*Evening*. We have had a long and satisfactory meeting – over 3,000 Blackfeet being present,' Lorne wrote to Queen Victoria after his day with Crowfoot. 'These people are much the best equipped we have seen, having many good ponies, and fine beaded dresses . . . The Yankees shoot them wherever they see them, which I think monstrous and abominable, & they have now sent troops to prevent them crossing the Line in pursuit of Buffalo. They always declare their only object in going is to get food and see their friends –

'I hope that all the assemblies we have had will do good in settling them. We do feed them here, but it is against our will, for we wish them to become independent through working on farms to which we appoint instructors. Little urchins, women and warriors are now at my window rubbing their stomachs to show they want food. The fine rifles and revolvers with which they are well armed wd make them a troublesome lot to deal with if they took it into their heads to make quarrels, for our force of Cavalry, called "Police" is small.'

On 15 September Lorne's expedition reached the site of today's city of Calgary – the furthest point fixed for the line of the new railway. There were five houses. Two or three white men were experimenting with raising cattle in the foothills of the Rockies, with startling success. 'Men hereabouts speak of it as "God's country",' the ranchers told him. Standing on top of a hill with a magnificent view of mountain and prairie, Lorne agreed. A year later he told a visitor to Rideau Hall, 'if I was not Governor-General of Canada, I would be a cattle rancher in Alberta'.

On 24 September Lorne's party crossed the American frontier into Montana where they boarded a train to Chicago. Within a fortnight he was back in Winnipeg. At a banquet of businessmen on 9 October he delivered a 'trumpet-tongued' address, telling his audience, 'you have a country whose value it would be insanity to question'.

Back in Ottawa Lorne told the Prime Minister, 'the inclination shown by [the Indians] to take advantage of farm instruction is marked'. Industrial schools should be established on every reserve, and implements, seed and stock supplied. He wanted permits to be issued to Indians to allow them to cross the US border freely. It was while travelling in the west that Lorne heard that the Smithsonian Institution in Washington had been gathering Indian artefacts. Now he drove forward the idea for the Royal Society of Canada, to which he would in due course bequeath his own collection of the artefacts he gathered on his journey.

Lorne's expedition was a modern royal progress, designed to promote growth, raise morale and unite the people, in the full glare of media attention. Charles Austin, Hamish MacGregor and Sydney Hall's illustrations for the *Graphic*; the reports in the *Globe* and the *New York Times*: for five months his journey was constantly in the news. Lorne's own drawings filled pages of the *London Illustrated News* in December 1881. He opened up the idea of the Canadian west as a land of unfathomable promise to the white man, but to the plight of the Indians he offered scant solution. The days of their glory had already diminished. Now they stood helpless before brutal forces of change – changes that Lorne, blind to their impact, was himself promoting.

It took just fifteen months to build the Canadian Pacific Railway across the prairies, in spite of Cree attempts to pull up the rails and set up camp on the line. Like a glittering spear it thrust its way across the ancient hunting grounds of the Blackfoot and the Cree. Now the Indians were moved to new reservations north of the rails – even further from the US border, on what was judged the best land for agriculture. By the winter of 1882, less than eighteen months after Lorne had seen them, 5,000 Indians were starving in the vicinity of Fort Walsh on the Manitoba/Saskatchewan border. Soon afterwards, thousands of new settlers moved on to the prairies. The grasslands were tilled and fenced and criss-crossed with barbed wire. Within a few years, the Plains Indians had been reduced from proud and fearless warriors, wearers of buckskin and hunters of buffalo, to a half-starved people, confined to reserves and living in poverty, completely dependent on government for relief.

For Lorne's part, his journey to the west marked him for the rest of his life. He never felt at home in Britain again. Two months after leaving Calgary, he was back in England, complaining of the dark, damp and unwholesome winter and making speeches on the attractions of emigration to Canada. In 1882 he and Louise travelled to British Columbia, where Lorne met the tribes of British Columbia and Vancouver Island. Lorne would have liked to stay in Canada 'all my days', as he told the Prime Minister, but in 1883, a year before his tour was up, he reluctantly resigned to return to Louise in England. There he returned to his Scottish estates, where he wrote poetry, produced travel books on Canada and promoted emigration. His books describing Indian life brought the Plains Indians into the drawing rooms of Britain, and recorded traditions that by then had all but died out.

11 Sweet talk and secrets – the rise and rise of Frank Athelstane Swettenham

Malaya 1874–1903

October 1875: Kuala Kangsar, in the noble state of Perak. In the heat of the jungle night a swirl of incense rose high into the timbers above a lofty hall. The end of Ramadan was near. In the heart of the *kampong* of Sultan Abdu'llah torchlight flickered; the jangle of tambourines sounded. Court women in coloured silks and favoured chiefs were ranged round the floor. Seated on a palm mat in the centre, a silk scarf of imperial yellow over his head, sat the Sultan himself.

Next to him, according to the witnesses, the state magician was beating a drum, his fingers brown and gnarled. Above the fevered drumbeat, his voice rose in incantation. Three times – again, according to the witnesses – spirits entered the body of the Sultan and three times the men around him promised to help him against the man with the light eyes. The state magician fashioned a figure of the British Resident out of flour. He and the sultan stabbed it three times. Then the magician struck the figure 'with a fan until there flew out of it a butterfly soul which he hit with a knife, drawing blood'. The day after the end of Ramadan, on 2 November 1875, forty-nine-year-old James Wheeler Woodford Birch, the British Resident of Perak, duly met his death – attacked by fearsome men wielding spears and crying '*amôk, amôk*' as he was washing before breakfast inside a floating bath-house in the river Perak. Three more of Birch's men were killed in the attack.

Now the Malays staked the river so no boats more could pass, for another Englishman was known to be paddling downstream. Unlike the schoolmasterly Birch, with his arrogance, persistence and scant knowledge of the people, Frank Swettenham spoke fluent Malay. He was young, eager and curious. He had lived among these strange, exotic peoples for almost four years, and he had been warned of danger. He travelled with his friend Mahmud, a war-like raja from the neighbouring province of Selangor, with an awesome reputation as a fighter. His boatmen knew the river. In the dead of night they approached the spot where Birch had been cut down two days before. Fires blazed and groups of armed men loomed huge in the shadows on the bank. Swettenham's frail white boat flying the Union Jack hugged the bank, trying to creep past beneath its shelter. All at once vapours seemed to rise from the water. Shrouded in mist, Swettenham and his men sailed silently past the village.

Frank Swettenham was just twenty-four years old when he buried Birch's battered body in the sandy soil beside the Residency. Since he was twenty he had roamed the Malay Peninsula, as interpreter, guide and fixer for the British governor of the Straits Settlements, based in Singapore. He was clever, a little brash, the product of an uneasy childhood in the north of England. His father had been a solicitor in Belper in Derbyshire, a small market town known for its cotton mills, a nail factory, and for being located – Swettenham would note proudly in his memoirs – on one of the first railway lines in the country. His family home, 'a queerly placed house', stood on the verge of a deep railway cutting: a perfect vantage point for a boy who loved watching trains.

The youngest child in a family of five, Frank saw little of his father, who was fifty when he was born on 28 March 1850. According to Frank he 'only appeared occasionally and without warning. His habit was to arrive late at night, and get in like a burglar through some unfastened window.' His father never said where he had been, never stayed for long. He had a mania for collecting antiquities of all kinds – furniture and guns, pictures, tackle, old clothes: shoes with paste buckles, long satin dresses. He would shut himself into his study, a chaos of treasures and secrets, locking it securely when he was gone.

By the time Frank was ten his mother had had enough. With her eldest son away at school, she packed up Frank, her 'spoiled darling', his older brother Alexander and two daughters and departed for Dollar, in Scotland. For several weeks they stayed in a hotel, 'and then tried to settle down and feel happy'. Frank was enrolled at the Dollar Academy – which, under the Reverend John Milne, provided free education to local children who could not afford to pay. Within a year his beloved mother was dead – an agonizing death from cancer of the womb. His elder sister took over the running of the house.

Now his father returned to live with them. He kept Frank by him, teaching him to hunt, shoot and fish. He never left Dollar again. Frank came to adore him. For two years he was dispatched to boarding school in York, where he learned to row, fence and play cricket. But the money ran out and Frank returned home to Dollar.

University was out of the question. His older brother, Alexander, who had had the good fortune to attend Clare College, Cambridge, was by then in Ceylon – today's Sri Lanka – in the government service. He encouraged Frank to try for an Eastern Cadetship in the Straits Settlements, headquartered in Singapore. Cramming under his father's eye in Dollar, Frank took the papers – in Latin, mathematics, history, and languages – and scored second out of twenty candidates for two places. It was a triumph. Frank sailed for Singapore on the *Pluto* – a small paddle-wheeled steamer, veteran of running blockades during the American Civil War, which had been recently purchased by the Colonial Office for the use of the governor in Singapore – in the autumn of 1870. He was just twenty.

All his life Swettenham could never get over the wealth of Singapore, 'this Far Eastern Clapham Junction', as he sardonically liked to call it. Beyond the lush intensity of its tropical heat and greenery, beyond the thrill of his ship's approach to the busy harbour and the beauty of its 'deep jade-coloured water', it was always Singapore's potential as a great shipping port that captured his imagination. He never cared for the Chinese who crowded into the place to make it their own, and gave up learning the language after a brief effort. The teeming life of their shops and bazaars held no allure for him. All his attention was focused on the affairs of the British, his rank among them, and what could be made of the place.

Young Swettenham was set to learn Malay – the language of the peninsula to the north – and to familiarize himself with government methods. Billeted with the army to save money, he had to hire a pony and cart, which cost him dearly, to get to the office every morning. In Singapore social distinctions were clearly defined. Everyone on the Chinese side of the Singapore River was intent on gain. The town, full of narrow Chinese shop-houses, banks and trading houses, throbbed with life, exotic sights and evil smells: there were Arabs and Jews in rich dark silks, Bombay merchants with huge white turbans, brown-skinned Malays in red sarongs, and everywhere the Chinese – limber, brown-backed coolies, plump, well-fed merchants in neat black caps and sombre crêpes, mandarins in sumptuous brocades.

Across the water ran the spacious British Esplanade, where white stuccoed government offices brooded behind jalousies, and the law courts and the cathedral dozed solemn in the heat. Quiet streets of spacious bungalows in abundant tropical gardens were overhung by luxuriant fronds of flowering trees. When the traveller Isabella Bird came there after meeting the Hennessys in Hong Kong, she remarked on how the wives of the British officials seemed to grow 'paler every week'. 'Kept alive by the efforts of ubiquitous "punkah-wallahs"; writing for the mail, the one active occupation', they led 'half-expiring lives'.

Every afternoon at five when the offices closed, English ladies with parasols in pale muslin dresses emerged to drive in state to watch their men at tennis and cricket on the Esplanade. Gossip turned on who was who, whose influence had procured which appointment, how so and so had been promoted, who was going on home leave. Young Swettenham caused a stir. He was dark and tall, with a wide fresh face and a handsome squared-off jaw. He was fit and athletic and a bold, if not especially gifted, cricketer. Off the pitch he cultivated a languid drawl and a detached air – in photographs his lanky figure is always leaning nonchalantly against some prop on the edge of the crowd. In the evenings there were dinner parties, concerts and theatricals, the occasional ball, and at the weekends house parties at seaside bungalows. Swettenham took special care to charm the governor's wife at dinners at Government House.

Within only fifteen months he had qualified as a court interpreter. Now, whenever the governor travelled for meetings with the Malay rulers on the peninsula, Frank went with him to translate. In the febrile circles of British Singapore envy stirred.

The British were very new to the Malay peninsula, a slim finger of land stretching from the regions of the ancient civilizations of Burma and Siam – today's Thailand – in the north, to the island of Singapore off its southern tip. To the east, the China Sea; to the west, the Straits of Malacca and the coastline of Sumatra. Singapore had been acquired on behalf of the East India Company from the Sultan of Johore in 1819. Since then it had prospered as a key staging post in Britain's trade with China. Apart from Singapore, only two tiny British outposts, at Malacca and Penang – 'the Straits Settlements' – had been settled along the whole length of the coast. Inland, beyond the inlets of the coastline, navigable by small craft, rafts and dugout canoe, lay a mysterious land of impenetrable jungle, known to be fraught with fratricidal quarrels between princes. Violent murder was the stuff of everyday. Piracy, robbery and plunder were rife, and an iniquitous

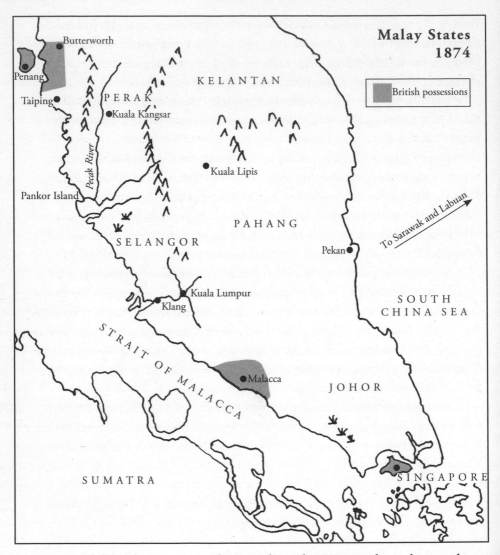

system of debt-slavery was endemic. The indigenous Malays, thirteenth-
century converts to Islam, were rumoured to be dying out.

Through all its recorded history, tin had been the Malays' most valuable
trading commodity. In the 1840s mining began on a large scale. While the
local princes were distracted by endless wars of succession, Chinese secret
societies who organized gang labour from the rural hinterlands of southern
China moved in to offer their services to competing Malay factions on the
peninsula. Meanwhile, British investors had begun putting large sums into
the mines. By 1870 the fight for control of the best concessions had become
especially bloody. In the mêlée, besieged rajas appealed for aid from the

British. By the time Frank Swettenham arrived in Singapore, the Colonial Office, which had been handed responsibility for the Straits Settlements from the India Office only three years before, was coming under pressure to change its policy to stay out of the Malay States.

Swettenham had still to qualify as an interpreter when he was invited to take his first trip up the coast. A British lawyer named James Davidson was defending the head of a Chinese secret society in Singapore, accused of abducting a young Chinese Catholic girl. In the drowsy heat of the court-room, Swettenham found himself transfixed by a large yellow-green emerald the accused was wearing on one finger. Davidson was convinced his client was innocent, and that the girl had been trafficked by a rival Chinese society to a mine near the village of Kuala Lumpur in the region called Selangor. He proposed that he and Swettenham should go to look for her.

It was 200 miles by filthy, cockroach-ridden steamer, crammed with coolies half-stupid with opium lying on the deck, on their way to the mines, up the coast to the fort of Klang. Then three days on the river, rowing and poling flimsy rattan craft upstream, the twenty miles to the grass-roofed Chinese village of Kuala Lumpur. The place was controlled by 'Capitan China', thirty-four-year-old Yap Ah Loy, one-time tin miner and petty trader, who had been in the region since the age of fifteen.

Yap entertained Davidson and Swettenham to a great dinner in the only solidly built house they saw. He had cast spoons and forks for them from Mexican dollars, so pure in silver they bent before they could use them. Violence was all around him. Wandering about the thatched *atap* hovels of Kuala Lumpur, Frank peered into a doorway to see a dead Chinese splayed across the red earth floor, a bullet hole through his chest. Walking in single file through the jungle to the tin mine, staring at the bare back of his Chinese bodyguard, he was mesmerized by a ten-chamber revolver hanging from a stick over his shoulder.

In the end, the journey was fruitless. He and Davidson could not find the girl. It was a twelve-hour hike with a guide back through the jungle to the banks of the river Klang – no path, up to their waists in water, torn by thorns, stung by blood-sucking insects, poisoned by the bites of scores of leeches.

This was Swettenham's first taste of the interior. That autumn he was appointed to his first post, working in the Land Office at Penang, a job that took him all over Province Wellesley, 'a mere strip, only thirty-five miles long by about ten broad', according to Isabella Bird, across the straits from

Penang. It was 'fertile, rich, prosperous and populous'. Swettenham spent his days visiting large sugar and tapioca estates, cultivating their owners and going snipe shooting in his spare time. He shared a large semi-derelict house in a compound of 'indescribable neglect' with the young head of the public works department. The 'Baronial Hall', as they called it, was managed by a Malay boy, a cook, and a drunken India syce who looked after their horses. Both men were working hard, daily riding miles along jungle paths haunted by tigers to visit outlying villages, returning to meet over brandy and sodas in the evening. But Swettenham, now the most accomplished Malay inter-preter in the Straits Settlements, stayed nowhere for long.

Serious fighting had broken out over the tin mines in the neighbouring province of Perak. Chinese pirates took the arguments to the waters of the Straits. Frank spent some weeks of scorching sun and long nights of drench-ing rain assigned to a Royal Navy gunboat – chasing fast-moving longboats manned by as many as twenty Chinese oarsmen. These would pull along-side a steamer or a small native boat, kill the crew and fire the vessels, before slipping into the maze of backwaters fringed by mangroves that lined the coast. For the navy, lost in the creeks in the darkness, catching them was a hopeless task.

Early in January 1874, Abdu'llah, one of several rajas who claimed the sultanate of Perak, wrote to the governor in Singapore – a flowery letter of potent phrases enveloped in imperial yellow silk – requesting a British officer 'to teach him how to rule the country'. It was the opportunity the British in Singapore had been waiting for. Within three weeks the governor had called Abdu'llah together with other Perak leaders and the key Chinese headmen in the state. They met on the island of Pangkor off the coast of Perak. It was young Frank Swettenham who translated the English/Malay negotiations and afterwards wrote the treaty in Malay that would change the region for ever. Abdu'llah would henceforth rule Perak as Sultan. By his side would be the first British resident in a Malay state.

Henceforth all matters relating to finance – the collection of taxes, the sale of land, leases to the mines – were to be decided by the British resident, whose advice, Sultan Abdu'llah agreed, must be asked and acted upon in all questions other than those touching Malay religion and custom. The treaty signed, a board of five commissioners was set up to travel through Perak to decide all claims to the mines. Swettenham, two other Englishmen, and two representatives of the Chinese factions were appointed. Their mandate included overseeing the disarming of Malays and Chinese, the destruction of stockades, and rescuing Chinese women and children who had been trafficked into the mines as prostitutes.

Travelling four to an elephant, by bullock cart and on foot, dragging boats up rivers, fording streams, swimming rivers, enduring plagues of mosquitoes and sand flies, and festering sores from the bites of leeches, the commissioners travelled through Perak over the next month destroying fortifications, collecting knives, guns and spears, and proceeding from one mine to the next. Every man they met was armed to the teeth. No papers in the shapes of land grants had ever been issued; no surveys had been made. Everywhere they discovered scores of Chinese women and children – small boys and girls as young as twelve – who had been kidnapped (many by Malays) and sold to Chinese in the jungle. Meanwhile, they were disconcerted to find that one ruler after another who had signed the Pangkor Engagement, as the treaty was called, now seemed oblivious to its terms.

'He would call for us when he had leisure', Swettenham was informed, when he called, fruitlessly for a second time, on the Mantri, one of Sultan Abdu'llah's four great chiefs, and the governor of Larut. They had already rescued a young Chinese girl – one of several the Mantri had purchased – angry and upset that she had been forced to submit to the Malay custom of female circumcision. When the commissioners discovered that the Mantri had also collected Abdu'llah's mining taxes the day before they arrived – in direct contravention of the Pangkor agreement – 'we could hardly believe it'. When the commissioners finally succeeded in gaining a two-hour interview with the Mantri, Swettenham did the talking. 'He said but little, but we told him a good many things, and I don't think he will easily forget us, for he did [not] seem at all comfortable.'

The Mantri – and he was not alone – had not understood the treaty he had signed. Frank was learning, but there was an abyss between him, young, unpolished and forthright, and the Malay rulers, measured, dignified and reserved – whose first rule of diplomacy was always to tell you what you wanted to hear. 'A Malay raja thinks himself to be the greatest man in the world,' wrote Emily Innes, in her memoir of life as the wife of the assistant resident. As the father of his people, the raja could exploit them at will.

The powers of a Malay sultan were derived from ancient Hindu ideas of kingship. The sultan ruled, the people obeyed; his subjects were his to order in any way he chose, everything they produced was his to claim. It was the rule for the poor to give to the rich. His chiefs, *datos,* ruled over his districts, his headmen, *penghulu,* kept order in his villages, *kampongs*. Justice was arbitrary and the opportunity for extortion rife. By the 1870s, this ancient system had become deeply corrupt. Self-proclaimed rajas wandered about the countryside with bands of armed followers, exacting tribute by force.

Meanwhile, every layer of society was shot through with systems of slavery: not just slaves who had been traded, purchased or captured as prisoners of war, but people who were held as bonds for debts, transferred from father to son, from mother to daughter, from generation to generation. It was no wonder, Swettenham thought, that ordinary Malays seemed so little inclined to work. The climate was warm. Fruit fell from the trees in the forest as it ripened, rice grew in abundance, and fish were plentiful. There was no need ever to suffer cold or hunger. To attract attention with any form of prosperity or success, a beautiful daughter or a gifted son, was to ask for trouble.

Travelling high on the back of his elephant, he was captivated by the jungle about him. The ground might be ridden with leeches, treacherous and swampy, but up here was a profusion of flowers: huge spreads of yellow blossom, scarlet flowers as big as breakfast cups, tamarind and mimosa, orchids, and mosses, trailers and lilies. Brilliantly coloured birds, which he called toucans – they were hornbills – parrots and kingfishers, glittered in the sun. Troops of monkeys flitted through the trees. Swettenham and the commissioners saw the footprints of elephant, tiger and rhinoceros, 'and speculated on the sport we might have some day in the hereafter', he wrote. They swam in the rivers, lived off the land. They had no plates, knives or forks, 'so we had leaves for plates and ate with our fingers, drinking out of preserved meat tins'. When they entered the valleys of the interior of Perak 'every turn of the river seemed more beautiful than the last'.

Almost a month after the commissioners left Pangkor they arrived at the village of Kuala Kangsar, a place of magical beauty at the head of a green valley. Here the Perak River flowed wide and clear from a purple range of distant hills. On either side of the crystal waters, villages of palm-roofed houses sheltered under clusters of coconut palms. Verdant rice-fields stretched inland. The headman was too unwell to see them ('I'm afraid there must be a very unhealthy atmosphere about us for all the headmen both Malays and Chinese get sick when we come'). But while the commissioners waited, the headman's mother, Che Mida, appeared, bringing them three Chinese women rescued from the mines, whom she had fed and clothed for months.

'She was very inquisitive and asked us any number of questions,' Swettenham said. Gracious, charming and hospitable, Che Mida was also a sound businesswoman. She owned several mines and knew where more could be developed. She was surprised to hear that Abdu'llah claimed the sultanate, and deeply interested in the news of the British agreement that had been signed at Pangkor. Complaining bitterly of the wickedness of the rajas, she deplored their discourtesy to the commissioners. She lent them a boat to help them on their way downriver, and Swettenham declared that 'she struck us as having more sense than most of the Malay men we have met'.

1 May 1874: 'The Merry May has pleasant hours and dreamily they fly.' Swettenham was lying comfortably in a boat gliding down the river, having said goodbye to Che Mida after a fortnight in Kuala Kangsar. 'It is indeed an enchanting place, and its praises cannot be too much sung.' The work of the Commission concluded, he was now travelling with J. W. W. Birch, the earnest and tactless nominee as the first resident of Perak. Before Birch could take up residence, he must succeed in the huge task of persuading Abdu'llah's rivals to accept the Pangkor Engagement and Abdu'llah's claim to the sultanate. These chiefs employed every ruse to avoid Birch and Swettenham, delaying the dispatch of promised elephants for their travels, refusing to acknowledge letters, and keeping them waiting for hours before telling them to go away.

'What? *Another* European? You travel about my country as if it were your own,' one told Swettenham. In spite of what Swettenham called their 'unvarying civility' these people 'are as stubborn as donkeys', he confided to his journal.

By the middle of June he was back with Che Mida again. 'She . . . gave herself no end of trouble in preparing a house, and did everything she could to make me comfortable.' Indeed. The principal room in her house was filled with an enormous bed-like platform on which she held court. Soothed and bathed, coaxed into a comfortable sarong, lounging beside her and feeding from a common dish, Swettenham found himself increasingly seduced by the magic of Che Mida's world.

'I have seldom slept in more curious company . . . myself and our own followers . . . the rest Che Mida's people of all ages, from a child of 4 months . . . to an old woman . . . [and] the rest were for the most part young men and women, boys and girls almost.' Most of them amused themselves during the night with smoking opium.

Che Mida herself was quick, intelligent, flirtatious and funny. Her talk was full of hidden meanings that Frank found irresistibly attractive. 'From Malay life it may be said that woman is never absent,' he would write later, while the Malay 'has soared into regions of matrimonial philosophy, and returned with such crumbs of lore as never fall to the poor monogamist'.

Of conversation, 'perhaps the chief characteristic is the fashion of speaking in parables, by innuendo, by the use of *doubles entrendres* and apparently meaningless suggestions, which are . . . well understood by those for whom they are intended'. It all gave zest and flavour to a game with 'a pleasurable sensation of risk'. In the process he was discovering a society which never turned its back on a man or a woman, 'however heinous their offences', a world in which 'the woman who has only known one husband, however attractive he may be, will come sooner or later to the conviction that life with another promises new and delightful experience'. This was the beginning of a love affair with Kuala Kangsar and its women that would last him all his life. Che Mida was extravagant, with a particular fondness for fine jewels and clothes, and fiercely jealous. As he wrote later, 'passions run high among a people living within a shout of the equator'.

Initiated in love, Swettenham's next assignment was politics. A nasty act of piracy brought him orders from the governor to proceed to Langat, a swampy village in the labyrinthine network of creeks and mangroves on the coast east of Kuala Lumpur. Swettenham was to act as assistant resident to the Sultan of Selangor, giving him informal advice, and coaxing him into the British fold.

He was still just twenty-four, the only white man in the state. He was nervous. 'I asked the Sultan repeatedly 4 or 5 times at least if he really wished me to stay with him . . . He said "Don't keep asking me that, you know I shall be only too glad . . ."'

'I have been in worse places,' Swettenham wrote later, but Langat was not good. 'The prospect was singularly unlovely: a few score blighted coco-nut palms, with broken and drooping fronds, like the plumes of a hearse . . . some particularly disreputable and tumble-down huts; the dark-brown waters of two deep and eddying streams; and all the rest mud and rank brushwood. When the tide went down, and the sun drew a pestilential vapour from the drying ooze, horrible, loathsome crocodiles crawled up the slimy banks to bask in the noisome heat.'

He lived with a guard of twenty Malays from the Malacca police force and a boy to look after him in an old stockade with a high pitched roof of palm leaves, infested with snakes. Twice a day the tide flooded the mud floor. It was infernally hot, and clouds of mosquitoes rose at sunset with a hum like a swarm of bees. In the heat, they had to light fires beneath the place to smoke them out. For his first six months, the rains were torrential.

Smoking the mosquitoes from a Malay house

The Sultan, Abdul Samad, lived in a dilapidated compound, surrounded, as befitted the 'father of his people', by hangers-on, waifs and strays, pariah dogs and stray cats. A considerable warrior in his youth – he claimed to have killed ninety-nine men with his own *kris* – the long dagger with distinctive curved blade which no man of a Malay state was ever without. Samad was now a small, curiously withered seventy-three-year-old man, 'so thin that every bone in his body stood out in bold relief against a background of loose skin'. He wore a scanty sarong, a coloured handkerchief on his head, and seemed content with his opium and his gardening.

The Sultan 'rather encouraged the somewhat prevalent idea that he was slightly imbecile and quite incapacitated for ruling, for by this means he saved himself all the trouble of keeping order', Swettenham reported to Singapore. In fact he was shrewd, and cynical. He and Swettenham got on.

'The people were strange and interesting, and made the place unusually exciting,' he said years later, when he was asked why he had liked it. Two thirds of the population of Langat were in some form of debt bondage;

every day another case was brought to him: a woman and her three children, her old father and mother, all at the mercy of one of the nobility for the sake of $56 owed by her husband, who had abandoned them. The Sultan's gatekeeper told him how he was gradually losing his only child, whom the Sultan had taken to live with him.

'She is now only about 6 years old, but he keeps her, and by the time she is 14 she will be indebted to him for 8 years food. That debt I shall never be able to pay.' Frank was beginning to identify with them, absorbing their customs, learning of their prejudices, 'getting into their hearts'. The more tales of abuse that were brought to him, the more angry he felt.

'It makes one feel . . .very "mean" that hearing of such wrongs one must hear and do nothing except mildly remonstrate, sit down and accept them as "adat Malayu" [Malay custom]. It is rather a travesty on the "English Protection" under which the Native States flourish. On occasion some particularly bad case exasperates one into action, flying right in the face of the Malay Rajas and their "adat Malayu" . . . a very "fig-leaf of pretence" to cover the exactions, oppressions, and cruelties which they heap on a long-suffering people.'

Meanwhile he was swapping myths and fairy tales, and making friends – especially with the fighter Raja Mahmud, the son of a close friend of the Sultan's, the man who would later save his life. Mahmud instructed him in the ways of young rajas: cockfighting, gambling, opium smoking – and of their aspirations to some kind of office that would give them the means of squeezing something out of those who dared not resist. Meanwhile, Frank was gentle with Abdul Samad, respected his dignity, gave him time to consider ideas. At the same time he mastered the Sultan's finances, and wrote letters full of flowery compliments at his dictation to the governor in Singapore. Frank suggested the Sultan built drains and improved the roads; meanwhile, he policed the coastline and travelled all over the state, inspecting its villages, mines, plantations and rivers. Selangor settled down.

'We are very much obliged to our Friend for the officer whom our Friend has chosen,' Abdul Samad told the governor in Singapore. 'He is very clever; he is also very clever in the customs of Malay government, and he is very clever in gaining the hearts of Rajahs and sons of Rajahs with soft words, delicate and sweet, so that all men rejoice in him as in the perfume of an opened flower.'

It was eighteen months later in November 1875 that the unfortunate Mr Birch met his death as the first British resident in Perak. To avenge his murder 1,600 British troops arrived from Singapore, Calcutta and Hong Kong, swiftly taking over the villages whose chiefs had conspired in Birch's death. Swettenham was a scout for the Hong Kong troops. By the end of 1876 the perpetrators of his murder had been tried – Swettenham testifying for the prosecution – and hanged. Sultan Abdu'llah and the Mantri were exiled to the Seychelles. Elsewhere in the peninsula other Malays opposed to the British intervention were forced to leave. Swettenham briskly concluded that this 'short occupation did more to secure permanent tranquillity than ten or fifteen years of "advice" by a British resident' could ever have done.

Swettenham was praised for his 'courage, ability and zeal' and promoted. He was now based in Singapore as assistant colonial secretary, with special responsibility for the Malay States. During these years the governors changed so rapidly that few had time to grasp the complexities of the Malay administration – one of them did not even attempt to visit the States – while Swettenham became the one constant on the scene, continually travelling to visit the new residents and their sultans, mapping the rules for the residents to follow, inspecting accounts and the workings of their offices.

In March 1877, after seven years of immersion in this rare and exotic land, Swettenham sailed for home in England and a year's leave. There he travelled around the country, visiting his relatives, played cricket with the Colonial Office team, and hunted with meets across the north of England.

He returned to Singapore with a wife.

Imagine the curiosity with which young Sydney Swettenham was greeted in Singapore, the clacking of tongues in the carriages on the Esplanade. She was just nineteen, with a cloud of dark hair, pretty and petite. She was the eldest of seven children of Cecil Holmes, a well-fed fifty-year-old housemaster at Harrow, and his handsome, but modest, suburban wife, Constantia. Even by the standards of his day Holmes was regarded as unusually stern and dictatorial. 'A churchman of the older type', his obituary drily put it ten years later. Justice of the peace, chairman of the Harrow Branch of the Conservative Association, cantankerous, quarrelsome and profoundly intolerant of any new idea, Holmes brooked no discussion – much less opposition – from his growing daughter.

Sydney was quick-witted and intelligent. But before her father she retreated, cultivating an attitude that was shy and retiring, mastering skills of subterfuge and deceit. The strain was trying, and from time to time her nerves spilled over into spectacular scenes of tears and resentment. 'Sydney is delicate', Swettenham, now twenty-seven years old, was led to understand.

His appearance – an introduction from one of his brothers – delivered Sydney's first chance of escaping home. He, on this rare home leave to England, was undoubtedly on the lookout for a suitable wife. To her he was handsome, confident and eligible. He, unused to pretty English girls of her age, was almost certainly infatuated. There was time for no more than a brief courtship.

They were married on a warm morning in late February 1878 in Harrow parish church. Sydney, tightly corseted in white silk trimmed with flowers, her veil descending from a plume of ostrich feathers, was attended by fourteen bridesmaids. The Bishop of Hereford and the Reverend Dr Butler, headmaster of the school, presided. A wedding breakfast for 150, a cake adorned with the monograms of the bride and groom; Frank's father had travelled from Scotland to be with him. After a brief honeymoon at Henley-on-Thames, the newlyweds sailed from Marseilles for the heat and greenery of Singapore, arriving early in May.

It was early days for the marriage, but already there were signs of trouble. Sydney, transplanted from the strict confines of her father's home, was immature, nervy and inhibited, prone to sudden outbreaks of frenetic energy that would turn, in the blink of an eye, to profound depression. Swettenham, big, strong and matter-of-fact, schooled in the subtle double-entendres of Che Mida and the girls of her household, was bold and experienced, eager to show his affection.

'The bachelor who marries,' Frank was to write in a rather louche, philosophical volume on affairs of the heart twenty years later, 'looks for reciprocation of his passion ... When he fully realises that his transports awaken no responsive feeling, but rather a scarcely veiled disgust, his enthusiasm wanes, he cultivates self-repression, and assumes a chilly indifference that, in time becomes the true expression of his changed feelings.'

Sydney was deposited in the green bower of Frank's bachelor bungalow in Singapore. Under the slow beat of the *punkah* scarcely moving the moist air, she wandered in the gloom of lofty rooms shaded by jalousies, tortured in the heat in her corsets and crinoline. She knew no one and had nothing to do. Some of the day could be got through by bathing – the habit in the heat of Singapore was three times a day – but as one Singapore wife, who might well have been Sydney, remarked to Emily Innes, the wife of the assistant resident who had by now succeeded Swettenham at Langat: 'What is the use of dressing three times a day if there is no one to look at you when it is done?'

Swettenham drowned his bitterness in work. He was constantly on the move, sometimes taking Sydney, often on his own: to Kuala Kangsar and evenings with Che Mida in Perak, to Penang, Kuala Lumpur, Langat and Klang in Selangor. In the evenings, he worked on a Malay dictionary and edited the *Journal of the Straits Branch of the Royal Asiatic Society*. He was determined to advance. He applied to be lieutenant governor of Malacca, then colonial secretary in Hong Kong, and cultivated Sir Frederick Weld, the new governor of Singapore, recently arrived from Tasmania.

Weld was well into his fifties, confident of his superiority, with a patriarchal approach to the Malays. He suffered painful attacks of gout. When, six weeks after he arrived in post in the summer of 1880, Frank and Sydney went with him on a tour of the Malay states, Frank teased him with a series of practical jokes, and carried him pig-a-back across a wide, rapid river. 'Taking him all round – with his sense of self-confidence (without which no man can do much) and somewhat unpleasant brusqueness of manner, he may formerly have made some enemies, but that is toning down,' Weld told Lord Kimberley, Secretary of State at the Colonial Office.

Weld shared Frank's vision of developing the rich natural resources of the peninsula. He decided to move the British Residency in Selangor, based at Klang, on the coast, to Kuala Lumpur. The place was now a Chinese boom-town riding high on the price of tin, still controlled by Capitan China, Yap Ah Loy, who had built himself a palatial residence close to the market, across from a collection of gambling dens.

The first British resident of Selangor, based at the seedy coastal port of Klang, was none other than William Bloomfield Douglas, who had founded Darwin in Australia's Northern Territories. Douglas had not changed his wild, dictatorial ways. Just as in Darwin, Douglas sited his new residency at Kuala Lumpur – laboriously transported plank by plank from Klang – on what he called a 'redoubt' on top of a hill overlooking the Chinese settlement across the river, and mounted a howitzer on the terrace for target practice into the jungle. His bluster cut no ice with Yap Ah Loy, who was bent on retaining the most valuable sites in Kuala Lumpur for himself. Early in 1880, Weld appointed Swettenham to investigate Douglas's activities and those of his son-in-law Dominic Daly, who had married Douglas's daughter, Harriet, and who was now in charge of the Land Office.

As in Darwin, so in Kuala Lumpur. Land office records 'were conspicuous by their absence', taxes were 'vexatious and unwise', and was it really necessary for Douglas to be accompanied on all occasions by a guard of five men? When Swettenham uncovered evidence that Douglas had deducted the cost of his own supplies from the Sultan's pay – his friend, Abdul Samad from Langat – Douglas was forced to resign.

'Might he not drive the coach a little too fast?' the Secretary of State inquired when Governor Weld proposed promoting Swettenham to the residency at Selangor. But doubts were set aside, and in 1882, at the age of thirty-two, Swettenham succeeded Douglas as resident.

Frank took over Selangor like the cocky heir to a decaying family firm, eager to sweep all away and begin all over again. He knew the country from end to end, and all the most important Malays from the Sultan down. Apart from thousands of Chinese crowded around the tin mines, the state was thinly populated in dilapidated *kampongs* along the rivers. Swettenham was convinced 'that acre for acre, above ground and below, the Malay Peninsula was a hundred per cent richer than any other country in the world'. He had plans for it.

Misery, squalor and neglect were rife. He began with Kuala Lumpur. The streets were pestilential, dangerous to health. Refuse from the drains was simply left beside the road. People bathed in the drinking wells, the brothels were 'as filthy as pig-sties', the squalor of the main market, stinking in a tumbledown shed, was 'indescribable'. Yap Ah Loy, who had run the place for years, was used to dispensing his own brand of very rough justice, protecting the Chinese secret societies and taking his cut from their monopolies on the gaming booths, opium dens and brothels. Swettenham was determined to show him who was in charge.

As for the British administration, the medical officer was a Sinhalese drafted from the island of Labuan who was drunk most of the time. The clerks in the Land Office never arrived before 10.30, while the heads of departments rolled in to work at eleven. The Residency was a barn of a place, with six bedrooms and five bathrooms, not a mat in the place, and a ground floor of bare concrete.

Over five short days of a visit from Governor Weld, Swettenham set out to replan the city. He negotiated with Yap Ah Loy for the sites the government wanted: a new hospital, a police station, a jail, new housing, and an

27. Government House, Labuan.

28. Hugh Low, 1869.

29. Kitty Low, at the time she first met Hennessy, in 1867.

30. John Pope Hennessy and his beloved first son, Johnnie, *c.*1872.

31. Government House, Hong Kong, with, to the left, bare rocks rising to the Peak above.

32. The drawing room of Government House, Hong Kong, *c.*1877.

33. The Marquess of Lorne, at the time he became Governor-General of Canada.

34. Princess Louise as a young woman.

5. Crowfoot, chief of the Blackfoot, addressing the Marquess of Lorne orth of the site of today's Calgary on 10 September 1881, drawn by Sydney 'rior Hall, of *The Graphic*, who accompanied Lorne on his expedition to the Jorthern Territories.

36. British officials in Malaya, 1874. Frank Swettenham leans against the balustrade. John Birch stands at the foot of the steps beside the Governor of the Straits Settlements, Sir William Jervois, seated. Behind Jervois's left shoulder is his private secretary, Henry McCallum, who would go on to become the Governor of Ceylon in 1909.

37. Swettenham, left, and forty-nine-year-old John Birch, showing the toll taken on a life spent in the tropics, not long before his murder as the first British resident of Perak.

38. Nineteen-year-old Sydney Holmes on her wedding day, 21 February 1878.

39. The view from the Residency, Che Mida's former home, at Kuala Kangsar, sketched by Frank Swettenham, *c.*1884.

40. In the garden of the Residency at Kuala Kangsar, July 1897. Swettenham, wearing a boater, stands to the left of the palm tree.

41 Sir Frank Swettenham, painted by John Singer Sargent, 1904.

42. The arrival of the Tennyson family at Adelaide Station, 10 April 1899.

43. The Tennysons explore Frenchman's Rock, commemorating the landing of Captain Nicholas Boudin and his expedition on Kangaroo Island, south of Adelaide, in 1903. Left to right: Mlle Dussau, Harold, Lionel, Aubrey and Hallam Tennyson. Audrey Tennyson is in the centre foreground.

44. Audrey Tennyson.

45. The Queen's Home, Adelaide.

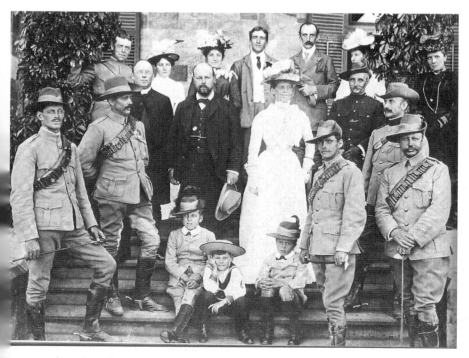

46. Lord and Lady Tennyson (centre), Lionel, Harold and Aubrey at their feet, with South Australian officers at Marble Hill as they were about to depart for the Boer War.

47. Flora Shaw, colonial editor of *The Times*.

48. Frederick Lugard, *c.*1895.

49. Lugard working at his desk in the Emir's palace immediately after the capture of Kano, 1903.

50. A ruler in Northern Nigeria arriving to meet Lugard.

extension to the main street. In the centre was to be the Royal Selangor Club, with a reading room facing a parade ground, playing fields and a pavilion for cricket and lawn tennis.

Swettenham spent half his day on correspondence – his reports 'remarkably careful and clear', Weld told Secretary of State Kimberley, 'such a relief after Douglas'. The rest was spent on inspecting the town: checking the prisoners had facilities for 'a soap and water bath' at least every second day, reprimanding a policeman caught gambling, checking supplies of bedding in the hospital, and viewing his construction projects: the clearing of swampland, clean new streets, substantial, brick buildings.

Meanwhile, he was planning Malaya's first railway line, writing for engineering advice from his older brothers in England and Ceylon: it was to be a single-track line from Kuala Lumpur to Klang, on the coast. He was overseeing a network of bridle paths through the jungle, and building a bridge. Traders were setting up shop along the new paths, which were soon widened to take bullock carts. Revenues were pouring in from the tin mines; there was no shortage of cash for his plans. Meanwhile, he was also taking advantage of the boom to buy up land himself.

Sydney was creating scenes. In Singapore, she had appeared to be almost well. She played tennis, won matches and took prizes at a flower show for a display – admittedly subdued – of ferns and moss. Six months before their move to Kuala Lumpur she hosted a fancy dress ball at which she chose to appear, redolent of opium, as 'Sleep'. She wore a straw-coloured ball dress wreathed with poppies, and powdered hair crowned with a scarlet poppy hat. Early in the new year of 1882, she taunted Swettenham at a Bal Costumé at Government House, coming up behind him dressed as 'Follow the Drum'.

Kuala Lumpur was a place so raw that Swettenham himself admitted it was scarcely suitable for ladies. Certainly he found it impossible to recruit a private secretary. The heat and humidity – ninety degrees during the day, down to the mid-eighties in the night – the snakes, the mosquitoes and flying insects, the white ants that devoured furniture, the earwigs, and yet more ants, some an inch long, which invaded the larders and storerooms, were a constant drain on the resources of the most resilient housewife. Then there was the ennui.

There was no place to go, nothing to do. There were only three British officials in the place and, on the outskirts, two British coffee planters recently arrived from Ceylon. Swettenham's number two was a bluff old Etonian of private means and a legal training, who served as the commissioner of lands. John Rodger was stuffy, 'a little overpowering at times', his wife – with whom Sydney was constantly thrown together – 'a grand dame'.

It was impossible for Swettenham to disguise the miserable state of his marriage. A year after they arrived in Kuala Lumpur, in October 1883, he dispatched Sydney to England for a break. Then he left on a three-month tour of India, taking an exhibition of Malay produce to Calcutta.

For a year, Swettenham revelled in freedom. Along with many other treasures acquired on his trip to India – for he had inherited his father's penchant for collecting – was an Anglo-Indian lady from Bangalore. When he returned to Singapore, Governor Weld directed him to Kuala Kangsar in Perak to relieve the resident, Hugh Low – Kitty Hennessy's father – who was to go on leave to England. When his mistress found herself with child, Swettenham arranged a marriage for her with a callow British clerk called Walter McKnight Young, working in the Perak government.

Now he found himself living in Che Mida's old house, which had been purchased for the Residency by Hugh Low. After a lifetime's experience in the east, Low had grown grey-bearded and venerable, the ideal British resident, and a man whose praise Swettenham particularly sought. He had a special sympathy for the Malays and, as he had shown in Labuan, a gift for making gardens. At Kuala Kangsar he had created a kind of Eden.

Low had staffed the house with impeccable servants from Java and China and furnished it beautifully: white painted walls, heavy wood beams on white fluted pillars, a dark polished floor covered with thick Persian rugs and the skins of tiger and black leopard. Silk hangings, rare prints on the walls, carvings and embroideries, a few well-chosen pieces of furniture. From its verandah, with its glorious views up the River Perak, hung baskets of orchids. The scent of jasmine and sweet chempak lingered in the air.

In the grounds, Low was experimenting with coffee from Arabia, quinine from Brazil, tea from Assam. He bred sheep and cows, turkeys from Malacca. But Low's most astonishing success was with a dozen unfamiliar plants sent from South America via Kew in 1877. Within a year, the first Para rubber tree had flowered in Kuala Kangsar; in two, the trees were twelve to fourteen feet high. The year Swettenham was living at Kuala Kangsar, 400 seeds – the genesis of Malaysia's largest industry of the twentieth century – were collected from the first twelve trees. 'Three hundred and ninety-nine germinated and I had the satisfaction of planting them on the sides of a small valley at the back of the Residency.'

Far from officialdom in Singapore, Swettenham lived with two like-minded male cronies: Martin Lister, one of the two coffee planters from Ceylon who had settled near Kuala Lumpur, and had become a close friend and his private secretary; and Hugh Clifford, only seventeen, a newly arrived cadet in the Malay States, who was rapidly coming to share Swettenham's love of Malay life. Together, they paddled down the river in dugouts, and swam there daily. Sultan Yusof, who had been put in place by the British following Birch's murder, was difficult and unpopular. But he was growing old. His son-in-law Raja Idris, intelligent, quick to absorb the ideas of others and groomed by Low, would inherit the sultanate. Swettenham got on with him well.

He painted, wrote and prepared the second edition of his English-Malay vocabulary, which Hugh Clifford would in future much expand. Meanwhile, Idris took him on jungle picnics, to collect the eggs of river turtles and to play *mêng-gêlunchor,* tobogganing down the smooth rock bed of a mountain waterfall on a plantain leaf, skittering into a pool below.

In September 1884 he set off with Lister and Clifford on a 200-mile tour of inspection of the villages of lower Perak, travelling by boat and trekking on foot through the jungle, re-entering the world of his 'real Malay'. Villagers lined the banks to greet him, registering grievances and complaining of miscreant *penghulus,* the local headmen, who continued to exploit them. At the village of Ipoh, on the banks of the Kinta River, the local chief laid on a splendid picnic party in the jungle. Fifty or sixty men and girls, mounted on a dozen elephants, made for a series of rock pools in the shadow of a cliff at the bottom of a hill. There they caught fish – first stunned by dynamite – with their hands, roasted them on fires, and ate them with rice, wrapped in plantain leaves. On the way home in the late afternoon, the elephant panniers were loaded with jungle fruit, for pelting one another on the way home. Once back in the village:

> There followed feast and revel
> *Melenggo* [lounging] on the floor
> *Melenggo* [sway dancing] led by Che Mat Nuh
> Who wedded his Malayan Ruth
> Despite her age, his early youth,
> And great Mahomed's law.

*Swettenham, right, at breakfast, which he liked to take about noon when
travelling, wearing a baju and matching trousers or sarong. The figure in
the centre is probably Martin Lister*

It was hardly the way for a British resident, acting or otherwise, to carry on.
But Swettenham – as Lister and Clifford would too – had developed a curious
double identity. Such was his sympathy and affection for the Malays that he
now deplored many habits of his countrymen. As Clifford would write later
of a fictional Englishman based in Malaya, Swettenham had been 'well-nigh
denationalised'. This was not, he said, 'a wholesome attitude of mind for any
European, but it is curiously common among such white men as chance has
thrown for long periods of time into close contact with Oriental races'.

'Have you come out to work or play? As long as you tell me, I can arrange
a programme for either,' drawled Swettenham, back in harness as the British resident of Selangor, as he greeted his new private secretary, young
Arthur Keyser, when he arrived in Kuala Lumpur, fresh out from England
in 1888. Frank was now thirty-eight: thick black moustache, white duck
suit, large white hat; wry, laid-back, just a touch disreputable.

He had spent the past two years on leave in England with Sydney. There had been moments of triumph: an award of the CMG by the Queen at Windsor Castle; dinner with the Prince of Wales following the opening of the Indian and Colonial Exhibition in London, and conversations with the painter Lord Leighton, whose eye was caught by the beauty of the silk and gold Malay sarongs which Frank had displayed. He hunted with his older brother in north Yorkshire in the winter, and played cricket with the Colonial Office team in the summer. He became firm friends with Charles Lucas, a brilliant Cambridge graduate of about his own age, now a rising star in the CO, working with him on *A Historical Geography of the British Colonies*, a text that would become one of the most authoritative sources on Empire of its day.

There was also fury and despair. One year after he and Sydney arrived in England, in April 1887, Sydney's tyrannical father contracted pneumonia and suddenly died. Her family seemed to fall apart. No one had told Swettenham that two years before their marriage, Sydney's mad uncle Arthur had slit his throat from ear to ear. Within a month of burying her father, Sydney was in an asylum. Swettenham wrote to the Colonial Office begging to extend his leave, on the grounds that his own health was fragile.

By early 1888, however, both he and Sydney had returned to Kuala Lumpur. There was much to do: laying out public gardens, starting work on a palatial new Residency and grand public offices, and working to woo senior Malays to the new capital of Selangor. For Frank, however, private life was becoming complicated. He was now one of two contenders to replace Hugh Low as the permanent resident of Perak, the most senior and highly paid post in the Malay States. His rival was William Edward Maxwell, the former assistant resident to Hugh Low in Perak, then commissioner of land in Singapore, now the resident of neighbouring Pahang, highly disciplined, scholarly, cautious and judicial, but also caustically critical and censorious. The son of the chief justice of Singapore, Maxwell had been born and brought up in Malaya. By the time Swettenham arrived to learn Malay in Singapore, Maxwell, who was four years older, was already the magistrate of Malacca. Equally at home and fond of the Malays, equally ambitious and obstinate, the two had never got on. Step by step, increasingly viciously – talk of tigers rampant and snakes in the grass littered notes on CO dispatches – they had dogged each other's climb up the Straits Settlements hierarchy, Maxwell always the senior.

Frank's unhappy marriage to Sydney might be common knowledge, but the truth of her mental fragility had to be disguised if his career was to have a future. At the same time, two of her brothers now requested his help to find posts in the Straits Settlements. Meanwhile, his son by his Anglo-Indian mistress was now nearly five years old, and the price of his maintenance – or was it his putative father's silence? – was becoming costly. Then, in the autumn of 1888, a beautiful young widow, Meta Rome, the wife of an old friend who had shot himself dead in their London flat when he contracted a fatal cancer, arrived on her way to Australia to claim her husband's assets.

Left, Meta Rome and, right, Sydney Swettenham. Both are thought to be copies of photographs, drawn by Swettenham

Meta was thirty-three, dark-haired and vivacious. Her departure for Melbourne was postponed. Before long she appeared to be running the Residency, partnering Swettenham at tennis, while Sydney played against them victoriously, going on to win the state championship. Stories gathered about how the resident could be seen in the company of a European lady in the vicinity of a faded bungalow in the forest near a lake.

Then there were questions over land deals. Purchases that Swettenham had made in Kuala Lumpur in the heady days of its early development five years before were coming under scrutiny in Singapore. In spite of regulations that prohibited all public officials from engaging in commercial undertakings without the approval of the Secretary of State, in spite of clear instructions from Governor Weld in Singapore, Swettenham had bought and continued to buy more land. Meanwhile, the decision as to who was to have the residency of Perak, Maxwell or Swettenham, was coming to a conclusion in London. Early in December 1888, as the recommendation in his favour penned by his friend Charles Lucas to the Secretary of State reached Malaya, Swettenham transferred the deeds of twenty-six land purchases in Kuala Lumpur — on which he had more than doubled his money — to Meta Rome.

1 June 1889: to the sound of marching pipes and drums and a splendid guard of honour of Perak Sikhs, in scarlet coats, curling black moustaches and whiskers, plaited and tucked up into big blue turbans, the new resident, Frank Swettenham, and his wife, Sydney, took up residence in Taiping, the new capital of Perak. Taiping — 'eternal peace' — was, like Kuala Lumpur, a thriving Chinese town built on tin mining, with large bazaars, curving roofs of gold and scarlet entrance arches. Nearby was the Malay village of Larut, the scene of Swettenham's difficult encounter with the Mantri, exiled fifteen years before. The town was set in the midst of tropical rainforest, planned and laid out by Swettenham during his year as acting resident while Hugh Low was in England. Magnificent trees soared towards the sky. Misty rain clouds descended almost every day. Here a railway that Swettenham had conceived ran away to the coast. High on top of the hills above, with fabulous views across the rainforest canopy to the sea in the west, was Malaya's first hill-station, open only to a privileged few in the colonial service.

A thoroughly British administration had been imposed. On Swettenham's agenda was development: roads, railways, water supplies, schools, hospitals — opening up the country, to entice British settlers and agricultural investment. British district officers now oversaw the village *penghulus*. The Sultan was Swettenham's old chum Idris, who, trained by Low, had by this time also visited England. On his return he had built a magnificent white stuccoed palace in Kuala Kangsar, furnished by Maples from London. When the Sultan's daughter was married, Swettenham hosted a dance for her at the Residency.

Sultan Idris chaired the meeting of the State Council – four or five chieftains and one or two leading Chinese – but it was Swettenham who managed the discussion, laying out the estimates, asking for views on capital sentences, legislation, appointments and new public works. 'The general affairs of the country were open to question and argument,' he wrote, but it was the British resident who set the agenda, and held all the cards in his hand.

England had indeed come to Malaya. 'Can he play cricket?' was the first question Swettenham demanded of a new candidate for a post. On Tuesday afternoons he was at home at 4.45 p.m. to welcome visitors. Social life was translated from the English Home Counties: the cricket ground was immaculate, the racecourse superb; Hugh Low had established a museum. Under Swettenham the Taiping season became the focal point of the colonial year, the excuse for the British to gather, filling every house in town, for days of racing and evenings packed with entertainment: gala dances in the Club reading room, tricked out in racing colours. There were cricket, golf and tennis, amateur theatricals, and concerts, billiards and bridge.

Still rumours of scandal and shady dealing dogged Swettenham. A full investigation into his Kuala Lumpur land dealings had been launched by his rival, Maxwell, who had replaced him as resident of Selangor. Meanwhile, Sydney's brother, M. E. Holmes (for whom Swettenham had found a place in the Perak treasury), was found to be fiddling accounts. Sydney herself was never about: off to Singapore, then to Kuala Lumpur, visiting Penang, then to Hong Kong with the Straits cricket team. She went on to China, then sailed for Brindisi. Swettenham chased after her to bring her home. His own health was coming under strain. In the autumn of 1891, he sailed for England on leave. During his stay he nearly died of pneumonia, and Sydney was once again certified and placed in an asylum. In London, a proposal that he be given a knighthood for his services in Malaya was turned down on the grounds that he was soon expected to be named in divorce proceedings.

Somehow the pair were reconciled again. Swettenham returned to Taiping with Sydney, and once again she tried to be a model resident's wife: energetic and gracious, presenting school prizes, singing at charity benefits, hosting dances and mounting amateur theatricals – in which her husband the resident played a starring role. He played cricket, she made teas. 'She . . . interests herself in everything,' reported the *Selangor Journal*. Sydney threw herself into the details of transforming exhausted tin mines into a series of artificial lakes surrounded by botanical gardens.

But it was no good. Swettenham had embarked on a provocative new flirtation. Isabel Caulfeild, dark-haired, dark-eyed and pretty, was the wife of the state engineer. 'You modern man, of modern times, with manner calmly cold,' she would write to him on Valentine's Day, 1895. 'No pretty trifling airy jests writ with a lover's pen would come from you, most self-possessed and cynical of men.' To win his heart and hold it: how arduous, but – what a prize.

In November 1893 Swettenham stood up to open the Taiping Lake Gardens, which Sydney had helped to create – today, the centrepiece of the city. In characteristically sardonic manner, he thanked the Chinese for their donations, and praised his wife for all her hard work. It proved the last straw for Sydney. Days later, at the St Andrew's Ball in Penang, she broke down. Isabel Caulfeild accompanied her on the steamer to Singapore. Now it was Sydney's turn to play fast and loose. Ten months after she left, a dreadful climax was reached. Swettenham returned from a trip to Singapore with Sydney on his arm. She was pregnant by another man. There were five days of appalling scenes at the Residency. On 1 November 1894, Frank dispatched his wife to England. Six months later, on 19 May 1895, she gave birth to a child. It was stillborn.

Swettenham was on leave in England in 1892 when he had several private discussions with his friend Charles Lucas in the Colonial Office on the possibility of uniting all the Malay States into one confederation. His argument was that no one in Singapore had the knowledge to challenge the actions of the residents successfully. Crucial to his proposal was the creation of a new post of resident general – answerable directly to the Secretary of State in London – to oversee the residents' activities, and rationalize their approach to the sultans. On his return to Perak, Swettenham began floating the idea of a centralized administration with united legal and administrative procedures for all the Malay states, in the *Straits Times*. In London, Lucas drafted the proposals. On 6 June 1895, the Secretary of State instructed the governor in Singapore to go ahead with the plan – providing the Malay rulers agreed.

By then Perak, under Swettenham's hand, had out-distanced all the other states in the race to modernization. 'The wealthiest Malays in the Peninsula are the Perak Malays,' Swettenham wrote in his annual report in 1894. 'It is they who vie with each other in the building of expensive houses and the possession of horses and carriages.' Swettenham's only possible rival for the post of resident general was William Maxwell, who had succeeded him in Selangor. But Maxwell, who was against the manner in which confederation had been designed, had no heart for the job. After years of effort harmonizing Malay legal codes and Asian custom with English law, and a lifetime devoted to the cause of Malaya, he confided to his friend Edward Fairfield at the Colonial Office, 'There is such a thing as knowing too much about things and people.' He decided to accept the CO's offer of the governorship of the Gold Coast. Within two years he was dead of blackwater fever.

One week after the Secretary of State's instructions were received in Singapore, Swettenham was dispatched to visit each of the states in order to gain the consent of the rulers to the new federation. As at Pangkor twenty years before, it was Swettenham who was to be responsible for 'a most careful' translation of the document of federation into Malay.

What would be the problem, Swettenham asked? It 'disturbs no existing arrangements, breaks no promises, doesn't alter the status of the Malay rulers'. Beginning with his friend Sultan Idris in Perak, with whom he had already had long talks about the scheme, within a fortnight Swettenham had obtained the signatures of all the Malays concerned – in Pahang, Selangor, Negeri-Sembilan and Perak. 'Nothing,' the treaty declared, 'is intended to curtail any of the powers or authority now held by any of the above mentioned Rulers in their respective States.'

Will these meddling English alter the ways of the very sun and moon?

After nine months' leave in England, Swettenham returned to Malaya as the first resident general in 1896, second only to the governor of Singapore in power in the region, and with 'general control', as he put it, 'over the Residents'. Swettenham set about designing a modern bureaucracy 'for and on behalf of the Rulers' that gradually put paid to the last notion of any powers of the sultans. A splendid Moorish Government Secretariat, in pink brick with minarets and an onion-domed clock tower described as 'Saracenic Moslem' style, began construction in central Kuala Lumpur to house the new Malay civil service. Its officers were to be recruited, as Swettenham himself had been, through examination and cadetships. By this time, the state councils of the sultans with their powers over finance, recruitment and local policy had become little more than rubber-stamping exercises. Residents would briefly explain in Malay the general outline of some intricate and technical measure drafted in English. It would then be passed, in English, by a state council whose members could not speak the language. Meanwhile, even the residents, brought together in 'Residents Conferences' to co-ordinate policy, found their own powers becoming merely nominal. New federal departments proliferated: railways, mines and surveys, post and telegraph, and schools.

In July 1897, Swettenham – at last, by the Queen's gift, Sir Frank – called together a grand conference of all the Malay rulers, sultans, members of the state councils and senior British officials at the palace of Sultan Idris in Kuala Kangsar in Perak. There had never been a gathering like it in Malaya before. After days of travelling by elephant and steamer, for the first time the sultans of the four Malay states – each attended by their own British resident – were able to meet each other. Even the proud, notoriously autocratic Sultan of remote Pahang attended. Abdul Samad, the Sultan of Selangor, now ninety-three, travelled from Langat, where he still lived in the same rural simplicity as he had done when Swettenham had served him twenty years before. There were massed bands and Chinese dragons, and telegrams of congratulations to Her Majesty the Queen; four days of feasting, music and dance; jungle picnics on elephant back, fishing, swimming, fireworks and amateur theatricals. The sultans were astonished at what was happening to their country.

'Until we visited Perak,' an old chief from the distant eastern state of Pahang remarked, 'we were like unto the frog beneath a coconut shell, not dreaming there were other worlds than ours.'

Tuesday, 23 April 1901: 'A busy morning. Since our arrival in Singapore I have been collecting information about the pacification of the Malay Peninsula which forms one of the most interesting and least known chapters in the history of British Colonial expansion in recent times,' wrote William Maxwell, a journalist travelling with the future King George and Queen Mary on a magnificent royal tour around the world.

'Thirty years ago the Malay Peninsula was practically a *terra incognita*. All we knew about it tended to prove that it was one of the most uninviting countries on the face of the globe – a swampy, mosquito-breeding, snake-infested region inhabited by a barbarous, warlike people that had the well-established reputation of being "treacherous by nature and pirates by trade . . ."

'In the short lifetime of a single generation all this has been completely changed by pacific means. A roadless, jungle-covered country, comprising an area of 25,000 square miles, inhabited by over half a million of warlike barbarians, has been placed, without the employment of a large, military force, under . . . a civilised, enlightened, progressive administration. The natives . . . now habitually go about unarmed.' More than 2,000 miles of excellent roads, a 200-mile network of railways, over 100 miles of telegraphs; lighthouses, wharfs, prisons, hospitals, schools, barracks, museums and handsome public offices had been constructed, and public gardens had been laid out.

'Surely it must have been very difficult to find men ready to go and live in a country . . . possessing [so] little to recommend it?' Maxwell asked his host, Sir Frank Swettenham.

'Not so difficult as you imagine,' Swettenham replied – unassumingly playing down his own role in the extraordinary success that he was nevertheless careful to portray as Malaya.

Swettenham had taken up his post as the new Governor of the Straits Settlements just two months before, on 17 February. Now he was working hard charming the royal party. The Sultan of Perak, now Sir Idris, had put his mounted Sikh escort and his state carriage at their disposal. There were audiences with the sultans, meetings with ordinary Malays, and a night visit to the Chinese town, driving about in rickshaws with scarlet-coated runners, lighted lanterns and sing-song girls.

'The Governor, a most attractive personage, fascinated all the party,' wrote Princess Mary's brother, the Earl of Athlone, to their older brother, Adolphus. 'I fear himself was attracted by "les beaux yeux" of Mrs DK [Derek Keppel], at least it appeared so to us . . . Having been told of his naughty little ways beforehand, we were naturally all on the "qui vive!" He is in fact a man with "a history" –'

The governorship of Singapore, with its magnificent and airy Government House, its deep shaded verandahs and glorious tropical gardens, its liveried servants and constant stream of illustrious visitors, was everything Swettenham aspired to. Isabel Caulfeild was there, her position remarked, ambiguous. Admirals of the fleet, Russian grand dukes, George Curzon, the Viceroy of India, Lord and Lady Lonsdale and the traveller Gertrude Bell all came to stay. But not everyone was sure they liked him.

'Sir F is a curious saturnine creature but very good company. We get on famously, I assuming a light and jocular tone,' wrote Gertrude Bell. 'I don't really like him, but I like a good many nice people a great deal less. You can't help feeling the undoubted power and ability of the Tuan under an almost comic self-absorption. I equally cannot help feeling that he has got a horrid inside.' In fact, she could not resist his wit and intelligence. They were friends for years.

For two and a half years as Governor of Singapore, all for Swettenham was glory, all was grand.

In the summer of 1903, a second conference was held with the Malay chiefs in Kuala Lumpur. It was a vast assembly. Each sultan and the members of his council were accommodated in temporary villages of pavilions set up in the Lake Gardens at Kuala Lumpur, each flying their state flags. Sultan Idris travelled from Kuala Kangsar with a retinue of 200. The rajas' swords and daggers of Swettenham's early days in Malaya had been replaced by tweeds and umbrellas. Not everyone, however, was happy with their new country, with its roads full of 'devil carriages', and a government service in which Malays were only permitted to be employed at the lowest level. Discreetly Swettenham soothed the sultans.

Sultan Idris was not prepared to let the Governor have the last word. In his closing speech he quoted a Malay proverb. Just as there cannot be two masters in one vessel, he said, 'neither can there be four rulers in one country'. Sir Idris could not see how the union was to work. What he wanted was that each state would be managed by its own officers, as a separate entity. When the conference broke up, Sir Idris rescinded the invitation he had previously made to Swettenham to travel back to Perak with him as his guest in his royal train.

Had Swettenham really intended to deceive the rulers? In his manner of negotiation, he was now a past master of Malay politesse, the habit of playing on the message the listener wanted to hear, that so many years ago the Malays had used with him. Or had his plans for federation, designed to put right a 'want of co-ordination' between the states, and to advance the means of progress, building roads and railways, clearing the rainforests – each a clear, straightforward object in itself, unleashed a host of implications he had not foreseen?

Now Swettenham's past was also beginning to catch up with him. For several years there had been signs that he was living beyond his means: his racehorses had been sold, a collection of Japanese porcelains, and lacquers, bronzes and his Malay weapons, had been auctioned; other assets realized. Concealing his affair with his Anglo-Indian mistress had become more and more expensive; his secret son, Walter Aynsley Young, was training expensively in England to be a doctor. Meanwhile, ever since they had parted nine years before, Swettenham had been cataloguing Sydney's infidelities and paying for her treatment. She had been certified insane again four years before. As Swettenham held his conference with the Malay sultans in Kuala Lumpur in the summer of 1903, Lady Swettenham, 'one of the handsomest women in London', was riding high in New York society. By the time it was over Swettenham had determined to divorce her. His position as governor of the Straits Settlements – the apogee of his ambition – was no longer tenable. For years he had been complaining to the Colonial Office that his health was not good. In September, he announced that he was to go to England for a short spell of leave.

No one in Singapore really believed that he would be back. There was a dinner at the town hall with flattering speeches, and a glittering party at Government House for him to say farewell to the Malay rulers. Then a brief salute on the wharf. With his ADC and private secretary, Swettenham watched from the deck as a crowd of his friends on the dock diminished, and the steamer pushed her way through the narrows of the winding passage to the open sea.

In January 1904 Swettenham sued Sydney for divorce. The application failed. The decision, and Frank's refusal to live with her again, put her back in an asylum, this time for seven years. Frank's life continued – seeing Gertrude Bell, collecting directorships of Malay rubber companies, and as head of the censorship office during the First World War. Sydney never entirely recovered her mental health, suffering further serious breakdowns, one after such a shocking scene in Saigon in 1928 that she had to be invalided back to England courtesy of the British government, again embarrassing Sir Frank. In 1938, at the age of eighty-eight, his bitterness unalloyed, Swettenham finally succeeded in divorcing his wife on the grounds of her incurably unsound mind – in spite of the evidence of one of Sydney's defenders, who cited his adultery with Meta Rome. 'Why, he drove her Ladyship mad with his badness.'

As a valedictory gift from the governorship of Singapore, the Straits Association commissioned a portrait of Sir Frank Swettenham by John Singer Sargent. Today it hangs in the National Museum of Singapore; a three-quarter-length copy is in the National Portrait Gallery in London. Standing beneath a huge globe tilted to show the lands of south-east Asia, beside his gilded seals of office, Swettenham leans with characteristic confidence against a chair covered in rich Malay silks. In a crisp white linen suit, the Order of St Michael and St George bold on his chest, a silver sword at his hip, his dark eyes glance sidelong out of the picture, sardonic, superior and strangely chilling.

12 Lady Tennyson at home

South Australia 1899–1903

By the end of the nineteenth century, a subtle shift had taken place in the role of the colonial governor. Now that so many colonies had developed representative government and prime ministers of their own, the requirement for administrative ability in a governor – particularly in the 'white' self-governing colonies of Australia, Canada, New Zealand and South Africa – was being overtaken by the need for aristocratic prestige, distinction and tact. Colonies with elected governments needed to be delicately handled, and new ways found to bind them to the motherland. A governor had always been the Queen's personal representative. Now he was becoming no less than the personification of monarchy itself. All the pomp and circumstance that could be mustered from London was brought to bear, and it was becoming rare for mere commoners to fill the role of such governors.

As the governor, his wife and family took on the mantle of royalty, an invitation to Government House, like Buckingham Palace at home, was confirmed as the *ne plus ultra* of social acceptance in the colonies. The role of the governor's wife in hostessing dinners, dances and other entertainments, opening bazaars, schools and hospitals, travelling as her husband's consort, and easing the way in challenging social circumstances was rarely discussed by the Colonial Office. It was critical to a governor's success, but that a wife would fulfil the role effectively was simply assumed.

Possessing an apparently inborn knowledge of etiquette, the governor's lady came armed with her clothes and her jewels. But she could only set the tone. Protocol was strict, orders of precedence strictly defined, invitations – so highly coveted – were issued accordingly. Who went in to dinner on the governor's arm, who was seated next to whom, was determined by guidelines laid down by the Colonial Office. The CO instructed who should wear what uniform on which occasion, and when Queen Victoria died in January 1901 governors' wives were given clear instructions. Full mourning, in deepest black, was to be observed for six months, and 'half mourning', in shades of grey and mauve, for a further half year. It was the responsibility of the ADC to make sure such details were correct, but any imperfections were sure to reflect on the governor's wife.

Audrey Tennyson could not have been more ideal for the role: in 1899 she was forty-five years old, and married for fifteen years to Hallam, eldest son of the great poet laureate Alfred, Lord Tennyson, hero of the nation. They had three attractive young sons: Lionel, ten, Aubrey, eight, and Harold, three. The great poet himself had always had a belief in the Empire, as 'a leader of all that is good'. Forty-seven-year-old Hallam, successor to the baronetcy, imbued with all the magic of his father's splendid name, had spent his adult life working as his father's companion and secretary. A man of unquestioned loyalty and with a nature suffused with tact, he was steady, reliable, and a great favourite of the Queen, whom he frequently visited with Audrey. Not exactly inspiring, Hallam was nevertheless a fine speaker and the perfect candidate for the role of governor of somewhere white and not too controversial, such as the distant colony of South Australia.

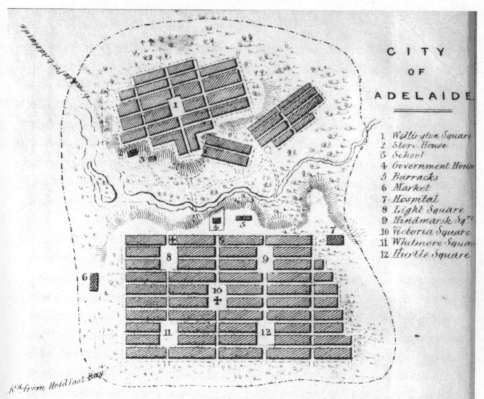

Plan of Adelaide, the ideal city, as laid out in 1837,
from a handbook of advice for colonists

Founded by an act of parliament in 1834, South Australia had been deliberately planned as a utopia, the personification of the best qualities of British society, with no religious discrimination, poverty or unemployment. Unlike New South Wales, Victoria and Queensland, South Australia suffered no taint of convict heritage. Adelaide, the capital, noted for its cleanliness, was laid out with wide streets, handsome public buildings and spacious gardens, and, by 1899, was a small city of 150,000 in a colony of less than 350,000. Society in Adelaide prided itself on its refinement and culture – and its democracy. In 1894 South Australia had become, after New Zealand, the second place in the world to grant universal adult suffrage – including votes for women.

With more than forty years' experience of representative government, Tennyson's role was to be no more than quietly advisory. But in the public eye, he and his family were as close to royalty as the people of Australia were ever likely to meet, the keepers of the standards of British life, the flame of British patriotism.

The word 'devoted' is hardly adequate to describe the degree to which Audrey Tennyson had so far submerged herself in the care of others. Warm and smiling, unassuming, infinitely patient, she had served as Hallam's faithful assistant, slaving – as his mother, Emily, had not hesitated to call it – for his famous parents. Willingly she had been drawn into the paradigm of cosy, united family life that the Tennysons had striven to create, and all that high Victorians regarded as most glorious and noble in the British way of life. Her absorption in her husband's family was resented by her mother, Zacyntha, once famous as a spirited beauty, but now, at seventy-five, dominating, possessive and sour.

'Your devoted child, Audrey', her daughter would sign over 260 letters from Australia, some of them sixty foolscap pages long, over the next four years. Somehow it had been Audrey's fate – Zacyntha would not do it – as the only daughter in a household with six sons, to take on the task of nursing her father, Charles Boyle. Audrey was just fourteen. Once handsome and dashing, Boyle had been a fellow of All Souls, then a junior official in the colonial service in the Cape and Mauritius. In 1868, at the age of sixty-two, he became an invalid. For fifteen years, Audrey's entire life revolved around him: cosseting him, reading to him, absorbing the literature he liked and the current affairs he talked about, until one day on holiday on the Isle of Wight with her jolly aunt, Mary Boyle, she was invited to dine with the Tennysons at Farringford House, where she met her future husband. A year later, in June 1884, aged thirty, she and Hallam were married. Audrey found herself plunged into a household in which every move turned around the whims of the great poet.

Farringford was a beautiful rambling Gothick house on the edge of a chalk down, with lovely views out to sea, and a vast spreading cedar in the garden. It was 'so deeply embowered in its surrounding trees and boskage that it seems, like some fairy palace, to disappear the moment it is left', Hallam was to write later. At its heart was Tennyson's great library, books overflowing from tables on to the floor. Alfred and Emily Tennyson's first casual visitor after they moved in, in 1853, was Prince Albert, who had driven over from Osborne.

Alfred had adored his two young sons, Hallam and Lionel, 'his little companions' as he called them, weaving them into adult life far more than was normal, taking them with him for walks, playing football, building them cities of bricks. Until they went away to school (Hallam to Marlborough, Lionel to Eton) they were dressed in romantic medieval costume. Their fair hair was long, and over full knee breeches and stockings they wore tunics of grey serge, trimmed with frilled collars and long scarves, belted on weekdays and crimson-sashed and stockinged on Sundays and holidays. In the evenings their mother, Emily, read to them. She was a relaxed mother who spent all her days working as Tennyson's manager and secretary. The boys were managed 'with kisses, diversions and uninhibited devotion'. Observer after observer commented on their high spirits and joy in life.

The house was full of interesting people. Their nearest neighbour was Emily's close friend, the photographer Julia Margaret Cameron. Charles Lutwidge Dodgson, later famous as Lewis Carroll, Edward Lear, and Robert and Elizabeth Browning and the Gladstones – even the Italian revolutionary Garibaldi – came to visit, while notes were regularly exchanged with the Queen.

By the time Hallam entered his final term at Cambridge in 1875, his mother had taken to her sofa as an invalid. Hallam quit university to take up his mother's place as his father's companion and secretary. Kind, gentle, contented, with a cheerful grace and humour, he was far more biddable than his younger brother, Lionel. As the years went by, his parents anguished over what Hallam was to do with his life. A career in the law had appealed, but had somehow come to naught. He wrote poetry. The poet, his father, who four times before had refused a peerage, was relieved when in 1883 he was again invited to take up the honour. 'I would fain see it bestowed on my son Hallam *during my lifetime,* if that could be done without embarrassment to you,' the poet laureate had told Gladstone three years before. Now it would descend upon his son, 'a cause of deep thankfulness to me', his mother wrote, and in due course, allow him to take up a public role in the Lords.

As the poet lay dying in the autumn of 1892, it was Audrey who recorded his every word, every action that took place in and around the sickroom – just as, for years, she had recorded notable things he said. The funeral, on 12 October 1892, at Westminster Abbey, took place before a vast crowd. The media coverage was extraordinary. Photographs of places where the poet had been born and lived and died; every portrait of him that could be got, pictures of all the family, masses of artist's impressions of his last days. This 'solemn ceremony', declared *The Times,* was 'the strongest possible testimony of the national belief that the late Lord Tennyson is distinctly and emphatically one of the Immortals'.

The poet buried, it was then Hallam's task – together with his mother and Audrey – to put together what was called the '*Memoir*' to his father. For four years after Tennyson's death, they pored over letters, documents, manuscripts and old diaries. They lived in the past, trying to recreate the life of the poet, Hallam and his mother methodically drafting and redrafting; Audrey faithfully making a fair copy. Meanwhile Hallam fended off gossip, false accounts, and the 'ghouls' who he imagined were waiting to devour his father's reputation, as he tried to carry out his father's 'exact' wishes. 'The work has been done with intensest anxiety on my part and with the intent to make it as exact and true as possible and pardon me if I say that I know better than anyone else what he wished me to do,' he wrote to his father's friend, James Knowles. The final, perfect edition of the book was at last published on 6 October 1897, five years after the poet's death, and a year after Emily died. It would shape the image of Alfred Tennyson for over 100 years.

From this peculiar, sheltered and introverted world, pushing back the pressures of fame, focused on the family and with poetry running through all its days, Lord and Lady Tennyson set sail for Australia.

Every servant from Farringford volunteered to come with them – even the kitchenman, who feared he might not be strong enough, and the second housemaid, who was 'in tears all day because she does not like to go so far'. Audrey herself was so overcome with breaking the news to the household that she broke down completely at prayers on the wintry morning in February when she told them.

First among them was her cook, Mrs Bates, a prodigious worker, unfailingly cheerful and utterly loyal, who would tell Audrey discreetly what all were saying below stairs; Clarke, her personal maid; Hitchman, the butler; and the head footman, Thomas, a bit of a lad. Horn was young Harold's nursemaid, whom he loved to wind up. Then there was Mlle José Dussau, the French governess from a well-to-do family of Bordeaux wine merchants, a woman in her prime, dark-haired, pretty, stylish and bright, and useful for delicate domestic tasks such as arranging the flowers and helping to entertain company.

The servants found the short voyage as far as Marseilles so bad that most of them said they would never come back to England again. By the time three weeks had passed, Audrey was longing for the voyage to be over. 'Here we are in the Red Sea,' she wrote on 18 March 1899. 'An old gentleman from Adelaide told Hallam, "I have been watching your lady & she'll do, I am sure of that, she plays with her children etc. and she won't be too stiff & the Adelaide people will like that."'

On Saturday 8 April they were at last drawing near to Adelaide. On Sunday the Governor's flag was run up. But the sea was very rough, the weather cold and blustery. Finally Monday 10 April dawned. 'The great day,' Audrey wrote. As they prepared to land, the ship rolling in the squalls, she felt increasingly nervous, fearing 'a most rough passage in the tender' and 'woe betide our poor smart clothes'.

Ultimately, however: 'it was all just as warm & splendid & enthusiastic a reception as you could have wished,' she told Zacyntha. The sun came out, the heat rose, the guns boomed and the crew cheered as the Governor and his family stepped down from the *Ophir* into the waiting tender. Thousands of people had been waiting for over two hours in the sun, packed close on the wharves at Port Adelaide, to greet them. After addresses of welcome, 1,500 children sang 'God Save the Queen' and the Australian national song. Then it was into a special train.

'We went to the windows & the children beamed & hundreds of hands were put up to wave to us, & along the line we again had fresh cheering till we arrived at Adelaide.' Flowers, greenery, red drugget, guards of honour, a great big coachman in Hallam's new red and yellow livery, and the drive to Government House, the children with Mademoiselle & Horn travelling behind, the streets full of people shouting 'Hurrah!'

'I can't help smiling often to myself at these moments which I think of myself as Audrey Boyle, & then driving thro' the streets in Australia with mounted escort, & the crowds shouting & cheering . . . children lifted up to see us, Hallam pulling off his hat & I bowing & smirking first one side, then the other . . . as we drive along at a snail's pace,' she was to write a year later. Meanwhile, the servants had all got to Government House before them, everyone feeling strange and out of place, not having understood that they should have brought the luggage. 'We had not even a sponge,' said Audrey.

All had been 'agreeably surprised' by the house, a long, low building of two storeys, painted a light buff. Inside were big square bright rooms, 'terribly bare of furniture but all *very* clean'. There were two entrances: one, for the public, where people wishing to call on the governor wrote their names 'in a huge red leather book', the other, for their private use. Big mahogany and gilt doors led into three drawing rooms – two in yellow, cream and gilt, and one, for the family's private use, in pale pink. A state dining room, a ballroom, Hallam's library and business room, the schoolroom, the billiard room. Beyond a green baize door were the staff rooms, with bedrooms over. Upstairs, a large, wide, carpeted passage with 'not a stick of furniture except some cupboards'.

Audrey's sitting room with a balcony was over the front portico; beyond it was her bedroom, and one for the two older boys. Then Harold's night nursery, a large day nursery, a dressing room for Hallam, and three spare rooms, and on: rooms for Mademoiselle and Clarke. Masses of cupboards, but 'not a single candlestick . . . not a flower glass, inkstand, blotting book, ornament of any kind . . . pictures, books . . . 2 single old table covers in the whole house etc etc.' Had she only known, 'I would have brought so much.'

There was a guardhouse with a sentry, and a flagstaff 'where of course the Union Jack always flies when H. is here'. The garden was 'extremely pretty', run by a head man from Sussex, and three or four gardeners. 'Brilliant borders of roses, plumbago, orange & lemon, great shrubs of verbena, oleanders, huge geraniums, & the grass with different palms very green from constant watering.' For lunch on that first day: 'oh, such luscious pears, figs, bananas & grapes'.

No sooner had they eaten than it was down to the Town Hall for Hallam's swearing-in, looking 'very well in his uniform', making 'a magnificent speech – not the slightest hesitation – his voice so strong it carried to the furthest end clear and slow'. The next day, a levée which Hallam held in the ballroom, beginning at 10.30 a.m. There were guards of honour, the band played on the lawn, and Hallam inspected the troops. On Thursday he and Audrey made a state appearance at the theatre. Friday was 'a great meeting in the town hall' for the twentieth anniversary of the Young Men's Christian Association. 'Saturday a garden party by the Mayor & Mayoress in our honour'. That night, a concert. On Monday, Hallam opened an enormous fair for the blind, which Audrey was to add to with 'a fresh fillip' a week later. All the while the weather was ' frantically hot', furniture had to be shifted and paintings hung. It was 'mail day' every fortnight. The pace seemed relentless.

At the opening of the fair for the blind, Audrey wore her 'grey foulard of Mrs Durrant's', and she wore a mauve one, for the garden party, by a Mrs Lane. For the 'stand-up' supper at their reception for the Queen's birthday a month later, she was in white satin, embroidered with pearls & crystals, her tiara, pearls around her neck, with a wonderful ornament, given to her by her brother Willy, that could be broken up into three brooches, a locket and a pendant, or worn, as on that evening, as a stomacher – 'with a few more diamond brooches'.

What she wore was constantly discussed in the newspapers. Her style was discreet, and, she liked to think, elegant, in contrast to what the women were wearing in Adelaide, 'the most gaudy dressing with brilliant colours'. But it was not appreciated. Poor Audrey. 'My lovely grey, & very smart gowns of Mrs Durrant's they make no remark about,' while the French governess, Mlle Dussau, 'who dresses in more colour – they admire very much'.

The daily routine in Adelaide was imported from Farringford: morning prayers for all the household at 9 a.m., breakfast directly afterwards. Then Audrey saw Mrs Bates, to settle orders for the day. At 10.30 she had the boys, whose tutoring she shared with Mademoiselle, for an hour or more; lunch was at 2 p.m. Dinner at eight – '& when we are alone soon after, H & I go to his room'. But it was rare that they were not joined by one of the ADCs for a chat: Captain Wallington, 'a *delightful*' man, Hallam's private secretary and general fixer, and Captain Lascelles, the ADC, who managed the money. Their monthly wages were so high, Audrey told her mother, that most of Hallam's salary would have to go to paying the staff that had now been augmented not only by Wallington and Lascelles, but an office porter, a messenger boy, a staff housemaid, coachman, groom, and two laundry maids.

Visits to the Fire Brigade, 'a really splendid force', entertaining actors at luncheon, two days of racing ('the boys went with us') and endless receiving lines. 'Everybody is introduced by their full names – the Honble, or Right Honble, etc. so & so, & then their occupation in full.' The ponderousness of it all made her laugh. 'The other night . . . Capt W called out in a loud voice as he always does, Mr So & So, Registrar of births, deaths & marriages – & the man would not advance to shake hands till this was done.' Young ladies solemnly signed 'the book' in the entrance hall at Government House, adding 'Debutante' to their names 'if she is just grown up, hoping for an invitation'. There was a visit from the governor and his wife from the neighbouring colony of Victoria, church services at the cathedral, and disconcerting remarks to cope with.

'I am not an Englishman, I'm a colonial,' the leader of the upper house, Sir Richard Baker, educated at Eton – and with his sons there too, told her. How could such apparently civilized people, she wondered, be 'so proud' of being 'colonials'?

Sunday, 25 June 1899: 'Tomorrow is our 1st ball; 450 people, & they say they eat like ogres at supper. Mrs Bates has got 22 turkeys, 10 tongues & 10 hams, *6 saddles of cold mutton*, a very favourite dish! 4 fillets of beef, 30 chickens, 6 dozen pigeons besides cutlets, sandwiches & soup & fish mayonnaise etc, & of course endless sweet things . . .'

It was a great success. Nearly 500 people came, more than anyone had ever had to an evening in Adelaide before. 'Mrs Bates did admirably. Nothing could have been better, everything good & pretty & well done.' Audrey could not imagine how she did it all: she had only had a charwoman for three days beforehand, and two on the day itself. 'She is quite insulted if I beg her to have help.'

While Hallam was conferring with the Prime Minister and taking on military inspections, Audrey was discovering the underbelly of Adelaide life. Audrey's life at Farringford had scarcely been touched by poverty. Once a week she had held a genteel 'mothers meeting' for fishermen and labourers' wives, at which she would read aloud to them while they did needlework. Now as the wife of the governor she was taken to the workhouse, 'just across the road outside Government House garden wall', where she was shocked to see nearly 500 men and women, 'so old and so destitute'

– 'here where labour is so scarce & wages so high'. She was even more scandalized to be taken to a separate building 'where no one is ever allowed except the clergy, doctor or relations', to meet young unwed mothers who were kept there.

'This is only for the first time of falling.' The girls – 'one as young as *fourteen*' – could stay until their babies reached six months. Meanwhile, at the general hospital patients told her about terrible conditions in the silver mines at Broken Hill, about 400 miles away in the remote outback: how badly paid the workers were, how expensive food was, '*everything,* even every vegetable, for nothing will grow there, comes from Sydney & has to come through Adelaide for duty'. At a 'club' for factory girls she was horrified to learn of 'the sweating' in the factories that went on. Female outworkers in the garment industry were paid no more than 1½d to make a shirt, which department stores sold for twenty times as much. She met Agnes Milne, the daughter of a Lambeth carpenter, now the government's factory inspector, 'a very interesting and sensible woman' who was battling sweatshop owners. Her stories roused Audrey. She was determined that the government should fund a centre for women that could cut out the middlemen exploiting the workers. She was furious that there were no penny banks, for the low-paid to save. 'Hallam is going to talk to the Government about it.' She did not know enough, yet, of what she might do.

She visited cottage homes for the elderly, and a crèche for babies and young children of working mothers. She went to the new telephone exchange in the post office, 'too intricate to explain by letter nor do I really grasp the working of it', and to the House of Assembly to listen to debates which Hallam, as governor, was not allowed to attend. She rehearsed his speeches with him. She decorated the winner of the Derby, opened bazaars, visited a convent and shook 'hands as fast as one could go with 1,500 people or more' at another garden party they hosted at Government House. (To Zacyntha: 'They ate & drank like ogres . . . ices & macedoine of fruit in custard glasses with ice cream on the top.')

14 October 1899: 'There is tremendous excitement all over Australia about the Boer war declared the day before yesterday. A great deal of cabling backwards and forwards to the Colonial Office. A great row in Parliament here . . . by the Labour Party who are furious at the money being voted and spent' – the premier had volunteered a contingent of soldiers to go to South Africa to fight without first putting a vote to the house.

A week later Audrey wrote: 'The troops sail on Monday . . . and we have the men, 150 including the band to dinner Saturday at 1 o'clock in the afternoon and Hallam will address them & bid them God speed on the lawn afterwards. Mrs Bates *delighted* of course at this unexpected pleasure!'

On the day, 'H and I met them at the main entrance and shook hands with them all as they marched in, and oh, the agony I suffered from the grip and Australian squeeze from all the men which made me many times almost disgrace myself by screaming out.' Three-year-old Harold stood beside the big drum, beating his own in time to the music of the band, and after Hallam had bade them farewell on the lawn, 'we rushed down to the parade ground to see them embark in the train. The crowds everywhere were something beyond description. The officers asked H to go with them to the port, so he told me to jump into a carriage with him, and we went down with the troops.'

Suddenly, she found herself 'marching to the drum at the head of the troops at a quick pace'. Cheering crowds, fit to bust, shedding tears of joy and pride – it was 'the greatest day South Australia has ever seen', Hallam reported, as he quoted his ministers to the Queen; 'a single thought seemed to pervade the whole atmosphere – and that was "For our Queen and mother-country"'.

This was a message that bolstered the Queen at home, but the reality for Audrey was not the high feast of patriotism it had seemed in the heat of the moment. 'Last Thursday I was on my sofa with a headache but *had* to look at the war news and then saw the call here for bandages & jackets had not been warmly responded to.' She sent at once for Mrs Bates and dispatched her to a wholesale warehouse for flannel. By 4 p.m. 'every woman in the house except for the kitcheners who were working hard for the men's dinner on Saturday was stitching at large red flannel jackets, [cutting and rolling bandages]. . .& 3 machines going hard'. The boys helped by oversewing seams.

'Children's lessons, everything, had to give way', for the next few days, right up to the moment before the ship sailed, when the lot was sewn up in canvas to go to the troops. Audrey herself worked every day until midnight. It was Audrey, five months later in March 1900, 'sick at heart' with the 'awful and appalling' news of the disaster at Ladysmith, where more than 1,500 British troops had surrendered to the Boers, who masterminded a series of letters in the British papers. Day after day she wrote for hours, so long that her back ached, asking for gifts for 'our South Australian soldiers'.

Audrey never questioned how she was to behave, or how she would run Government House. 'It is a most curious sensation being treated as royalty,' she confessed not long after she arrived. Stateliness, dignity, kindness and warmth: 'queenliness' was what she strove for. Mlle Dussau, the governess, stepped up to the role of lady-in-waiting. Before long she too was bearing high the standard of Government House by delivering a set of lectures on French literature to the university. Audrey was amazed at her aplomb. But what a struggle it was to keep the peace behind the scenes, to 'study the different tempers & temperaments, first the children, then the staff, then the servants', she told her mother.

'I have to superintend *everything* and everybody. Hitchman, the butler, was 'very worthy', but 'too blind & deaf to be very much good'. Her maid Clarke was getting terribly slow and deaf, constantly worrying Audrey about what clothes to pack, what hat to bring, what shoes went with what. The footman, Thomas, was just sufficiently unreliable to be maddening. He had not disgraced himself – yet.

She had to order all her gowns and hats, medicines for Hallam and clothes for the boys from England, from Harrods or her dressmaker, through her mother. As with any mail order service, things went wrong. No kilts had arrived for the boys, who were still in their sailor suits, but 'two pairs French kid *girls* high boots' had come. Alas, all the gowns (there were four) 'are no good to me except the black serge'. Mistakes could take half a year to rectify. And now that they were at war, 'I am in despair about my mourning,' she told Zacyntha. With the royal opening of the Federal Parliament in Melbourne planned for the following May, she expected to need at least four new evening gowns, yellow satin shoes and yellow stockings. But she had fallen out with her dressmaker, to whom she had returned things that did not fit. What was she to do?

Doings with 'her chicks', fair-haired, brown-eyed, flowed through her days. Lionel, so like herself, 'just as harem scarum & persistent for what he wants as ever'. He was so good at games that by the age of fourteen he was scoring ninety runs at cricket, outplaying all the young men enlisted to play at Government House. Aubrey, a typical middle child, absorbed her attention more for his dramas (scarlet fever, a fall from his horse) than his character. Her youngest, Harold, ' a little imp on springs' who called himself 'a soldier of the Queen', was the one she adored. The children were swept up in as much as she could manage: attending, whenever possible, inspections of the troops, watching dances from the gallery behind the palms, playing cricket steadily every day, 'scampering' off with her on their ponies whenever she had a spare moment.

After they had been in Australia six months, Audrey asked her mother to begin looking for a tutor for the boys, someone who, she hoped, would also be able to double as Hallam's aide-de-camp. From the moment Zacyntha's chosen candidate, Mr Maurice, set foot in Government House in April 1900, he and Mlle Dussau had eyes for no one else. Audrey warned her governess not to go about alone with him, or to sit up talking after ten at night, when the lights were generally put out. 'People would talk at once.' Hallam forbade Maurice to have Mlle Dussau in the staff quarters. By October, as the temperature rose and the leaves of the eucalyptus trees drooped in the heat, Maurice had become a 'rather irritating person from being such a terrible prig'.

By December he was 'absolutely useless'. By then Maurice and Mademoiselle had become inseparable, Audrey wrote, 'on too intimate terms to be good for them'. The children 'are always making signs at each other, & looking and laughing across the table – making it odious for everyone else'. Audrey was furious. Mademoiselle 'is so much older than him and should have known better'. In January, Hallam at last gave Maurice his notice. By then Mademoiselle was wearing a gold ring on her left hand, and 'no one knows what the true situation is'. Audrey would never have a tutor in the house with a governess again.

By the following July, however, Mr Maurice had long gone and, whatever Mademoiselle's secret heartbreak, all was merry at Government House again. The Duke and Duchess of York, in Australia to open the new Federal Parliament in Melbourne, had come to stay. Mlle Dussau was at her most charming, flirting discreetly with one of the ADCs and invited by the Duke to sit next to him at luncheon.

Each December, when the heat rose to 114 degrees in the shade, the family would retreat until April to a house at Marble Hill, about an hour and a half out of town. There would be no meetings of the legislature or entertaining until May. The dust and heat were terrible at first in the carriage, Audrey wrote, '& then a lovely drive all up hills with sheep, green hills with gum trees, & *such* wild roses'. Marble Hill had a white painted gate to a wide drive through woods. The house, with a tower, was built of stone. The verandahs were enormously wide and the rooms were large and airy, with lovely views of woods all round. There was only one store nearby. All their supplies were brought up from Adelaide twice a week on a laundry cart.

One Monday evening towards the end of April 1900, Audrey told Mrs Bates that 200 soldiers of the Imperial Contingent would be coming to dine on Friday.

'Delighted,' Bates answered.

'But can you be ready? Mind, 200 hungry thirsty men?'

'Oh, yes, that will be all right, don't you worry.'

Through it all, the one person that Audrey could rely on was Mrs Bates, 'the help & comfort of my life'. She would rise from her sickbed when taken ill, never seemed to lose her composure, refusing Audrey's suggestions that they should hire chefs to help out, working to produce astonishing feasts with only two girls and occasional extra charwomen to do the washing up.

'If you could see *how* they eat & about 900 people for the two!' Audrey was talking about a great house party in October 1900, and two balls they had just had: one on a Wednesday, the next the following Monday. Each day it took her and Mlle Dussau all day to arrange the flowers. After dancing most of the night at the first ball, the next morning Audrey was on a train by 9 a.m. for a three-hour journey with Hallam to open an agricultural show at Strathalbyn.

'All the wonderful inventions were shown & explained to me which was mostly gibberish, but I have learned to be a terrible humbug & sometimes manage to make a sensible remark & they think her ladyship most intelligent. I always live in terror for fear they should ask me afterwards if I could repeat their explanation, & then I should be famously up a tree.' Cringing amateur plays, dreary school performances, 'the Admiral of the Fleet & his flag lieutenant to stay; official luncheons, & the house 'full & valets & endless waiters & workpeople to feed'.

From the kitchen Bates calmly kept up a steady stream of 'endless cakes for refreshments, coffee, tea & two or three kinds of ices going fast the whole time'. After the house party ended Audrey wrote, 'Bates told me this morning she had made 20 lbs of butter from all the cream left over.' She then started making the cakes for two garden parties they were giving the following week.

Audrey was exhausted. 'I feel tired & weary & am yearning for a little real rest,' she wrote her mother in the middle of it all. 'It is terribly hard work, day after day, public functions, & when you go to bed & feel one is over & dead tired, that the next day you must begin again . . . the last fortnight has been a great strain.' Incessant talking, to endless people, 'generally a good many new ones who are brought up & Presented & one has to be pleasant'. Audrey was prone to headaches, and devastating migraines that could last for days. Nor was she easy on herself. 'I am writing rather under difficulties as I am dictating Roman history to Lionel at the same time,' she said.

Even as Audrey and Hallam were giving their first ball as governor and lady of South Australia in June 1899, a referendum was carried throughout the five Australian colonies of New South Wales, Victoria, South Australia, Tasmania and Queensland to create a federation. No one knew now what would happen to the governorships. Audrey was not keen on Lord Hopetoun, the current governor-general, and his wife. They were much too full of themselves, much too showy, wasteful and extravagant, and never thanked the servants. They came to stay in Adelaide, in May 1902.

'I am afraid their visit will cost us a fearful amount, for they in themselves were a party of 7 & the menservants were a fearful expense.' For the overnight journey from Adelaide on their return to Melbourne, Lord and Lady Hopetoun and their two staff required '2 bottles of whisky, 2 bottles of claret, 1 bottle port, 9 bottles Spa water (which costs I don't know what out here!). Then [their valet] took a menu to Mrs Bates, saying they required fish, 2 chickens, a tongue, ham, fillet of beef, & other things I forget – dessert, pears, apples, grapes & bananas; bacon & eggs to fry for their breakfast, tho' they stop at an excellent station for breakfast & are due at Melbourne at 10.'

Hopetoun's governor-generalship was marked by a series of blunders. Soon after his visit to the Tennysons, he resigned. Hallam Tennyson was named to succeed him, and the family moved to Melbourne in August 1902. Government House, Melbourne, was famously grand, complete with proper state apartments and a ballroom the size of the one at Buckingham Palace. There were special entrances and cloakrooms for the public. Quite away from these: 'We have a beautiful suite of rooms, a row opening into each other – my bathroom, sitting room, bedroom, H's dressing room, his bathroom – a delicious sitting room.' But Melbourne was freezing. The house was so cold, she wore her outdoor coat and hat 'till dressing time'.

Government House, Melbourne

The servants were pleased. 'Old Hitchman in all his glory & delighted with the grandeur. Mrs Bates, slaving away. They find it very difficult to address me as "Your Excellency" & I *long* to say, "don't" for it gets on my nerves.'

The permanent household now numbered forty. The establishment, in Audrey's view, was becoming much too large and unwieldy – five men in the stables alone, and Hitchman, rather doddering, who insisted on keeping all drink under strict lock and key, was quite unable to cope.

The whirl of events stepped up. The Tennysons were now constantly travelling: Adelaide, Brisbane, Sydney and Queensland, in a royal train built for the Duke and Duchess the previous year. 'No words can describe the luxuriousness of it,' wrote Audrey. Luncheons, dinners, teas, and talking, talking, talking. Whenever she set foot outside, 'one is instantly a public character & has to make conversation & smile & bow etc which is all very well now & again but one gets very sick of it'.

'Lady Tennyson, may I present so & so?' Audrey could no longer, as in Adelaide, take up any interest that caught her eye; her and Hallam's doings were reported daily in newspapers all over Australia: planting trees, giving out school prizes, going to plays and concerts, attending balls. Who she danced with, sat next to at dinner; the heliotrope silk muslin she wore to a ball; presenting certificates to newly qualified nurses, helping raise funds for one needy cause after another, attending the annual show of the Sheep-breeders Association.

By now, however, Audrey had learned how to use her influence. She had taken up Agnes Milne's sweatshop campaign in Adelaide, and urged the premier of South Australia to establish tribunals to improve seamstresses' pay and conditions. It was soon after a visit to struggling villagers along the Murray River in dust-storms and drought that she conceived the idea, in December 1900, for a 'lying-in hospital' in Adelaide. It would serve the lonely, overworked mothers she had found living in the bush, and provide them with 'rest & quiet & the best trained nursing and food' until they were fit to cope with their new baby alone at home. She found the site, raised the money and fought the doctors who boycotted the project. To her rage, they insisted on charging even the poor several guineas to attend home births. She oversaw the construction down to the last detail, and hired her own staff. She refused to have any doctors on the governing committee.

At the end of May 1902, she opened the new hospital, called the Queen's Home. Fifteen hundred people grouped in front of the building; long lines of carriages, endless flags and flowers. She got through her speech without a break, 'but I was trembling all over when it was done'. Though people could not hear most of the men, 'they could hear every word I said', she told Zacyntha. 'What it is to be a woman, and the Governor's wife!'

Now, as the wife of the governor-general, she started work on the premiers and governors of all the five states, to instigate a closed season all over Australia to protect the indigenous animals – opossums, wallabies, platypus, kangaroos, which 'otherwise will soon be extinct'.

For all Audrey had experienced, she remained true to her roots. By the time she addressed the Mothers' Union in Sydney in May 1903, she had become a practised and inspiring speaker, relaxed, confident and amusing – but she was not in favour of radical change. Speaking on the role of motherhood, the plight of Adelaide's poor and unwed mothers stayed with her.

'The most dangerous years of an Australian girl's life are from 14 to 18,' she declared. Only if they were carefully guarded and guided until the age of twenty were they then 'generally capable of looking after themselves'. Mothers of Australia must watch and guard, and, above all, pray 'against the insane love of excitement' – the 'base of most of the evil of the present day' – which was doing such immeasurable harm to their young sons and daughters.

The speech caused uproar and made national news. Editorials declared that in excitement, the women and girls of Australia were finding freedom, experiencing the thrill of the new, the dawn of the future. 'You were a bold woman, Lady Tennyson, to say all you did,' the premier of Australia told her. In spite of this, as the wife of the governor-general Audrey had made herself much loved. Her maternity home in Adelaide, spotlessly clean and filled with fresh flowers, set a new standard for the nation.

It was her mother, Zacyntha, who brought about the early return of Hallam and Audrey from the governor-generalship of Australia at the end of 1903. She never ceased reproaching Audrey for deserting her in her old age. She never had anything positive to say, always slightly ticked her off. Tennyson had been governor-general for little more than a year – the Colonial Office wished him to stay for five – by the time they came to leave.

'There goes the nicest woman we have ever had in Australia,' declared the Lady Mayoress of Melbourne as she bade her farewell. Audrey was heartbroken. 'We have just come back from a long expedition to the top of a range of hills called the Black Spur . . . Such a glorious day, hot sun with delicious air and the scenery gorgeous,' she wrote in November 1903, a few weeks before she was due to sail. 'Thousands of tree ferns and magnificent huge gumtrees 200 to 300 feet high and 50 to 60 feet round – great giants. The tree cicadas are perfectly deafening. We heard the whip-bird quite close in the bush track we walked along . . . Oh, I do love all this Australian bush, and it just tears my heart to think I shall never see it again.'

Hallam, Audrey and the boys returned to live at Farringford. Zacyntha's reproachful tone continued after the family's return, until her death in 1907. Tennyson, offered the governorship of Madras, turned it down. He continued to take an active interest in the Empire, but never undertook another governorship. Instead, he went on to edit nine volumes of his father's poetry, and write a second memoir, *Tennyson and His Friends*.

With the outbreak of the First World War, Audrey threw herself into running a military hospital on the Isle of Wight. In January 1916 their cherished youngest son, Harold, was killed when his ship struck a mine in the Channel. Ten months later, exhausted with grief and overwork, Audrey succumbed to pneumonia and died at the age of sixty-two, on 7 December. Fifteen months later, in March 1918, Aubrey was killed in action. Although Lionel was wounded three times, he went on to fulfil his youthful promise as a cricketer, playing for England, and serving as captain of the team in Australia in 1921.

In 1995 the maternity hospital that Audrey founded in Adelaide was amalgamated with the Children's Hospital in North Adelaide. The building she had so carefully overseen was sold. Escaping conversion into an abortion clinic, it was remodelled as luxury apartments.

Mlle Dussau never ceased her flirtations. She cast her eye over Mr Maurice's successor as tutor, and several of the Governor-General's ADCs. But her triumph was to have captured the attention of the Duke and Duchess of York during their stay at Government House in Adelaide in 1901. In February 1903, the Duke, now the Prince of Wales, cabled a request to her to come as governess to their daughter, Princess Mary. Audrey was at once flattered and cross that her governess should be poached. But she agreed to let her go when they returned to England. Thirty years later, Mlle Dussau was still making an impact as an elderly spinster, dining with the bon viveur and leader of the British wine trade, André Simon. She was still a governess in Buckingham Palace, where the young man who had once been the Duke of York was now King George V.

13 A marriage of imperialists
Northern Nigeria 1901–6

On 11 June 1902 a private wedding took place in the small English church in the flowery port city of Funchal on the island of Madeira – a convenient calling point between the ports of the British Isles and the west coast of Africa. The bride, slim, auburn-haired and vividly attractive, was almost fifty. The groom was a British army officer six years her junior: fox-faced and slightly built, loaded with a kind of barely suppressed energy, with swirling moustaches and intense brown eyes. The quiet ceremony united two of the most influential imperialists in the history of the British Empire: the writer and journalist Flora Shaw and Sir Frederick Lugard, soldier, adventurer, explorer – and now High Commissioner of Northern Nigeria.

'Not *the* Miss Shaw?' Lord Curzon, the Viceroy of India, had written to Lugard on hearing of his engagement. 'If she be another, may she be equally brilliant and not less charming.' Was there anyone, indeed, whom Flora Shaw did not know and had not charmed in the corridors of power in Westminster? Lord Cromer, Viscount Milner, Cecil Rhodes – Joseph Chamberlain, of course, and Sir George Goldie, the handsome, discreet founder of the Royal Niger Company, the man who had given Lugard his first job in west Africa, and with whom she had been in love. Flora was elegant and warm. Time after time, men of experience seemed to lose their discretion before her wide expressive eyes and keen interest in their affairs. Until two years before her marriage she had been the colonial editor of *The Times*: the first woman on the permanent staff of the paper. She championed British expansionism and the British right to rule. The circulation of *The Times* in the 1890s may have been limited to only 35,000, but its influence was recognized around the globe. Even the great Abraham Lincoln had called it 'one of the greatest powers of the world', as he put aside time for an interview with one of its correspondents.

'A fine, handsome, bright upstanding young woman, as clever as they make them, capable of any immense amount of work, as hard as nails and talking like a *Times* leader all the time.' Thus the west African traveller and writer Mary Kingsley. Kingsley was no friend of Flora, who refused to review her books in *The Times*. 'She is imbued with the modern form of public imperialism,' said Kingsley. 'It is her religion.' She always dressed in black.

Few women of any era have enjoyed such a brilliant career as Flora Shaw. She was born in December 1852, in Woolwich, the third child of an Anglo-Irish captain in the Royal Artillery and his beautiful, if delicate, French wife, Marie. Her parents had met while he was serving in Mauritius in 1848; Marie was the daughter of the Governor. Flora grew up moving between winters near the Royal Military College in Woolwich, and the family seat in Kimmage, near Dublin, in Ireland in the summer. Her mother taught her French; she told her tales of her grandmother's courage before the Paris mobs during the French Revolution; a beloved governess supervised a gentle, female education. As her father rose to the rank of major-general and commandant of the Royal Military College, her mother, who gave birth to a child every year, declined. By the age of thirteen, Flora and her elder sister, Mimi, were running the household, looking after their mother and a dozen children. Flora sought escape in the books of the Woolwich Arsenal library.

It was while attending a lecture at Woolwich that Flora came to the attention of the famous art and social critic John Ruskin. She was seventeen; he was fifty. 'Such a pretty lady', he was to write to her five years later. She had looked so grand and sophisticated coming into the lecture hall, he had not realized he had met her at dinner a little while before. Ruskin took her up, directed her reading, and introduced her to Thomas Carlyle. 'When you are as old as I am, you can say that you knew a man who knew Goethe,' Carlyle told her. She in turn read his *French Revolution*.

In February 1870, just before Flora turned eighteen, Ruskin delivered his inaugural lecture as Slade Professor of Art at Oxford. It was a speech that would define an era. 'Will you, youths of England, make your country again a royal throne of kings, a sceptred isle, for all the world a source of light, a centre for peace; mistress of Learning and of the Arts . . .?'

'Reign or Die': this was what England had to do or perish. 'She must found colonies as fast and as far as she is able, formed of her most energetic and worthiest men . . . teaching these her colonists that their chief virtue is to be fidelity to their country, and that their first aim is to be to advance the power of England by land and sea.' The national impact of the lecture was momentous. Ruskin's injunction was to become Flora's creed.

That year Mimi married, and their mother died. Within two years, Flora's father, always aloof and unapproachable, had married again – to an unsympathetic stepmother. For a time Flora took refuge with her mother's sister in France, returning to stay from time to time with Mimi and the Ruskins. She was starting to write. Ruskin of course advised her, but before long she was invited to become housekeeper/governess to Mimi's husband's cousin, Colonel Charles Brackenbury, his wife Hilda, and their nine children in Aldershot. Brackenbury had served with General Wolseley in his campaign on the Gold Coast, and later as *The Times* correspondent during both the Austro- and Franco-Prussian wars. Until recently he had been working in the newly established intelligence branch of the War Office. He was also a close friend of the novelist George Meredith. Thanks to them, Flora's first children's story, *Castle Blair,* was published to enthusiastic reviews.

Flora left the Brackenburys when the youngest children left school. She became a social worker and teacher in the slums of the East End. Four more novels were published. In 1882, at the age of thirty, she was finally able to live independently. She rented a room in a cottage, Little Parkhurst, at Abinger in the Surrey woods.

'To me you would be sunshine,' George Meredith, who lived nearby, wrote to welcome her to the neighbourhood. 'The life here is lonely and monotonous, but you have that in the mind which can kindle dullness.' She often walked from Abinger to his house at Box Hill, and had long conversations with his visitors, people like Robert Louis Stevenson and Charles Eliot Norton from Harvard. She was keeping a diary, planning a history of England, thinking about the life she had seen in the slums, wondering whether the answers to poverty and overcrowding might not be migration to colonies overseas.

In the winter of 1886, she was invited to Gibraltar by friends. To finance the trip, Meredith introduced her to one of the greatest newspaper editors of the day, W. T. Stead of the *Pall Mall Gazette*. Stead – who would end his life going down on the *Titanic* – made no allowance for women. He told her she could expect foul language, scathing editorial criticism, demeaning assignments and unchaperoned nights. For Flora, the rest was history. She came home from Gibraltar with a scoop: a lengthy interview with Zobehr Pasha, a Sudanese political prisoner who might have saved the life of the mighty General Gordon at Khartoum, had not the British arrested him. Within six weeks of her article, which featured on the front page, Zobehr was free and on his way back to Cairo.

Eighteen months later she was reporting on the British occupation of

Egypt, as a correspondent not only for the *Gazette* but the *Manchester Guardian*. From then on she began reporting on all manner of foreign affairs: Persia, heavy guns, the army as a career. She was in and out of the Colonial Office, regularly briefed by the Permanent Secretary, Sir Robert Herbert, meeting the Secretary of State, invited to receptions and dinners. She was rapidly becoming an authority on the politics of the Mediterranean and, increasingly, on Africa. 'Home after midnight – wrote column of report,' she recorded in her diary. 'Bed four o'clock.'

In the summer of 1889, she met Cecil Rhodes. Big, bluff and confident, he was thirty-six, founder of the de Beers diamond mines, a multi-millionaire, and one of the wealthiest men in Africa. By this time he was moving north on the back of his British South Africa Company from South Africa across the Zambezi, staking out today's Zimbabwe, Zambia and Malawi, beginning to open up a vast ill-defined area of southern and central Africa. Rhodes made other men seem 'like thread-paper beside him', she wrote. As she quizzed him, he walked 'like a caged lion all the time through two rooms'. Why was he willing to chance such immense sums on the potential of Africa?

'Some men collect butterflies,' he said. 'I do this. It interests me.'

The scramble for Africa was in full spate. Flora's work was taking off. She was the only woman at a conference in Belgium to formulate an international law outlawing the slave trade. For the first time, European nations were co-operating on something greater than their own national interests. More and more, she was becoming committed to the idea of Empire, of the need to rouse the British public to a sense of imperial responsibility. When Moberly Bell, a correspondent for *The Times* whom she had met in Egypt in 1888, became managing editor of the paper, he determined to commission her. She dusted down a previous article on Egyptian financial reform and submitted it.

'Whoever wrote it [is] the sort of fellow we ought to get on *The Times*,' declared the paper's proprietor. Bell told her if she were a man she 'would be Colonial Editor tomorrow'. As it was, even as a freelance, her influence immediately began to make its impact on the paper. The 'Foreign and Colonial' column was changed to 'Colonial and Foreign' (it would later be headed 'Imperial'): a serious, reasoned mix of news and commercial information. Meanwhile, C. P. Scott kept her on at the *Manchester Guardian*, even though he deplored the growth of British influence in Africa and had no faith in emigration as a cure for British social problems.

'I am not so good a John Bull as you,' he told her, while giving her free rein to rouse commitment to the Empire in what she called this 'stronghold of the Liberal camp, supposed to be anti-imperial'. She was delighted.

In January 1892 she came down with influenza. Exhausted from over-work, she was confined to bed for almost two months. The doctor prescribed a long holiday. Knowing this was beyond her means, Moberly Bell offered to dispatch her to South Africa as a special correspondent. She landed in Cape Town with excellent introductions, an intriguing curiosity as a woman on business, elegantly dressed in black, vivacious and intelli-gent. At Government House, the Governor, Sir Henry Loch, and his wife were kind and helpful, consumed with running what 'Mr Rhodes calls the Circus Show part of their business and [making] themselves proportion-ately popular'. As far as Flora was concerned, it was only Cecil Rhodes, now in the Cape Cabinet, and two of his colleagues who were in earnest over plans to develop the country.

'Up to the Karoo! It means up from Cape Town . . . to a plateau topping the summit of Table Mountain,' she told her readers in *The Times* as she left by a night train for Kimberley to see Rhodes's de Beers diamond mines. She began underground, braving 'the slush and heat and drip of the 800 ft level' while she splashed, candle in hand in the darkness. 'Above, below, on every side you hear the sound of pick and rock drill and rolling trucks. Black figures glue themselves against the walls to let you pass.'

Here Rhodes had implemented a system of managing black labour that would inspire the notorious pass laws of apartheid in the twentieth century. Fourteen hundred white men, many with their wives, lived on a comfort-ably planned estate a mile and a half from the mines, while 6,000 black African workers were confined to a locked compound directly connected to the mine by a covered way. Strip-searched on entering and leaving, the black men could not leave the premises without formal permission. They could only see their wives and family through a grille, in the presence of an overseer. Seeing all the men digging, loading trucks and sorting diamonds, 'you can never doubt any more that the African native is able to work', Flora wrote. They were paid £1 a week; one third of the lowest wages paid to the white workers. The strictures of their lives, even 'under liberal man-agement', made her uneasy. 'The conditions of seclusion are as absolute as those of the life of any monk,' she wrote, concluding that the system was unnatural – 'far too artificial to be universally applied'. She was ignored.

She went on to Johannesburg and its gold mines – the town very new, growing at an alarming rate, dirty, disorderly, and full of 'luxury without order . . . display without dignity'. She contrasted the slow-moving, conservative Dutch Boer, obsessed with 'pasturage for his cattle and earth for his corn seed . . . no need of hurry, no need to keep pace with modern inventions', with the hustling Englishman bent on making a fast profit. She went on to Pretoria, where she descended from the coach 'in a state of powderous dirt . . . hair, eyes, teeth . . . full of gritty sand', so filthy 'you might be carted away by mistake for a roadside sweeping'. She could not get over the wealth of the country.

Flora met everyone of importance, catalogued all the issues of the day. 'Material is the subject of daily talk and daily effort. The opening of means of communication, the development of mines, the settlement of land . . . the task . . . is nothing less than Titanic.' How to make the black man work? This was the burning issue. 'The difficulty, it is often said,' she wrote, 'is that the native has no wants. If we could give him wants he would work to satisfy them. This is the object of the most enlightened missionary efforts . . .'

Every three or four days she produced a major article over 3,000 words long – clear, readable, taking her reader with her on her travels. 'We began our journey by starlight . . . within four hours of Bloemfontein the veldt took the aspect of a yellow land upon which a child's Noah's ark had been set out. Herds of cattle and horses and flocks of sheep, with here and there a quaint figure wrapped in a blanket watching them, were scattered thickly over the landscape.' Three weeks later: 'I came down from De Aar Junction . . . to Port Elizabeth, and from Port Elizabeth by sea to East London. The descent is made in five great steps, through wild, but no longer treeless, scenery. Mountain passes, covered with euphorbias, flowering aloes, and aromatic herbage, alternate in succession with plateaux that widen out to farm and pasture lands.' Her articles were bringing the Empire into the drawing rooms of England, shaping what the British were thinking.

'Never have I so often heard the word "remarkable" applied so generously and by so many different sorts of people as to your letters [from Africa].' Moberly Bell was delighted with her dispatches. He amused her with talk of how amazed important men were to find that 'Our Correspondent' was a woman – in print Flora was always 'he'. Meanwhile, Bell instructed her to 'get some ordinarily trustworthy but not brilliant man who can be trusted to send short telegrams giving actual news from all parts of South Africa', which she could then recast into articles from her desk back in London. Then he asked her to travel on: to Australia, New Zealand and Canada – continuing the series of 'Letters' she had begun.

Flora was away for over a year. Her only lightweight silk dress caught fire in the heat of Australia; landslides blocked her train in the Rocky Mountains. She travelled endlessly by post-cart and buggy and stayed in some very bad hotels. She met prime ministers and governors, millionaires and bushrangers, Canadian Mounties and government officials; visited sheep stations, mines and factories, schools and evangelical societies, plantations and Quebec farms so meagre 'they might almost have been in Ireland'. New Zealand she found hopelessly provincial: 'they are dreadfully pleased with themselves in the towns'. The Canadians were even more so.

By the time she returned home, Flora was over forty. She was more than ever convinced that London was the centre of the world, and that a flourishing Empire revolved around it. *The Times* rewarded her with a full-time job as colonial editor, an office in Printing House Square and a salary of £800 – over £65,000 today. While she was away, her father had died. Two of her sisters had been widowed. She had become the family's main breadwinner. Giving part of her income to her older sister, Mimi, she invited her three younger sisters to live with her. They set up home in a tall, narrow house in Pimlico. As she called it, Flora played 'master of the house' and grumbled 'at the bills and the dinner'.

Frederick Lugard gave no thought to who one 'F. Shaw', the editor of the 'Colonies' column of *The Times*, might be. What he wanted was a decent review of the book he had just written. While Flora was travelling around the world in the autumn of 1892, Lugard had returned to England after almost three years in East Africa. His mission was to persuade the British government of the urgency of annexing the territory of Uganda – and to defend his reputation.

Lugard was thirty-five, small, tough and wiry. His exploits in Africa had captured the attention, if not yet of the general public, of the War and Colonial Offices. Quick, fiery and intense, eager to act and take command, he had been the child of impoverished evangelical missionaries in Madras and had no doubts of his own righteousness. His father, Frederick, the gently reared son of the secretary of the Royal Military Asylum for the children of soldiers in Chelsea, had grown up profoundly scarred by the stories of losses at Waterloo to become a devout army chaplain to the East India Company. Based in the lovely, timber-vaulted English church, with its louvred shutters and over-wrought stone memorials, in the company's compound in Madras, by 1854 he was forty-six, an impecunious widower with five children by two marriages. That year he married Lugard's mother, Mary Jane Howard. She was neat, dark-haired and pretty, the thirty-six-year-old daughter of a Cambridge-bred clergyman, and a missionary of the Church Missionary Society. Frederick, their third child and eldest son, was born in 1858.

Mary Jane was not strong; there was a child every year. After bearing five, two of whom died, Lugard's father sent her to England with all the younger children for her health. The voyage was hell. A single cabin, stiflingly hot and airless, alive with cockroaches, overrun with red ants, and six children, two of them sickly. 'Most days the sun struck vertically down upon the unshaded deck,' she wrote. Clouds of mosquitoes bred in the water-butts, the poop steps were steep and difficult with a babe in arms; the male passengers cursed wailing children. Fred, who was five, was bullied. In England, they settled near her mother in a tiny house in York. There, Mary Jane prayed daily to God to help her. Young Fred bore witness. 'Make me a clergyman when I am a man,' he prayed, 'and make my dear Papa rich, and let us all be rich . . .' When Fred was seven his mother died.

His father returned to England broken by grief. There was a move into lodgings, and a series of schools: at ten a prep school run by Moravians near Worcester, where Fred's ears were boxed so often for punishment, his hearing was permanently damaged; at thirteen a Church of England school for boys at Rossall, on a gale-ridden stretch of the chilly Lancashire coast. Slight but sinewy, Fred was bullied, constantly late for chapel, and punished with endless 'drills' of 'lines'. Then his closest friend, who would take him home in the holidays, died of 'cold and exposure'.

When Fred was seventeen, a new headmaster arrived to overhaul the school. He introduced competitive games and an emphasis on scholarship. More interestingly – even more so because Lugard remembered it so vividly – he had emotions and was not afraid to show them. 'A man need not be afraid to wear his heart on his sleeve, it is only [jack] daws will pick at it,' he told the boys. Lugard finished school with prizes in divinity and history, and a hero in Livingstone – the missionary in Africa who faced every kind of danger 'for the sake of the truth'.

With no allowance from his father and no idea what to do, he was taken in hand by two of his father's younger brothers. Both had been in the army; one of them, Sir Edward Lugard (the Sikh Wars and the Indian Rebellion) had recently spent ten years as Under-Secretary for War. Fred sat the exams for Sandhurst and came out sixth of nearly 1,000 candidates.

He was there for eight weeks. Early in 1878, war with Russia threatened in Turkey. All the Sandhurst cadets were hastily commissioned. Lugard could not afford to serve with a regiment in England. He sailed for India and the 2nd Battalion in Peshawar on the North-West Frontier.

Lugard was turning out to be a man who did nothing by halves. He mastered Hindustani and Urdu and developed the habit of working long into the night. He threw himself into the life of an army officer in the cantonment with his horse and his dog: drill on the parade ground, evenings of whisky and soda, smoking and bridge at the club and dinners in the mess; games of polo, racing horses and above all, reckless tiger hunts and pig-sticking on his grey mare 'Delusion'. There was a year, early on, spent in England to recover from fever. There he realized finally that, without any money from his father, he would never have enough money to marry. 'I wish my own chance of having little ones were not among the impossibles,' he told his half-sister, Emma. But 'an officer's life is the best, bar none, in the world', he told his younger brother, Ned. 'If one has to face a bad climate or find oneself in a hold for coin . . . the whole system of Mess life, especially in India, is a grand one. You get your racquets, polo, pig-sticking, riding – *chacun à son goût* – to the extent he can afford etc.' Nothing could beat life in the army.

He was playing bridge one evening when he was handed a telegram ordering him to the Sudan, in charge of transport for an Indian contingent sent to relieve Khartoum. From there he wrote to Ned in March 1885. 'Do not tell father, that I was in the fight on March 23rd.' Five thousand dervishes had attacked. The action had been desperate, full of confused hand-to-hand fighting – 'like demons, even *women!*' – and sobering. Nearly 2,000 men – 315 of whom were British – were killed. 'The stench when we left of *hundreds* of human corpses plus *hundreds* of camels and mules was suffocating.' Lugard escaped with a shoulder wound. A year later, he was back in India in command of a transport unit based at Lucknow. It was there, in the heat and dust of the summer of 1886, that he fell passionately in love with a beautiful divorcee, Frances Gambier.

Little is known of the romance, only its effect. Lugard had been posted onwards to Burma when a year later, news reached him that Frances lay dying from injuries in a carriage accident. He fled back to Lucknow to find she had sailed for England. Chafing at the delay, he hastened to London, where he found her fit and well, in the arms of another man. Lugard went crazy with grief.

'Fred turned up last evening looking better than when he first came home but I thought rather *wild!*' his uncle, Sir Edward, told Ned. He had joined the London Fire Brigade. Night after night he deliberately hurled himself into the flames of fires, refusing to come home, or explain to his baffled uncle why his career should 'end like the stick of the previously brilliant rocket . . . I cannot understand it!' He applied for sick leave from the army, collected his entire savings of £48, and like the hero of Rider Haggard's *The Witch's Head*, which he had recently read, took ship for Zanzibar, with a vague notion of fighting the slave trade. Lugard's penury – he'd travelled on the deck – and apparent aimlessness did not impress the Consul there. He drifted south along the coast, until he landed in Mozambique. There, the British Consul had several ideas for what an experienced British officer might do.

This was the age of freebooters and mercenaries all over Africa, moving through deserts and jungles unknown to the white man, on the lookout for all kinds of natural resources, wealth and opportunity. Like Cecil Rhodes's British South Africa Company, all kinds of syndicates were exploring, making treaties with chieftains who had no idea what they were signing, laying down claims to vast sources of mineral wealth. In April 1888 Lugard was hired by the African Lakes Company, operating between the Mozambique coast and Lake Nyasa – now also known as Lake Malawi. He was to mount an expedition against Arab slave traders who had attacked their small trading post and a Scottish mission at Karonga, in the north-west corner of the lake. He was thirty.

After India, the Sudan and Burma, the fevered delta of the Zambezi, with its shallow, silted waters infested with crocodile and hippopotamus, its banks lined with creeper and dark jungle trees, its stands of elephant and buffalo and its gliding white-headed fish eagles, was a new experience. Egrets and kingfishers flashed in the sunlight. Lugard was travelling alone in a dugout canoe, paddled by peoples he knew nothing of, sleeping at night under shelters of sticks and grass among clouds of mosquitoes, soon suffering from fever.

His position was hazardously ambiguous. 'The Foreign Office learnt from the consuls near you that you were knocking about in East Africa and they wrote to the War Office asking who you were and what you were doing,' his cousin was to write him later. No one was prepared *officially* to countenance his acts. But arriving in Blantyre – with its small square of houses, a manse and a high brick church, a little piece of Scotland in the midst of Africa – he met Scottish missionaries and representatives of the company whom he liked and respected. They told him how Arab and Swahili slavers had been exploiting tribal conflicts around Lake Nyasa, systematically exporting the weak to the coast for the past thirty years. Everyone was convinced that unless the Arabs were stopped, a huge slave route would be opened along the north of the lake. Would Lugard take command? He was joined by fourteen Scots from the African Lakes Company, including John Moir, the man in charge, seven mercenaries from Natal, the mission doctor and a couple of white hunters. Ten days later, on 28 May, the party arrived at Karonga. Lugard staked out the Arab stockades, seven miles away.

It was a story of settling in, and recruiting and instructing over 300 'naked fighting men' wearing haloes of pig-bristles around their heads. The men had seen their wives and children stolen from them, or were themselves refugees from slaving. 'Finding out their war cry, I said that when I shouted they must charge side by side with the white man,' Lugard recorded. At 1 a.m. on the morning of 16 June, he raised a British 'Hurrah!' and charged the stockade. It all went horribly wrong. The explosives set to blow up the stockade did not go off. Lugard and another man were seriously wounded; a third was killed. The British retreated. Over the next year Lugard would attack a dhow, and make two more attempts to blow up the Arab stockades at Karonga. Defeated, troubled by his wound which periodically robbed him of the use of his left arm, appalled by the slaving he had seen, he determined to tell his story in England, and bring back reinforcements.

It was the summer of 1889 and Cecil Rhodes was in London, bent on getting a royal charter for his British South Africa Company, and government endorsement for the push he was making into central Africa. Three weeks after Lugard landed in England, Rhodes bought the African Lakes Company. Flora was not yet working for *The Times,* but she might as well have been. The paper was excited, bullish. The same kind of chartered company that had won India for Britain was to be used in central Africa! Rhodes's scheme was one of the greatest ever, declared the *Pall Mall Gazette.* This may well have been Flora at work. The paper ran a leader headlined, 'Painting the African Map Red', crying, 'Chartered Adventurers, go ahead!'

There was no place for Lugard in Rhodes's, and the Foreign Office's, plans for the region around Lake Nyasa. This was a man who was a little too passionate, a little too unreliable, altogether too ready to take action into his own hands. However, these attributes did not daunt the founder of the Imperial British East Africa Company, William Mackinnon. When Mackinnon asked him to explore a new route from Mombasa to the interior of East Africa, a bitter, chastened Lugard said 'yes'.

Travelling with mules, camels, donkeys and 120 Swahili porters, Lugard was three months out of Mombasa in March 1890 when new instructions arrived. The twenty-four-year-old Kabaka, the King of Buganda (in today's Uganda), had been recently reinstated on his throne with the help of European missionaries and a British trader. Mwanga was a man of whom no contemporary European had other than the most disagreeable things to say. Cruel and capricious, he was openly homosexual, a smoker of *bhang,* and responsible for not only the torture and murder of scores of Christians, but numerous conspiracies and other killings. Thirteen years before, Buganda had welcomed its first Anglican missionaries, dispatched from Britain at the instigation of the journalist and explorer Henry Morton Stanley. They were followed two years later by two French Catholic priests. With Mwanga's accession to the throne at the age of eighteen in 1884, the people of the country had rapidly become riven by religious faction, between French-inspired Catholics, British-led Protestants, and the northern Muslims, who had been converted by the Arabs. Mwanga, caught between the novelty of the new Christian religions and the pagan worship in which his own authority was embedded, was faced with a confused and highly volatile situation, threatened by Arabs, Germans and British. In the five years before Lugard arrived one religious group after another had fought for control.

Now there were fears that the powerful influence of French priests in the country could lead to German – rather than British – annexation. Lugard was to obtain a treaty 'to regularise' the position of the Imperial British East Africa Company in the kingdom of Buganda: in short, obtain 'control of all White affairs', conciliate the warring religious factions (while remaining 'perfectly impartial', he was to 'point out the scandal which their differences present to the cause of Christianity'), stop the import of arms, and impress on Mwanga 'a sense of power of the Company'.

He arrived in Kampala in December 1890, his boots broken, his clothing in rags, with three Europeans, a superb Somali interpreter, and a battered Maxim gun. Anxious though he was, Lugard was determined to take no nonsense from Mwanga. As he entered the town he was disconcerted by a surprising aura of civilization, as Mwanga's royal band of flutes and drums greeted him.

Lugard had no sooner crossed the Nile north of Lake Victoria into the kingdom of Buganda when he began to become increasingly impressed by an atmosphere of orderly cultivation and prosperity. There were roads and fences, and the people were clad in spotless imported cotton. The chiefs he met were intelligent; the place was structured and civilized. Lugard determined to keep the initiative, bringing his own chair and sitting on it before the Kabaka. His first meeting, however, was disconcerting and fraught with tension. Mwanga giggled as he stroked a boy beside him, while his chieftains asked lengthy, detailed and intelligent questions. Five days later, having briefed the French White Fathers and the chiefs of different persuasions on the treaty he had drafted, Lugard met Mwanga for a second time. Again he was determined to retain control of the meeting.

'After some discussion I asked if the King were ready to sign . . . he shuffled and I got more determined and rapped the table and told him to sign if he wanted peace.' Just as Mwanga seemed about to agree, rifles were cocked, and 'a clamour went up from the crowd at the entrance that their country was being sold'. It took Lugard three more days to obtain his signature. As darkness fell, the sound of war drums rose from the surrounding hills.

Lugard was now marooned in a fragile stockade with no more than 100 men capable of firing a rifle. It was three months' difficult march back to the coast at Mombasa. He dispatched a runner to the coast with news of his success, and a request for a British resident and a unit of 500 trained soldiers for Kampala. It took nearly a year for a reply to arrive from the company. Uganda offered no source of income beyond a few ivory tusks; the company was in serious financial difficulty. Lugard was instructed to renegotiate a treaty that would put its rights in perpetuity, and withdraw to the coast.

He was furious. 'What was the object of starting this Company on an apparently impossible basis?' he wrote in his diary. He was bitter that such a retreat would mean breaking faith with a people whose trust over the past year he had laboured to win. During his time in Uganda, Lugard had tried to broker peace between the Catholics and the Protestants, in what he called 'this hornets' nest of Uganda'. Meanwhile violence had continued. Catholics and Protestants had taken to murdering those who converted from one faith to another, caravans arrived from the coast carrying arms, and Mwanga vacillated between one faith and another.

As news of Lugard's instructions to leave Uganda leaked out, Mwanga attended Christmas Mass with the White Fathers. In retaliation the Protestants sacked the French mission. Lugard fired two rounds from the Maxim, and rode into the mission to rescue the priests. Fighting broke out.

'Missions wiped out by Protestants. Six fathers prisoners . . . Catholics killed, dispersed enslaved . . .' ran the cable that the French Ambassador presented in London. It took four months for Lugard to calm the situation. 'Extermination by fanatics was not my view of God's will for his creatures,' he told them. 'I am here not as a teacher of religion, not as a Protestant, but as a legislator.' He had learned that there were as many Muslims in Uganda as Catholics and Protestants. Gradually he was able to bring the Muslim chief Mobogo, whose trust he had earned, together with his nephew, Mwanga. They agreed a delineation of areas in which those of each faith should live, and signed a new declaration with the British East Africa Company. When Lugard set off for the coast, he bore a magnificent royal war-drum, presented to him by Mobogo, and a letter to Queen Victoria from Mwanga, signed by all his chiefs.

'I earnestly beseech you to help me,' Mwanga told the Queen. 'Do not recall the Company from my country. I and my chiefs are under the English flag . . . we desire very, very much that the English should arrange this country.' Should the company's agents be recalled, 'my country is sure to be ruined, war is sure to come'. He wanted Lugard back.

Lugard landed in England in the autumn of 1892 accused by the French of war crimes and suspected by the British government of provoking a war. A commission of investigation was launched. Meanwhile, Lugard embarked on a public relations campaign to clear his name. He wrote a long letter to *The Times*. Commercially, politically and for humanitarian reasons, Britain could not abandon Uganda. Not only was the country rich in ivory, it had great potential for coffee, rubber, wheat and cotton. Here was the source of the Nile, the command point of the waterways from the lakes of southern Africa, to the Nile in the north, and the gateway to Egypt and the Sudan. If Britain abandoned Uganda, another foreign power was bound to step in; Britain's influence on the east coast of Africa would become worthless. Meanwhile, the place was teetering on the brink of anarchy. Britain had a responsibility to safeguard the missionaries, Catholic and Protestant, and the mass of ordinary people who would be sold as slaves should civil war break out. In honour, the nation could not abandon Uganda.

For the next nine months he worked ferociously, producing a book, and giving public lectures all over the country: Manchester, Edinburgh, Glasgow, Aberdeen, Newcastle, Cambridge, Liverpool, Birmingham, Norwich and London. More than 300 people, 'Lords and Dukes and all sorts of swells', had to be turned away from his address at the Royal Geographical Society. Arguing passionately for Uganda, he was fast becoming a celebrity.

His book, a 350,000-word epic, was called *The Rise of Our East African Empire*. Compiled from his diaries, it is anecdotal, fact-filled, argumentative, revealing a man of principle; courageous, dogged and uncompromising.

'F. Shaw' ticked Lugard off for his 'literary impropriety' in requesting a review of his book in *The Times*. She then proceeded to call it 'the most important contribution that has yet been made to the history of East Africa'. When he wrote to thank her, she told him, 'if we could stir the country to feel more than it does the importance of dealing in the best way with our African possessions it would be a real gain'. She added, 'I am nearly always at home late in the afternoon –'

Lugard was a hero. Piles of cards were left at his club, political hostesses vied for his attention, the newly elected Prime Minister, Lord Salisbury, invited him to spend a weekend at Hatfield; the new Secretary of State for the Colonies, Joseph Chamberlain, had him to Highbury, his country house on the outskirts of Birmingham. 'I've been plunging tremendously, advertising myself and my book everywhere,' he wrote to Ned on 20 December 1893. After a lifetime surrounded by men and roughing it in Africa, society came as a shock: ladies smoking, talking of things like metaphysics, house parties at which everyone 'does exactly as they like . . . I don't mind fast *ladies* – but fast *men* are hateful to me. I find myself gasping at their audacity like a fish on a bank.

'It's amusing to see the Duchess and diamonds side, after trying the other however I can't run to this – I had to buy a new hat today, someone boned my good one at this damned club and left me a *beast* in its place . . . I shall have to buy a new overcoat, and goodness knows where it will stop for my dress suit isn't as new as it might be.'

Flora took up Lugard's campaign for the annexation of Uganda in *The Times* while he worked on the Secretary of State himself. The weekend before parliament scheduled a major debate on Africa in June 1895, Lugard

stayed at Highbury to coach Chamberlain. The Secretary of State rose to a
packed house. Treaties, legal statuses, names of peoples and places – MPs
quoted them familiarly. Contrast 'the intimate knowledge shewn by the
whole House on the question', Lugard told Ned, and a debate on African
affairs when he had first come home two years before, 'and you'll see that
my ceaseless efforts . . . *have* produced a wonderful result'. Uganda was to
become a British protectorate. The Crown would safeguard it from hostile
invasion or civil disturbance, while interfering as little as possible in its
domestic affairs.

Lugard, the celebrity, by Spy, December 1895

'Miss Shaw, the specialist of *The Times,* told me that the conversion of
Chamberlain was indeed notable, that in 1890 he had twice taken her to
dinner, and he was quite half-hearted about Africa, now he is the leading
enthusiast and goes further than anyone else in the House.' It was a triumph
for both of them.

Shaw and Lugard were now in constant touch. Over the next five years
they wrote to each other constantly – long, intense discussions of African
affairs. They did not always see eye to eye. He didn't like Cecil Rhodes and

deplored her admiration for him. 'A woman's emotion always will dominate her intellect,' he told Ned. Flora would have laughed. In 1897 she was summoned before a select committee of the House of Commons inquiring into the disastrous Jameson Raid into the Transvaal which Rhodes had masterminded. She was to explain incriminating telegrams to and from *The Times* which suggested she knew about it beforehand. Cool, dressed in black silk and white pearls, she was eloquent and well prepared. At *The Times* she had been aware of 'a plan' – but not 'a raid'. She was frank and lucid, and in her manner 'the Lady witness beat all the men', recorded Chamberlain.

In spite of his successful campaign to annex Uganda, Lugard had not been rewarded with the job he had longed for: running the new protectorate as its commissioner. Once again he had to look for employment. He was offered a job in west Africa, working for Sir George Goldie's Royal Niger Company. Lugard was to proceed to Borgu, a remote place in the north of today's Nigeria, to secure a treaty with its ruler. Physically, just getting there was a feat of superhuman endurance: through extreme heat, torrential rain, coping with occasional ambushes and frequent attacks of fever, which he battled with antipyrin and thirteen-mile marches in the blazing sun. But he succeeded in his task. His next contract was with the new British West Charterland Company: a 700-mile trek across the Kalahari desert in the southern African region of Bechuanaland – now Botswana – to explore a mineral concession. None of this was what he wanted: to work for the Colonial Office, running a colony or a protectorate such as Uganda in East Africa.

Early in 1897, Flora ran a series of long articles on west Africa, putting the name 'Nigeria' for the first time to the territory of the Niger delta. In July Chamberlain wrote to Lugard commanding him to proceed without delay to raise a West African Frontier force of 2–3,000 men, and occupy the hinterland of the Gold Coast and the Niger, 'which otherwise may be occupied by the French'. If Lugard could take care of the French, Chamberlain told him, the country would buy out Sir George Goldie's Royal Niger Company. Lugard did 'take care of the French', and on 1 January 1900 he was at last rewarded with the kind of position he had dreamed of as Her Majesty's High Commissioner, to take over from where Sir George Goldie's Royal Niger Company had left off, to run the show in the region called Northern Nigeria.

Some fifteen months later, in the spring of 1901, Lugard arrived home on six months' leave. At Abinger he and Flora walked up and down between the azaleas, where they 'tired the sun with talking . . . of her work and my work'. By the time he left to go back to Nigeria that October, she had promised to marry him.

Flora was not sure she loved him. 'We cannot force it. Let us not try on either side: but let us be content to marry as friends.' But with the wedding and the intimacy of the honeymoon in the hills above Funchal, clinging to him for support on a steep path, she was won over by his kindness and sensitivity. She wrote to her niece, Hilda – Mimi's daughter – 'I can hardly tell you how easily and naturally I have taken to this *vie à deux*. I am astonished myself to feel how little I am disturbed by it . . . he is never in my way.' Now, instead 'of not seeming to know me by sight as of old, Fred notices everything I put on', and she thought he was pleased that she had now taken to wearing 'pretty white things'. Fred, too, had experienced a modest improvement: 'he too is feeling just a little naturally happy'.

On 20 June 1902 they embarked for the Niger with Flora's forty-six trunks and cases, and her maid. Neither Flora nor Fred enjoyed good health: years of stress and overwork laid her open to exhaustion; he was subject to constant attacks of fever. Already on the voyage he was suffering from a bout of malaria and its consequent depression. Yet, wrote Flora, as they steamed south along the coast of Africa, 'for the first time in my life I am in no particular hurry for the voyage to end'.

The aura persisted as they sailed on, up the Niger, past the overhanging jungle of the delta, the river now so wide the distant shores seemed like a lake. They had to take out their binoculars to look at the hippopotami and crocodiles on the banks. 'Time passes on board rather like a dream. We get . . . often an illusion that we are ourselves standing still and that the scenes on the bank are defiling before us . . . Fred is of course at work again and plods in these hours through the piles of papers which form the machinery of office work. Some of them are interesting and then he hands them over to me to read too . . .'

They finally reached Lokoja, the sky white with heat, to wait for the river to rise, and took up temporary residence in an empty Government House. From the verandah Flora had a wide view of a circle of hills and the confluence of two great muddy rivers, the Niger and the Benue.

28 July 1902: 'The days as they pass at present are absolutely without incident. I wake between four and five. Early tea is brought at six. I send round to Fred's room to let him know that it has come. He comes in very

sleepy to have a cup and then goes away to his office where piles of papers await him . . . At six [in the evening] Fred stops work. The sun then is just on the edge of setting and we go for a tearing walk in the dark which gives us exercise and brings us in streaming with perspiration to an extent which makes all my clothes seem exactly as if they had been dropped in the wash-tub . . . After dinner there is an hour on the verandah and between ten and eleven we usually separate for the night.'

The 'black labourers' were 'absurd, just like a crowd of children'. But she thought she could get on with them. In the house, they were learning her ways 'wonderfully fast' and Fred was finding the little dinners they were giving, with their white linen, fresh flowers and a new lampshade, 'better than anything he had ever had in Nigeria'. Some of the staff 'are hardly perhaps what we should call gentlemen', but they were intelligent, well-mannered and keen on their work. On King Edward VII's Coronation Day the Lugards hosted a dinner for twenty, the table decorated with artificial roses from Flora's 'band-boxes', as none grew there. They 'drank the King's health, the band played "God save the King", and a black crowd of servants and others clustered round the open windows crying "Good King! Good King!"'

A month later they reached their final destination, Lugard's headquarters at Zungeru, on the banks of the Kaduna, a tributary of the Niger. Government House was 'a big airy bungalow raised on piles with a twelve-foot verandah all round' with views towards distant hills. Zungeru itself, which a little more than a year before had been undiscovered jungle, was a little town of white houses 'like a pretty English suburb', Flora wrote, 'rushing up like a crop of mushrooms. Every day new houses begin to appear and new roads are cut.' The electric light plant was getting into order. In the distance, hills rose against the sky. There were thirty civil and military officers, and a few dozen non-commissioned officers. 'Everyone now is asking me about bringing their wives out,' Flora told Moberly Bell at *The Times*. But things were not perfect: Zungeru, even today, is known as the hottest, most humid place in Nigeria. Puff adders and hyenas prowled in the garden, Fred never worked less than a twelve-hour day, and the doctor had persuaded him that she should on no account be permitted to go out in the sun.

'I spend the greater part of my time in solitary confinement,' she told Moberly Bell, writing long letters, and getting down to reading the books which for years she had not had time for. Since she was eighteen, Flora had been in charge of her life. For years she had been at the centre of affairs. She had revelled in her reputation as a woman who could go anywhere, and 'write three columns of good copy for a newspaper on the back of portmanteau in a desert'. Now she was finding life as the high commissioner's wife very hard. When she came down with malaria in October, the doctor ordered her home without delay.

'From us to you. I do not consent that any one from you should ever dwell with us. I will never agree with you. I will have nothing ever to do with you. Between us and you are no dealings except as between Mussulmans and Unbelievers, War, as God Almighty has enjoined us. There is no power or strength save in God on high.' Thus the Sultan of Sokoto, 'King of Kings', in Northern Nigeria wrote to High Commissioner Lugard in the spring of 1902, not long before he sailed to marry Flora in Madeira. Lugard took the message as a denunciation of three treaties the Sultan had made with the Royal Niger Company in 1885, 1890 and 1894.

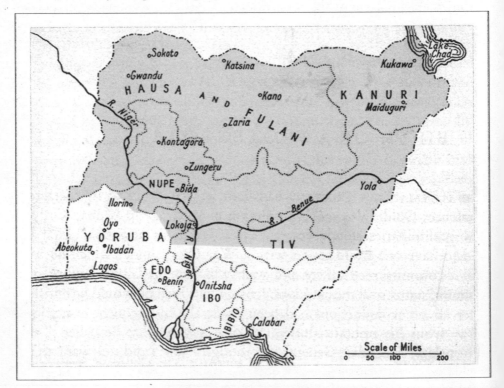

The Niger region as Lugard took it over, 1901

It is almost impossible today to imagine the fragility, the sheer effrontery, of the British government's position in Northern Nigeria at the time they took over responsibility from the Niger Company. The British flag had been run up above a makeshift parade ground on the banks of the Niger River on 31 December 1899. The next day, Lugard penned a note on a map: 'Northern Nigeria as we took it over 1.1.1900.' The map was vague, to say the least: an arbitrary bulk of land north of the confluence of the Niger and Benue Rivers, covering almost 300,000 square miles – one third the size of India, three times the size of the United Kingdom – lying south of the country that is Niger today; Lake Chad to the north-east, Benin to the west. Most of this was quite unexplored: in only a few places beyond the Niger and Benue had the Niger Company's agents penetrated more than fifty miles from the banks. One hostile emir suggested white men were a species of fish that would die if they went too far from the water.

The general population was entirely ignorant of the existence of Britain. There was a British population of just fifty, a handful of Royal Niger Company trading stations on the Niger – some of them merely hulks anchored in the water – and communication was only by runner or canoe. To the north, beyond the river's reach, lay the southern Sahara provinces of the Hausa and Fulani, still ruled by the great Sultan of Sokoto and the Emir of Kano, a city famed for its market in slaves, its great wall and an army of mailed horsemen. Both men were bitterly hostile to the British.

It was clear that Lugard would never have enough staff, revenue or military to hold the country. Only by retaining 'the native authority' could Britain hope to rule. He had begun by designing an administration modelled on his experience in India, seating young British residents on the right hand of emirs. The Nigerian chiefs were to have 'clearly defined duties and an acknowledged *status* equally with the British officials'; Lugard's power as High Commissioner was discharged through them. As far as possible, indigenous institutions were to be used to govern.

He himself was constitutionally unable to stop work, rarely putting in less than sixteen hours a day, and eleven while on leave: writing letters, reports, instructions, and dispatches; drafting laws, estimates, reviewing judicial decisions and interviewing all manner of men. At one point his dispatches to the Secretary of State alone averaged twenty-five a week – in addition to correspondence with other west African governors, and internal correspondence with seventeen residents and various departments.

As residents he selected men who were beginning to emerge from

Oxford and Cambridge to train for the colonial service: men who were sympathetic to the Africans and who knew how to play the game – educated at public school, tough, gallant and decisive, who could assert the kind of superiority that commanded respect. They needed to. He could only afford to put one or two in each of the immense provinces he was creating.

'It is difficult for you home-folk to realize what communication is in this country,' one young officer told his mother: 'Kontagora, 9 days off, Bauchi, 10 days and Keffi 10 or 11 days, all by runner.' Three murders had followed the Sultan of Sokoto's communiqué: the first a British administrative officer, next a Nigerian missionary and finally, the British Resident of the small Fulani emirate of Keffi. Tension was rising. 'It just shows what a policy of bluff it is out here,' the officer went on. 'The Fulani could have done the same in every station wherever they liked.'

The murderer of the British Resident fled to Kano, where the Emir gave him succour. 'If a little town like Keffi could do so much, what could not Kano do?' the Emir declared.

So long as the Emir of Kano and the Sultan of Sokoto were recalcitrant, Lugard believed the Fulani would be troubled by a 'double allegiance' to the British Crown. Spies and agents would travel from palace to palace, fomenting resistance. Meanwhile, even further north, an Anglo-French boundary commission was in the field, surveying a borderline thousands of miles long that would run between Northern Nigeria and the southern reaches of French West Africa – today's Niger. As Flora sailed for home in November, there were rumours that the Emir of Kano was preparing for war. Lugard strengthened the small British garrison at Zaria, 100 miles south-west of the city.

What happened next was pure Lugard. The first the Colonial Office knew of impending action was a Reuters report in *The Times* on 5 December. Hasty telegrams demanded explanations from Lugard. He replied with a series of passive/aggressive replies, full of self-righteous justification. A fine officer had been murdered. Deferring action would show signs of fear. 'Safety of garrison of Zaria, prestige of British Government, possibility of delimitation of frontier, depend on energetic action,' Lugard wired London.

'The advocates of conciliation at any price who protest against Military Operations in Northern Nigeria appear to forget that their nation has assumed before God and the civilized world the responsibility of maintaining peace and good order [in a] British Protectorate and that the towns of

Kano and Sokoto are ruled by an alien race who buy and sell the people of the country in large public slave markets daily,' he went on. Public mutilations took place in the marketplace, the heads of the executed were mounted on stakes, there was bribery in the courts: 'the whole scheme of rule' was marked by oppression and extortion. The Secretary of State, however, remained cool. His Majesty's government regretted the necessity for taking action against Kano; Lugard should have kept them better informed. The communiqué arrived too late. The day after this rebuke was penned in London on 29 January 1903, Lugard dispatched a force of 800 officers and men with four guns and four Maxims to Kano. Three days later he followed himself.

He marched at speed, half on foot, half on horseback: eight miles one day, twenty-five the next, his private secretary fainting in the heat in the saddle. Every day he rose at 4 a.m., stopping only for the 200 bearers following with food and tents to catch up. While they did so, he dictated dispatches and wrote nightly to Flora.

Ahead of him, the troops had passed the Kano frontier. After a single shell killed the chief of the first town, the gates of all the others opened one after the other. Their Fulani headmen fled to Kano. Far across a great plain the troops could see the high red walls of a vast city. Kano was eleven miles around. There were thirteen gates in its fifty-foot-high walls. As the troops charged through the first gate they found themselves in a great open space, more than a mile from the city proper. Here the Maxims did their stuff. Twelve hundred of the Kano garrison fell before the troops marched unopposed into the town and took the Emir's palace. 'A brilliantly conducted affair,' Lugard told Flora.

A week later, having covered eighty-two miles in three and a half days, Lugard rode into Kano in the hot sand-charged wind of the *harmattan* and set up office in the Emir's private audience chamber. 'A marvellous place. 18 ft square – walls of mud very thick,' he told Flora. It was beautifully decorated 'in quaint designs and shapes in black, white, pale blue and yellow', with gilded arches beneath a dome, and splendidly carved doors. (He sent them to Flora.) Lugard had never imagined there could be anything like this city in Africa, with its fine mud buildings, splendid fortifications, large, handsome population and its 'quantities' of Arabic writings. Or its cruelty: the slave market in its centre, the Emir's stinking dungeons, so overcrowded there was no room for the prisoners to stand without trampling others to death, the ghastly methods of torture and execution.

A view towards Kano, a city that astonished the few Europeans who managed to reach it with its civility, throbbing industry, and the constant coming and going of caravans carrying salt, slaves and goods from Tripoli

Within three days of its capture, except for the slaving, it was business as usual in Kano's markets. A single British outrage, in which a soldier killed a civilian, was dealt with by Lugard sitting in court-martial before the chiefs. The soldier was condemned to death and executed. Then, beneath the gilded arches and high dome of his chamber, he met the chiefs of Kano, with their new emir-elect wearing a snow-white *pugari*, lined with yellow. The others were in embroidered gowns and high, indigo-coloured turbans, which swathed their heads and necks and hid their mouths. They sat on a Turkish carpet while he, wearing a suit 'much torn and mended', sat in his old deckchair with his officers beside him.

Lugard took particular care that the translation of the treaty should be accurate. He told them the British government would retain their existing rulers, and customary rights of succession and nomination or election, subject to veto by the high commissioner. Mohammedan law would continue, so long as it was not contrary to the law of the Protectorate; trade would be encouraged, but slave raiding and trading were to stop; mutilation, imprisonment under

inhumane conditions would no longer be allowed; sentences of death were only to be carried out with the consent of the British resident. Otherwise they were to be absolutely free in the exercise of their religion. 'I added at the close of my remarks that it was not the desire of Government to upset and to change such native laws and customs as were good, and that it would be our desire to study them so as to understand the people . . .'

Two weeks later he delivered a similar speech in Sokoto. Before the British guns the Sultan's army of 15,000 horsemen had broken up and dispersed. The Sultan fled.

'The old treaties are dead,' he told the new Sultan and his chiefs. 'Now these are the words which I, the High Commissioner, have to say for the future. The Fulani in old times . . . conquered this country. They took the right to rule over it, to levy taxes, to depose kings and to create kings. They in turn have by defeat lost their rule which has come into the hands of the British. All these things which I have said the Fulani by conquest took the right to do now pass to the British.'

'Why are we fighting Kano?' A week before Lugard dispatched his troops, Flora published her (unsigned) article in *The Times*. It was a masterful setting of the scene: the alluring and mysterious walled city 'established before the Tower of London was built', centre of religion, learning and a trade rich in cottons, leathers, gum Arabic and ivories. She told of its uneasy allegiance and 'the duty' of Sir Frederick Lugard, 'first High Commissioner under the British Government', to bring 'some form of British administration' to this country of millions – with a valiant staff of no more than '165 white men', civilian and military. Her arguments were a mirror of his own: the threat of the French to the north ('irregular border actions'), the need to suppress slave trading and establish a 'civilized system of law'. So far British success had depended on the maintenance 'of an almost phenomenal prestige', and it was for this, 'the unbroken record of dignity and authority', that the expedition was necessary.

While she was in Nigeria, Flora had written as Flora Shaw to Joe Chamberlain, her old friend, and in the name of Lady Lugard to him in his capacity as Colonial Secretary. Within days of landing in England she was calling at the Colonial Office to tell Assistant Under-Secretary Reginald Antrobus how hard Lugard and his staff were working. She had seen how fever afflicted him, how depressed it made him; and how hard he pushed himself at work in a climate known to be a killer. The next week she was back, for a long interview with the Permanent Under-Secretary, Sir Montagu Ommanney, carefully guarding herself against 'speaking in any way definitely for you', she told Lugard. She heard that Chamberlain was so concerned about what she had been saying about the dangers of the climate upon his health that the Colonial Office was thinking of asking him to take up the governorship of Western Australia.

'I said, "Frankly, what would a man of his ability do in such a place?" Sir Montagu pointed out in a tentative sort of way that these state governorships are regarded as prizes and are greatly desired by many people. I said, "Yes, doubtless, and they should be left to those who desire them, and feel themselves fitted to 'footle about to the tune of God save the King'." He laughed and said that to tell the truth both he and Mr Chamberlain had anticipated the answer . . .'

Already Flora was trying to find some way to keep Lugard at home in England. A week before Christmas she 'happened to meet' the acting Colonial Secretary Lord Onslow – Chamberlain was in South Africa – at dinner. She turned the conversation 'to what an advantage it would be to the public service . . . to bring the men who have served with distinction on the outskirts of the Empire [home] to work at the centre . . . Our conversation was interrupted but he asked if he might motor over from Clandon – where as he reminded me he is our country neighbour – and lunch some day at the cottage where we will talk further.'

In May, Lugard came home on leave. They had six months together, living between a small flat in Chelsea and Little Parkhurst, Flora's cottage at Abinger, 'all paint and shavings' as they extended it. They egged on the builders, and went for long walks in the woods. Every day Lugard spent hours at his desk, writing reports, corresponding with Nigeria. He visited the Colonial Office and lectured widely, while Flora introduced him to society. In November 1903 he returned to Northern Nigeria, taking his younger brother Ned with him. The tour was to be seventeen months.

'But the separation is far too long,' Flora wrote. 'It must perforce teach both of us to live alone, and that is not what we meant to learn when we married.' She continued converting Little Parkhurst into a home where they could hold small weekend house parties, decorating it with his collection of African weapons, trophies from big-game hunting and the Emir's doors from Kano. Socially, she was in demand. 'A most interesting dinner,' recorded the Prince of Wales, when she dined with him, together with the Curzons, Conan Doyle, Baden Powell, Lord Roberts and the Aga Khan. She promoted her husband indefatigably, discussed his policies over dinner, gave lectures on Nigeria at the Society of Arts and the Royal Colonial Institute, and started work on a major history of Northern Nigeria.

Daily, they wrote to each other, letters pages long, trying to figure how they could be together without giving up his control of Nigeria. Passion, energy and conviction burn off the page. Though for Flora's sake he would attempt most things, he could not take on a governorship like Jamaica, Ceylon, or part of Australia. Meanwhile they teased the issues: the incompetence of the officials in the Colonial Office, the 'ignorant and more or less obstructive clerks', the 'nameless boys' with power who knew nothing of the situation in the field; Antrobus, 'such an enormous ass' for thinking the administration of Northern Nigeria ought to be the same as the Gold Coast; the growing complexity of administering west Africa – for example should not Northern Nigeria, the southern provinces and Lagos be united under a single government?

At last they hit on the germ of a solution. Now that the telegraph had delivered instant communication between Zungeru and London, why should not Lugard become a governor who spent the winter in Northern Nigeria and the summer in London, in charge of a new department of

'Tropical Administration', dedicated to the problems of Africa, with an expert like himself at its helm?

Chamberlain had resigned from the Cabinet in 1903. Now Flora went to work on his successor as Secretary of State, Alfred Lyttelton, on the project that she and Lugard now called, between themselves, 'the scheme'. Lyttelton was handsome and athletic, a man with wit and charm to match her own. But he had none of her experience in colonial affairs. Flora wrote to him, she met him, he came with his wife for a weekend in Abinger. By the time Lugard returned on leave in May 1905, four Cabinet ministers had been converted to 'the scheme'. The clerks in the CO, however, 'never will accept it', Flora told him. 'The remedy will be to promote them with KCMGs to be Governors themselves, whereby these birds will be killed with one stone, for they will be both got rid of and converted.'

In England Lugard went to work on Lyttelton himself. By the time he sailed for Africa in November, 'the scheme' was in the bag. Lyttelton had agreed to an experiment. Lugard was to return from Nigeria in six months' time, to try it.

'We have together achieved the impossible and got the CO to undertake a most radical and disturbing reform,' he told Flora as he sailed from England. Nevertheless, he counselled caution. The government was weakening; there was bound to be an election.

Flora did not rest. Her book on Nigeria, *A Tropical Dependency,* had just come out. She dispatched beautifully bound copies with notes to the King, the Prime Minister, Lyttelton, and a dozen other important statesmen. By the beginning of December, she was expecting a communiqué from Lyttelton announcing 'the scheme' every day. On 3 December, Prime Minister Balfour resigned. She dispatched an article explaining a 'reform' in tropical colonial administration to *The Times*. Two days later it was published, accompanied by a leader endorsing 'a far-reaching scheme of administrative rule'. At the Colonial Office, Reginald Antrobus was furious that such an announcement had been made without his knowledge. The next day, a new prime minister, Henry Campbell-Bannerman, announced the names of his new, Liberal Cabinet. The Secretary of State for the Colonies was to be Lord Elgin.

Elgin? Flora knew nothing about him. A retired Indian Viceroy, the father of many children, undistinguished – 'four foot high, four foot broad, but stuffed four foot full of solid sense', she reported to Lugard – he was very antisocial, very shy and notoriously inaccessible. His deputy was Winston Churchill. 'Bad news,' replied Lugard.

The general election of January 1906 delivered the Liberals an overwhelming majority. Like the great reversals of power in 1945, 1979 and Tony Blair's victory in 1997, it was the sign of a sweeping change in public opinion. The country, exhausted with the Boer War in South Africa, was losing its taste for wars, expansion and great exploits of colonial acquisition. A more sympathetic approach to poverty and new social priorities was emerging. The first Labour MPs, under Ramsay MacDonald, were elected. Flora predicted that the country had given Campbell-Bannerman such a strong mandate that the Liberals were likely to be in power for twenty years.

Meanwhile, Antrobus had marshalled his forces. Early in February, Flora's informants were telling her that the officials in the Colonial Office were practically unanimous against 'the scheme'; Churchill had joined them, famously minuting, 'I can see no reason why the Colonial Office should become a Pantheon for Pro-Consuls.' She was trying every avenue to meet Elgin herself. On Tuesday 6 February she set out for the Colonial Office without an appointment, sent in her card and asked to see Churchill. 'Of course to you it must seem ridiculous that a boy of his age [he was thirty-one] – and ignorance –should have the power and influence that he has,' she prefaced her account to Lugard.

Flora had met a worthy opponent. They argued for an hour. She: 'the scheme' had been decided and agreed. Under it Sir Frederick would be home the following summer. Churchill: that he was expecting Lugard, but only on leave as usual. 'The idea of a Governor-General responsible for groups of colonies pleases me,' he said. But that responsibility for west Africa should be carried on from London did not. He insisted: 'the man on the spot must be responsible'. Flora argued that breaks in continuity, caused by the ill health of British governors, had hampered west African development for 300 years. Now, with the telegraph, what was the difference of dealing with affairs in places at two months' distance from headquarters, from London or Zungeru?

'I see,' said Churchill. 'So, it becomes really a question of the definition of "the spot".'

He paid Lugard every tribute. He was most anxious for his advice. It did not matter that 'the scheme' had left all the officials in the Colonial Office 'spluttering and protesting'.

'But, there are men of knowledge and men of power. In this office there are men of knowledge, of extraordinary ability and industry, but – they have no power. There is only one individual in this Office who has power and that is the Secretary of State.' He went on:

'On the borders of the Empire there are men like your husband who have made the Empire by their energy, their courage and inventive genius. These are men of power. Now what you want to do is to bring a man of power and put him in here amongst these men of knowledge. He has knowledge of his own subject as well as power. A man like that is an expert. He knows more than any of us. He can with his knowledge override the Secretary of State himself. Don't you see that you want to endow him with a double position? He is to have power as well as knowledge? Surely this is an anomaly?'

'*Everything* is urgent, and one is kept at high pressure from morning till night . . . I love this turgid life of command, when I can feel that the sole responsibility rests on me for everything,' Lugard told Flora. As she was arguing his case in London, in Nigeria he was entertaining Lord Scarborough, the new head of the Royal Niger Company in Zungeru. He was taking him over the work of his government, flicking through a sample of his latest telegrams before dinner, when he found himself reading the following: 'Whole of C Company, Mounted Infantry, defeated and annihilated at Satiru . . . Hillary and Scott, Residents; Blackwood, West African Frontier Force; are, I fear, killed. Dr Ellis severely wounded, Sergeant Slack and myself and doctor only men remaining: most urgent. Signed Gosling, Sergeant.'

Satiru was a well-known centre of Islamic fanaticism twelve miles south of Sokoto. A man had declared himself to be the prophet Jesus. From there, religious ecstasy escalated into killing every white man that could be found. Lugard's nearest troops – twenty-five African infantry and five Europeans – were at the end of a telegraph line eighty miles from the disaster. He ordered them to get out, and then waited to learn whether the Emirs of Sokoto and Kano, so recently brought into line, would rise. Religious fervour swept the country. The newly proclaimed prophet Jesus was preparing to march on Sokoto. Meanwhile, Lugard's main body of troops were 500 miles to the south-west, at the opposite end of the country, dealing with the razing of a Niger Company depot on the Benue River. It took three weeks for him to muster 600 men – thirty of them European officers – and several Maxims.

Then the Sultan of Sokoto cabled his loyalty. Together his forces marched with the British on Satiru. Two thousand rebels armed with hoes and axes met them before the town. 'They came on, and the horsemen gave way and went back; no one took any notice,' recorded one Sokoto chief. 'Someone gave an order, everyone fired, then a whistle blew; everyone stopped and there was no one left alive in front.' The troops piled into the town, killing civilians as they went. In due course the bodies of the British were recovered and buried with full military honours. 'Jesus' was captured, tried in the local court with those who first proclaimed him, and executed in the marketplace. Their heads were set up on spears.

The Sultan did not stop there. Calling out the whole population of Sokoto, he ordered Satiru razed to the ground. He pronounced a curse on anyone who rebuilt its walls. That more than 2,000 people had been killed was an underestimate, Lugard's officers reported. The people had been exterminated.

News of the slaughter reached an appalled Colonial Office on 13 March – just as a scandal was breaking over the sanctioning of the flogging of Chinese 'slaves' by the High Commissioner of South Africa, and Churchill was furiously protesting to the Natal government, which had executed twelve leaders of a black rebellion.

'How does this extermination of an almost unarmed rabble . . . compare with the execution of twelve Kaffirs in Natal after trial . . . I confess I do not at all understand what our position is, or with what face we can put pressure on the Government of Natal while these sorts of things are done under our direct authority.' Lugard seemed to be behaving like some kind of African tsar, Churchill said. Four days before the slaughter, Elgin had cabled Lugard informing him that 'the scheme' was rejected. Now he was summoned home for talks.

'The fateful cablegram arrived today,' Lugard told Flora. For weeks he had been thinking about retiring. His post was no sinecure, 'and were I not a very rapid worker as well as one who does long hours I should find little time to write "Special Memos" and "Standing Orders" on important subjects, or deal with new and difficult Legislation'. He had done his best for six and a half years, and 'the time has perhaps come for a move to something else'. 'From the health point of view', it was high time he was in England.

Friday, 25 May 1906: 'This must go before the afternoon post comes in,' Flora wrote. 'It will greet you at Grand Canary, dear, with welcome, but that will be two weeks hence. What I am thinking of now is that tomorrow you leave the coast and begin your journey home. You are on the Niger now, working hard I expect to finish off papers which you wish to leave in order. I hope there will be no sticking on a sand-bank this year, and perhaps on Sunday I may have a cable saying "sailed". I see nothing beyond three months now, but I hope that before they are over we may see life laying itself out a little more clearly before us, and that in the new chapter there may be less of this sorrowful separation.

'Perhaps – who knows? – this may be the last of the series of long letters which we have written to each other . . .'

A year later Lugard was installed as the Governor of Hong Kong. Flora was by his side. The routine and ceremony, to say nothing of the entertaining, in which Flora delighted – galled him. The tiny size of the place cramped him. A year after they settled into Government House, Flora was taken seriously ill and returned to England. Lugard took refuge in matters of education, and helped found the university. In 1911 the Colonial Office began to sound him out on whether he would consider returning to Nigeria again – to plan and implement the unification of northern and southern Nigeria with the colony of Lagos – a vision he and Flora had imagined in their 'scheme' five years before.

'We are agreed that you are the right man,' Antrobus – now Sir Reginald – told him, while the Secretary of State, now Lewis Harcourt, wrote to persuade Flora personally. How could Lugard resist? Here, as he told Ned, was 'the biggest job in the whole empire'. As for Flora, she saw that he would be able to set his seal on the work he had begun in Nigeria. 'Our personal happiness must not stand in the way,' she told him. As for the terms: the post was to be for four years only, the first of which would be administered six months in Nigeria, and six months in London. Under Governor-General Lugard, on New Year's Day, 1914, a united Nigeria was inaugurated.

Lugard retired to live with Flora at Little Parkhurst at the end of the First World War. From then until his death at the age of eighty-seven, in April 1945, he never stopped working: writing, lecturing, speaking, recording details of his amalgamation of Nigeria, polishing the instructions to his staff that formed the basis of administration of Nigeria, and sending hundreds of articles and letters to the press. In 1922 he became Britain's member on the Permanent Mandates Commission of the League of Nations. The same year he published *The Dual Mandate in British Tropical Africa,* essentially a distillation of all that he had learnt throughout his career in Africa, a handbook on how to govern Africa, according to ethical principles of what he called 'indirect rule' – preserving indigenous institutions and customs and acting through local rulers. In it he attacked those – principally members of the Labour Party – who doubted the value of Empire. To Lugard, it was 'the greatest engine of democracy the world has ever known', laden with opportunity – but also responsibilities. Lugard was under no illusion 'that European brains, capital and energy [would ever] be expended in developing the resources of Africa from pure philanthropy'. But he believed the benefits to Africa should be mutual. Under the British, famine and disease had been checked; the slave trade, wars and human sacrifice had ended. Railways, roads, the reclamation of swamps and deserts, and a system of fair trade: all could bring prosperity to ordinary Africans. Britain's ultimate goal was to prepare those who had been colonized for self-rule. *The Dual Mandate* won him international recognition and laid the ground for British colonial policy until the end of Empire in the 1960s.

Flora died in January 1929, aged seventy-six, and almost blind. 'My precious darling,' she wrote to him, 'in case I should ever leave you alone I want this to be a word of farewell and love and gratitude for all these last happy years that we have enjoyed together – I want you never to remember anything but the love and the joy and the peace of it . . . think only of how happy you have made me and of the joy we have realized together – such deep sweet true joy that I never can thank you enough for it –' Until the end of his life Lugard kept her room exactly as she left it.

14 Where the land was bewitched

Uganda 1906–10

TENS OF THOUSANDS
KILLED BY A TINY FLY

MODERN SCIENCE DISCLOSES
CAUSE OF THE SLEEPING SICKNESS.

Scourge Which Has Swept Along
the Congo River for 1,200 Miles and
Puzzled Missionaries and Natives
Is Likely to Be Ended by Investigation of Experts.

It is no exaggeration to say that the civilized nations find
themselves today in the presence of a terrible evil that is
beginning to oppose a powerful barrier to their colonial
enterprises in tropical Africa. A malady which up to the
present time has been sure death to every person attacked
by it has been making fearfully rapid progress . . . Not until
the past few months has the world begun to realise the
appalling nature of the plague that is killing tens of thousands in Equatorial Africa.

New York Times, 20 March 1904

One chill January morning in England in 1899 a dapper fellow turned half
left to face a camera. Dressed in a tweed suit in bold windowpane check and
matching bowler hat, cane in hand, thirty-year-old Henry Hesketh Bell
was immaculate: blond, handsome, moustachioed, bespectacled. He had
just been appointed administrator of the tiny island of Dominica in the
West Indies, the apogee of his ambition so far. 'I'd like to rule a tropic isle,
not very big – say one square mile', he might have been humming to himself. There was a look of bravado in his eye, a hint of smugness in the curl
of his lip.

To his left a more sober group fanned out in the embrace of the stone
door of Highbury, Joseph Chamberlain's beloved country house on the
southern outskirts of Birmingham: Mr and Mrs Chamberlain, the Duke

and Duchess of Devonshire, the latter rouged and rich in furs and diamonds, Lord and Lady Bradford, well-fed and self-satisfied, and a couple of desiccated under-secretaries of state from the Treasury and the Foreign Office.

The photograph commemorated a weekend house party at the home of the Secretary of State for the Colonies. Bell meticulously recorded every detail in fourteen pages of his diary: the lunches, the teas, the dinners and 'smokes and whiskey' in the library; the silly games, the monosyllabic Duke with his 'alcoholic laugh', the Duchess's 'elaborately curled auburn wig' and magnificent collar and chain of diamonds; Chamberlain's geniality, but also the flash in his eye, his lack of scruple and refinement. 'There is still an undefinable something which places him outside the ranks of those whose ancestors were in the upper classes,' recorded Bell.

It was Chamberlain's younger son, Neville, who was responsible for Bell's invitation. Four years before, twenty-five-year-old Neville had been dispatched to manage the large sisal plantation in the Bahamas in which his father had invested over £50,000 – over £4 million today. Bell had been the energetic treasurer of the islands. Not only were both men interested in making money, they were both enthusiastic entomologists. In the Bahamas, the air was ripe with speculation; Bell himself was playing the stock market, buying land, growing pineapples, selling them on. The islands, however, were not ideal for large-scale sisal cultivation; in 1896 the price collapsed. Chamberlain's investment plunged. The loss nearly broke him. But Neville's and Bell's friendship survived.

Bell was a man who all his life would keep his antecedents quiet. His father was hopeless at money; his mother 'generally ailing or unhappy about something or other'. Bell had been born in France, among the hills and half-timbered cottages of Chambéry in Savoie. His childhood had been spent discreetly on the Continent, moving from one small private school to another in the Channel Islands, Brussels and Paris. 'Les affaires mauvais comme toujours,' he would write after visiting his parents in Paris a year later, in 1900. For Bell the higher reaches of English society represented some kind of nirvana. Harry, as he was known at home, was ill at ease and lonely in the crowd at his London club. The invitation to Highbury – home of the great Chamberlain, the man who could make or break his career – to say nothing of 'the idea of mixing in such very great society', made him acutely nervous.

'I don't think I made any faux pas.' Bell reckoned afterwards he had made a good impression, but felt himself strangely let down. 'There was nothing to show that [these great men] knew much more than the generality of newspaper reading people' on the political topics of the day. He tipped the valet ten shillings, the butler ditto, and after calling on Mrs Chamberlain in London the following Sunday, sailed for his new post in Dominica.

Seventeen years earlier Harry Bell had been a fastidious youth of wide curiosity with a taste for design and invention. Fluent in French, educated in music and drawing, he had a fine singing voice and a talent for turning an elegant phrase. He was lodging with family friends in Stuttgart and learning German when another family friend – no less than Sir William Robinson, the Governor of Barbados – wrote to offer him the post of third clerk in his office at a salary of £100 a year.

Bell had not lasted long in Robinson's office. After ten months he was transferred – his eyes were weak and the work would be outdoors – to the revenue department of the island of Grenada, an English colony 'about the size of the Isle of Wight'. He had begun the habit of keeping a commonplace book and a diary. Bell was fascinated by the superstition of the former African slaves whom he met on the island. In his spare time he began work on a series of sketches about black superstition, part memoir, part paean to the loveliness of Grenada.

Reading *Obeah, Witchcraft in the West Indies* today is not a comfortable experience. Bell wanted to dispel the Victorian stereotype of the West Indies as full of 'yellow fever, rum, slaves and buccaneers', and capture 'negro life and character'. *Obeah,* the first of seven books he was to publish, was accorded considerable acclaim in London at the end of 1889. Going to England on home leave, he found his name was becoming known. Today we can thank him for articulating the kind of cosy stereotypes that colour racial prejudice to this day. He was still just twenty-five.

Bell was promoted to the Gold Coast as supervisor of customs. Little had changed there since the days when Lord Carnarvon had begged George Strahan to build a hill station to safeguard the health of his officers fifteen years before. 'The Gold Coast,' Bell quipped, 'is a country where "How do you do?" is not a mere formality.' Within two months, he was down with his first case of malaria. His job required him to travel up and down the coast, inspecting customs points, and trying to catch rogues who were defrauding the revenue. As horses could not survive on the Gold Coast, he rode about in the only form of transport available: a hammock carried by eight bearers, fourteen hours a day, thirty-five miles, with the 'thundering surf on one side and low dismal bush on the other'.

He travelled light with his servant Sam, 'the Kruboy' Tom Walker, and his interpreter, Abiobissa, in his spare time designing inventions (games, patent collar studs, tropical chest-protectors, water-closet guards), studying snakes and spiders, and advising European botanists on the planting of cocoa. Meanwhile he was at work on a novel. *A Witch's Legacy* was a romantic adventure of a young West Indian planter saved from bankruptcy by his pal, his noble black overseer, who recovers a secret legacy in diamonds from thieves.

Bell spent four years on the Gold Coast, marked by the deaths of a close friend and more than a dozen colleagues from fever, by the terror of shipwreck in the Irish Sea – 'I landed the next day in pyjamas, an overcoat and one shoe' – and by the horrific experience of presiding over an execution when he was acting magistrate of Accra. Bell had to signal the hangman to draw the bolt that would drop four fetish priests condemned for the ritual murder of four traders into the void. He enjoyed two periods of six months' leave in London and on the Riviera – where he experimented with systems to beat the gaming tables – with his mother and sister Nellie. But these breaks could not recover his health. In May 1894, aged twenty-nine, he was so ill with fever he was carried on board ship, not expected to survive the voyage to England.

But he did. Bell was posted as treasurer to the more clement Bahamas, and on, as the administrator, to Dominica.

'I am really very lucky to get an administrative post at this stage of my career and before I am 35,' Bell wrote as he sailed from England after his weekend with the Chamberlains in 1899. He loved Dominica. He attacked the administration with energy. He built the 'Imperial Road' from one side of the island to the other, and founded his own model plantation, 'Sylvania', in the virgin forest of the island to grow cocoa, limes, oranges and vanilla, leading the way for more British planters to follow. He promoted the island's virtues in the British press, and, significantly, put forward the idea of insuring property in the West Indies against hurricanes to the London insurance market.

Government House became the centre of Dominica's social life – white social life, that is. Bell gave brides away, judged children's fancy dress parties, held garden parties, and captured the heart of the future novelist Jean Rhys, whom he singled out at a ball he held. For Bell not only had charm and cut an elegant figure, he was a wonderful dancer. 'I longed for that waltz to last forever, to skim forever round and round with Mr Hesketh's arm about me,' Rhys wrote, 'looking in the glass I knew that that night had changed me.'

It was some five years later, at the end of November 1905, that Bell was telephoned as he came in from a ride through the orange groves at Sylvania to be told that a 'secret and personal' telegram had arrived from the Secretary of State. He had been offered the appointment of commissioner of Uganda at a salary of £2,000 a year – £160,000 today. Here at last was a proper promotion! But governing an obscure African protectorate was far from the job he desired; what he wanted was the governorship of some gentle colony with a decent climate. All he knew of Uganda was that it was somewhere in the centre of Africa, undoubtedly primitive, and, for a man like himself who had twice nearly died of malaria, almost certainly deadly.

From what little he could glean from the books at his disposal, Bell was further disturbed to find that Uganda was also magnificent, nearly the size of France, with huge possibilities for development. Blackwater fever might flourish but 'there are no Councils or anything of that sort to hamper rapid action'. Although a commissioner was not a pukka governor, Bell noted, he was a 'Commander-in-Chief, and consequently must have all the usual powers'.

Bell could not resist the upward thrust, the siren call of power. This was the chance of a lifetime: complete responsibility, the prospect of 'Empire building' on a fine scale. A knighthood was sure to follow. He cabled his acceptance.

Bell liked to take stock of himself at the beginning of each New Year, weighing and measuring himself (five feet eight inches, 145lb; from time to time taking the length of his torso, his calves and his thigh), assessing his financial position, weighing up how he appeared in the eyes of the world. Now, on board the *Orinoco* en route from Dominica to London early in January 1906: 'Otherwise than financially, my progress has been exceptionally good & even beyond my expectations. I am now appointed to an office equal to that of a Governor with a salary of £2000 a year & extras. I ought to get a knighthood in a few months time & my prospects (provided my health holds out) are excellent. More than that: Je crois que je suis maintenant "a mon mieux". Belle position, bonne santé, not "quite middle aged", chante bien, danse bien, agile, et de figure agreeable, je trouve persona grata partout. Si je me sentais d'humeur matrimoniale, je crois que je pourrais choisir presque n'importe [qui].' He felt himself quite at the summit of his life.

The passage was fine, the weather fair. He spent his time playing bridge, chess, 'reading by snatches and playing various infantile deck games'. He read to a little circle after lunch from the draft of his latest novel, *Love in Black*, he paraded the deck with his little terrier Lottie, 'the pet of the ship'. Of the passengers, none except for Sir William Ingram, owner of the *Illustrated London News*, were of much interest: 'told me today that Harmsworth paid £200,000 for his peerage and the King got the money . . . he himself had been approached with a barony in view, but that he thought the price too high'. Bell – who in his enthusiasm to record the gossip in his diary must have added an extra nought on to the number – £20,000 would be about £1.5 million today – did not doubt him.

The 31st of January found him at the Colonial Office. 'Saw Harris to thank him for my promotion. Said it was due to Chamberlain. I told him that I rather funked the climate. He expressed concern & should so unfortunate a necessity arise I think he will help me to another billet.' A few days later he saw the Secretary of State himself, Lord Elgin, 'a pleasant nonentity', and was warned that he could expect a summons to the palace to meet the King any day. Meanwhile, he was pursuing the issue of his knighthood and could not understand why the official he saw at the CO 'at once began to look uncomfortable'.

News of his insurance scheme for hurricanes was all over the press. Bell was in demand. Invitations crowded in. 'I find myself now approaching without the slightest awe the so-called "great ones" of the Earth. Who would have believed it a few years ago?' He was lunching daily at the clubs, calling on the Chamberlains, speaking at the Church Missionary Society, going to a diamond sale at Christie's, invited to Lady Campbell-Bannerman's official reception at 10 Downing Street.

'Very few fine jewels . . . no Garters & very few people who appeared of consequence . . . Rather the crowd one might expect to see at the Prime Minister's under a Republic . . . [the Prime Minister] looked old but hearty & his wife, a common looking old party, received her guests sitting: a bourgeois looking couple.'

As for Uganda: he found that the Colonial Office knew little more than he did. His first concern was the state of Government House at Entebbe: 'looks dreadfully rough & ugly. Hideous galvanised roof & no attempt at decoration', and the list of furniture was 'purely elementary'.

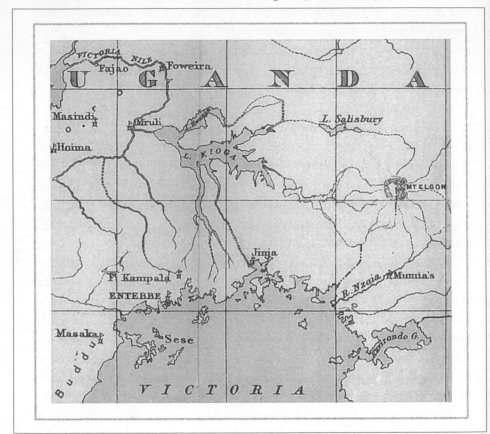

Bell was taking on the job that Frederick Lugard had wanted, after he had persuaded the British government to annex Uganda just over ten years before, in 1895. Since then vast energies had been employed in building a railway from the east African coast at Mombasa to the shores of Lake Victoria. It was the only sensible way to reduce an 800-mile journey that took three months on foot across hugely difficult terrain. The project took eight years.

Meanwhile, the Kabaka Mwanga, with whom Lugard had had such difficult dealings, had staged a revolt against the British two years after the protectorate was declared. Deported to the Seychelles, he had died. In 1903 the gargantuan railway construction was completed. A prefabricated steamer was hauled up the line to carry passengers across Lake Victoria to the British capital, Entebbe. The place lay square on top of the equator. In

1906 the population of Uganda was estimated by the Colonial Office at 3,520,000, of whom 240 were European.

This was virgin territory. Its boundaries were still uncertain. The soil was immensely fertile. Cotton grew wild in parts. If the climate was not exactly suitable for permanent settlement by English families, the place was nonetheless ripe for further exploration and who knew what kinds of enterprise? The only problem with Uganda that Bell could see was that everyone who was not white was dying.

It was in the blaze of heat that followed the rains in July 1901 that thirty-one-year-old Dr Albert Cook, who had founded the Church Missionary Society Hospital at Kampala five years before, first noted eight cases of a mysterious new disease. Patients were coming to him with symptoms of fever, headaches and pains in their joints; some with terrible vomiting. Emaciated, confused, full of lethargy and longing for – but unable to – sleep, the worst went mad before they died. Six months later came news of more than 200 deaths on Buvuma, one of a group of islands near the (northern) Busago shore of Lake Victoria. In the weeks that followed more and more reports of the sick and dying came in. Dr Aubrey Hodges, a forty-year-old medical officer based at the tiny port of Jinja, on the north-west shore of Lake Victoria, was faced with queues of hundreds of people: mothers thin and wasted, infants in arms, children languid and thin, men with faces stark with pain. Meanwhile in Kampala every kind of treatment Albert Cook tried on the disease he now called 'sleeping sickness' failed.

When the rains began again in April 1902, the British called on the Uganda chiefs to segregate the sick – to no effect. The Buyama of Busago refused, while the Baganda, the princely peoples whose Kabaka ruled from Kampala, drove their sick into the bush where they died of starvation or were eaten by wild animals. People were terrified. Evil spirits possessed those who were sick and dying. Even the land was bewitched. When villagers abandoned their homes, leaving their sick to die, they carried the disease with them. Meanwhile, over the western frontier, the scourge was sweeping 1,200 miles of the Congo River. The British authorities feared the plague would spread via the Ugandan railway to the sea coast at Mombasa, and north to the banks of the Nile.

Three medical officers were dispatched from the Royal Society in London on a six-month contract to begin a bacteriological study of the disease at a laboratory at Entebbe. Early in October 1902, a young researcher called

Aldo Castellani spotted a 'fish-like parasite darting about' in the cerebro-spinal fluid of sufferers. But by the end of the year there was still no clue as to what was causing the disease. The death toll rose to more than 30,000.

The laboratory where the causes of sleeping sickness were traced to the tsetse fly

In February 1903 a Colonel David Bruce and his wife Mary arrived from England to bolster the research team. Bruce was forty-eight, a former assistant professor at the Army Medical School, and one of the most remarkable scientists of his day. Tough, instinctive and meticulous, he and Mary had spent two years in an isolated bush camp in Zululand, studying a fatal disease attacking the cattle. Together they uncovered the transmission of microscopic parasites – trypanosomes – from tsetse fly to animals. Two months after they arrived in Kampala, the Bruces became convinced that sleeping sickness was caused by a trypanosome carried by *Glossina palpalis,* a species of tsetse fly that infested the whole region of the lake.

Still the people died. In view of the Bruces' discovery, a plan to segregate the sick on one of the islands in Lake Victoria was abandoned. Not a single patient could be saved at a mission hospital near Entebbe established by the White Fathers, the French Roman Catholic order.

The counting of bodies had become impossible. Cook instructed the chiefs in Busoga in the north to send a twig for the death of everyone known to have succumbed to the disease. In twenty-four hours, over 11,000 twigs arrived. By the end of 1903, the death toll had reached over 90,000. Whole villages had been wiped out, and tracts of land renowned for cultivation had reverted to bush and forest. An eerie silence crept over the land. The people could not bring themselves to believe that bites from the common tsetse – a fly that they had known for generations without causing any harm – could be causing the disease.

By the time Bell prepared to leave London in the spring of 1906, the death toll in Uganda had climbed to 200,000. Sleeping sickness had reached the banks of the Nile and was creeping towards the Sudan, while in the Congo the pestilence ran unchecked. At the headquarters of the Royal Society in Albemarle Street, Bell met its president and Colonel Bruce. The doctors were not getting enough help from the Ugandan administration in the battle against the disease, he was told. What more could he do?

Bell promised to look into it.

Bell landed in Mombasa at the end of March with quantities of provisions from the Army & Navy Stores, a new set of guns, and his new private secretary, Frank Burton, whom he'd found through the personal columns of *The Times*. Burton was in the militia, 'a nice fresh young Irish giant . . . very good tempered and willing'. For the next three years he rarely left Bell's side.

On the journey from London Bell had travelled to Nice to see 'the Pater', on to Monte Carlo to stay with the Ingrams of the *Illustrated London News* for the gaming, and thence to Cannes, where he was smitten with the last girl who would seriously take his fancy.

They were watching tennis. She was twenty-six, blonde 'but not too much so', blue-eyed, 'not remarkably pretty, but quite good looking & with an especially charming expression. A delightful voice & evidently amiable.' She sang prettily, danced divinely, and played tennis 'quite above the average. Very intelligent, well educated, & sympathique.' In fact, he began to feel 'quite spoony', stayed two days longer to see more of her, and 'had serious matrimonial thoughts'.

But for one 'desiderata' she failed to rise to his ideal. Unable to get any hint of her social position, he discovered: 'they live at "Brightside", Stroud, Gloucester. Tout ça est assez bourgeois.' If only he could have been satisfied that her social position would be better than his, he believed he would have taken the plunge. Then it struck him: what if the girl was merely interested in *his* prospects?

Bell embarked for Mombasa from Venice on 28 March. The voyage was smooth, the weather, until they reached the coast of Africa, delightfully cool. He was learning Swahili. It was beneath a sun of shining pewter in the dusty haze of Aden that he received a letter from Uganda informing him that one of the doctors on the sleeping sickness team had been bitten by a fly and 'caught trypanosome'. A white skin was no longer any protection against sleeping sickness. Bell's blood ran cold.

In Mombasa he stayed at Government House – luncheon and dinner parties every day, a guard of the King's African Rifles always standing about. 'Kept on presenting or saluting every time one passed. I could not move out my room without hearing a slap on the butt of a rifle, & I won't have that sort of tomfoolery at Entebbe.'

He thought the servants very black and much more ugly than the West Indians. They could hardly speak a word of English, while the white population mostly looked washed out. He was feeling seedy, troubled by his liver. Mombasa was muggy, possibly feverish. Before he left he hired a Goan steward and a cook, muttering about the wages 'absurdly high – 55 rupees (about £4) for a steward & nearly £6 for a cook'. Besides these he would want two or three 'houseboys' for about £1 [£80 today] each.

But all at once, stepping into the comfort of his Pullman car on the night train to Nairobi, the magic of East Africa began to play. 'I wondered what [the] others who, in days not so long ago, had had to tramp wearily the whole of the 600 miles, from the coast up to Uganda, would think if they saw us today, whizzing through the country, during the night, in a train full of electric light and every convenience of civilisation!' The first morning he woke at six to a glorious day, 5,000 feet above sea level, to be offered a seat on a big bench with cushions fitted over the front of the engine, above the cowcatcher at the front of the train.

Great rolling plains opened out before them. Magnificent antelope gazed at the passing train, a mob of ostriches leapt out of the way, and as they travelled on the game became ever more plentiful. Vast herds of hartebeest, zebra and gazelle. On the horizon, pale violet mountains rose, and 'far up in the sky above a blank of haze' he was shown the peak of Kilimanjaro. With the air 'like ether', it was impossible to imagine that they were virtually on the equator. Except for one or two small parties of Kikuyu working on the track who salaamed deeply to him – 'very black and ugly . . . wearing all sorts of queer rings and metal plates' – he imagined the region devoid of population.

He was almost sorry to reach Nairobi. 'A lot of white men about, mostly in Khaki with puttie leggings', typical settlers, good public school types, 'in the prime of life and looking wonderfully fit'. The views from the officials' houses, strung on a ridge overlooking vast plains, were beautiful, but the town itself, 'composed almost entirely of ugly galvanised houses', was not. His second night on the train as it climbed further into the highlands was bitterly cold.

He awoke the next morning to wondrous views of the Rift Valley and Lake Naivasha – where Lords Delamere and Hindlip and other white settlers were taking up the land. Beyond – 'the view from the brink of the Mau escarpment was a dream of beauty. Four thousand feet below us the vast Kavirondo plain lay spread out like a gigantic carpet of every tone of verdant colour: green upon green, with amethyst and a wealth of tawny shades, stretching away to a far horizon where pearly grey and mauve melted into a sky of tender blue. I could have spent exquisite hours gazing at this amazing panorama.

'But I knew that, in this case especially, did distance lend enchantment to the view. The gently undulating plain . . . was the real Africa of the Equator; the Africa of malaria, of insects, of torrid heat and of disease of many kinds.' As he stood upon that wonderful plateau, in an atmosphere 'full of spring-like life and energy', Bell felt as if his feet were in 'white man's country' and what he was looking down on was the real Africa, the 'typical home of the African negro', the one that he half dreaded, half knew could fulfil his ambition, his dreams of power and prestige.

The approach to the great lake named for Queen Victoria – for Bell, so full of associations with the great explorers of Africa, Speke and Burton, Grant and Stanley – had been so flat that he barely glimpsed it until he reached its shores at Kisumu. There he boarded the steamer *Winifred*. He had been astonished: a 600-ton steamer, 'as smart as if she had only just left the Clyde', lit by electricity, fitted with electric fans in the cabins 'and we had ices for dinner!'

The lake, Bell wrote, was almost as big as Scotland, 'so vast that one gets the impression of travelling on a great sea'. On its coast to the south was German East Africa, today's Tanzania; on the east today's Kenya. The milky waters merged into the haze above. Night fell. In the morning, the sky was

blue. The heat rose. Now the steamer was hugging the Uganda shore, covered with dense masses of tropical vegetation. Bell looked about and
realized they were sailing among islands of desolation. Bush and scrub rose
on abandoned fields of banana and coffee. Once healthy villages were over-
grown with jungle. Masses of tangled liana were festooned from tree to
tree. Mud walls were sinking back into the earth, grass roofs collapsed. The
few people whom he saw bore all the signs he had been warned of: wasted
bodies, faces of pain, a look of intense fatigue.

On they sailed. The shores rose in a succession of gently rolling hills,
dense and green, covered in jungle, the branches of trees overhanging the
water. Late in the afternoon the steamer approached the British settlement
of Entebbe.

'So peaceful and serene was the aspect of the place in the soft afternoon
light, with its rose red roofs peeping out from masses of splendid trees, that
I found it hard to realise that I was in the centre of "darkest Africa" . . . the
surrounding country might have been the coast of Hampshire.' The bush
had been cleared, but magnificent trees remained, casting shade over what
looked like parkland.

There was not much to Entebbe – a small fort, a few military buildings,
a police station, some native huts, a handful of officials' houses and a newly
built sports club with tennis courts and playing fields. The real capital,
home of the Kabaka – a twelve-year-old boy named Daudi Chua – was at
Kampala, twenty-five miles south. British policy was to run the territory,
as far as possible, 'as a purely native state'. Five days after Bell landed, the
three regents of the kingdom of Buganda came to call, bringing nearly all
the chiefs of the twenty *zazas* (the English called them 'counties') with
them.

'They all live near Kampala, and had travelled . . . on bicycles, in rickshaws or on foot.' The avenue up to Government House was lined by Sikh
troops, and the drawing room had been fitted up with a dais, as if for an
Indian durbar, or *baraza* as they were called in Uganda. The chiefs towered
over the diminutive Bell, natty in his new white uniform. The three regents,
gowned in resplendent black and brown silk *kanzus* trimmed with gold
braid, especially impressed him. They were intelligent and distinguished,
particularly the Katikiro, or Prime Minister, Sir Apolo Kagwa – 'KCMG,
if you please and an absurd bungle of the FO to have given him that', Bell
confided to his aunt. All the men had taken leading parts in the wars of
religion that had devastated Buganda in Lugard's day. Now that each of

them possessed large land holdings and were paid generous salaries from the British, Bell judged them loyal and dependable.

'I have now been here a week and am still delighted with almost everything I find here,' Bell wrote to his aunt on 6 May. He could not say the same for Government House, a large wood and iron bungalow surrounded by verandahs. Bell thought it 'as ugly and prosaic a building as one would not wish to see'. Already he had spotted a hillside with wonderful views of the lake for a new residence. Meanwhile, the roads were made of gravel, 'excellent for cycling', he told her. Everything grew. 'Never was there such a place for roses; there are almost too many of them, and such blossoms as you hardly ever see out of a show in England.'

He was getting rapidly into the run of things, impressed with nearly all the men who filled the official posts. 'Most of the seniors have considerable experience of the country ... their subordinates appear to have been carefully selected, and most of those in the Political branch are Oxford or Cambridge men.' His deputy, George Wilson, bluff, verbose but dependable, had come to Uganda when Lugard was there more than ten years before. Dr Aubrey Hodges, in charge of investigating and treating sleeping sickness, had his whole heart in his work. Bell thought he would get on with them.

Their wives were another matter. Few of the senior officials were married, or had their wives with them. 'Those who are have very dowdy or suburban wives. There are not more than three or four of the womenfolk who are in the slightest way interesting or good looking.' He began to regret that he was to operate without a council. 'The responsibilities ... are enormous ... The Commissioner is a complete autocrat and has powers far greater than those of any Colonial Governor.'

Entebbe might look charming, but Bell feared the place was malarious. Within days of arriving, three cases of blackwater fever, which turns urine the colour of stout, had been reported and three of his servants were sick. Privately, he was depressed and out of sorts. He had not felt well from the time he landed in Mombasa. Now he was running a low-grade fever, had no appetite, and complained of a great lassitude and what he described as a 'tired feeling in my brain'. He consulted Hodges: 'Said that I wanted mental rest' and prescribed exercise. Early in June, his secretary, Burton, began running a temperature of 103. By the end of that month there had been seven cases and two deaths from blackwater fever, and Burton was ill again. Hodges diagnosed dengue fever.

'One more for our collection,' quipped Bell.

Bell and Hodges were now deep in talks about sleeping sickness. Bell found him wise, modest and loyal. Hodges was supervising six young medical officers. The science of tropical diseases was at the cutting edge, one of the most exciting fields in modern medicine. Not only were the men able, they were keen, and had been working tirelessly since the beginning of the year – travelling constantly to investigate the spread of the disease, the distribution of the fly and, with elementary knowledge of the language, to gain the trust of the people. They were operating in the wild, among elephant, rhino, hippo and crocodile, with the most primitive of equipment, in regions yet to be explored. Meanwhile the different peoples they encountered had at least half a dozen different names for illnesses that might or might not be sleeping sickness. An epidemic of *ruhinyo*, for example, which caused chronic disability and occasional death, was found to be beri-beri, a disease that had never been encountered in Uganda before.

The team had already observed that the tsetse fly flourished near open water overhung by shady scrub. Now they were just beginning to conclude that sleeping sickness was conveyed from place to place by man, and from man to man by the fly. The tsetse could bite through clothes, but preferred bare skin. The flies loved the heat of the sun, were seldom seen early in the morning or late in the afternoon, and disappeared in rain or high wind.

There was still so much they did not know. It was only recently that one of the team had discovered the pupae of *Glossina palpalis*. Another was investigating its flight patterns, and the presence of trypanosomes in dogs. They knew nothing of the life cycle of the fly, at what stage it became infectious, or how long it remained so.

If they could just find out where exactly the fly was distributed, Hodges told Bell, they might be able to make a plan to segregate the sick. Meanwhile, he said, as fast as trees and scrub were cleared from the waterside, the jungle grew back again. Bell ordered the planting of citronella grass on cleared ground.

A few days later Bell met his first victims of sleeping sickness. Travelling in state to Kampala – sixty-six porters, a double rickshaw, he himself in blue uniform and solar topee riding in a mule-drawn tonga, followed by his cook and servants – he stopped en route to see the White Fathers, who were treating almost 100 patients with the disease.

The hospital consisted of a group of large thatched *banda* huts. The sun was blazing; it was very hot. 'Playing in the shade of a banana grove [were] a dozen boys and girls, from three to seven years old, oblivious to the first stages of the disease: enlarged glands at the base of the neck. Forty or fifty more, sitting in the sun in front of their houses, their features drawn, eyes haggard, very sleepy and apathetic, and evidently in constant pain. They shivered in the heat of the blazing sun, wrapping brown rags around them, complaining of the cold, and of a drying-up sensation in their skin – they had great fear of being touched. They had probably been ill for two years and would die within twelve months.'

The fathers told him how the people feared the white doctors, how they refused to believe the tsetse could be the cause of this appalling plague, and how the course of sleeping sickness was so enigmatic – it could take two or three years to gestate.

In the last *banda* he came upon the dying. Lying on beds of withered leaves, they had reached a ghastly stage of emaciation. The air was full of the sound of moaning. Half a dozen, tethered to logs of wood, uttered peals of frenzied laughter.

Meanwhile, back at Government House, Bell set up a routine: fortnightly 'At Homes' in the afternoon, a dinner party for fourteen every Monday evening. The Goan cook he had hired in Mombasa had turned out to be 'really first-rate', but the small boy, Sulimani, 'who appeared to be such a treasure and so wonderfully intelligent', had relieved him of all his best silk underwear, while the butler was caught taking half a dozen bottles of drink from the storeroom, for what he called a 'big night'.

But he was getting them into order. Some had been marched down to the lake and ordered to scrub themselves clean. The Goan servants wore European dress, but the 'boys' wore long white *kanzus*, with red fezzes. His table servants wore scarlet cummerbunds and red, gold-laced Zouave jackets, with the royal monogram on their fezzes.

In the garden, there was a head gardener and no less than twenty-four men. 'They pick out the weeds as if they were doing lace work,' Bell wrote to Auntie. Beside two police orderlies, always sitting on the verandah, ready to carry messages or accompany him, he had a military guard of four Sikhs – out of 200 in the country, the backbone of the British forces – 'very fine fellows who do nothing but strut up and down on sentry-go all day, and whenever I put my nose out of doors, I hear a shout of "Gartinart" – which means "guard turn out", and the other three rush out of their guard-house and present arms as I go by'.

Beyond the house, he was *Bwana Balozi*, 'Great Master'.

By late July the thunder season was over. The weather had turned chilly. Bell was wearing 'exactly the same clothes . . . that I would wear in Spring at Home'. At the end of the month, he embarked on a two-month tour inland, moving north up Lake Victoria beyond Kampala to Jinja, the source of the Nile, where Dr Hodges was based, and then on, in a great circular loop to the west, via Murchison Falls, a 'leisurely steam down Lake Albert', a quick march through to Hoima, 'already an important station', and then a straight push back by bicycle – 'the roads are in excellent condition' – to Entebbe. He was taking with him a doctor, Wiggins, one of Hodges's team, to investigate the occurrence of sleeping sickness on the Nile and other waterways.

Besides talking to the chiefs about what could be done to tackle sleeping sickness, Bell's object was to test a cheap and easy means of transport between British East Africa, Uganda and the Sudan by way of Lake Kioga and the Nile. This was part of an even larger scheme that he wanted to investigate: a link between the Indian Ocean and the Mediterranean, without using the Suez Canal. Imagine being able to travel, Alexandria to Mombasa, by rail, river and lake, in just eighteen days!

Accordingly, 1,000 men had now created thirty-five miles of road where once there had only been a foot-wide track through elephant grass, so that a one-and-a-half-ton steam launch could be transported overland from Jinja to Kakoge. There the Nile 'is believed', Bell wrote – so far only one or two Europeans in a canoe had done the journey – 'to be a clear open river with no obstacles to navigation'.

'Our "safari" or caravan looked most imposing as we started on our way,' Bell wrote to his sister Nell, in Dominica. Two hundred and ten porters carried tents, furniture and stores; crockery, plate, linen, tables, beds, chairs. Ten servants came with him, and forty men of the constabulary as his guard. They had brought enough sweet potatoes and millet to feed 500 men. 'As for "roughing it" there is absolutely none. As carriers are paid only about three pence a day, there is no necessity to go without one's usual comforts . . . Half way we found a breakfast table laid under a charming natural arbour, and there we pitched into an excellent feed of beefsteaks, and fried eggs.'

The journeys were short and easy: for three or four hours from the early morning Bell rode a mule or his bike or was carried in a sedan chair, slung on poles. Wherever they stopped, the local chief had laid out long rows of huge clusters of bananas to feed the men in his caravan. For him, there was breakfast or tea, and a beautifully thatched *kibanda* of logs and reeds, the floor strewn with lemongrass, as shelter for the night. In the heat of the day he could get through a lot of work on his papers. The late afternoon was spent stalking game – the grass was much too high to bag any – or going down to the river to see if they could get 'a hippo or a croc or two'. Then Bell would come back, ready for 'a nice warm tub' and an evening of dinner and cards, sitting round a fire, listening to the sounds of the wild and telling tales of leopard kills.

He was deeply impressed with the country. 'I used to think the soil of Dominica very fertile,' he told Nell, 'but if a West Indian could see the land here, he would like to eat it.' His vision was to extend the Ugandan railway north towards the Nile, clear the rivers of weed and form a network of canals to feed the railway and the steamers that would ply a route into Egypt. As the local population was far too small to develop this great territory, they could set up agricultural settlements using Indian and Chinese labour. He planned to ask the Colonial Office to send him trained agriculturalists to instruct the Baganda, and set up model plantations to show how crops could be grown and prepared for export.

Bell never thought of Uganda as becoming anything other than a 'black man's country'. He intensely disliked the white settlers and the way they were taking over Kenya. In Uganda, the British had 'an unrivalled opportunity to see whether a stable African State can be built up by its own people under straight and disinterested guidance'. He was thinking cotton, rubber, tobacco and tea in the higher altitudes.

But still he was not well. He was feeling wretched, tired and so depressed at times he had to take himself off away from the others. At night he could not sleep. None of his great plans for Uganda could go forward until the dreaded sleeping sickness was stamped out. He turned again to the files.

Bell's safari was travelling through Busogo, the region worst affected by the disease. At Kakoge he transferred to the small steamer that had been hauled overland. Along the riverbanks, the signs of the sickness were everywhere about him. One of the six doctors serving with Hodges's investigation landed to see him from the other side of the Nile. 'A most nervous man & quite unstrung. He has cause enough . . . as he seems convinced he has got the disease – Dr Wiggins tells me that his is a very suspicious condition; his glands are enlarged & he has low fever.' Bell ordered him to Entebbe. On 20 August the tsetse were all over them, many in the boat. Bell himself was bitten by the flies but the party trusted that as they were far from any settlement, the flies were not infected. 'I thereupon donned my veil & gloves,' he wrote.

It was on this journey that Bell began to think in detail about how to tackle the disease. Hodges's team of doctors had almost finished mapping the habitat of the tsetse. The chiefs whom he was meeting were much more ready to accept any proposals he might make for repressing the disease than they would have been two or three years before. The time was ripe for energetic action. The more he thought about sleeping sickness, the more he realized that the only way to stop its spread was to break the links in its transmission.

But how? Several schemes to isolate the sick had been put to London in the past, but had been set aside from lack of practicality or expense. It was impossible to destroy the swarms of flies that infested the Lake Victoria shoreline; impossible to clear so much jungle. If these steps were out of the question, Bell reasoned, 'we must withdraw from the insects the source of their infection'. All the sick had to be put beyond the reach of the tsetse.

But millions of flies were already infected – and countless thousands of people who were apparently well were gestating the disease. If something radical was not done soon, everyone living around the lake would soon be dead. There seemed to Bell no solution but to remove *everyone* from the reach of the fly: 100,000 people from over 200 miles of shoreline.

Bell's theory was that two miles inland from the lake shore, tsetse flies were rare and people would be safe. Moving the sick, shunned by their villages, was unlikely to be controversial. The compulsory evacuation of the healthy, however, away from the homes they knew and loved, the lands they tilled, and where their ancestors were buried, would be tough. But virtually all the land belonged to the chiefs; the people were their tenants. Provided the people could be offered equally valuable land inland from the lake shore, Bell thought he might be able to pull off the scheme. 'I am going to assume that, in the days to come, the tsetse flies, being unable to find fresh sources of infection, may gradually become as harmless as they were before the disease was introduced . . . and that the *tabu* districts may then again be fit for population.'

Dr Hodges backed him up. The medics were no closer to finding a cure.

So too did Dr Koch, a doctor sponsored by the German government to experiment with an arsenic-based drug, atoxyl (developed by the Liverpool School of Tropical Medicine but rejected by the Royal Society's committee overseeing the sleeping sickness experiments) on his patients. Hundreds were flocking to him every day for treatment – he and his assistants were at the limits of their endurance. Koch's opinion was that everyone still alive on the islands on the lake was infected, and would die within a year or two. It was high time for administrative action to deal with the problem.

Bell quailed as he drafted his plan for London. The plans were so drastic, the costs of moving the people and creating four great hospital camps to accommodate 20,000 sick 'very considerable'. He would need a special grant by parliament.

Bell counted on support at the Colonial Office. But he knew London would be wary of his strategy. Shortly after he left England, the Under-Secretary of State for the Colonies, Winston Churchill, declared in the Commons that isolating infected districts was not an option. Only the discovery of some treatment, 'capable of being applied to man', would be practicable.

Bell's deputy, George Wilson, was instructed to begin negotiating Bell's plans with the chiefs. By November, Bell and Aubrey Hodges were ready. He ordered the clearance to begin on one area near the lake, and work to begin on building three of the largest segregation camps. He wanted them in full operation before the end of the year. On 23 November, a dispatch 'as good as anything I have ever done' was sent to London.

'I submit, that, failing the discovery of a therapeutic cure,' Bell told the Secretary of State, Lord Elgin, 'it is only by the complete removal of all sick persons from the fly-infested districts that we can arrest the spread and progress of the disease, and I recommend to your Lordship the transfer to fly-free areas of the whole remaining population of the districts in the immediate vicinity of the Lake shore.'

Bell's dispatch arrived in London just after Christmas. His plan was immediately recognized as being of vital importance 'to all of tropical Africa'. Sleeping sickness was not only decimating Uganda and the Congo Free State, but was spreading towards the Sudan and south to today's Kenya and Zimbabwe. Its implications were in fact so massive that officials at the Colonial Office seemed temporarily paralysed. They were going to need international co-operation to co-ordinate research and administrative measures. They were going to need a second opinion on Bell's plan. But the Committee for Tropical Diseases at the Royal Society, which had been overseeing the scientific investigation, was virtually in collapse due to the insults hurled by Colonel Bruce at the Colonial Office's distinguished medical adviser, Sir Patrick Manson. No one in Britain had the practical knowledge to know if Bell's plan would work; none of the experts agreed with each other. 'It seems hopeless for us laymen to try to decide on all these conflicting views,' minuted one Colonial Office official on Bell's dispatch. They wanted another 'competent advisory committee' to advise them. And so they nattered on until the end of January, planning the meeting of a new committee early in April. No one wrote to Bell.

At the white settlements of Entebbe and Jinja, Bell instituted a kind of apartheid. Only essential black labour was to be permitted within the settlements. All workers had to be registered, and were to live in a supervised labour camp outside the settlement boundaries. Badges had to be worn at all times.

The chiefs along the lake shore in Buganda and Busoga were given three months to move their people inland. Bell promised that resettlement would take place as soon as the scientists could confirm the life cycle of the sleeping sickness trypanosome in the fly. Slowly, reluctantly, people gathered their food, packed what they could carry on foot and moved to one of the 'healthy' regions that had been allocated, or went to relatives away from the lake shore. To allow access to the shoreline, land was stripped of vegetation 200 yards back from the water, and half a mile in either direction along the shore. Early in March police parties began firing the abandoned villages, to deter illegal return. Only one small disturbance took place; three people were wounded.

'Everyone was leaving. No one would stay behind alone,' remembered one man more than eighty years later. Some villagers crept back to hunt or fish, but the laws were strict. Trespassers were sentenced to imprisonment with hard labour.

Nine months after arriving in Uganda, in February 1907, Bell had another terrible attack of fever. On Dr Hodges's advice he was living almost entirely on milk and soup. Meanwhile he fretted that there was still no word from London on his sleeping sickness plans. Scores were dying daily. He could not go on indefinitely waiting for formal sanction from London. 'The Chiefs are playing up splendidly, and I have promised that, in exchange for their depopulated estates on the lake shore they will receive equally valuable ones inland.' The risk was considerable: 'but I have some good friends at the CO . . .'

At the end of April, Lord Elgin's response to Bell's dispatch finally arrived in Entebbe. 'Some of your proposals are of a far reaching nature,' he commented mildly. He wanted to discuss them with his expert advisers before he would ask the Treasury for funding. By then Bell was already on his way to London – on leave to consult doctors in Harley Street. He was also coming to the Colonial Office. On 7 June he faced the committee of medical experts considering his sleeping sickness proposals.

'It soon became evident . . . that there was a fear that the rather violent steps that I proposed to take might provide a great disturbance among the people and lead to serious trouble. Old Sir Patrick [Manson, the most prominent authority at the meeting] . . . considered that it would be impossible to remove, more or less forcibly, from their farms and ancestral homes on the lake shore, anything like 100,000 people and felt sure that we would be let in for a serious native war . . . a much better plan would be to clear completely of forest the whole of the fly-infested belt.' Bell pointed out this would mean clearing 'something like 1,000 square miles of land and an immense expenditure'.

'After a good deal of desultory talking I decided that the moment had come for telling them what the present situation actually is. Gentlemen,' he announced, 'I am glad to be able to tell you that some of you are arguing against what is a *fait accompli.*' Given the appalling mortality, he had taken the responsibility of going ahead with his plans himself. 'Already, almost half the fly-infested lake shore has now been completely cleared of its inhabitants . . . [who] have been settled in fly-free areas.' All at once Bell found himself the hero of the hour. The funds he needed from the Treasury would be forthcoming.

Bell returned to Entebbe on 5 November. He landed on the jetty, lined with a Sikh guard of honour, decorated with arches, flags and greenery, to a seventeen-gun salute. His deputy, George Wilson, and all the heads of departments were there in uniform to greet him. A week later, Winston Churchill, Under-Secretary of State for the Colonies, arrived, keen to see all.

Though they disagreed on issues, they got on well, having a 'great pow-wow' in their rickshaws as they were wheeled the twenty-six miles to Kampala to call on the Kabaka. Bell was challenged to keep Winston to his programme ('he is a difficult fellow to handle') and was surprised to overhear him dictating an article to a clerk in his bath. 'He was very unreserved . . .'

'How old are you?' he said.

'On my admitting that I am 43, he exclaimed, "Do you know I am ten years younger than you? I wonder where I shall be when I am your age," looking at me as if I was Methuselah! "Where do you think you will be?" said I. "P.M.," he replied.'

Churchill wrote stirringly of the riches and beauty of Uganda, 'an island of gentle manners' where 'an amiable, clothed, polite and intelligent race dwell together in an organised monarchy'. Leaving it to sail down the White Nile to the Sudan and Egypt, he wrote how 'the best lies behind one. Uganda is the pearl.' Thanks no doubt to Churchill's endorsement, Bell finally got the knighthood he had coveted for so long in the King's birthday honours in 1908. He noted every letter of congratulation. Soon afterwards his new Government House at Entebbe was completed. He and Captain Usborne of the Royal Engineers had concluded that 'as Entebbe did not strike one as a tropical place, they would design a large villa, a really comfortable English house, such as one might find in the southern counties'. The result, built of red brick with white timber trim, gabled roofs and verandahs, was stunningly suburban: 'just such a house as the mayor of a provincial town would build for himself when he retired from business', wrote one visitor. In spite of his private feelings of shame whenever he shot a splendid animal, Bell furnished the drawing room with his game trophies, framing the door with magnificent elephant tusks. The cost of lighting an evening gathering – with kerosene lamps – was 'ruinous'.

From the house he could look down over his settlement at Entebbe to see 'men and ladies dotted over the golf course; [and] a little to the right, the tennis courts of the Club, all full of players'. Now, in spite of its drawbacks, it was proving 'one of the most healthy places in tropical Africa', where 'even the white babies look fairly rosy'. A new Anglican church had replaced the old mud-walled and grass thatch hut, and a monorail to Kampala had been completed. Bell collected a considerable private menagerie in the grounds of Government House: a pair of warthogs, four ostriches, a large chimpanzee, a tame leopard, a pair of lions, a porcupine and two owls. He tried to teach the Ugandans to train their elephants to work by importing a large female elephant and a *mahout* from India to demonstrate, and brought the first motor car and a lorry from England to the land. He never stopped making plans for the future of Uganda: new roads and a railway to the Nile; growing cotton, coffee, rubber, and tea. He planned elegant new towns – at least on paper. His relations with people in Uganda were almost solely with white officials; he could not feel the same affection for the Africans as he did for the people of Dominica. He made no intimate friends.

Days after the people living on the 150 islands on Lake Victoria were ordered to abandon their settlements and move to safe regions on the mainland, Bell left Government House at Entebbe for the last time. On 3 May 1909 he travelled to hold a farewell *baraza* with the Kabaka, the chiefs and all his officials in Kampala. At 9.30 in the evening, a big drum was beaten on one of the Kampala hills, and on the instant, thousands of torches lit up in a blaze. Bell and Burton, in black tie and evening dress, climbed into Bell's open car to drive to the jetty on the first leg of his long journey back to England. The whole of the six miles of road to the port was lined with Baganda holding flaming torches, crying, '*We Wale! We Wale!*'

Sir Henry Hesketh Bell seems an unlikely African hero. Vain and snobbish, but with a delightful sense of humour, only someone as convinced of his own righteousness as Bell could have carried off the feat of saving so many lives. He gave full credit to the team around him – Aubrey Hodges and his small band of medics, his district officers and his deputy commissioner, George Wilson. All had been essential for the success of his sleeping sickness scheme, while without the goodwill of the Ugandan chiefs he would have been powerless. But Bell was the person who digested the medical research and saw a way forward. He devised the plan, raised the funding, and drove it through.

By 1910 there were six 'infected areas' in Uganda, the most virulent remaining the two-mile-wide strip that ran the entire length of southern Uganda along the Lake Victoria shore. Within two years of implementing Bell's measures, deaths from sleeping sickness in the kingdom of Buganda fell to just eighty-two. In time the infection disappeared from the lake shore tsetse, and the people were permitted to return to their ancestral villages. Bell's method of declaring infected areas, and making them illegal to occupy, went on repeatedly in Uganda until independence in 1962. Segregating people from infected tsetse fly is still the main means of containing the disease in Africa, where it remains endemic. Various drug treatments have been developed, but they have proved toxic and unreliable, especially in the later stages of the disease, when the parasite invades the brain. It was only in July 2009 that a team of doctors working for Médecins Sans Frontières in the Congo completed a study showing that they have succeeded at last in the long search for a cure for sleeping sickness.

Bell was promoted to become governor of Northern Nigeria in succession to Frederick Lugard. He still dreamed of a post in a warm, gentle island like Cyprus. He did not want Northern Nigeria, but the terms of his letter of appointment were so flattering he could not turn it down. No sooner did he arrive than he found himself out of his depth. A querulous note creeps into his diary. He was bullied by a team of tough, Lugard-trained, independent-minded district officers. He did little but question and delay their recommendations, while they mocked his lack of social background and his fear of the climate. After three miserable years he was recalled to London, and, to his appalled chagrin, demoted to be governor of the Leeward Islands. But he was soon reconciled to his beloved West Indies. In 1916 he moved to his last post as governor of Mauritius.

Bell's retirement was long and agreeable, a ceaseless round of elegant luncheons, dinners, cocktails, golf and travel in London and the French Riviera. He wrote to *The Times,* protested about cruelty to animals, dabbled in evening séances, propelled beautiful women gracefully round the dance floor. He never ceased to monitor his health, or to try to perfect a winning system at the gaming tables of Monte Carlo. He died in 1952, in his eighty-eighth year. He never married.

15 A socialist in the West Indies
Jamaica 1907–12

The Fabian lecturers are famous throughout the world. Their women are beautiful; their men brave. The executive council challenges the universe for quality. . . Join the Fabian, and you will find its name a puissant protector.

George Bernard Shaw

On Monday, 14 January 1907, the day dawned on perfect weather in Kingston, Jamaica. From the shore, the waters of the Caribbean Sea were clean and clear, sapphire blue in the distance. At the dockside United Fruit Company lighters rocked gently alongside the jetty. A steady stream of black figures, ragged and dirty, moved easily up the gangways from the jetty to the hatches, and then wound back to the white sheds along the wharf for another load: women steadying heavy stems of green bananas on their head clouts with the tips of their fingers, their long cotton dresses streaked with dark stains of juice; men in singlets, greasy with sweat, carrying barrels of oranges, crates of grapefruit in their arms. As they swung them into the hatches, the rhythm of plantation songs filled the air. 'All-do'h I had so many, many sins . . . He has taken dem away and pardon'd me . . .'

A couple of blocks inland, a crowd of MPs and businessmen from Manchester and Liverpool revelled in the warm sunshine and the clear light air, enjoying the quaint old town of Kingston, with its white timbered houses and soft tiled roofs, and congratulating themselves on escaping from the dark and cold of the English winter.

Over 100 experts in horticulture, planters from Barbados and Jamaica, even a merchant from west Africa, had gathered for a major conference on agriculture. As the meeting broke for lunch, the Governor of Jamaica, Sir Alexander Swettenham – elder brother of Sir Frank, who had stepped down in such haste from Singapore not long before – invited ten of the delegates to lunch at the Jamaica Club. Three hours later those left in the club uttered ghastly shrieks. Beneath their feet the floors leapt, the roof fell in, and walls and pillars collapsed on top of them.

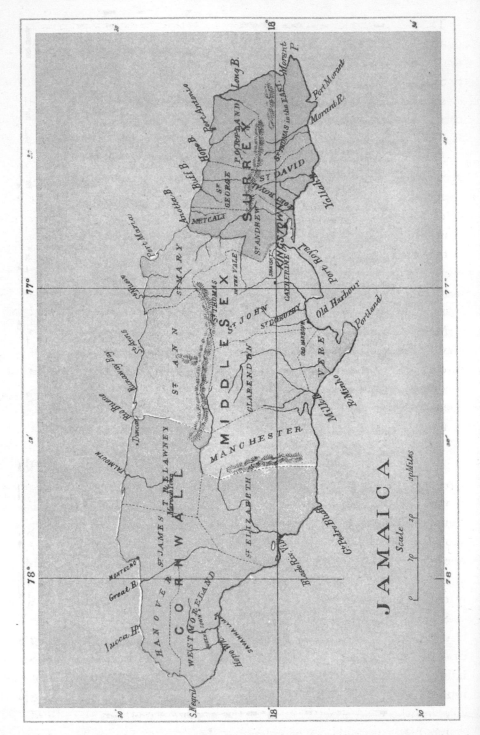

The huge earthquake that hit Kingston at 3.42 that afternoon measured 6.5 on the Richter scale. In not much more than a minute the city was razed to the ground. The fire that followed burned out of control for at least the next two days. 'Brigade helpless from the start; no water; trains toppled over, poles crashed across roads; everyone felt sickening helplessness, people kneeling, crying "O God save us!" impossible to quiet them. Heartbreaking wailing,' Hamar Greenwood, MP, telegraphed the Secretary of State.

At the Constant Spring Hotel, five miles out of town, the ladies who had been having their afternoon rests gathered on the lawn with blankets and their bed things around them. Miraculously, all but one of the conference delegates had survived, although a number had been injured. Along the coast, a huge wave rolled inland. That night more than 200 slept on the lawn of the hotel. There were a series of aftershocks, while the blaze of the raging fire over the city was plainly visible. King's House, where the Governor lived, had been shattered; the Governor and his family were reported to be living in tents.

Meanwhile Governor Swettenham had cabled the British Minister at Havana. Within hours the American torpedo-boat *Whipple* had been dispatched from Guantanamo. It reached Jamaica two days after the quake, on Wednesday evening, the 16th. The next morning, Thursday, the traumatized conference delegates sailed for New York. As they did so, two American battleships, the *Missouri* and the *Indiana,* under the command of US Admiral Davis, arrived in port.

The chaos was indescribable. The ruins smouldered. The stench was awful. No one had any idea how many people might be dead. Maybe 1,000? All the shops, warehouses and banks had been destroyed. There was worry about the security of their safes. There was no food. Men in singlets were looting. Over 500 prisoners were said to be on the brink of mutiny in the penitentiary. No one knew where the Governor was. Admiral Davis ordered the landing of an armed force and working parties of marines. After an hour or so, at 10 a.m., he came face to face with Governor Swettenham.

Swettenham was sixty-one. That he may have been unhinged by the trauma of these events was not at first apparent, although his surviving cable to Havana, merely requesting 'bandages, lint and wool for those injured by the earthquake, at cost of colony', suggests that he may not immediately have appreciated the scale of the disaster. But with the reeking city and the dead about him, early the following morning he ordered Admiral Davis to withdraw his American forces and return to Cuba.

The Americans nursed the insult at this brusque rejection of their offer of aid. At least $1,000,000 to help with relief of Jamaica was stopped. President Roosevelt congratulated Davis on 'his distinguished contribution to humanity'. It took the first British warship four more days to arrive – one week after the earthquake. That day Swettenham tendered his resignation.

'Send Mr Olivier!'

Jamaica's archbishop, leading lawyers, the newspapers, and many ordinary people on the island were united. Although there were reasons why the Colonial Office might have been reluctant to do so, in the circumstances there was no one else they could have dispatched. Sydney Olivier had returned to London from Jamaica only a little more than two years before, after a four-year term as Colonial Secretary. During this time he had been acting governor of the island three times. Before that he had more than ten years' experience specializing in West Indian affairs at the Colonial Office. He had been dispatched to serve in the colonies three times: short fire-fighting stints, admittedly, but still – he had seen the places and knew what went on. Six months as colonial secretary in British Honduras, six months as auditor-general of the Leeward Islands, and in 1896–7 secretary to a royal commission on the conditions of the sugar colonies.

Now, as the principal clerk in the Colonial Office in charge of West Indian affairs, Olivier was senior. He had been following every detail of the disaster from London, already meeting the Lord Mayor of London to implement a huge fund-raising campaign and summoning aid for relief. At forty-eight, he was a striking man: tall, elegant, curling grey hair receding, his black beard trimmed to a neat point. 'Like a Spanish grandee in any sort of clothes, however unconventional,' his old friend George Bernard Shaw described him. In Downing Street, Olivier scandalized Chamberlain by appearing for a meeting wearing a grey flannel suit, flannel shirt, tan shoes and a derby hat.

There was not much, in fact, about Olivier that was conventional. Born in 1859, he was one of eight children of Arnold Olivier, a stern, dedicated, Anglican clergyman with whom, Sydney found as he grew, he was increasingly at odds. Sent to board at a preparatory school at the age of eight, then to Tonbridge School, he emerged an atheist, and very keen on girls, with an exhibition to Corpus Christi, Oxford. He wanted to become an architect; his mother wanted him to go to the bar. Outside the porter's office at college, he saw an advertisement for clerkships starting at £250 a year in the

Treasury and the Colonial Office, subject to competition. In 1882, he sat one of the first CO entrance exams.

By the early summer, aged twenty-three, he found himself living in a dingy square in Paddington and sharing an office with an unprepossessing clerk of his own age, Sidney Webb. Olivier thought of himself as strapped for cash; Webb was much poorer than he was. Born and schooled near Leicester Square, Webb had arrived at the Colonial Office via clerkships in the War Office and the Inland Revenue a year before. A bulky, shambling figure with a Cockney accent, and sharp eyes that missed nothing, he possessed a mind like a computer, clever, fact-collecting, earnest. Every moment of his spare time was spent in study at the British Library, reading voraciously, and taking evening courses. He was a friend of George Bernard Shaw.

Shaw was three years older, earning his living writing serialized stories and reviews. Olivier took to breakfasting with him at his home in Fitzroy Street as he walked on his way to work; the three young men frequented anarchist communist clubs in Clerkenwell. In January 1884, the Fabian Society was formed. In May 1885, Shaw persuaded Olivier to join it.

Fabians wanted equal rights and equality for all. They wanted the ownership of land and industry 'socialized' – made the property of the people – to do away with idle owners, so that profits were paid to those who worked to produce them. Fabians were not revolutionaries in the voguish mode of the Marxists, who recruited converts against the time they could take out capitalists on the barricades. They worked by subtler means, permeating other groups with the reason and good sense of their ideas.

'Gentle habits and trained reasoning powers may achieve a complete Revolution without a single act of violence,' Shaw declared. Their goals were long-term, gradual. In the Fabians it was Webb who had the ideas, produced the statistics and laid out their policy, Shaw who established the tone and did the talking. Olivier played the long game, got them organized and did the planning. He and Webb, with Graham Wallas, a schoolmaster at Highgate School, Olivier's closest friend from Oxford, became known among the Fabians as the 'Three Musketeers'. Shaw was their d'Artagnan, and the celebrity campaigner for the rights of women workers, Annie Besant, got them out on the street.

In the same month that Olivier joined the Fabians, he married Margaret Cox. Her older brother Harold had been one of his closest friends at Tonbridge

School. They first met when, as head boy and president of the debating society, Olivier was chairing a school debate in 1877. He was eighteen; she three years younger. He was tall and authoritative, calm and decided; she was tiny, with soft, delicate features and lovely blue eyes, diffident and unsure. Her family called her 'Meg'.

Her father, Homersham Cox, was a circuit judge. Margaret was brought up in small, impoverished, Surrey country villages. She remembered her mother, with her fine, glossy black hair, wearing a loose white cotton wrapper, bathing her children every morning after breakfast. There were ten of them – and one who did not live. Margaret was about fourteen when, after three weeks of constant nursing by her mother, 'this child died. I think that after the child died my mother did not believe in a God anymore.' It was at that time that Margaret too lost her faith.

Harold would bring Olivier home in the holidays. Together he and Margaret would slip her sister's chaperonage to go for long walks through the countryside, making for Penshurst, Hever or Chiddingstone, talking all the time of what they saw around them, flowers, birds, trees, the soils. In August 1883, 'I rushed my fence on Thursday last at Tonbridge,' Olivier told his friend Graham Wallas. He had asked her to marry him.

'If you are anxious to receive a really inspiring batch of letters I should recommend you to write and inform your parents and your eldest sister that you have engaged yourself for marriage with a young lady of unorthodox religious opinions,' he went on. 'Without reservations' his father regarded the step as 'a wanton burning of my ships'. Margaret might have given up religion, but she despaired that Olivier wanted to do away with all ceremony for the wedding, even the bridesmaids and a cake. 'It is very sad that we should live in a time when the old sacraments have come to have no strength or meaning for us . . . What are we to do? Must we go through all the most important acts of our lives without any consecration of them beyond that which our own feelings at the time can give?'

In spite of this, she couldn't quite believe her wonderful fortune. 'Looking back, now,' Margaret was to write almost forty years later, 'I wonder what on earth I was doing with a king like that!' He was always working 'for a greater world than mine could ever be'. Intellectually, she felt she could not begin to match him, nor, with his obliviousness to the feelings of others, did he encourage her confidence. But gamely she tried, reading John Stuart Mill, discussing Boswell, Kant and Hegel with him.

Rooms in West Kensington; fortnightly meetings of the Fabians, Sunday evenings with William Morris at his Kelmscott House room, an addition to his home in Hammersmith; the Oliviers met anarchists and Russians and took holidays – 'bicycles not yet being general' – tricycle riding in the Kentish countryside. They went to Germany: Weimar, Dresden and the Wagner festival at Bayreuth with George Bernard Shaw. Harold wrote from India, where he was teaching maths at an Islamic college in Aligarh, of his socialist qualms over employing a *punkawallah*, 'but it is just so hot . . . and after all it is just a job like any other'. Then, a small house in Maida Vale, and the birth of four daughters: Margery, tall, brown-eyed and brown-haired, in 1886; Brynhild, who would become an outstanding beauty, a year later; Daphne, dark and dreamy; and Noel, the youngest, quiet and inconspicuous, born on Christmas Day, 1892.

All around them they were aware of horrible poverty, an atmosphere of restlessness and fear. The unemployed marched through London. In 1889 the Fabians published *Fabian Essays in Socialism*. Olivier contributed a piece on the moral basis of socialism. In Shaw's words, the edition 'went off like smoke'. Suddenly Fabianism was famous. By 1893 the membership had risen to over 500, many of them influential people like Keir Hardie, Ramsay MacDonald and Emmeline Pankhurst. Seventy local societies, with hundreds more members, grew up around the country.

Olivier, said Shaw, was always half a dozen paces ahead in any argument. With a mind 'like a champion chess player', 'he was a law to himself and never dreamt of considering other people's feelings'. He dealt with any opposing prejudice by 'walking through it as if it wasn't there'.

Olivier's Fabian activities ought to have put an end to serious prospects of promotion. But in 1890, after eight years in the West India department of the Colonial Office, he was eager to see the realities of the peoples and places he was constantly reading about. He took the first opportunity of getting out to a colony: a crisis in British Honduras between the governor and his council. Its finances were in a mess. In the autumn of 1890 Olivier was dispatched to Belize as acting colonial secretary, up until that time an unprecedented step for a junior clerk from the Colonial Office. So that he would be able to master the numbers in Belize, he taught himself double-entry bookkeeping on the voyage out.

'Approaching the long, low bank of dark mangrove bushes, fronted with mud, we were beached against the garden palisade of King's House. The Private Secretary promptly took me for a walk through the town, showing,

as I thought, an amazing cheerfulness at the most depressing surroundings
I have ever seen. I was really frightened. This was worse than any tropical
place I had ever imagined and all tropical places had, at that time, a deadly
reputation.' Belize was built on mudflats, laid down by the Belize River
about nine miles from solid land. Wide ditches were filled with black swamp
water, squalid houses balanced on piles. 'A strong acrid odour hung in the
fog,' Olivier wrote. But such was his success in reorganizing the administration and balancing the books that he returned to London in the spring of
1891 to be regarded as something of a magician, that rare being: a financial
authority and business head in Downing Street.

Upon his return, the Oliviers moved to a converted pair of cottages in
Limpsfield, a scattered hamlet with a big wooden windmill, overlooking
the Weald of Kent. Olivier took a room in London for two or three nights
a week. Fellow Fabians and good friends lived in and around Limpsfield:
the Edward Peases, Edward and Constance Garnett, Henry Salt, founder
of the Humanitarian League, and his wife Kate, and the social reformer
Octavia Hill. There were the novelists Ford Madox Ford and E. V. Lucas.
The Olivier girls were free to roam where they liked through the wood-
lands with the children of their parents' friends: climbing trees, skinning
rabbits, collecting birds' eggs and putting on plays. H. G. Wells taught
them croquet; they picnicked with the Russian revolutionaries Prince
Kropotkin and Sergius Stepniak, who had killed the chief of the Russian
secret police in 1878. It was from here, in the autumn of 1899, that Olivier
set off for the first time to live in Jamaica. Margaret and the children followed a year later.

Olivier brought to Jamaica, or so it seemed to Herbert de Lisser, a twenty-
one-year-old journalist on the weekly *Jamaican Times*, 'an entirely new
element in the social life of the community'. De Lisser was the son of the
African-Jewish editor of a small local newspaper, who had died when he
was fourteen. He was soon to become the editor of Kingston's *Daily Gleaner*,
a post he was to hold for forty years.

'So strenuous was his energy, so original his point of view, so penetrat-
ing were his dark flashing eyes', Olivier began 'gradually changing the *ethos*
or character of Jamaica permanently,' de Lisser wrote. Where everyone else
was wearing starched collars, he wore a relaxed greyish morning coat and
soft shirts. Alone of white people of rank, the new colonial secretary – the
de facto head of the administration – was remarked for being seen actually

walking about Kingston, even in the heat of the day, through the dust of the soft limestone that rose from the pavements. In the office, 'he moved like lightning'. He tolerated no delays and no red tape. He was quick, nervy, idiosyncratic, restless and impatient, intolerant of shortcomings in those immediately surrounding him. He launched into an investigation of every-thing to do with Jamaica, pouring himself into the details of the island. Who owned the land? Who were the people?

Jamaica had been a British colony for so long – over 250 years – that the nation had come to regard it as a vague, rather hopeless, part of its birth-right. Olivier knew the headlines: discovered by Columbus in 1494, captured from the Spanish under Oliver Cromwell in 1655 as a base to chal-lenge the sea roads from Spanish Central America; then, a lair for pirates, a hideout for swashbuckling buccaneers, who preyed upon Spanish galleons full of gold.

Among the earliest English settlers were several who had signed Charles I's death warrant. They established a tradition of obstruction to the Crown that had continued down the centuries. Meanwhile, under treaty with Spain, Port Royal, at the narrow entrance to Kingston harbour, had been awarded a monopoly for the slave trade from west Africa for the whole of the Caribbean and the southern United States. But, on 7 June 1692, the capital was struck by one of the most violent earthquakes in history. In two minutes, the whole town sank beneath fathoms of water.

The capital and the slave mart moved to Kingston, laid out on a tidy grid of streets by the Royal Engineers. Meanwhile sugar cane planted on the coastal plains thrived. Coffee was planted and flourished. By the end of the eighteenth century, Jamaica was in its glory days: over 1,000 large sugar plantations, gracious houses, and, at the rear, quarters for hundreds of black slaves.

Nine-tenths of their owners, however, were living in Britain. There they squandered the profits of their Jamaican estates. In order to keep their jobs, plantation managers had to remit a certain profit to England; mean-while, they creamed as much as they could for themselves so that they in turn could become proprietors and go home to star in society. Olivier described them as 'West Indian nabobs'. White British overseers and book-keepers were wretchedly underpaid. To Olivier the system was iniquitous. It bred every kind of cruelty and depravity – 'domineering autocracy, dis-honesty, sexual exploitation and over-driving of slaves'.

An idealized vision of a sugar cane plantation, published in Britain in 1883

With the coming of abolition in 1834, Jamaica's prosperity collapsed. People who had once been slaves no longer cared to work for white masters. Exports in sugar had already been in decline; coffee plantations could no longer survive without the nimble fingers of women and children to harvest the crop. In 1846 British protection of the West Indian sugar tariff was abandoned. Meanwhile production of European sugar beet was rising. Plantation after plantation was deserted. Still, owners in England, and even local planters, clung on to their properties, convinced that in time the Eldorado of previous generations would return.

By 1865, half of the 600 estates that remained were in ruins. Poverty and malnutrition had spread. There was a clear hierarchy of race and caste: a white ruling elite, and a second tier of free people of colour and Jews – both of whom had had the vote since 1831 – and on the bottom, former slaves of different skin tones: blacks, mulattos, quadroons, and mustees.

That year, Jamaica's worst rebellion broke out in the remote mountains in the centre of the island. Here lived the Maroons, the last descendants of the island's indigenous Indians who had formed unions with former Spanish and runaways. Years of poverty and injustice, of arrests and imprisonment on trumped-up charges, reached breaking point on 11 October 1865. Four days before, a group of former slaves had broken a man who had been unjustly sentenced for trespass out of prison. Warrants had been issued for their arrest. Now, backed by hundreds of others, they marched in protest to the courthouse in Morant Bay, capital of the sugar-growing parish of St Thomas, on the south-east tip of Jamaica. Fearing what might happen, the militia opened fire; the protesters rioted; twenty-five people, black and white, were killed. Over the ensuing days 2,000 black vigilantes took to the countryside, killing two white planters. The Governor's reaction was savage. In the ensuing fighting, nearly 450 people were killed and over 350 arrested and executed. Six hundred men and women were flogged or imprisoned, and over 1,000 homes razed to the ground. The Governor was recalled to England and Jamaica's constitution was suspended. Until the Morant Bay rebellion Jamaica – like Barbados – had been governed as the colonies of North America had been until the American revolution of 1776. There were two house legislatures: one Crown-appointed, the other an assembly elected by colonists qualified by property to vote. The Jamaica assembly, once free to determine its own laws, was now replaced by Crown Colony government with power vested in the governor and his Executive Council.

Meanwhile conditions for the mass of the people – former slaves, free coloured and poor whites – continued to deteriorate. Whole families were left to squat or starve, while gangs of vagrant youths and young girls began to move about the island in search of labour. Thousands went to work on the railway building in Panama. Others drifted towards the towns, to Spanish Town, Montego Bay and Kingston. There was work for perhaps one quarter of those who arrived. Young men especially seemed aimless and delinquent. Kingston sank into squalor.

'There are no persons of indigenous race in Jamaica,' Olivier was to write later. Africans and Europeans had been interbreeding for so many generations that almost everyone was made of a mixture of races. In a population of almost 650,000 there were not more than 15,000 – including Jews – who claimed to be unmixed white. What impressed him was how many of the 'coloured' class were landowners, commercial clerks, lawyers, doctors, artisans and tradesmen and how many blacks owned substantial smallholdings, or were schoolteachers, Protestant clergymen and even magistrates. It was in the agricultural districts where the sugar industry still held sway that they were poorest and most degraded. Yes, there was prejudice, but there was not the bitter racial hostility of the southern United States or South Africa.

Until Olivier arrived, the purpose of the government was simply to provide law and order. No one with any influence in Jamaica had ever seen the point of public expenditure on education, health and public works. 'The task of implementing . . . reforms, with a Governor and a civil service . . . discredited [by] subservience to time honoured procedures, and the elected element in the Legislative Council determined to weaken the power of the state, would not be easy,' Olivier told Shaw shortly after his arrival in December 1899.

As colonial secretary, Olivier overhauled the civil service, and by underwriting loans to private investors set up central factories for processing raw cane sugar. Fulminating at the loss to the economy of so much land in the hands of absentee landlords, he changed the law to permit the sale of Crown lands to black smallholders. When, in April 1902, three days of rioting broke out in Montego Bay, Olivier, as acting governor, went to help quell them himself. 'Not since Morant Bay has there been such a rising against constituted authority,' claimed the *Daily Telegraph*. Fuelling the unrest was a new property tax that had aggravated the riots, which he saw was impossible for ordinary people to pay. When the Governor returned to the island, he persuaded him to remit the tax. Only the humanity of the Colonial Office, it seemed to him, stood between the planters and the black population of the islands.

Olivier could not live without debating ideas. Continuing the Fabian tradition, he set up a series of lectures on socialism at the Institute of Jamaica. Today it is a collection of museums and the national library; then it was the one place in Kingston where a black man could come to learn, prepare to apply for a place at university in England, and read books. Talk by the most senior man in the government service of equality for all and the need for the working classes to take control of the means of production had never been heard in Jamaica before. Almost certainly in his audience would have been a schoolmaster, Robert Love, editor of the *Jamaican Advocate*. Love was a rousing orator whose speeches captured the young. 'We love the white man because he is a brother, we love the coloured man because he is a son; we love the black man because we love ourselves,' he would memorably declare. Four years later, Love would become the second black man elected to the Legislative Council.

Early in 1902 Olivier delivered an after-dinner speech at the Kingston Athenaeum entitled 'Socialism and its advantages'. 'The people must learn to help themselves,' he told his audience. Most of what he said went over the heads 'even of the gentry', Herbert de Lisser said. But in London Chamberlain heard the news with fury. Only a few weeks before, Olivier had published an article in England on 'Liberalism and the Fabians'. It included an attack on Chamberlain's colonial policy.

'I will not have any politics in the Colonial Office,' declared Chamberlain, 'and if Mr Olivier cannot keep his personal views to himself while he remains a public servant, he had better resign and the whole world may have the benefit of his socialism.' Olivier had broken the unwritten law upon which the civil service depended for loyalty. He was barely saved by his colleagues.

Olivier was vain and he was arrogant, but by the time he was due to go home in April 1903, Jamaicans were petitioning the Secretary of State to keep him there. Olivier had taken more pains to make himself 'personally acquainted with the affairs of Jamaica, its people, their condition of life, than any other previous official within our recollections or knowledge', and while 'some among us have not been able to concur in all Mr Olivier has done and said during his term of office here, his abilities – of such original and independent thought – of marvellous capacity for work – and untiring and unselfish interest in the well-being of the Island' were exceptional. The petition was signed by twenty-three merchants, landowners and justices of the peace. It took an earthquake, but four years later they got their wish.

Report of Major E. E. Chown, Royal Marines, 23 February 1907: 'It may be said that the whole of Kingston and its suburbs are either destroyed or in ruins. A very few of the substantially built houses are still standing but so shaken and injured by the shocks that it will be impossible to repair them.' Chown said it was impossible to estimate the total loss of life. Inhabitants had been called upon to register the names of their killed and missing 'but up to this date there has been little response . . . Of the injured the daily number of in-patients at the hospital is about 300, mostly cases of concussions and legs amputated.

'Directly after the earthquake, the greater portion of the black and coloured population were stupefied by terror and amazement . . . Vast numbers of them fled from the city. Some became frenzied and ran here and there declaring the end of the world had arrived, impeding the work and terrifying the workers. Others formed groups and commenced praying.' At the penitentiary, the prisoners spent the time singing hymns. As the first panic subsided, the government was able to help and clear the streets only with difficulty, and even now 'a considerable portion of able-bodied black men may be seen lounging about the streets or basking in the sun on the Race Course, although labour is still in demand'.

Chown concluded: 'There are several statues in Kingston, but they are for the most part unhurt. That of Queen Victoria in front of the Public Gardens is untouched, but the figure has been slewed round on its pedestal towards the S. E. It originally faced South.'

'Even the basement walls, about 2 ft 6" thick, are cracked up like biscuits.' Five months after the earthquake, on 16 May, Olivier had landed. Now he was making a thorough inspection of King's House, the governor's residence. It would have to be demolished, he told Margaret. She was still in England. 'So will the ballroom so there's an end to that.'

Olivier had had just a month before leaving England to find an architect to rebuild Kingston. He persuaded his forty-year-old brother-in-law, Charles Nicholson – a coming architect with a passion for ecclesiastical design – to come with him to oversee the design of new public buildings. There were grumblings about nepotism at this appointment but Olivier's allies at the CO saw them off. Ted Scott, the son of the editor of the *Manchester Guardian*, was appointed to be his private secretary. Margaret and the girls would follow after she had packed up Limpsfield and his flat in London and tied up their affairs.

The wind had come on so strong the night before he sailed from Avonmouth that the ship had stayed in dock for an extra half a day. The voyage had been so rough that no one could go on deck for five days. 'The boat plunged and rocked a good deal,' he told Margaret, 'but it did not incommode me in my large bed . . . nor badly enough for ones trunks to slide and charge about across ones cabin.' He'd had a big cabin, with a private bathroom, 'a great convenience: I have two baths a day, and no scuttling about passages half-dressed.' He had spent his time reading Boswell's *Life of Johnson,* 'again', and making plans with Nicholson for improving King's House. 'He has designed a church whilst on board . . .'

'I hope you have not been much harassed with the household, and the business of getting out of the flat. Remember I do depend on you.' He began by instructing Margaret on how much rent to charge on letting the house in Limpsfield. He'd left behind the key, 'quite tiny', to an account book 'which may still be in one of my pockets', and she was not to forget to tell their daughter Daphne to keep her shoulders back.

'Begin by getting rid of all my old shoes that I left behind – except the large boots . . . I forgot to ask Hoad if he would like to have my bicycle . . .' Another thing was the broken mirror that was in the lavatory. 'There is a large piece of it put away somewhere (I think in the storeroom – wrapped in brown paper) which it could be worthwhile to have cut down and fitted into the frame, reduced for that purpose . . .' She was to forward some suits he had ordered, take more pictures to the framer, pack up some others to bring out, and collect some books he had left at the Colonial Office.

To prepare herself for her new role as governor's lady, he told her she should read the diaries of Lady Nugent, who had been the wife of the governor of Jamaica 100 years before, which had only just been published. As if Margaret had no ideas for herself, as if she had never seen the governor's wife in Jamaica in operation before, he warned her that she would have to devote herself to good works. But, mind: 'all social work in Jamaica is so parsonified, and the black people are so religious, you must manage to work without scandalizing them. They have got quite used to me: but then I keep my mouth shut a good deal.'

It was not until some weeks later that he thought to tell her that the Secretary of State, Lord Elgin, had proposed him for a knighthood. 'So you may have to alter the labels on your luggage before you start. I ought to give you a diamond necklace or something else suitable', but he couldn't get anything like that in Jamaica. 'Also, will you be surprised that I have bought a house? It is a little place on Stony Hill called Fort George, with a beautiful view and reputed to be very cool.'

Huge crowds had greeted him on landing. He had immediately begun touring Kingston. He found the hospital in ruins. 'The patients are in tents, rather hot but looking comfortable enough . . . The club consists now of only a buggy-shed boarded in but as there is nowhere else in town where lunch can be got it is much frequented.' Then he drove along the harbour to look at the town. 'Certainly the spectacle is extraordinary. One wonders where all the people are living, a tent or two in the gardens looks so small.' For the first month after he arrived Olivier had no time to ride out into the hills beyond Kingston to see the damage. House after old house where their friends used to live had collapsed and were falling down.

In June a second earthquake hit. It was especially severe at Port Royal, where forty men of the garrison were injured. By the middle of July, famine was overtaking the eastern section of the island. In New York, the papers were predicting that Jamaica would be given to the United States, in exchange for the Philippines.

Olivier's main task was the restoration of calm, the feeding of the people, and the rebuilding of Kingston. He would drive into Kingston in the early morning, his beloved Great Dane, Loge, bred at Kingston's Botanical Gardens, loping beside him. On the way, he would pass women from the hills 'swinging down to market, each with a wide, round basket on her head full of yams, gourds, mangoes, bananas [and] truncheons of sugar-cane'. His day was spent first at his desk, then out and about, assessing and inspecting, active and practical. There were trips by train to Montego Bay and Spanish Town, and long journeys across the island on horseback, and by buggy, Loge beside him or riding on the seat; tossing lumps of sugar to children as he passed, stopping to talk to people sitting by their huts along the road. In the autumn, Meg and the girls arrived.

Margaret was now forty-five; their eldest daughter, Margery, twenty-one. The following spring, Bryn would return to England to go to the Royal College of Art and Daphne to Newnham College, Cambridge; Noel, who would be fifteen, would be dispatched to board at Bedales. While King's House was being rebuilt, the family lived in a small bungalow in the grounds, but Fort George, the little coffee house on top of a hill, which Olivier had bought soon after he landed, was so close, only forty-five minutes from 'the big house', that they could spend much of their time there.

For now, the girls were learning shorthand in the morning. They went sailing, played tennis and challenged visiting officers from the fleet to polo matches on their ponies. In the evenings, Margery played the piano; Daphne sang. They played bridge and occasionally entertained a few guests to dinner, but large-scale entertaining was out of the question. In the morning Margaret briefed the old butler, Rodrigues, who was 'lachrymose or cheerful' depending on his mood, and accompanied Olivier on various visits in the afternoons: the prison, the cathedral, Montego Bay and the new constructions in Kingston.

The following spring, Margaret and the girls sailed for England together. At the beginning of December she returned alone. 'All these passages to & fro across the Atlantic are to my thinking a great waste. If we had stayed here all these years we should by now have built up an interest in the island . . . we should also have made a home . . . Anyhow, here we are.' After nearly twenty-five years of marriage, Margaret still doubted her worth, was still consumed by shyness. Like Olivier, she gloried in the beauty of Jamaica, its early golden mornings and its purple mountains, the blue of the sea and the sky, and the sunsets flaming red. But she never felt at home. Olivier, who she dubbed 'the Strenuous One', in his shabby jackets with his pockets torn, was not easy to live with. He could be by turns demanding, condescending, prickly and taciturn. With her girls at home in England, her life in Jamaica seemed increasingly futile.

She took to spending more and more time alone at Fort George. She loved waking in her 'wonderful little room with windows on all sides . . . from which I can see hills on the east . . . blue sea to the south . . . the smell of early morning . . . the sense of freedom!' There, she lived 'a detached sort of life'. There was no one about except the servants – and her animals. She gardened in the morning, working with 'a tall black man called Stan', would have another bath and change. 'S comes in the evenings – or sometimes the later afternoon. It is peaceful & not at all boring & I very seldom have that horrible feeling that I ought to be doing something else. It is a great effort to "go down".'

Margaret did not find the Jamaican 'aristocracy' easy. 'The ladies were finely got up all very smiling & pleasant . . . The first remarks, even to people you have not seen before are easy enough, but it is difficult to carry on a long conversation with a Jamaican lady or Gentleman whom you do not know.' When she did go down to a function in Kingston, she generally came back feeling that she had accomplished very little, '& it was hardly worth the great effort that it cost'. 'A governor's wife has few friends outside her family,' she wrote. She felt as lonely as anyone in a London street.

The rebuilding of Kingston went on. Breeding grounds for malaria were cleared. The streets were widened, contractors were compelled to put up buildings that were earthquake-proof, trees were planted along the sidewalks, parks were laid out, and the foreshore improved. By May 1910, King's House was nearing completion, and Charles Nicholson's massive new white blocks of government offices – made of reinforced concrete to withstand the next earthquake – were finished.

'I am very well and as usual very full of work,' Olivier told Graham Wallas. He was inspecting the clearing of swamps on the north side of the island, overseeing the building of roads – 'new deviations' to avoid dangerously steep gradients. He implemented a new public health law, the first comprehensive sanitary code for Jamaica, and was reducing taxes – to increase consumption, and build the revenues. The American United Fruit

Company was leasing or buying up neglected plantations to cultivate bananas. Olivier was frustrated. He wished that British companies shared the Americans' grasp of efficiency and new business methods; and dreamed that black smallholders would unite to sell their bananas en masse, and to ship them to markets abroad themselves. Nevertheless, the island was prospering.

The Fabians had little to say on how the Empire should be run – only that colonial governments should be democratized and that governors should act with local councils as prime ministers, rather than despots. Olivier, however, had no confidence that Jamaica's uneducated population was ready for democracy. His approach as governor was cerebral and superior; he was outspoken and careless of giving offence – and by his own admission was little short of dictatorial.

'I shall never cause any proposals to be made in the House in the expectation of meeting a combined opposition, because my proposals will never be made in any sectional interest,' he told the Legislative Council in 1908. Everything he did would be done with 'sincere devotion to the general interests of the Island'. In fact, as he told Bernard Shaw when he and his wife came to stay with the Oliviers in Kingston in 1911, people in Jamaica could not see further than the ends of their noses.

'I now do not consult them. I do what is needed. In eighteen months or so they see that I was right, and stop howling about it.'

> Never would an English mind
> Bow beneat' such tyranny;
> Rise, O people of my kind!
> Struggle, struggle to be free!
>
> Shake de burden off your backs,
> Show de tyrants dat you're strong;
> Fight for freedom's rights, you blacks,
> Ring de slaves' old battle-song!

There was a change in the mood of Jamaica around that time, hard to track – a conjunction of people and ideas, the product of long evenings spent in talk, of literature and politics, one way or the other, for or against, a common thread, not quite a catalyst: Olivier. The lines from this poem celebrate the hero who inspired the Morant Bay rebellion, George William Gordon, who had been executed. They were written by the well-known Jamaican poet Claude McKay, who was just twenty when Olivier first met him at the home of one his closest friends on the island, Walter Jekyll. (Jekyll's sister, Gertrude, was to become the famous garden writer and designer.) Jekyll was a wealthy, eccentric, Cambridge-educated Buddhist, an exile from British society, who lived a reclusive life in a remote valley in the Blue Mountains. In sandals and a white suit, he would climb up on foot to visit the Oliviers at Fort George, to eat red pea soup and avocado pears. He and Olivier talked Fabianism and German philosophy, Kant, Nietzsche and Hegel. It was Olivier who encouraged him to publish the first authoritative collection of Jamaican folk songs and stories, *Jamaican Song and Stories*, in 1907.

He also encouraged McKay, whom Jekyll tutored and whose talent he nurtured. Olivier helped McKay edit his first collection and encouraged him to publish. *Songs of Jamaica,* which came out in 1912, was dedicated to Olivier. In the same way, Olivier encouraged Herbert de Lisser, editor of the *Daily Gleaner,* who had begun taking down stories of everyday Jamaicans, which he serialized in the paper, to turn them into books.

The seeds of black consciousness were scarcely beginning to form when Olivier first delivered his Fabian lectures on the island as colonial secretary in 1902. In the United States legal segregation – Olivier called it apartheid – was at its height following the Civil War. In 1903, the American writer W. E. B. Dubois published his seminal *The Souls of Black Folk*, outlining the struggles of 'the massed millions of the black peasantry', declaring that 'the problem of the Twentieth Century is the problem of the colour line'.

Jamaica's problems of poverty and race had stayed with Olivier while he was in London. In 1906, not long before he returned to Jamaica following the earthquake, he published a small book entitled *White Capital and Coloured Labour*. It came out under the small imprint of the 'Independent Labour Party'. Its subject was racism, and it tackled it head on.

'The colour line is not a rational line, the logic of neither words nor facts will uphold it,' he wrote. It was a man's personality that defined him, not the colour of his skin. Men could no longer be treated unequally, and no stable mixed community could hope to grow up so long as colour prejudice and 'race antagonism' maintained their supremacy, he said. The fact of racial prejudice – 'superstitious, if not hysterical' – had to be recognized and faced, and steps taken towards inter-racial understanding. He judged 'negrophobia . . . in the United States [as] the most active source of danger', and if there was no change in the way white men regarded black, he predicted an apocalyptic outbreak of race wars, in parts of the United States and South Africa. In Britain he was dismissed as a crank. In Jamaica, black men read him differently.

Towards the end of the hurricane season in the autumn of 1908, Olivier had a series of furious confrontations with a former government legal clerk who that July had been admitted to the bar after returning to Jamaica from studying law at the Middle Temple. Thirty-eight-year-old Sandy Cox, 'the People's Sandy', had been elected a member of the Legislative Council almost at once, and appointed to the deputy clerkship of a court. In January 1909 Olivier charged him with being absent without leave and removed him from his post. Cox protested to London. Meanwhile, from his first moment as a member of the Legislative Council, Cox began challenging Olivier's authority as governor. Two months after Olivier sacked him, he set up the National Club, Jamaica's first nationalist political organization. The National Club's manifesto declared that only native-born Jamaicans could be members and that each member must pledge himself to Jamaican self-government. It would be surprising if its other founders – Alexander Dixon, the first black Jamaican to be elected to the Legislative Council in 1899, and Hubert Simpson, a thirty-seven-year-old lawyer and Kingston councillor, had not attended Olivier's Fabian lectures at the Institute of Jamaica in 1902 nor read his *White Capital*.

Cox was unseated in elections for the Legislative Council in 1911, on technicalities over his residence and his income, and the National Club faded away. But its secretary was a twenty-two-year-old printer called Marcus Garvey, a man hungry for ideas and advancement, who even then was taking elocution lessons from Dr Robert Love, the powerful orator and editor of the *Jamaica Advocate*. Garvey was to go on to become the founder of the 'Back to Africa' movement in the United States, an inspiration of the civil rights movement, and Jamaica's first national hero.

By late 1912, Olivier's term of five years had already been exceeded. Cox was still agitating, and a wealthy, well-connected, liberal female plantation owner was also suing the governor for libel.

26 December 1912. Fort George.

Dearest Meg this is Monday morning: tomorrow the Leg Council meets and I have still to write most of my speech: so I shan't have any time for a letter unless I make it now . . . I came up here by myself on Saturday . . . I was very busy with papers here yesterday, and in the afternoon I went for a drive along the new road beyond to Christiana. It is getting on well. But it is very dreary work being here all by oneself and I wish I were at home.

I hear there was a riot, or something like it in Kingston yesterday evening. The Car company [has raised the fares] which has caused great dissatisfaction, and last night a lot of roughs got together and fired the Power House and pulled some of the cars out and smashed them and set them on fire. I am going down now to inquire about it . . .

Months before, the Canadian-owned West India Electric Company had put tram fares up by 14 per cent. People had protested by slowing down the transport: paying in farthings and asking for receipts – a slow protest of mounting attrition, rising from the bitter ground of poverty and despair in the Kingston slums. As Olivier told Margaret, he had no sympathy with the company. He had heard that a good many police were involved. 'But they ought to have been able to prevent the pulling out and destruction of cars.' By the time Olivier got down to the streets of Kingston, a full-scale riot was in progress. One person had been killed and over thirty wounded. In the street – according to Bernard Shaw – Olivier found 'an insurgent negro battering in the door of a newspaper office'. He grabbed him by the scruff of the neck and hurled him out of the way.

Olivier climbed back into his car, but got out again when he heard the bellows for help of several policemen whom the crowd had locked in a rum shop. 'You people should know better than this,' he admonished them. 'You are a brave man,' people told him, 'but we mean to get square with these policemen.' Two men went for the Governor. Olivier was hit on the back of the head with a brick. Marcus Garvey stepped in and hauled him out of the way.

'As you steam into Kingston Harbour,' Olivier wrote later, 'you have on your left hand a desolate mass of hills that at sundown stands black-purple against an incredible glory of crimson and orange and ochre and delicate apple-green . . . the emerald of the mangrove fringe of the beaches is drenched with floods of scarlet; the opal of the huge lagoon, dead calm between day breeze and night breeze, is burnt into its depths with strange, dull lilac tinctures.'

On just such an evening, not long after the tramcar riots on the streets of Kingston, in January 1913, Olivier left Jamaica at the end of his term as governor. He had been given a final dinner at the Club. As he told it afterwards, the loading of banana bunches into the holds of cargo ships – the work of women and girls – had finished for the day. Men were unloading orange barrels from vans on the floor of the goods shed, 'white flimsy-looking barrels drilled full of holes, which crackled and creaked' as they were rolled across the planking, down the gangway, into a fore hatch. Under the arc lights, he saw women and girls, 'propped up along the outer wall of the shed . . . some chattering a little in sudden bursts, now and again, like sparrows settling to roost, but most of them silent, relaxed, fast asleep. They slept as they had dropped there in their rags, here singly, there together . . . on the scattered banana trash between the railway sidings, against the ties . . . [in] formless heaps . . . But presently there would be more fruit to load . . .

'I climbed on board the steamer, and when she began to cast off went below and turned in.'

Olivier had 'no Kiplingesque idolatry of the Empire', as Shaw put it. Its break-up would not be the end of the world. 'His Fabian grasp of the appalling social danger of the imperial instincts that were keeping Downing Street under the thumb of a handful of planters in the face of millions of black proletarians, reduced official Kiplingism, in his view, to negligible poppycock.'

The more Olivier wrote, the plainer it was to the Colonial Office that he was pro-black and not pro-planter. On his return to London, he was appointed Secretary to the Board of Agriculture and Fisheries. He never worked for the Colonial Office again.

Jamaica would not leave him. Now he spoke out at every opportunity on the subject of race: in letters to the newspapers, in speeches, and in books. 'Says Color Line Must Be Abolished', ran the headline in the *New York Times* after Olivier told the Anglican Church Congress in 1913 that desegregation could be the only solution to the 'negro question'. He shocked American opinion. It would be through him that Marcus Garvey applied to the Colonial Office for funds to study at Birkbeck College, and he to whom he came in London for introductions to British politicians. When Garvey set up his Universal Negro Improvement Association, aimed at uniting all of Africa and its diaspora, Olivier wrote to wish him well. From then, until his retirement as assistant comptroller and auditor to the Exchequer in 1920, he continued to speak out against racial discrimination. In 1924, when the Labour Party came to power under Ramsay MacDonald, 'its lack of representation in the House of Lords compelled it to hand out peerages to any presentable members within its reach', wrote Shaw, 'and Olivier, being eminently presentable and much more aristocratic-looking than most of the hereditary nobles, became Lord Olivier. Being also the only available overseas diplomat, he was made Secretary of State for India.'

'We . . . are not a little disturbed at the prospect of Sir Sydney Olivier at the India Office,' the commander-in-chief in Delhi reported to King George. '[He is] said to be a faddist of the bull in the china shop order . . . may do an infinity of harm . . . knows nothing about India, but a good deal about Jamaica.'

In 1927 Olivier published a fierce polemic on racism in South Africa called *The Anatomy of African Misery. White Capital and Coloured Labour* was reissued in 1929. He never got over his love for Jamaica. He returned many times: investigating again the conditions of the sugar industry in 1929, and to write. 'The blessed island', he would call it in the profile he wrote of the island in 1936.

For years, speaking in the Lords, he tried to persuade the government to take more interest in Jamaica's problems, and those of black people in South Africa and Kenya. Increasingly he was regarded as a crank and an eccentric. In August 1942, in the midst of the Second World War, he wrote angrily to H. G. Wells over the non-publication of the Moyne Commission report into the Jamaican riots of 1938: 'Of course, as I am eighty-three years old . . . my opinions count for nothing, but I am of the opinion . . . that nothing short of expropriation of the large sugar estates in Jamaica, Trinidad and British Guiana will help the West Indies.'

Six months later, he died. Almost thirty years later, in 1971, the majority of Jamaica's sugar production was nationalized.

16 Letters from Nairobi

British East Africa 1909–12

The retirement of Sir Percy Girouard adds another name to the growing list of able public men who have exchanged the service of the Crown for private business. "Personal reasons" are stated to be the cause of his resignation; and it is an open secret that he has been offered, and has accepted, an important position with Messrs. Armstrong. It is possible that a further reason may be found in the health of Lady Girouard, who has never been able to spend very much time in East Africa. In any case, there is no question of friction either with the Colonial Office or with the people of the country. A Reuter telegram from Nairobi states that a mass meeting was convened for 5 o'clock yesterday to discuss the Governor's resignation, "which is apparently viewed with consternation by the settlement."

The Times, 17 July 1912

'When events occur, only part of the truth is sent abroad; the rest is kept back': so says a Maasai proverb. And so it was with Sir Percy Girouard, Governor of British East Africa – the country we know today as Kenya – the man who gave away the rich pastures of Laikipia, the northern homelands of the Maasai, to the white settlers.

In 1883 a Royal Geographical Society expedition, which was trying to find an overland route from Mombasa on the coast of East Africa to Uganda, first brought back news of a land ideal for European settlement. 'A more charming region is probably not to be found in all Africa,' its leader, Joseph Thomson, wrote. Park-like, cool and green, it was blessed with familiar-looking flowering shrubs, noble forests, and 'pine-like woods [where] you can gather sprigs of heath, sweet-scented clover, anemone, and other familiar forms'. Here, 'great herds of cattle, or flocks of sheep and goats are seen wandering knee-deep in the splendid pasture'. What would Thomson have made of a lone Maasai herder, etched against the horizon? 'The greater part of Lykipia – and the richer portion – is quite uninhabited,' he declared.

In 1890 Frederick Lugard also reported finding these magnificent uplands and that they were uninhabited. 'Covered with luxuriant pasture throughout the year . . . the specialty of this district would, I think, be the establishment of ranches and cattle-runs,' he said. With the acquisition of Uganda in 1895, and the decision to build a railway from the coast at Mombasa to the shores of Lake Victoria, the Foreign Office took over responsibility for the territory in between: British East Africa, the country we now call Kenya.

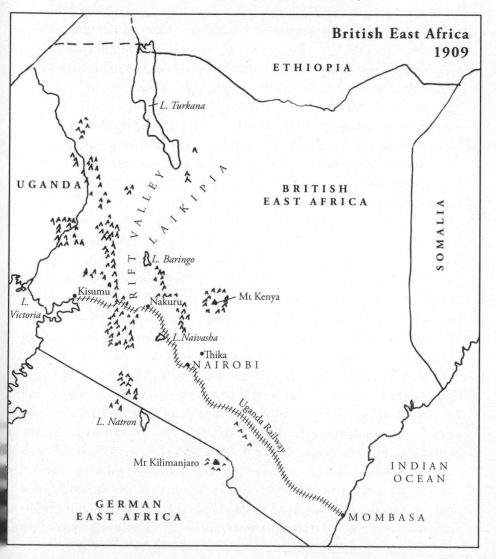

After years of huge and dangerous toil on the railway – by thousands of imported Indian labourers – the 'great snake stretching from sea to lake' was finished at last. Foretold by a prophet of the Maasai, the Ugandan railway sliced through their finest grazing grounds, in the Rift Valley. For the Maasai, who had grazed their flocks in these regions since time out of mind, nothing would ever be the same again.

In 1897 one of the first of the great flock of 'large white birds' the prophet had also foretold made his appearance. Twenty-seven-year-old Hugh Cholmondeley, third Baron Delamere, was well over a year into his fifth expedition hunting lion and elephant in Somaliland. After a 1,000-mile trek from Berbera on the Gulf of Aden through the deserts of Somalia, and into what is today northern Kenya, Delamere climbed the 4,000-foot escarpment from the hot basin around Lake Baringo, to come upon the vast open pastures of Laikipia. After a year in the grim desolation of the desert, his first glimpse of the grassy downs of the highlands sweeping towards the lush foothills of Mount Kenya was a revelation. To him, too, the region seemed empty. Clear, cool water ran in the streams; the breeze was fresh; banks of cloud massed on the horizon. Here, surely, was the promised land, a rich and fertile country that a man like him could make his own.

After his first sight of Laikipia, it took Delamere almost six years to return to East Africa to settle. In the meantime, he had mortgaged the estate in Cheshire that had nurtured his family since 1615 and collected a wife. He was thirty-three. Small, ginger-haired and immensely tough, Delamere was wilful and reckless, charming, flamboyant and extravagant, with a temper he had never been taught to control. He had been in trouble at Eton – racing at Ascot, wrecking a boot shop in Windsor – and had a passion for hunting, speed and adventure. After coming into his inheritance at the age of seventeen, he spent no more than two years of conventional landowning life in England – winters of hunting and the 'season' in London – before setting off to travel: Corsica, New Zealand and work on an Australian sheep station. In 1892, at the age of twenty-one, he made his first trip to Somaliland on a quest for big game. For four years he returned, each time mounting more and more lavish expeditions. In vain did his trustees write him dignified letters warning him of imminent bankruptcy.

In January 1903, Delamere walked into the small tin shed that served as the land office in the middle of Nairobi. In Maasai, '*nairobi*' means 'cold'. Here, on a bleak, windswept and treeless veldt, the feeding place for thousands of wild animals, was the last open space with room for trains to shunt before the railway set off on its steep climb up the Kikuyu escarpment towards Lake Victoria. When Delamere arrived the place consisted of a sprawl of hasty sheds and a squalid quarter of about 5,000 Indian railway workers. The permanent European population numbered a few dozen. Delamere put in a formal application for 100,000 acres of sheep-grazing land in Laikipia, and set up camp outside. With him were his wife, Florence, twenty-five, the daughter of the Earl of Enniskillen, and her two brothers, Galbraith and Berkeley Cole.

The British High Commissioner, Sir Charles Eliot, rejected Delamere's request for land at Laikipia on the grounds that it was too far from the railway. Undaunted, Delamere next applied for a vast block in the Rift Valley running down from the Aberdares to Lake Naivasha. But this, he was told, might cause hardship to the Maasai. On his third attempt, he was permitted to purchase 100,000 acres to the north-west, at Njoro.

Apart from the railway line, none of East Africa had been surveyed; no one knew what land was occupied by what kind of Africans. British East Africa was scarcely regarded even as a protectorate; in London, responsibility for it lay in the Africa department of the Foreign Office, currently run by little more than one man. There was no land policy.

It was left to the commissioner, the man on the spot, somehow to muddle through. Sir Charles Eliot was the son of a Wiltshire clergyman, a brilliant scholar, linguist and diplomat, who had served in Russia, Tangier, Constantinople and Washington. While the railway to Uganda was still under construction, he took charge of a region that was fast becoming known among the world's millionaires as the best big-game shooting-ground on earth. Eliot could not abide big-game killing, and could not cope with Africans. The 'astonishing exhibitions of nudity' of the Maasai disgusted him; he found their customs of war horrific and brutal.

'Their habits may be interesting to anthropologists, but they are socially and politically abominable,' he wrote. Their love of cattle raiding was a danger to the public peace, the arrangements whereby their young warrior castes lived unmarried in villages with immature girls was 'a moral scandal . . . physically disastrous for the race'. Segregating them in separate reserves would simply isolate them, and confirm them in degenerate habits.

'We have in East Africa the rare experience of dealing with a *tabla rasa,* an almost untouched and sparsely inhabited country, where we can do as we will,' he went on. Much better to mix the Maasai up among Europeans and civilize them. He set up grants of 640 acres in the region next to Delamere's farm, free to any white settlers who applied. While Delamere began doing all he could to promote these gifts in England, Eliot dispatched his commissioner of customs on a marketing expedition to South Africa. The news of free land grants was eagerly received in the depression and general discontent of the end of the Boer War. Was British East Africa to become the last refuge of the *voortrekker*? By early 1904, hundreds of families began crowding into Nairobi, eager to take up free lands, while from England sailed a growing stream of titled aristocrats down on their luck. The land office was besieged.

When Lord Lansdowne, the Foreign Secretary in London, went over Eliot's head to grant a syndicate of South African and London financiers *five hundred square miles* of prized Maasai lands in the Rift Valley to prospect for minerals, Eliot, who had been waiting months for permission from London to make two modest grants to two South African farmers, resigned. Was this newfound land to be solely the possession of the white man? The position of the Maasai had to be clarified. In the summer of 1904, his successor, Sir Donald Stewart, opened negotiations with their elders.

From first contact, around 1885, relations between the British and the Maasai had been friendly, even admiring. In the years that followed, they often sought refuge at British forts from warfare that threatened to engulf them. For their part, the British prized the Maasai as first-rate interpreters and guides. Of all the peoples along the railway line to Uganda, only the Maasai left materials and supplies untouched. The British often employed their warriors as mercenaries in helping suppress other uprisings. One of their elders, Ole Gilisho, had led some of these warriors. Unaware that by tradition the Maasai had no one leader, the British elevated the prophet Olonana to the position of 'paramount chief'. Both he and Ole Gilisho were put on the government payroll.

By 1904 Maasai stocks had been devastated by rinderpest and the people themselves decimated by smallpox, and years of drought and famine. Stewart proposed that the Maasai relinquish their grazing grounds between today's towns of Naivasha and Nakuru in the central Rift Valley and move to two reserves: one in Laikipia in the north, the other, south on the border with German East Africa – today's Tanzania. Five square miles near Naivasha, the sacred site of Kinangop, was to be reserved for Maasai circumcision ceremonies, which were held every eight years, and a road along a half-mile strip between these two reserves was to be constructed for their use. The

Maasai were in no position to argue. Stewart swore to them that this agreement 'would endure so long as the Masai [*sic*]as a race shall exist'.

Stewart was fully aware of Delamere's and his two brothers-in-laws' desire for land in Laikipia, and knew how powerful they could be. 'I cannot express too strongly to your Lordship, the absolute necessity of making these Laikipia lands an absolute native reserve for the Masai,' he wrote to the Secretary of State at the Foreign Office. In February 1905, the Maasai began their move out of the Rift Valley. On 1 April, the Foreign Office in London handed a single volume of correspondence to the Colonial Office – and with it responsibility for British East Africa.

The CO was far from clear what should be done with this promising new territory. African policy was balanced between protecting black interests in the colonies of west Africa, and promoting those of white settlers in the south. The magnificent central highlands of British East Africa were clearly an enviable resource. But ought they really to be settled by Europeans? The presence of thousands of labourers who had been brought in from the vastly overcrowded continent of India to build the Uganda railway suggested that surely here was a natural outlet for Indian emigration?

Meanwhile, in the burgeoning town of Nairobi, all the talk, fuelled by Lord Delamere, was of building a white man's country. Unpleasant incidents took place, such as when the president of the newly formed Colonists Association publicly flogged three black men in the front of the courthouse. Exchanges of dispatches to London took weeks. The issue of who should settle the country, who should live where, dragged on. Stewart died – of complications of pneumonia and drink. The first full governor, Colonel James Hayes-Sadler, arrived, ex-India army, ex-Uganda, amiable, industrious and completely incapable of making decisions. The officials he inherited had worked in the field for years with African communities. They firmly believed that black interests had to be protected from the pressures of white settlers. The Colonial Office agreed.

At the end of 1907, Winston Churchill, Under-Secretary of State at the Colonial Office, on his way to see Hesketh Bell in Uganda, came to see for himself. Nairobi was filled with raw energy and tension. 'A typical South African township', he declared – rent with political and racial discord: 'the white man *versus* the black; the Indian *versus* both', officials versus settlers, the railway administration versus the protectorate generally.

Churchill the politician soothed and placated, but refused to commit himself to a vision of what kind of country this might be. Poor Hayes-Sadler

– 'Flannelfoot' as Lady Delamere christened him – was no match for the demands of what Churchill described as 'unruly' settlers. Many of them were struggling after two terrible growing seasons, in what was, for all its beauty, a strange, cruel and unpredictable land. The Africans, by whom work with hand tools was regarded as degrading, did not care to supply them with labour. The situation needed a firm hand. In April 1909 the Colonial Office relegated Hayes-Sadler to the Windward Islands.

His replacement, Sir Percy Girouard, by contrast, was a man to conjure with. Over the past twelve years he had laid down a network of railways in north, south and west Africa. Exceptionally for a governor of a British colony, he was a colonial himself – and the white settlers of East Africa liked that idea. A Roman Catholic French Canadian, whose forefathers had settled in Quebec in the early eighteenth century, his father was an eminent Montreal lawyer, a member of the federal parliament, and had just been appointed deputy governor-general of Canada.

Such antecedents would have made Girouard an unusual man to be found in the British army at any time: young 'Gerry', as he was known in the family, grew up in a substantial stone house near McGill University in what is now downtown Montreal, a serious, sensitive child with a precocious interest in geography and world trade. At the age of twelve his family was fractured by the death of his beloved mother. Within three months, in September 1879, he and his older sisters had been dispatched to boarding schools: he to Trois Rivières – a crude pulp and paper town on the banks of the St Lawrence River in Quebec – where he was enrolled in the Collège St Joseph. The college was a seminary under the strenuous spiritual direction of a radical conservative bishop whose message of faith depended upon the preservation of the French language and culture that had been imported to French Canada in the time of Louis XIV. The regime was built on self-denial, frugal and strict in the extreme: up before dawn, Mass twice a day, long retreats of prayer, silence and contemplation. For Girouard, whose mother had been the gentle daughter of an Irish doctor, it was a harsh and lonely existence, designed to nurture either a deep sense of guilt – or rebellion.

Girouard adopted the discipline of the seminary, but left French Canada behind. Thanks to strenuous lobbying by his father, he scraped into the Royal Military College at Kingston – and engineering. Then it all began: his love affair with railways. There was mapping and surveying, laying out the final stages of the Canadian Pacific Railway, west of Winnipeg. Girouard loved nothing better than the sight of virgin land to be laid bare, levelled, trammelled and tracked. He won his way to the Royal Arsenal at Woolwich. Then in July 1895 he was introduced to the Sirdar of the Egyptian army, the great Sir Herbert Kitchener himself.

Kitchener invited him to join his railway party, which was preparing to advance south from Egypt into the Sudan. 'I felt that my hour had come,' he recalled in the dry, unfinished memoir of his life. The War Office refused to let him go. But, having flouted the priests who would have kept him in the church, and his father, in the law, Girouard's attitude to British military authority was cavalier. When news came the following spring that Kitchener was advancing south towards Dongola in the Sudan, he had the audacity to cable him personally. 'May I come now?'

Build a desert railway from Wadi Halfa (south of Abu Simbel) to Berber (north of Khartoum)? Ridiculous! Impossible! But Lieutenant Girouard took it on. 'Rock and Sand, Dust Storms, Heat and Flies,' he wrote. A mile a day, for 250 miles. Kitchener could scarcely contain his impatience. Girouard's preparations were so meticulous they filled a volume several inches thick, 'and such was the comprehensive accuracy of the estimate that the working parties were never delayed by the want of even a piece of brass wire'. Thus wrote Winston Churchill, who at the age of twenty-two interviewed a bronzed and confident thirty-year-old Girouard in Cairo. Girouard, with his humour and trans-Atlantic bravado, inspired a contagious sense of personal invincibility that young Winston could not resist. By then no member of Kitchener's famous 'Band of Boys' was quite so close to the great general as this young Canadian.

From the railways of Sudan to the presidency of the Egyptian State Railway at the age of thirty-one; the following year, 1899, Girouard was dispatched to the Boer War in South Africa, in charge of the railways for the South African Field Force. And who else could have delivered the trains on time, and kept them running – the crucial means of communication – through weeks of incessant bomb blasts and guerrilla sabotage? At one place he laid eighty miles of track in forty-eight hours. He brooked no interference. When the War Office queried his estimates, Girouard went over its head to Joe Chamberlain himself. By the time the war was over in 1902, 'the famous Girouard', as Arthur Conan Doyle called him in his history of the Boer War, had been knighted, and invited to stay on as commissioner of railways for the Transvaal and Orange River colonies.

He was exhausted. It was in Pretoria, in the comfortable home of Sir

Richard Solomon, Attorney-General and Lieutenant Governor of the Transvaal, and his wife, Elizabeth, that he found respite. Here, thirty-six-year-old Sir Percy first met their twenty-one-year-old daughter, Gwendolen. Slim, dark-haired and shy, she was their much-loved only child. Sir Richard and his wife were children of nonconformist missionaries. Having grown up among the Griqua, Sir Richard was known for his principles and liberal sympathies for the black and dispossessed.

One evening Gwen sat listening to all the troubles Sir Percy was having trying to persuade hard-bitten members of his railway board in Johannesburg – owners of gold companies and hostile Afrikaners – to agree the costs of running the railways. The cost of freight was seen as the main cause of the rising cost of living in the Transvaal. The next day she wrote to him. 'I am only a child in some ways, and you are a very clever man, but . . . you told me last night that no-one in this world cares whether you live or die, or whether you do well or badly. Never think that again because there is one person who cares more than a little and who would give a great deal to be able to help a little . . .'

Their wedding on 10 September 1903 was all that could be wished for: the cathedral at Pretoria massed with tropical palms and arum lilies, Girouard in scarlet dress uniform, Gwen demure in white veil. Swords flashed, trumpets blared, the wedding cake was imported from London, and fifty brawny Royal Engineers pulled the bridal carriage to the station draped with flags and bunting. A cheering crowd of 2,000 saw the bridal couple off on the first leg of their honeymoon in England.

They stayed at Brown's Hotel in London. Girouard spent the day visiting the Colonial Office and the clubs. 'I generally say goodbye to him after breakfast and never see him again till dinner-time when we nearly always dine out,' Gwen told his father in Montreal. 'We meet some interesting people but they talk of nothing in the world but this Fiscal Question, till one gets quite tired of it.' Gwen enjoyed politics – up to a point. She and Girouard returned to South Africa in December. He was immediately summoned to the Cape to discuss railway finances.

It seems Sir Percy was not quite the financial genius Churchill had suggested. In June 1904 Lord Milner, High Commissioner of South Africa, sacked him as head of the railway board: 'With every recognition of your great service and your eminent ability in *your army line,* I do not think [finance and general business] are your strong points,' he told him. In December 1904, Girouard sailed for England grimly determined to lobby for something more interesting than the 'regimental grind' as a staff officer he had been offered at Chatham. Perhaps he might stand for parliament? Gwen, pregnant with their first child, followed with her parents in the spring. Sir Richard was to be High Commissioner for South Africa in London. They settled in a house at Studland Bay in Dorset; Girouard stayed in London during the week, commuting home to see them at weekends.

Girouard's friend Winston Churchill was in the Colonial Office as Under-Secretary of State for the Colonies when Sir Frederick Lugard resigned as high commissioner of Northern Nigeria in the summer of 1906. His Kano to Sokoto campaign had demonstrated the imperative need for a 350-mile railway line from Baro in the south to Kano in Northern Nigeria. What was wanted was 'a no frills' effort, but the work of an expert. Churchill called him in, metaphorically flung the files at him and asked for the answers. Who else now for Northern Nigeria but Sir Percy? 'On Christmas day I received a very nice present in the shape of an offer from Lord Elgin of the high commissionership of Northern Nigeria,' he told his father.

'Napoleonic both in compass and precision!' This was Churchill's view of Girouard's 'comprehensive analysis of the Baro–Kano Railway and the Niger River Transport System', which he delivered after six months in Nigeria. In other areas, Girouard followed Lugard's instructions to the letter, implemented a land policy that safeguarded it for the people, and established 'native' treasuries. He returned to London on leave in April 1909, his reputation as a man of action redeemed, just as 'Flannelfoot' Sadler was moved from Nairobi to the West Indies. Churchill was keen to keep Girouard in Northern Nigeria until the railway line, the costs of which he had personally guaranteed, was complete, but the new Secretary of State, Lord Crewe, concerned about economic stagnation in East Africa, considered Girouard 'the most likely man . . . to set things going'. He sounded Girouard out. Girouard replied tactfully that he would leave the question of transfer from west to East Africa 'to the public interest'. By August he was writing: 'I am on a German boat a disgrace to a British Colony that we should have no British line.'

He was bound for Mombasa, and hard at work on a book which he called 'The Imperial Idea', a historical analysis of the evolution of government in British colonies, keeping a new ADC, John Murray, and his private secretary, Captain Pat O'Brien, typing all day. Gwen, Lady Girouard, with whom he had perhaps spent five months in the past three years, was to follow him to

Kenya in November. They had taken the difficult decision to leave their four-year-old son, Dickie, with her parents in England.

Sir Percy Girouard disembarked at Mombasa in sweltering heat in September 1909: a slight, rounded figure wearing a cork helmet and carrying a swagger stick, a conspicuous row of medals and clasps pinned to his white uniform. He was forty-two. Beneath the brim of his helmet, his monocle seemed to dominate his face: pudgy, rather ugly, moustached, and unyielding. His manner was gruff. He had developed a tendency to bark. When he took his hat off, his thinning fair hair seemed plastered to his head.

Secretly the idea of East Africa unnerved him. Running Northern Nigeria, 'a purely native protectorate' of civilized and sophisticated emirs, had been a relatively clear-cut operation. Lugard had bequeathed him a meticulous set of instructions, a well-ordered administration and a cadre of trained and experienced officers. Government took place through the Nigerian rulers, using African ideals. In fact it left him free to do much as he liked. 'Excepting for the hold of the Secretary of State, I am a little independent king,' he had told his father. There had certainly been no councils to bother with, or bolshie white settlers.

Gwen would follow in two months' time. In the meantime, his schedule was prodigious: Mombasa, then to Nairobi to settle into Government House, followed by a four-week tour of the protectorate and Uganda. British East Africa presented a complex scenario: 200,000 square miles, roughly the size of France, much of it a mix of highland and dry savannah. Beyond a strip along the coast, hot, humid, fever-ridden, belonging to the Sultan of Zanzibar was the 'Northern Frontier', a great lawless swathe of country to the north-west that had scarcely been explored, much less brought into administration. Here borders were undefined, subject to raids by Ethiopians and Somalis armed with guns. There were 4 million people, of whom no more than 2,000 were European; peoples of all kinds, speaking Arabic, Swahili, Bantu languages; former Indian railway workers, speaking Hindi; the Maasai, the Kikuyu, and the Luo. For British defence, there were two battalions of the King's African Rifles and a couple of handfuls of British officers.

The British had defined seven provinces, each headed by a provincial commissioner. These were divided into districts and sub-districts, headed by district officers, most of them old hands from before the days of the protectorate, used to autonomy, sympathetic to the Africans they lived among, and who had the habit, disconcerting to a man in Girouard's position, of calling in at the Colonial Office whenever they were in London to organize changes to their own district.

Girouard had not built his railways with sweet talk, or by permitting insubordination. 'He shakes hands in a funny way. He gives you his hand, gives you a good look out of one of his eyes, which one you cannot make out, that's all. Not a word does he utter,' recorded one assistant commissioner who never got over his fear of Girouard. Soon after he took over in Nairobi officials were seen to be scurrying into their offices at unusually early hours.

Lord Delamere was waiting for him. By now his ginger hair grew long over his shoulders. He wore an enormous sun helmet, old khaki breeches and a woolly cardigan. He was the undisputed leader of the settlers; politics surrounded him: questions of labour, land laws, water rights. Delamere and his cronies – they now included thirty-year-old Lord Cranworth and his wife Vera, Lord Hindlip and half-a-dozen sons of other peers of the realm – were self-reliant, disparaging of British convention, impatient of bureaucracy, set on making East Africa their own, and above all, capable of making a big fuss at the centres of power in London.

Within six weeks of arriving in East Africa, at the end of October, Girouard was staying as Delamere's guest at his house at Elmenteita, on the first stage of his journey to Uganda. There were few white men who could tell him more about the Maasai. As Delamere liked to tell it, a small party of them had walked up to his first farm at Njoro soon after his first sheep arrived from England.

'We have heard that a white man has come who is bringing many sheep and cattle and that he claims to know better how to herd them than we do. We wish to see,' they told him. As his fences went up, and his ewes began to breed, they asked him how long he would stay.

'I shall stay for ever.'

'Then we will look after your sheep. You do not understand the pastures. You do not understand sheep. We will help you.' From that time the Maasai had worked for him as herdsmen, gathering to squat on the floor in his tin house in the evenings, discussing the habits of the animals, the character of the pasture, into the night.

How much time Girouard would have had to talk politics on this visit is debatable, for staying too were former US President Teddy Roosevelt and his son Kermit – on a hugely publicized expedition to collect specimens of big game and other mammals for the Smithsonian Institution in Washington.

Over drinks before dinner, Delamere and Roosevelt made a heady mix. But Girouard, noted in London for rather vulgar manners, but also for brains and wit, held his own. 'At last we have a man at the head of affairs who is really interested in the country and wants it to prosper,' wrote Lady Delamere, while Girouard reported to the Colonial Office: 'I really believe that Delamere will become a firm friend.'

Girouard was already bombarding London with telegrams urging immediate staff changes. By the middle of November, he had put the final touches to a monumental dispatch on British East Africa. 'No one can quite guess the administrative chaos of this place,' he told the Secretary of State. General policy was 'practically non-existent'. There was one judicial approach to African issues in Nairobi; others in the provinces. He wanted immediate improvements: a new economic strategy based on exports; the creation of a strong administrative machine and everything possible that could be done – as in Northern Nigeria – to develop African institutions. Meanwhile, the white settlers had to be encouraged to take active participation in government. That there might be a contradiction between these two strands of policy seems not to have occurred to him. It took the officials at the Colonial Office some weeks to digest his dispatch – the most detailed document on the region they had ever received. When they did so, they were impressed. Girouard wanted a free hand, and he wanted to get on with it. If they didn't like what he wanted to do, he told them, he would resign.

Government House, Nairobi, 22 November 1909: 'My own Darlings,' Gwen wrote to her parents. 'Here we are arrived quite safely . . . First of all I must tell you both that Gerry had been his very sweetest and nicest ever since we came . . . and that, as far as it is possible away from you three darlings, I am happy and *very* well . . . Gerry met me at Mombassa, came on the boat about seven o'clock full of spirits . . . I had been up for hours watching us steam into the harbour, it is the prettiest island like a fairy tale, all palms and so green and tropical but oh! The heat. One mops oneself all the time. We went off in a little Government launch straight to our own house which is charming . . . looking over the sea and a flagged courtyard and a great comfy hall and easy chairs, punkas going everywhere.'

Gwen was now twenty-seven. She had travelled out from England with her cousin Anna Walton, who was two years younger, her maid Bird, and Bobbie Oppenheim, son of the well-known banker and art collector Henry Oppenheim. Bobbie was a second lieutenant in the Dragoon Guards. He

51. Henry Hesketh Bell among his animal trophies, Uganda, *c*.1909. He hated hunting.

52. The view of Entebbe and Lake Victoria from Government House, Uganda, 1908.

53. One of the first medical missionaries in Uganda, dispensing medicine, 1892.

54. 'Just such a house as the mayor of a provincial town would build for himself when he retired from business': Bell's new Government House at Entebbe, with his pet lion cubs on the lawn.

55. The drawing room and hall at Government House, Entebbe.

56. 'We Wale! We Wale!' Sir Henry Hesketh Bell departs from Kampala 3 May 1909.

57. Sir Sydney Olivier as Governor of Jamaica, 1907.

58. Margaret Olivier in Jamaica, c.1908.

59. The Olivier girls with their father in Kingston, Jamaica, c.1901. Left to right, Margery, aged fifteen, Daphne, twelve, Bryn, fourteen, and Noel, nine.

60. Earthquake damage, Jamaica, January 1907.

61. Loading bananas at Kingston, Jamaica, c.1900.

62. Sir Percy Girouard and his syce in British East Africa, 1909.

63. Gwen Girouard on safari, 1909.

64. Mr Elkington's hunt ('a very rich man, a real Sussex country squire') assembles before Government House, Nairobi. He arranged to hold it on Wednesdays, rather than on Sunday mornings, so that the Governor's wife, Gwen, could join them.

65. Staying with the Delameres at Elmenteita, December 1909. From second left: Girouard's ADC John Murray, Gwen Lady Delamere, Anna Walton, Percy Girouard, Lord Delamere.

66. Fording a river on safari, December 1909.

67. Hugh Clifford, soon after he arrived in the Malay States, aged twenty-four.

68. Clifford, back right, towered over the Malays in the province of Pahang.

69. Hugh Clifford and his new wife, Elizabeth de la Pasture, on honeymoon in Devon, September 1910.

70. Sir Hugh Clifford, his eyes luminously vacant, in full gubernatorial regalia, not long before retirement.

71. Where Clifford loved to spend time as acting Governor of Ceylon: the King's Pavilion, Kandy.

was coming to stay with the Girouards in East Africa for six months to recover his health.

'We were met at the wharf by all the ladies of Mombassa and three children with a gigantic bouquet! And in the afternoon we went and opened a fancy fair.' Gwen could not contain herself. She always wrote in one long, unstoppable sentence. 'All our gallant soldiers in full uniform and Anna and I in white muslin and sun helmets were motored down in little trolleys, there are no horses in the whole of Mombassa and everyone drives in these things guided by their black boys most perilously fast going down hill. There were three thousand Arabs at the Fair and the whole of the white residents . . . they played "God Save the King" and they all cheered and I felt a thousand cameras clicking at me when Gerry was making his speech, and I was shyer than I have ever been in my life before!'

Early the next morning they started off by train to Nairobi. 'We have a very comfy coach and travelled up in a special with every luxury and were up about five the next morning and on the cowcatcher to see what game we could see. We prayed to find a lion but there were not any, but we saw three giraffes quite near the line and hundreds of hartebeest and wildebeest and zebra. They don't even stop grazing as the train goes by and they are so pretty. I don't believe I shall ever have the heart to shoot any . . .

'All the ladies of Nairobi met me here and a guard of honour and a bouquet and I was introduced to them all. I really hardly know myself! It is just like a very small, very straggly Pretoria, this place.'

Nairobi was growing fast. Thick red dust clogged the streets in the dry season, which turned to a sea of mud in the rains. But trees were springing up, and hotels were being built. The Norfolk Hotel, 'The True Home of the Big Game Shooter' – boasted that it had played host to one marquis, three earls, five lords and three foreign counts 'and many others of the World's finest Sportsmen' in its first season. Two hundred and fifty *voortrekkers* had just arrived. The population – mainly Indian – had risen to 16,000. The European population was still only a few hundred.

Government House was two miles outside the town, a spreading stone-built house, half-timbered in mock Tudor style; capacious and substantial, with wide lawns and spreading views from the verandah. Gwen thought it *'hideous* inside and out, like the most appalling suburban villa, but one must confess it is comfortable, my bedroom is charming. I am writing there now. It's the best room in the house and has its own bathroom and everything next door.'

Bird took care of her clothes, dressed her hair, guarded the door if she felt 'seedy' – and when she came down with malaria. She never shared a room with Girouard – on safari, she roomed with Anna, while Bird was left in Nairobi. She had nothing to do with running the house, which was looked after by Girouard's thirty-year-old ADC, John Murray. She liked him. He 'is splendid, he simply works all day long and against enormous difficulties, the boys are legion. I never get to the end of them all, and they won't work, we have a magnificent youth black as your hat, called Oussimi or "all that is beautiful" who is supposed to work under Bird and each of the men has their own boy besides the stable ones and the kitchen ones and a Hindoo butler and Monkton as a sort of steward! What the cost of it will all be I simply can't conceive.'

Within her first day she had seen the stables ('I've got a darling little racing pony called Silvermane'), called on their nearest neighbours, Lord and Lady Cranworth ('I felt so sorry for them in their tiny little house rather unhealthy with their two little children'), and had the Delameres to dinner. On day two, she had her first callers, thirty women, all afternoon. 'It really was awful. All these strange women came in and stayed hours and hours. I have now found out that Lady Sadler used to be at home every afternoon between three and five, so I have decided to say "not at home" to everyone unless they are especially asked to tea.'

Gwen was merely a consort: a flighty, volatile consort for Girouard. She was young, smart and well dressed – with a tendency to alarm the South Africans with her liberal views, inherited from her father. She was selfish and tactless, telling off Lord Delamere for infringements of etiquette, while Girouard 'sizzled in his chair', and a merciless snob. 'Some of the people were *so* funny . . . Two women curtsied quite low to me and oh! their clothes!' But she was full of life and laughter.

'I can't say the people here are exciting and very few of the officials strike me as being clever,' Gwen told her father. Everyone she met seemed to have ended up in East Africa because they were broke. Mr Jackson, the Lieutenant Governor, 'came to this country to shoot, lost all his money and stayed on as an official'. Mr Elkington 'was a very rich man, a real Sussex country squire with an awfully nice ugly wife who lives for hunting – and they lost all their money and are breeding horses'. Anna was shocked by another white settler, who cheerfully declared: 'We're all black sheep and ne'er do wells out here!'

The talk was all of big-game hunting. An American millionaire had come to inspect the country with a balloon and a group of photographers to take pictures of animals in the wild; a doctor, Atkinson, who had accompanied Lord Delamere on his early expeditions in Somalia 'was here last week. He has been in the country for twelve years and he once shot 21 elephants in a fortnight – his stories made us gasp simply.' Sometimes they danced, but the best part of dinner parties was when Anna sang afterwards.

How she missed her parents, how she longed to be with them for Christmas! It had cost her more than she could ever say to part with them and Dickie, she had told them as she sailed, 'a little stranger going out into the wilderness', promising 'to try and make a success of it all'.

She and Anna spent two hours every morning doing the flowers, fresh for every room in the house. Within less than a fortnight, she was hosting an 'enormous' reception. 'About 300 people and a black band and the most gorgeous tea and I have *never* seen such an odd collection in all my life, every tradesman in the place and all their wives . . .' But then she *had* to practise with her rifle, 'and there are all these new and unbroken ponies to try'. The altitude was 'trying', it tired her out, and gave her and Anna 'real bad blues'. As for Girouard, 'his nerves have been very bad for the last two days and he was rather bad last night at dinner – the first time he has made a scene'.

The arrival of Gwen, with Anna and Bobbie, young, fun-loving and frivolous, was doing nothing for Girouard's nerves. Quite apart from the age difference between them, in their six years of marriage the Girouards had only spent weekends and brief holidays in Spain and Italy together. He was used to command, to living entirely in the company of men. Yet it was Gwen's vulnerability and shyness that had first attracted him to her. He wrote illustrated letters to Dickie, which today remain striking for their humour and a tenderness, which, on the rare occasions on which she tried, Gwen could never match. He could be charming and funny, a clever mimic who never failed to get an encore for his singing of the French-Canadian 'Alouette' after dinner. At the same time he was a martinet, intensely driven, a perfectionist who was unable to endure opposition. Now he was anxious to get on with the reforms he had outlined to the Colonial Office in his long dispatch, worried about money (apart from his salary, he had no income, and Gwen was extravagant); irritated to distraction over not hearing from London on a grant to extend Government House – absolutely essential if everyone was not to live in tents – for a visit planned by the Duke and Duchess of Connaught early in the new year.

*'Mummy and the dead buffalo': Girouard's sketch for his son,
Dickie, of one of Gwen's early hunting triumphs*

Three weeks after Gwen arrived, on 14 December, the household set off for a month's safari: Gwen, Girouard, Anna, Bobbie and John Murray, a holiday for the ladies, a working trip for Girouard. 'I wish you could see Anna and me in our safari clothes . . . the very shortest skirts to our knees, a Norfolk coat, bandanna handkerchiefs round our necks. Leather gaiters and huge khaki sun helmets, we look just like bush rangers!' she told her parents. She had learned to ride astride and was getting quite good with her gun. They travelled through 'glorious green country', stopping for Girouard to interview South African farmers, and to visit a mission where chiefs' sons were being taught. Gwen went off to shoot buck with Bobbie – 'the first shot I fired I was so excited that my gun kicked and hit me on the nose until I bled like a *pig* – but I hopped off my pony and tore after another and didn't mind a bit – it was all so thrilling! I wish you could see our safari, over 300 carriers, the wildest looking warriors with hardly any clothes on, and then the cooks and people on mules and all our ponies.'

They met 500 'wild Lumbwa people in all their war-paint, mostly beads and savage spears and shields and they make a red paint out of castor oil and pigment which goes over all their heads and faces. Really very fine they looked – and in the evening they did us a wonderful war dance – hundreds of them with feathers in their heads and chanting and making fierce noises.'

Sunday, December 19th

Near Sotik

It is pouring with rain and I am sitting in a grass hut in a clearing in the middle of the bush. We started at six o'clock this morning and rode 15 miles in the blazing sun with a break for breakfast and I have been asleep for *two* solid hours and feel much revived and rested. We really had had the most delicious time so far . . .we met [two officers] coming back from their shoot [who] looked the most awful ruffians with enormous beards and open shirts and football shorts and very brown legs. Not the least like smart Guardsmen . . . They [had] got several lion and put up a herd of 300 elephant not very far from where we are going . . . Wherever we go they have a grass hut . . . to feed in and all our tents grouped round it, the flag in the middle and camp fires round us at night. Sentries walking up and down . . . we sit round the fire in the evenings and spin yarns and listen to the gramophone! I *do* love it so . . .

All our men except Gerry are growing beards and look the most awful ruffians. Bobbie is a different creature and I think this life may be the making of him. Anna is happy and so sweet and good. I keep wanting you and longing to tell you things and sometimes when I am sitting by the fire in the evenings I get such a craving on me for you all, my darlings – just a feeling that I want to be loved – oh! dear . . . God bless you all and kiss my little boy.

For two days they stayed with the Delameres at Elmenteita. 'They have a dear little shanty looking right over a lake with the loveliest range of mountains and great trees and tropical flowers,' Gwen wrote. She and Anna stayed in the house, while the men slept in their tents in the garden. Lady Delamere is 'so plucky and clever and amusing. I have never seen anything like her appearance. She wears any sort of clothes and her hair just tied with a ribbon and an old red kimono in the evenings. The lake was all covered with flamingoes and we went out in a little boat to shoot some to make a fan for me. Then we had a tremendous day pig-sticking, galloped down some eland and shot two.'

It was in these days before Christmas that talk turned again to the Maasai and the delicious pastures to the north in Laikipia. Vets had observed how the East Coast fever that decimated the cattle settlers were trying to breed in the Rift Valley seemed curiously absent from the Maasai pastures in

Laikipia. Would it not be for the best to unite the Maasai in a single large reservation in the south, away from the finest land in Kenya, so obviously designed for white agriculture? The idea had been floating about the Land Office for months. Indeed, Girouard's safari was intended to take him into the region proposed as an extension to the existing southern reserve. There was no doubt that administratively things would be easier for the government if the Maasai were settled in one region.

The Maasai ceremonies of circumcision were due to take place the coming spring. Hundreds would be gathering from north and south at Kinangop in the Rift Valley. Would this be a good time for talks? Girouard drafted a dispatch to London.

22 January 1910: 'I *am* astonished at what you say about people here criticising me for not being "at home",' Gwen wrote to her parents. 'I have had one big reception and two big tea-parties. I am always in every Sunday afternoon and very often on the other days as well – but one can't go out in the middle of the day here so between four and 6.30 is our only time for getting any exercise – so we always walk or ride or play tennis then and I *have* to say not at home.'

On their return to Nairobi, her packing cases had arrived. She was decorating the house for the imminent visit of the Duke and Duchess of Connaught, scheduled for the middle of Race Week in Nairobi. 'I have put all the tulip chintz in the drawing room, and the hall is blue.' The staircase had been polished. 'Then I have had Anna's room and mine all done in white – white matting on the floor and white linen on the chairs. The garden is ablaze with roses & carnations & we have them all over the house.' The prospect of the royal visit was putting everyone on edge. Anna – 'free love under one arm and anarchy under the other' – was 'going to wear a red tie when they come "to declare her Socialism" but as red does not suit her & she has a strong vein of vanity – I do not think she will do it', wrote Gwen. But Gerry was very nice, the visit went well, the races continued, and a day or two after the Connaughts departed, she gave a great ball, for 285.

'And all the settlers we asked came, people who would never go inside the Sadlers house – so I do think they must like us – we all danced until three o'clock and then talked it over for another hour!'

Girouard was proceeding rapidly on the Maasai front. On 2 February, the paramount chief Olonana visited him at Government House to request the Governor's support over trouble he was having with the *moran* – young male warriors – from the southern reserve. Olonana had been faithful to the British ever since a judicial inquiry into a massacre in 1895, in which an English trader was murdered, found that the Maasai had been so provoked that their only punishment ought to be the confiscation of cattle that had already been captured from them. But since the signing of the treaty of 1904, the open track that had been promised between Laikipia and the southern reserve had never become a reality. In the middle of 1908, the British government imposed quarantine restrictions to prevent the spread of East Coast fever in livestock; the Maasai had been forbidden to move their cattle along its course; hence they did not move at all. Girouard floated his proposal of moving the Maasai of Laikipia to the southern reserve. Would not uniting all his people in a single reserve strengthen Olonana's authority? Olonana agreed.

'Things are going fairly well enough,' Girouard told his father. 'I have settled down well and got a grip. Met my Legislative Council twice and found the unofficials not too refractory. It is a hard country to handle, so many divergent interests and a lot of discontent. The country itself is wonderful in beauty and possibilities and as I feel the best elements are with me hope to see material progress before too long.' Three weeks later, Girouard took time out from a lion-hunting trip in the Ngong hills – 'an enormous party', wrote Gwen; 'The food was simply awful . . . and not a lion did we see' – to hold talks with Delamere at Olonana's kraal. There he met the old warrior Legalishu, and Masikonde, the most senior elder of the Laikipia Maasai. Details of what exactly took place that day were never recorded – only that Legalishu and Masikonde consented to the Maasai move from Laikipia.

Girouard was jubilant. 'The result was a strikingly unanimous decision in favour of concentration in the Southern Reserve,' he wrote to London. This had not been a case of mere acquiescence, but real enthusiasm: 'a result – highly satisfactory to me'.

In Nairobi the weather had turned very hot. The wind was ceaseless, whipping up the dust, howling into corners. 'Everyone is sitting waiting for the rains to come,' wrote Gwen. 'Gerry has been extraordinarily trying and irritating just lately.' During the previous autumn he had applied for funds from the Treasury to build a branch line off the Uganda railway, from Nairobi north to Mount Kenya. The Colonial Office turned his plans down. Girouard shifted monies around in his budget, and by early March had started work on the earthworks for what he casually described as a forty-mile 'tramway' to Thika – a sparsely inhabited, but promising new district for white farmers, part of the way to Mount Kenya. Among the settlers, the project 'is seen as a big "coup" and has pleased everyone enormously', wrote Gwen, 'and it opens the country up'. Girouard's dilemma now was: how could he come clean with London about it, and secure the remaining funding? First in dispatches, then in telegrams, his arguments for the railway continued to be firmly rejected. Colonial Office officials were becoming concerned at Girouard's repeated assaults. 'It is becoming difficult to retain unimpaired confidence in Sir PG's judgement,' George Fiddes, the permanent under-secretary, observed. Moreover, administering a distant protectorate by telegram, interspersed by pages of detailed dispatches that took three weeks to arrive, was proving chaotic.

The day after Girouard's first meeting with Olonana, a medical officer wrote to his old professor at Oxford. Like many of the 'rank and file' in East Africa, he said, he was incensed at the wrong being dealt the Maasai. At the heart of the proposal to move the Maasai from Laikipia were the pressures of the settlers, not the wishes of the people themselves. Water was scarce in the southern reserve; the grazing could not compare with the lush pastures of Laikipia. 'If the Maasai knew enough they would appeal to the courts and win. Because they don't,' he demanded, 'we are going to wrong them?'

The letter landed at the Colonial Office like a small grenade. On 19 April the Secretary of State cabled Girouard. Any move by the Maasai was to be halted at once. He was to await instructions by dispatch.

In Kinangop, the circumcision ceremonies were nearly over. Many of the Maasai, having heard news of the new agreement and that the rains, which had been scanty in Laikipia, had been unusually abundant in the southern reserve, had already set off.

LARGE NUMBER ALREADY MOVED, ACTING ON ORDERS FROM LENANA. QUARANTINE WILL PREVENT ANY RETURN, Girouard replied by cable. It infuriated the CO. Who was telling the truth, the Governor or the doctor? It was 'amazing' that the Governor should have taken such an irrevocable step as moving the people without first obtaining permission from the Secretary of State. At the Colonial Office the whole business was beginning to take on 'a very ugly look'. It 'might easily become a very awkward question'. What credence had Girouard given to Stewart's binding treaty with the Maasai, guaranteeing them their lands for as 'long as the Maasai as a race exist'?

Gwen had returned to England with Anna and Bobbie, to be reunited with her son in the middle of April. In November Girouard arrived in London for talks with the Colonial Office. Over the summer he had produced a massive document proposing sweeping changes in the East African administration. In a private dispatch, he had excoriated his staff, arguing that many of them should be removed. They were an 'old gang' who thought their position unassailable. 'The situation had grown up to consider Joe or Brown or Robinson as the true exponent of policy on a particular line,' he complained. This would not do. Meanwhile, an Indian member of the Legislative Council, Alibhai Mulla Jeevanjee, who had made a fortune out of constructing the Uganda railway, had been making speeches in London claiming that a deliberate attempt was being made to debar Indians from commerce and agriculture in East Africa. At the same time, Delamere had merged various settler organizations into a single 'Convention of Settlers Committees' and had begun agitating for popular representation. Besides the treatment of the Maasai, all kinds of issues – the high cost of freight, the shortage of labour, and questions over development priorities such as tramways, port facilities, water supplies, postal services and codified laws – needed to be sorted out.

Britain was in the middle of a general election. As Girouard kicked his heels in London, all significant decisions had to be put on hold. In spite of this, he worked ceaselessly, generating enough paperwork to keep two officials and a private secretary busy. Discreetly a friend in the Colonial Office mentioned that an important shipbuilding and engineering company in Newcastle, Armstrong Whitworth, which also produced armaments and cars, was looking for a new managing director. Would Girouard be interested if he were able to put the job his way? Girouard was intrigued. He was apparently too busy to join Gwen, Dickie and her parents in the country until Christmas Eve.

Gwen had found his moods and bad temper increasingly difficult to tolerate. A carefree week spent with Anna, Bobbie and John Murray at Elementeita, just before she had sailed for England, had shown her a side of life that she had never known before. It was so good 'not to be scolded & found fault with and not to have to sit up on one's hind legs & entertain strangers!' It was only after serious discussion with her father that she was persuaded to return to Africa with her husband in February 1910. Anna came with her. At Aden the heat was almost unbearable. Girouard picked up a cable from the new Secretary of State for the Colonies, Lewis Harcourt: IT HAS BEEN DECIDED THAT THE MASAI SHALL NOT BE MOVED FROM THE NORTHERN RESERVE.

Girouard took his fury out on Gwen, whom he attacked before everyone at the lunch table for leaving a report he had written on her deckchair. 'Never tell my wife a thing you don't want the whole of London to know,' he said scornfully. She was too hopeless to be trusted with anything.

They landed at Mombasa to a nineteen-gun salute. At Nairobi 'there were 500 people on the station to meet us, including the soldiers, and as [Gerry] stepped out of the train the band played God Save the King and I thought they would never stop cheering'. She was determined to be on good behaviour.

26 February 1911: 'I go in to see Gerry every morning after breakfast now and talk business. I am being just as nice to him as I know how. He had a great explosion of wrath yesterday morning before breakfast because his photo was not on my dressing table – but I am beginning to think he is not responsible. He says the most impossible things and five minutes later he is ready to swear he never said them! On the whole he is very nice to me and you need not be afraid that I will play the game, my Dad – I have given you my promise.'

Gwen was miserable. She could never bear to see Vera Cranworth and her little boy – frequently down with malaria – without thinking of Dickie. But she was glad for his sake that she did not have him with her. The house – immaculately run by their butler, Monkton – was 'too much of a pandemonium', a constant stream of guests coming and going. She never had time alone. Nothing had really changed, but all of a sudden the pace seemed to have stepped up: the flowers, writing invitations, menus and dinner-cards; at night, dancing to the gramophone, learning the one-step and the Boston, keeping up with the new settlers arriving with young wives, the new romances, the new babies, and a stream of game-shooting guests. One of the ladies 'is very anxious to shoot a zebra for each of her sons so that they can have the skins in their rooms at Eton . . . [while] Prince Arthur is trying to get a lion on his way home . . .'

It was Gwen, not Girouard, who had become aware that many of the settlers did not like Lord Delamere, and increasingly distrusted his influence over the Governor. Pressure was mounting on Girouard. His old boss, Kitchener, was touring the country, demanding he put together for him 'the largest possible free grant of Crown Lands' in the country. For the first time, two white settlers had been murdered. Meanwhile, Girouard was expected to make a major speech to the annual gathering of settlers at the Nakuru Agricultural Show. There he knew he would have 'to confess he had done practically nothing at home and had been refused the alteration to land laws and the Maasai move – but', Gwen recorded loyally, 'he spoke with great firmness and they cheered him to the echo –'

Girouard, however, wasn't sleeping. He and Harcourt were spatting by cable. Delamere was being rude and distant, cold-shouldering him socially, arguing with him in public, co-ordinating opposition among the settlers towards him. Behind the scenes in Government House, John Murray, his ADC, was moody – 'always sparring with Gerry' – and talking of going home. Into this highly charged mix came the news that his chum in the Colonial Office was definitely putting the job with Armstrong Vickers (£5,000 a year for six years or £3,000 with a share in the profits) his way. On 20 March, the same day that Girouard and Delamere held a furious confrontation in the council chamber, news of the death of Olonana arrived at Government House. With his dying words he had exhorted the northern Maasai to abandon Laikipia and move to the south.

Early in April, the rains began in earnest. The weather was bitterly cold. On the fifth, a meeting of elders of the northern and southern Maasai was held in Ngong. According to Girouard, the Maasai declared that they wished to leave Laikipia of their own free will, and go to the southern reserve. First, all Europeans would have to be removed from that region, and better water supplies put in. He reported that a new agreement quite as formal and solemn as Stewart's of 1904 had been drawn up and signed.

10 April 1911: '[To dinner] we also had Mr & Mrs David Davies, the richest of the Welsh MPs & a radical and ardent supporter of Lloyd George – Gerry has got it into his head that he will attack him in the House of Commons over the native question – the Masai, you know, have just had a meeting to elect their new chief and they said at the meeting that they *wished* to move – Gerry has cabled this home to Harcourt but he says they are sure to think he is sacrificing the natives to the white settlers and refuse to allow it – personally I would give just anything if this Armstrong scheme came off. I think Gerry is at a far-end of his patience and I am sure this country does not suit him.'

Just as before, an unpleasant letter found its way to the Colonial Secretary's desk, this time via the leader of the Labour Party, Ramsay MacDonald. 'Our Governor is not playing fair; his mind and ambitions lead him into intrigues

and bluffing. It is freely said that he does not mean to listen to Colonial Office
admonitions. He thinks himself safe in the favours of wealthy planters and
investors.' Harcourt demanded that Ramsay MacDonald produce more evidence. Nothing was forthcoming. As the Colonial Office saw it, Girouard
had done what had been asked and produced a new treaty with the Maasai.
Uneasily, Harcourt telegraphed his consent to the move.

1 June 1911: 'Gerry is most awfully pleased because the CO have at last
decided to let him make the Masai move – it will make an enormous difference in the country and everyone will be delighted and he has now gained
every point he went home for except the alteration in the land laws.'

Life for Gwen was all a breathless rush: 'We had such a lot of people to tea
on Sunday and the three tennis courts going.' A big garden party the day
before, the King's birthday, and they were to dine with the Cranworths that
night. Her pony Silvermane was in training for the races that summer. She had
got into the habit of reading novels, then sitting up and chatting until all hours.
Up at six, never in bed before one: she was thin, tired, and smoking too much.
But still, they were to visit Uganda, 'be on Safari all July only be back in time
for the races on August 2nd, then we are going down to Mombasa to give
some dinners and a small dance there – and then home on the 12th'.

It had been at the end of April that ' a horrid thing has happened. Galbraith Cole [Lady Delamere's brother] shot a black man dead whom he
found trying to steal his sheep, instead of reporting the matter to the Police
at once, he left the body there for a week until it was found. Now they will
have to arrest and try him, of course a white jury will acquit him . . . Lord
Delamere was here yesterday . . .' Of all the Delamere clan, the only one
Gwen really liked was Galbraith Cole. He was twenty-nine, and suffered
from arthritis, stooped and so weak he could sometimes hardly walk. Gwen
was deeply shocked. But Girouard seemed to abdicate as governor. Rather
than put him in prison, Cole was reported to be ill and put into hospital.

On 7 June she wrote that the jury had acquitted him unanimously, 'so he
escapes scott-free although there is no doubt he behaved in a very brutal
way . . . – he shot the native as he was in the act of stealing his sheep and
though he saw the man was dying he left him out there all night and never
reported the matter to the police at all.' All Gerry cared for was whether
the news would get out in the House of Commons.

Four days later they started on their journey to Uganda. At Njoro, Delamere met them at the head of a large group of angry settlers. The Maasai

were moving through their farms. Within days, they themselves were in the midst of crowds of Maasai, men, women, children, and countless hundreds of sheep, cattle and goats. 'Today we have been through a great forest and met all the Masai beginning their move, it was most interesting, they are fine looking people, the men with great head-dresses of ostrich feathers & very little else, and the women with solid amulets & bracelets of silver and brass and huge rings in their ears, they had their herds with them. I have never see so many sheep & goats and cattle and calves in my life, we literally rode past miles of them,' Gwen wrote.

It was on this safari, at a place called Aruba, that Gwen finally came to the realization that she could not live with Girouard any more. The safari had collapsed. They were stranded sixty miles from anywhere, the ponies had stampeded and four of them had got right away. They had no option but to walk, sharing the remaining ponies. Years of difficult relations with her husband came to a head in a furious row. 'He is actually jealous because I go out shooting with John [Murray, his ADC], John of all people . . . Sometimes I feel it is just hopeless. I have simply busted myself to be sweet to G this time but he's impossible,' she told her parents.

On 30 July Girouard received a cable from the Colonial Office ordering him to deport Galbraith Cole. Typically, he argued. There would be an uproar in the country, he warned. In London, Harcourt was furious. He accused Girouard of shirking responsibility. As Girouard buckled down to obey, he meekly announced in Nairobi that he was only acting on the orders of the Imperial government. Lord Delamere cabled the London papers to protest.

The case of Galbraith Cole was far from the only issue immediately troubling the Colonial Office over Girouard's administration. Up in the Northern Frontier district, on the border with Somaliland, Girouard's policy of keeping raiding factions 'under observation' threatened to break down into the need for full-scale military action. With news of the Maasai move from Laikipia, speculation in land in East Africa's most fertile region took off. A farm bought from the government for $55 at the beginning of 1910 now sold for $500. Question after question about what was happening in East Africa was raised in the House of Commons. Then, on 21 August, Girouard was forced to cable London. Heavy rain, showers of hail and freezing temperatures on the Mau, a high range of hills rising to 10,000 feet, had brought the Maasai move to a halt. Harcourt could not believe it.

An estimated 10,000 men, women and children, 200,000 cattle, and a million sheep were on the move. Nothing had been planned. Grass was scarce, the track a muddy morass. The result was chaos and tragedy. When the weather changed for the worse, some Maasai turned back to Laikipia, others pressed on. Stories reached London of the dead and the dying: photographs of skeletons scattered in the bush were published. Those Maasai who reached the promised land of the southern reserve discovered that in fact, the land was dry and the grazing poor.

Girouard was no longer rational on the subject. 'They are today the richest Africans I have come across but they are not one whit more advanced than 100 years ago, their immorality or rather immoral habits are a crying danger. The havoc has been checked by fortuitous circumstance . . . but I will have croakers who certainly don't know a Masai from a Fulani howling what a cruel beast I am. If we don't move them and forcibly turn them into traders it will . . . mean a bloody war and who will come out of that best?' he wrote to the influential journalist Edmund Morel on 1 October. To the Colonial Office he went further: he would change the Maasai's marriage customs, and put an end to the warrior system. He would turn them into cattle traders and bring them into line with modern times.

Again, Harcourt could not believe what his Governor was telling him. The issue of future policy was irrelevant. The Maasai move had clearly been grossly mismanaged. Girouard's response was scarcely coherent: the Maasai had endured no hardship, he was adamant. Yet he was unable to say what had happened to all those who were missing. Had they gone to the north? The south? Or had they stayed on settlers' farms? In the meantime, an aggrieved district commissioner – whom Gerry had described as 'self satisfied, pig headed and highly unpopular' in his proposals to overhaul his staffing – had called at the Colonial Office. Farms in the northern reserve *had* been promised to white settlers, he told officials. This intelligence confirmed Harcourt's worst suspicions. He cabled Girouard: had any land been promised to white farmers in Laikipia?

Girouard's response was an unambiguous 'No'.

8 May 1912: London. The final scene in the panelled office of the Secretary of State for the Colonies cannot have been pleasant. Faced with Viscount Harcourt's questions, Sir Percy Girouard prevaricated. He could not seem to remember the content of his cable assuring the Secretary of State that no land in Laikipia had been promised to white settlers. After the interview,

there could be no question that he could continue as governor of East Africa. By then, his long-awaited offer from Armstrong-Vickers had been secured. Sir Percy resigned. Not long afterwards, an investigation by his successor in Nairobi, Henry Belfield, revealed that during 1909 negotiations had been conducted with settlers for land in Laikipia. In April 1910 – a year before the Maasai signed the new agreement – Girouard had confirmed twenty-seven offers of land, amounting to almost 200,000 acres, in Laikipia. Twenty-four were made to settlers from the southern reserve as compensation for moving. The remaining three were to Lord Delamere and his brothers-in-law Galbraith and Berkeley Cole.

When the northern Maasai finally saw the lands that had been offered them in the southern reserve it became clear they had been tricked. The soil was dry and much less fertile than Laikipia. Legalishu was not happy. But the new treaty had been signed with Girouard. There could be no turning back. In May 1912 preparations were made for the final move. Officers in charge of overseeing the transfer were instructed as follows:

'The elders will be informed that the Government has issued orders for the move to be carried out, and that they are expected to co-operate. Every endeavour will be made not to wound their feelings or lower their prestige, but if they refuse to assist, Ngaroya will be placed in charge of the northern reserve, and Legalishu and Masikonde will be told they will have to forgo their subsidies. They will also be informed that if the Masai refuse to move, troops will be sent to Laikipia. Legalishu will be allowed to move first of all if he so desires, in which case he will be given the Lemek Valley.'

Legalishu and his elders consulted lawyers. Early in 1913 they sued the Crown for the enforcement of the treaty of 1904, the restoration of Laikipia, and for damages suffered during the moves. The suit was dismissed on the grounds that the Maasai were not British subjects; that the treaty of 1904 was a contract between two sovereign nations, not cognizable by any British court. Counsel for the Maasai dismissed this. They appealed to the Privy Council. But the pressures persuading them to take no further action were too great. They lost heart. In March 1913, the Maasai left Laikipia for ever.

The Maasai have never agreed among themselves on the nature of the agreements that their elders signed, the wisdom of the second move, or which leader they should have followed. Girouard's breaking of the 1904 contract and their eviction from Laikipia have by now become deeply entangled with issues of lack of development, poverty and marginalization. The injustice rankles to this day.

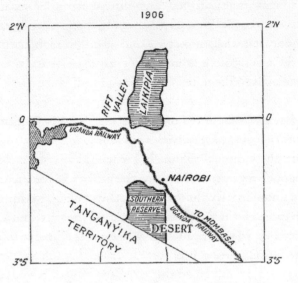

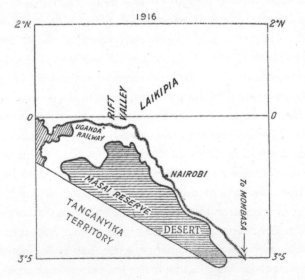

*Norman Leys's sketch maps showing how the lands of the
Maasai altered between 1906 and 1916*

After the First World War the Kenya government promised free land in the region that had become known as the 'white highlands' on 999-year leases at an annual rent of just ten cents an acre. Farms of less than 160 acres were given away free. By June 1919 over 2,000 applications had flooded into Nairobi. A year later, the country ceased to be a protectorate and became a fully-fledged Crown colony. Europeans – but not the Indians or the black Africans – were given the vote.

In August 1911, Gwen returned to her parents' home in England, and reunion with Dickie. She never lived with Girouard again. After his final meeting with the Colonial Office, he returned to Canada for the second time in twenty-five years. The next year, Sir Richard Solomon died. Free of her father's potential disapproval, Gwen sued Girouard for divorce. The decree came through the day before the Grand Duke of Austria was assassinated in Sarajevo. In January 1915, her divorce was finalized. By that time Bobbie Oppenheim had been posted to Cairo, to await orders to sail for Gallipoli.

Exactly when Gwen discovered that she was in love with him no one knows. One evening she suddenly left home, abandoning Dickie and her mother, and travelled to meet him in Cairo, where they were married. A little more than a year later, in May 1916, Gwen died giving birth to twins, who perished with her. She was just thirty-four. Girouard was heartbroken.

For a moment during the First World War, his fortunes rose again. He became director-general in charge of British munitions supply. 'The greatest authority in the British Empire upon the use of railways in war,' declared the *Newcastle Chronicle,* 'the Man who was Unafraid of Kitchener'. But once more Girouard could not brook control and fell foul of his superiors. He returned to the board of Armstrong Vickers until 1919, when he was forced, again, to resign. On 26 September 1932 he died in a nursing home in London at the age of sixty-five. His obituary in *The Times* ran over two columns, under the headline: 'a great railway engineer'. No mention of discord, no mention of divorce. His policy for East Africa had been clear, but entirely contradictory: preserving the country 'for white supremacy combined with absolute justice to the coloured races'.

17 Running the show
Ceylon 1907–12

In 1907, Ceylon – today's Sri Lanka – was a jewel, the nation's premier Crown colony, to a governor, the 'blue ribbon of the Service', as those at Buckingham Palace liked to describe it. Rather like India, but not quite: this teardrop-shaped island off its southern tip was rich and fertile, the well-advertised source of the Empire's teas and, increasingly, of rubber. Ceylon was a source of rare gems and spices, pearls and coconut. To anyone travelling to the east from Europe, its capital, Colombo, was an essential stopover. From here, steamers sailed onward to Singapore and Hong Kong, Shanghai, Japan, Australia and New Zealand.

What a tropical paradise greeted the weary voyager after three long weeks at sea! In contrast to the barren wastes of the Red Sea port of Aden, the last port of call, passengers walking down the gangway were assaulted by damp heat, glaring sunlight, and tall palms towering over luxurious mounds of fabulous greenery. Dark-skinned people wore sarongs vibrant with colour; the roads were full of rickshaws, coolies and bullock carts. For the traveller with twenty-four hours to spare, a day trip to Kandy, high in the mountains in the centre of the island, was a popular excursion by train. Rising from the heated lowlands of the western coast, it seemed to the visitor as if a vast garden extended up the mountain slopes inland. High into the hills, past green rice fields tucked into valleys, villages half hidden under palm and fruit trees, through clearings of young rubber trees, the train ran; up a narrow gauge past sheer drops of rock faces, to cocoa gardens, cinnamon trees, and finally, to the centre of the tea plantations, where row upon row of low bushes were spread in the cool of the higher slopes. Here at Kandy was a beautiful lake, and lovely, shady paths for riding. To the north, hidden in the jungle, lay the ruins of a Buddhist civilization of great antiquity, Anuradhapura, from where Sinhalese embassies had departed to Rome in the days of the Emperor Claudius.

To the Hindus, Ceylon was the semi-mythical 'Lanka', scene of the heroic combats of the Ramayana, inhabited by apes, giants and devils. To ancient Arabia and Persia it was a paradise of gems and spices. The native

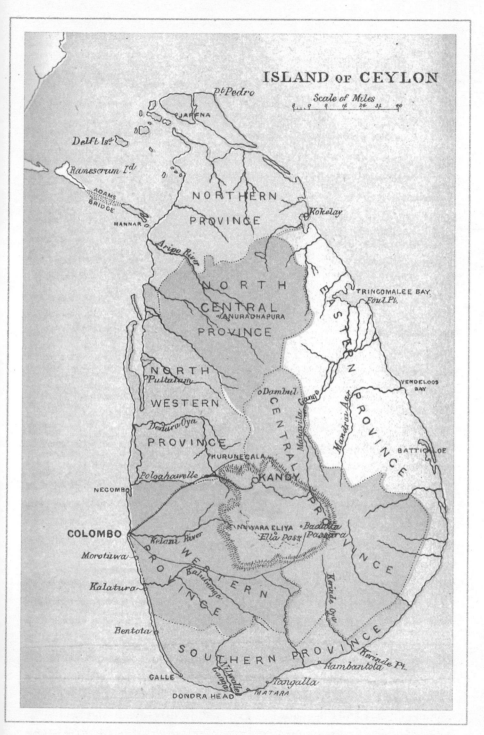

ISLAND OF CEYLON

Scale of Miles

Sinhalese, however, were 'people of lion's blood': they fought off the Hindu Brahmans who menaced them from India's neighbouring Malabar Coast, and the Portuguese who sought to gain a foothold there in the sixteenth century. The Dutch had managed to establish a presence at Colombo in 1658. But it took another century before the British East India Company began to intrigue with the inland kingdom of Kandy in 1766. Another fifty years of wars and skirmishing, unscrupulous dealings and the depositions of kings took place before the British finally wrested control of the island – and its dependent islands, the Maldives – in 1815.

There were a few more upsurges of resistance, but by the turn of the twentieth century, almost sixty years of peace had reigned on the island. Meanwhile, metalled cart roads had been built beyond the railways, through the thirsty, meanly forested foothills of what the British authorities called the eastern 'dry zone', on to the wastes of the northern Jaffna Peninsula, home to the Tamils, waterless, stony and barren. There, and to the east and south, where the coast was hot and parched, ancient systems of irrigation were being restored.

Everywhere, British progress was being made. Schools were springing up. Forests were being preserved, game reserves established; the antique ruins of Anuradhapura were beginning to be excavated, and their ancient inscriptions translated.

To this 'wonderland of tropical Asia', as he called it, a new colonial secretary, Hugh Clifford, arrived to head the administration on 11 July 1907. A new governor, Sir Henry McCallum, was also due to come into post, but not for another six weeks. In the meantime, Clifford was to be acting governor.

He was forty-one, a big man, well over six feet tall, with a large bald head and an expansive personality. Clifford was one of those men who fill a room, magnetically theatrical, charming, witty and clever. A first-class civil servant, he was incisive, efficient, with a huge capacity for work. He was also a well-known novelist, vain, sensitive, and with a sardonic brand of humour. In this short history of colonial administrators, Clifford stands, Janus-like, a lofty master in the art of colonial service, looking back to the sensitive young men who lived alone in the jungle and the swashbuckling adventurers of the Victorian era; and forward to the rational, imperialistic bureaucrats of the twentieth century.

He was a man full of contradictions. He was fascinated by the idea of Britain's Empire and the public servants at the centre of it, and would imagine himself as a young Roman, sent to colonize the valley of the Thames.

How uneasy these people must have felt as they encountered the ancient backward Britons, Clifford thought: homesick, frightened, and so far away from home. But look at the miracle of civilization they had wrought! Clifford never thought of himself as one of those colonized Britons. He was the man who would take responsibility for the uncivilized races. He liked to think of himself as in the vanguard of all that was new, taking the wheel of a car – and later, aeroplanes – himself. Dominating and highly effective, with a man like Clifford at the head of a Crown colony's civil service, there might be much less work for the governor to do, but a tussle for control when he chose to do it.

On the afternoon of Clifford's first day in Ceylon, he was sworn in as acting governor in the Legislative Chamber. Surrounded by judges of the Supreme Court in white wigs and black gowns, colonial officials in the navy tailcoats and elaborate gold braid of the 'Windsor uniform', and Sinhalese princes in brocaded hats and colourful silk pantaloons, he took his oath of office. In the harbour, a battery of guns saluted. Soon after, Clifford left on a tour of the southern half of the island. By the time the new Governor Sir Henry McCallum and his wife, Dolly, arrived six weeks later, he was fully briefed on the state of Ceylon. It was clearly prosperous. A full survey of the island still needed to be completed. The administration and taxes needed to be reformed. This was a bland statement issued from Clifford's office for the press. In fact, things were not as settled as they looked. Nascent political associations were discussing constitutional reforms and preparing disturbing petitions to the Secretary of State for the Colonies for changes in the way Ceylon was governed.

As His Excellency the Governor and Lady McCallum moved into the governor's official residence at Queen's House in Colombo, grand, white-stuccoed and porticoed, Clifford took up residence in Temple Trees, an old Dutch-built house with a lovely garden, facing the sea. Apart from his staff, he was alone. Six months before, his beloved wife, Minna, thirty-six years old, had died as the result of complications following injuries in a carriage accident. His three young children were with relatives in England.

Clifford's house in Colombo was named for two ancient 'temple' trees – fragrant frangipanis, with yellow and white flowers – which stood beside the gate. Its blossoms are liberally strewn with jasmine and oleander in Buddhist temples across Ceylon. There is no flower with a heavier fragrance, no other scent that so evokes the colour and intensity of southern

Asia. Not least to Clifford, who all his life was fond of talking of the power of smell to conjure up 'old thoughts, old memories, and old desires'.

Clifford was the eldest son of Major-General Sir Henry Hugh Clifford, and a grandson of the seventh Baron Clifford of Chudleigh, in Devon. By the time he was born his father was forty. The general had spent his life in big military campaigns overseas: South Africa, the Crimea – winning the Victoria Cross at the battle of Inkerman – and in China, capturing Canton. As the third son of the seventh baron, he had never had much money. At an early age young Hugh was sent to board at a day school which he described as 'a small hell on earth' in Coventry, while his parents and his five younger brothers and sisters retreated from England to the town of Dinan in Brittany to save money. There he would join them for the summer.

The family was devoutly Roman Catholic. There were private Masses and weekly confessions, stone churches clouded with incense. One of Clifford's uncles was a priest; his aunt was a nun; his younger brother Everard was to become a Carthusian monk, taking a vow of silence that cut him off from his family for ever. He adored his mother, Josephine. While his father, Clifford recorded, 'never, if he could avoid it, read any book save those that deal with the technique of his profession,' his mother was a gifted writer of whom Dickens expected great things. In due course, Clifford was dispatched to a small, eccentric school at Woburn Park run by a cousin, Monsignor William Joseph Petre, a prelate of the church. Petre instilled in the boys a sense of their destiny as rulers, of futures in public service. He trained them in debate and argument in their own school parliament. At the age of thirteen, his father took Clifford on his first visit to Ugbrooke, the family's handsome stone-built seat in the rolling Devon countryside.

Driving round the estate with his father in a dog-cart, watching the tenants and servants receive his father, it seemed to Clifford as though 'I had suddenly become a part of a great family-congregation, the existence of which I had up to that time been ignorant. It imbued me, even at that very early age, with a tremendous sense of responsibility – as though one's actions during all one's lifetime must, in some measure, be regulated by the manner in which they might perhaps affect this great body of interested spectators.'

In April 1883, a month after Clifford turned seventeen, his father died as the result of stomach cancer. Clifford had passed for Sandhurst, to follow him into the army. His dream, however, had always been to become a journalist.

Now that his mother was left with five younger children to support, both were out of the question. 'You will have to make your tea before you try and pour it out,' she told him. Fortunately, his father's closest childhood friend, a cousin, Sir Frederick Weld, Governor of the Straits Settlements in Singapore, wrote to her. He had an Eastern Cadetship in his gift: would young Clifford like to take it up? Within weeks he had landed in Singapore, and before six months were out he had become private secretary to Hugh Low, Kitty Hennessy's father, the British resident in Perak. By that time Low had become a legend in Malaya, venerable and grey-bearded. He lived in the beautiful house that had once belonged to Frank Swettenham's first amorata, Che Mida, in Kuala Kangsar. The house was surrounded by grounds where Low carried out botanical experiments with coffee from Liberia, tea from Assam, tomatoes, pink pineapples, roses and rubber trees.

Clifford's next two years were spent in Perak – passing language exams and becoming the collector of land revenues. Everyone in Low's considerable establishment knew his place, managed with a stately efficiency by a local Malay – 'a big, fat Klinn' – two valets (a pair of twins from Java), a Chinese cook, and a Malay *punkah* puller. Three Sikhs in scarlet turbans armed with Malacca canes saluted the resident and his guests as they passed, and marched in solemn procession with him on inspections to the barracks. Every night at 9 p.m. a cannon boomed out from the parade ground to signal the end of the day.

Meetings of the State Council were held with due pomp: 200 red-uniformed troops welcomed the Raja. M. Brau de Saint-Pol Lias, a guest of Low's, recorded the scene. 'The Resident goes towards him and receives him amidst the troops. The music plays, the cannons thunder; it is all very solemn! The Raja and the Resident, heading the procession, climb the hill and arrive in the big room where the Council table has been prepared.' The Raja took the president's seat; Low sat on his right. 'But no matter where Mr Low sits . . . it is obvious that he is the one who constantly conducts the debates and does it as a man who is perfectly used to dominating his audience.' Low managed the council, focusing on how various rules and regulations could best be fitted in with rural Malay customs and routine. Would vaccinations against smallpox offend Islamic law? Should abducting a girl under sixteen for marriage be a punishable offence? Low took them through the issues, his tone persuasive.

'If an objection occurs it is answered with good sense; if it persists at the risk of time being wasted, a suitable friendly jest is ready, a subtle sentence that assures his audience's laughter, and the incident is forgotten. The objector remains confused on the spot and does not dare say more; the Resident relieves him with a kind word.' These were the lessons in government which would serve Clifford in future.

In the autumn of 1884, he travelled across the province with Frank Swettenham, who was acting as resident while Hugh Low was on leave, and his private secretary, Martin Lister. They left him behind to stand in for a sick district collector in the remote village of Tanjong Malim, with no European clothes. For weeks Clifford went about 'dressed in the queer garments purchasable in one or another of Tanjong Malim's three Chinese shops, and was presently compelled to do all my jungle tramping barefoot'. In 1887, Sir Frederick Weld trusted him with a mission to the remote east coast state of Pahang, to persuade its powerful and unpredictable ruler to accept British control of his external affairs. A year later, at the age of twenty-one, Clifford was posted to his court as an 'agent'.

'As you crush your way out of the crowded roadstead of Singapore, and skirting the red cliffs of Tanah Merah, slip round the heel of the Malay Peninsula, you turn your back for a space on the seas in which ships jostle one another, and betake yourself to a corner of the globe where the world is very old,' Clifford was to write later. From Singapore to the capital of Pahang at Kuala Lipis was a voyage of a fortnight. Except for an occasional 'sea tramp', there was nothing to show that white men had ever visited the eastern shores of Malaya – more than ever remote from the rest of the peninsula because the fierce monsoons of the China Sea close the ports for six months in every year.

Clifford was young and eager. Tall and lean, he was fresh-faced and already beginning to lose his hair. He towered over the Malays, whose heads reached only to his chest. He set up home in 'a big, rambling native hut' on the main street, once lived in by a concubine of the King. The back of the house 'straggled out over the river, on half a hundred crazy wooden piles'. It had four main rooms: a reception room; the former boudoir of the concubine, almost entirely filled by a platform on which she had held court and slept. Here he squatted to eat his rice, 'to yarn with his own people', or to receive those 'who could be given a more or less public audience'. To the left was a bedroom/study, heaped with piles of books, his luggage, and a table for writing, which overlooked the river. To the rear of his bedroom was a room for his 'native followers', and the kitchen with a ladder down to the bathing-raft for the house, where he would wash in the morning.

Clifford lasted no more than a year before he was invalided home with fever. When he returned to Pahang, he was made superintendent of the interior of the province. Here, for four years, he led the suppression of armed resistance – just how ruthlessly, we do not know – until, in 1896, he was promoted to the post of resident to the Sultan of Pahang. His roles were similar to Frank Swettenham's in his early years in Selangor and Perak. Dressed in a sarong, with a band of faithful Malay retainers, two of them of raja rank, Clifford was advising a sultan who for all intents and purposes was living in the Middle Ages, under what Clifford described as 'a complete feudal system'.

Like Swettenham, Clifford had been invited to write about the life he was seeing in Pahang for the *Singapore Free Press*. He needed no second invitation, pouring his thoughts down in a series of vignettes of rural Malay life and in the process, trying to come to terms with the life he was leading.

'A white man, who has lived twelve consecutive months in complete isolation, among the people of an alien Asiatic race, is never wholly sane again for the remainder of his days,' he wrote. 'For the life he learns to live, and the discoveries he makes in that unmapped land, the gates of which are . . . barred and chained against all but a very few of his countrymen, teach him to love many things which all right-minded people very properly detest.' One of his early heroes was Jack Norris, a young Englishman like himself in an outpost just beyond the British border, 'sent there to see fair in places where fair dealing formed no essential part of the local polity'. He wrote of the thrill of expeditions to 'benighted lands', the spice of danger and the chance of adventure, and life in poorly paid billets; how boys with 'pluck and brains', with 'good knowledge of the natives and of the vernacular, [and] a tough constitution' scrambled for the jobs.

Meanwhile Pahang and its people were creeping into his soul. Clifford loved his forced marches, hours of fast pacing through the jungle with his trusted men beside him. The great Malay rain forests were 'among the wonderful things of the Earth'.

Here the air 'hangs heavy as remembered sin', and 'the gloom of the great cathedral is on every side'. His writing is full of Catholic allusion, of secret sins and private guilt. Clifford was writing too many stories of forbidden love, too suggestively, for anyone to avoid the conclusion that more than one Malay woman had stolen his heart and introduced him to customs that played no part in European convention – ways of life he found increasingly difficult to give up. 'All these things come to possess a charm the power of which grows apace, and eats into the very marrow of the bones of the man who has once tasted this particular fruit of the great Tree of Knowledge.' The divides between east and west, the rulers and the ruled, the complicated life of the lonely colonial servant, half in, half out of their society, and the curse of modernity on the Malays, had begun to haunt him.

Soon, with his mother's help in England, he was submitting pieces to literary magazines. In his first collection of essays and short stories, *East Coast Etchings,* published in 1896, he wrote of the dangers inherent to colonialism, where Europeans could spend weeks 'without coming into contact with any Asiatics save those who wait at table, clean his shirts and drive his car', years 'without acquiring any profound knowledge of the natives of their country or [their] language', and how they could not hope to engage with the people they ruled with empathy and understanding. To Clifford, the ideal way to govern, was 'to instinctively feel the native Point of View', to be in such 'complete sympathy'; he had become one with them and 'in a manner, they [had come to] love him'.

It was while on his way home on leave with this manuscript in late 1895 that he read Joseph Conrad for the first time. *Almayer's Folly,* which he had bought for the voyage, struck him as a work in a class of its own. Conrad was achieving, 'with extraordinary success', something for which he, 'in a much humbler sphere, was also aiming'. All the same, Clifford concluded that Conrad had nothing but 'a superficial acquaintance' with Malayan customs, language and character. Clifford gave Conrad's book a mixed review in the Singapore press; from that point the two men began to follow one another's work closely. It was also during that leave in England that Clifford married Minna, the twenty-five-year-old, dark-haired and vivacious daughter of Gilbert à Beckett, a playwright and satirist on the staff of *Punch*. Minna's mother was a composer; their household was full of parody, music and laughter. After the wedding in April 1896, Minna sailed with Clifford for Singapore, travelling on to live with him in remote Pahang. By now he was thirty.

During these years, during which his two eldest children – a son, Hugh, and a daughter, Mary – were born, Clifford developed a stringent writing discipline, rising at three in the morning, brewing his own tea, and spending two or three hours at his desk before settling down to his official work.

In Court and Kampong, his second volume of short stories, was published in 1897, dedicated to Minna. In it he tried to give 'some idea of the lives lived in these lands by Europeans whose lot has led them away from the beaten track . . . above all, by those Malays who, being yet untouched by contact with white men, are still in a state of original sin'. He was dealing with all classes, 'dwellers in the courts of kings, peasants in their kampongs, fisher folk'.

It was on his next leave in England, in the spring of 1899, that he and Conrad met for the first time. Over the past six years, Clifford had produced a stream of articles and short stories for literary magazines like *Blackwood's* and *Cornhill.* By now, every book he produced was widely reviewed on both sides of the Atlantic. The milieu in which he moved in England, peopled by writers, artists and playwrights, was an unconventional one for a colonial servant. Among his friends were Rudyard Kipling and the poet Sir Edmund Gosse, George Meredith, Thomas Hardy and H. G. Wells, but it was Conrad and his wife, Jessie, with whom Clifford and Minna particularly got on. He and Minna would cycle the seventy miles from Dorking to stay with the Conrads for weekends at their home at Pent Farm in Kent. The two men were attracted by the same themes, the dark interaction of Europe and Asia, the rulers and the ruled. Conrad marvelled at Clifford's sure grasp of non-European characterization, while Clifford never doubted that Conrad was the better writer. He, however, had a surer grasp of the business of getting published. It was with difficulty that, in 1903, Clifford persuaded Conrad to come to London and allow him to introduce him to George B. M. Harvey, the editor and owner of the American publisher Harper's. In the course of a brief, stilted meeting, Harvey commissioned the 100,000-word book that would become Conrad's masterpiece, *Nostromo.*

Clifford was acting as resident of Selangor in Kuala Lumpur in September 1901 when he was poisoned with a potion of ground glass, by the hand of someone, his family always believed, with whom he had lived in Pahang. Invalided to Singapore General Hospital, he was so ill that he, Minna and the children were dispatched to England. In London he was treated by the eminent specialist in tropical medicine Sir Patrick Manson, the doyen of Colonial Office medical officers. He recorded his treatment: 'Tonight – no food after 5 pm; at 9 pm mustard poultice to pit of stomach & 10 drops of laudanum; at 9.20 pm six pills. Lie flat on back, low head. Neither eat, drink speak or move till 6 am. Tomorrow night the same but only 5 pills. Wednesday night no laudanum & only 4 pills & so on dropping a pill daily. Food: meagre. Arrowroot, chicken broth, barley water, and milk.' Manson's dictum was to keep him hungry; some sustenance 'every 3 hours'. For months he recuperated in his mother's grace-and-favour apartment in Hampton Court Palace.

Clifford supplemented his half pay from the Colonial Office by writing. His daughter Mary was four. All her life she remembered her father, pale and drawn, propped up by pillows, with a strong light behind the bed, as he wrote. At last, in the summer of 1903, he was passed fit to return to Malaya. Sir Frank Swettenham, now risen to become governor of the Straits Settlements in Singapore, offered him a job. Clifford was longing to get back. He was grouse shooting in Scotland when Charles Lucas, Swettenham's crony at the Colonial Office, cabled him to come to London for urgent talks.

That March there had been serious riots on the West Indian island of Trinidad. Since the early 1890s, radical agitation for reform of both central government and the capital Port of Spain's Municipal Borough Council had been growing. On 23 March, a committee of the ratepayers' association, backed by a crowd of over 1,000, demanded entry to a Legislative Council debate on a new ordinance to do with water works, and changes to water rates.

The meeting was held at the Red House, the centre of government. As the council proceeded, the noise of the crowd outside increased. Stones were hurled through the windows, breaking a stained-glass memorial of Columbus's landing in Trinidad. Before long, the smoke of burning timber filled the chamber. The Riot Act was read; but still the angry mob came on. The Governor was reported to have lost his nerve; the police opened fire into the crowd. By the time the riot was over, nine people had been killed and forty wounded. The Governor's landau had been destroyed, the police barracks set alight, and the Red House, containing all the government's records, had been burnt to the ground.

A commission of inquiry dispatched from England recommended fundamental reforms for Trinidad. The Governor was gently eased out with a medical certificate that declared him unfit for future tropical service; the colonial secretary was in disgrace, and about to be sent on leave. Clifford's excellent work in bringing peace in Pahang and the nature of his writing had meanwhile furnished him with a reputation for being good with unfamiliar peoples. Charles Lucas was asking him to take on the role of colonial secretary in Trinidad. His instructions were 'to get as much controversial matter off the slate as soon as possible', so as to give the incoming governor 'a fair and square start'.

Clifford accepted the post with the greatest reluctance. Not only was he longing to return to Malaya, but wide discrepancies in pay and conditions of service had grown up between different regions of the Empire. Clifford had to take a significant drop in salary, sacrifice his pension rights and pay his own fare across the Atlantic. A refusal, however, would seriously damage his prospects in the colonial service.

He left Minna, who had just given birth to their third child, Monica, and Hugh and Mary in England. Landing in Port of Spain that autumn, he began the work of superintending the government of an island of which he knew nothing, in a highly volatile atmosphere, and where almost all of the government's records had been destroyed. His first task was to oversee the trials of the ringleaders of the riot, and draft a new bill for the waterworks. His next was to put together a memorandum for the incoming governor on how to improve relations between the government and the population. Clifford concluded there were too many white planters on the Legislative Council, and not enough blacks; too many non-Creoles and not enough Creoles; too many Protestants, and not enough Roman Catholics. He recommended sweeping changes to representation. He warned that they would 'offend many of the rooted prejudices of the white population of this Island', but he was convinced that 'certain sections of the population should be adequately represented who hitherto have been more or less [inarticulate]'.

Clifford was interested in good government. He was wary of those who manipulated crowds, and anxious to protect his people from themselves. Like Sydney Olivier in Jamaica, Clifford thought the black population too politically immature to allow it too much power; otherwise, he was convinced, a minority of clever, articulate spokesmen, out for their own interests, would attempt to delude the majority. 'The only salvation for the Colony,' he wrote, 'lies in the administration of its affairs being entrusted to men who are free from all local ties and interest.' This was paternalism – government by objective people like himself: 'selected white officials, who are instructed to acquaint themselves in the most painstaking fashion with local needs and requirements, to give a sympathetic hearing to all parties, and to decide every question to the best of their ability for the good of the community as a whole . . .'

★

Clifford had little time to write in Trinidad – 'a regret for this place is crammed with copy', he wrote to his publisher, William Blackwood. Some months after he arrived, Minna and baby Monica had followed him to the island. But the anguish of separation from their two oldest children had been too much for Minna to bear. After no more than a year, she returned to England. Clifford recorded the pain of his deprivation in *Rachel,* a heart-breaking story of the damage done to a man and his family by prolonged separation, published in 1904.

In the spring of 1906, Minna and Monica returned to Trinidad. That August, the three of them spent a delightful month on Tobago. In the autumn, Clifford applied to succeed Lugard as high commissioner of Nigeria, but while serious consideration was given to his candidacy – Sir Montagu Ommanney, Permanent Under-Secretary at the Colonial Office, described him as 'one of the very few men in the colonial service having a real and responsive insight into the genius of alien races', he was rejected. Instead, he was offered the colonial secretary's job in Hong Kong. Then, suddenly in December, the more prestigious position of colonial secretary of Ceylon was vacated; Clifford was asked if he would take this post instead.

As news of his promotion came, Minna was fighting for her life. In November, she had fallen from a pony cart as it turned a sharp corner. This was followed by an attack of meningitis and pneumonia. On 14 January 1907, she died. Clifford had lost 'the sweetest, purest, truest and most loving spirit' he had ever known. In February, he sailed for England alone with his tiny daughter, to spend the Easter holidays with his 'poor motherless bairns' – his ten-year-old son, Hugh, and nine-year-old Mary. In the late spring, he sailed for Ceylon, to face 'the empty, empty life which is now mine'.

By the time Clifford got to Ceylon after four years in the government offices of Trinidad, he had few illusions about what he was doing as a British colonial administrator. Years before, he had deplored 'the boot of the ubiquitous white man', crushing down forests, beating out roads, kicking down native institutions, stamping out 'much of what is best in the customs and characteristics of the native races', reducing them 'to that dead level of conventionality, which we call civilization'. He had become the kind of white man he had detested in Malaya: he spoke no Tamil or Sinhalese; he knew nothing of the peoples of Ceylon. The closest he came to the ordinary people of the country was when he talked to his driver. Although he might, at best, be respected for his wisdom, he knew he would be 'hated for his airs of superiority, pitied for his ignorance [and] feared for what he represents'. By now he had become a master of 'the caustic minute to the suffering subordinate', and learned how to strangle any idea he did not approve of 'with swaddlings of red tape'. His letters were strictly businesslike, imperious – or long-winded and abstruse when it suited him. He created systems, delegated tasks and shifted paper at speed.

In 1907 there were three and a half million people in Ceylon, of whom just over 6,000 were European. The British ran the country as an autocracy, according to a constitution established in 1833. The island was divided into nine provinces, each headed by a British government agent with two or three district assistants – each of whom had anything from six to twenty years' experience in Ceylon. Based in their provincial *kacheri,* or government offices, they handled not only day-to-day administration – land ownership, registration of births, marriages and deaths, and the collection of revenues – but also justice, making the hand of the British government in the control of the population ubiquitous. Meanwhile, reports on a myriad of affairs, from land sales and the health of the population, to the state of the crops and the weather, were fed into the Government Secretariat in Colombo, a long low white building lined with verandahs, centred on a portico beneath a low clock tower. Here was a vast machine, a civil service largely worked by Sinhalese, where the labour of co-ordinating policy was carried out under British direction. From here the *Government Gazette* was published weekly. Its constant replaying of the phrase 'by authority' above Hugh Clifford's name made it clear that the Colonial Secretary was the man in whose name all work was done: land was sold, tenders were issued for building contracts, statistics collected, new ordinances drafted and published, and roads were constructed.

Meanwhile, behind the scenes, Clifford oversaw all important correspondence. He decided what to bring before His Excellency the Governor's attention or to forward to the Secretary of State in England. He set the agenda for the Legislative and Executive Councils – which advised the Governor. Deferential white faces of the most senior British officials surrounded him. Behind his back, however, he was always the 'novelist'. His biggest fault, according to his former boss in Trinidad, Governor Sir Henry Moore Jackson, was his tendency to form conclusions too rapidly, and his unwillingness to compromise. This was a characteristic he shared with his new chief.

Sir Henry McCallum was fifty-five, one of many governors whose unimaginative and obstructive roles are perhaps best consigned to obscurity. He trained as a military engineer at the Royal Military Academy, Woolwich, and mastered telegraphy before working in the office of the inspector-general of fortifications. In 1875, at the age of twenty-three, he was posted as the private secretary to the governor of the Straits Settlements in Singapore. Over the next twelve years he worked as an engineer in and around the Malay Peninsula, for the likes of Frank Swettenham, and met Hugh Clifford for the first time. From Malaya he had been posted as governor of Lagos in 1897. New to west Africa, McCallum proved tactless and unreceptive to African advice. Transferred as governor to Newfoundland, the friction between McCallum and the elected prime minister of the colony led to his recall in 1901. Next he was appointed governor of Natal, where he proved even more unsympathetic to the Zulus. Finally – for reasons which appear inexplicable here – he had been appointed to be governor of Ceylon.

Over the next five years, McCallum's wife, Dolly (who, on the eve of her marriage to McCallum in 1897, was seeing rather a lot of the man who would in due course become the eighth Duke of Atholl) was to find the climate in Ceylon increasingly 'difficult'. Clifford would find himself standing in for McCallum as acting governor three times – altogether for just over a year. According to newspaper reports, in the early days of their relationship, the Governor and his Colonial Secretary operated on the basis of 'mutual esteem and friendship'. The statement could hardly be further from the truth.

Where Clifford was large and jovial, fond of wearing bow ties, playing a round of golf and chain-smoking cigarettes, he was also cocky, 'showy', as Frederick Bowes, whom Clifford appointed in August 1908 to be his principal assistant in the Secretariat, put it. 'His fatal weakness was an unfathomable vanity. He loved himself, and he loved listening to himself.' By contrast, McCallum was florid, beak-nosed, well-fed and moustachioed, blunt, businesslike and exuberant. 'Somewhat boisterous', he was said to be 'at his best when he adjourned to the bar'. Arriving one day by car from Kandy to open an agricultural show at Matale, in the tea-planting district, McCallum's greatest anxiety before he undertook the arduous duty of following a procession and receiving addresses of welcome was for immediate refreshment. 'However, all went well,' reported Bowes, who on that day was on duty in his former post as the assistant government agent, 'though during the reception I had hastily to intervene when I found His Excellency sapping the sense of discipline of my local Board members by telling them how he had told the [Secretary of State] that he would be damned if, etc. etc', while the Sinhalese were shocked by his boorishness.

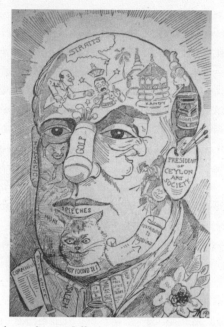

How the British saw him: Clifford, one of the great celebrities of Ceylon

Later, whenever he met Bowes as Clifford's assistant, McCallum would 'shake his fist in friendly warning and tell me to mind never to "trust a damned Papist"', while if he mentioned McCallum to Clifford, he would 'wonder how I could bring myself to go near such an old bounder'.

Underlying the green tranquillity of Ceylon and the gentle charm of its people was a growing sense of grievance against the British. Ten years before, the manner in which the British had begun excavating the ancient Buddhist city at Anuradhapura had alarmed and offended local Buddhists. Plans to build an Anglican church near two holy sites also caused distress. In 1903, when a Buddhist woman was killed during a crowded pilgrimage, these tensions erupted into a riot. Meanwhile, the mighty revelations emerging from the uncovering of Ceylon's ancient heritage fuelled national pride and a drive for education. Now Governor McCallum was having to forward a steady stream of petitions to London requesting Sinhalese representation on the Executive Council and begging the reform of the Legislative Council.

Clifford dubbed these first political agitators 'the little core of rot'. Publicly, he was a master of the soothing word, the solemn assurance. But

anyone arguing for wider Sinhalese participation in government was kept
securely at arm's length. Clifford could not accept that the world about him
was changing; that those whom the British had taken care to educate were
now wanting a say in the running of their own land; or that the frank
expression of public opinion was something to be valued, rather than suppressed. The stunning Liberal victory in the general election of 1906 had
unnerved him. 'This new parody of a House of Commons', full of an
'appalling collection of extremists, cranks, faddists, false-sentimentalists',
depressed him unutterably. Earlier, in Trinidad, Sir Henry Jackson, who
was his boss as governor, had been dismayed by Clifford's 'strong objection
to the elective principle', when it was proposed to hold a ballot for town
councillors in Port of Spain.

As in Trinidad, the issue in Ceylon in 1908 was power. The population
was dominated by roughly 2.3 million Sinhalese – mostly Buddhist – living
in small rural villages. In the north lived just under a million Tamils, fer-
vently Hindu. Elsewhere on the island were a strong Dutch trading
community, a large portion of Christians – mainly Roman Catholic – and
a quarter of a million Muslims. Meanwhile, not even mentioned as eligible
for a voice, half a million Indian indentured workers laboured in near
slaving conditions on the tea estates.

As for the British – some 6,300 strong – class war simmered within the
tight confines of the ruling community. At its apex were the civil servants,
highly paid, with good prospects. Next down were the planters, who considered themselves socially equal to the officials – they played tennis
together and belonged to the same clubs – but their prospects, relying as
they did on the vagaries of weather, soil and market prices, were never as
secure. Apart from the wealthiest business tycoons, banking clerks and
businessmen were never seen in 'polite' society. In Ceylon all the British
were grand – 'a good deal grander than we could have been at home in London or Edinburgh, Brighton or Oban', wrote Leonard Woolf – later to
marry the writer Virginia Woolf – who was a twenty-seven-year-old office
assistant in Kandy during Clifford's first year as colonial secretary. He
described Clifford's circle as 'exalted'.

Neither Governor McCallum nor Clifford saw any reason to change a
system that had been stable so long. After all, the village remained the principal political entity for the majority of the population. Their only desire
'is to be suffered to till their fields in peace and security and to be saved from
exaction and oppression', wrote Clifford. Meanwhile, the Legislative

Council, consisting of ten top government officials (the governor, the commander of troops, the colonial secretary, the attorney-general, treasurer and controller of revenue, two heads of departments, and the government agents from the West and Central provinces) was bolstered by eight 'unofficials' representing the key groups of people on the island. There were three representatives of the white planters, merchants, and 'general Europeans'; one for the Dutch, known as the 'burghers'; and one each for the 'low country' Sinhalese, the Kandyans, the Tamils and Muslims. Each unofficial was nominated by a group of his peers, who were self-selecting. Each tended to be automatically reappointed when his term came to an end. The Legislative Council was no more than advisory. The real decisions were taken by the eight-member Executive Council – the government's top officials plus one 'ex-officio' observer from the Legislative Council. Even these, the governor could override.

Clifford had spent his first year in Ceylon overseeing countless issues regarding personnel, changes to the excise system, the extension of port facilities in Colombo, sales of Crown lands and other matters of administration, from schooling to telegraphs, and extending electricity further into the hills. Always, however, he craved escape from the 'ordered present with its conventions, its formalities, its duties, its burdens and its petty responsibilities'. Whenever possible he got away to Kandy, with its lovely lake centred in a hollow of the hills. There, in the spring of 1908, he had entertained the tiny, aged Empress Eugénie of France, ushering her solicitously to the inner sanctum of the temple of the Buddha's Tooth, the Dalada Maligawa, one of the most sacred shrines in Buddhism. Meanwhile, he was conducting an affair with the glamorous wife of an absent British officer, to whom he lent his official residence, the Lodge. He had furnished it comfortably with books and a piano; it had a garden filled with flowering trees, where gardenias thrived, and huge bamboos. The air sparkled.

In November 1908 questions were raised in the House of Commons on the subject of changing the constitution for Ceylon. As word of the debate arrived in Colombo, Clifford sailed for a six-week trip to Malaya and Cambodia. He was seeking loneliness and peace, 'to get once more into tune with the Asia of olden days'. In Phnom Penh, 'half of which is a modern French town', he was 'jarred by the incongruity which results from grafting on to the gnarled trunk of Asia, the rank products of latter-day Europe'. Alone, he climbed the great Phnom above the city, losing the urban dross beneath him, to the top of the pagoda, where he revelled in what he called 'the East – the real East, mysterious and very ancient – waiting with her immense and measureless patience to catch the awful whisper that shall reveal the secrets of life and birth and death'.

Upon his return in the new year of 1909, influential Sinhalese were demanding elections to the Legislative Council. 'Seeing how undesirable it would be from a political point of view to give encouragement to any such idea for – I venture to say – some considerable time,' McCallum told the Secretary of State, he and Clifford embarked on a slow campaign of resistance. It was not until the end of May that Clifford drafted a reply to London in response to the questions raised in the Commons six months before. Five Sinhalese organizations begged for reform. All representatives should be elected; furthermore, the indigenous populations of Ceylon ought to be regarded as a single 'nation'. Suggestions of 'widespread dissatisfaction' and 'seething discontent' were 'to the last degree inaccurate and misleading'.

'A soothing draught': Clifford's condescension to the concerns of the Sinhalese permeated every debate in the Legislative Council

Clifford made every effort to discredit the Sinhalese proposals. 'These memorials emanate not from "the people of Ceylon", but from certain well defined classes of the native population ... a very small minority [of] natives who have assimilated an education of a purely Western, as opposed to Oriental, type, and who are to be regarded, not as representative Ceylonese, but as a product of the European administration of Ceylon on lines approved by British tradition.' They came from the towns, had no 'intimate experience' of the colony as a whole, or the rural population, the bulk of the people. They would not be representative. 'I do not consider the masses of people are in a position to perform this duty wisely or efficiently for themselves.' It was – and this is Clifford speaking – the government agent, the 'experienced civil servant', 'the best part of whose lives have been passed in Ceylon', who had spent their lives protecting the people from themselves, who were the best representatives of the people. The only change that McCallum and Clifford were prepared to make was the introduction of one new member, nominated from those representing European-trained and educated Sinhalese – the chief source of dissent. In London, some at the Colonial Office would have liked to open up the whole system to free elections. But if they granted representative government to the Crown colony of Ceylon, they might have to do it elsewhere . . .

So the business of the government in Ceylon ran on, keeping Clifford busy: a durbar of the Sinhalese chiefs in June; inspections of the pearl banks, where thousands of fishermen from India and Arabia came to dive for six weeks every year, in July. Reports of resignations, retirements and petitions from Sinhalese civil servants begging for rises in pay or reinstatement were forwarded to London; details of the parcel post were approved with Australia. There were cases of fraud in the department for public instruction; ordinances protecting wild animals and for preventing the cultivation of water hyacinth, which – as it still does today – 'causes so much damage by infesting waterways here'. An employee who it was feared might have sleeping sickness was found to be afflicted by syphilis, and the committee on Indian emigration reported that Ceylon could take another 20,000 immigrants from southern India every year for employment on rubber and tea estates. There was a conference on leprosy, work on malaria prevention, a mineralogical survey. All these apparently random pieces of business: step by step, Ceylon progressed. In June, it was announced that Clifford had been knighted in the King's birthday honours.

Clifford could not resist the temptation of making showmanlike speeches and public pronouncements on policy before Governor McCallum had approved them. In vain, his principal assistant, Frederick Bowes, tried to curb what he called Clifford's 'peacocking impulse'. Increasingly,

McCallum reported privately to London, Clifford was trying to sabotage any proposal that did not emanate from himself. In the meantime London had digested the issue of representation on the Legislative Council. The Sinhalese were to gain an extra seat, chosen by election, while the number of European representatives was to be reduced from three to two, also elected by popular franchise. They were no longer to be selected by class, but from two constituencies: urban and rural. Clifford could not accept these proposals.

Early in 1910, he took the unprecedented step of sending his own dispatch to London on the reform of the constitution, spelling out his objections to elections, rather than nominations, of European representatives to the Legislative Council. 'Astounding', minuted one official; 'enough to make one despair of Sir H. Clifford's sanity', recorded another.

Meanwhile, Clifford's rearguard action on the reform of the constitution was causing havoc in Colombo. Europeans were up in arms because London had decreed that their number on the council be reduced. McCallum was no better – 'I think it especially necessary to leaven the large number of Native Unofficials with a sufficient number of unofficial white blood.' He was having an anxious and difficult time fighting 'the battles of HM Government practically single handed'. He begged for a decisive statement from London on future representation in Ceylon. Meanwhile, Clifford 'will not see that he is backing the wrong horse and still endeavours to force my hand which I will not have'. Early in April, Clifford was still inviting public criticism of the scheme proposed by London. 'He has overreached himself entirely,' bleated McCallum. 'I can never again have the same confidence in him.'

At the end of April 1910, Clifford sailed for England on leave. The *Ceylon Morning Leader* bade him bon voyage. 'Clever, fluent, versatile, ready, "retortful" and resourceful in debate', Clifford was 'the most literary Colonial Secretary Ceylon had ever had'. Underneath the banter ran a caustic theme. Clifford's 'mordant wit, his pungent sarcasm, his acid criticism of other men's opinions, his clever facility in satire' and his 'breezy contempt for the beaten paths of official diplomacy' were making people squirm. Clifford had no interest in Ceylon's affairs or its politics. 'He loved to distress the unready simpletons of our little Parliament,' the paper said. The people were eagerly awaiting the first meeting of the 'reformed' Legislative Council, when they could at last pit against him 'men of our own choice, foemen worthy of his steel'.

★

In England, Clifford was summoned to see Lord Crewe, the Secretary of State. 'He had no thought of acting with any disloyalty to the Governor or HMG,' Crewe laconically recorded. Clifford was blind to any dismay he might have caused. Within days he was writing from the Travellers Club to apply for the post of resident-general of the Federated Malay States – the post Frank Swettenham had dreamt up for himself in Malaya. He might speak Malay, and know all the Sultans – it was the scene of the most productive years of his life – but officials at the Colonial Office brushed the application off without a second thought. Clifford had shown he could not be trusted to obey orders he didn't like. 'An attitude of that kind in the FMS will do inconceivable harm.'

Clifford meanwhile was absorbed in courtship. Elizabeth de la Pasture was the same age as he, forty-four. She was also dark-haired and glamorous, a famous best-selling novelist and playwright, whose husband, a French count, had died eighteen months before. Two of her plays had been performed at major London theatres; one had been staged at Sandringham by command of Edward VII. Elizabeth had two daughters: Edmée, who was twenty, would in due course become the well-known writer E. M. Delafield, author of *Diary of a Provincial Lady*; and eighteen-year-old Yolande. The wedding was private, early in the morning of Saturday, 24 September, in the crypt of Westminster Cathedral. Its announcement in the papers the same day caused a literary sensation. It was followed by a quiet honeymoon in Devon, and a few more weeks in London. Clifford made further calls at the Colonial Office, spoke on 'Old Malaya' at the Working Men's College and at the Ceylon Association dinner. On 3 January 1911 he and Elizabeth, with her daughter, Yolande, sailed for Colombo via Marseilles. Both writers were at work on new novels.

The new Lady Clifford proved to be one of Clifford's most important assets in his final eighteen months in Ceylon. 'She was charming,' wrote Frederick Bowes, 'the only official lady of gubernatorial rank who ever did anything to pull people together in Ceylon.' Betty, as Clifford called her, teased him and brought him down to earth. She encouraged his writing, and gave him a happiness he had not known since Minna had died. She was sophisticated and clever, a woman of the world, who knew how to entertain with warmth and grace. 'She caught hold of the European women in Ceylon, and the native ladies too,' said Bowes, 'and shook them together so effectively that they have kept the mould to this day.'

Clifford's latest book, *The Downfall of the Gods,* inspired by his visit to Cambodia and the collapse of the Khmer empire, came out to reviews around the world. At the end of June 1911, McCallum and his wife, Dolly, who had been in 'indifferent health' for some time, sailed for England on six months' leave. Clifford stepped into his shoes as acting governor and he and Elizabeth moved into the Queen's House in Colombo. 'August Week', the annual gathering for the British community from 'up-country' in the capital, came and went 'with a scream of joy like a freshly burst monsoon', as Lady Clifford presided over a 'perfect' ball at Queen's House, danced every night elsewhere, and presented cup after cup at the races, cricket and polo matches, rugby and boxing tournaments. Clifford complained afterwards to London of the expense.

The tensions between educated Sinhalese and the administration continued to rise. Prejudice against promoting Sinhalese to higher appointments – they lack 'grit, self-help, confidence in themselves and shirk taking responsibility', declared the director of public works – was endemic. It was only with considerable reluctance that the first Sinhalese – 'we cannot pass him over, as the most senior member of the civil service' – Ponnambalam Arunachalam, the Registrar-General, was invited to take the seat to which he was entitled on the Executive Council. A new excise bill to reform the country's liquor traffic was being driven ruthlessly through by Clifford, in spite of the fact that it would do nothing to curb the availability of drink – which is what the mass of the people wanted – but would only divert more money into the government's coffers. Debate on the issue, on 17 April 1912, coincided with the arrival of the Registrar's older brother, sixty-year-old Ponnambalam Ramanathan, as the first elected Sinhalese member on the Legislative Council.

It is difficult to imagine a more distinguished or less controversial man than Ramanathan. A barrister and King's Counsel of more than thirty-five years' standing, Ramanathan's second wife was an Australian. Both his grandfather and a grand-uncle had been among the first Sinhalese appointed to the Legislative Council in the past; he himself had served on the Legislative Council for thirteen years, from the age of twenty-eight, and had served the British administration for more than sixteen years as solicitor-general.

But on that day Clifford's ire was up. When Ramanathan began demanding details of how the new excise system would work in practice, Clifford refused to tell him. Ramanathan accused him of trifling, and declared his withholding of information 'an act of misgovernment'. Clifford told him he was out of order and demanded an apology, and then went on, supported by a brief interjection or two from McCallum, scathingly rejecting each of Ramanathan's attempts to apologize, steadily escalating the man's humiliation. The session ended with a thorough mortification of Ramanathan, shocking to read today. The headlines told a different story: 'Ceylon's Governor insulted by Hindu', ran the headline in the *New York Herald*.

Clifford, meanwhile, continued to keep his eye out for a better posting. The year before, he had applied to become governor of Mauritius. Again his application was blocked. By the middle of 1912, he had served as colonial secretary for five years: the prominent governorships of Jamaica and Fiji were vacant. It was time for a promotion. 'Frankly, we are quite as anxious as [the Secretary of State] that our Colonial Secretary should have an adequate field for his genius, provided our own island is spared the distinction,' jibed the *Ceylon Morning Leader* at the end of June. At the end of August, Clifford accepted the governorship of the Gold Coast, and on 17 September, a 'large and representative gathering' said farewell to Sir Hugh and Lady Clifford at the Grand Oriental Hotel.

In May 1915, three years after Clifford left the island, ten days of Sinhalese Muslim riots erupted in Ceylon, quelled by martial law. It was Ponnambalam Ramanathan who travelled to England to argue for the release of the Sinhalese leaders held in detention. Not until 1920 was the 'official' majority of government officers on the Legislative Council replaced by an unofficial one that represented the Sinhalese. In the meantime, every reform proposed was blocked.

What had happened to the youthful Clifford's claims to understand the masses of Asia even better than themselves? Clifford left no family letters that let us into his innermost thoughts: only his fiction speaks. A year after he left Ceylon, one of his most poignant short stories was published. 'Our Trusty and Well Beloved' is the story of a distinguished governor, lauded with honours, who returns to a colony he knew as a young man. Pursued by restlessness and insomnia, and memories, 'memories that mocked his present eminence – tore at the heart of him', he tries for a brief evening to step back into the days of his youth. He slips away into the back streets of the town he used to know so well, only to find himself unable to regain the will and trust of the people he loved in time to stop a violent uprising.

For seven years, until 1919, Clifford was governor of the Gold Coast, so notorious for the toll it had taken on the lives of British administrators throughout the nineteenth century. With a free hand to do as he would, he was the first British governor to bring real progress to the territory. The kingdom of the Ashanti at Kumasi had been added to the Gold Coast in 1900; but even by the time Clifford arrived wheels were scarcely known, and no pack animals could survive. He overhauled the administration, and invested heavily in public works, vastly improving the living conditions, and therefore the morale, of public servants. In July 1916, his only son, Hugh, was reported missing in the trenches in France, believed killed in action. That August he was photographed in Togoland, now the Volta region in eastern Ghana, looking grim and old. Ten days later, his younger brother, Henry, was killed. In 1919, Clifford succeeded Lugard as governor of Nigeria, where he served until 1925.

For years, there had been signs that Clifford's behaviour was becoming increasingly eccentric: he once greeted a visitor wearing only his socks. By the time Clifford returned to England from Nigeria, he was showing signs of delusions. In 1925 he was sent again to be governor of Ceylon for a wildly erratic two years, and then on to the dream he had wanted all his days, to be governor of Malaya, in 1927. By this time, he was over sixty, chain-smoking and exhausted, his eyes luminously vacant. The following year, his health completely collapsed. In the summer of 1928 he was shipped home to retirement in England, where from time to time he could be found sitting in a Malay sarong on the steps of the Colonial Office. In 1930 he was confined to the Priory in Roehampton. He died there on 18 December 1941, ten days after the start of the Japanese invasion of Malaya. Elizabeth died four years later.

18 Going home

They that dig foundations deep,
Fit for realms to rise upon,
Little honour do they reap
Of their generation
Any more than mountains gain
Stature till we reach the plain.

Rudyard Kipling, 'The Pro-Consuls', 1906

Sir Hugh Clifford's episode in Ceylon is a fitting illustration of the conflicts and tensions governors would continue to face. Such was his later celebrity as a governor, so adamant his refusal to cover his bald head in the sun (one of the reasons his physician on his second tour in Ceylon explained his tendency to delusion), that he inspired Noël Coward's famous song, 'Mad Dogs and Englishmen'. For years Clifford may have suspected he was descending into madness. In spite of numerous reports to the Colonial Office from those who encountered him, including a warning from King George V to Leo Amery, the Colonial Secretary, about his manic energy and eccentric behaviour, Clifford was offered the post of governor of Ceylon for a second time in 1925. He invited his former principal assistant, Frederick Bowes, to go with him as a sort of unofficial adviser. When Bowes met him, Clifford was in a state of super-excitement. He told him he needed him: he had no memory of the people of Ceylon.

'Poor man – he was very ill,' Bowes wrote. Meanwhile Lady Clifford, apparently in a state of terror, pulled him behind a door to ask him secretly how she found her husband. Clifford told Bowes he had seen an eminent specialist who had passed him as perfectly fit: there were few men like himself who after forty years in the tropics could still enjoy a cold bath, loop the loop or drive their car though London traffic – an experience that as his passenger had distinctly unnerved Bowes.

By the time Clifford reached Malaya in 1927 he was quite mad. 'Most of us do like a personality,' pronounced *British Malaya* cheerfully, after the Governor astounded crowds in Singapore by running up and down the

'Tropical Life': such was Clifford's eminence that by 1925, talk was that he might be offered the Viceroyalty of India, a promotion that was virtually unheard of for a colonial governor

wings of a seaplane in mid-air, to save it from coming down in a squall. 'I have been up very often and enjoy climbing outside during a flight,' he said afterwards. Yet word of more alarming eccentricities – regular night-time telephone conversations with a dead mistress – never appeared in the press. None of his colonial secretaries had the courage to report to London on the true state of his mental health. Even as the fluency of his written dispatches petered out, the failure of the Colonial Office to sense the deteriorating state of his mind was typical, not only of the reluctance of the times to acknowledge mental infirmity, but of the detachment from the day-to-day life in the colonies it was responsible for administering – 'a measure of that Ministry's fitness to guide the Colonial Empire', Bowes bitterly concluded.

Clifford was not the only one who was unsuitable for governorship in his later years. Often the Colonial Office continued to promote those who had seen noble service when they were younger, reluctant to acknowledge shortcomings or that ill health had worn them out. A blind eye was turned to the dubious case of Governor Goldsworthy of British Honduras – today's Belize – a heroic army officer who had fought in the Indian Rebellion, commanded John Glover's Hausa in Lagos and served as his second-in-command on the assault at Kumasi. Goldsworthy had gone on to be president of Nevis, colonial secretary of Western Australia, and administrator of St Lucia. While on home leave from the Honduras in 1885 – now aged forty-six – he was arrested for assaulting a police officer while flirting with a prostitute in Mayfair at two o'clock on an October morning. His brother, an MP, testified on his behalf. Fortunately the arrest of a governor was only reported in one newspaper; after a warning to Goldsworthy, the Colonial Office let the matter drop. But within five years, his increasingly arbitrary and high-handed behaviour in Honduras was causing difficulties for London. Goldsworthy was demoted to the remoteness of the Falklands Islands, from where he retired, three years before his death in 1900.

The governor who lost his nerve when a mob burned down the Red House in Trinidad was Cornelius Moloney, who had a lifetime's experience as a colonial official. Following his father into the 1st West India Regiment, his first posting, at the age of nineteen, was to Sierra Leone as a civil commandant. Seven years later, he was serving as private secretary to George Strahan during his term as governor of the Gold Coast, and was with Strahan when he was stranded for days on the Volta River, struck down like him with a virulent case of malaria.

Moloney was to live in the fevered climate of west Africa for almost twenty-five years, going on to become administrator of the Gambia, and then governor of Lagos in 1886. The peoples, plants and animals of the region fascinated him. He set up a botanic garden and a forestry department in Lagos, and on visits to England cultivated the leading botanists of the day at Kew, sending them samples of plants. While acknowledging the wealth of west Africa's rainforests, Moloney hated to see the death of these majestic trees. In his *Sketch of the Forestry of West Africa*, published in 1887, he pointed out the crucial role of the forests in regulating the climate, pleading for a stop to the wholesale felling of timber that was transforming the wealth of the land into desert wastes and barrenness.

By 1891 Moloney was forty-three. The Colonial Office had accepted his application for a long period of leave to recover his failing health, when all at once there was a change of mind. Moloney was asked to step into Goldsworthy's shoes as governor of British Honduras. He had been in Belize no more than two weeks before his wife was dead of yellow fever. Heartbroken, Moloney begged the Colonial Office to let him retire or, at the least, move him away from the tropics. He was refused. Moloney buckled down to govern for a full five-year term, and built his second botanical station in the grounds of Government House, Belize. The end of 1900 found him in Port of Spain, a victim of recurring attacks of fever, as governor of Trinidad and Tobago, until the fateful day that his order to fire on rioters brought an end to his career.

Overworked, often ill, experienced governors could never get over London's inability to understand the situations they faced on the ground. Glover, Gordon, Bell, Swettenham and, most persistently, Lugard: none believed that those in the Colonial Office knew best what to do. Doubts about the effectiveness of the Colonial Office, more gravely, doubts about the whole mission of Empire, deeply troubled many governors and senior officials who served. What was the real impact they were having on the peoples and the territories they administered?

Soon after Britain annexed Lagos, Frederick Elliott, Permanent Secretary in the Colonial Office, recorded his thoughts. 'Wherever we go in Africa, our views are as enlightened and lofty, compared with those of the barbarous peoples amongst whom we find ourselves, as those of a superior race of beings, and if we choose to employ steamers and a few disciplined troops, our influence is paramount. The apparent good is so great that it is fascinating. But still one cannot help occasionally asking oneself, where is it to end?' Elliott worried about the disparity between Britain's power and her knowledge. 'The first is so tremendous that we can at will, exalt or destroy, but who is to ensure us a corresponding discrimination?'

If Sir Bartle Frere had no doubts about his policies towards the blacks in South Africa, many of those immediately below him did. Captain Charles Warren, whom Lady Frere ensnared to stay on in South Africa against his will, had serious reservations about the legality of the settlement that took the wealth of the Kimberley diamond mines from the Griqua. The liberal Anglican Bishop of Natal, John Colenso, mounted a fierce campaign challenging Frere's actions over the Zulus. Colonel Anthony Durnford, killed on the field at Isandlwana and on whose shoulders most of the blame for the disaster was laid, was horrified at the persistent wrongs done to black Africans: 'I blush for my *white skin* often here,' he wrote in his letters, published in a posthumous memoir by his brother; 'there is little justice for the Natal natives, who, if they but knew their own strength, could hurl the white race into the sea'. One of Lugard's first residents in Northern Nigeria, Charles Orr, wondered if the Fulani emirs were not using the British to abuse the peasantry even more than they had before their arrival.

'Obviously the whole position is utterly hopeless unless one can trust the emir . . . If he is using me to oppress the people, how must they feel towards the government? An alien race, different in colour, ideas, character, habits, religion, backing up the other alien race in oppression – what must they feel? If I am merely an instrument of injustice and oppression, what is the use of my working myself to death in an unhealthy climate amid intense discomfort in exile from home and friends?'

Whatever their private griefs and disillusions, as their careers overseas came to an end governors dreamed of going home at last to Britain, to the old haunts of their youth and the tranquillity of its green countryside, to reward and recognition and comfortable retirement in fashionable parts of London or the Home Counties. Time and again they had been uprooted and transferred across the world. Now their careers of travel and unortho-dox experience, of status and being at the centre of affairs in places and among peoples they had grown to know and perhaps to love, must come to an end.

In 1883, seventy-three-year-old Lord Napier of Magdala faced retire-ment as governor and commander-in-chief of Gibraltar after a lifetime of distinguished service overseas. He had first sailed for India as a Royal Engi-neer at the age of eighteen, served alongside Sir Bartle Frere on the Council of India some thirty years later, and gone on to capture the fortress of Magdala at the head of a heroic Abyssinian campaign in 1868, to become the foremost soldier of his day. Constantly asked to advise the government on every kind of international issue in places from Turkey and Egypt to South Africa, in 1876 he was invited to take on the vital task of overseeing the gar-rison at Gibraltar – key to control of the Mediterranean and beyond, through the Suez Canal to India. There he lived in imperial style with a battery of servants and a large personal staff in the staterooms and private apartments of the Convent, commuting frequently by ship to attend com-mittees in London.

Napier had fifteen children by two wives; now as he contemplated retire-ment he was more and more uneasy at the prospect of returning to live in England. How was he to manage on an income that would be less than two-thirds of the salary to which he was accustomed? Daily, sometimes twice, he wrote to his wife Mary, thirty-two years his junior, carefully revising his sums, recalculating the costs of educating their nine boys (the youngest was two), estimating their tax, trying to work out how they were going to manage and still save money that would provide her with an income once he was dead. The prospect of a future in an unfashionable part of London was galling. He and Mary were going to have to be content to stay quietly at home wherever they settled, he told her, pleading, as they batted back and forth plans of possible places to live, not to 'commence on a heavy Establishment before I return'.

It was not only the money. While Indian viceroys could generally expect a peerage on their retirement to England, it was virtually unheard of to award one to a colonial governor. Of the sample in this book, only Arthur Gordon and Frederick Lugard were raised to the peerage – neither in reward for their services as colonial governors. Gordon, who had gone on from Fiji to govern Ceylon until his retirement in 1890 at the age of sixty, was awarded a peerage three years later by his old mentor, Gladstone, on the understanding that he would support home rule for Ireland in the Lords. Lugard's award was made in 1928, ten years after he left his final posting in Nigeria, largely for his contribution to colonial policy, and his work with the League of Nations. For many, like William des Voeux, retirement to England was soured by lack of recognition and the modesty of pensions.

Once they had been important men, leaders in their society. Like richly paid expatriates of our own day, return to everyday life in England was disillusioning. 'So few of the people one meets take a deep interest in things that do not affect themselves personally or concern their own world beyond the strip of sea that encircles our shores, and are bored if other than local affairs are discussed. Men who have made history, and whose lives have been bound up with practical politics and big undertakings, must suffer from intense loneliness when placed among people who hold narrow views and contracted ideas,' concluded Lady Glover.

By the turn of the twentieth century most of Africa had been conquered; the nation's responsibilities towards her colonies were becoming clarified. There was a clear sense of being in charge of what was officially described as 'the British Colonial Empire'. Including India, Britain was now mistress of an empire that that extended over 11 million square miles – '91 times the area of the Mother Country', of which the 'Colonial Empire' – some forty-nine 'distinct and independent Governments' – was more than eighty times that of the United Kingdom.

Joseph Chamberlain's eight-year term as colonial secretary marked the beginning of slow change at the Colonial Office. He gripped the issue of the devastating numbers of deaths of Europeans from tropical diseases, appointing Sir Patrick Manson, one of the finest experts in tropical medicine, to be his adviser, and founded hospitals for tropical diseases in London and Liverpool. Teams of medical researchers were dispatched to the tropics to investigate the origins of malaria. When, in 1902, a West African Medical Staff was started, it met with amazing success. The death rate of European officials in west Africa fell dramatically from 20.6 per thousand in 1903, to 12.8 in 1924 and 5.1 in 1935.

In 1899, Chamberlain initiated a survey to discover who worked for the Crown in all the colonies around the world: who were they and what did they do? It turned out there were over 400 staff from Britain, some of whom had been selected by the Colonial Office through 'patronage'; others were Far Eastern cadets, admitted by examination. Chamberlain dreamed of a coherent system of colonial administration, with proper staff training and a career structure, to service all Britain's dependencies outside India. He encouraged communication, gave small dinner parties for officials home on leave, and backed the establishment of the Corona Club for officials to meet one another while on leave in London. 'Got an axe to grind?' Chamberlain would say, as he took a seat beside the youngest official in the room to sip his glass of port after dinner.

By 1910, two assistant private secretaries in the Colonial Office dealt with appointments full-time. They sat in a small, very high room, sifting applications made on printed forms boldly headed 'Patronage', interviewing candidates, and making recommendations to the Secretary of State in short memos entitled 'Submission'. 'He wrote his initials at the bottom and the man was in,' wrote Ralph Furse, one of those secretaries, who would go on to develop the Colonial Office's final systems of recruitment over the next thirty years. It was personality and character – above all, the ability to command respect – rather than brains or personal connections that tipped the scales in a candidate's favour. By the outbreak of the First World War the number of university graduates, mainly from Oxford and Cambridge, entering the service had begun steadily to increase. A system of training of colonial officers was implemented in 1924. It was not until 1931, however, that the system of 'patronage' came to an end, and an independent appointments board was created.

Beyond Britain, the Empire was changing. Canada, Australia, New Zealand and South Africa all fought as independent entities during the First World War. Elsewhere, British education systems exported to the colonies were bearing fruit. Black Africans and West Indians, Chinese, Malays and Sinhalese were entering universities. Among the elite, there was a budding sense that however different their societies and cultures, there were bonds that they shared in common. At a three-week Imperial Conference of twenty-six colonies held in 1926, the notion that autonomous countries, equal in status, might be united by allegiance to the Crown sowed the first seed of the Commonwealth. Today there are fifty-four nations.

By 1939, the Colonial Service had mushroomed into a vast machine: 200,000 men and women – not including those 'locally employed' – were working in fifty different colonies around the world, more than twice the size of the British administration in India. Life for the British governor in the tropics was much more civilized. Pith helmets, mosquito nets, firearms and camping equipment remained necessities, and in places like the Gold Coast, where tours of duty were still not much more than a year without a break, wives could only come with official permission. Now, however, governors and their staffs golfed, hunted and played polo, while kerosene fans cooled their houses and motor cars were collected and shipped virtually anywhere in the world. In Hong Kong, the British were advised to wear tinted glasses, and ladies to bring fur coats to wear in winter. Fiji was one of the few places where, while children did not have 'the red cheeks of a more bracing climate', they could safely remain 'until adult life without physical deterioration'.

In Africa white uniformed governors continued to retain autocratic power until the day their colonies became independent from the late 1950s. Elsewhere they were seen as figureheads. Communications improved and the management of Empire was rationalized. The stories of bungling conquest, of accident, amateur improvisation and confrontations of personality that gave rise to the colonies became glossed over by the myths of time. Items of day-to-day administration were forgotten as files were closed. The toll taken on the private lives of colonial governors and their officials from illness, death, separation from loved ones and sheer hard work has never been catalogued. In the popular imagination today, the building of the British Empire is seen as the construction of a machine for power and control in the world.

The lives of these governors show how imperfect this machine was. Greed, ambition, commerce, and politics – to say nothing of religion and a sense of righteousness – all played their part in the story of Empire. But like most of history, the building and running of Britain's colonies was ad hoc and messy. Where there was a vision it was jeopardized by unintended consequences, personality and circumstance.

★

One autumn evening while researching this book I visited the Foreign and Commonwealth Office, where responsibility for the few fragments of the colonial Empire that remain today came to rest in 1968. Tucked away in a corner, beyond the magnificent offices designed by Sir Gilbert Scott for the Foreign Office, with their high, imposing proportions and elaborate decoration, you come to the plain, unadorned corridors that once housed the Colonial Office and the tall corner office where Lords Carnarvon and Kimberley, Joseph Chamberlain, Lewis Harcourt and, later, Winston Churchill laboured. To the left of the door as you enter is a high burr-walnut map case, with pull-down maps labelled in gold: the Seychelles, Mauritius, South Asia and Pakistan, all the names of former colonies around the world. Opposite is a marble fireplace, decorated in scarlet and white, with Queen Victoria's monogram. The room is so vast that on summer evenings before the First World War, when the Secretary of State was safely occupied in the House of Commons, juniors used to play games of stump cricket from the great door to the fireplace. In those days, there was no such thing as dictation. Minutes were written by hand and only the Secretary of State himself was permitted to use red ink. Leather dispatch boxes in red, black and green and bundles of brown folders tied up with red tape stood on a heavy mahogany sideboard. The office had the smell of an old library.

A few months before my visit, in March 2007, an advertisement had appeared in the newspapers, inviting applications for the governorship of St Helena, one of the ten posts of governorship that remain, in places like Gibraltar, the Virgin, Cayman and Falklands Islands, Pitcairn and Bermuda. 'South Atlantic,' it read. 'Attractive Package, 3 year fixed term appointment.' The governor was to be responsible for the good governance of St Helena, Ascension Island and Tristan da Cunha. 'An airport is due to be opened by 2012; the Governor will continue developing the economy to support the opening up of access to the island.' Besides being able to engender 'the right climate for investment', a strong leader and a good strategic thinker 'with the capacity to maintain effective relations with a range of people' was required.

At first glance it seemed as if what was wanted was a chief executive of a modern multinational organization. Reading between the lines, however, I caught a glimpse of the kind of conundrums that faced the governor of old: how to build an economy out of next to nothing, how to work with an elected council, to mix the good of the community while winning and keeping the confidence of the people, in one of the most isolated places on the globe. It was going to take ingenuity, skill, imagination and guts. Whoever got that job was going to be on their own. I thought I might send them this book.

Acknowledgements

For helping me realize an idea: my agent, Bill Hamilton, and my editor, Eleo Gordon.

For signposts: Henry Barlow, Olivier Bell, Kathleen Burk, Else Churchill, Robert Clifford-Holmes, Jack Cross, A. J. Christopher of Nelson Mandela Metropolitan University, Laurence Davies, Kathy de la Rue, Pippa Harris, Jill Hasell at the British Museum, Chantal Knowles, Arthur Lucas, Tamsin Majerus, Dr Anthony Morton, curator of the Sandhurst Collection at the Royal Military Academy, Michael Moss, Sabera Shaik, Colin Studd, Tony Stockwell, Anne Trebilcock and Nick Weekes.

For sharing their private papers and granting me permission to quote from them: Jack Cross of Adelaide, Australia, for his unpublished manuscript, *Facing Asia – the Foundation of the Northern Territory*; Anthea Holmes for Sir Hugh Clifford's papers; the late E. Douglas Potter and his son, Bill, for William Bloomfield Douglas's diary; Sarah Frere for her family's letters; Mark Girouard, Michael Smith and Ian and Pam Reid for the papers of Sir Percy and Lady Girouard, and Her Majesty the Queen.

For help tracking materials: the staff of the British Library, the Royal Geographical Society, the Museum of Archaeology and Anthropology at Cambridge University, the National Archives of Canada and Northland International University in the United States. Many at the National Archives, John Cardwell and Rachel Rowe of the Royal Commonwealth Society Collection at Cambridge University, Pamela Clark and her team at the Royal Archives, Lucy McCann and her staff at the Bodleian Library of Commonwealth & African Studies at Rhodes House, Oxford, and all at the London Library.

For research: Jacqueline Day, Barbara and Phillipa de Lacy, Joseph McAuley, Charlotte Lydia Riley, Sarah Ross-Goobey and David Souden.

For help with the maps: Zoë Shinnick.

For inspiration and encouragement: Roland Chambers, Anne Chisholm, Sybil del Strother, Michael Holroyd, Anthony Kirk-Greene, Sam Knight, Ag MacKeith, Hilary Mantel, Heidi Mirza, Geoff Mulgan, Siriol Troup, Ian Wright and my father, Jeffery Williams.

For respite: Crispin and Shaunagh Latymer.

Finally, for faith. Through all the day-to-day drudgery and the highs and the lows, and without whom I could not possibly have completed this book, my indispensable and adored Sarah, Ian and Sam. Hero of it all, my beloved husband, William.

Notes

My intention in writing this book has been to capture the atmosphere of the times and the voices of the governors and other main protagonists. Wherever possible I have used contemporary phrases to describe people, weather and scenery. In chapters where I have largely depended on a single source to produce the narrative, this will be cited at the beginning of the chapter and, except in the case of quotations which support important statements of fact, these will not be referenced in detail.

Conversions to today's prices come from Lawrence H. Officer, *Measuring Worth*, Measuring Worth, 2010, http://www.measuringworth.com/ukcompare/index.php.

Key to archives

Bodleian Library of Commonwealth & African Studies, Rhodes House, University of Oxford: BOD
British Library: BL
Cambridge University Library: CUL
Canadian National Archives: CNA
National Archives: NA
Royal Archives: RA

Introduction

p. 2 The survey of 1879: all details of descriptions of Government Houses, conditions and living and comments from the governors are from NA CO 537/156 A, B, C, D, where they can be found, catalogued by colony.

p. 2 'These wretched colonies': Disraeli to Malmesbury, 1852, quoted in Stanley R. Stembridge, 'Disraeli and the Millstones', *Journal of British Studies*, 5 (November 1965), pp. 122–39.

p. 9 'The whole tone of the white population': A. J. Stockwell, 'Hugh Clifford in Trinidad', *Caribbean Quarterly*, 24 (March–June 1978), pp. 8–33.

p. 10 'Why, some of them seem to think': Henry Hesketh Bell, *Glimpses of a Governor's Life*, London, 1946, p. 79.

p. 10 'the officer appointed by the Crown': *Colonial Office List*, 1862, p. 75.

p. 11 'the single and supreme authority': Charles Jeffries, *The Colonial Empire and its Civil Service,* Cambridge, 1938, p. xxiii.

Chapter 1: Dispatch

p. 13 'drawn from a rank in society'; 'prepared in the kitchen': John W. Cell, *British Colonial Administration in the Mid-Nineteenth Century: The policy making process*, London & New Haven, 1970, p. 26. Some twenty years later, Sydney Olivier, who would go on to govern Jamaica, spent most of his first three years after taking a degree from Oxford registering dispatches and filling in forms granting extensions of leave to British officers. Officially, the hours had not changed, but they usually did not leave until 7 or 7.30 in the evening, performing the bulk of their work after tea.

p. 14 'an approximation of what they at first expected': *Colonial Office List*, 1862, preface; 'so strangely various': Edward Beasley, *Mid-Victorian Imperialists: British gentlemen and the empire of the mind*, London, 2005, p. 31.

p. 15 'His Lordship regrets that the vacancies': Robert Heussler, *Yesterday's Rulers*, London, 1963, p. 7.

p. 16 'but this he has in common': Sir William des Voeux, *My Colonial Service*, vol. I, London, 1903, p. 254.

p. 16 'There could be no better school': Sir Bartle Frere to Carnarvon, 22 May 1874, *Carnarvon Papers,* BL, vol. lxi, ADD 60797.

p. 17 'Victoria, by the Grace of God': in this case, taken from the draft letters patent for Henry Stanhope Freeman at Lagos, 13 March 1862, NA CO 380/63.

p. 17 'in inverse rather than in direct proportion': Des Voeux, *My Colonial Service*, vol. 1, p. 144.

p. 17 'brittle if too heavily pressed': John Buchan, *Lord Minto: A memoir*, London, 1924, p. 122.

p. 18 Des Voeux is frank: Des Voeux, *My Colonial Service*, vol. 1, p. 148.

p. 20 'Persons entitled to precedence', *Colonial Office List*, 1879.

p. 20 'I have elaborate instructions': H. G. Stanmore, *Fiji: Records of private and public life. 1875–1880*, Edinburgh, 1897, vol. I, p. 124.

p. 20 'of remarkable trees and plants': NA CO 854/21, Circular dated 24 April 1880.

p. 20 'revoltingly botched executions': NA CO 854/21, Circular dated 27 June 1880.

p. 21 'The territory occupied': C.3797 *Census of England and Wales* (43 & 44 Vict. Co. 37) 1881, vol. IV. General report, p. 81. House of Commons Parliamentary Papers Online, 2005.

p. 22 'Up to now I have been entitled': Bell, *Glimpses of a Governor's Life*, p. 99.

p. 23 'Complete India Outfit'; 'Ellis & John's new long cloak' and other advertisements from *Colonial Office List,* 1879.

p. 24 'Look upon the sun' Kerr D, Cross, *Health in Africa*, London, 1897, p. 4.

p. 24 'each dish costing the life of a tree': Lady Glover, *Memories of Four Continents*, London, 1923, p. 97.

p. 24 'To protect the region': Cross, *Health in Africa,* p. 4.

p. 24 'Every article of furniture': At first Denison was prepared to let it slide – 'as an inconvenience, a sort of purchase of an annuity' – but by the time he landed he realized how unfair it was to men sent out as governors 'by compelling them to start their careers under the pressure of debt' and the government 'by limiting its choice of men'. Sir William Denison, *Varieties of Vice-Regal Life*, 2 vols, London, 1870, p. 2.

p. 25 'no small portion . . . one felt there could be but little hope': ibid., p. 4; 'Alas! Our northern stars': ibid., p. 5.

Chapter 2: Commander Glover on the Slave Coast

For an introduction to Sir John Glover see the *Life of Sir John Hawley Glover,* written by his wife, and published in London in 1897. His diary and letters from the voyage on the *Dayspring* were edited by A. C. G. Hastings, and published in various editions up until 1926. Only significant passages of general description have been annotated.

p. 26 'as smooth as a lake'; 'This morning': A. C. G. Hastings, *Voyage of the Dayspring,* London, 1926, p. 47.

p. 26 'A man of dash and daring': Lady Glover, *Life of John Hawley Glover,* London, 1897, p. xix.

p. 27 'All day we were steaming along': Hastings, *Voyage*, p. 51.

p. 27 The following day, the *Dayspring* and ff.: ibid., pp. 53–5.

p. 30 'I liked Mr Crowther's appearance': ibid., p. 59.

p. 30 'I was seized': ibid., p. 61.

p. 31 'The whole is one entire swamp': ibid., p. 70.

p. 31 No one was well: ibid., p. 95.

p. 32 'This is a land of war, distrust and rapine': Glover, *Life,* p. 55.

p. 32 'I am almost mahogany in colour': Glover, *Life*, p. 57.

p. 33 'Christmas morning': ibid., p. 68.

p. 34 'thirsting for his blood, yet not one daring to touch him': Glover, *Life*, p. 80.

p. 34 'Those were the merry days': R. Burton, *Wanderings in West Africa,* London, 1863, vol. II, p. 234.

p. 35 In 1853 Akitoye's son Dosunmu succeeded him: according to Burton, Akitoye poisoned himself in the presence of two slave boys for having failed to give satisfaction to his subjects – in what sense we do not know.

p. 36 'a growth of gigantic trees indicated holy ground': R. Burton, *Abeokuta and the Cameroons Mountains,* London, 1863, p. 17.

p. 37 'amadavats, orioles and brilliant palm birds': ibid., p. 17.

p. 37 'the Governor and his guests': Glover, *Life*, p. 104.

p. 38 'much given to pomp': Mrs Foote, *Recollections of Central America & the West Coast of Africa,* London, 1869, p. 202.

p. 39 Major Leveson, 'a decorated officer': Glover to Cardwell, 6 December 1865. NA CO 147/9.

p. 40 'to some one Person': Blackall to Carnarvon, and minutes, 18 August 1866, NA CO 147/9.

p. 40 'The natives consider exchanging men': Foote, *Recollections*, p. 220.

p. 41 In 1865 a Select Committee: *Report from the Select Committee on Africa (Western Coast),* House of Commons, 26 June 1865.

p.41 'system of Pawns [slaves]': Glover to Cardwell, 7 December 1865, NA CO 147/9.

p. 41 'From the enclosed statement of the woman "Awa"': Glover to Cardwell, 6 December 1865, NA CO 147/9.

p. 42 'Golobar, Chief of the Forces'; 'Emir of Eyo'; 'Commander of all the Great Fire Ships': Hennessy to Kimberley, 31 January 1873, NA CO 147/27.

p. 42 'So great was the consternation': Glover, *Life*, pp. 111–12.

p. 42 'killed and sacrificed': Glover to Cardwell, 7 September 1865, NA CO 147/9.

p. 43 'a want of patience': Blackwell to Glover, 12 April 1867, NA CO 147/13.

p. 43 'How long ought a man': minute by Elliott, 12 July 1862, on Freeman to Newcastle, 4 June 1862, NA CO 147/1.

p. 43 'These literally are the only recent cases'; 'Sheep?' minuted another official: ibid.

p. 44 'The king and his partisans': Glover to Blackall, 16 January 1866, NA CO147/11.

p. 44 'When I showed [the Bashorun]': Glover to Blackall, 14 February 1867, NA CO 147/13.

p. 44 'a neat and tidy African town': Hennessy to Kimberley, 27 April 1872, NA CO147/23.

p. 45 'in order that he might': 'The Condition of Lagos', reprinted from the *Manchester Courier*, 5 November 1872, in NA CO 147/25.

p. 45 'It is impossible not to see': Hennessy to Kimberley, 30 April 1872, NA CO 147/23; 'not to listen to the white merchants'; 'could lead to the closure of that market': Disposition of traders, 29 April 1872, enclosed in ibid.

p. 46 'the question of Slavery': Glover to Livingstone, 11 May 1872, NA CO 147/23.

p. 46 'Your good friend': Hennessy to the Alake, Ogbonis, Baloguns & Parakoyes of Abbeokuta [*sic*], 30 April 1872, NA CO 147/23.

p. 46 'a public declaration': Hennessy to Glover, 18 May 1872, NA CO 147/23.

p. 47 'Captain Glover': Glover to Kimberley, London, 7 November 1872, NA CO 147/26.

p. 47 'appears to have misunderstood': Hennessy to Hopkins, 18 June 1872, NA CO 147/23.

p. 48 'I discerned the sturdy form': Glover, *Life*, p. 177.

Chapter 3: The loneliness of the righteous governor

All quotations in this chapter, unless otherwise indicated, have been taken from the first volume of Sir William des Voeux's account of his life, *My Colonial Service*, published in London in 1903.

p. 50 'The planters were again doomed': Cmd 3165. Blue Book report for St Lucia 1861, *Accounts and papers of the House of Commons*, vol. XXXIX, London, 1863.

p. 59 The Court of Policy: until the British were ceded control of the colony at the end of the Napoleonic wars in 1814, it had been Dutch, and little reform had taken place since. Power rested with the Governor, a Court of Policy, and a combined court. Control of the unofficials of the Court of Policy rested with nominations by two ancient bodies of 'Kiezers', appointed for life, whose past qualification was to be elected by the votes of those who had not owned fewer than twenty-five slaves. *Colonial Office List* 1867, pp. 23–4.

p. 64 Christmas Day, 1869: 'My Lord, I should not more delay' and ff.: Des Voeux to Granville, 25 December, 1869, 'Report of the Commissioners appointed to enquire into the Treatment of Immigrants in British Guiana', *Parliamentary Papers*, vol. 20 [C.393] (1871).

p. 65 'so appalling and involving such cruelty': *The Times,* 17 October 1871.

p. 66 'Your Commissioners we give God the Glory': E. Jenkins, *The Coolie, His Rights & Wrongs*, London, 1871, p. 150.

p. 68 'The continual presence in the house': Des Voeux, *My Colonial Service*, p. 264.

Chapter 4: Captain Douglas settles Palmerston

Captain Douglas's daughter, Harriet, who married Dominic Daly, the son of the Governor of South Australia, while the family was stationed at Palmerston, left a fine account of the earliest days of the settlement in *Digging, Squatting, and Pioneering Life in the Northern Territory of South Australia,* published in London in 1887, from which general descriptions are taken.

p. 70 'It is evident that, of this great continent': Denison, *Varieties,* 8 January 1857, p. 374.

p. 72 'The water of this river': William Hardman, ed., *The Journals of John McDouall Stuart,* London, 1865, p. 314; 'Delighted and gratified': ibid., p. 328; 'If this country is settled': ibid., p. 328.

p. 76 'The cooking-establishment was perfect' and ff.: Sir Henry Keppel, Sir James Brooke, Walter Keating Kelly, *The Expedition to Borneo of HMS Dido for the Suppression of Piracy,* vol. II, London, 1847, p. 17.

p. 76 'to extirpate piracy': Brooke to Templer, 31 December 1844, in John C. Templer, *The Private Letters of Sir James Brooke,* vol. II, London, 1853, p. 42.

p. 77 'which would be an excellent thing provided it was permanent': Brooke to Templer, 4 October 1843, in ibid., vol. I, London, 1853, p. 299.

p. 77 Initial news of Douglas's appointment: Mrs Dominic C. Daly, *Digging, Squatting, and Pioneering Life in the Northern Territory of South Australia,* London, 1887, p. 10.

p. 77 'He never said a word about the £100 I lent him': 28 April 1870, Captain John Hart, diaries, quoted in Jack Cross, *Facing Asia – the Foundation of the Northern Territory,* unpublished mss.

p. 77 Annie, whose '*affaires de coeur*' : Daly, *Digging*, p. 13.

p. 78 'The place looked what it was' and ff.: ibid., pp. 44–6.

p. 80 'additional measures for promoting immigration': Granville to Fergusson, 9 February 1870, and minute, quoted in Cross, *Facing Asia*.

p. 83 'a classical but strictly Larrakiah name': Daly, *Digging*, p. 66.

p. 83 'Douglas kept track of their comings and goings: one of the old blacks': Kathy de la Rue, *The Evolution of Darwin 1869–1911*, Darwin, 2004, p. 29. A man speared Dr Millner's favourite hack; the offender, Binmook, had, it turned out, taken action after his dog was shot by a settler, for killing some of his fowls. Douglas sentenced him to a dozen strokes across his shoulders with a riding whip and released him. Douglas noted that the Aborigines were less offended by this kind of physical punishment than by incarceration, which they regarded as barbaric. Cross, *Facing Asia*.

p. 84 'Can it be credited that the whole Franco-Prussian war': Daly, *Digging*, p. 126.

p. 84 Meanwhile, inland: 'He sometimes almost sentences men': 5 June 1871, *Diaries of Edward Napoleon Buonaparte Catchlove,* State Library of South Australia; 'lolling about': 11 October 1871, ibid.

p. 85 'A really payable gold field': Douglas to Commissioner of Crown Lands, 29 August 1871, enc. in Ferguson to Kimberley, 11 October 1871, NA CO 138/128.

p. 86 'Clouds and close': 16 January 1872, *Douglas Diary*; Douglas Papers.

p. 86 'with prickly heat': 12 February 1872, *Catchlove Diaries*.

p. 86 In the diary: 'settled into the accounts': 15 January 1872, *Douglas Diary*; 'Pickles': 17 January, 1872, ibid.; Mr Little's [a telegraph officer] manner': 2 May 1872, ibid.

p. 86 'very ill all day': 15 May 1872, ibid.

p. 86 'on a medical certificate': 25 May 1872, ibid.

p. 86 'vomiting, [with] dreadful depression': 18 June 1872, ibid.

p. 87 'nothing would persuade me to the contrary': 20 June 1872, ibid.

p. 87 Douglas barricaded himself: 20 June 1872, ibid.

p. 87 'I shall have to give up': 24 July 1872, ibid.

p. 87 Douglas's trip : 'Not having during my long experience': 26 September 1872, ibid. ; '*I am 50*': 25 September 1872, ibid.

p. 88 'the shamefully disorganised state': Report on Northern Territory, 30 July 1873, NA CO 15/62.

pp. 88–9 For months Douglas had realized: 'The division of authority': Douglas to Reynolds, 2 June 1873; 'to be free': Douglas to Reynolds, 4 June 1873, quoted in Cross, *Facing Asia*.

p. 89 'a familiar figure': John Gullick, 'Biographical note on Bloomfield Douglas', *Journal of Malaysian Branch of the Royal Asiatic Society*, vol. 48 (2), 1975.

Chapter 5: Fever and delusion

The correspondence between Lord Carnarvon and Captain George Strahan is taken from 'Carnarvon's personal correspondence with the Governors of the West Africa Coast, 1874–1878' at the National Archives, PRO 30/6/24.

p. 92 'I hardly remember a time': Arthur Hardinge, *The Life of Henry Howard Molyneux Herbert, Fourth Earl of Carnarvon, 1831–1890*, Oxford, 1925, p. 58.

p. 94 'A very evil choice': W. E. F. Ward, *A History of the Gold Coast*, London, 1948, p. 257.

p. 94 'What this place wants': Wolseley to Duke of Cambridge, 27 February 1874, Ian F. W. Beckett, ed., *Wolseley and Ashanti*, Stroud, 2009, p. 409.

p. 95 'He is a very nice fellow': Wolseley's Journal, 22 September 1873, Beckett, *Wolseley and Ashanti*, p. 82.

p. 95 'selfish interests or the ambition for larger empire': W. D. MacIntyre, 'Commander Glover and the Colony of Lagos, 1861–73', *Journal of African History*, 4, no. 1 (1963), pp. 57–79.

p. 96 'sick and weakly': Albert Augustus Gore, *Medical History of Our West African Campaigns*, London, 1876, p. 5. Studies showed that although the death rates were far lower among black troops from the West Indies and those recruited locally, the incidence of sickness was still very high: twice as many West Indian troops were admitted with fever as Fantees from the Gold Coast – but, curiously, the mortality rate of the Fantees was higher.

p. 96 'Why ought we perversely': *The Times*, 16 April 1874.

p. 96 'Pestilential morasses': Glover, *Life*, p. xxi.

p. 96 'exhalations from the wet earth': Mr C. A. Gordon, MD, letter to *The Times*, 29 August 1873.

p. 96 'the new-comer imagines'; 'a scorching fever': ibid.

p. 97 'wretched sallow look': Gore, *Medical History*, p. 149.

p. 97 'for reasons that are still not fully understood today, only a large dose of quinine might stop the course of fever in its tracks: basically, quinine interrupts the process by making the young parasites choke on the products of their own digestion.

p. 98 'the heated men'; 'prevent annoyance': 'Preservation of Health on the Gold Coast', *The Times*, 16 January 1874.

p. 98 The campaign only lost fifteen men: Gore, *Medical History*, p. 140.

p. 99 'the deadliness of the climate': Carnarvon to Wolseley, 27 February 1874, NA PRO 30/6/24.

p. 99 'for one person to dine': Frederick Boyle, *Through Fanteeland to Coomasie*, London, 1874, p. 33.

p. 100 'Never did I leave any spot': Wolseley's Journal, 4 March 1874, Beckett, *Wolseley and Ashanti*, p. 411.

p. 100 'a spot saturated with filth': Sale: Report on the future recommending Accra, 5 March 1875, NA CO 96/117.

p. 100 There were pleasures: 'casting languishing glances around': A. B. Ellis, *West Africa Sketches*, London, 1881, p. 192; 'really a very good looking girl': Wolseley to Louisa Wolseley, [17]–26 October 1873, *Wolseley and Ashanti*, p.174; 'divine' Sunday: Hardinge, *The Life*, p. 67.

p. 102 What about the 'rising ground' at the back of Elmina: Carnarvon to Strahan, 16 August 1874, NA PRO 30/6/24.

p. 102 'I trust that I may soon have at my disposal the services of an efficient staff': Strahan to Carnarvon, 20 September 1874.

p. 103 'a powerful element': Strahan to Carnarvon, 7 August 1874, no. 93, *Correspondence relating to the affairs of the Gold Coast*, 1875, C.1139; C.1140; House of Commons Parliamentary Papers Online.

p. 103 the situation of domestic slaves, treated almost like family, was such that few would 'avail themselves of opportunities for self-redemption': Strahan to Carnarvon, 19 September, 1874, no. 5, ibid.

p. 104 'on negotiations with the native Kings': Carnarvon to Strahan, 30 October 1874 , no.118, *Correspondence relating to the affairs of the Gold Coast*.

p. 104 'I need hardly say': Carnarvon to Strahan, 6 November 1874, NA PRO 30/6/24.

p. 104 'In no country': Rowe to Carnarvon, 1 July 1874, no. 50 in *Correspondence relating to the affairs of the Gold Coast*.

p. 105 'where Mangrove bushes grow'; 'in their own persons': Memorandum of sanitary conditions of certain places on the Gold Coast by Dr Samuel Rowe, 13 February 1875, NA CO 96/117; 'valuable services of Dr Rowe': Carnarvon to Strahan, 9 March 1875, NA CO 96/117.

p. 105 'the most unhealthy stations': Carnarvon to Strahan, 28 May 1875, NA PRO 30/6/24.

p. 106 *'as soon as possible'*: Freeling to Carnarvon, 17 March 1877, NA PRO 30/6/24.

p. 107 'attacked with a fatal cold': *New York Times*, 12 March 1887. His legacy, the two ordinances on the abolition of slavery, which, although scholars disagree, seem to have made little impact: see McSheffrey, Gerald M., 'Slavery, Indentured Servitude, Legitimate Trade and the Impact of Abolition in the Gold Coast, 1874–1901: A Reappraisal', *Journal of African History*, 24, no. 3 (1983), pp. 349–68.

Chapter 6: *White stalkers on the beach*

Both Arthur Gordon, later Lord Stanmore, and his wife, Rachael, kept most of their letters and diaries from their time in Fiji. H. G. Stanmore, *Fiji: Records of private and public life. 1875–1880* was published in four volumes in Edinburgh in 1897. The second volume is almost entirely devoted to 'The Little War' that broke out in the highlands of Viti Levu ten months after Gordon landed. Descriptive quotations not noted below come from these volumes.

In Fiji, 'B' is pronounced 'MB', 'C' is 'TH' and 'Q' is 'NGG'. Thus Cakobau is sometimes written, and pronounced, 'Thakombau' and the drink '*yaqona*' is 'yangona'.

p. 108 *A Fijian Glossary:* from Deryck Scarr, *Fiji: Politics of Illusion, the Military Coups in Fiji,* Sydney, 1988, p. xi.

p. 109 'The Great Chief who has charged me': (Mrs C.) H. B. Richenda Parham, *Fiji Before the Cession,* printed in the *Fiji Times,* 1933–41 (manuscript copy in the British Library).

p. 111 After ten months on the islands: Mrs (Sarah Maria) Smythe, *Ten Months in the Fiji Islands, with an introduction and appendix by Col. W. J. Smythe,* London, 1864, p. 207.

p. 111 As for the task of civilizing the natives: ibid., p. 208.

p. 112 'If matters remain as they are': J. D. Legge, *Britain in Fiji*, London, 1958, p. 151.

p. 112 'You won't eat *me*': C. F. Cumming, *At Home in Fiji*, London, 1881, p. 18.

p. 113 'You have been a Hot House plant': J. K. Chapman, *The Career of Arthur Hamilton Gordon*, Toronto, 1964, p. 4.

p. 113 'an excessive desire to be eminent': ibid., p. 6.

p. 113 'I am *always* awkward': F. M. G. Willson, *A Strong Supporting Cast: The Shaw Lefevres, 1789–1936*, London, 1993, p. 279.

p. 114 Gordon fell in love: 'wild, free forest life': Chapman, *The Career*, p. 44; 'Thy servant Arthur': *Oxford Dictionary of National Biography;* 'Socially I don't suppose': Willson, *A Strong Supporting Cast*, p. 194.

p. 114 He was lonely: 'essentially foreigners'; 'Blue-noses': Chapman, *The Career,* p. 18; 'I won't marry'; 'Why don't you come': Willson, *A Strong Supporting Cast*, p. 194.

p. 114 As a trustee of University College London, Rachael's father was outspoken in his support for women taking university degrees; in 1879 her closest sister, Madeleine, seven years younger, would become the first head of Somerville College, Oxford.

p. 114 'that a lady's voice': Willson, *A Strong Supporting Cast*, p. 279.

p. 115 'utterly unfit . . . to be the Governor of a Constitutional Colony': ibid., p. 201. He felt himself a mere puppet 'dragged helpless through the degrading dirt [by] the cobblers, tinkers, tailors and thieves who, with few exceptions were the politicians of that region': Chapman, *The Career*, p. 46.

p. 115 'very small and wretched': Gordon to Gladstone, 26 March 1866, Paul Knapland, 'Gladstone–Gordon Correspondence, 1851–1896: Selections from the Private Correspondence of a British Prime Minister and a Colonial Governor', *Transactions of the American Philosophical Society* (American Philosophical Society), New Series 51, no. 4 (1961), pp. 1–116.

p. 115 He landed to a crowded and enthusiastic reception: Gordon to Lady Gordon, 7 December 1868, Stanmore Papers, BL, 49,225, f. 57.

p. 116 'It is almost necessary to have been Governor': Chapman, *The Career*, p. 45.

p. 116 The voyage was so awful: Gordon to Gladstone, 3 and 30 May 1871, Knapland, 'Gladstone–Gordon Correspondence'.

p. 117 'You will I am sure': Gordon to Gladstone, 26 July 1874, ibid.

p. 117 'The prospect of *founding* a colony': Gordon to Lady Gordon, 15 July

1874, Arthur Hamilton Gordon, *Mauritius. Records of private and public life, 1871–1874,* 2 vols, Edinburgh, 1894, II, pp. 646–9.

p. 117 Still, Gordon argued: Stanmore, *Fiji,* vol. I, p. 43.

p. 118 'I was to call the chief place Patteson': Bishop Patteson was murdered by islanders in the Solomons in September 1871 in revenge for 'recruiting' labour for Queensland's plantations. In England, bodies like the Aborigines Protection Society and missionary societies organized a campaign during 1872–3 to persuade Gladstone's Cabinet to annex Fiji.

p. 118 It was not until . . . March, 1875: Stanmore, *Fiji,* vol, 1, p. 65.

p. 118 'a regular globe trotter': Alfred Maudslay, *Life in the Pacific,* London, 1930, p. 84.

p. 119 'Some pleasant fellow-passengers': Stanmore, *Fiji,* vol. I, p. 72; 'Somaulis, and Arabs, Hindoos': ibid., pp. 79–83.

p. 119 'But it is, oh! so hot': ibid., p. 83; 'I longed to stop and pick up all kinds of curiosities': ibid., p. 97.

p. 120 'I do not much like Sydney': ibid., p. 111.

p. 120 "*You* won't like it, Lady Gordon": ibid., p. 238.

p. 120 Measles had killed more than 40,000: these are Gordon's figures. See ibid., p. 121.

p. 120 'The canoe of our death': traditional *meke* quoted in Parham, *Fiji Before the Cession.*

p. 121 'bringing back baskets full of all sorts of curious, rainbow coloured fish': Cumming, *At Home in Fiji,* p. 37.

p. 122 'Everything here far exceeds my expectations': Stanmore, *Fiji,* vol. I, p. 125.

p. 122 Three days later Cakobau came: ibid., p. 127.

p. 122 'strapping Tongan women': Deryck Scarr, *The Majesty of Colour,* Canberra, 1973, vol. II, two tons of yams were collected, and sent to the starving islanders.

p. 123 'He is a far more striking man than the photographs' and ff.: Stanmore, *Fiji,* vol. I, p. 127.

p. 124 'the whole of the land within the limits of Fiji': Chapman, *The Career,* p. 203.

p. 125 It would be impossible 'to deny to the natives a large measure of self-government': Stanmore, *Fiji,* vol. I, p. 197.

p. 125 'there is a charming fellow here – Olive, of the marines': ibid., p. 124.

p. 125 The new Attorney-General, de Ricci: 'shifty, intriguing': ibid., p. 138; '*on the shoulders* of some native policemen', ibid., p. 224.

p. 125 Gordon was revelling in Fiji: ibid., pp. 160–61.

p. 126 Gordon had taken immediately to this rite, and ff.: ibid., pp. 161–2.

p. 126 'Have you learnt enough Fijian to know what *malua* means?': ibid., p. 150; 'The town (which I rarely enter)' and ff.: ibid., p. 138.

p. 127 'First I went all over the house': ibid., p. 269.

p. 128 None of them was over thirty: Maudslay, *Life in the Pacific*, pp. 86–9.

p. 128 Nurse came down every morning to dress Rachael: Stanmore, *Fiji,* vol. I, pp. 171–2.

p. 129 'We constantly have three or four extra *men*': ibid., p. 172.

p. 129 By the middle of October: ibid., p. 273.

p. 129 'Sometimes I am afraid he will get ill': 2 November 1875, ibid., p. 297.

p. 129 'I have given up the idea of having things nice': ibid., p. 345; 'our expenses are enormous': ibid., p. 308.

p. 130 The sacred attachment which the Fijians felt for their lands: Sir William des Voeux, who succeeded Gordon, wrote that Fijians held ownership of land 'to be so sacred a nature that permissive occupation for any length of time had no effect in prescribing the rights of the original proprietors. In one case ... the occupiers of certain land were asked if they were the owners; to which the reply was that at a period long past, having been driven out of their own territory by a hostile tribe, they were allowed to settle upon it by the true owners; that they had, therefore, no right in it themselves, and still regarded themselves as "vulgagi" or strangers.' Des Voeux, *My Colonial Service*, vol. II, p. 358.

p. 130 Every week or so he set off on another trip: Stanmore, *Fiji,* vol. I, p. 388.

p. 131 For Rachael, it was a relief: ibid., p. 345.

p. 131 Gordon was once more glorying in the strange life: ibid., vol. II, p. 12.

p. 131 Dressed in a pair of unbleached drill trousers: ibid., p. 129; 'We get up when it feels warm enough': ibid., p. 96.

p. 132 'I wish I could give you some idea': ibid., p. 71.

p. 132 'I miss all reference to Major Pratt and his soldiers': Carnarvon to Gordon, 14 September 1876, ibid., p. 222.

p. 133 It had been Maudslay, and ff.: Lady Gordon to Madeleine Shaw Lefevre, 10 July 1877, ADD49234, Stanmore papers, BL, vol. XXXII.

p. 133 'The house now moves like a clock': Cumming, *At Home in Fiji*, p. 250; 'William and Moses are so handsome and graceful': Stanmore, *Fiji,* vol. II, p. 38; 'the Governor and staff all wear': ibid., p. 180.

p. 133 'rather a large pill': Chapman, *The Career*, p. 199.

p. 134 'I am not given to screaming hysterics': Gordon to Herbert, 22 January 1878, Stanmore, *Fiji,* vol. II, pp. 704–5.

p. 134 Meanwhile, the traders and planters hated Thurston and Gordon's new system of taxation: 'native' taxes rose in Fiji from £6,000 in 1873 under King Cakobau's poll tax to £19,885 in 1879 under Gordon's regime. It would have reached Gordon's estimate of £21,000 in 1880 had there not been a drastic decline in prices due to a general depression. Gordon preferred a drop in revenue to a forced increase in Fijian production. Chapman, *The Career*, p. 170.

p. 134 'What uphill work it all is': Stanmore, *Fiji,* vol. II, p. 324.

p. 135 'What I should *like* would be, everything clean twice a day': Lady Gordon to Mary Shaw-Lefevre, 25 January 1876, Stanmore, *Fiji,* vol. I, p. 402.

p. 135 Eka didn't 'mind any amount of roughing': ibid., vol. II, p. 123; 'dressy, affected, [and] silly': 23 November to 1 December 1877, ibid., p. 643.

p. 135 Meanwhile, Rachael watched the Fijian women: ibid., p. 150.

p. 135 By December 1877 she was writing: 'I don't think we have ever had such a dull time': 23 November to 1 December 1877, ibid., p. 641; 'dread . . . going among people again': Stanmore, *Fiji,* vol. III, p. 140.

p. 136 'literary occupation, pleasant society, my books round me': Willson, *A Strong Supporting Cast*, p. 282.

p. 136 'I quit my wife, my children': ibid., p. 282.

p. 136 His system of taxation in kind: Sir William des Voeux, his successor, remarked that it was a 'remarkable and probably unprecedented fact [that] we are able to raise such a sum from a race like the Fijians without the presence of either soldiers or of armed vessels': Chapman, *The Career*, p. 170.

p. 137 'There was no longer the same passive waiting for suggestions which had been shown on previous occasions': Stanmore, *Fiji*, vol. IV, pp. 199–200.

p. 137 'a puppet – a leaden seal – the mere instrument of his Ministers': Stanmore, ibid., p. 500.

p. 137 He never ceased to worry what would happen to Fiji: ibid., p. 246.

p. 137 'the free unconventional dress': [Letter to Lady Gordon, 29 October 1880], ibid., p. 475; 'above all, the men': ibid., p. 500.

Chapter 7: The washing of the spears

The authorized biography of Sir Bartle Frere, produced from his papers, assembled faithfully by Lady Frere and his two eldest daughters, May and Catherine, is the two-volume *The Life and Correspondence of Sir Bartle Frere,* written by John Martineau and published in London in 1895.

p. 139 'Dead was the horse': Muziwento, who as a boy lived near Isandlwana, quoted in J. Laband, *Fight Us in the Open: the Anglo-Zulu War through Zulu eyes*, Pietermaritzburg, 1985, p. 21.

p. 140 'a very important and critical matter': Carnarvon to Frere, 13 October 1876, NA PRO 30/6/33.

p. 140 'Your letter found me here': Frere to Carnarvon, 18 October 1876; 'nor would it do for me', Frere to Carnarvon, 6 November 1876, NA PRO 30/6/33.

p. 141 Frere 'is to try & set matters right': 6 March 1877, RA VIC/MAIN/QVJ/ 1877.

p. 141 'very long & rather twaddling': Sir Henry to Lady Ponsonby, 28 August 1873, RA VIC/ADDA36/616; 'a dear old patapouf': Sir Henry to Lady Ponsonby, 12 September 1875, RA VIC/ADDA36/95 ; 'said to be a superior person': Sir Henry to Lady Ponsonby, 1 October 1876, RA VIC/ADDA36/1143.

p. 141 Within a year: John Martineau, *The Life and Correspondence of Sir Bartle Frere,* London, 1895, vol. I, p. 43.

p. 143 'I noticed also his lover-like devotion': ibid., p. 53.

p. 146 'It is still Summer here': Frere to Victoria, 10 April 1877; RA VIC/ MAIN/O/32/104.

p. 146 'Then there is the Hottentot admixture': Anthony Trollope, *South Africa*, London, 1878, p. 70.

p. 146 'sleepy and slipshod': Martineau, *The Life*, vol. II, p. 164.

p. 147 'What can be worse than this?': H. A. Bryden, *The Victorian Era in South Africa,* London, 1897, p. 7.

p. 147 'Every available minute': Frere to Carnarvon, 10 June 1877, NA PRO 30/ 6/33.

p. 148 'nothing but annexation': Martineau, *The Life*, vol. II, p. 181.

p. 148 'as of everything else': Frere to Ponsonby, 1 May 1877, RA VIC/ MAIN/O/32/105.

p. 149 'I was fully intending': Sir Charles Warren, *On the Veldt in the Seventies,* London, 1902, p. 205.

p. 149 'Lady Frere finds me plenty to do': ibid., p. 207.

p. 149 'We all went for a walk': ibid., p. 210.

p. 150 'there are so many rumours': ibid., p. 216.

p. 150 'I have had an ominous letter': ibid., p. 384.

p. 150 'by no means bad fellows': Frere to Duke of Cambridge, 27 May 1878, RA VIC/ADDE/1/8323.

p. 150 'Sir Bartle says': Lady Frere to Carnarvon, 28 August 1877, NA PRO 30/6/33.

p. 150 'in which Elephants': Frere to Carnarvon, 30 August 1877, NA PRO 30/6/33.

p. 150 'so favoured by nature': Frere to Victoria, 14 October 1877, RA VIC/MAIN/O/32/123.

p. 150 'the houses too far apart': Martineau, *The Life*, vol. II, p. 193.

p. 151 'very rambling': Frere to Carnarvon, 3 October 1877, ibid., p. 194.

p. 151 'Unless I had seen it myself': Frere to Ponsonby, 17 October 1877, ibid., p. 199.

p. 151 'the smouldering discontents': Frere to Victoria, 13 February 1878, RA VIC/MAIN/O/33/8.

p. 152 'the Dutch Command system': Frere to Victoria, 14 October 1877, RA VIC/MAIN/O/32/123.

p. 152 'Even as far down as Algoa Bay': Lady Frere to Carnarvon, 20 November 1877, NA PRO 30/6/34.

p. 152 'every ounce of flour': H. H. Parr, *Sketch of Kafir and Zulu Wars,* London, 1880, p. 77.

p. 152 'We do not seem to have had much decisive news': Eliza Frere to Anne Frere, 7 January 1878, Frere papers.

p. 153 'It suited the . . . Ministry': Frere to Duke of Cambridge, 20 February 1878, RA VIC/ADDE/1/8245.

p. 153 'You may confidently contradict': Frere to Lady Frere, 3 February 1878, RA VIC/MAIN/O33/3.

p. 153 'the Prime Minister told me': Frere to Duke of Cambridge, 20 February 1878, RA VIC/ADDE/1/8245.

p. 154 This news 'has, without any figure of speech': Frere to Carnarvon, 17 February 1878, Martineau, *The Life*, vol. II, p. 219.

p. 156 'Did I ever tell Mr Shepstone': H. Rider Haggard, *Cetywayo and His White Neighbours*, London, 1888, p. 13.

p. 156 'come with the next full moon'; memorial to Sir T. Shepstone from Reverend Mr Filter and 19 others praying for protection against the Zulus, May 1878, NA CO 879/14.

p. 157 'Zulus had been found': Parr, *Sketch*, p. 99.

p. 157 'a general and simultaneous rising': Frere to R. W. Herbert, 18 March 1878, Martineau, *The Life*, vol. II, p. 223.

p. 157 'Urgent summonses': Frere to Victoria, 17 September 1878, RA VIC/MAIN/O/33/21.

p. 157 'a very dreary life': Frere to HRH Prince of Wales, 9 November 1878, RA VIC/ADDA5/136.

p. 158 'every form of selfish and narrow-minded difficulty': Frere to Herbert, 12 January, 1879, Martineau, *The Life*, vol. II, p. 239.

p. 158 'almost fanatically just and loyal': Frere to Hicks Beach, 30 September 1878, Martineau, *The Life*, vol. II, p. 238.

p. 158 'as one might a tame wolf': Frere to Ponsonby, 23 December 1878, RA VIC/MAIN/O/33/34.

p. 158 'properly treated, the Natal Kaffir': Frere to Duke of Cambridge, 28 December 1878, RA VIC/ADDE/1/8486.

p. 158 'the Zulus are now quite out of hand': Frere to Hicks Beach, 30 September 1878, Martineau, *The Life*, vol. II, p. 244. He went on: 'I assure you the peace of south Africa for many years to come seems to me to depend on your taking steps to put a final end to Zulu pretensions to dictate to Her Majesty's Government . . . unless you settle with the Zulus you will find it difficult, if not impossible to govern the Transvaal without a considerable standing force of Her Majesty's troops.'

p. 158 'the demon king', Cetewayo: Frere to Hicks Beach, 28 October 1878, NA CO 879/14.

p. 159 'into a position clearly subordinate': Frere to Hicks Beach, 8 December 1878, ibid.

p. 160 'Still no news on C's compliance': Frere to Hicks Beach, 6 January 1879, ibid.

p. 160 'As soon as the cavalry': Parr, *Sketch*, p. 180.

p. 161 'South Africa has reached its crisis': Thomas B. Jenkinson, *Amazulu*, London, 1882, p. 81.

p. 162 'whom you are bound': Frere to May Frere, received 3 March 1879, RA VIC/MAIN/N/36/7.

p. 162 'Ketchawayo is said': Jenkinson, *Amazulu*, p. 82.

p. 162 'the very serious damage': Frere to Hicks Beach, 3 February 1897, NA CO 897/14.

p. 162 'You must not be anxious': Colonel Lanyon to Lady Frere, 8 April 1879, RA VIC/MAIN/O/34/36.

p. 162 'I was glad': Sir Bartle to Lady Frere, 10 April 1879, RA VIC/MAIN/O/34/49.

p. 163 'their fear and hate of a savage race': quoted from an article in the *Daily News,* Martineau, *The Life*, vol. II, pp. 312–13; 'very careful consideration . . . reposed in you': Hicks Beach to Frere, 19 March 1879, NA CO 879/14/13.

p. 164 'Throughout the whole of South Africa': speech by Sir Bartle Frere, and others delivered at Cape Town, 11 June 1879, published by John Murray, London, 1879, RA VIC/MAIN/O/35/11.

p. 164 'In both Houses of Parlt' : 19 March 1879, RA VIC/MAIN/QVJ/1879.

p. 164 'Why is [he] considered': telegram from Queen Victoria to Lord Beaconsfield, 23 May 1879, RA VIC/MAIN/O/34/87.

p. 164 'I am waiting to know': Frere to Prince of Wales, 5 August 1879, RA VIC ADDA5/189.

p. 164 'Irresponsible radicals': Frere to Prince of Wales, 30 October 1879, RA VIC/MAIN/T/7/109.

p. 165 'an animal long indulged': Frere to May Frere, 7 March 1879, RA VIC/MAIN/O/34/57.

p. 165 'He told me': Frere to Victoria, 15 September 1879, RA VIC/MAIN/O/36/32.

p. 165 'undoubtedly presented a ridiculous appearance': Ponsonby to Frere, 15 November 1879, RA VIC/MAIN/O/36/86.

p. 165 'poor Sir Bartle': 10 October 1880, RA VIC/MAIN/QVJ/1880.

p. 166 'They would surely understand': Martineau, *The Life*, vol. II, p. 451.

Chapter 8: 'The mind of heaven and earth'

Virtually all Sir John Pope Hennessy's papers were burnt by his wife, Kitty, after his death. In 1964, his grandson, James Pope-Hennessy, published a wry memoir of him, *Verandah,* based on family lore, Hennessy's few surviving personal papers and his correspondence with the Colonial Office. Pope-Hennessy's notes and his grandfather's handful of private papers are now at the Bodleian Library of Commonwealth & African Studies, University of Oxford, where I have consulted them to verify the accuracy of Pope-Hennessy's treatment of Hennessy's career, specifically in Hong Kong. Unless otherwise indicated, all quotations in this chapter are from *Verandah,* pp. 185–228.

p. 169 'an impassable fence': Geoffrey Robley Sayer, *Hong Kong, 1862–1919,* Hong Kong, 1975, p. 9.

p. 170 'You will like to know who have got the nicest houses here': Jan Morris, *Hong Kong,* London, 1988, p. 83.

p. 170 'Obey and remain': G. B. Endacott, *A History of Hong Kong,* Hong Kong, 1964, p. 6.

p. 170 'A harmless luxury': ibid., p. 11.

p. 171 'There can be neither safety nor honour': ibid., p. 14.

p. 171 'to this fascinating vice': Morris, *Hong Kong*, p. 83.

p. 172 According to the *New York Times*: 'The Troubles in Barbados', *New York Times*, 29 April 1876.

p. 172 Training as a doctor was his parents' idea: James Pope-Hennessy, *Verandah*, London, 1964, p. 35.

p. 173 'My dear fellow, you will die in a ditch': ibid.

p. 173 'Everybody here says I am the most successful new member': ibid., p. 37.

p. 173 'I often think of you, Hennessy': ibid., p. 49.

p. 174 'some lucrative but quiet Governorship': ibid., p. 50.

p. 176 'a cheery wedding': Emily Hahn, *James Brooke of Sarawak*, London, 1953, p. 132.

p. 176 'a marriage likely to provide *Brio* to the East': Pope-Hennessy, *Verandah*, p. 96.

p. 179 'All dem Governor': Krio song recorded in 1965, quoted in Odile Goerg, 'Between Everyday Life and Exception: Celebrating Pope Hennessy Day in Freetown, 1872–c.1905', *Journal of African Cultural Studies* (Taylor & Francis Ltd), 15, no. 1 (June 2002), pp. 119–31.

p. 180 'to make the life of prisoners': Linda Pomerantz-Zhang, *Wu Tingfang (1842–1922): Reform and modernization in modern Chinese history*, Hong Kong, 1992, p. 51.

p. 180 'Hers is not a common character & her beauty is quite out of the ordinary': Pope-Hennessy, *Verandah*, p. 97.

p. 182 'in larger quantity': G. B. Endacott, *An Eastern Entrepot: A collection of documents illustrating the history of Hong Kong*, London, 1964.

p. 182 'A considerable social disturbance': 'China and Japan', *New York Times*, 19 October 1877.

p. 183 The crime rate rose: by 13 per cent in Hennessy's first year, to 40 per cent in the second.

p. 183 'Damned Chinamen': Pomerantz-Zhang, *Wu Tinfang*, p. 53.

p. 183 'We cannot speak Chinese': ibid.

p. 183 By their own account, the Chinese 'swallowed the insult': ibid.

p. 186 To the Legislative Council, ff: 'any respectably dressed': ibid., p. 60; 'If the principle of class distinction: ibid., p. 61.

p. 186 'Such was the mutual incompatibility': Ernest Eitel, *Europe in China: The history of Hongkong from the beginning to the year 1882*, London, 1895, p. 63.

p. 187 'over the smooth wide roads': John Y. Simon, ed., *The Personal Memoirs of Julia Dent Grant* (Mrs Ulysses S. Grant), New York, 1975, p. 275.

p. 188 'the insane and violent demeanour': Hayllar to Secretary of State, 27 July 1881, NA CO 129/193, in Hennessy Papers, BOD, MSS Brit Emp S.409.

p. 189 In one of his last speeches: Statement of His Excellency Governor Sir John Pope Hennessy, KCMG, on the Census Returns and the Progress of the Colony, House of Commons Papers, 1881, vol. LXV, no. 42.

p. 190 'Sir John carried with him'; 'want of temper and judgment'; 'vexatious and unjustifiable': Eitel, *Europe in China*, p. 567.

Chapter 9: The Death of Thomas Callaghan

p. 192 'to Monte Video': Callaghan to Hicks Beach, secret and confidential, 9 July 1879, NA CO118/54.

p. 192 'I have the honour': Callaghan to Hicks Beach, 13 May 1879, no. 20, *Papers relating to Her Majesty's colonial possessions* [C.2444] 1878–79, House of Commons Parliamentary Papers Online.

p. 195 'experience in the subtleties of Chinese character': Christopher Munn, *Anglo-China: Chinese people and British rule in Hong Kong, 1841–1880*, Richmond, 2001, p. 117.

p. 195 'to break down': Mitchell to Fortescue, 29 July 1862, NA CO 129/90.

p. 195 'Bring warm clothing': Callaghan to Secretary of State, 9 August 1879, NA CO 537/160B.

p. 196 'tolerably comfortable'; 'even of an inferior description': ibid.

p. 198 'Poor D'Arcy': Callaghan to Meade, 6 February 1878, NA CO 78/68.

p. 000 But he saw no reason: Callaghan to Carnarvon, 15 February 1878, NA CO 78/68.

p. 198 How to raise money?: ibid.

p. 198 'to reduce by one farthing': note by R. Meade, 10 May 1878, on Callaghan's dispatch of 6 May 1878, NA CO 118/54.

p. 198 'in this paradise of cattle': ibid.

p. 199 He did not give up: Callaghan to Meade, 6 February 1878, NA CO 118/54.

p. 199 From the Falklands Islands Blue Book 1878: Callaghan to Hicks Beach, 13 May 1879, no. 20, *Papers relating to Her Majesty's colonial possessions* [C.2444] 1878–79, House of Commons Parliamentary Papers Online.

p. 200 'For the first time in the annals': Callaghan to Secretary of State, 9 August 1879, NA CO 118/54.

p. 200 'to withstand the strong pressure': Callaghan to Hicks Beach, secret and confidential, 9 July 1879, NA CO 118/54.

p. 200 Callaghan's own health was suffering: ibid.

p. 200 Confidentially: notes on Callaghan to Hicks Beach, 9 July 1879, NA CO 118/54.

p. 201 'I can assure your Lordship that it is with the utmost pain': Callaghan to Kimberley, 1 June 1881, NA CO 23/221.

p. 201 'paralysis of the heart': 'Cause of Gov. Callaghan's Death', *New York Times,* 11 July 1881.

p. 201 'virtually sacrificed his life': Alice Callaghan to Lord Kimberley, 5 June 1882, NA CO 23/221.

p. 201 'He was not an eminent man': Arthur Arnold MP to [illegible], 29 August 1881, NA CO23/221.

Chapter 10: The Marquess of Lorne and the Indians

p. 202 These were lands: http://www.collectionscanada.gc.ca/canadian-west.

p. 204 'Dust, sun and speechifying': Lorne to his father, George, 8th Duke of Argyll, 19 July 1881, Lorne Papers, CNA.

p. 205 'People have Manitoba . . . on the brain': *The Times,* 10 August 1881.

p. 205 'We can go nowhere without seeing the head of an American': Gary Pennanen, 'Sitting Bull, Indian without a country', *Canadian Historical Review,* LI, no. 2 (June 1970), pp. 123–40.

p. 205 All the same, Canadians were nervous: ibid.

p. 206 'Looks like you're expecting Indian trouble' and ff. to 'surrender of their horses': taken from Lorne's note of his meeting with Evarts, 11 September 1879, Sir John A. Macdonald Papers, vol. 80, CNA.

p. 207 Like previous meetings, the talk accomplished nothing: Pennanen, 'Sitting Bull'.

p. 207 'I shake hands': ibid. At the end of the nineteenth century, a small remnant of Sitting Bull's band continued to live at Wood Mountain in the summer, and in the winter worked for the townspeople of Moose Jaw in the new province of Saskatchewan.

p. 207 'Westward Ho! for the great plains and rivers': Duke of Argyll, *Passages from the Past,* London, 1907, p. 459.

p. 208 'A thrill of joy': Charles Tuttle, *Royalty in Canada embracing sketches of the house of Argyll, the Right Honourable the Marquis of Lorne, (governor-general of Canada), Her Royal Highness the Princess Louise*, Montreal, 1878, p. 17.

p. 208 In fact, there was not much to distinguish Lorne: Frances Balfour, *Obliviscaris. Dinna Forget,* London, 1930, pp. 80–81.

p. 208 'someone from her own country': Robert M. Stamp, *Royal Rebels*, Toronto, 1988, p. 82.

p. 209 'looked upon him as a regular outsider': ibid., p. 112.

p. 209 'if anything too chivalrous': Balfour, *Obliviscaris*, p. 87; 'for his manly beauty of a fine Celtic type': Stamp, *Royal Rebels*, p. 42; 'In the ball rooms of that date': Balfour, *Obliviscaris*, p. 87.

p. 209 '"One of 'our great Viceroyalties' was vacant"': Argyll, *Passages*, p. 394.

p. 209 'The view of Ottawa': Lorne to his father, George, 8th Duke of Argyll, 4 December 1878, Lorne Papers.

p. 210 'Of all things, finance is the most puzzling': Argyll, *Passages*, p. 438.

p. 211 'a wonder that her skull was not fractured': ibid., p. 153.

p. 211 'I fear the NW journey would certainly be too fatiguing': Lorne to his father, 13 May 1881, Lorne Papers.

p. 212 The chief: 'very Indian in face and physique' and ff. to 'His claim would be investigated': *The Times*, 17 August 1881.

p. 213 'But [this is] not much to their taste': *Scotsman,* 18 August 1881.

p. 213 'Out of sight of shore, Lake Superior': Argyll, *Passages*, p. 463.

p. 214 'Far away from the noise and dust of civilisation': *The Times,* 3 September 1881.

p. 214 'A night camp': The Marquis of Lorne, *Canadian Pictures*, London, n.d., p. 135.

p. 214 For three days they paddled, off-loaded, portaged, and ff: *The Times,* 3 September 1881.

p. 215 'Winnipeg is in a fever': Lorne to Kimberley, 3 August 1881, Lorne Papers.

p. 215 'In 18 months the Railway': Lorne to Victoria, n.d., RA VIC/ADDA 17/1801.

p. 216 'You gaze and the intense clearness': Stamp, *Royal Rebels*, p. 171.

p. 216 'much better than Ontario, it's dry': *The Times*, 15 September 1881.

p. 217 'You would never complain of the want of bird life': Argyll, *Passages*, p. 465.

p. 217 'Here they come, as I write, to the Great Pow-Wow', and ff: *Scotsman*, 16 September 1881.

p. 218 In the intervals, warriors came forward, and ff: *The Times,* 21 October 1881.

p. 218 'The Indian would not touch the food supply of a friend': Lorne, *Canadian Pictures,* p. 171.

p. 218 It was at that great pow-wow: Argyll, *Passages,* p. 471.

p. 219 1 September: 'It is bitterly cold today, and freezing hard' and ff.: *Scotsman,* 18 October 1881.

p. 219 'at last came the welcoming ring of a rifle shot': *The Times,* 9 November 1881.

p. 220 After a while tom-toms sounded, and dancing began, and ff: Lorne, *Canadian Pictures,* pp. 162–4.

p. 221 'Next summer, or at latest next fall': Pierre Berton, *The Last Spike,* Toronto, 1971, p. 233.

p. 221 '*Evening.* We have had a long and satisfactory meeting'; 'I hope that all the assemblies': Lorne to Victoria, n.d., RA VIC/ADDA 17/1803.

p. 221 'Men hereabouts speak': Stamp, *Royal Rebels,* p. 177.

p. 221 '[I]f I was not Governor- General': ibid.

p. 221 'You have a country whose value': ibid., p. 179.

p. 221 'the inclination shown': Memorandum to the Privy Council on subjects brought to His Excellency's notice during his tour in the North-West, 20 October 1881, Lorne Papers.

Chapter 11: *Sweet talk and secrets – the rise and rise of Frank Athelstane Swettenham*

For notes on Frank Swettenham's youth and early childhood, and his first few years as a young interpreter, see the first twenty pages of his memoir, *Footprints in Malaya,* published in London in 1942.

p. 224 'with a fan until there flew out of it a butterfly soul': Pat Barr, *Taming the Jungle: The men who made British Malaya,* London, 1977, p. 138.

p. 227 'Kept alive by the efforts of ubiquitous "punkah-wallahs"': Isabella Bird, *The Golden Chersonese,* London, 1883, p. 118.

p. 230 'to teach him how to rule': Frank Swettenham, *British Malaya,* London, 1948, p. 175.

p. 231 Everywhere they discovered scores of Chinese women: Chow Ah Yeow's testimony was typical: 'I am the wife of a Si Yip named Li Yii. Malays took me to Kurow and sold me to Gho Quan for $30 and he took me to Kota. I want to go anywhere to be quiet.' Testimonies in P. L. Burns and C. D. Cowan, eds, *Sir Frank Swettenham's Malayan Journals 1874–1876*, Oxford, 1975, p. 50.

p. 231 'He would call for us when he had leisure': 31 January 1874, *Malayan Journals*, p. 20; 'He said but little': 9 February 1874, ibid.

p. 231 'A Malay raja thinks himself': Emily Innes, *The Chersonese with the Gilding Off*, London, 1885, vol. I, p. 89. 'The relation between a raja and a *ryot* seems to be a truly paternal one,' she went on. A raja passing a poor man's garden, orders his men to break through the fence and tear up the corn, and bring it to him, 'while the unfortunate owner, attracted by the noise, humbly bows and smiles as he sees the raja had condescended to appropriate his corn.' In the same way, a fisherman might be deprived of his catch. 'The raja may take from the latter . . . but is bound in return not to let the *ryot* starve, and to stand by him in danger. If a Malay *ryot* commits murder, or any other crime for which he is "wanted" by the police, the raja whom he follows – if he be a fine old Malay raja . . . screens him. He would no more think of handing him over to justice than an English father would think of handing over his own son.' ibid., p. 183.

p. 232 Travelling high on the back of his elephant: *Malayan Journals*, p. 33.

p. 232 'I'm afraid there must be a very unhealthy atmosphere': 15 February 1874, ibid., p. 36.

p. 233 'She was very inquisitive': ibid.

p. 233 'The Merry May'; 'It is indeed an enchanting place': 1 May 1874, ibid., p. 85.

p. 233 'What? *Another* European?': 30 April 1874, ibid., p. 84.

p. 233 'She . . . gave herself no end of trouble', and ff: 13 June 1874, ibid., p. 91.

p. 234 'From Malay life it may be said that woman . . . passions run high among a people living within a shout of the equator': Frank Swettenham, *The Real Malay*, London, 1900, pp. 267ff.

p. 234 Many were jealous of Swettenham's promotion. 'What then are we to think of the appointment of Mr F. A. Swettenham to be Assistant Resident and virtually Resident, to the State of Salangore [*sic*]?' sniped the *Singapore Daily Times*. 'Here we have a cadet of four years experience as a subordinate clerk in the Settlements, raised at a bound [to a post equal] to an official of nearly 30 years experience . . . This lucky "Dowb", moreover, is sent to the most turbulent state in the Peninsula.' Henry S. Barlow, *Swettenham*, Kuala Lumpur, 1995, p. 99.

p. 234 'I asked the Sultan repeatedly': 19 August 1874, *Malayan Journals*, p. 109.

p. 234 'I have been in worse places'; Swettenham, *Footprints*, p. 42.

p. 235 The Sultan, Abdul Samad, lived in a dilapidated compound: Innes, *The Chersonese*, vol. I, p. 40.

p. 235 The Sultan 'rather encouraged the somewhat prevalent idea': Barlow, *Swettenham*, p. 73.

p. 235 'The people were strange and interesting': William Maxwell, *With the 'Ophir' round the Empire*, London, 1902, p. 105.

p. 236 'She is now only about 6 years old', and ff.: 22 August 1875, *Malayan Journals*, p. 283.

p. 236 'We are very much obliged to our Friend': Barlow, *Swettenham*, p. 80.

p. 237 'short occupation did more to secure': Barr, *Taming the Jungle*, p. 20.

p. 237 'A churchman of the older type': Barlow, *Swettenham*, p. 185.

p. 238 'The bachelor who marries': Frank Swettenham, *Unaddressed Letters*, London, 1898, p. 109.

p. 239 'What is the use of dressing three times a day': Innes, *The Chersonese*, vol. I, p. 35.

p. 239 'Taking him all round – with his sense of self-confidence': Barlow, *Swettenham*, p. 204.

p. 240 As in Darwin, so in Kuala Lumpur: ibid., p. 208.

p. 240 'Might he not drive the coach a little too fast?': ibid., p. 212.

p. 240 'acre for acre': Arthur Keyser, *People and Places*, London, 1922, p. 101.

p. 240 Misery, squalor and neglect were rife: Barr, *Taming the Jungle*, p. 70.

p. 241 'remarkably careful and clear': Barlow, *Swettenham*, p. 233; 'a soap and water bath': Barr, *Taming the Jungle*, p. 71.

p. 242 John Rodger was stuffy, 'a little overpowering': Barlow, *Swettenham*, p. 232.

p. 243 'Three hundred and ninety-nine germinated': Barr, *Taming the Jungle*, p. 101.

p. 243 'There followed feast and revel': Barlow, *Swettenham*, p. 323.

p. 244 'well-nigh denationalised', and ff.: Hugh Clifford, 'A Freelance of To-day' in William R. Roff, *Stories by Sir Hugh Clifford*, Kuala Lumpur, 1966.

p. 244 'Have you come out to work or play?': Keyser, *People and Places*, p. 100.

p. 246 Meta Rome: from the 1890s his publishers also were instructed to conduct correspondence to him through her in England.

p. 246 'The general affairs of the country': Swettenham, *Footprints*, p. 103.

p. 248 'Can he play cricket?': Keyser, *People and Places*, p. 101.

p. 248 'She . . . interests herself in everything': Barlow, *Swettenham*, p. 394.

p. 249 'You modern man, of modern times': ibid., p. 403.

p. 249 No one in Singapore had the knowledge to challenge the actions of the residents successfully: 'Having for six years seen the system of "Protection" at work in the Malay States,' wrote Emily Innes, bitter at the way Bloomfield Douglas had exploited his position as resident in Selangor, 'I am inclined to think that the only persons protected by it are [the] Residents. Everyone else . . . is practically at their mercy . . . rumours may reach the Singapore officials . . . of their doings, and their characters may be thoroughly well known at headquarters; but such rumours, proceeding as they do from natives only, are of no avail . . . the mouths of the only people who could give trust-worthy evidence – namely the Assistant Residents, Collectors, and Superintendents – are carefully closed by etiquette.' Innes, *The Chersonese*, vol. II, p. 247.

p. 249 'The wealthiest Malays in the Peninsula': Barr, *Taming the Jungle*, p. 122.

p. 250 'There is such a thing as knowing too much': ibid.

p. 250 What would be the problem, Sweetenham asked: 'disturbs no existing arrangements': Barlow, *Swettenham*, p. 448; 'Nothing is intended to curtail': Treaty of Federation, NA CO 273/205, received in London 7 September 1895.

p. 250 'Will these meddling Engish . . .': Innes, *The Chersonese*.

p. 250 After nine months' leave in England, Swettenham returned: 'general control': Barr, *Taming the Jungle*, p. 124; 'passed in English': J. M. Gullick, *Rulers and Residents*, Oxford, 1992, p. 52.

p. 251 'Until we visited Perak': Barr, *Taming the Jungle*, p. 128.

p. 251 'A busy morning', and ff: Maxwell, *With the 'Ophir'*, pp. 99ff.

p. 252 'The Governor, a most attractive personage': Alexander George, Earl of Athlone, to Prince Adolphus of Teck, 30 April 1901, RA QM/PRIV/CC53/31–35.

p. 253 'Sir F is a curious saturnine creature but very good company': Barlow, *Swettenham*, p. 524.

p. 253 'neither can there be four rulers in one country': Gullick, *Rulers*, p. 60.

p. 254 'one of the handsomest women': *New York Times,* 30 August 1903.

p. 254 'Why, he drove her Ladyship mad with his badness': Barlow, *Swettenham*, p. 720.

Chapter 12: Lady Tennyson at home

The basis of this chapter is *Audrey Tennyson's Vice-Regal Days*, a collection of her letters written to her mother, Zacyntha Boyle, from Australia, edited by Alexandra Hasluck and published in Canberra in 1978. Notes from other sources are cited below.

p. 257 'a leader of all that is good': Hallam Tennyson, *Alfred Lord Tennyson, a Memoir by his son*, London, 1899, vol. II, p. 605.

p. 259 'so deeply embowered in its surrounding trees': 'A Friend', *Harold Tennyson RN*, London, 1918, p. 3.

p. 259 Alfred had adored his two young sons : Thwaite, *Emily Tennyson*, p. 270.

p. 260 'I would fain see it bestowed', Alfred Tennyson, *Oxford Dictionary of National Biography*.

p. 260 'a cause of deep thankfulness to me': ibid.

p. 260 'solemn ceremony': Thwaite, *Emily Tennyson*, p. 15.

p. 260 The poet buried, it was then Hallam's task: ibid, p. 26.

p. 266 'the greatest day South Australia has ever seen': Tennyson to Victoria, 29 January 1900, RA VIC/MAIN/P30/39.

p. 272 At the end of May 1902, she opened the new hospital: 'A Friend', *Harold Tennyson*, p. 48.

p. 272 'The most dangerous years': *Sydney Morning Herald*, 6 May 1903.

Chapter 13: A marriage of imperialists

Extracts from the letters and diaries of the Lugards, and all otherwise unattributed references in this chapter, have been taken from Margery Perham, *Lugard*, 2 vols, London, 1960, the comprehensive account of Frederick Lugard's life. Flora Lugard's early life comes from E. Moberly Bell's *Flora Shaw*.

p. 275 'Not *the* Miss Shaw?': Karl E. Meyer and Shareen Blair Brysac, *Kingmakers*, New York, 2009, p. 62.

p. 275 'one of the greatest powers of the world': ibid., p. 61.

p. 275 'A fine, handsome, bright upstanding young woman': *Oxford Dictionary of National Biography*.

p. 276 It was while attending a lecture at Woolwich: E. Moberly Bell, *Flora Shaw*, London, 1947, pp. 20, 21.

p. 276 'Will you, youths of England, make your country again a royal throne': John Ruskin in *Lectures on Art,* online at *The Norton Anthology of English Literature,* www.wwnorton.com/college/english/nael/20century/topic_1/jnruskin. htmwww.

p. 277 'To me you would be sunshine': Bell, *Flora Shaw*, p. 41.

p. 278 Rhodes made other men seem 'like thread-paper beside him', and ff.: ibid., p. 80.

p. 279 'I am not so good a John Bull': ibid., p. 90.

p. 279 'Up to the Karoo! It means up from Cape Town': 'Letters from South Africa', *The Times*, 22 July 1892.

p. 279 'you can never doubt any more that the African native': ibid., 28 July 1892.

p. 279 She went on to Johannesburg and its gold mines: Bell, *Flora Shaw*, pp. 104–7.

p. 280 'Material is the subject of daily talk': *The Times*, 2 September 1892.

p. 280 Every three or four days she produced a major article: 'We began our journey by starlight': ibid., 2 September 1892; 'I came down from De Aar Junction': ibid., 20 September 1892.

p. 280 'Never have I so often heard the word "remarkable"': Bell, *Flora Shaw*, p. 119.

p. 282 'Mary Jane was not strong', and ff: Perham, *Lugard*, vol. I, pp. 8–19.

p. 282 'A man need not be afraid to wear his heart': ibid., p. 33.

p. 283 'I wish my own chance of having little ones': ibid., p. 60.

p. 283 He was playing bridge one evening: ibid., p. 51.

p. 284 'The Foreign Office learnt from the consuls near you': ibid., p. 114.

p. 287 'After some discussion I asked if the King were ready to sign . . . he shuffled': ibid., p. 230.

p. 287 'What was the object of starting this Company': ibid., p. 313.

p. 288 'Missions wiped out by Protestants. Six fathers prisoners': ibid., p. 328.

p. 288 'I earnestly beseech you to help me': ibid., p. 320.

p. 290 'Miss Shaw, the specialist of *The Times*': ibid., p. 461.

p. 291 'the Lady witness beat all the men': Meyer and Brysac, *Kingmakers*, p. 82.

p. 296 'It is difficult for you home-folk to realize what communication is in this country': Perham, *Lugard*, vol. II, p. 94.

p. 296 'The advocates of conciliation at any price': ibid., p. 100.

p. 299 'The old treaties are dead': ibid., p. 128.

p. 299 'Why are we fighting Kano?': *The Times*, 20 January 1903.

p. 300 'speaking in any way definitely for you', and ff.: Flora to Frederick Lugard, 6 December 1902, MSS Perham 309/1 BOD; 'I said, "Frankly, what would a man of his ability do in such a place?"': ibid.

p. 300 Already Flora was trying to find some way: Flora to Frederick Lugard, 18 December 1902, ibid.

p. 301 'But the separation is far too long': Bell, *Flora Shaw*, p. 250.

p. 301 'A most interesting dinner': 19 May 1904, RA GV/PRIV/GVD/1904, 19 May.

p. 301 'ignorant and more or less obstructive clerks': Flora to Frederick Lugard, 5 December 1904; 'nameless boys': 10 February 1905; 'such an enormous ass': 11 March 1905, MSS Perham 309/1.

p. 302 'never will accept it . . . The remedy': Flora to Frederick Lugard, 6 April 1905, ibid.

p. 302 'a far-reaching scheme of administrative rule': *The Times,* 5 December 1905.

p. 303 'Of course to you it must seem ridiculous': interview with Churchill, in Flora to Frederick Lugard, 6 February 1906, MSS Perham 309/1.

p. 304 'Whole of C Company, Mounted Infantry defeated and annihilated: Perham, *Lugard*, vol II, p. 252.

p. 305 'How does this extermination': ibid., p. 271.

p. 305 'The fateful cablegram arrived today': Lugard to Lady Lugard, 15 March, 1906, MSS Perham 309/1.

p. 307 'the greatest engine of democracy the world has ever known': Charles Lucas, quoted by Frederick Lugard in *The Dual Mandate in British Tropical Africa,* 1922, p. 608.

p. 307 'My precious darling': Flora to Frederick Lugard, 19 October 1927; MSS Perham 312/3.

Chapter 14: *Where the land was bewitched*

The basis of this chapter is Sir Henry Hesketh Bell's memoir, *Glimpses of a Governor's Life,* published in London in 1946, from which I have taken quotations and descriptions that I have not attributed elsewhere.

p. 309 The photograph commemorated a weekend house party: 23 January 1899, *Diary*, vol. I, Hesketh Bell Papers, BL.

p. 309 Bell was a man who all his life would keep his antecedents quiet: 1 January 1900, ibid., vol. II.

p. 309 'I don't think I made any faux pas': 23 January 1899, ibid., vol. I.

p. 310 Bell was promoted to the Gold Coast, and ff: *Synopses of Diaries*, vol. I, 1890–99, Sir Henry Hesketh Bell Collection, CUL, Y3011C-N.

p. 310 'I longed for that waltz to last forever': Jean Rhys, *Smile Please,* London, 1979, p. 91.

p. 312 'Otherwise than financially, my progress': 12 January 1906, *Diary,* vol. V.

p. 313 The passage was fine: ibid. The *New York Times* noted the price of a peerage on 6 January 1895 as £10,000; during the Lord Levy scandal in 2006, the price was said to be £1 million.

p. 313 The 31st of January found him at the Colonial Office, and ff: 31 January 1906, *Diary*, vol. V.

p. 313 'I find myself now approaching without the slightest awe': 9 February 1906, ibid.

p. 313 ' Very few fine jewels . . . no Garters & very few people who appeared of consequence': 18 February 1906, ibid.

p. 313 As for Uganda: 26 January 1906, ibid.

p. 317 They were watching tennis, and ff: 4 April 1906, ibid.

p. 318 'Kept on presenting or saluting every time one passed': 8 April 1906, ibid.

p. 318 wages 'absurdly high': 18 April 1906, ibid.

p. 319 'But I knew that, in this case especially, did distance lend enchantment': Bell, *Glimpses*, p. 106.

p. 320 'They all live near Kampala': Bell to his aunt, 5 May 1906, *Letters, Sir Henry Hesketh Bell Collection*, CUL, RCMS 36.

p. 321 'Never was there such a place for roses': Bell to his aunt, 20 May 1906, ibid.

p. 321 'very dowdy or suburban wives': Bell to his aunt, 24 July 1906; 'The responsibilities . . . are enormous': Bell to his aunt, 10 May 1906, ibid.

p. 321 Entebbe might look charming, and ff.: 12 May 1906, *Diary*, vol. V.

p. 323 'Playing in the shade of a banana grove': Bell to his sister, Nell, 24 May 1906, *Letters*.

p. 323 Meanwhile back at Government House, and ff: Bell to his aunt, 9 July 1906, ibid.

p. 324 'exactly the same clothes . . . that I would wear in Spring at Home': ibid.; 'leisurely steam down Lake Albert', and ff: Bell to Nell, 28 July 1906, ibid.

p. 324 'Our "safari" or caravan looked most imposing': ibid.

p. 325 'I used to think the soil of Dominica very fertile': ibid.

p. 325 Bell never thought of Uganda as becoming anything other than a 'black man's country': Bell, *Glimpses*, p. 159.

p. 325 'A most nervous man & quite unstrung': 31 July 1906, *Diary*, vol.V.

p. 326 'I thereupon donned my veil': ibid.

p. 326 'we must withdraw from the insects the source of their infection': Bell, *Glimpses*, p. 135.

p. 326 'I am going to assume': Bell, *Glimpses*, p. 136.

p. 327 On 23 November, a dispatch 'as good as anything I have ever done', and ff.: Bell to Secretary of State, 23 November 1906, NA CO 536/8.

p. 328 'It seems hopeless for us laymen': Minutes on Bell's dispatch, ibid.

p. 328 'Everyone was leaving': J. Bulobo, interviewed 11 November 1993 at Bugoto, cited in Kirk Arden Hoppe, 'Lords of the Fly: Colonial Visions and Revisions of Sleeping-Sickness Environments on Ugandan Lake Victoria, 1906–61', *Africa: Journal of the International African Institute*, Edinburgh University Press, 67, no. 1 (1997), pp. 86–105.

p. 328 'The Chiefs are playing up splendidly': Bell, *Glimpses,* p. 151.

p. 329 At the end of April, Lord Elgin's response to Bell's dispatch, and ff.: ibid., p. 163.

p. 329 Though they disagreed on issues, and ff.: ibid., p. 168.

p. 330 Churchill wrote stirringly: Winston Churchill, *My African Journey,* London, 1989, p. 118.

p. 330 'just such a house': Frederick Treves, *Uganda for a Holiday,* London, 1908, p. 204.

p. 332 In July 2009 a team of doctors working for Médecins Sans Frontières completed a study: 'Nifurtimox-eflornithine combination therapy for second-stage African *Trypanosoma brucei gambiense* trypanosomiasis: a multi-centre, randomised, phase III, non-inferiority trial', *Lancet*, 374, issue 9683, pp. 56–64, 4 July 2009.

Chapter 15: A socialist in the West Indies

My chief source for Sydney Olivier is taken from his wife Margaret's collection of his papers, published as *Sydney Olivier* in London in 1948. General descriptions not cited below are taken from this volume.

p. 333 'The Fabian lecturers': Michael Holroyd, *Bernard Shaw: The search for love,* Vol. I, London, 1988, p. 171.

p. 335 "O God save us!" impossible to quiet them': Hamar Greenwood to Colonial Office, 15 January 1907, NA CO 884/9/14.

p. 335 'bandages, lint and wool': Truman H. Newberry (Acting Secretary to the US Navy Department) to the Secretary of State for the Colonies, 25 April 1907, NA CO 137/661.

p. 336 'his distinguished contribution to humanity': *New York Times*, 25 August 1907.

p. 336 'Like a Spanish grandee': George Bernard Shaw, 'Some Impressions', in Margaret Olivier, ed., *Sydney Olivier*, London, 1948, p. 9.

p. 337 'Gentle habits and trained reasoning powers may achieve': Holroyd, *Bernard Shaw*, p. 175.

p. 338 'this child died': Margaret Olivier, *Diary*, Olivier Papers, BOD.

p. 338 'I rushed my fence on Thursday'; Olivier to Wallas, 10 July 1883, ibid.

p. 338 'It is very sad': Margaret Cox to Olivier, 6 January 1884, ibid.

p. 338 'Looking back, now I wonder what on earth': Margaret Olivier, 'A sort of account of married life,' *c.* 1920, ibid.

p. 339 'but it is just so hot': Harold Cox to Margaret Olivier, Feb 1886, ibid.

p. 339 'went off like smoke': Holroyd, *Bernard Shaw*, p. 188.

p. 339 Olivier . . . was always half a dozen paces ahead: Shaw, 'Some Impressions'.

p. 340 Olivier brought to Jamaica, and ff: Herbert de Lisser, 'Notes on Lord Olivier's Official Career in Jamaica', in Olivier, ed., *Sydney Olivier*.

p. 341 'he moved like lightning': Christopher Lynch-Robinson, *The Last of the Irish R.M.s,* London, 1951, p. 90.

p. 342 Nine-tenths of their owners: Sydney Olivier, *Jamaica: The blessed island,* London, 1936, p. 23.

p. 343 'There are no persons of indigenous race in Jamaica': ibid., p. 11.

p. 344 'The task of implementing . . . reforms': Francis Lee, *Fabianism and Colonialism,* London, 1988, p. 90.

p. 344 'Not since Morant Bay has there been such a rising against constituted authority': http://www.jamaica-gleaner.com/pages/history/story0026.html.

p. 344 'We love the white man because he is a brother': S. Hurwitz and E. Hurwitz, *Jamaica, a historical portrait,* London, 1971, p. 190.

p. 344 Early in 1902: De Lisser, 'Notes' in Olivier, ed., *Sydney Olivier*.

p. 345 'I will not have any politics in the Colonial Office': Lee, *Fabianism*, p. 105.

p. 345 'personally acquainted with the affairs of Jamaica': 21 April 1903. Enclosure from Chairman and Secretary of West India Committee to Chamberlain, 12 June 1903, NA CO 137/638.

p. 345 Report of Major E. E. Chown: 23 February 1907, NA CO 137/660.

p. 346 'Even the basement walls': Sydney Olivier to Margaret Olivier, 16 May 1907, Olivier Papers.

p. 346 The wind had come on so strong . . . I keep my mouth shut a good deal': Sydney Olivier to Margaret Olivier, 4, 9 May 1907, Olivier Papers.

p. 347 'So you may have to alter the labels on your luggage': Olivier to Margaret Olivier, 23 June 1907, Olivier Papers.

p. 347 'The patients are in tents': ibid.

p. 348 'lachrymose or cheerful': Daphne Olivier to Margaret Olivier, 21 October 1910, Olivier Papers.

p. 348 'All these passages to & fro': Margaret Olivier, *Diary*, December 1908, Olivier Papers.

p. 349 She took to spending more and more time alone', and ff.: Margaret Olivier, *Diary*, 17 May, June, 1909, Olivier Papers.

p. 350 'I shall never cause any proposals': Olivier, ed., *Sydney Olivier*, p. 240.

p. 350 'I now do not consult them': Shaw, 'Some Impressions'.

p. 350 McKay, Claude, *Gordon to the Oppressed Natives*, quoted in Winston James, *A Fierce Hatred of Injustice: Claude McKay's Jamaica and his poetry of rebellion*, London, 2000, p. 89.

p. 351 'The colour line is not a rational line': Sydney Olivier, *White Capital and Coloured Labour*, London, 1906, p. 58.

p. 352 'Dearest Meg this is Monday morning': Sydney Olivier to Margaret Olivier, 26 December 1912, Olivier Papers.

p. 353 'But they ought to have been able to prevent': ibid.

p. 353 'an insurgent negro': Shaw, 'Some Impressions'.

p. 353 Olivier climbed back into his car: James, *A Fierce Hatred*, p. 84.

p. 353 'As you steam into Kingston Harbour' . . . and turned in': Olivier, *Jamaica*, p. 441.

p. 354 Olivier had 'no Kiplingesque idolatry': Shaw, 'Some Impressions'.

p. 354 'Says Color Line Must Be Abolished ': *New York Times*, 3 October 1913.

p. 354 'its lack of representation in the House of Lords': Shaw, 'Some Impressions'.

p. 355 'We . . . are not a little disturbed': Commander-in-Chief, Lord Rawlinson, to Col. Clive Wigram, assistant private secretary to the King, 23 January 1924, RA PS/PSO/GV/C/N 2555/ 52.

p. 355 'Of course, as I am eighty-three years old': Olivier, ed., *Sydney Olivier*, p. 182.

Chapter 16: Letters from Nairobi

Michael Smith's unpublished biography of Sir Percy Girouard, *The Lily and the Rose,* together with the letters of his wife, Lady Girouard, make up most of the content of the family papers lent to me by Mark Girouard and provide the basis of my account here. Descriptive phrases in quotations have been taken from Smith's mss, unless otherwise indicated.

p. 356 'When events occur': quoted in Lotte Hughes, *Moving the Maasai*, London, 2006, p. 23.

p. 356 In 1883 a Royal Geographical Society expedition, and ff.: ibid.

p. 358 'great snake stretching from sea to lake'; 'large white birds': ibid., p. 27.

p. 359 Eliot had had a brilliant career at Balliol, taking a first in Greats, and prizes for essays in Sanskrit and Syrian. Sent to St Petersburg, he learned Russian in two months, and published a Finnish grammar at the age of twenty-five. Mastering Arabic in Morocco took him three months; he arrived in Nairobi having finished a history and philosophy of the Ottoman Empire that became a standard work. He was also to write a standard work on British nudibranchiate molluscs. Elspeth Huxley, *White Man's Country*, London, 1953, p. 76.

p. 359 'astonishing exhibitions of nudity'; 'Their habits may be interesting': Huxley, *White Man's Country*, p. 82.

p. 359 'We have in East Africa': ibid., p. 131.

p. 361 'would endure so long as the Masai as a race shall exist'; 'I cannot express too strongly to your Lordship': G. H. Mungeam, *British Rule in Kenya 1895–1912*, Oxford, 1966, p. 122.

p. 361 'A typical South African township': Churchill, *My African Journey*, p. 20.

p. 363 Kitchener invited him to join his railway party: A. H. M. Kirk-Greene, 'Canada in Africa: Sir Percy Girouard, Neglected Colonial Governor', *African Affairs* (Oxford University Press on behalf of the Royal African Society), 83, no. 331 (April 1984), pp. 207–39.

p. 363 Build a desert railway: Michael L. Smith, *The Lily and the Rose* (unpublished mss), Girouard Papers.

p. 364 'I am only a child in some ways': ibid.

p. 364 'I generally say goodbye to him after breakfast': ibid.

p. 364 It seems Sir Percy was not quite the financial genius: ibid.

p. 365 'On Christmas day I received': ibid.

p. 365 'Napoleonic both in compass and precision!': ibid.

p. 366 Secretly the idea of East Africa unnerved him: ibid.

p. 367 'He shakes hands in a funny way': ibid.

p. 367 'We have heard that a white man has come', and ff.: Huxley, *White Man's Country*, p. 152.

p. 368 'At last we have a man at the head of affairs': ibid., p. 240.

p. 368 'No one can quite guess the administrative chaos of this place': Smith, *The Lily and the Rose*.

p. 368 'My own Darlings . . .very straggly Pretoria, this place': Lady Girouard to Sir Richard and Lady Solomon, 22 November 1909, *Letters,* Girouard Papers.

p. 369 '*hideous* inside and out': ibid.

p. 370 Bird took care of her clothes: ibid.

p. 370 Within her first day: ibid.; 'It really was awful', and ff.: 24 November, 1909, *Letters,* Girouard Papers.

p. 370 'I can't say the people here are exciting': 29 November, 1909, ibid.

p. 371 Atkinson'was here last week': ibid. 4 November [*sic*] should be December 1909.

p. 371 How she missed her parents: 30 October 1909, ibid.

p. 371 She and Anna spent two hours every morning: ibid. 4 November [*sic*] should be December 1909; The altitude was 'trying', and ff.: 29 November 1909, ibid.

p. 372 Three weeks after Gwen arrived, and ff.: 19 December 1909, ibid.

p. 373 'It is pouring with rain': 19 December 1909, ibid.

p. 373 'They have a dear little shanty': Smith, *The Lily and the Rose.*

p. 374 'I *am* astonished': 22 January 1910, ibid.

p. 374 On their return to Nairobi . . . talked it over for another hour!': 17 February 1910, ibid.

p. 375 'Things are going fairly well enough': Smith, *The Lily and the Rose.*

p. 375 The food was simply awful': 26 February, 1910, *Letters,* Girouard Papers.

p. 375 'The result was a strikingly unanimous decision': Smith, *The Lily and the Rose.*

p. 375 In Nairobi the weather had turned very hot: 26 February 1910, *Letters,* Girouard Papers; the project 'is seen as a big "coup"', and ff.: Smith, *The Lily and the Rose.*

p. 376 'If the Maasai knew enough': Hughes, *Moving the Maasai,* p. 41.

p. 376 LARGE NUMBER ALREADY MOVED: Smith, *The Lily and the Rose.*

p. 376 Girouard replied by cable: Mungeam, *British Rule in Kenya,* p. 262.

p. 377 'The situation had grown up to consider Joe or Brown': Smith, *The Lily and the Rose.*

p. 377 'not to be scolded & found fault with': 3 March 1910, *Letters,* Girouard Papers.

p. 378 IT HAS BEEN DECIDED: Smith, *The Lily and the Rose.*

p. 378 'Never tell my wife a thing': 18 February 1911, *Letters,* Girouard Papers.

p. 378 '26 February: I go in to see Gerry every morning': 26 February 1911, ibid.

p. 378 Gwen was miserable: 1 March, 1911; 'is very anxious to shoot a zebra': 29 March 1911, ibid.

p. 379 'the largest possible free grant': Smith, *The Lily and the Rose*.

p. 379 'to confess he had done practically nothing': 7 March 1911, *Letters,* Girouard Papers.

p. 379 '[To dinner]': 10 April 1911, ibid.

p. 379 'Our Governor is not playing fair': Mungeam, *British Rule in Kenya*, pp. 263–4.

p. 380 '1 June 1911: Gerry is most awfully pleased', and ff., 1 June 1911, *Letters,* Girouard Papers.

p. 380 ' a horrid thing has happened. Galbraith Cole': 27 April 1911, ibid.

p. 380 'so he escapes scott-free': Lady Girouard to Sir Richard and Lady Solomon, 7 June 1911, ibid.

p. 381 'Today we have been through a great forest': 27 June 1911, ibid.

p. 381 'He is actually jealous': 6 July 1911, ibid.

p. 382 'They are today the richest Africans': Smith, *The Lily and the Rose*.

p. 382 'self satisfied, pig headed and highly unpopular': Mungeam, *British Rule in Kenya*, p. 215.

p. 383 'The elders will be informed that the Government': Norman Leys, *Kenya*, London, 1924, p. 113.

p. 385 'The greatest authority in the British Empire': Kirk-Greene, 'Canada in Africa'.

p. 385 His obituary in *The Times*: 27 November 1932.

Chapter 17: Running the show

Clifford's childhood and early life are taken from H. A. Gailey, *Clifford: Imperial Proconsul*; unless otherwise indicated I have used the 1966 edition of *Stories by Sir Hugh Clifford,* edited by William R. Roff, for copies of Clifford's short stories.

p. 386 'blue ribbon of the Service': Lord Stamfordham, George V's private secretary, to J. A. P. Edgcumbe at the Colonial Office, 24 February 1927, RA PS/PSO/GV/C/L/2107/2.

p. 388 'wonderland of tropical Asia': Hugh Clifford, 'The Premier Crown Colony', *The Times,* 24 May 1911.

p. 390 'old thoughts, old memories, and old desires': Hugh Clifford, 'Our Trusty and Well-Beloved'.

p. 390 'a small hell on earth' and ff.: taken from a fragment of autobiography, quoted in H. A. Gailey, *Clifford: Imperial Proconsul*, London, 1982, pp. 5–9.

p. 391 Clifford's next two years were spent in Perak . . . the Resident relieves him with a kind word': Barr, *Taming the Jungle,* pp. 97–8.

p. 392 'dressed in the queer garments': Gailey, *Clifford,* p. 15.

p. 392 'As you crush your way out': Clifford, 'The East Coast'.

p. 392 Clifford was young and eager: Clifford, 'At the Court of Pĕlĕsu'.

p. 393 'A white man, who has lived twelve consecutive months': Clifford, 'Up Country'; 'sent there to see fair': 'At the Court of Pĕlĕsu'.

p. 393 'among the wonderful things of the Earth': Hugh Clifford, *In Court and Kampong,* London, 1897.

p. 393 Here the air 'hangs heavy as remembered sin': ibid.

p. 394 'without coming into contact with any Asiatics': Hugh Clifford, *East Coast Etchings,* London, 1896.

p. 394 Conrad was achieving 'with extraordinary success': Hugh Clifford, 'The Genius of Mr Joseph Conrad', *North American Review* (University of Northern Iowa), 178, no. 571 (June 1904), pp. 842–52.

p. 395 'some idea of the lives lived in these lands by Europeans': Clifford, *In Court and Kampong.*

p. 395 'Tonight – no food after 5 pm': A. J. Stockwell, 'Sir Hugh Clifford's early career (1866–1903) as told from his private papers', *Journal of the Malaysian Branch of the Royal Asiatic Society,* 49, no. 1 (1976), pp. 89–112.

p. 397 'to get as much controversial matter off the slate': A. J. Stockwell, 'Hugh Clifford in Trinidad', *Caribbean Quarterly,* 24 (March–June 1978), pp. 8–33.

p. 397 'offend many of the rooted prejudices': ibid.

p. 397 Clifford was interested in good government: ibid.

p. 398 'a regret for this place is crammed with copy': ibid.

p. 398 'one of the very few men in the Colonial Service': ibid.

p. 398 As news of his promotion came: Clifford to Clemens, 31 January 1907, Institute of Commonwealth Studies, correspondence with Theodor Clemens, CS 96 3/11/3.

p. 398 By the time Clifford got to Ceylon: 'the boot of the ubiquitous white man . . . civilization': Clifford, *In Court and Kampong*; 'hated for his airs of superiority'; 'the caustic minute'; 'with swaddlings of red tape': Clifford, 'Up Country'.

p. 399 the 'novelist': Frederick Bowes, 'Bows and Arrows', unpublished autobiographical journal, 1867–*c.*1943, BOD.

p. 400 'mutual esteem and friendship': *Ceylon Morning Leader,* 1 July 1907, Sir Hugh Clifford Papers.

p. 400 Where Clifford was large and jovial: 'His fatal weakness was an unfath-
omable vanity': Bowes, 'Bows'; 'Somewhat boisterous': H. A. J. Hulugalle,
British Governors of Ceylon, London, 1963; 'However, all went well': Bowes,
'Bows'.

p. 401 Later, whenever he met Bowes: Bowes, 'Bows'.

p. 401 Clifford dubbed: 'the little core of rot': the Padikara Mudaliyar of
Ceylon, *The Government of the Island of Ceylon*, London, 1938; 'This new
parody of a House of Commons': Gailey, *Clifford*, p. 56 ; 'strong objection
to the elective principle': Stockwell, 'Hugh Clifford in Trinidad'.

p. 402 'a good deal grander': Woolf, Leonard, *Growing: An autobiography of the
years 1904 to 1911*, London, 1964, p. 24; 'exalted': ibid., p. 138.

p. 402 Neither Governor McCallum nor Clifford: McCallum to Crewe, 26
May 1909, NA CO 54/72.

p. 403 'ordered present with its conventions': Clifford, 'Our Trusty and Well-
Beloved'.

p. 403 'to get once more into tune with the Asia of olden days', and ff.: Hugh
Clifford, *Downfall of the Gods,* London, 1911, preface.

p. 404 Upon his return in the new year of 1909: 'Seeing how undesirable':
McCallum to Crewe, 29 January 1909, NA CO 54/723; 'widespread dissatisfaction': McCallum to Crewe, 26 May 1909, NA CO 54/725.

p. 404 Clifford made every effort to discredit: ibid.

p. 405 But if they granted representative government to the Crown colony of
Ceylon, they might have to do it elsewhere: Minutes on dispatch from
McCallum to Crewe, 26 May 1909, NA CO 54/725.

p. 405 So the business of the government in Ceylon: index NA CO 54/725.

p. 405 'peacocking impulse': Bowes.

p. 406 London had digested the issue of representation on the Legislative Council:
'The European population [eligible to vote] at the last census was only 6,300
including a considerable number of Govt servants. If 6,300 Europeans ought
to have 3 members, surely 953,000 Tamils ought to have more than five and 2¼
million Sinhalese more than 3. There is such a large European element in the
Council already owing to the fact that all the official members are white, that
I am inclined to doubt whether, if the native community really bestirred themselves we should not find it difficult to justify the existence of two European
officials.' Minute by CO official, on dispatch of 23 March 1910, NA CO 54/732.

p. 406 'Astounding', minuted one official; 'enough to make one despair':
Minutes on Reform of the Legislative Council, 19 January 1910, NA CO
54/732.

p. 406 Meanwhile, Clifford's rearguard action: 'I think it especially necessary to leaven': McCallum to Hopwood, private, 30 March 1910, NA CO 54/733; Clifford 'will not see that he is backing the wrong horse', and ff.: McCallum to Hopwood, 15 April 1910, NA CO 54/733; 'He has overreached himself entirely': McCallum to Hopwood, 6 April 1910, NA CO 54/733.

p. 406 At the end of April 1910, Clifford sailed for England: *Ceylon Morning Leader,* 27 April 1910, Clifford Papers.

p. 407 In England: 'He had no thought': note by Lord Crewe on confidential dispatch from McCallum, 6 April 1910, NA CO 54/733; 'An attitude of that kind in the FMS': minute on Clifford's application to be Resident-General of Federated Malay States, 19 May 1910, CO 54/740.

p. 407 The new Lady Clifford: Bowes, 'Bows'.

p. 408 'August Week', the annual gathering: newspaper clippings in Clifford Papers.

p. 408 'grit, self-help, confidence': MacCallum to Crewe, 26 May 1909, NA CO 54/725; 'we cannot pass him over': McCallum to Crewe, 28 January 1912, NA CO 54/750.

p. 409 'Ceylon's Governor insulted by Hindu': 17 April 1912, *New York Herald,* in Clifford Papers.

p. 409 'Frankly, we are quite as anxious': 29 June 1912, *Ceylon Morning Leader,* in Clifford Papers.

p. 409 'memories that mocked his present eminence': Hugh Clifford, 'Our Trusty and Well Beloved'.

Chapter 18: Going home

p. 411 'Poor man – he was very ill': Bowes, 'Bows'.

p. 411 'Most of us do like a personality': A. J. Stockwell, 'Sir Hugh Clifford in Malaya, 1927–9', *Journal of the Malaysian Branch of the Royal Asiatic Society*, vol. 2, no. 53 (1980); 'a measure of that Ministry's fitness to guide': Bowes.

p. 414 'Wherever we go in Africa': Minute by Elliott, 12 July 1862, on Freeman to Newcastle, 4 June 1862, NA CO 147/1.

p. 414 'I blush for my *white skin* often here': E. Durnford, *A Soldier's Life and Work in South Africa 1872–1879*, London, 1882, p. 97.

p. 414 'Obviously the whole position is utterly hopeless': Letter written 10 March 1907, in Perham, *Lugard*, vol. II, p. 264.

p. 416 'commence on a heavy Establishment before I return': Napier to Lady

Napier, 20 March 1883, and ff., Napier Papers, BL, MSS EUR F/ 114/53, nos 81–4.

p. 416 'So few of the people one meets take a deep interest in things that do not affect themselves personally': Lady Glover, *Life of Sir John Hawley Glover*, p. 288.

p. 416 By the turn of the twentieth century: *Colonial Office List*, 1906.

p. 417 'Got an axe to grind?' Ralph Furse, *Aucuparius: Recollections of a recruiting officer*, London, 1962, p. 26.

p. 417 'He wrote his initials at the bottom': ibid., p. 17.

p. 417 'the red cheeks of a more bracing climate': Colonial Office, *Information as to the conditions and cost of living in the Colonial Empire, 2nd edition*, HMSO, 1935, p. 30.

p. 417 the governorship of St Helena: *Sunday Times*, 4 March 1907.

Bibliography

Unpublished sources

Private Papers

Douglas Papers
Frere Papers
Girouard Papers

Libraries

BRITISH LIBRARY

Carnarvon Papers
Hesketh Bell Papers
Napier Papers
Stanmore Papers

CAMBRIDGE UNIVERSITY LIBRARY: ROYAL COMMONWEALTH SOCIETY COLLECTIONS

Correspondence between Sir Henry McCallum and Lord Crewe 1902–12
Sir Henry Hesketh Bell Collection

NATIONAL ARCHIVES CANADA

Lorne Papers
Sir John A. Macdonald Papers

Oxford University: Bodleian Library of Commonwealth and African Studies (Rhodes House)

'Frederick Bowes, Bows and Arrows', unpublished autobiographical journal, 1867–*c.*1943

Sir Hugh Clifford Papers

Sir Edouard Percy C. Girouard Papers

Sir John Pope Hennessy Papers

Lugard Papers

Sir Sydney Olivier Papers

Perham Papers

Cross, Jack, *Facing Asia – the Foundation of the Northern Territory,* unpublished mss.

Smith, Michael L., *The Lily and the Rose,* unpublished mss, *Girouard Papers.*

Stratton-Brown, Mrs W. A. H., 'Long Ago in Selangore', unpublished memoir, Bodleian.

State Library of South Australia

Diaries of Edward Napoleon Buonaparte Catchlove

National Archives

Colonial Office Records: CO series

Correspondence with Lord Carnarvon PRO 30/6

Foreign Office Records: FO series

Blue Books: Falkland Islands, 1878, CO 81/33; St Lucia 1861, CO 258/57

Published sources

'A Friend', *Harold Tennyson RN,* London, 1918.

Argyll, Duke of, 'Passages from the Past', London, 1907.

Balfour, Frances, *Life of Dr MacGregor,* London, 1912.

—— *Obliviscaris. Dinna Forget,* London, 1930.

Banton, Mandy, *Administering the Empire, 1801–1968,* London, 2008.

Barlow, Henry S., *Swettenham,* Kuala Lumpur, 1995.

Barr, Pat, *Taming the Jungle: The men who made British Malaya,* London, 1977.

Beasley, Edward, *Mid-Victorian Imperialists: British gentlemen and the empire of the mind,* London, 2005.

Beckett, Ian F. W., ed., *Wolseley and Ashanti,* Stroud, 2009.

Bell, E. Moberly, *Flora Shaw,* London, 1947.

Bell, Henry Hesketh, *Glimpses of a Governor's Life,* London, 1946.

—— *Obeah, Witchcraft in the West Indies,* London, 1899.

Berton, Pierre, *The Last Spike,* Toronto, 1971.

Best, Nicholas, *Happy Valley,* London, 1979.

Bird, Isabella, *The Golden Chersonese,* London, 1883.

Blakeley, Brian L., *The Colonial Office, 1868–1892,* Durham, N.C., 1972.

Boyle, Frederick, *Through Fanteeland to Coomassie,* London, 1874.

Boyson, V. F., *The Falkland Islands,* Oxford, 1924.

Bryden, H. A., *The Victorian Era in South Africa,* London, 1897.

Buchan, John, *Lord Minto: A memoir,* London, 1924.

Burns, P. L. and Cowan, C. D., eds, *Sir Frank Swettenham's Malayan Journals 1874–1876,* Oxford, 1975.

Burton, Richard, *Abeokuta and the Cameroons Mountains,* London, 1863.

—— *Wanderings in West Africa,* London, 1863.

Calvert, James, *Fiji and the Fijians,* ed. George Stringer Howe, vol. II, London, 1860.

Cannadine, David, *Ornamentalism,* London, 2001.

Cawkwell, M. B. R., Maling, D. H. and Cawkwell, E. M., *The Falkland Islands,* London, 1960.

Cell, John W., *British Colonial Administration in the Mid-Nineteenth Century: The policy making process,* London & New Haven, 1970.

Chapman, J. K., *The Career of Arthur Hamilton Gordon,* Toronto, 1964.

Churchill, Winston, *My African Journey,* London, 1908.

Clifford, Hugh, *East Coast Etchings,* London, 1896.

—— *Freelance of To-day,* London, 1903.

—— *In Court and Kampong,* London, 1897.

—— *Sally: A study, and other tales of the outskirts,* Edinburgh, 1904.

—— *The Downfall of the Gods,* London, 1911.

—— *The House of Clifford: From before the conquest,* Chichester, 1987.

Clifford, Lady, *Our Days on the Gold Coast,* London, 1919.

Colonial Office, *Information as to the Conditions and Cost of Living in the Colonial Empire, 2nd edition,* HMSO, 1935.

Colonial Office List, London, 1866–1917.

Conrad, Jessie, *Joseph Conrad and His Circle*, London, 1935.

Conrad, Joseph, *Heart of Darkness*, London, 1902.

Cranworth, Lord, *Profit and Sport in British East Africa*, London, 1939.

Cross, Kerr D., *Health in Africa*, London, 1897.

Crowther, Samuel, *The Gospel on the Banks of the Niger, Journals 1857–1859*, London, 1859.

Cumming, C. F. Gordon, *At Home in Fiji*, London, 1881.

Cundall, F. S. A., ed., *Lady Nugent's Journal*, London, 1907.

Daly, Mrs Dominic D., *Digging, Squatting and Pioneering Life, in the Northern Territory of South Australia*, London, 1887.

Dance, Daryl Cumber, *Fifty Caribbean Writers: A bio-bibliographical critical sourcebook*, London, 1986.

Delafield, E. M. *Beginnings*, London, 1935.

De la Rue, Kathy, *The Evolution of Darwin*, Darwin, 2004.

Denison, Sir William, *Varieties of Vice-Regal Life*, 2 vols, London, 1870.

Des Voeux, Sir William, *My Colonial Service*, 2 vols, London, 1903.

Dimbleby, Josceline, *A Profound Secret*, London, 2004.

Donovan, P. F., *A Land Full of Possibilities, a History of South Australia's Northern Territory*, St Lucia, Queensland, 1981.

Dryden, Linda, *Joseph Conrad and the Imperial Romance*, London, 2000.

Duff Gordon, Lady, *Letters from the Cape*, London, 1927.

Durnford, E., *A Soldier's Life and Work in South Africa 1872–1879*, London, 1882.

Eitel, E. J., *Europe in China*, London, 1895.

Elliott, Philip, *The Making of the Memoir*, Lincoln, 1995.

Endacott, G. B., *A History of Hong Kong*, Hong Kong, 1964.

—— *An Eastern Entrepot: A collection of documents illustrating the history of Hong Kong*, London, 1964.

Evans, Harold, *Men in the Tropics*, London, 1949.

Ferguson, Niall, *Empire: How Britain made the modern world*, London, 2003.

Foote, Mrs, *Recollections on Central America & the West Coast of Africa*, London, 1869.

Fortescue-Buckdale, Sir Charles, *Major-General Sir Henry Hallam Parr*, London, 1917.

Frere, B S., *A Record of the Family of Frere of Suffolk and Norfolk*, privately printed, 1982.

Frere, Mary, *Old Deccan Days*, London, 1868.

Gailey, H. A., *Clifford: Imperial Proconsul*, London, 1982.

Glover, Lady (Elizabeth Rosetta), *Life of Sir John Hawley Glover*, London, 1897.

Glover, Lady, *Memories of Four Continents,* London, 1923.

Gordon, Arthur Hamilton, *Mauritius. Records of private and public life, 1871–1874,* 2 vols, Edinburgh, 1894.

Gore, Albert Augustus, *Medical History of Our West African Campaigns,* London, 1876.

Graham, Jeanine, *Frederick Weld,* Auckland, 1983.

Gullick, J. M., *Rulers and Residents, Influence and Power in the Malay States 1870–1920,* Oxford, 1992.

Haggard, H. Rider, *Cetywayo and His White Neighbours,* London, 1888.

Hahn, Emily, *James Brooke of Sarawak,* London, 1953.

Hardinge, Arthur, *The Life of Henry Howard Molyneux Herbert, Fourth Earl of Carnarvon 1831–1890,* Oxford, 1925.

Hardman, William, ed., *The Journals of John McDouall Stuart,* London, 1865.

Harris, Pippa, ed., *Song of Love: The Letters of Rupert Brooke and Noel Olivier,* London, 1991.

Hasluck, Alexandra, ed., *Audrey Tennyson's Vice-Regal Days,* Canberra, 1978.

Hastings, A. C. G., *Voyage of the Dayspring,* London, 1926.

Heussler, Robert, *Yesterday's Rulers,* London, 1963.

Hill, Robert A., ed., *The Marcus Garvey and Universal Negro Improvement Association Papers,* vol. I, Berkeley, 1983.

Hollett, Dave, *Passage from India to El Dorado,* London, 1999.

Holroyd, Michael, *Bernard Shaw: The search for love,* vol. 1, London, 1988.

Honigsbaum, Mark, *The Fever Trail,* London, 2001.

Hooper, Steven and Roth, Jane, eds, *The Fiji Journals of Baron Anatole von Hügel 1875–1877,* Cambridge, 1990.

Hughes, Lotte, *Moving the Maasai,* London, 2006.

Hulugalle, H. A. J., *British Governors of Ceylon,* London, 1963.

Hurwitz, S. and Hurwitz, E., *Jamaica, a historical portrait,* London, 1971.

Huxley, Elspeth, *White Man's Country,* London, 1953.

Innes, Emily, *The Chersonese with the Gilding Off,* London, 1885.

James, Lawrence, *The Rise & Fall of the British Empire,* London, 2005.

James, Winston, *A Fierce Hatred of Injustice: Claude McKay's Jamaica and his poetry of rebellion,* London, 2000.

Jeffries, Charles, *The Colonial Empire and its Civil Service,* Cambridge, 1938.

Jenkins, E., *The Coolie, His Rights & Wrongs,* London, 1871.

Jenkins, Thomas B., *Amazulu,* London, 1882.

Karl, Frederick and Davies, Laurence, eds, *The Collected Letters of Joseph Conrad,* Cambridge, 1988.

Keppel, Sir Henry, Brooke, Sir James, and Kelly, Walter Keating, *The Expedition to Borneo of HMS Dido for the Suppression of Piracy*, vol. II, London, 1847.

Keyser, Arthur, *People and Places,* London, 1922.

Kirk-Greene, A. H. M., *Britain's Imperial Administrators, 1858–1966*, Basingstoke, 1999.

Knapman, Claudia, *White Women in Fiji,* London, 1986.

Laband, John, *Fight Us in the Open: The Anglo-Zulu War through Zulu eyes,* Pietermaritzburg, 1985.

—— *Isandlwana,* Pietermaritzburg, 1992.

Lee, Francis, *Fabianism and Colonialism,* London, 1988.

Legge, J. D., *Britain in Fiji,* London, 1958.

Lethbridge, H. J., ed., *The Hong Kong Guide,* Hong Kong, 1982.

Lewis, Gordon K., *The Growth of the Modern West Indies,* Kingston, 2004.

Leys, Norman, *Kenya,* London, 1924.

Lorne, The Marquis of, *Canadian Pictures,* London, n.d.

Lovat, Alice, Lady, *The Life of Sir Frederick Weld,* London, 1914.

Lugard, F. D., *The Rise of Our East African Empire,* London, 1893.

—— *The Dual Mandate,* London, 1922.

Lynch-Robinson, Christopher, *The Last of the Irish R.M.s,* London, 1951.

Mann, Kristin, *Slavery and the Birth of an African City: Lagos 1760–1900,* Bloomington, 2007.

Martineau, John, *The Life and Correspondence of Sir Bartle Frere,* London, 1895.

Maudslay, Alfred, *Life in the Pacific Fifty Years Ago,* London, 1930.

Maxwell, William, *With the 'Ophir' round the Empire,* London, 1902.

Meyer, Karl E. and Brysac, Shareen Blair, *Kingmakers,* New York, 2009.

Mills, L. A., *Ceylon under British Rule 1795–1932,* London, 1933.

Morris, Donald R., *The Washing of the Spears,* London, 1966.

Morris, James, *Farewell the Trumpets; Heaven's Command; Pax Britannica,* London, 1981.

Morris, Jan, *Hong Kong,* London, 1988.

Morris, Mervyn, *Making West Indian Literature,* Kingston, 2005.

Mungeam, G. H., *British Rule in Kenya 1895–1912,* Oxford, 1966.

Munn, Christopher, *Anglo-China: Chinese people and British rule in Hong Kong, 1841–1880,* Richmond, 2001.

Olivier, Margaret, ed., *Sydney Olivier,* London, 1948.

Olivier, Sydney, *Jamaica: The blessed island,* London, 1936.

—— *White Capital and Coloured Labour*, London, 1906.

Ondaatje, Christopher, *Woolf in Ceylon,* Toronto, 2005.

Padikara Mudaliyar of Ceylon, The, *The Government of the Island of Ceylon*, London, 1938.

Pakenham, Valerie, *The Noonday Sun, Edwardians in the Tropics*, London, 1985.

Parham, (Mrs C.) H. B. Richenda, *Fiji before the Cession*, printed in the *Fiji Times*, 1933–1941.

Parr, Henry Hallam, *Sketch of Kafir and Zulu Wars*, London, 1880.

Perham, Margery, *Lugard*, 2 vols, London, 1960.

Pomerantz-Zhang, Linda, *Wu Tingfang (1842–1922): Reform and modernization in modern Chinese history*, Hong Kong, 1992.

Pope-Hennessy, James, *Verandah*, London, 1964.

Porter, Andrew, ed., *The Oxford History of the British Empire; The Nineteenth Century*, vol. III, Oxford, 1999.

Purvis, John B., *Handbook to British East Africa and Uganda*, London, 1900.

Rhys, Jean, *Smile, Please*, London, 1979.

Roff, William R., ed., *Stories by Sir Hugh Clifford*, Kuala Lumpur, 1966.

Rosenzweig, Paul A., *The House of Seven Gables – A History of Government House*, Darwin, 1996.

Savory, Elaine, *Jean Rhys*, Cambridge, 1998.

Sayer, Geoffrey Robley, *Hong Kong, 1862–1919*, Hong Kong, 1975.

Scarr, Deryck, *The Majesty of Colour*, Canberra, 1973.

—— *Fiji: Politics of illusion, the military coups in Fiji*, Sydney, 1988.

Selzer, Anita, *Governors' Wives in Colonial Australia*, Canberra, 2002.

Simon, André L., *In the Twilight*, London, 1969.

Simon, John Y., ed., *The Personal Memoirs of Julia Dent Grant* (Mrs Ulysses S. Grant), New York, 1975, p. 275.

Smythe, Mrs (Sarah Maria), *Ten Months in the Fiji Islands, with an introduction and appendix by Col. W. J. Smythe*, London, 1864.

Stamp, Robert M., *Royal Rebels*, Toronto, 1988.

Stanley, Henry M., *Coomassie*, London, 1866.

Stanmore, H. G., *Fiji: Records of private and public life. 1875–1880*, Edinburgh, 1897.

Stark, James H., *Stark's Jamaica Guide*, Boston, 1902.

Statham, Pamela, *The Origins of Australia's Capital Cities*, Cambridge, 1990.

Swettenham, Frank, *Also and Perhaps*, London, 1912.

—— *British Malaya*, London, 1948.

—— *Footprints in Malaya*, London, 1942.

—— *Malay Sketches*, London, 1896.

—— *The Real Malay*, London, 1900.

—— *Unaddressed Letters* , London, 1898.

Tatham, David, ed., *Dictionary of Falklands Biography*, Ledbury, 2008.

Templer, John C., *The Private Letters of Sir James Brooke,* vol. II, London, 1853.

Tennyson, Hallam, *Alfred Lord Tennyson, A Memoir by his son*, London, 1899.

Thomson, Alice, *The Singing Line,* Vintage, 1999.

Thwaite, Ann, *Emily Tennyson: The poet's wife,* London, 1996.

Tidrick, Kathryn, *Empire and the English Character,* London, 1990.

Treves, Sir Arthur, *Uganda for a Holiday,* London, 1908.

Trollope, Anthony, *South Africa,* London, 1878.

—— *The Letters of Anthony Trollope,* ed. John Hall, Stanford, 1983.

Tuttle, Charles, *Royalty in Canada embracing sketches of the house of Argyll, the Right Honourable the Marquis of Lorne, (Governor-General of Canada), Her Royal Highness the Princess Louise,* Montreal, 1878.

Ward, W. E. F., *A History of the Gold Coast,* London, 1948.

Warner, John, *Fragrant Harbour,* Hong Kong, 1976.

Warren, Sir Charles, *On the Veldt in the Seventies,* London, 1902.

Wheatcroft, Andrew, *The Tennyson Album: A biography in original photographs,* London, 1980.

Williams, Thomas, *Fiji and the Fijians,* London, 1860.

Willson, F. M. G., *A Strong Supporting Cast: The Shaw Lefevres, 1789–1936,* London, 1993.

Wilson, A. N., *The Victorians,* London, 2002.

Winstedt, R. O., *A History of Malaya,* London, 1935.

Wolfston, Freda, *Pageant of Ghana,* London, 1958.

Woolf, Leonard, *Growing: An autobiography of the years 1904 to 1911,* London, 1964.

Journals

Allen, J. de V., 'Two imperialists: a study of Sir Frank Swettenham and Sir Hugh Clifford', *Journal of the Malaysian Branch of the Royal Asiatic Society*, 37, no. 1 (1964), pp. 41–73.

Anderson, Catherine E., 'A Zulu King in Victorian London: Race, Royalty and Imperialist Aesthetics in Late Nineteenth Century Britain', *Visual Resources*, 24, no. 3 (2008), pp. 299–319.

Clemens, Florence, 'Conrad's Malaysia', *College English*, 2, no. 4 (Jan. 1941), pp. 338–46.

Clifford, Hugh, 'Some facts concerning the Gold Coast', *Journal of the Royal African Society*, 14, no. 53 (Oct. 1914), pp. 15–23.

—— 'The Genius of Mr Joseph Conrad', *North American Review* (University of Northern Iowa), 178, no. 571 (June 1904), pp. 842–52.

Girouard, Sir Percy, 'The Development of Northern Nigeria', *Journal of the African Society*, VII, no. XXVIII (July 1908).

Goerg, Odile, 'Between Everyday Life and Exception: Celebrating Pope Hennessy Day in Freetown, 1872–c.1905', *Journal of African Cultural Studies* (Taylor & Francis Ltd), 15, no. 1 (June 2002), pp. 119–31.

Gullick, John, 'Biographical note on Bloomfield Douglas', *Journal of Malaysian Branch of the Royal Asiatic Society*, 48 (2), 1975.

Hoppe, Kirk Arden, 'Lords of the Fly: Colonial Visions and Revisions of African Sleeping Sickness Environment on Ugandan Lake Victoria, 1906-61', *Africa: Journal of the International African Institute* (Edinburgh University Press), 67, no. 1 (1997), pp. 86–105.

Illustrated London News.

Kirk-Greene, A. H. M., 'Canada in Africa: Sir Percy Girouard, Neglected Colonial Governor', *African Affairs* (Oxford University Press on behalf of the Royal African Society), 83, no. 331 (April 1984), pp. 207–39.

Knapland, Paul, 'Gladstone–Gordon Correspondence, 1851–1896: Selections from the Private Correspondence of a British Prime Minister and a Colonial Governor', *Transactions of the American Philosophical Society, New Series* (American Philosophical Society), 51, no. 4 (1961), pp. 1–116.

McIntyre, W. D., 'Commander Glover and the Colony of Lagos 1861–73', *Journal of African History*, IV, no. 1 (1963), pp. 57–9.

McSheffrey, Gerald M., 'Slavery, Indentured Servitude, Legitimate Trade and the Impact of Abolition in the Gold Coast, 1874–1901: A Reappraisal', *Journal of African History*, 24, no. 3 (1983), pp. 349–68.

Pennanen, Gary, 'Sitting Bull, Indian without a country', *Canadian Historical Review*, LI, no. 2 (June 1970), pp. 123–40.

Priotto, G. et al., 'Nifurtimox-eflornithine combination therapy for second-stage African *Trypanosoma brucei gambiense* trypanosomiasis: a multicentre, randomised, phase III, non-inferiority trial', *Lancet,* 374, Issue 9683, 4 July 2009, pp. 56–64.

Smith, Robert, 'The Lagos Consulate 1851–1861: An Outline', *Journal of African History*, 15, no. 3 (1974), pp. 393–416.

Soff, Harvey G., 'Sleeping Sickness in the Lake Victoria Region of British East Africa, 1900-1915', *African Historical Studies* (Boston University African Studies Center), 2, no. 2 (1969), pp. 255–68.

Spafford, Ronnie, 'Jeremiah Thomas Fitzgerald Callaghan CMG, Governor of the Falkland Islands 1876–1880', *Falkland Islands Journal*, 1994.

Stembridge, Stanley R., 'Disraeli and the Millstones', *Journal of British Studies* (University of Chicago Press), 5, no. 1 (Nov. 1965), pp. 122–39.

Stockwell, A. J., 'Hugh Clifford in Trinidad', *Caribbean Quarterly*, 24 (March–June 1978), pp. 8–33.

—— 'Sir Hugh Clifford's early career (1866–1903) as told from his private papers', *Journal of the Malaysian Branch of the Royal Asiatic Society*, 49, no. 1 (1976), pp. 89–112.

Websites and electronic resources

Australian Dictionary of Biography – online edition, National Australian University, 2006. www.adbonline.anu.edu.au.

Australian Newspapers. www.newspapers.nla.gov.au.

Library and Archives Canada: www.collectionscanada.gc.ca/canadian-west.

Dictionary of Canadian Biography Online. www.biographi.ca.

Lawrence H. Officer, *Measuring Worth*, Measuring Worth, 2010, www.measuring worth.com/ukcompare/index.php.

House of Commons Parliamentary Papers Online. ProQuest Information and Learning Company, 2005:

> Blue Book report for St Lucia 1861. Cmd 3165. *Accounts and papers of the House of Commons*, vol. XXXIX, London, 1863.

> *Census of England and Wales*, C.3797 (43 & 44 Vict. Co. 37), 1881, vol. IV, General report, p. 81.

> Correspondence relating to the affairs of the Gold Coast [C.1139] [C.1140], 1875.

> Further papers relating to the Ashantee Invasion [C.890] [C.891] [C.892] [C.893] [C.894], 1874.

> Gold Coast. Further correspondence respecting the Ashantee invasion [C.921] [C.922] [C.1006], 1874.

> Papers relating to Her Majesty's possessions in West Africa. Sierra Leone and Gold Coast Colony, including Lagos [C.1402], 1876.

> Royal Commission on fugitive slaves. Report of the commissioners, minutes of evidence, and appendix, with general index of minutes of evidence and appendix [C.1516-1], 1876.

> 'Report of the Commissioners appointed to enquire into the Treatment of Immigrants in British Guiana', vol. 20 [C.393], 1871.

Papers relating to Her Majesty's colonial possessions [C.2444], 1878–9.

Papers relating to Her Majesty's colonial possessions, Reports for 1879, 1880 and 1881 [C.3218], 1882.

Select Committee on Africa, *Report from the Select Committee on Africa (Western Coast),* House of Commons, 26 June 1865 (Parliamentary Papers), V (1865).

Statement of His Excellency Governor Sir John Pope Hennessy, KCMG, on the Census Returns and the Progress of the Colony, House of Commons Papers 1881, vol. LXV, no. 42.

Oxford Dictionary of National Biography, 2009. www.oxforddnb.com.

Royal Family of Jaffna, The, 2010. www. jaffnaroyalfamily.org/ponnambalan. php (accessed 29 August 2010).

The New York Times, Article Archive. www.nytimes.com.

The Times Digital Archive 1785–1985. http://infotrac.galegroup.com.

Norton Anthology of English Literature, www.wwnorton.com/college/english/ nael/20century/topic_1/jnruskin.htm.

www.jamaica-gleaner.com/pages/history/story0026.html.

Index

Page references in *italic* indicate text illustrations.

Abbey, Mr (butler) 119, 127, 129, 131
Abbey, Mrs 119, 131
Abdul Samad, Sultan of Selangor 234,
    235, 236, 240, 251
Abdu'llah, Sultan of Perak 224, 230, 233,
    237
Abeokuta 30, 34, 35, 38, 41, 46
Aberdeen, George Hamilton Gordon,
    4th Earl of 8, 113
Abinger 277, 291–2, 301, 302
Abiobissa (interpreter) 311
Aborigines 21, 78, 79, 82, 83–4, 90
Aborigines Protection Society 65
Aburi 105
Accra 105, 107
    fort 93, 101, 104
ADC (aide-de-camp)
    holders of the post *see* Burton, Frank;
        Knollys, Captain; Lascelles,
        Captain; Murray, John; Olive
        (chief of police, Fiji); Parr, Henry
        Hallam; Wallington, Captain
    role 18–19, 256–7
Adelaide 70, 72, 73–4, 77, 81, 257, 258,
    261–70, 272, 273
Aden 119
Africa
    East *see* British East Africa; Mauritius;
        Uganda; Zanzibar
    South *see* South Africa
    West *see* Cape Coast; Gold Coast
        (Ghana); Lagos; Nigeria; Northern

        Nigeria; Sierra Leone; the Gambia;
        West Africa
African Lakes Company 284
Aga Khan III, Sultan Mahommed Shah
    301
Akitoye, King of Lagos 34–5
Ambriz 95
Amery, Leo, Secretary of State for the
    Colonies 411
Anatomy of African Misery (Olivier) 351
Anti-Slavery Society 65
Antigua 10, 24
Antrobus, Sir Reginald 300, 302, 303, 306
Anuradhapura 386, 388, 401
Armstrong Whitworth 377, 379, 383,
    385
Arnold, Alice (later Alice Callaghan) 196
    see also Callaghan, Alice
Arnold, Arthur 201
Arthur, Catherine *see* Frere, Lady
    Catherine
Arthur, Sir George 142
Ashanti 93, 94, 410
    map *92*
    wars 3, 11, 16, 28, 48, 91, 93–4, 96,
        97–9
Athill, John 63
Athlone, Alexander Cambridge, 1st Earl
    252
Atholl, John George Stewart-Murray,
    8th Duke of 400
Atkinson, Dr 371

Austin, Alfred 173
Austin, Charles 204, 212, 214, 218, 222
Austin, Gardner 167–9
Australia 2, 6, 17–18, 21, 70, 417
  map 71
  North Australian Expedition 70
  Northern Territory 71, 72, 89
  South Australia *see* South Australia
  Sydney 70, 120, 127, 272
  Western 21, 179, 413
Awa (slave woman) 41

'Back to Africa' movement 352
Baden Powell, Robert 301
Baganda 315
Baikie, William Balfour 27, 32, 33, 34, 98
Bailey, Arthur 196, 200
Baker, Sir Richard 264
Balfour, Arthur James, 1st Earl 302
Barbados 64, 69, 107, 171–2
  map 52
Barkly, Sir Henry 145, 147
Baro–Kano Railway 365
Barry, Charles 92
Barter, Mr (botanist) 33, 34
Bates, Mrs (cook) 261, 263, 264, 266, 269, 271
Beaumont, Chief Justice 61
Beausoleil, Monsieur 51
Beckett, Gilbert à 394
Beckett, Minna à (later Minna Clifford) 394
  see also Clifford, Minna
Beecroft, John 35
Belfield, Henry 383
Belize *see* British Honduras
Bell, Gertrude 252–3, 254
Bell, Henry Hesketh (Harry) 12, 22, 308–10, 312–13, 414
  as administrator of Dominica 311–12
  as Commissioner of Uganda 312, 313–15, 320–32
  early life 310

final posts and retirement 332
  in the Gold Coast 310–11
  as Governor of Northern Nigeria 332
Bell, Moberly 278, 279, 280–81, 293
Bengal 78, 81
Besant, Annie 337
Bight of Benin 35
Bijapur 142–3
Birch, James Wheeler Woodford 224–5, 233, 236–7
Bird, Isabella 185, 227
Bird (maid) 368, 370
Birkhall 139, 141
Black Hawk 197
Black Watch 91
Blackfoot people 205, 206, 220, 221
blackwater fever 250, 312, 321
Blyden, Edward Wilmot 179
Boer war 265–6, 303, 363
Boers 140, 147, 148, 150, 156, 158, 162–3
  Great Trek 147
Bombay 143–4
Bosphorus (mail steamer) 77
Boussa 27, 33
Boussa, King of 33
Boutwell, Commander 109
Bowes, Frederick 400–401, 405, 407, 411, 412
Boyle, Charles 258
Boyle, Frederick 99–100
Boyle, Mary 258
Boyle, Zacyntha Antonia Lorinzina 258, 268, 273
Brackenbury, Charles (Col.) 277
Brackenbury, Hilda 277
Bradford, George Bridgeman, 4th Earl of 309
Bradford, Lady Ida Frances 309
British Australian Telegraph Company 81, 85, 86
British Commonwealth 1, 418
British East Africa 356–85
  Maasai *see* Maasai

map 357
Mombasa *see* Mombasa
Nairobi *see* Nairobi
British East India Company *see* East India
  Company
British Empire 2, 11, 21, 417–18
  'Colonial Empire' 416
  map *xii–xiii*
British Guiana (Guyana) 8, 49, 54–62,
  64–7
  map 55
British Honduras (Belize) 21, 142,
  339–40, 412–13, 414
British Malaya 411
British South Africa Company 278, 285
British West Charterland Company 291
Brooke, Charles 176
Brooke, Emma 75
Brooke, James, Raja of Sarawak 75–6,
  77, 175
Browning, Elizabeth 259
Browning, Robert 259
Brownlee, Charles 151, 153
Bruce, David (Col.) 316, 317, 328
Bruce, Mary 316
Buchan, John 17–18
Buckingham, Richard Temple-Grenville,
  3rd Duke of, Secretary of State for
  the Colonies 174
Buganda (Uganda) 286, 287, 320–21, 328
Bulwer, Sir Henry 148, 156, 157, 158, 159
Burdett-Coutts, Lady Angela 173, 176
Burton, Frank (ADC) 317, 321, 331
Burton, Richard (traveller) 34, 36–7
Busoga 315, 317, 325, 328
Butler, Rev. Dr (missionary) 238
Butterworth (Natal) 150, 151
Byron, John (sea captain) 191

Cakobau, King of Fiji 109, 112, 120, 122,
  123, 123–24, 125, 129, 137
Callaghan, Alice (née Arnold) 192, 196,
  200, 201

Callaghan, Thomas 11, 192–201
  as Governor of Labuan 195
  as Governor of the Falkland Islands
    192–5
Cambridge, Prince George, 2nd Duke of
  153, 154
Cameron, Julia Margaret 259
Campbell, Elizabeth 209
Campbell, Frances 209
Canada 6, 17–18, 21, 115, 202–23, 417
  des Voeux in 54
  Girouard's upbringing in 362
  Lorne in 202–5, 206–23
  map *216–17*
  New Brunswick 114, 115
  Flora Shaw in 281
Canadian Indians 205–8, 212–13, 217–19,
  220–21, 222
  see also Blackfoot; Cree; Ojibeway;
    Sioux
Canadian Pacific railway 202, 222, 362
Canning, Miss 174
Canton (Guangdong) 170, 171
Cape Coast 44, 93, 95, *99*, 99–100, *101*,
  102, 103, 106–7
  see also Ashanti; Gold Coast
Cape Colony 140, 147, 148
  under governorship of Frere 145–65
Cape Frontier, 9th 154
Cape of Good Hope 140, 146–7
  under governorship of Frere 145–65
Cape Town 144–6, 152, 154, 162, 163–4,
  279
Cardigan, James Thomas, 7th Earl of 4
Cardwell, Edward, 1st Viscount,
  Secretary of State for the Colonies
  112
Carew, Walter 125, 128, 133, 134
Carlyle, Thomas 276
Carnarvon, Henry Howard Molyneux
  Herbert, 4th Earl of, Secretary of
  State for the Colonies 13, 91–3,
  112

and Frere 140, 146, 147, 149, 151, 154
and the Gold Coast 16–17, 94, 95,
101–4, 105
and Gordon 117, 124, 125, 132
and Hennessy 173, 179, 182
Carroll, Lewis (C. L. Dodgson) 259
Castries 49, 50, 51, 67, 68
Catchlove, Edward Napoleon Buonaparte 84–5, 86
Caulfeild, Isabel 249, 252
Cavendish, Frederick 64–5
Cecil, Robert, 3rd Marquis of Salisbury
289
census 20–21
Cetewayo, King of the Zulus 155–7,
158–9, 160, 163, 164–5
Ceylon Morning Leader 406, 409
Ceylon (Sri Lanka) 6, 8, 15, 21, 386–8,
399, 401, 402, 409
under governorship of Clifford
388–90, 398–409, 410, 411
map *387*
Challenger, HMS 197
Chamberlain, Harriet 308
Chamberlain, Joseph, Secretary of State
for the Colonies 11, 21, 107, 302,
308, 416–17
and Girouard 363
and the Lugards 275, 289–90, 291, 297,
300
and Olivier 336, 345
Chamberlain, Neville 309
Charles I 341
Charles II 203
Charterhouse 54, 63
Che Mida 232–4, 239
Chelmsford, Frederic Augustus
Thesiger, 2nd Baron 153–4, 161,
164–5
Chief Justice, post of 15, 18
abuse of role 63, 129–30
holders of the post *see* Athill, John;
Beaumont, Chief Justice;

Callaghan, Thomas; Glover, Sir
John Hawley
China Mail 169
Cholmondeley, Florence *see* Delamere,
Lady Florence
Cholmondeley, Hugh *see* Delamere,
Hugh Cholmondeley, 3rd Baron
Chown, E. E. (Maj.) 345–6
Christianburg castle 57
Chua, Daudi, Kakaba of Uganda 320
Church Missionary Society 30, 41–2,
315
Churchill, Winston 303–4, 305, 327,
329–30, 361–2
and Bell 329–30, 361
and Girouard 363, 365
and Lugard 303, 305
and Flora Shaw 303
City Hall Museum, Hong Kong 186
Clarke, Miss (maid) 261, 267
Clifford, Lady Elizabeth (née de la
Pasture) 407, 408, 410, 411
Clifford, Everard 390
Clifford, Henry 410
Clifford, Sir Henry Hugh (Maj.-Gen.) 390
Clifford, Sir Hugh 9, 12, 243, 244,
388–410, *401*, *404*, 411–12
as Colonial Secretary in Trinidad
396–8
In Court and Kampong 395
Downfall of the Gods, The 408
early life 390–91
East Coast Etchings 394
as Governor of Ceylon 388–90,
398–409, 410, 411
as Governor of Malaya 410, 411–12
as Governor of Nigeria 410
as Governor of the Gold Coast 409,
410
in Kuala Lumpur 395
'Our Trusty and Well Beloved' 409
in Pahang 392–4
in Perak 391–2

poisoned 395–6

Clifford, Hugh (son of Sir Hugh) 394, 397, 398, 410

Clifford, Hugh Charles, 7th Baron Clifford of Chudleigh 390

Clifford, Josephine 390, 391

Clifford, Mary 394, 396, 397, 398

Clifford, Minna (née à Beckett) 394, 395, 397, 398

Clifford, Monica 397, 398

Co-Hongs 170

Cody, Bryan 175, 176, 178

Cody, Willie 178

Cole, Berkeley 359, 383

Cole, Galbraith 359, 380, 381, 383

Colenso, John, Bishop 414

Collins, William 192

Colombo 386, 388, 389, 403, 406

colonial governors 8–11, 14–25, 256–7
  post of Chief Justice *see* Chief Justice, post of
  post of Colonial Secretary 15, 18, 19
  post of Governor *see* Governor, post of
  see also specific governors

Colonial Office List 14, 24

Colonial Office, London 9, 10, 13–14, 21, 91–3, 414, 416–17, 419
  and Bell 313–14, 325, 327–8, 414
  Blue Books 19, 192–4, *199*, 200
  and British East Africa 361–2, 375–6, 377, 380, 381
  and Ceylon 405, 406
  Chamberlain *see* Chamberlain, Joseph
  and Clifford 406, 407, 411, 412
  colonial appointment system 15–17, 417
  and Fiji 109–11, 132, 133–4, 136
  and Gordon 116, 117, 414
  and Lagos 40, 41, 42–4, 45, 47–8
  and the Malay States 229
  and Olivier 345, 354
  patronage 15, 417

and the post of Governor 18, 20, 21–2, 256
  promotion of unsuitable elder governors 412–14
  protocol and dress instructions for governors' wives 256
  under-secretaries *see* Antrobus, Sir Reginald; Carnarvon, Henry Howard Molyneux Herbert, 4th Earl of (later Secretary of State); Churchill, Winston; Cox, Charles; Elliott, Frederick; Fairfield, Edward; Fiddes, George; Furse, Ralph; Herbert, Sir Robert; Merivale, Herman; Ommanney, Sir Montagu
  Secretary of State *see* Secretary of State for the Colonies
  and Flora Shaw 278, 300, 302, 303–4

Colonial Secretary, post of 15, 18, 19
  London-based Secretary of State *see* Secretary of State for the Colonies

Columbus, Christopher 50, 341

Commonwealth 1, 418

Complete India Outfit 22–3

Conan Doyle, Arthur 301, 363

Congo 317, 332
  Free State 327

Congo River 315

Congo (steamer) 99

Connaught, Prince Arthur, Duke of 374

Connaught, Princess Louise, Duchess of 374

Conrad, Jessie 395

Conrad, Joseph 394, 395

Conyngham, A. M. 174

Cook, Albert 315, 316

Cook, James 2

Cooper, Fenimore 220

Corona Club 417

Coulson, William 197

In Court and Kampong (Clifford) 395

Cox, Charles 21

Cox, Harold 337–8, 339
Cox, Homersham 338
Cox, Margaret (later Margaret Olivier) 337–8
    see also Olivier, Margaret
Cox, Samuel 51, 68, 69
Cox, Sandy 352
Cranworth, Bertram Gurdon, 2nd Baron 367, 370
Cranworth, Lady Vera Gurdon 367, 370, 378
Cree 205, 206, 217–18, 221, 222
Creole, The 64
Crewe, Robert Crewe-Milnes, 1st Marquess of, Secretary of State for the Colonies 365, 407
Cromer, Evelyn Baring, 1st Earl of 275
Cromwell, Oliver 341
Crosby, James 61, 66
Crowfoot, Blackfoot chief 220
Crown Prince 197
Crowther, Samuel 30, *31*, 32, 34, 47–8, 93
Cruikshank, Jessie 100
Cumming, Constance Gordon, 'Eka' 118, 119, 121, 127, 133, 135
Curzon, George, 1st Marquess Curzon of Kedleston 252, 275, 301
Custer, George Armstrong (Gen.) 205

Dahomey (Benin) 38
Dahomey, King of 38, 41, 42
Daily Gleaner 340, 351
Daily Press 186
Daily Telegraph 344
Daly, Dominic (Dominick's son) 74, 77, 89, 240
Daly, Dominick (Governor, South Australia) 73
D'Arcy, Colonel 196, 198
Darwin, Charles 73
Darwin, Australia 90
    Port Darwin 73, 78–9, 81

    see also Palmerston
Darwin, Falkland Islands 197
Davidson, James 229
Davies, Mr and Mrs 379
Davis, Admiral C. H. 335
Davis (police trooper) 80
Dayspring (steamer) 26, 27, 30–31, 32, 33
de la Pasture, Elizabeth (later Lady Clifford) 407
    see also Clifford, Lady Elizabeth
de la Pasture, Yolande 407
de Lisser, Herbert George 340–41, 345, 351
de Ricci (Attorney-General, Fiji) 125, 127
Dean, Messrs 197, 198–9, 200
debt bondage 235–6
Delafield, E. M. 407
Delamere, Lady Florence 359, 362, 368, 373
Delamere, Hugh Cholmondeley, 3rd Baron 358–9, 360, 361, 367, 370, 373, 377, 378, 379, 380, 383
Delane, John 112
Demerara River 55, 56, 58, 59, 61
dengue fever 321–2
Denison, Caroline 24, 25
Denison, George 53
Denison, Julia 53
Denison, Sir William 24–5, 53–4, 70
Derby, Edward Geoffrey Stanley, 14th Earl of 173
des Voeux, Marion (née Pender) 68, 69
des Voeux, Sir William 16, 17, 18, 137, 416
    as administrator of St Lucia 53, 62–9
    arrival in St Lucia 49–50, 51–3
    in British Guiana 49, 54–62, 65–7
    career after leaving St Lucia 69
    early life 53–4
Devonshire, Louisa Cavendish, Duchess of 309
Devonshire, Spencer Compton Cavendish, 8th Duke of 308–9

Dewdney, Edgar 216
diamonds/diamond mines 147, 279, 414
Dickens, Charles 390
Dido (gunboat) 76
disease *see* fevers; malaria; measles;
    sleeping sickness
Disraeli, Benjamin, 1st Earl of Beacons-
    field 3, 161, 164, 173, 174, 209
    1874 election victory 91
Dix, Macnamara 50, 51, 62
Dixon, Alexander 352
Dodgson, Charles Lutwidge 259
Dominica 308, 311–12, 325
Dosunmu, King of Lagos 35, 36, 38,
    39–40, 44, 46, 47
Douglas, Ellen (Elli) 74, 77, 79, 84, 89
Douglas, Harriet 74, 77, 78, 79, 81, 82,
    83, 84, 89, 240
Douglas, Johnnie 77
Douglas, Mrs (W. B. Douglas's mother)
    75
Douglas, Nell 77, 79, 81, 83, 84, 85, 89
Douglas, William Bloomfield 8, 73–90,
    239–40
    early life 73–7
    as first Government Resident of the
        Northern Territory 74–5, 77–90
    life after leaving Palmerston 89
Doyle, Arthur Conan 301, 363
dress
    Colonial Office instructions 256
    Complete India Outfit 22–3
    in Fiji 133
    Governor's uniform 19
    Governors' wives 256
    soldiers' 98
    use of flannel 24
Dual Mandate in British Tropical Africa,
    The (Lugard) 307
Dubois, W. E. B. 351
Dundas, George 3
Durnford, Anthony (Col.) 414
Dussau, José 261, 262, 263, 267, 269, 274

Dutch East India Company 146
Dyak people 76, 77

East Africa *see* British East Africa;
    Mauritius; Uganda; Zanzibar
East Coast Etchings (Clifford) 394
East India Company 2, 5–6, 141, 170,
    227, 281, 388
    see also Dutch East India Company
Edijan, Kobina 94
education 116, 181, 306, 401, 404–5,
    417
    for women 144
Edward, Prince of Wales 139, 141, 157,
    164, 165, 209, 245, 259
Egba 34, 38, 42, 44, 45, 46, 47
Eitel, Ernst Johann 184, 186–7, 187,
    188–9, 190
Elgin, Victor Alexander Bruce, 9th Earl,
    Secretary of State for the Colonies
    302–3, 313, 327, 329, 347
Eliot, Sir Charles 359
Elizabeth II 1
Elkington, Mr 370
Elliott, Charles (Capt.) 171
Elliott, Frederick 43, 96, 414
Elmina Castle/fort 48, 94, 100, 101, 104,
    178
Ely, Jane Loftus, Marchioness of 173,
    174, 180
Eminsang, George Emile 94
Entebbe 7, 12, 314, 315–16, 320–24, 328,
    329, 330
Eugénie, Empress of France 403
Evarts, William 206–7
Eyo (gunboat) 42, 45, 46

Fabian Society/Fabians/Fabianism 337,
    339, 340, 350, 351
Fairfield, Edward 250
Falkland Islands 6, 21, 191–4, 196–201
    Blue Book 192–4, *199*, *200*
    map *193*

Falkland Islands Company 197, 198–9, 200

Farringford House 259, 260–61, 264, 273

Fergusson, Sir James 80, 85

Fernando Po 30–31

fevers 9, 14, 27, 32, 33, 51, 62, 82
  blackwater fever 250, 312, 321
  dengue fever 321–2
  East Coast fever in livestock 373–4, 375
  on the Gold Coast 12, 96–7, 102, 104, 105, 107
  malarial 9, 14, 39, 48, 53, 87–8, 96–7, 107 *see also* malaria
  in Mauritius 116
  yellow fever 55, 58–9

Fiddes, George 376

Fiji 8, 9, 69, 108–38
  Fijian council (*Bose*) 136–7
  Gordon's governorship of 119–27, 129–34, 136–8
  map *110*
  measles carried to 120, 124, 131
  taxation 130, 134, 136
  Viti Levu uprising 131–2

Filter, Rev. 156–7

Fingoe 150, 152, 154

flogging 180, 182, 184, 195

Foelsche, Paul 78, 80, 87

Foote, Mrs (consul's wife) 38, 40

Ford, Ford Madox 340

Fowler, Henry 47

France
  claim on Newfoundland fisheries 14
  Seven Years War 2
  war on Upper Niger 45

Franco-Prussian war 84

Freeling, Sandford 106

Freeman, Henry Stanhope 36, 37

Freetown, Sierra Leone 30, 33, 44–5, 178–9

Frere, Sir Bartle 11–12, 16, 94, 139–46, 147–54, 156–66, 414

early life 141–2
  as Governor of Bombay 143–4
  as Governor of the Cape and High Commissioner for South Africa 140, 145–54, 156–65
  in India 139, 141–4
  life after leaving South Africa 165–6

Frere, Bartle (son of Sir Bartle) 143, 145, 154

Frere, Lady Catherine ('Kate', née Arthur) 139, 141, 142–3, 145, 148, 149, 150, 152, 154, 162, 165, 166

Frere, Catherine ('Katey', daughter of Sir Bartle) 143, 144, 145, 166

Frere, Eliza (Lily) 145, 152, 154

Frere, Georgina 143, 145

Frere, John Hookham 142

Frere, May 142, 144, 145, 166

Fulani 295, 296, 297, 414–15

Furse, Ralph 417

Gambia, the 44, 178, 179, 196, 413

Garibaldi, Giuseppe 259

Garnett, Constance 340

Garnett, Edward 340

Garvey, Marcus 352, 353, 354

Gcaleka people 150, 151–3

George III 2

George, Prince of Wales 274, 301
  see also George V

George V 274, 411
  see also George, Prince of Wales

Georgetown (Guyana) 55–6, 59, 65–7

Ghana *see* Cape Coast; Gold Coast

Gibb, Livingstone 171

Gibraltar 2, 6, 10, 14, 145, 277, 415

Girouard, Dickie (son of Sir Percy) 366, 385

Girouard, Lady Gwendolen (née Solomon) 364, 365, 365–6, 368–73, 374, 375, 376, 377–78, 380–81, 385

Girouard, Sir Percy 12, 356, 362–9, 371–85

as Commissioner of Railways for
Transvaal and Orange River
colonies 363–4
early life 362–3
as Governor of British East Africa
365–9, 371–83
in Northern Nigeria 365
retirement 383, 385
in South Africa 363–4
Gladstone, Agnes 113
Gladstone, Mary 113
Gladstone, William Ewart 95, 112, 113,
116, 118, 259, 416
Glover, Lady Elizabeth Rosetta Scott 24,
26, 48, 416
Glover, Frederic 28, 29
Glover, Sir John Hawley 3, 8, 11, 26–48,
91, 98, 178, 414
as administrator/Governor of Lagos
37–48
and the Ashanti 28, 48
early life 28–9
journey and introduction to Africa
26–8, 29–33
Glover, Mary 28–9
Glyn, Richard (Col.) 151
gold 84, 85, 89, 90, 93
Gold Coast (Ghana) 6, 12, 16, 21, 28, 48,
91–107, 178–9, 418
Bell in 310–11
Governor Clifford 409, 410
Governor Hennessy *see* Hennessy,
John Pope
Governor Strahan *see* Strahan, George
(Capt.)
map 92
riots 46
see also Ashanti; Cape Coast
Goldie, Sir George 275
Goldsworthy, Sir Roger 412–13
Goodman, John 67
Gordon, 'A.G.', cousin of Sir Arthur
Gordon 118, 119, 125, 128, 130, 131

Gordon, Sir Arthur Hamilton Gordon,
later 1st Baron Stanmore 8, 11, 20,
65, 112–18, 416
early life 113–15
as Governor of Fiji 69, 119–27,
129–34, 136–8
as Governor of Mauritius 116–17
as Governor of New Zealand 137
as Governor of Trinidad 115–16
Gordon, Charles George (Gen., 'Chinese
Gordon') 187, 277
Gordon, George William 350
Gordon, Jack 116, 118, 128, 136
Gordon, Nevil 115, 118, 128, 136
Gordon, Lady Rachael (née Shaw-Lefe-
vre) 65, 114–16, 116, 119–20, 127,
128–9, 131–3, 134–6
Gore, Albert 97
Gosse, Sir Edmund 395
Gothenburg (steamer) 90
Government Gazette (Ceylon) 399
Government House
Adelaide 262, 267–8
Cape Coast 100
Cape Town 145–6, 148–9, 279
Dominica 311–12
Entebbe 314, 320, 321, 323–4, 330
Fiji 112, 121, *121*, 122–3, 127–8, 134
Hong Kong 169, 185, 187, 306
Labuan 176
Lagos 37, 39–40
Melbourne 6, 270, *271*
Mombasa 318
Nairobi 366, 369–71, 374–5, 379
Rideau Hall, Ottawa 209, 210
St Lucia 53
Stanley 196–7
Tasmania 7
Governor, post of 15, 17–21
uniform *19*
Goyder, George 73, 78–9
Grahamstown (South Africa) 150
Grant, Mrs Ulysses 187

Grant, Ulysses S. (Gen.) 187
Granville, George Leveson Gower, 2nd
    Earl Granville, Secretary of State
    for the Colonies 62, 64–5, 80, 173
The Graphic 204, 216, 222
Gray, William Henry 80–81
Greenwood, Hamar 335
Gregory, Augustus Charles 70
Griqualand West 3, 140, 147, 149
Gulnare (schooner) 77–8, 83–4, 85

Hall, Sydney 204, 216, 222
Hamilton Gordon, Arthur Charles *see*
    Gordon, Sir Arthur Hamilton
    Gordon, later 1st Baron Stanmore
Handy (gunboat) 36
Harcourt, Lewis, Secretary of State for
    the Colonies 378, 379, 380, 381
Hardie, Keir 339
Hardy, Thomas 395
Hart, John 74, 77
Harvey, George B. M. 395
Hassim, Raja Muda 75
Hausa
    freed 33–4, 38
    province 295
    troops/police 37, 40, 41, 42, 43, 44, 46,
        91, 99
Hayes-Sadler, James (Col.) 361–2, 365
Hayllar, Thomas Child 184–5, 188, 189
Heligoland/Helgoland 4–5, 5
Hennessy, Bertie 167, 180, 188
Hennessy, John Patrick (Johnnie) 177,
    178
Hennessy, John Pope 12, 171–9, 180,
    189–90
    in Barbados 171–2
    early life 172–4
    as Governor-in-Chief of the West
        African Settlements 44–5, 46–7, 94,
        178–79
    as Governor of Hong Kong 167, 169,
        181–9

as Governor of Labuan 174–8
Hennessy, Lady Kitty (née Low) 45, 167,
    176, 177, 178–9, 180, 185, 187, 188,
    189–90
Hennessy, Mary 174–5, 176
Henry, Prince of Prussia 187
Herbert, Sir Robert 93, 134, 179, 189,
    200, 278
Hicks Beach, Sir Michael, Secretary of
    State for the Colonies 2, 158, 159,
    160, 163, 186
Highbury 289–90, 308–10
Highclere, Hampshire 92, 101
Hill, Octavia 340
Hincks, Francis 56, 59, 60, 61–2, 64
Hindlip, Charles Allsopp, 3rd Baron 319,
    367
*Historical Geography of the British Colonies,
    A* 245
Hitchman, Mr (butler) 261, 267, 271
Hodges, Aubrey 315, 321, 321–2, 326,
    327, 331
Holmes, Cecil 237, 245
Holmes, M. E. 248
Holmes, Sydney (later Sydney Swetten-
    ham) 237–8
    see also Swettenham, Sydney
Hong Kong 6, 8, 15, 21, 167–71, 179–81,
    181, 418
    Callaghan in 195
    des Voeux in 69
    Hennessy's governorship 169, 181–9
    Lugard in 306
    map *168*
Hong Kong and Shanghai Bank 171
Hongs 170, 171, 189
Hopetoun, John Hope, 7th Earl 270
Horn (nursemaid) 261, 262
Hudson's Bay Company 202, 203

Ibadan 38, 41, 43, 46
Idris, Raja (Sultan of Perak) 243, 247–8,
    250, 252, 253

Illustrated London News 91, 204, 222
Imperial British East Africa Company
    286–7, 288
indentured labour 59–60, 64–5, 66, 136,
    137
India 5–6
    Complete India Outfit 22–3
    Frere in 139, 141–4
India Office, London 10, 15
Indiana (battleship) 335
Ingram, Sir William 313
Innes, Emily 231, 238, 250
Ionian Islands 6, 95
Isandlwana 161, 164, 414

Jackson, Sir Frederick 370
Jackson, Sir Henry Moore 399, 402
Jamaica 6, 9, 21, 340–55
    1692 earthquake 341
    1907 earthquakes 333–6, 345–6, 347
    map *334*
    Morant Bay rebellion 116, 343
Jamestown 2
Jane, Marchioness of Ely 173, 174, 180
Jardine Matheson 170, 182
Java 81, 85
Jeevanjee, Alibhai Mulla 377
Jekyll, Gertrude 351
Jekyll, Walter 351
Jenkins, Edward 65, 66
Jenkinson, Thomas 161–2
Jinja (Uganda) 324, 328
Jocelyn, Lady Francis Elizabeth 62
Johannesburg 279–80, 364
John Adams 109
Joseph, Franz 173
*Journal of the Straits Branch of the Royal
    Asiatic Society* 239

Kader, Abdul 32, 33
'Kaffirs' 157, 158
    wars 147, 152, 153
Kagwa, Sir Apolo 320

Kampala 286–7, 315, 316, 320, 329, 331
Kandy, Ceylon 386, 388, 403
Kano 297–300, *298–9*
Kano, Emir of 295, 296
Karikari, Kofi (Ashantehene) 91, 94, 101
Kennedy, Sir Arthur 179–80, 184
Kent, John 92
Kenya *see* British East Africa
Keppel, Henry (captain) 76
Keswick, William 170, 182–3, 186, 188
Keyser, Arthur 244
Kikuyu 366
Kimberley, John Wodehouse, 1st Earl of,
    Secretary of State for the Colonies
    20, 117, 184, 215, 239, 241
Kimberley, South Africa 140, 149, 414
Kinangop 360, 376
King Williams Town (South Africa) 151,
    153, 154
King's House, Jamaica 6
Kingsley, Mary 275–6
Kingston 333–5, 341, 343, 344, 345–6,
    347–8, 349, 353
Kipling, Rudyard 395
Kitchener, Sir Herbert 363, 378–9
Klang (Malaysia) 229, 239, 241
Knollys, Captain (ADC) 119, 128, 131,
    133
Knollys, Sir Courtenay 10
Knowles, James 260
Koch, Dr 327
Kosoko, usurper to throne of Lagos 35
Kreli, Gcaleka chief 151, 154
Kropotkin, Prince 340
'Krumen' 27–8, 32
Kuala Kangsar 224, 232–4, 239, 242–3,
    251
Kuala Lumpur 229, 239, 240, 241–2, 245,
    247, 250, 253, 395
Kumasi 91, 93, 97–8, 101, 410

Labour Party, British 265, 307, 354–5
Labuan 4, 174–8, 195

Lagos 33–48, 413

Laikipia 356, 358, 359, 360, 361, 373–4, 375, 376, 379, 381, 382–3

Lake of the Woods 214, *214*

Langat (Malaysia) 234–6, 239

Lansdowne, Henry Charles Petty-Fitzmaurice, 5th Marquess 360

Lanyon, Colonel Sir William Owen 3–4, 103, 104, 162

Larrakeyah 88

Larrakia 78, 79, 80, 82, 83–4

Lascelles, Captain (ADC) 262

Le Hunte, George Ruthven (lawyer) 119, 128, 133

Lear, Edward 259

Lees, Charles (Capt) 101, 105

Legalishu (Maasai warrior) 375, 383

Leighton, Frederic Leighton, Baron 245

Levuka 109, 121, 127, 131, 135

Liberal Party, British 303, 402

Lincoln, Abraham 275

Lisser, Herbert George de 340–41, 345, 351

Lister, Martin 243, 244, *244*, 392

Little Big Horn, Battle of 205

Littleton, William 148, 150, 161

Loch, Sir Henry 279

Loftus, Jane, Marchioness of Ely 173, 174, 180

Lokoja 292–3

London School of Hygiene and Tropical Medicine 107

Lonsdale, Hugh Lowther, 5th Earl 252

Lonsdale, Lady Grace Gordon 252

Lorne, John Campbell, Marquess of, later Duke of Argyll 12, 202–5, 206–23, *210*

Louise, Princess, Marchioness of Lorne and Duchess of Argyll 12, 202, 208–9, 210, 211, 223

Love, Robert 344, 352

Low, Hugh 175–6, 177, 180, 188, 242, 391

Low, Kate (née Napier) 175–6

Low, Kitty (later Kitty Hennessy) 176
see also Hennessy, Lady Kitty

Lu K'u (Lu Kun) 170

Lucas, Charles 245, 247, 249, 396–7

Lucas, E. V. 340

Lugard, Edward (Sir Frederick's brother) 283, 289, 290, 291

Lugard, Sir Edward (Sir Frederick's uncle) 282–3, 284

Lugard, Sir Frederick John D., later Lord Lugard 12, 275, *290*, 290–302, 303–7, 357, 365, 414, 416
Dual Mandate in British Tropical Africa, The 307
early life 281–5
as Governor-General of Nigeria 306
as Governor of Hong Kong 306
as High Commissioner of Northern Nigeria 291, 292–302, 303–5
retirement 306–7
and Uganda 281, 286–9

Lugard, Lady Flora *see* Shaw, Flora

Lugard, Mary Jane (née Howard) 282

Lugard, the Rev. Frederick G. 281–2

Lumbwa 372

Luneberg 156–7

Luo 366

Lyttelton, Alfred, Secretary of State for the Colonies 302

Ma'afu (Tongan chief) 125, 129, 138

Maasai 358, 359, 360–61, 366, 367, 373–5, 376–7, 378, 379, 380–83
lands 12, 356, 360–61, 373–5, 376–7, 378, 382–3, *384*, 385

McCallum, Lady Dolly 389, 400, 408

McCallum, Sir Henry 388, 389, 399–401, 402, 404, 405–6, 408, 409

McCoskry, William 36, 39, 41

MacDonald, Ramsay 339, 379–80

MacDonnell, Sir Richard 72, 73

MacGregor, Hamish 204, 212, 213, 216, 217, 219, 222

MacGregor, William 124, 134, 137–8
McKay, Claude 350–51
Mackinnon, William 286
MacLachlan, George 78, 80, 81, 84, 85
MacLeod, James Farquharson (Col.) 205
McNair, A. L. (Capt.) 16
Madeira 275, 294
Mahmud, Raja 236
Malacca 75, 227, 245
  see also Straits Settlements
malaria 9, 32, 96–7, 107
  malarial fevers 9, 14, 39, 48, 53, 87–8,
    96–7, 107
Malaya (Malaysia) 224–55
  Clifford in 391–5, 410, 411–12
  Kuala Lumpur *see* Kuala Lumpur
  Malay States 8, 89, 228, 229, 237, 239,
    249–50
  Pahang 245, 250, 251, 392–4
  Perak *see* Perak
  Singapore *see* Singapore
  Straits Settlements 15, 21, 227, 229–30
    see also Malacca; Penang; Singapore
Maldives 388
Malta 6
Manchester Guardian 278
Manitoba 203, 205
Manson, Sir Patrick 328, 329, 395,
  416–17
Maori wars 109
Maroon 342
Mary King 87
Masikonde (Maasai elder) 375, 383
Maudslay, Alfred, later Sir Alfred
  Maudslay 128, 130, 133, 137
Maurice, Mr (tutor) 268
Mauritius 8, 21, 67, 116–17, 190, 332
Maxse, Sir Henry Fitzhardinge 4, 5
Maxwell, William Edward 245, 248, 250
Maxwell, William (journalist) 251–2
measles 120, 124, 131
Melbourne 6, 270–71
Meredith, George 277, 395

Merivale, Herman, Under-Secretary of
  State 14
Merriman, John Xavier 151, 153
Métis 203
Mfengu 150
Millner, Dr 78, 79, 81, 83, 86, 87, 88, 90
Milne, Agnes 265
Milne, John 225
Milner, Alfred, 1st Viscount 275, 364
missionaries 35, 43, 93, 109, 156
Missouri (battleship) 335
Mobogo, Ugandan Muslim chief 288
Moffat, J. S. 51
Moloney, Cornelius 413–14
Molteno, John Charles 145, 147, 148, 153
Mombasa 314, 315, 317, 318, 366, 369, 378
Monkton (butler) 370, 378
Montego Bay riots 344
Morant Bay rebellion 116, 343
Morris, William 339
Morrison, Walter 65
Morton, Henry 91
Murchison, Sir Roderick 27, 70
Murray, John (ADC) 365, 370, 372, 377,
  379, 381
Mwanga, King of Buganda 286, 287,
  288, 314

Nairobi 7, 319, 358–9, 360, 361, 366, 368,
  369–71, 375, 378
Napier, Kate 175–6
Napier, Lady Mary 415–16
Napier, Robert Cornelis, 1st Baron
  415–16
Napier, William 175
Napoleon III 173
Natal 140, 147, 150, 154–62, 305
National Club, Jamaica 352
New Brunswick 114, 115
New York Herald 91
New York Times 172, 182, 222, 354
New Zealand 6, 134, 137, 281, 417
Newcastle Chronicle 385

Newcastle, Henry Pelham-Clinton, 5th
    Duke of Newcastle-under-Lyme,
    Secretary of State for the Colonies
    72, 113–14
Newfoundland 2, 3
  des Voeux in 69
  fisheries 14
Ng Choy (Wu Tingfang) 181–2, 183–4,
    185–6, 190
Nicholson, Charles 346
Niger delta 31, 34, 291
Niger, River 26–7, 291, 292
  war on Upper Niger 45
Niger River Transport System 365
Nigeria 291
  Clifford as Governor of 410
  freed slave returning to 30
  Lagos *see* Lagos
  Lugard as Governor-General 306
  Northern Nigeria *see* Northern
    Nigeria
  unification of 306
Nightingale, Florence 145
Nile, River 288, 315, 317, 324
North Australian Expedition 70
North, Marianne 20
Northern Nigeria 291, 292–305
  Bell as Governor of 332
  Girouard in 365
  Hausa *see* Hausa
  Lugard as High Commissioner of 291,
    292–302, 303–5, 306
  map 294
Norton, Charles Eliot 277
Nugent, Lady Maria 347

O'Brien, Pat (Captain) 365
Ojibeway 212–13
Old Deccan Days (May Frere) 144
Ole Gilisho 360
Olive (chief of police, Fiji) 125, 128
Olivier, Arnold 336
Olivier, Brynhild 339, 340, 348

Olivier, Daphne 339, 340, 346, 348
Olivier, Margaret 337–8, 346–7,
    348–9
Olivier, Margery 339, 340, 348
Olivier, Noel 339, 340, 348
Olivier, Sydney, 1st Baron 12, 336–41,
    346–55
  Anatomy of African Misery 351
  in Belize 339–40
  as Colonial Secretary in Jamaica
    340–41, 343–5, 346–54
  early life 336–9
  White Capital and Coloured Labour 351,
    355
Olonana (paramount chief of the Maasai)
    360, 374–5, 379
Omeo (steamship) 81, 82
Ommanney, Sir Montagu 300, 398
Onslow, William Hillier, 4th Earl
    300–301
opium 170–71
Oppenheim, Bobbie 368–9, 371, 372,
    373, 377, 385
Oppenheim, Henry 368
Orange Free State 140, 149
Orr, Charles 414
Ottawa 6, 18
Ovalu, island 120–22, *121*

Pahang 245, 250, 251, 392–4
Pall Mall Gazette 277–8
Palmer, Roundell 112
Palmerston 73, 79–90
Palmerston, Henry John Temple, 3rd
    Viscount 73
Pangkor Engagement 230–31, 233
Pankhurst, Emmeline 339
Park, Mungo 26–7, 33
Parr, Henry Hallam (ADC) 148, 150,
    161
Parr, Katherine 28
Pease, Edward 340
Pease, Marjory 340

Penang 75, 227, 229, 239, 248
  see also Straits Settlements
Pender, Sir John 68, 69
Pender, Marion (later Marion des Voeux) 68
  see also des Voeux, Marion
Perak 180, 224–5, 230–33, 236–7, 239, 242–5, 247, 248–53, 391–2
Petre, William Joseph 390
Phnom Penh 403–4
Pietermaritzburg 157–9, 161–2
Pluto (steamer) 226
Ponnambalam Arunachalam 408
Ponnambalam, Ramanathan 408–9
Ponsonby, Sir Henry 141, 145, 165
Port Darwin 73, 78–9, 81
Port Elizabeth 150
Port Essington 73
Port Moresby 7
Port of Spain 396, 397, 402, 414
Port Royal 341, 347
Port Stanley 191–2, 194, 196–7, 198
Porto Novo 38, 43, 44, 45
Porto Novo, King of 42, 43
Pottinger, Brabagon (Maj.) 16
Poundmaker, Cree Chief 219, 220–21
Pratt, Major 131
Pretoria 162, 163, 363–4
Prior, Melton, MP 91
Prometheus, HMS 36
Province Wellesley 229

Quebec 2, 362
Queen 29
Queen's Home hospital, Adelaide 272
quinine 9, 20, 27, 31–2, 97, 98
Quittah, fort 93

racism 9, 64, 354, 355
  Jamaica 351–2, 354
  South Africa's black labour management 279
  United States 351

Rafael 197
Rawson, Sir Rawson W. 15–16
Reynolds, C. S. (Capt.) 16
Reynolds, Thomas 88–9, 90
Reynolds, W. (Capt.) 16
Rhodes, Cecil John 275, 278, 279, 290–91
Rhys, Jean 312
Rideau Hall, Ottawa 6, 209–10
Rift Valley 319, 358, 359, 360, 361, 373, 374
Rise of our East African Empire, The (Lugard) 289
Robbin, Henry 41, 42
Roberts, Frederick Sleigh, 1st Earl 301
Robinson, Sir Hercules 112, 120, 195
Robinson, Sir William 310
Rodger, John 242
Rome, Meta 246, *246*, 247, 254
Roosevelt, Kermit 367
Roosevelt, Theodore 336, 367–8
Roper River 72, 82, 85, 87
Rorke's Drift 161
Rowe, Samuel 38, 41, 44, 103–4, 105
Royal Geographical Society 26, 27, 70, 356
Royal Niger Company 275, 291, 294, 295
Royal Society, London 315–16, 317
  Committee for Tropical Diseases 328
Royal Society of Canada 222
Royalist (former schooner) 75, 77
Rupert's Land 202, 203
Ruskin, John 276, 277

St Elmo 197
St Helena 6, 419–20
St Lucia 49–53, 62–9
  Pitons 49, *49*, 51
Saint-Pol Lias, M. Brau de 391–2
St Vincent Island 3
Sale, Captain 104
Salisbury, Robert Cecil, 3rd Marquis of 289

Salt, Henry 340
Salt, Kate 340
Sam (Bell's servant) 311
Sarawak 75–6, 176
Sargent, John Singer 254
Saro 30, 38, 39
Saskatchewan, Johnnie 219
Sassoon, Sons and Co. 171
Satiru 304–5
Sattara 142–3
Scarborough, Lord, chairman, Royal
　　Niger Co. 304
Schmidt, Christian 82
Scotsman 204, 216
Scott, C. P. 278–9
Scott, Elizabeth (later lady Elizabeth
　　Glover) 48
　　see also Glover, Lady Elizabeth Rosetta
　　Scott
Scott, Sir George Gilbert 21, 144
Scott, Ted 346
Secretary of State for the Colonies
　　creation of post 10
　　holders of the post *see* Amery, Leo;
　　　　Buckingham, Richard Temple-
　　　　Grenville, 3rd Duke of; Cardwell,
　　　　Edward, 1st Viscount; Carnarvon,
　　　　Henry Howard Molyneux Herbert,
　　　　4th Earl of; Chamberlain, Joseph;
　　　　Crewe, Robert Crewe-Milnes, 1st
　　　　Marquess of; Elgin, Victor
　　　　Alexander Bruce, 9th Earl;
　　　　Granville, George Leveson Gower,
　　　　2nd Earl Granville; Harcourt,
　　　　Lewis; Hicks Beach, Sir Michael;
　　　　Kimberley, John Wodehouse, 1st
　　　　Earl of; Lyttelton, Alfred; New-
　　　　castle, Henry Pelham-Clinton, 5th
　　　　Duke of Newcastle-under-Lyme
Selangor 89, 229, 236, 239–42, 244, 245,
　　247–8
Selborne, Roundell Palmer, 1st Earl of
　　112

servants
　　of Bell 311
　　of the Girouards 368, 370, 378
　　of the Gordons 119, 127, 129, 131
　　interpreters 287, 311, 360
　　of Lady Tennyson 261, 262, 263, 264,
　　　　266, 267, 269, 271
Seven Years War 2
Shaw, Flora (later Lady Lugard) 12,
　　275–81, 289, 290–94, 299–301,
　　302–4, 305–6, 307
Shaw, George (Maj.-Gen.) 276–7
Shaw, George Bernard 336, 337, 339,
　　350, 353, 354–5
Shaw-Lefevre, Sir John 114
Shaw-Lefevre, Madeleine 115
Shaw-Lefevre, Rachael (later Rachael
　　Gordon) 114–15
　　see also Gordon, Lady Rachael
Shaw, Marie 276
Shaw, Mimi 276, 277, 281
Shepstone, John 159
Shepstone, Sir Theophilus 147–8, 150,
　　154–5, 156
Sherbo (steamer) 45
Sierra Leone 6
　　Freetown 30, 33, 44–5, 178–9
Simon, André 274
Simons Bay 149
Simpson, Hubert 352
Sind 139, 143
Singapore 6, 8, 226–7
　　Clifford in 391, 395
　　Douglas in 89
　　Swettenham in 226–7, 237–8,
　　　　252–3
Singapore Free Press 393
Sioux 205–7, 217–18
Sitting Bull, Chief 205, 206, 207
Sketch of the Forestry of West Africa
　　(Moloney) 413
slavery
　　abolition in the Cape Colony 147

abolition in Zanzibar 139
and aftermath of abolition in Jamaica
    341–3
child 41
debt bondage 235–6
fight against 2, 8, 14, 34–5, 37
Fiji and 111
on the Gold Coast 102
Hausa *see* Hausa
indentured labour 59–60, 64–5, *66*,
    136, 137
labourers in British Guiana following
    end of 59–60, 64–7, *66*
Lagos 34–5, 37, 38, 40–42, 45, 46, 47
Lugard and Arab slave traders 284
Malaya 231, 235–6
Mauritius 117
slave woman 'Awa' 41
sleeping sickness 315–17, 318, 322–3, 324,
    325, 326–7, 328–9, 331–2
Smithsonian Institution, Washington 222
Smythe, Colonel 111
Sokoto 297, 299, 304
    Sultans of 294, 295, 296, 299, 304–5
Solomon, Lady Elizabeth 364
Solomon, Gwendolen (later Gwen
    Girouard) 364
    see also Girouard, Lady Gwendolen
Solomon, Sir Richard 364, 385
Soufrière 50, 63, 67
South Africa 17–18, 140–66, 417
    Boer war 265–6, 303, 363
    Boers *see* Boers
    Cape Town *see* Cape Town
    Frere as High Commissioner 140,
        145–54
    Girouard in 363–4
    map *144*
    Orange Free State 140, 149
    Flora Shaw in 279–80
    see also Cape Colony; Griqualand
        West; Natal; Transvaal
South Australia 258

Adelaide *see* Adelaide
    Douglas settles Palmerston (1870–73)
        70–90
    Lady Tennyson at home (1899–1903)
        260–74
    map *71*
Sphinx 29
Sri Lanka *see* Ceylon
Stanley, Falkland Islands 191–2, 194,
    196–7, 198
Stanley, Henry Morton 48, 286
Stanmore, Sir Arthur Hamilton Gordon,
    1st Baron *see* Gordon, Sir Arthur
    Hamilton Gordon, later 1st Baron
    Stanmore
Stead, W. T. 277
Stepniak, Sergius 340
Stevenson, Robert Louis 277
Stewart, Sir Donald 360, 361
Strahan, George (Capt) 12, 94–5, 107
    early life 95
    as Governor of the Gold Coast 99,
        100–101, 102–3, 104–6, 107
Straits Settlements 15, 21, 227, 229–30
    Governor Swettenham 252–4 *see also*
        Swettenham, Sir Frank Athelstane
    Province Wellesley 229
    see also Malacca; Penang; Singapore
Straits Times 249
Stuart, John MacDouall 70–72
Sulimani (boy in Entebbe) 323
Swettenham, Sir Alexander 225, 226,
    333, 335–6
Swettenham, Sir Frank Athelstane 12,
    224–55, *244*, 392, 396, 414
    early life 225–6
    in Selangor 89, 240–42, 244, 245,
        247–8
    in Singapore 226–7, 237–8, 252–3
Swettenham, Sydney (née Holmes)
    237–9, 241, 245, *246*, 248–9, 254
Sydney 70, 120, 127, 272

Table Bay 146, 149
Taiping (Malaysia) 247–8, 249
Tanjong Malim 392
Tasmania 7
Taylor, Dr (missionary) 30
Tennyson, Alfred, 1st Baron 259–60
Tennyson, Aubrey 257, 273
Tennyson, Lady Audrey Georgiana 12,
  257–74
Tennyson, Baroness Emily 259
Tennyson, Hallam 12, 257, 258, 259–60,
  262–3, 266, 268, 270, 273
Tennyson, Harold 257, 261, 266, 267, 273
Tennyson, Lionel 257, 259, 267, 273
Thesiger, Frederic Augustus, 2nd Baron
  Chelmsford 153–4, 161, 164–5
Thomas (footman) 261, 267
Thompson, David 203
Thompson, Juliana 38
Thompson, Marian 38
Thomson, Joseph 356–7
Thurston, John Bates 122, 125, 126, 130,
  137
Times, The 65, 69, 91, 117, 212, 218, 260,
  275–6, 356
  Charles Austin 204, 212, 214, 218, 222
  Moberly Bell 278, 279, 280–81, 293
  and Flora Shaw 278, 279–81, 289, 291,
    299–300, 302
tin mining 228, 230, 239, 241, 247
Townsend, Harry (missionary) 30, 34
Transvaal 3, 140, 147, 148, 156–7, 158,
  160, 162, 364
  see also Boers
Treacher, John 4
Trinidad 9, 67, 115–16, 396, 413
  Clifford as Colonial Secretary in
    396–8
  des Voeux appointed Governor 69
  Gordon as Governor of 115–16
Trollope, Anthony 9, 146, 154, 172
tsetse fly 316, 317, 322, 326, 328, 331–2
Tugela River 157, 159, *159*, 160

Tung Wah hospital 183, 184, 189
Tuttle, Charles 208

Uganda 281, 286–9, 312, 313–32
  map *314*
  Uganda railway 314, 315, 325, 357–8,
    375, 377
Ugbrooke 390
United Fruit Company 333, 349–50
United States of America
  'Back to Africa' movement 352
  and the Canadian Indians 203–4,
    205–7
  civil war 111
  colour and segregation 351
  Evarts (Secretary of State) 206–7
  offer to help with Jamaican earth-
    quake 335–6
Universal Negro Improvement Associa-
  tion 354
Usborne, Captain 330

Vanu Levu 136
Victoria, Lake 314, 315, 316, 319–20, 331
Victoria, Queen 6, 11, 17, 32, 109, 112,
  118, 141, 164, 165, 184, 209, 245, 256,
  257, 288
Viti Levu 128, 131–2
von Hügel, Anatole, Baron 128, 133, 138

Walker, Tom (servant) 311
Wallas, Graham 337, 349
Wallington, Captain (ADC) 263, 264
Walton, Anna 368, 369, 370, 371, 372,
  373, 374, 377, 378
War Office 39, 94, 101, 103, 177, 187,
  363
Warren, Charles (Capt), later Sir 148–50,
  414
Webb, Sidney 337
Weld, Sir Frederick 7, 239–41, 242, 247,
  391, 392
Wells, H. G. 340, 355, 395

West Africa 3, 8, 14
    Cape Coast *see* Cape Coast
    the Gambia *see* Gambia, the
    Gold Coast *see* Gold Coast (Ghana)
    Lagos *see* Lagos
    Nigeria *see* Nigeria; Northern Nigeria
    Sierra Leone *see* Sierra Leone
West African Medical Staff 417
West India Electric Company 353
West Indies 6, 10, 14, 15
    Barbados *see* Barbados
    Jamaica *see* Jamaica
    St Lucia *see* St Lucia
    Trinidad *see* Trinidad
    Windward Islands 52, 107, 171, 362
Whipple (torpedo boat) 335
White Capital and Coloured Labour
    (Olivier) 351, 355
Wiggins, Dr 324, 326
Wilberforce, Samuel 112, 114, 115
Willoughby, Henry 39, 47
Wilson, George 321, 327, 329, 331
Windward Islands 107, 171, 362
    map 52
Winifred (steamer) 319, 320
Winter, Francis 7
Winton, Sir Francis Walter de (Col.) 204

Wolseley, Garnet (Maj.-Gen.) 91, 93, 94,
    95, 97, 100, 164, 203, 277
Wolverine, HMS 75
Woolf, Leonard 402
Wu Tingfang *see* Ng Choy

Xhosa 150, 151–3, 154

Yap Ah Loy, 'Capitan China' 229, 239,
    240–41
York, George, Duke of (later George V)
    268, 274
York, May (Mary), Duchess of 268
Yoruba people 34, 38, 42, 45, 46
Young, Walter Aynsley 254
Young, Walter McKnight 242
Yusof, Sultan of Perak 243

Zambesi (mailboat) 167
Zanzibar 7, 139
Zaria 296
Zobehr Pasha 277
Zomba 7
Zulu 161
Zululand 158, 160–61, 316
Zulus 155–62, 164–5, 414
Zungeru 293–4, 301, 304